EXS 67

DNA Fingerprinting: State of the Science

Edited by S. D. J. Pena
R. Chakraborty
J. T. Epplen
A. J. Jeffreys

Birkhäuser Verlag
Basel · Boston · Berlin

Editors

Prof. Dr. S. D. J. Pena
Núcleo de Genética Médica
de Minas Gerais (GENE/MG)
Av. Afonso Pena 3111/9
30130-909 Belo Horizonte
Brazil

Prof. R. Chakraborty
Genetics Center
University of Texas
Health Science Center
PO Box 20334
Houston, Texas 77225
USA

Prof. Dr. J. T. Epplen
Molekulare Humangenetik, MA
Ruhr-Universität
Universitätsstr. 150
44780 Bochum
Germany

Prof. Alec J. Jeffreys
Department of Genetics
University of Leicester
Leicester LE1 7RH
England

Library of Congress Cataloging-in-Publication Data
DNA fingerprinting: state of the science/edited by S. D. J. Pena . . . [et al.].
    p.   cm.—(EXS; 67)
    Includes bibliographical references and index.
    ISBN 3-7643-2781-2 (hardcover).—ISBN 3-7643-2906-8 (softcover).—
    ISBN 0-8176-2781-2 (hardcover).—ISBN 0-8176-2906-8 (softcover)
    1. DNA fingerprints—Congresses. I. Pena, S. D. J. (Sergio D. J.) II. Series.
    [DNLM: 1. DNA Fingerprinting—Congresses. W1 E65 v.67 1993 / W 750 D6291 1993]
RA1057.55.D637   1993
575.1—dc20
DNLM/DLC
for Library of Congress

Deutsche Bibliothek Cataloging-in-Publication Data
DNA fingerprinting: state of the science/ed. by S. D. J. Pena . . . – Basel; Boston; Berlin;
Birkhäuser, 1993
    (EXS; 67)
    ISBN 3-7643-2906-8 (Basel . . .) brosch.
    ISBN 3-7643-2781-2 (Basel . . .) Gb.
    ISBN 0-8176-2906-8 (Boston) brosch.
    ISBN 0-8176-2781-2 (Boston) Gb.
NE: Pena, Sergio D. J. [Hrsg.]; GT

© 1993 Birkhäuser Verlag, PO Box 133, CH-4010 Basel, Switzerland
Printed on acid-free paper produced from chlorine-free pulp
Printed in Germany
ISBN 3-7643-2781-2   ISBN 3-7643-2906-8
ISBN 0-8176-2781-2   ISBN 0-8176-2906-8
(Hardcover)   (Softcover)
9 8 7 6 5 4 3 2 1

Contents

**Part III Application of DNA Fingerprinting to the Study of
Microorganisms, Plants, and Animals**

A Plants

D Mammals

Preface

DNA fingerprinting had a well-defined birthday. In the March 7, 1985 issue of *Nature*, Alec Jeffreys and coworkers described the first development of multilocus probes capable of simultaneously revealing hypervariability at many loci in the human genome and called the procedure **DNA fingerprinting**. It was a royal birth in the best British tradition. In a few months the emerging technique had permitted the denouement of hitherto insoluble immigration and paternity disputes and was already heralded as a major revolution in forensic sciences. In the next year (October, 1986) DNA fingerprinting made a dramatic entrée in criminal investigations with the Enderby murder case, whose story eventually was turned into a best-selling book (*"The Blooding"* by Joseph Wambaugh). Today DNA typing systems are routinely used in public and commercial forensic laboratories in at least 25 different countries and have replaced conventional protein markers as the methods of choice for solving paternity disputes and criminal cases. Moreover, DNA fingerprinting has emerged as a new domain of intense scientific activity, with myriad applications in just about every imaginable territory of life sciences. The Second International Conference on DNA Fingerprinting, which was held in Belo Horizonte, Brazil in November of 1992, was a clear proof of this. One hundred and fifty researchers from more than thirty countries gathered to discuss their technical and methodological advances and their new results with the successful application of DNA fingerprinting to the study of a wide reach of specific genetic and population problems in microorganisms, plants and animals, ranging from protozoa to man. The conference was also a success in that a cohesive vision of biology emerged under the unifying concept of the ubiquitous presence of polymorphic tandem repeat regions in eukaryotic genomes. The articles that compose this book were chosen among the papers presented at the Second International Conference on DNA Fingerprinting. They were selected and prepared with this cohesive vision in mind. Some are reviews and some present new research data. All are highly informative in their specific target areas. We can only hope that this volume will not only serve as a source book of DNA fingerprinting knowledge but will also constitute a platform from which new research is launched.

The Editors

DNA Fingerprinting: State of the Science
ed. by S. D. J. Pena, R. Chakraborty, J. T. Epplen & A. J. Jeffreys
© 1993 Birkhäuser Verlag Basel/Switzerland

Brief introduction to human DNA fingerprinting

A. J. Jeffreys[a] and S. D. J. Pena

[a]*Department of Genetics, University of Leicester, Leicester LE1 7RH, England, and Núcleo de Genética Médica de Minas Gerais (GENE/MG), Av. Afonso Pena 3111/9, 30130-909, Belo Horizonte, Brazil*

Introduction

In early 1985, Jeffreys et al. (1985b) described the first development of multilocus DNA fingerprints and speculated that these individual-specific DNA patterns might provide a powerful method for individual identification and paternity testing. At the time, it was thought that the implementation of these applications would be protracted, and that major legal problems would be encountered as DNA evidence proceeded from the research laboratory to the court room. Subsequent history showed that this prediction was unduly pessimistic. By April 1985 the first case, involving a UK immigration dispute, had been satisfactorily resolved by DNA fingerprinting (Jeffreys et al., 1985a). Shortly thereafter, DNA evidence in a paternity dispute was admitted in a UK civil court. DNA typing in criminal investigations saw its debut in October 1986 with the Enderby murder case, an investigation which led to the first instance of the release of a prime suspect proved innocent by DNA evidence (Gill and Werrett, 1987; Wong et al., 1987; see Wambaugh, 1989). By 1987, DNA typing results had been admitted in evidence in criminal courts in the UK and USA, and in 1988 the UK Home Office and Foreign and Commonwealth Office had ratified the use of DNA fingerprinting for the resolution of immigration disputes which hinge upon disputed family relationships (Home Office, 1988). 1989 saw the first major attack, in the USA, on the procedural and scientific validity of DNA typing in forensics (see Lander, 1989), resulting in a major independent review carried out by the US Congress Office of Technology Assessment (1990) which concluded that DNA-based identification was scientifically valid provided that appropriate technology, quality control and quality assurance procedures were implemented. However the question was far from settled. Further strong attacks were made in the United States on the statistical aspects of DNA typing for the positive identification of criminals (for instance, see Lewontin and Hartl, 1991) leading to equally strong rebuttals

(Chakraborty and Kidd, 1991). In May 1992, a US National Research Council Commitee issued a report stressing the scientific validity of DNA-based identity testing and setting guidelines (National Research Council, 1992). For paternity testing there has been rather less dispute and even major critics of the forensic use of DNA tests have endorsed the use of DNA fingerprinting with multilocus probes for this purpose (Lander, 1991). Today DNA typing systems are in place in public and commercial forensic laboratories in at least 25 different countries, with many other countries actively considering DNA analysis in forensic and legal medicine.

Together with this extraordinarily rapid spread of DNA typing, the last few years have been major developments in the underpinning technology and our understanding of the genetics of hypervariable DNA. We will review here the various "classical" DNA test systems available and will discuss the biological properties of the highly variable DNA regions which provide the basis for DNA typing. Major current topics such as internal variation in minisatellites, the role of transcribed microsatellite expansion in the genesis of some genetic diseases, and aspects of the population genetics of mini- and microsatellites, will be covered in depth in other chapters of this book and will not be dealt with in this review.

Multilocus DNA fingerprinting

The most variable loci discovered in the human genome consist of tandemly-repeated minisatellites, otherwise known as VNTR (variable number of tandem repeats) loci (Nakamura et al., 1987), and provide the basis for most currently used DNA typing systems. Surprisingly, there are clear DNA sequence similarities amongst the tandem repeat sequences of many human minisatellites, which define the minisatellite "core" sequence (Jeffreys et al., 1985b). The core is presumably involved in the generation of minisatellites and/or maintenance of variability in allelic repeat unit copy number at these loci, possibly by promoting unequal crossing over between tandem repeats. Direct evidence for the recombinational proficiency of minisatellites has come from studies of inter-plasmid recombination in transfected mammalian cells (Wahls et al., 1990). Recently, we and others have discovered several DNA binding proteins which interact with high affinity with minisatellite tandem repeats (Collick and Jeffreys, 1990; Collick et al., 1991; Wahls et al., 1991; Yamazaki et al., 1992) which may provide a route to unravelling the biochemical processes which operate at these extraordinary VNTR loci.

Whatever the role of the minisatellite core sequence, its discovery immediately suggested that DNA hybridization probes comprised of tandem repeats of the core sequence should detect multiple variable human DNA fragments by Southern blot hybridization, to produce an individual-specific DNA "fingerprint". Jeffreys et al. (1985b, c) have developed two such multilocus probes, termed 33.6 and 33.15, which vary in the length and precise sequence of the core repeat and which are the ones most used around the world in casework analysis, primarily in parentage testing (Jeffreys et al., 1991). Each probe detects typically 17 variable DNA fragments per individual in the size range $3.5-20+$ kb, plus many smaller DNA fragments which are too complex to resolve electrophoretically and which are not used in the statistical evaluation of casework data. Extensive pedigree analysis shows that 33.6 and 33.15 detect independent sets of variable DNA fragments, with only approximately 1% of fragments codetected by both probes (Jeffreys et al., 1986, 1991). Incidentally, these probes cross-hybridize to variable loci in a wide range of animal, bird and plant species, though the many applications of non-human DNA fingerprints in breeding, population genetics and conservation biology will not be discussed here.

Following the development of multilocus probes 33.6 and 33.15, many other tandem-repeated DNA fingerprinting probes have been reported (see for example Ali et al., 1986; Vassart et al., 1987; Fowler et al., 1988; Pena et al., 1990). Indeed, Vergnaud (1989) has shown that almost any tandem-repeated sequence can, to some extent at least, detect multiple variable human DNA fragments. However, the most effective multilocus probes all tend to be G-rich and similar in sequence to the original minisatellite core sequence. Most importantly, little research has been done on establishing the degree of independence of the sets of loci detected by different multilocus probes (other than 33.6 and 33.15), and indeed there is now clear evidence that signficant overlap between different probes may exist (Armour et al., 1990; Julier et al., 1990). It is still unclear what molecular features are essential to an efficient multilocus probe, although the idea of the minisatellite core sequence remains as the only conceptual basis for understanding probe effectiveness.

Properties of human DNA fingerprints

The statistical evaluation of multilocus DNA fingerprint evidence, whether in comparing a forensic specimen with a criminal suspect or in determining paternity, rests on a single parameter, namely the proportion of bands x which on average are apparently shared between unrelated people (Jeffreys et al., 1985c). x has been estimated at 0.14 for probe 33.6 and 33.15 from extensive Caucasian casework, with no evidence for significant shifts in the value of x between different ethnic groups. A conservative value of x of 0.25 is deliberately used in casework evaluation, to prevent over-interpretation with respect to the defendant and to allow for reduction in variability due to inbreeding ($x = 0.25$ is equilvalent to an assumption of first cousin relationship in an outbred Caucasian population). Assuming statistical independence of bands, then the chance that n bands in individual A would all be matched by bands of similar electrophoretic mobility in B is given by x^n. This probability is not of full identity, since (a) individual B may have additional bands not present in A, (b) non-scored bands smaller than 3.5 kb would also have to correspond between A and B, (c) for identity, bands would have to match in precise relative position and relative intensity, a criterion far more stringent than used in determining in band-sharing coefficient x. The statistical estimator x^n is therefore extremely conservative. Note incidentally that the individual specificity of multilocus DNA fingerprints is derived, not from the (modest) statistical weight attributed to a given band, but from the large number of bands scored.

Statistical evaluation of DNA fingerprints, whether using the estimator x^n or more formal Bayesian analyses (Hill, 1986; Brookfield, 1989; Evett et al., 1989a, b), makes a number of critical but testable assumptions. First, the band sharing frequency x is assumed to be constant for all bands (or more correctly molecular weight intervals on the DNA fingerprint). In fact, x decreases with increased DNA fragment size (Jeffreys et al., 1985c), and algebraic considerations show that this heterogeneity in x results in x^n being a conservative match estimate. Second, all bands are assumed to be statistically independent. Non-independent could in principle arise through linkage or allelism between bands, and through inbreeding leading to relatively homogeneous sub-populations within the global population from which x was estimated. Extensive analyses of pedigrees and of loci cloned from DNA finger-prints shows widespread dispersal of the variable DNA fragments around the human genome, and enormous allelic length variability, resulting in very low levels of allelism and linkage between human DNA fingerprint fragments, and therefore substantial independence of bands (Jeffreys et al., 1986; 1991). This is not necessarily true for all species, and indeed there is clear evidence of major linkage and, probably, linkage disequilibrium between different DNA fragments detected in mice (Jeffreys et al., 1987) and cattle (unpub. data). In man, the sole residual concern is therefore that of inbreeding. While non-random mating obviously occurs, the relevant question is whether human inbreeding in practice could result in a significant increase in the band sharing frequency within a local community. This is unlikely. The band sharing frequency x is largely dictated by gel electrophoretic resolution, with many of the underlying loci showing far higher levels of variability. As a result, many different variable loci can, and do, contribute bands to a given gel interval (Wong et al., 1987), thereby providing a buffer against shifts in allele frequency at individual contributing loci due to inbreeding. In practice, the band sharing frequency x in Caucasians remains the same if comparisons are restricted to husband-wife pairs (who by definition are representatives of local breeding communities), with as yet no evidence for a subset of consanguineous marriages which might signal significant inbreeding (Jeffreys et al., 1991). In only one instance, involving a highly inbred small community from the Gaza strip where consanguineous marriages are a cultural norm, was the band-sharing coefficient between "unrelated" individuals significantly increased (Bellamy et al., 1991). However the magnitude of the increase in x (approximately 0.2 per probe) was modest and still resulted in DNA fingerprints which are essentially completely individual-specific.

Extension of multilocus DNA fingerprints to paternity disputes raises one other concern, namely the effect of germline mutation of DNA fingerprints bands on the efficiency of parentage estimation. Such mutation will generate one or more offspring bands which cannot be attributed to either genuine parent, providing evidence which could be interpreted as an exclusion. The incidence of mutation at these highly unstable loci is not insignificant; using both 33.6 and 33.15, 27% of offspring show one mutant band, 1.2% show two mutations and an estimated $<0.3\%$ show three unassignable bands. To determine whether this level of mutation significantly blurs the discrimination of fathers from non-fathers, we have determined the proportion of non-maternal bands in a child which cannot be attributed to the alleged father. For a sample of 1419 true fathers, this proportion was, as expected, low (mode $= 0$, range $= 0 - 0.18$). For a corresponding sample of 283 falsely accused non-fathers, this proportion was much higher (mode 0.77, range $0.43 - 1$). Thus this proportion provides a single statistic which efficiently distinguishes fathers from non-fathers, even in the presence of mutation (Jeffreys et al., 1991) (In practice paternity disputes, particularly those showing mutant bands, are further tested using single locus minisatellites probes, see below). For a given paternity case, statistical evaluation uses the x^n statistic or Bayesian analysis combined with the empirically observed frequency of new mutant bands to determine an appropriate paternity index.

Multilocus human DNA fingerprinting is thus supported by a substantial body of genetic and population data, and is now routinely used in paternity and immigration testing. These probes have proved particularly useful in the latter disputes, where no prior assumptions about claimed family relationships (for example between the UK sponsor, his alleged wife and alleged children) may be made, and where one is sometimes required to prove for example that a man is the family's father, rather than the brother of the true father. All of these analyses use pristine DNA obtained from fresh blood and do not involve inter-blot comparisons, thereby minimizing problems in data production and interpretation. In contrast, DNA fingerprints have proved less powerful in routine forensic testing, due to the relative lack of probe sensitivity, problems in interpreting incomplete patterns resulting from partial DNA degradation and/or poor DNA recovery, inter-blot comparison problems due to subtle variations in hybridization stingency and in the resulting patterns, the (not insurmountable) difficulty of data banking the complex patterns, and the inability to detect mixed DNA samples originating from more than one person. Nevertheless, DNA fingerprints have been used successfully in a number of criminal investigation (see for example Gill and Werrett, 1987), and provide rich patterns in which electrophoretic band shift, which has bedevilled some single locus probe analyses (Lander, 1989), is readily identifiable and correctable.

Single locus minisatellite probes

DNA fingerprints provide DNA phenotypes, not genotypes, in which information on loci and alleles is unavailable. In contrast, cloned human minisatellites can produce locus-specific DNA hybridization patterns from which genotypic information can be deduced, of critical importance in for example linkage analysis. Hundreds of cloned minisatellites have now been isolated, either by chance, by screening human genomic libraries for clones which detect hypervariable loci (Knowlton et al., 1986), or by hybridization screening of libraries using oligonucleotides based on known VNTR sequences (Nakamura et al., 1987, 1988) or by selective cloning of DNA fingerprint fragments into λ bacteriophage vectors (Wong et al., 1986, 1987) or more efficiently into a charomid vector followed by ordered-array library screening with a range of multilocus probes (Armour et al., 1990). This latter approach has proved to be very effective both on humans and on other mammalian and avian species.

Many of these cloned minisatellites have been localized in the human genome (and indeed provide critically informative landmark loci in human linkage maps). They have been found on essentially every human chromosome, including the X chromosome and the X-Y pairing region. Minisatellites are however not randomly distributed in the genome but instead preferentially localize near the ends of human chromosomes (Royle et al., 1988). DNA sequence analysis of these proterminal minisatellites and their immediate environs shows that they are frequently closely linked to other hypervariable loci (sometimes within a few base pairs) and to dispersed repeat elements such as Alu, L1 and proretroviral LTRs (Armour et al., 1989b). In two instances, a human minisatellite has been shown to have evolved by tandem-repeat amplification from within such a dispersed element. The clustering of minisatellites in these proterminal chromosomal regions is intriguing, particularly in view of the role of these regions in chromosome pairing and recombination. However, there is no clear evidence as yet for the direct involvement of minisatellites in these aspects of chromosome mechanics, and instead it is possible that their presence in these regions may reflect the existence of relatively unstable DNA domains adept at accumulating elements such as minisatellites and retroposons. Finally, there is no evidence for expression, function or coding potential of human minisatellites; one exception is the hypervariable MUC1 locus which, remarkably, encodes a highly polymorphic mucin (Swallow et al., 1987). It is therefore extremely unlikely that genotypic data gleaned from the minisatellites used in forensic medicine will ever provide phenotypic information, for example on disease liability. In this regard, the situation is quite different for some trinucleotide variable tandem repeats that can be transcribed and occasionally translated, and which have been implicated in the etilogy of some important human genetic dieases (Wrogemann et al., this book; Riggins et al., 1992).

Given the large number of cloned minisatellites, it is possible to select a combination of probes appropriate for forensic analysis. The probes should be unlinked to minimize the risk of allelic association (linkage disequilibrium) between different loci. Each probe must be locus-specific and detect, by Southern blot hybridization analysis, a hypervariable locus with one band per allele, giving two-band patterns (heterozygotes) or one-band patterns (presumptive homozygotes or heterozygotes with alleles of similar size). We have established a set of 5 hypervariable loci conforming to these requirements and all typable on *Hin*fI blots (Wong et al., 1987; Smith et al., 1990). In the United States the FBI led the way in evaluating a corresponding set of loci, using *Hae*III as a standard restriction enzyme. Presently, which enzyme is used is primarily a matter of choice, each one having particular advantages and drawbacks.

The single locus minisatellite probes chosen for forensic casework all show extraordinary level of allelic variability. The most variable and informative locus described to date is MS1, with alleles ranging from 1 to 23 kb long, and with >99% of individuals showing two resolvable alleles by Southern blot hybridzation. The repeat unit is 9 bp long yielding in principle 2400 different allelic length states. Genomic DNA mixing experiments (Wong et al., 1987) and determination of allele length frequency distributions at MS1 in human populations (Smith et al., 1990) show that there are no common alleles at this locus, and theoretical considerations suggest that most or all of the 2400 possible allelic length states exist in human populations. Of course, not all alleles can be electrophoretically resolved, resulting in the allele length frequency distributions being quasi-continuous. In contrast, loci with lower variability (<96% heterozygosity) tend to show a more limited number of distinct alleles with real and measurable population frequencies (Wong et al., 1987; Smith et al., 1990); allele length frequency distributions at such loci tend to be discontinuous or "spiky", rather than smooth, with the result that small errors in allele sizing can result in large errors in allele frequency estimates. Such loci will also tend to be more vulnerable to genetic drift and inbreeding effects (see below), and are best avoided for forensic use, if possible.

Single locus minisatellite probes provide a very powerful tool for forensic analysis provided that DNA of sufficient quality and quantity can be recovered from the forensic specimen. Detection based on ^{32}P-label or enhanced chemiluminescence is sensitive, the limits being approximately 10 ng genomic DNA. Mixed DNA samples (e.g. semen bearing vaginal swabs, blood from more than one victim) can be readily identified. The individual specificity achievable amongst unrelated people with a battery of four sequential single locus probe tests is comparable to that achievable using one multilocus probe. This follows, not from the large number of bands scored as with multilocus probes, but from the low population frequency of each of the single locus probe alleles. However, these probes are relatively poor at discriminating between close relatives. For example, a single probe has, at best, only a 75% chance of distinguishing two siblings (<99.6% for 4 probes). For this reason, we prefer the term "DNA profiling", rather than DNA fingerprinting, to describe single locus probe analysis.

Evaluation of single locus probe profiles

The statistical evaluation of DNA profile evidence requires knowledge of allele frequencies and assumptions about population structuring. Suppose that a single locus probe yields two alleles a and b, with frequencies q_a and q_b measured in the reference population. Suppose further than the forensic profile is indistinguishable from that of the suspect (allowing for the occasional instance of minor electrophoretic band shift, within an acceptable range established from extensive casework experience). The probability of chance "match", under the assumption that alleles associate at random in the population, is given under the Hardy-Weinberg equilibrium by $2q_a q_b$. However, the sizes of the alleles are not known with absolute precision, either in the casework samples or in the reference database, and thus some form of allele pooling or "binning" is required to estimate appropriate values of q_a and q_b and to correct these values for sampling errors arising from the finite size of any population database. It is important that allele pooling is conservative relative to the criteria used to declare a forensic match, such that the statistical weight of the evidence is biased in favour of the defendant (equivalent to the use of a conservative band-sharing frequency in the evaluation of multilocus DNA fingerprints). It is also important to appreciate that there is not necessarily a sharp distinction between "match" and exclusion in forensic analysis, and that severe cases of electrophoretic band shift could yield results that would have to be declared inconclusive. The obvious solution to this problem is to identify and eliminate the causes of such shifts (which in our experience have very rarely proved to be a significant problem).

The only biological problem to emerge from the recent debate is whether appropriate ethnic reference databases are used and whether the assumption of Hardy-Weinberg equilibrium is valid. This problem resolves into two questions. First, do significant differences in allele length frequency distributions exist between different ethnic groups? Second, do localized inbred subpopulations exist within a given population in which the chance of allelic identity is far higher than estimated from allelic frequencies derived from the population as a whole? The answers to these questions are not simple. They are discussed in depth in three reviews in this book (Chakraborty and Jin, 1993; Budowle et al., 1993; Balazs et al., 1993).

Minisatellite mutation

Assuming that the vast majority of minisatellites are without phenotypic effect, a reasonable assumption, high allelic length variability at these loci must reflect high rates of the de novo mutation producing new length alleles. Direct measurement of minisatellite mutation rates, both in the germline and in somatic tissue, is not only important for unravelling the molecular processes which generate variability at these loci, but is also of direct relevance to forensic and legal applications of single locus probes. Germline mutation will produce apparent exclusions in paternity testing, and somatic mutation could in principle produce divergence in DNA phenotypes between different tissues (e.g. blood and sperm) in the same individual.

Germline length change mutation rates at human loci have been directly measured in human pedigrees (Jeffreys et al., 1988a). As expected from the neutral mutation – random drift hypothesis, mutation rate increases with variability and become significant above approximately 96% heterozygosity. For the most variable human minisatellite used in forensic analysis, MS1, the mutation rate is an extraordinary 0.05 per gamete. Offspring are as likely to inherit a mutant allele from their mother as from the father, and mutant alleles can be, with equal frequency, either larger or smaller than their progenitor allele. Mutation events can sometimes result in the gain or loss of kilobases of the tandem repeat array, though most mutation events are small, involving the gain or loss of only a few repeat units. Mutation rates of approximately 10^{-2} per gamete do not significantly interfere with the use of these probes in paternity analysis, provided that mutation rates are known and can be incorporated into statistical likelihood ratio analyses of paternity against non-paternity. Less variable loci with unknown mutation rates will, in contrast, generate the occasional paternity case where "exclusion" with one probe, but inclusion with remaining probes, will lead to an inconclusive result where the relative likelihood of paternity with mutation against non-paternity cannot be determined, except by indirect estimation of mutation rates from locus heterozygosity (Jeffreys et al., 1988a).

In pedigree analysis, mutant offspring provide indirect information on the incidence of mutant parental gametes. An alternative strategy to estimating mutation rates is to determine the density of new mutant minisatellite molecules directly in gametic (sperm) DNA. This can be achieved by fractionation of sperm DNA by gel electrophoresis to remove progenitor alleles, followed by single molecule PCR analysis to count directly the number of new mutant molecules of abnormal length (Jeffreys et al., 1990). This approach is exquisitely sensitive, being capable of detecting mutation events as infrequent as 10^{-7} per gamete, and yields an estimate of MS32 minisatellite mutation rate comparable with that obtained by pedigree analysis. This approach could in principle be used to estimate mutation rates at less variable loci where pedigree analysis is not feasible.

Minisatellite mutation is not restricted to the germline, but also occurs somatically, as shown by the analysis of clonal tumour cell populations and lymphoblastoid cell lines (Armour et al., 1989a) and by single molecule PCR analysis of normal somatic DNA (Jeffreys et al., 1990). As a result, any tissue will contain a majority of cells with the two progenitor minisatellite alleles, plus a diversity of cells containing various mutant new length alleles. While the proportion of cells harboring new mutant alleles can be significant, the heterogeneity in new mutant allele length will prevent their detection by conventional Southern blot hybridization. This however will not necessarily be true for PCR analyses operating at, or close to, the single DNA molecule level, a consideration of relevance to PCR analysis of minute forensic specimens. Also, it will not be true if a mutation occurs in a very early stem cell lineage, which will create a tissue either mosaic for original non-mutant cells plus cells descended from the same mutant progenitor cell (creating a tissue with three alleles) or tissue homogeneously composed of mutant cells. Such a process could result in the divergence of single locus profiles between different tissues of the same individual (e.g. blood and sperm), of obvious concern in forensic analysis. To date, we have seen only one instance of an early stem cell event in man (A.J.J., I. Patel, L. Henke, unpublished data), though very low-level mosaicism can be routinely detected in blood and sperm DNA (Jeffreys et al., 1990). In contrast, two highly variable and unstable minisatellites have been identified in mice at which a significant proportion of new mutations occur very early in development, within the first few cell divisions following fertilization, to produce 3-allele mice globally mosaic for similar numbers of original and new mutant cells. This process also creates mice with 3 alleles in the germline which segregate in a non-mendelian fashion into offspring, and can also generate differences in DNA profiles between for example embryonic and extra-embryonic tissues of the same individual (Kelly et al., 1989; 1991). It still remains to be seen whether this process is unique to mice, or can occasionally occur in man.

Investigation of new mutant minisatellite alleles also sheds light on the molecular processes generating these new length mutants. Early analyses involving the study of genetic markers closely flanking the new mutant allele (Wolff et al., 1989, 1990) or internal analysis of new deletion mutant alleles recovered by size-selection and single molecule PCR (Jeffreys et al., 1990) suggested that mutation seldom if ever involves crossing over between the tandem-repeat arrays of different alleles in an individual. However, more recent analysis combining the detection of new mutant alleles in pedigrees and in sperm with internal mapping by MVR-PCR (Jeffreys et al., 1991; unpublished data) has shown clear evidence that inter-allelic gene conversion is a major process in mutation at some minisatellite loci at least. This topic is discussed in more detail in the chapter on MVR-PCR in this book.

Amplification of minisatellites by PCR

Single locus minisatellite probes can be used to type as little as 10 ng human genomic DNA, corresponding to 1700 diploid cells. To improve sensitivity, we and others have shown that it is possible to amplify minisatellites by the polymerase chain reaction (PCR; Saiki et al., 1988), using amplimers designed from the unique sequence DNA flanking the minisatellite tandem repeat array (Jeffreys et al., 1988a, 1990; Boerwinkle et al., 1989; Horn et al., 1989). Subnanogram amounts of genomic DNA can be readily typed using this approach, and multiple hypervariable loci can be simultaneously amplified using appropriate combinations of amplimers. Alleles up to 10 kb long can be faithfully amplified and detected by Southern blot hybridization with the appropriate tandem-repeat probe. By limiting the number of cycles to the exponential phase of PCR, the yield of product becomes proportional to human DNA input, an important consideration in forensic analysis. If the PCR cycle number is increased, alleles up to 6 kb long can be directly visualized on ethidium bromide stained agarose gels, without any need for blotting/hybridization. However, at such high cycle numbers, the relationship between DNA input and product yield can be lost, and collapse of these tandem-repeat alleles to give complex profiles of spurious minisatellite products can occur, particularly with large and inefficiently-amplified alleles. Also, spurious DNA products may arise through mispriming elsewhere in the genome. PCR typing of minisatellites can also be extended with good efficiency and fidelity to the single molecule/single cell level (Jeffreys et al., 1988, 1990). While such sensitivity dramatically increases the potential range of forensic analysis to hair roots, saliva, urine and skeletal remains (see below), it also brings in formidable problems of sample contamination, both by carry-over of previous PCR products and by inadvertent contamination of evidentiary material with extraneous human cells (remember, for example, that saliva and nasal mucus can contain hundreds of cells per microlitre!). In casework the three human minisatellites most commonly typed by PCR ("Amp-FLPs") are ApoB (Boerwinkle et al., 1989), D17S5 (also known as D17S30; Horn et al., 1989) and D1S80 (Budowle et al., 1991). These minisatellites are relatively simple to study, because they amplify very easily on PCR (most alleles are shorter than 1 Kb) and can be detected following simple polyacrylamide gel electrophoresis by ethidium bromide or silver staining. However, their variability (and consequently their information content) is much lower than the much larger minisatellites conventionally typed by Southern blotting. In the Brazilian Caucasian population, the average heterozygotes of ApoB (13 alleles), D17S5 (13 alleles) and D1S80 (23 alleles) are respectively 0.82, 0.84 and 0.84 (S.D.J.P., unpublished observations). Correspondingly, mutations are very rare in these minisatellites. In spite of some claims to the contrary, absolute allele classification is not possible with Amp-FLPs due to microvariation in repeat unit type within alleles.

Microsatellites

Microsatellites – also known as simple sequence repeats or short tandem repeats (STR) – are genomic sequences that consists of a mono-, di-, tri- or tetra-nucleotide motif repeated in multiple tandem copies. Although microsatellites containing all nucleotide combinations have been identified, the class most abundant in the human genome contains a $(CA)_n \cdot (GT)_n$ dimer and is more frequently referred to as CA-repeat. The existence of CA-repeats, their presence in high copy number and their dispersion throughout the genomes of all eukaryotes tested were first demonstrated more than ten years ago (Hamada et al., 1982; Tautz and Renz, 1984). In the human genome there are approximately 50–100,000 copies of CA-repeats, which occur every 30 kb in euchromatic DNA (Stallings et al., 1991). In 1989 three groups simultaneously reported the detection by PCR of variability in these microsatellites (Weber and May, 1989; Litt and Luty, 1989; Tautz, 1989). They proved to be frequently polymorphic in CA repeat copy number, and provided PCR-typable markers with alleles in the 70–200 bp range. CA-repeats can be ascertained through computer-aided searches in known human DNA sequences in databases or through screening of libraries of short genomic sequences with a poly(dC-dA)·poly(dG·dT) probe. Weissenbach et al. (1992) used the latter strategy to identify 2,995 such microsatellites in the human genome. 84% (2,506) of these regions were successfully amplified and 93% (2,327) of the amplified markers were polymorphic. However, of a selected subset of 814 chromosomally mapped microsatellites, only 605 (74.4%) had heterozygozites above 0.7. These 814 mapped markers span 90% of the human genome at an average distance between adjacent markers of 5 cM. Thus they constitute an invaluable resource for genome studies. Nevertheless, the forensic informativeness of such loci is relatively low, with <90% heterozygosity, small number of alleles and "spiky" allele frequency distributions potentially vulnerable to inbreeding and ethnic group divergence effects. Although all allele length states, including alleles which differ by a single CA repeat, can be resolved by DNA sequencing gel analysis (Litt and Luty, 1989; Weber and May, 1989), rather fuzzy phenotypes consisting of several bands per allele are produced, apparently as a byproduct of the PCR reaction. This limits even further the forensic applicability of CA-repeats.

Another group of microsatellites involves tri- and tetranucleotide repeats. The first reported family of simple repeats, the GATA/GACA sequences, was originally identified and isolated from snake satellite DNA (Epplen et al., 1982). Subsequently it was found that these simple quadruplet repeats are present throughout the eukaryotes. Oligonucleotide probes made up of tandem arrays of these sequences generate multiband DNA fingerprints in humans (Ali et al., 1986). In 1990 Peake et al. amplified by PCR a GATA repeat region in intron 40 of the von Willebrand factor gene and showed that it was polymorphic. In contrast to the CA-repeats, there was no need for resolution of the PCR products in sequencing gels, since alleles differed by four base pairs. Thus, the fuzzy bands that complicate the analysis of 2 bp microsatellites were not a problem. Similar results had been obtained in 1989 by Yandell and Dryja, working with another tetranucleotide repeat, $(CTTT)_n$, closely linked to the retinoblastoma gene in chromosome 13.

Trimeric and tetrameric tandem repeats were shown to occur every 300 to 500 kb in the human X chromosome and appear to be interspersed at this frequency (approximately 10,000 loci) throughout the genome (Edwards et al., 1991). Typing of these regions, particularly the tetranucleotide repeats, has great potential usefulness because they combine the short allele sizes, essential for the study of degraded DNA samples (see below), with the analytical simplicity of Amp-FLPs. Many such polymorphisms have now been described, including a particularly useful one located in the short arm of the Y chromosome (Santos et al., 1993). Unfortunately, as described above for the CA-repeats, the forensic informativeness of these loci is often limited by low variability. However, at least one hypervariable tetranucleotide region has already been described, namely an $(AAAG)_n$ stretch located at a human β-actin-related processed pseudogene (Polymeropoulos et al., 1992). This has an average heterozygosity of 0.94 and more than 23 alleles. It is very likely that by intensive search, other highly variable microsatellites will be discovered. An alternative way to increase the informativeness of these polymorphisms is to perform the typing of two closely linked loci, thus obtaining a large number of haplotypes. For instance, we have amplified simultaneously by PCR two GATA-repeat polymorphic sites that are physically separated by 212 base pairs in intron 40 of the von Willebrand factor gene (Pena et al., 1993). Although the average heterozygosites of the individual loci were only 0.72 and 0.78 respectively, the diversity value was 0.93 at haplotype level.

Forensic analysis of degraded DNA

Frequently, the DNA recovered from forensic specimens is too degraded to allow single locus minisatellite analysis, either by Southern blotting procedures or by PCR. The recent development of PCR-typable DNA marker systems based on much shorter segments of human DNA provides a solution to this problem. Saiki et al. (1986) and Higuchi and Blake (1989) have developed a marker system based on the polymorphic HLA-DQα locus, involving PCR amplification of a short DNA segment followed by allele classification by dot-blot hybridization with a range of allele-specific oligonucleotide probes. This system can currently distinguish 6 alleles and thus 21 different genotypes. However, only one locus is analyzed, allowing exclusion but not definitive inclusion in casework analysis. As discussed above, another potentially very useful set of markers has been developed from short simple sequence regions or "microsatellites", particularly tetranucleotide tandem repeats which are simpler to analyse. The third class of marker system is based on DNA sequence analysis of the highly variable control region of mitochondrial DNA (Greenberg et al., 1983), which should prove to be particularly useful for minute degraded DNA samples where the yield of nuclear DNA is too small for typing; in such samples, multicopy mitochondrial DNA may still survive in PCR-typable amounts. The amplification and sequencing of the control region of mtDNA can be automated (Sullivan et al., 1991; Hopgood et al., 1992). It should be noted that mitochondrial DNA is strictly maternally inherited and can give no information in paternity analyses. However it is extremely useful for the identification of human remains from comparative studies with matrilineal relatives.

One area of considerable forensic and anthropological interest is the possibility of typing DNA from skeletal and dental remains. Mitochondrial DNA has been shown to be amplifiable from teeth (Ginther et al., 1992) and from bones, even ancient ones (Hagelberg et al., 1990). Several groups have recently extended this analysis to nuclear DNA markers in skeletal remains exhumed several years after interment. As expected, most of the DNA recovered (usually >99%) is of non-human origin, and presumably arises from bacteria and fungi in the remains. The human DNA component, detected by hybridization with an Alu probe, is generally severely degraded. Despite this degradation, contamination with non-human DNA and the presence of PCR inhibitors in skeletal DNA extracts, typing of nuclear microsatellite markers has proved possible. Furthermore, in several cases analyzed to date, the bone DNA typing information has been shown to be authentic (Hagelberg et al., 1991; S.D.J.P. unpubl. data).

Future perspectives

The scientific and legal framework of DNA typing in forensic and legal medicine has now been firmly established. A summary of the available "classical" marker systems and their range of applicability is given in Tab. 1. There are four major areas of future development. First, using the extreme sensitivity of PCR, to what extent can DNA testing be extended from the traditional forensic samples such as blood, semen stains and vaginal swabs to more esoteric samples such as saliva traces (for example on blackmail letters) and skeletal remains? Second, what improvements in DNA marker systems and marker detection are possible? An ideal marker would perhaps have the following features: (a) alleles limited in size to $100-500$ bp, such that all alleles can be efficiently amplified by PCR, even in degraded DNA, (b) all allelic length states resolvable, such that precise allelic classification is possible, (c) large numbers of alleles, with no common allele, (d) a quantifiable and sufficiently high mutation rate (perhaps in the range $10^{-2} - 10^{-3}$ per gamete) to ensure insulation against genetic drift effects. No such marker has yet been identified, and may actually not exist in the human genome. One novel alternative to "classical" typing based on allele size is the use of MVR-PCR to develop digital DNA typing systems based on the analysis of repeat unit sequence variation *within* minisatellite alleles; this is discussed in this book in the chapter on MVR-PCR.

Table 1. Summary of available "classical" typing systems and their range of applicability

		Technical Simplicity	Informativeness	Genotype	Paternity Testing	Degraded DNA	Mixed Samples
Probe Systems	Multilocus Probes (DNA Fingerprints)	+	+++	–	+++	–	–
	Single locus probes	++	++	(+)	++	–	++
PCR Systems	Minisatellites	++	+	+	+	++	+
	Microsatellites (2-bp repeats)	++	+	++	(+)	++	+
	Microsatellites (3- and 4-bp repeats)	+++	+	++	+	++	++
	HLA DQα	+++	(+)	+++	–	++	+
	Mitochondrial DNA	+	++	+++	–	++	–

In terms of DNA marker detection, highly sensitive non-isotopic probes detected by enhanced chemiluminescence are rapidly replacing radioisotope-based detection systems. Many aspects of PCR-based typing should be amenable to automation, particularly using automated gel electrophoretic or micro-capillary electrophoretic analysis of fluorescence-tagged PCR products. The third area of development concerns databasing of criminal offenders or potentially entire populations, which raises considerable problems, not only of a social and legal nature but also in relationship to standardization of DNA markers and analytical procedures. The final area relates to the potential of human molecular genetics to deliver DNA markers capable of giving phenotypic information from forensic DNA samples where there is no suspect; such information might include sex (already testable), ethnicity, and visual appearance (e.g. hair colour, eye colour, stature). The latter characters, in particular, present a far-from-trivial problem and will require a profound revolution in our ability to dissect the molecular genetics of quantitative characters in man; indeed such DNA analyses may eventually prove in practice to be impossible.

Acknowledgements

A. J. J. is a Howard Hughes International Research Scholar. Research was supported by grants to A. J. J. from the Medical Research Council, the Lister Institute, the Wolfson Foundation and the Royal Society and to S. D. J. P. from CNP$_q$ and FAPEMIG. The 33.6 and 33.15 minisatellite probes described in this paper are the subject of Patent Applications, and commercial enquiries should be addressed to Cellmark Diagnostics, 8 Blacklands Way, Abingdon Business Park, Abingdon, Oxfordshire, OX14 1DY, UK.

References

Ali S, Muller CR, Epplen JT (1986) DNA fingerprinting by oligonucleotide probes specific for simple repeats. Hum Genet 74: 239–243

Armour JAL, Patel I, Thein SL, Fey MF, Jeffreys AJ (1989a) Analysis of somatic mutations at human minisatellite loci in tumours and cell lines. Genomics 4: 328–334

Armour JAL, Wong Z, Wilson V, Royle NJ, Jeffreys AJ (1989b) Sequences flanking the repeat arrays of human minisatellites: association with tandem and dispersed repeat elements. Nucleic Acids Res 17: 4925–4935

Armour JAL, Povey S, Jeremiah S, Jeffreys AJ (1990) Systematic cloning of human minisatellites from ordered array charomid libraries. Genomics 8: 501–512

Balazs, I (1993) Population genetics of 14 ethnic groups using phenotypic data from VNTR loci. *In* Pena SDJ, Chakraborty R, Epplen JT, Jeffreys AJ (Eds), DNA fingerprinting: State of the Science. Basel: Birkhäuser Verlag

Bellamy RJ, Inglehearn CF, Jalili IK, Jeffreys AJ, Bhattacharya SS (1991) Increased band sharing in DNA fingerprints of an inbred human population. Hum Genet 87: 341–347

Boerwinkle E, Xiong W, Fourest E, Chan L (1989) Rapid typing of tandemly repeated hypervariable loci by the polymerase chain reaction: application to the apolipoprotein b 3′ hypervariable region. Proc Nat Acad Sci USA 86: 212–216

Brookfield JFY (1989) Analysis of DNA fingerprinting data in cases of disputed paternity. IMA J of Mathematics Applied in Medicine Biology 6: 111–131

Budowle B (1993) VNTR population data from various reference groups and the significance of application to identity testing. *In* Pena SDJ, Chakraborty R, Epplen JT, Jeffreys AJ (Eds), DNA Fingerprinting: State of the Science. Basel: Birkhäuser Verlag

Budowle B, Chakraborty R, Giusti AM, Eisenberg AJ, Allen RRC (1991) Analysis of the VNTR locus D1S80 by the PCR followed by high-resolution PAGE. Am J Hum Genet 48: 137–144

Chakraborty R, Jin L (1993) A unified approach to study hypervariable polymorphisms: statistical considerations of determining relatedness and population distances. *In* Pena SDJ, Chakraborty R, Epplen JT, Jeffreys AJ (Eds), DNA Fingerprinting: State of the Science. Basel: Birkhäuser Verlag

Chakraborty R, Kidd KK (1991) The utility of DNA typing in forensic work. Science 254: 1735–1739

Collick A, Dunn MG, Jeffreys AJ (1991) Minisatellite-binding protein Msbp-1 is a sequence-specific single-stranded DNA-binding protein. Nucleic Acids Res 19: 6399–6404

Collick A, Jeffreys AJ (1990) Detection of a novel minisatellite-specific DNA-binding protein. Nucleic Acids Res 18: 625–629

Edwards A, Civitello A, Hammond HA, Caskey CT (1991) DNA typing and genetic mapping with trimeric and tetrametric tandem repeats. Am J Hum Genet 49: 746–756

Edwards A, Hammond HA, Jin L, Caskey CT, Chakraborty R (1992) Genetic variation at five trimeric and tetrameric tandem repeat loci in four human population groups. Genomics 12: 241–253

Evett IW, Werrett DJ, Buckleton JS (1989a) Paternity calculations from DNA multilocus profiles. J Forensic Sci Soc 29: 249–254

Evett IW, Werrett DJ, Smith AFM (1989b) Probabilistic analysis of DNA profiles. J Forensic Sci Soc 29: 191–196

Fowler SJ, Gill P, Werrett DJ, Higgs DR (1988) Individual specific DNA fingerprints from a hypervariable region probe: alpha-globin 3'HVR. Hum Genet 79: 142–146

Gill P, Werrett DJ (1987) Exclusion of a man charged with murder by DNA fingerprinting. Forensic Science International 35: 145–148

Ginther C, Issel-Tarrver L, King M-C (1992) Identifying individuals by sequencing mitochondrial DNA from teeth. Nature Genetics 2: 135–138

Greenberg BD, Newbold JE, Sugino A (1983) Intraspecific nucleotide-sequence variability surrounding the origin of replication in human mitochondrial DNA. Gene 21: 33–49

Hagelberg E, Gray IC, Jeffreys AJ (1991) Identification of the skeletal remains of a murder victim by DNA analysis. Nature 352: 427–429

Hagelberg E, Sykes B, Hedges R (1990) Ancient bone DNA amplified. Nature 342: 485

Hamada H, Petrino MG, Kakunaga T (1982) A novel repeated element with Z-DNA forming potential is widely found in evolutionary diverse eukaryotic genomes. Proc Natl Acad Sci 79: 6465–6469

Higuchi R, Blake ET (1989) Applications of the polymerase chain reaction in forensic science. *In* Banbury Report 32: DNA Technology, Forensic Science (eds J Ballantyne, G Sensabaugh, J Witkowski; Cold Spring Harbor Laboratory Press, 1989) pp 265–281

Hill WG (1986) DNA fingerprint analysis in immigration test-cases. Nature 322: 290–291

Home Office (1988) DNA profiling in immigration casework. Report of a pilot trial by the Home Office and Foreign and Commonwealth Office (Home Office, London)

Hopgood R, Sullivan KM, Gill P (1992) Strategies for automated sequencing of human mitochondrial DNA directly from PCR products. BioTechniques 13: 82–92

Horn GT, Richards B, Klinger KW (1989) Amplification of a highly polymorphic VNTR segment by the polymerase chain reaction. Nucleic Acids Res 17: 2140

Jeffreys AJ, Brookfield JFY, Semeonoff R (1985a) Positive identification of an immigration test-case using human DNA fingerprints. Nature 317: 818–819

Jeffreys AJ, Wilson V, Thein SL (1985c) Individual-specific "fingerprints" of human DNA. Nature 316: 76–79

Jeffreys AJ, Wilson V, Thein SL, Weatherall DJ, Ponder BAJ (1986) DNA "fingerprints" and segregation analysis of multiple markers in human pedigrees. Am J Hum Genet 39: 11–24

Jeffreys AJ, Wilson V, Kelly R, Taylor BA, Bulfield G (1987) Mouse DNA "fingerprints": analysis of chromosome localization and germ-line stability of hypervariable loci in recombinant inbred strains. Nucleic Acids Res 15: 2823–2836

Jeffreys AJ, Royle NJ, Wilson V, Wong Z (1988a) Spontaneous mutation rates to new length alleles at tandem-repetitive hypervariable loci in human DNA. Nature 332: 278–281

Jeffreys AJ, Wilson V, Neumann R, Keyte J (1988b) Amplification of human minisatellites by the polymerase chain reaction: towards DNA fingerprinting of single cells. Nucleic Acids Res 16: 10953–10971

Jeffreys AJ, Neumann R, Wilson V (1990) Repeat unit sequence variation in minisatellites: a novel source of DNA polymorphism for studying variation and mutation by single molecule analysis. Cell 60: 473–485

Jeffreys AJ, McLeod A, Tamaki K, Neil DL, Monckton DG (1991) Minisatellite repeat coding as a digital approach to DNA typing. Nature 354: 204–209

Jeffreys AJ, Turner M, Debenham P (1991) The efficiency of multilocus DNA fingerprinting probes for individualization and establishment of family relationship, determined from extensive casework. Am J Hum Genet 48: 824–840

Julier C, de Gouyon B, Georges M, Guenet J-L, Nakamura Y, Avner P, Lathrop GM (1990) Minisatellite linkage maps in the mouse by cross-hybridization with human probes containing tandem repeats. Proc Nat Acad Sci USA 87: 4585–4589

Kelly R, Bulfield G, Collick A, Gibbs M, Jeffreys AJ (1989) Characterization of a highly unstable mouse minisatellite locus: evidence for somatic mutation during early development. Genomics 5: 844–856

Kelly R, Gibbs M, Collick A, Jeffreys AJ (1991) Spontaneous mutation at the hypervariable mouse minisatellites locus Ms6-hm: flanking DNA sequence and analysis of germline and early somatic events. Proc R Soc Lond B 245: 235–245

Knowlton RG, Brown VA, Braman JC, Barker D, Schumm JW, Murray C, Takvorian T, Ritz J, Donnis-Keller H (1986) Use of highly polymorphic DNA probes for genotype analysis following bone marrow transplantation. Blood 68: 378–385

Lander ES (1989) DNA fingerprinting on trial. Nature 339: 501–505

Lander ES (1991) Research on DNA typing catching up with courtroom application. Am J Hum Genet 48: 819–823

Lewontin RC, Hartl DL (1991) Population genetics in forensic DNA typing. Science 254: 1745–1751

Litt M, Luty JA (1989) A hypervariable microsatellite revealed by in vitro amplification of a dinucleotide repeat within the cardiac muscle actin gene. Am J Hum Genet 44: 397–401

Nakamura Y, Leppert M, O'Connell P, Wolff R, Holm T, Culver M, Martin C, Fujimoto E, Hoff M, Kumlin E, White R (1987) Variable number of tandem repeat (VNTR) markers for human gene mapping. Science 235: 1616–1622

Nakamura Y, Carlson M, Krapcho K, Kanamori M, White R (1988) New approach for isolation of VNTR markers. Am J Hum Genet 43: 854–859

National Research Council (1992) DNA Technology and Forensic Science. National Academy Press, Washington DC

Peake IRRR, Bowen D, Bignell P, Liddell MB, Sadler JE, Standen G, Bloom AL (1990) Family studies and prenatal diagnosis in severe von Willebrand disease by polymerase chain reaction amplification of a variable number tandem repeat region of the von Willebrand factor gene. Blood 76: 555–561

Pena SDJ, Macedo AM, Braga VMM, Rumjanek FD, Simpson AJG (1990) F10, the gene for the glycine-rich major eggshell protein of Schistosoma mansoni recognizes a family of hypervariable minisatellites in the human genome. Nucl Acids Res 18: 7466

Pena SDJ, Souza KT, Andrade M, Chakraborty R (1993) Allelic associations of two polymorphic microsatellites in intron 40 of the human von Willebrand factor gene. Submitted for publication

Ploos van Amstel HK, Reitsma P (1991) Tetranucleotide repeat polymorphism in the vWF gene. Nucl Acids Res 18: 4957

Riggins GL, Lokey LK, Chastain JL, Leiner HA, Sherman SL, Wilkinson KD, Warren ST (1992) Human genes containing polymorphic trinucleotide repeats. Nature Genetics 2: 186–191

Royle NJ, Clarkson RE, Wong Z, Jeffreys AJ (1988) Clustering of hypervariable minisatellites in the proterminal regions of human autosomes. Genomics 3: 352–360

Saiki RK, Bugawan TL, Horn GT, Mullis KB, Erlich HA (1986) Analysis of enzymatically amplified β-globin and HLA-DQα DNA with allele-specific oligonucleotide probes. Nature 324: 163–166

Saiki RK, Gelfand DH, Stoffel S, Scharf SJ, Higuchi R, Horn GT, Mullis KB, Erlich HA (1988) Primer-directed enzymatic amplification of DNA with a thermostable DNA polymerase. Science 239: 487–491

Santos FR, Pena SDJ, Epplen JT (1993) Genetic and population study of a Y-linked tetranucleotide repeat polymorphism with a single non-isotopic technique. Hum Genet 90: in press

Smith JC, Anwar R, Riley J, Jenner D, Markham AF, Jeffreys AJ (1990) Highly polymorphic minisatellite sequences: allele frequencies and mutation rates for five locus specific probes in a Caucasian population. J For Sci Soc 30: 19–32

Stallings RL, Ford AF, Nelson D, Torney DC, Hildebrand CE, Moyzis RK (1991) Evolution and distribution of $(GT)_n$ repetitive sequences in mammalian genomes. Genomics 10: 807–815

Sullivan KM, Hopgood R, Lang B, Gill P (1991) Automated amplification and sequencing of human mitochondrial DNA. Electrophoresis 12: 17–21

Swallow DM, Gendler S, Griffith B, Corney G, Taylor-Papadimitriou J, Bramwell ME (1987) The human tumour-associated epithelium mucins are coded by an expressed hypervariable gene locus PUM. Nature 328: 82–84

Tautz D (1989) Hypervariability of simple sequences as a general source for polymorphic DNA markers. Nucl Acids Res 17: 6463–6471

Tautz D, Renz M (1984) Simple sequences are ubiquitous repetitive components of eukaryotic genomes. Nucl Acids Res 12: 4127–4138

US Congress Office of Technology Assessment (1990) Genetic witness: forensic uses of DNA tests, OTA-BA-438 (Washington DC: US Government Printing Office)

Vassart G, Georges M, Monsieur R, Brocas H, Lequarre AS, Christophe D (1987) A sequence in M13 phage detects hypervariable minisatellites in human and animal DNA. Science 235: 683–684

Yamazaki H, Nomoto S, Mishima Y, Kominami R (1992) A 35-kDa protein binding to a cytosine-rich strand of hypervariable minisatellite DNA. J Biol Chem 267: 12311–12316

Yandell DW, Dryja TP (1989) Detection of DNA sequence polymorphisms by enzymatic amplification and direct genomic sequencing. Am J Hum Genet 45: 547–555

Wahls WP, Swenson G, Moore PD (1991) Two hypervariable minisatellite DNA binding proteins. Nucleic Acids Res 19: 3269–3274

Weissenbach J, Gyaypay G, Dib C, Vignal A, Morisette J, Milasseau P, Vaysseiz G, Lathrop M (1992) A second generation linkage map of the human genome. Nature 359: 794–801

Wrogemann K, Biancalana V, Devys D, Imbert G, Trottier Y, Mandel J-L (1993) Microsatellites and disease: a new paradigm. *In* Pena SDJ, Chakraborty R, Epplen JT, Jeffreys AJ (Eds), DNA Fingerprinting: State of the Science. Basel: Birkhäuser Verlag

DNA Fingerprinting: State of the Science
ed. by S. D. J. Pena, R. Chakraborty, J. T. Epplen & A. J. Jeffreys

Notes on the definition and nomenclature of tandemly repetitive DNA sequences

Diethard Tautz

Zoologisches Institut der Universität München, Luisenstr. 14, 80333 München, Germany

Summary
Tandemly repetitive DNA is a major component of all eukaryotic genomes. This fact has been known for almost 30 years and research on this class of DNA is still being done. Its biology and evolution are therefore now becoming fairly well understood. DNA-fingerprint techniques rely very much on this knowledge. However, the large amount of research on these sequences has inevitably led to a large number of different concepts and theories about their nature. This has also resulted in some confusion as to the nomenclature. The following notes are intended to resolve this confusion somewhat and to give some definitions for the major classes of tandemly repetitive DNA.

Satellite sequences

Satellites were named before they were known to consist of tandemly repetitive DNA. They were found when the first buoyant density gradients were run on ultracentrifuges. Genomic DNA forms a band in such gradients, the position of which depends on the G-C content of the DNA. It was quickly noted that prokaryotic genomic DNA would normally form a single peak, while eukaryotic DNA would either show a very broad peak, or even multiple peaks. The extra peaks found were called "satellite" peaks and the corresponding DNA "satellite" DNA. Renaturation kinetics with such satellites showed that these peaks consisted of highly repetitive DNA, usually of millions of tandem repeats of a relatively short sequence motif (reviewed in Britten and Kohne, 1968). Thus, the explanation why these DNAs form satellite peaks in the gradients is that their sequence complexity is very low and their average GC-content can therefore deviate easily from that of the rest of the genome. However, not all satellites need to show such extra peaks, since they may equally well have the same GC-content as the rest of the genome. Satellites of this type have been called "cryptic satellites" since they lie within the bulk of the DNA in the gradients.

Satellite DNA has become a synonym for tandemly repeated DNA sequences with repetition grades of $10^3 - 10^7$. Usually, the repeat units have a length of up to 300 bp, but they may sometimes be also larger. Satellites with very short repeat units (2–6 bp) have sometimes been named "simple sequence satellites". This nomenclature has unfortunately led others to call all satellites "simple sequence DNA" (e.g. Lewin, 1990). This leads to some confusion, since "simple sequence DNA" is also being used for a different class of sequences (see below). I would therefore propose that the term "satellite DNA" is only used for sequence classes which fall under the following definition:

Definition: Satellite-DNA

Degree of repetition: 10^3–10^7 at each locus

Number of loci: usually few, at most one or two per chromosome for a given type of repeat unit; the different loci may have locus-specific repeat variants

Repeat unit length: two (one?) to several thousand bp

Location: usually in the heterochromatin, mainly in centromeres

Minisatellites

Minisatellites are distinctly different from satellites in that each cluster has only a moderate degree of repetition. Furthermore, the length of the repeat units is apparently also somewhat more restricted and they are more dispersed throughout the genome, though they tend to cluster towards telomeric regions, at least in humans (Royle et al., 1988). Minisatellites were first detected by chance by various groups, and it was quickly noted that such regions may be associated with length polymorphisms (e.g. Bell et al., 1982). Alec Jeffreys was the first to discover that they are a general phenomenon and gave them the generic name "minisatellites" (Jeffreys et al., 1985a). Most importantly, he showed that they were useful for a technique that he called "DNA fingerprinting"* (Jeffreys et al., 1985b). It was originally suggested that many minisatellites share some sequence similarities, namely a so-called "core sequence" (Jeffreys et al., 1985a). This sequence is part of the repeat unit of each minisatellite locus and appears to have some similarity with the Chi-recombination signal known from *E.coli*. However, even though there are good arguments for the (functional) existence of such a core sequence in minisatellites, the issue is not finally settled. Thus, the presence or absence of a core sequence is probably not a good basis for a definition of this class of sequences.

*Nowadays a distinction is made between "DNA fingerprinting" and "DNA profiling". "DNA fingerprinting" is used for applications where multiple loci are revealed at the same time, e.g. when using multilocus probes. These are potentially useful in uniquely identifying an individual, but they do not allow to infer its genotype. In contrast, single locus probes usually allow to score the genotypes, but are less likely to discriminate (related) individuals unequivocally. It was therefore suggested to use the term "DNA profiling" for this latter type of application (Jeffreys et al., 1991a).

Nakamura et al. (1987a) have independently found a number of minisatellite loci and have shown that they are useful to reveal polymorphisms. They have suggested a different name for this class of sequences, namely "variable number of tandem repeat" loci, or in short "VNTR" loci. This term is more descriptive and more generally applicable. However, since any locus showing variable tandem repetition could be interpreted as falling within this broad definition, it does not appear to be a good choice for a limited class of sequences.

I should like to suggest therefore that the term "minisatellites", rather than VNTR, be used for the class of sequences defined below, in particular since the term "minisatellites" is a proper name and it has been derived from a related, existing name for a class of sequences, namely from "satellites".

Definition: Minisatellites

Degree of repetition: two to several hundred at each locus

Number of loci: probably many thousands, but each locus showing a distinctive repeat unit

Repeat unit length: 9 (or shorter?) – 100 bp

Location: interspersed, but often clustered in telomeric regions

Simple sequences

Some types of simple sequences were indirectly detected already in the 1970's and became known as "polypyrimidinic stretches" (Birnboim and Straus, 1975) although they were not recognized to be part of a more general class of sequences in eukaryotic genomes before the advent of sequencing techniques. Other subclasses of simple sequences were also independently described. One of these were the GATA or GACA repeats, which were found by crosshybridization with a simple sequence satellite from the heterogametic chromosome of a snake (Epplen et al., 1982). A substantial amount of work has focussed on the question whether these sequences might have a specific role in sex-determination, but convincing proof has not been obtained and any effects seen in these experiments appear now to be incidental (Levinson et al., 1985). Another class of simple sequence repeats, the GT repeats, were detected at a time when it was shown that DNA may form a left handed helix, so-called Z-DNA (Hamada et al., 1982). Z-DNA forms preferentially in tracts of alternating purine-pyrimidine nucleotides such as GT repeats. This raised speculations that GT repeats may have something to do with Z-DNA formation and indirectly with gene-regulation or recombination, though convincing proof for any of such functions was not found.

However, it soon became clear that not only the few classes of simple sequences mentioned above existed in eukaryotic genomes, but that apparently all other types of simple sequence repeats occurred as well (Tautz and Renz, 1984). They were therefore defined as a new general class of sequences and the generic name "simple sequences" was given. This designation was derived from the term "simple sequence satellites" (see above) but implied that they were different from these types of satellites.

Simple sequences were suggested to arise by slippage mechanisms which implied that they should be polymorphic (Tautz and Renz, 1984; Levinson and Gutman, 1987a) but it was not before the advent of PCR that this could be shown. However, with the use of PCR, it was quickly clear that simple sequence loci have a number of advantages for DNA fingerprinting (or DNA profiling) and genome mapping (Weber and May, 1989; Litt and Luty, 1989; Tautz, 1989). This has caused a revived interest in this class of sequences. Litt and Luty (1989) suggested therefore a new name, namely "microsatellites". This term is of course a homage to the ingenious term "minisatellites" chosen by Alec Jeffreys, and it is certainly a good name for this class of sequences. However, this puts us into a situation where we have two names for the same class of sequences; the term "simple sequences" which was applied before mini-satellites were known and with the name "microsatellites" which is nowadays the better name, since it establishes the connection to mini-satellites and DNA fingerprinting. To make things worse, Edwards et al. (1991) have come up with yet another name, namely "short tandem repeat" or "STR" loci. However, the acronym "STR" is alternatively used for the term "synthetic tandem repeats" which have been shown to be useful for DNA fingerprinting (Vergnaud et al., 1991). To avoid further confusion, I would suggest therefore to stick either to the original name "simple sequences" or to "microsatellites", whereby the latter name is the most widely used nowadays.

Definition: Simple sequences or microsatellites
Degree of repetition: five to about hundred at each locus
Number of loci: 10^4-10^5 for short motifs, less for longer motifs
Repeat unit length: one to six bp
Location: more or less randomly scattered throughout the genome; frequently also in transcription units

Cryptically simple sequences

In large sequencing projects one frequently finds regions of DNA which are composed of internal repeats which are not necessarily in tandem and which can be intermingled with other types of repeats. Such regions were called "cryptically simple sequences" (Tautz et al., 1986) since they hide within the bulk of the DNA. It is however difficult to provide a unique definition for such sequences, since it is not clear what the upper and lower bounds for such a definition would be. There may be a continuum between simple sequences, cryptically simple sequences and random sequences. In fact, if one analyzes eukaryotic genomes with appropriate computer algorithms, one finds that probably most of the genome is cryptically simple, at least at a low degree (Tautz et al., 1986; Smillie and Bains, 1990). Cryptically simple sequences have not yet been systematically exploited for DNA fingerprinting, though it has been shown at least for *Drosophila* that they can be polymorphic in populations (Kreitman, 1983; Tautz, 1989).

Tandemly repeated genes

The classes discussed so far are in all probability non-functional DNA sequences in the sense that they do not exist because selection for a function has created them. This does however not preclude that they may have effects on some functions in some cases. There are on the other hand tandemly repetitive DNA elements with a clear genetic function, namely the tandemly repeated genes. Best known are the repeats coding for the ribosomal RNAs and for the histone genes. These tandemly repeated regions are shaped by the same genomic turnover mechanisms as the other classes of repeats discussed. They provide therefore also a potential source for polymorphisms which has not yet been systematically tapped. Experiments are however under way to make use of the information hidden in these classes of sequences (Schlötterer and Tautz, in prep.).

Other classes?

It is not yet clear whether all phenomena of tandemly repetitive DNA in eukaryotic genomes can be described within the framework of the sequence classes listed above. It seems possible that further classes may have to be defined. Jörg Epplen has shown that simple sequence oligonucleotide probes reveal DNA fingerprint patterns that are very similar to those obtained with minisatellite probes, i.e. polymorphic DNA fragments with a size of up to 20 kb or even larger (Epplen et al. 1991). It is however as yet unclear how the polymorphism of these fragments is generated. Zischler et al. (1992) have analysed such loci in more detail and found long stretches of various simple sequence motifs mixed together. It appears that these loci may have been derived from simple sequence or microsatellite loci, but undergone further expansion processes which are more reminiscent of minisatellites. Thus, in strict terms, such loci would not fall under either definition. It must therefore remain open whether it will be necessary to define a new class for them. I would suggest that they be given a generic name, if it could be shown that a particular genomic mechanism creates these types of loci. For the time being, though, they may be called VNTR loci, since this is the most neutral term (see above) and the probes that are used to detect them sould be called "simple sequence (oligonucleotide) probes".

Nakamura et al. (1987b) have characterized a locus in humans which they called "midisatellite". This locus is apparently too large to fit the minisatellite definition and too small for a true satellite. However, the repeat units found are very reminiscent of minisatellites and one could treat this locus therefore as a particularly large minisatellite.

It should be generally noted that the upper and lower bounds of the above definitions are of course not absolutely fixed and that there are also overlaps between the definitions. There will always be extreme cases of loci which fit more than one definition. Yet I believe that the definitions provide some guidelines for assigning particular loci to particular sequence classes. They should also discourage the invention of new names, unless one can make a case for a truely new class of sequences.

Conclusion

The many different types of tandemly repetitive DNA elements reflect the general propensity of genomic DNA to become internally repetitive, a propensity which is due to internal genomic mechanisms such as unequal crossover and slippage (Smith, 1976; Stephan, 1989; Tautz et al., 1986). These mechanisms produce length polymorphisms which can be exploited in DNA fingerprinting techniques. This general propensity is probably the reason why it is possible to use basically any internally repetitive DNA probe to produce DNA fingerprint patterns. Accordingly, even random short oligonucleotides which are ligated together to yield tandem repeat probes can reveal polymorphic bands (Vergnaud et al., 1991).

The understanding of how the different classes of tandemly repetitive DNA-elements arise and how they produce polymorphisms is continuously growing (Levinson and Gutman, 1987b; Jeffreys et al., 1990; Jeffreys et al., 1991b; Schlötterer and Tautz, 1992). However, much of this understanding is still based on speculation and theory rather than on sufficient experimental proof. In particular, the question which of the genomic mechanisms – mitotic recombination, meiotic recombination, gene conversion, replication slippage, DNA repair mechanisms or others – are most important for the shaping of each of the different classes of tandemly repetitive DNA elements is still largely open. These questions may not seem to be so important for those who simply want to apply DNA fingerprinting techniques. However, a detailed analysis of DNA fingerprint data may eventually require some assumptions on how the polymorphisms arise and how they have to be interpreted in the population context. Further research in this direction will therefore be necessary.

Acknowledgements
I should like to thank Hans Zischler for his comments on the manuscript and Sergio Pena for his patience and encouragement.

References

Bell GI, Selby MJ, Rutter WJ (1982) The highly polymorphic region near the human insulin gene is composed of simple tandemly repeating sequences. Nature 295: 31–35

Birnboim HC, Straus NA (1975) DNA from eukaryotic cells contains unusually long pyrimidine sequences. Can J Biochem 53: 640–643

Britten RJ, Kohne DE (1968) Repeated sequences in DNA. Science 161: 529–540

Edwards A, Civitello A, Hammond HA, Caskey CT (1991) DNA typing and genetic mapping with trimeric and tetrameric tandem repeats. Am J Hum Genet 49: 746–756

Epplen JT, McCarrey JR, Sutou S, Ohno S (1982) Base sequence of a cloned snake W-chromosome DNA fragment and identification of a male specific putative mRNA in the mouse. Proc Natl Acad Sci USA 79: 3798–3802

Epplen JT, Ammer H, Epplen C, Kammerbauer C, Mitreiter R, Roewer L, Schwaiger W, Steimle V, Zischler H, Albert E, Andreas A, Beyermann B, Meyer W, Buitkamp J, Nanda I, Schmid M, Nürnberg P, Pena SDJ, Pöche H, Sprecher W, Schartl M, Weising K, Yassouridis A (1991) Oligo-nucleotide fingerprinting using simple repeat motifs: a convenient ubiquitously applicable method to detect hypervariability for multiple purposes. *In* Burke T, Dolf G, Jeffreys AJ, Wolff R(Eds), DNA Fingerprinting: Approaches and Applications (pp. 50–69). Birkhäuser Verlag, Basel

Hamada H, Petrino MG, Kakunaga T (1982) A novel repeated element with Z-DNA forming potential is widely found in evolutionary diverse eukaryotic genomes. Proc Natl Acad Sci USA 79: 6465–6469

Jeffreys AJ, Wilson V, Thein SW (1985a) Hypervariable minisatellite regions in human DNA. Nature 314: 67–73

Jeffreys AJ, Wilson V, Thein SL (1985b) Individual-specific fingerprints of human DNA. Nature 316: 76–79

Jeffreys AJ, Neumann R, Wilson V (1990) Repeat unit sequence variation in minisatellites: a novel source of DNA polymorphism for studying variation and mutation by single molecule analysis. Cell 60: 473–485

Jeffreys AJ, Royle NJ, Patel J, Armour AL, MacLeod A, Collick A, Gray IC, Neumann R, Gibbs M, Crosier M, Hill M, Signer E, Monckton D (1991a). Principles and recent advances in human DNA fingerprinting. *In:* Burke T, Dolf G, Jeffreys AJ, Wolff R (Ed.), DNA Fingerprinting: Approaches and Applications (pp. 1–19) Basel: Birkhäuser Verlag

Jeffreys AJ, MacLeod A, Tamaki K, Neil DL, Monckton DG (1991b). Minisatellite repeat coding as a digital approach to DNA typing. Nature 354: 204–209

Kreitman M (1983) Nucleotide polymorphism at the Adh locus of Drosophila melanogaster. Nature 304: 412–417

Levinson G, Marsh JL, Epplen JT, Gutman GA (1985) Cross-hybridizing snake satellite, Drosophila and mouse DNA sequences may have arisen independently. Mol Biol Evol 2: 494–504

Levinson G, Gutman GA (1987a) Slipped-strand mispairing: a major mechanism for DNA sequence evolution. Mol Biol Evol 4: 203–221

28

Levinson G, Gutman GA (1987b) High frequencies of short frameshifts in poly-CA/TG tandem repeats borne by bacteriophage M13 in Escherichia coli K-12. Nucleic Acids Res 15: 5323–5338

Lewin B (1990) Genes IV, Oxford University Press, Oxford

Litt M, Luty JA (1989) A hypervariable microsatellite revealed by in vitro amplification of a dinucleotide repeat within the cardiac muscle actin gene. Am J Hum Genet 44: 397–401

Nakamura Y, Leppert M, O'Connell P, Wolff R, Holm T, Culver M, Martin C, Fujimoto E, Hoff M, Kumlin E, White R (1987a) Variable number of tandem repeat (VNTR) markers for human gene mapping. Science 235: 1616–1622

Nakamura Y, Julier C, Wolff R, Holm T, O'Connell P, Leppert M, White R (1987b) Characterization of a human "midisatellite" sequence. Nucleic Acids Res 15: 2537–2547

Royle NJ, Clarkson RE, Wong Z, Jeffreys AJ (1988) Clustering of hypervariable minisatellites in the proterminal regions of human autosomes. Genomics 3: 352–360

Schlötterer C, Tautz D (1992) Slippage synthesis of simple sequence DNA. Nucleic Acids Res 20: 211–215

Smillie F, Bains W (1990) Repetition structure of mammalian nuclear DNA. J Theor Biol 142: 463–471

Smith G (1976) Evolution of repeated DNA sequences by unequal crossing over. Science 191: 528–535

Stephan W (1989) Tandem repetitive noncoding DNA: forms and forces. Mol Biol Evol 6: 198–212

Tautz D, Renz M (1984) Simple sequences are ubiquitous repetitive components of eukaryotic genomes. Nucleic Acids Res 12: 4127–4138

Tautz D, Trick M, Dover GA (1986) Cryptic simplicity in DNA is a major source of genetic variation. Nature 322: 652–656

Tautz D (1989) Hypervariability of simple sequences as a general source for polymorphic DNA markers. Nucleic Acids Res 17: 6463–6471

Vergnaud G, Mariat D, Zoroastro M, Lauthier V (1991) Detection of single and multiple polymorphic loci by synthetic tandem repeats of short oligonucleotides. Electrophoresis 12: 134–140

Weber JL, May PE (1989) Abundant class of human polymorphisms which can be typed using the polymerase chain reaction. Am J Hum Genet 44: 388–396

Zischler H, Kammerbauer C, Studer R, Grzeschik KH, Epplen J (1992) Dissecting $(CAC)_5/(GTG)_5$ multilocus fingerprints from man into individual locus-specific hypervariable components. Genomics 13: 983–990

DNA Fingerprinting: State of the Science
ed. by S. D. J. Pena, R. Chakraborty, J. T. Epplen & A. J. Jeffreys
© 1993 Birkhäuser Verlag Basel/Switzerland

On the essence of "meaningless" simple repetitive DNA in eukaryote genomes

C. Epplen, G. Melmer, I. Siedlaczck, F.-W. Schwaiger, W. Mäueler and J. T. Epplen

Molecular Human Genetics, Ruhr-University, 44780 Bochum, Germany

Summary

Various kinds of simple tandemly repetitive DNA sequences are abundantly interspersed in the genomes of practically all eukaryotic species studied. The comparatively elevated mutation rates of simple repeat blocks result in highly polymorphic and therefore extremely informative investigation systems for studies on forensic, ecological and genetic relationship questions. Recently the techniques for analyzing simple repeats have achieved great effectivity and simplicity. Beyond their utility as tools for differentiation and individualization, certain of these repeated elements harbor quite unexpected qualities which may be discussed in the context of their biological meaning. i) A specific subset of simple $(cac)_n$ or $(gtg)_n$ repeats is expressed in mature mRNA and total cellular RNA. ii) Despite the apparently high mutation rate certain $(gt)_n$ or mixed $(gt)_n/(ga)_m$ stretches of intronic simple repeats are preserved in immunologically relevant genes for at least 70×10^6 years and they bind nuclear protein molecules with high affinities. Consequently in addition to their tool character, the biological aspects of simple repeated DNA should be taken into consideration.

Introduction

Genome organization in eukaryotes is characterized by one prominent feature that separates these mostly complex organisms from their equally successful counterparts in evolution, the prokaryotes. Genomic **redundancy** is by and large restricted to the eukaryotes, at least above a threshold of meaningful quantity. Some principles of eukaryotic genome structure were evidenced already by the early studies on DNA dissociation and reassociation kinetics (Britten and Kohne, 1968). Two different principles described the overall periodicity with which the predominant part of these unique and more or less abundant elements are interspersed with each other: the so-called short period interspersion ("Xenopus" type) and the long period interspersion patterns ("Drosophila" type) of single copy and repetitive DNA sequence organization were distinguished. At that time the foundation of DNA sequence information was lacking. Therefore these interspersion pattern data have been perceived widely as molecular anatomy of the genomic desert. Nevertheless the crude molecular architecture of the eukaryotic genomes has been interpreted by their discoverers (and a small community of followers) as possibly bearing also some functional significance.

In conclusion from the aforementioned genome organization models, several of the pertinent properties of the eukaryotic genome were ascribed to certain subsets of the repetitive DNA sequences. In addition, theoretically appealing functions were attributed to short interspersed repetitive sequences, e.g. the concerted regulation of the expression of multigene families and interrelated genetic cascades (Britten and Davidson, 1973). Though intellectually most stimulating, the practical meaning of these proposed organizational principles and derived theories has hardly survived the beginning of thorough genome fine analysis by modern molecular cloning and sequencing techniques. Rather, the early collective analytical approach has necessarily kept hidden the unforeseeable complexities of the eukaryotic genome. In addition, the relationships of cytogenetically demonstrable euchromatic and heterochromatic chromosome organization principles in the human genome are nowadays becoming clearer. Large chunks of repetitive DNA constitute the bulk of the (mostly silenced) heterochromatic material. As exemplified from data on human chromosomes 21 and Y (Chumakov et al., 1992; Foote et al., 1992), the intricacies of longer stretches of repeat sequences are still not amenable to analysis by techniques representing the state of the art in modern genome mapping research. Needless to say, approaches for sequencing human genomes *in toto* are not yet available, thus leaving plenty of room for speculatory ideas about the genomic "desert" (Ohno, 1972).

Apart from these basic considerations, repeated DNA in general has turned out to represent a versatile tool for investigating different aspects of eukaryotic genomes, not only for structural questions but e.g. for disease diagnostics in man (Epplen, 1992a). In this context one particular component of the repetitive sequences has gained considerable attention because these repetitive DNA blocks are ubiquitously interspersed and highly informative: longer stretches of simple, tandemly organized repetitive sequences with motifs of 2 to 6 (or 10) bases (Epplen, 1988; Beckman and Weber, 1992). Amenable to amplification by the polymerase chain reaction (PCR), their high polymorphism information content (PIC) makes these simple sequences superior to other possible polymorphic targets such as conventional restriction fragment length polymorphisms. The ongoing simplification and automation of diagnostic and research procedures provides additional considerable advantages in utilizing these tools collectively. This fact reflects the newly pronounced interest of the genome research community in these interspersed simple sequence blocks because of their applicability to all kinds of polymorphism studies.

Recently, DNA sequence data banks have become loaded with data entries harboring repetitive sequences. The representation of a subset of the simple repeats in the EMBL/GenBank data banks are shown in Tab. 1: Except for $(CG)_{15}$ all mono to quadruplet motifs are

Table 1. Representation of selected simple tandem repetitive DNA sequence motifs in the EMBL/GenBank data bank

(November 1, 1992)

Simple repeat motif (monomer)	Number of occurrences in n bases			
	n = 25	30	50	100
(a)		489		3
(c)		8		
(at)		454		
(ca)	2284	1859	1164 (>160)*	2
(cg)	1	0 (106/120)*		
(ct)		292		2
(ca)(ct)		16		
(ct)(ca)+	97	72	18	4
(cac)#	40	14		
(cgg)&	36	23		
(ctc)&	51	31		
(ctg)%		61		
(gaa)%		32		
(gaca)$		18		
(gata)$	59	67		0(379/400)*
(ggat)		10		
(gggca)°		1		
(ttaggg)§		17		
(gtggaggcct)		0 (112/120)*		
Randomized				
$a_{15}\ t_{15}$		0 (92/120)*		
$c_{15}\ a_{15}$		0 (76/120)*		
$c_{15}\ g_{15}$		0 (84/120)*		
$g_{15}\ a_{15}$		0 (88/120)*		
$c_{15}\ a_8\ c_7$ +		0 (96/120)*		
$c_{20}\ a_{10}$ #		0 (88/120)*		
$c_{10}\ g_{20}$ &		0 (96/120)*		
$c_{20}\ t_{10}$ %		0 (92/120)*		
$g_{10}\ a_{20}$ $		0 (84/120)*		
$g_8\ a_{15}\ t_7$ $		0 (74/120)*		
$g_{18}\ c_6\ a_6$ °		0 (78/120)*		
$t_{10}\ a_5\ g_{15}$ §		0 (70/120)*		

*Score defining highest similarity found, e.g. 120/120 = identity

abundantly present as perfect 30 bases long simple repeats (in the total of roughly 1.2×10^8 base pairs). It is well known that, because of CpG methylation and deamination of 5′-methylcytosine, this dinucleotide motif is generally under-represented in the human genome. Thus the simple tandem $(CG)_n$ stretches are also subject to this elimination principle. But the over-representation of the other simple repeat motifs is surprising on the basis that a random 30mer is expected only once in

10^{18} nucleotides. The data banks currently contain roughly 1.2×10^8 base pairs of synthetic, prokaryote and eukaryote nucleic acid sequences. A more meaningful evaluation of the over-representation of simple repeats can thus be tried by comparing the occurrence of random 30mers with the same net base constitution as the simple sequences. As expected, none of these random oligonucleotides was identified even once. In this context it is also noteworthy that $(CA)_n/(GT)_n$ repeat blocks increased in the EMBL/GenBank files from 1057 (September 1, 1992) over 1343 (October 1, 1992) to 1859 (November 1, 1992). Meanwhile, a second generation linkage map of man has been established employing more than 800 of these $(CA)_n/(GT)_n$ polymorphic markers (perfect simple repeats equal or longer than 24 base pairs; Weissenbach et al., 1992). In contrast, the more complex and longer variable number of tandem repeats (VNTR) will probably always remain underrepresented in the data banks since they tend to escape conventional cloning and sequencing strategies where prokaryotic vectors are employed. In addition, stretches of hypervariable repeats with longer periodicity are often too long to be amplified by PCR efficiently (Zischler et al., 1992). Finally, in humans these genomic elements are preferentially located at the telomeres – in contrast to the ubiquitous interspersion of simple repeat stretches (Zischler et al., 1989, see below).

Is multilocus DNA fingerprinting still the first choice for most individualization purposes and genetic relationship studies?

In all investigated animal and plant genomes one or more kinds of *simple* repetitive DNA sequences are present in such quantities and sequence organization that they can be demonstrated with routine molecular biology techniques (Epplen, 1989; Epplen et al., 1991). Chemically synthesized oligonucleotide probes are an efficient means to arrive at such conclusions, also in previously completely uncharacterized species. This statement can be aggravated by the fact that base-specific hybridization is achieved under standard conditions such that single mismatches would prevent stable probe hybridization and signal detection. In consequence of the aforementioned general genome organization facts, it is not too surprising that oligonucleotide probes carrying simple repeat motifs are adequate if not optimal tools for multilocus DNA fingerprinting in a wide variety of different eukaryotic species from fungi to plants and primates (Beyermann et al., 1992; Epplen, 1992a; Weising et al., 1991, 1992). Advantages of hybridization technology directly in the gel have been discussed in detail elsewhere (Epplen, 1992b). For humans questionable paternity cases with false classical exclusions can be solved (Bender et al., 1992) to the extent that civil suits where monozygotic twins are named as putative fathers are now admitted in court for multilocus DNA fingerprint analyses. The aspect of efficient genome screening via a collection of multilocus probes is particularly interesting in tumor research, where genomic changes are often not predictable (Nürnberg et al., 1991, in press; Bock et al., 1993). For routine purposes, non-radioactive multilocus DNA fingerprinting (Zischler et al., 1989) has recently been evaluated using AMPPD-evoked chemoluminescence (Epplen and Mathé, 1992). This procedure is much faster for blotted nucleic acids; however, chemo-luminescence is trapped in the gel matrix preventing signal development directly in the gel.

The application of multilocus DNA fingerprinting to ecological studies in avian and primate species is covered elsewhere in this volume (Lubjuhn et al.; Nürnberg et al.). Suffice it to state here that also in fish (Schartl et al., 1991, in press) including Latimeria (Schartl et al., in preparation) and all other species studied to date (Epplen et al., 1991) including a variety of insects (see e.g. Achmann et al., 1992), the panel of simple repeat oligonucleotide probes has proven sufficiently informative and discriminating to answer the various ecological and behavioral scientific questions raised.

In our laboratory all routine relationship studies in man, animals, plants and fungi are performed by multilocus DNA fingerprinting. In the last few months for example some hundred paternity cases in horses have been settled using probes $(GGAT)_4$ and $(GTG)_5$ after *Hae*III digestion of genomic DNA. Most of these cases would have been impossible to clarify without the informativity and power of multilocus probes; the frequent occurrence of incest relationships or closely related putative sires greatly weaken classical blood group and monolocus system evidence. It turned out to be absolutely essential to have the blood drawn and to have ensured the identity of the equine individuals by officially recruited veterinarians. Since data protection is "built into the multilocus fingerprint", no additional information other than individuality and relationships can be interpreted from the patterns.

By using the multilocus fingerprinting probe $(CAC)_5$ the first well-documented case of monozygotic twins was detected harboring differences in their otherwise identical genomes (amongst about 30 pairs; Hundrieser et al., 1992). Fortuitously the respective monolocus probe HZ4103 had independently been developed for the locus D9S128 (Zischler et al., 1992). The genomic organisation of this locus is shown in Fig. 1. PCR using the oligonucleotide primers P1 and P2 as well as P2 and P3 resulted in the expected fragments of about 350 bp and 150 bp. Using the oligonucleotides P1/P4 and P3/P4 yielded also the expected fragments of about 1 kb and 0.8 kb for the twins as well as several unrelated individuals for control. These results demonstrate that the apparently increased allele size in one of the twins is not a result of various lengths of the repetitive sequences between P3 and P4. There-

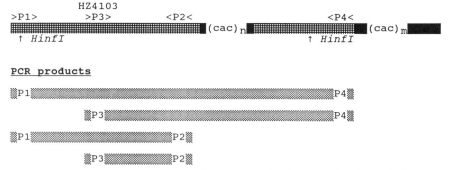

Figure 1. Schematic representation of the $(CAC)_n/(GTG)_n$-containing locus D9S128 as detectable with the oligonucleotide probe HZA4103. This locus varies in the multilocus fingerprints of one pair of monozygous twins with otherwise identical genomes. Primers (P1–4) were synthesized which attach to various regions of the locus. The PCR products obtained with the primer pair P1/P4 are unexpectedly identical in length for all individuals investigated as are the other PCR products. This result excludes at first sight that the $(CAC)_n$ stretch between P2 and P4 generates length variability in the locus D9S128. Predigestion of the genomic DNA with the restriction enzyme HinfI prevents amplification of the P3/P4 product.

fore the allele size variations can only be due to insertions outside the primer sites of the oligonucleotides P3 and P4. Yet these allele sizes are demonstrable after digestion with Sau3AI, MboI and HinfI. Because there are two HinfI sites in the cloned fragment of the locus HZ41 insertion outside of P3 ↔ P4 does not appear a priori to represent a valid explanation. However, we cannot exclude methylation of the HinfI sites rendering them undigestible under standard conditions. In order to test the methylation hypothesis we digested human genomic DNA with HinfI prior to PCR amplification using the P3/P4 primer pair. As expected no amplification was observed demonstrating that the site is not methylated in genomic DNA. Therefore the differential methylation of at least one HinfI as well as the Sau3AI (MboI) sites must have happened upstream of P3. Further experiments to identify the methylated sites are currently under way. Concomitantly we are also investigating possible tissue differences in this pair of twins. The molecular basis for variability generation and mutational events in such loci of the $(CAC)_n/(GTG)_n$ multilocus fingerprint should thus be enlightened.

Human autosomal and Y chromosomal simple repeats

The subject of perfect simple repeat sequences on the primitive heteromorphic sex chromosomes of several vertebrate species such as fish, reptiles and birds has been covered in detail recently (Nanda et al.,

1990b, 1993). Considerable accumulations of particular simple repeat motifs occur especially on largely heterochromatic gonosomes. Yet they are not stable – even not during short evolutionary time spans in closely related species (Nanda et al., 1992, 1993). The heterochromatic part of the long arm of the human Y chromosome is packed with repetitive DNA structures (Schmid et al., 1990; Foote et al., 1992). Large parts of this classical satellite-like sequence may have descended from pentameric simple repeats (Nakahori et al., 1986). In man, extended stretches of certain simple sequences have not been demonstrable so far by fingerprinting or hybridization *in situ*. Only Y chromosomal $(GATA)_n$ repeats have been examined to a limited extent in cosmid clones (Roewer et al., 1992). Therefrom a most useful system has been developed for investigating a particular Y chromosomal $(GATA)_n$ repeat (see contribution by Roewer et al. in this volume). When investigated by *in situ* oligonucleotide hybridization usually quite a few simple tandem sequences are detected more or less evenly spread over the autosomal supplement of various animal species and man (Zischler et al., 1989; Nanda et al., 1991). In contrast, particular accumulations of a subset of the repeats can occur without doing any harm to the organism (Nanda et al., 1990b, 1993). For example in man and primates, major perfect $(GACA)_n$ stretches are aggregated marking the nucleolus organizer regions (Nanda et al., 1990a). The mechanisms that generate variability in simple repeats result in similar polymorphisms on the autosomes and the gonosomes (Roewer et al., 1992; Santos et al., 1993). For a comparison with autosomal simple repeats we have also analyzed about 350 cosmid clones from human chromosome 7 (Melmer et al., 1990) for the presence of such repetitive sequences (Melmer, unpublished data). Nearly half of them contained $(CA)_n/(GT)_n$ blocks ($n > 7$), and 50–60 hybridized to the probes $(TCC)_5$ and $(CAC)_5$. About 5% were $(GAA)_6$ positive, whereby strong intensity differences indicated that the simple repeat lengths varied by a factor of 10 to 100 – or the repeat sequence is different. For example, human genomic DNA from unrelated individuals was hybridized with the probe $(GAA)_6$ after digestion with various restriction enzymes (Fig. 2). Upon *BamH*I digestion, clustering of $(GAA)_n$-containing, repetitive DNA is seen at about 6 kilobases whereas frequently cutting restriction enzymes produce the expected smaller fragments. In pulsed field gel electrophoresis after digestion with the rarely cutting restriction enzyme *Mlu*I human DNA appears as a smear ranging from 50 kb to over 1000 kb (Fig. 1); after hybridization with $(GAA)_6$ predominant hybridization signals range around 50 kb. *Sal*I-digested DNA rendered additional smaller fragments. In summary the organization of $(GAA)_n$ repeats in the human genome is characterized by relatively intense interspersion of smaller $(GAA)_n$ units and very few DNA fragments with extremely high amounts of poly (GAA).

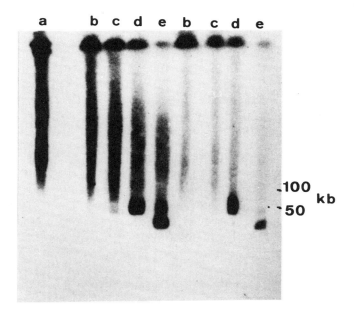

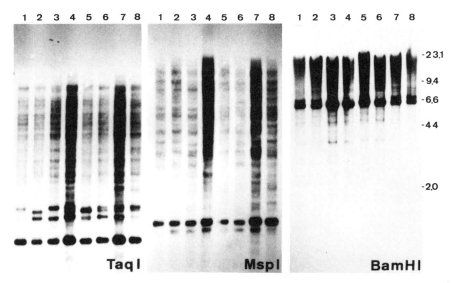

Figure 2. Genomic organization of simple repetitive $(GAA)_n$ loci as demonstrated after digestion with various restriction enzymes recognizing 4–6 bases and hybridization with the oligonucleotide probe $(GAA)_6$. 8 different individuals were investigated each with the respective probe enzyme combination. The restriction enzymes used are indicated in the bottom of the figure. The data imply that – independent of the restriction enzyme used – large chunks of more or less perfectly organized $(GAA)_n$ units are localized on one to a few DNA fragments. Loading order for the pulsed field gel: **a** yeast chromosomal DNA; for both individuals, 1 and 2, the DNA was digested with the restricted enzymes: **b** *Apa*I, **c** *Sac*II, **d** *Mlu*I and **e** *Sal*I.

On the biological meaning of simple repeated sequences:
(1) cDNA expression and preservation in evolution

Recently the mRNA expression of simple repetitive DNA sequences has unexpectedly gained considerable attention (for a review see Sutherland and Richards, 1992): GC-rich trinucleotide repeats are represented in the mature transcripts of genes responsible for extraordinarily inherited diseases like fragile-X syndrome (*FMR-1* gene), myotonic dystrophy (*DM-1* gene) and Kennedy disease (androgen receptor gene). While the amplified $(CCG)_n$ repeat in the fragile-X syndrome appears to reside in the 5' untranslated region of *FMR-1* (fragile X mental retardation 1) mRNA, the unstable simple $(CAG)_n$ trinucleotide is contained in the transcribed part of the androgen receptor gene (X-linked spinal and bulbar muscular atrophy, Kennedy disease) or the 3' untranslated region (Dystrophia myotonica 1; *DM-1*), respectively. Reduced penetrance in *DM-1* has also been attributed to the unstable $(CTG)_n$ repeat (Shelbourne et al., 1992). Prior to this interest from medical geneticists, we had started to investigate individual simple repeat transcription like $(GATA)_n$, $(CAC)_n$, $(GTG)_n$ (Schäfer et al., 1986; Epplen, 1988; Epplen et al., 1991; Zischler et al., 1992): Using 15–20mer oligonucleotide probes specific for various simple repeat motifs, we have observed only very rarely **prominent** and **distinct** species of mRNAs that harbor perfectly repeated simple elements in Northern blot hybridizations using several different tissues. Nevertheless the screening of cDNA libraries from lymphocytes with the $(CAC)_5/(GTG)_5$ [and in one instance $(TCC)_5/(GGA)_5$] probes revealed 40 independent clones exhibiting specific hybridization signals (Tab. 2). Whereas $(TCC)_n/(GGA)_n$-containing sequences are represented more than twice as much as $(CAC)_n/(GTG)_n$ in the data banks (see Tab. 1), at least in our T lymphocyte clone A9.C4E cDNA library perfect $(TCC)_5/(GGA)_5$ transcripts are nearly completely lacking.

Among the $(cac)_n/(gtg)_n$ containing clones transcripts of one gene encoding the *MHC* class I promotor binding protein were identified (*MHC*-PBP: Epplen and Epplen, 1992) in independent B- an T-cell derived libraries from unrelated individuals. The 3'-untranslated region of the human *MHC*-PBP harbors a $(GTG)_5$ repeat whereas the mouse homologue exhibits at the respective location a single "gtg" trinucleotide unit. The immediately flanking single copy portions were quite similar in the two species yet completely unrelated to the simple $(GTG)_n$ repeat of man. This situation is apparently characteristic for the large bulk of all the transcribed simple repetitive DNA elements: they bloom in one species and vanish in the other. $(CAC)_n/(GTG)_n$ containing transcripts of two other human genes were identified, hnRNP and tissue plasminogen activator (TPA). Here short exonic (hnRNP) and intronic (TPA) simple repeat stretches were present. Table 2 gives a survey of

Table 2. cDNA library screening for $(cac)_n/(gtg)_n$ containing sequences

LIBRARY SOURCE (AMPL/NA)	INDEPENDENT CLONES	LENGTH	GENE IDENTIFIED/ SIMILARITY[x]/ HOMOLOGY	SIMPLE REPEAT LENGTH/ HIGHER ORDER STRUCTURE	ADDITIONAL SIMPLE REPEATS/REMARKS
CE 29 TCC (NA) 0.6x10[5] PFU	3.2	120 bp	RAT α-2 MICROGLOBULIN[1]	$(GTG)_3$-$(GTG)_4$-$(GTG)_8$ / YES	
	5.1	225 bp	NOT SIGNIFICANT	$(GTG)_7$ / NO	
	8.1	1026 bp	PSEUDORABIES VIRUS[2] MOUSE NUCLEOLIN[3] HUMAN NUCLEOLAR PROTEIN (B23)[4]	$(GTG)_5$ / NO	
	7.2	1350 bp	INTRON HUMAN TPA[5]	$(GTG)_4$ / NO	
	4.1	1400 bp	WF ANTI FREEZE PROTEIN[6]	$(GTG)_2$-$(GTG)_4$-$(GTG)_2$ / YES	$(GCC)_6$
A9A2Br TCC (AMPL) 1.7x10[5] PFU	5, 9, 14, 18,	1753 bp	MHC PROMOTOR BINDING PROTEIN	$(GTG)_5$ in 3'-UT/NO	NO $(GTG)_n$ REPEAT IN MOUSE SEQUENCE
		1753 bp	MHC PROMOTOR BINDING PROTEIN	$(GTG)_5$ in 3'-UT/NO	"
		1756 bp	MHC PROMOTOR BINDING PROTEIN	$(GTG)_5$ in 3'-UT/NO	"
		1753 bp	MHC PROMOTOR BINDING PROTEIN	$(GTG)_5$ in 3'-UT/NO	"
	17	1800 bp	SO FAR NOT SIGNIFICANT	PRESENTLY UNDER INVESTIGATION	$(TTGC)_3$
	22	1900 bp	SO FAR NOT SIGNIFICANT	$(GTG)_5$ / NO	$(CAG)_4$, $(GGC)_6$
	2, 11	1900 bp	SO FAR NOT SIGNIFICANT	$(CAC)_5$ / YES	$(GCC)_6$, $(CA)_4$, PALIND. $(CAG)_5(CTG)_4$, $(CTG)_4$
A9A2Br (NA) 1.8x10[5] PFU	B2	1400 bp	SO FAR NOT SIGNIFICANT	$(CAC)_3$ / NO	$(ATT)_3$, $(AT)_3$, $(GA)_3$
	B6	2000 bp	SO FAR NOT SIGNIFICANT	$(CAC)_4$, $(CAC)_{14}$/NO	$(CTC)_{11}$
	B7	1100 bp	SO FAR NOT SIGNIFICANT	$(GTG)_5$ / NO	$(GAA)_3$, $(GT)_5$
	B8	830 bp	NOT SIGNIFICANT	$(GTG)_6$ / NO	ALU REP.$(GT)_8GC(GT)_{13}$
	B9	1696 bp	MHC PROMOTOR BINDING PROTEIN	$(GTG)_5$ in 3'-UT/NO	NO $(GTG)_n$ REPEAT IN MOUSE SEQUENCE
	B3	900 bp	YEAST mtDNA[7]	$(CAC)_6$ / NO	
	B5	2000 bp	YEAST mtDNA[7]	$(CAC)_6$ / NO	
	B11	2100 bp	YEAST mtDNA[7]	$(CAC)_6$ / NO	
	B13	2000 bp	SO FAR NOT SIGNIFICANT	$(GTG)_4$ / NO	ALU REPEAT, $(GAAAA)_4$
A9.C4E TCC (NA) 2.4x10[5] PFU	16.1	1800 bp	NOT SIGNIFICANT	$(CAC)_8$ / NO	ALU REPEAT ELEMENT
	5.1	800 bp	NOT SIGNIFICANT	$(CAC)_6$ / NO	$(GT)_4$
	17.1	800 bp	NOT YET ANALYZED		
	3.2	1500 bp	hnRNP A1	$(CAC)_4$ / NO	IN EXON 7; ALSO E.G. PRESENT IN RAT
	5.3	2500 bp	hnRNP A1	$(CAC)_4$ / NO	
	16.3	3500 bp	HUMAN UBIQUITIN[8]	$(GTG)_5$ / NO	$(TGGGGG)_2$, $(ATC)_3$
	20.1	3500 bp	NOT YET ANALYZED		
KDB BCL (NA) 3.4x10[5] PFU	5.1	1400 bp	RODENT ENOLASE[9]	$(GTG)_{15}$/ NO	IN THE 5' UT
	2.1	1800 bp	HEMAGGLUTININ (E.CORREDENS)[10]	$(CAC)_7$ / NO	
	1.2	3500 bp	SO FAR NOT SIGNIFICANT	$(CAC)_5$ / NO	ALU REPEAT ELEMENT
	B6	2100 bp	SO FAR NOT SIGNIFICANT		
	B9	2000 bp	SO FAR NOT SIGNIFICANT		
	B12	2000 bp	MOUSE LORICRIN GENE[11]		$(GCC)_6$, $(CAG)_3$, $(CAG)_4$
	B1	1753 bp	MHC PROMOTOR BINDING PROTEIN	$(GTG)_5$ in 3'-UT/NO	NO $(GTG)_n$ REPEAT IN MOUSE SEQUENCE
	B7	1753 bp	MHC PROMOTOR BINDING PROTEIN	$(GTG)_5$ in 3'-UT/NO	"
	B14	1753 bp	MHC PROMOTOR BINDING PROTEIN	$(GTG)_5$ in 3'-UT/NO	"

[1] [$(cac)_n$ 85% FOR 85 bp]
[2] [81% FOR 48 bp]
[3] [90% FOR 39 bp]
[4] [90% FOR 39 bp]
[5] [70% FOR 227 bp]; TPA = TISSUE PLASMINOGEN ACTIVATOR
[6] [60% FOR 246 bp]; WF = WINTER FLOUNDER
[7] [71% FOR 49 bp]
[8] [100% FOR 107 bp]
[9] [89% FOR 211 bp]
[10] [63% FOR 280 bp]
[11] [65% FOR 63 bp]

A9.C4E			
TCC	15.3	1200 bp	NO SIGNIF. HOMOL.
(NA)	6.1	2000 bp	NO SIGNIF. HOMOL. $(TCC)_5$
2.4x10[5] PFU			$(TCC)_5^+$ cDNA CLONES

other $(gtg)_n/(cac)_n$ containing cDNAs isolated including their sequence similarities/homologies as revealed by data bank searches (Epplen and Epplen, submitted). As expected in expressed sequences the perfect simple $(gtg)_n/(cac)_n$ repeats are comparatively short. In addition, some of the isolated clones represent "illegitimately" expressed genomic sequences. Such transcripts are present in cDNA libraries from total cellular RNA; the larger the library the more of these hnRNA equivalent clones are likely to be detected.

For a detailed description of one specific hypervariable monolocus system based on simple repeats see the chapter Immunoprinting... (Buitkamp et al., this volume). Here a highly polymorphic *MHC-DRB* gene contains an intronic simple $(GT)_n(GA)_m$ repeat that varies in the different alleles of one species. The principal $(GT)_n(GA)_m$ repeat is preserved for at least 7×10^7 years from ungulates to primates (Ammer et al., 1992). The whole *MHC* itself appears as an example of dissimilar genes locked in close linkage by "condensation" of the genome (Fisher, 1958). Polymorphisms of individual *MHC* genes on the other hand are usually generated by genetic exchange. Recombination and gene conversion like events tend to be limited to restricted areas in the *MHC*. For the *MHC-DRB* genes the 3'-site that restricts the exchange appears to coincide with the simple repetitive stretch (Schwaiger et al., 1993, in press, Fig. 3). As noted before, simple repeat loci tend not to be stable over extended evolutionary periods ($>10^7$ years).

On the biological meaning of simple repeated sequences:
(2) Protein binding to simple repeat sequences

It has been demonstrated recently that certain nuclear proteins bind to mixed simple repetitive $(gt)_n/(ga)_m$ sequences (Mäueler et al., 1992a, b) which reside in intron 2 of the *MHC-DRB* genes in vertebrates (Rieß et al., 1990; Ammer et al., 1992; Schwaiger et al., in press). In order to evaluate the meaning of this protein binding property to simple repetitive DNA it is necessary to clarify certain definitions and parameters: i) Is a purely operational definition of DNA-binding specificity sufficient or meaningful? ii) What properties characterize an appropriate unspecific competitor for protein binding? iii) How many different proteins are involved in specific shifted bands?

Unfortunately, PCR-generated products are not appropriate for binding studies (Mäueler et al., 1992b). Protein binding to such target DNAs is unpredictable and not reproducible probably because of slippage artifacts introduced during PCR plus the presence of variable amounts of single-stranded DNA. Since eukaryotic DNA of many species contains simple $(GT)_n$ and $(GA)_m$ repeats, it can not be used as an unspecific competitor. In our system, as with most other DNA-bind-

Sequence exchanges in the evolution of *MHC-DRB* exon 2/intron 2 regions

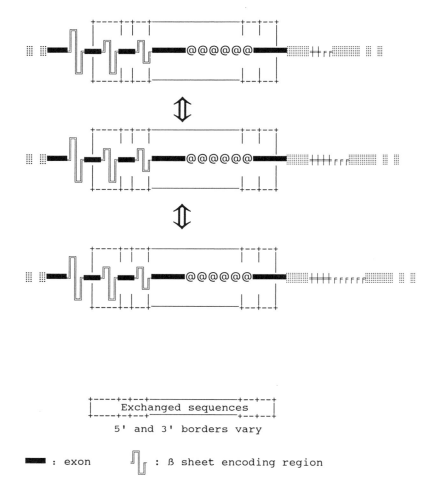

Figure 3. A model explaining intra-/inter-exon exchanges in the evolution of *MHC-DRB* genes. The exon can be subdivided into portions encoding β-pleated sheets (β1, β2, β3) and α-helical portions of the *MHC-DRB* protein chain. Note that the locations of the switched sequence boundaries are not narrowly restricted but fluctuating. The intronic simple repeat appears to define the 3′-endpoint of the exchanged sequences. The symbols used are explained at the bottom of the figure. For a detailed discussion of the implications with respect to the function of the immune system see Epplen (1992c).

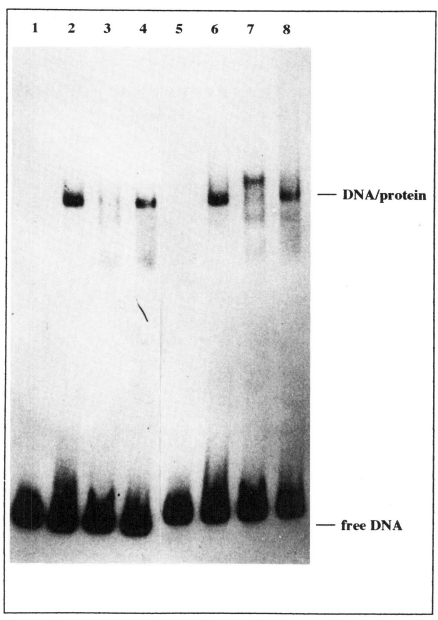

Figure 4. Gel retardation analysis using different $(GT)_n(GA)_m$-containing, simple repetitive target DNA sequences and total cellular protein extracts. Lanes (1–4) contain $(GT)_{22}(GA)_{15}$ and lanes (5–8) $(GT)_{25}(GA)_{10}CA(GA)_3CA(GA)_6$ targets. Lanes (1 and 5) contain DNA without protein; (2 and 6) HeLa cell extract; (3 and 7) Daudi cell extract; (4 and 8) A9 cell extract. The gel shift system and the radiolabeling procedure were carried out as described previously (Mäueler et al., 1992a). Daudi and A9 cells are EBV-transformed B lymphocytes. Note the differences in the shifted target bands.

42

ing proteins, the unspecific competitor of choice is poly dI/dC (Mäueler et al., 1992a). Many additional double-stranded DNA fragments were evaluated as non-specific competitors revealing that 75% of some 20 cloned plasmid sequences (without apparent similarity) compete with about 5-fold lower affinity compared to the unlabeled specific competitor. These data suggest that the protein(s) in question bind to a distinct secondary DNA conformation rather than to a defined sequence. In our DNA binding studies preliminary but substantial evidence was generated that several protein components are binding in combination or interaction to generate the shifted DNA fragment pattern (Mäueler, unpublished data). The binding constants amount to $5 \times 10^{-9}–5 \times 10^{-10}$ M. Thus the DNA/protein interaction does not appear unspecific. As can be inferred from Fig. 4 different protein extracts cause slightly different band shift patterns. Do these differences relate to the differences in the gene expression status in tumor cells versus EBV-transformed lymphocytes? Clearly the Daudi cell extract does not display the most intense, impressively shifted band. Using the more complex and elongated simple repeat $(GT)_{25}(GA)_{10}CA(GA)_3CA(GA)_6$ as target, a novel band shift signal appears which is not observed in HeLa or A9 extract. The less prominent shift bands are in good agreement in both B lymphocyte extracts. The role of simple repeats as target structures for proteins involved in recombination and gene conversion mechanisms requires further evaluation.

Conclusions

The presence and ubiquitous interspersion of simple repetitive DNA sequences throughout eukaryotic genomes leaves many questions open but offers unprecedented opportunities. The practical meaning of simple repeats is not confined to their usefulness as tools for differentiation and identification of individuals. At present we cannot decide what part of the pool of simple repetitive DNA sequences is endowed with which biological meaning. Apparently not all of these elements represent pure evolutionary junk. A small subset is expressed in mature mRNA. Research hints at influences on gene expression as well as structural properties in the nucleus, perhaps via DNA/protein interaction. Yet in addition it appears necessary to develop other and comprehensive investigative strategies to differentiate between all these appealing but essentially hypothetic possibilities.

Acknowledgements
Supported by the Deutsche Forschungsgemeinschaft (Ep 7/5-2), the BMFT and the VW-Stiftung. We thank Dr. Alec J. Jeffreys for his valuable improvements in reviewing this manuscript. Oligonucleotide probes are subject to patent applications. For commercial enquiries contact Fresenius AG (Oberursel, Germany).

References

Achmann R, Heller K-G, Epplen JT (1992) Last-male sperm precedence in the bushcricket *Poecilimon veluchianus* (Orthoptera, Tettigonioidea) demonstrated by DNA fingerprinting. Mol Ecol 1: 47–54

Ammer H, Schwaiger F-W, Kammerbauer C, Arriens A, Lazary S, Epplen JT (1992) Exonic polymorphism versus intronic hypervariability in *DRB* genes: Evolutionary persistence and group specific organization in simple repeat sequences. Immunogenet 35: 330–337

Beckmann JS, Weber JL (1992) Survey of human and rat microsatellites. Genomics 12: 627–631

Bender K, Kasulke D, Mayerova A, Hummel K, Weidinger S, Epplen JT, Wienker TF (1991) A problematical exclusion case involving the PI locus: a multifaceted approach. Hum Hered 41: 1–11

Beyermann B, Nürnberg P, Weihe A, Meixner M, Epplen JT, Börner J (1992) Fingerprinting plant genomes with oligonucleotide probes specific for simple repetitive DNA sequences. Theor Appl Genet 83: 691–694

Bock S, Epplen JT, Noll-Puchta H, Rotter M, Höfler H, Block T, Hartung R et al. (1993) Detection of somatic changes in human renal cell carcinomas with oligonucleotide probes specific for simple repeat motifs. Genes Chromosomes Cancer 6: 113–117

Britten RJ, Kohne DE (1968) Repeated sequences in DNA. Science 161: 529–540

Britten RJ, Davidson EH (1973) Organization, transcription and regulation in the animal genome. Quart Rev Biol 48: 565–613

Chumakov I, Rigault P, Guillou S, Ougen P, Billaut A, Guasconi G, Gervy P et al. (1992) Continuum of overlapping clones spanning the entire human chromosome 21q. Nature 359: 380–387

Epplen JT (1988) On simple repeated GATA/GACA sequences in animal genomes: a critical reappraisal. J Hered 79: 409–417

Epplen JT, Ammer H, Epplen C, Kammerbauer C, Roewer L, Schwaiger W, Steimle V et al. (1991) Oligonucleotide fingerprinting using simple repeat motifs: a convenient, ubiquitously applicable method to detect hypervariability for multiple purposes. *In*: Burke T, Dolf G, Jeffreys AJ, Wolff R (eds) DNA-fingerprinting: Approaches and applications, Birkhäuser, Basel, pp 50–69

Epplen JT (1992a) Diagnostic applications of repetitive DNA sequences. Clin Chim Acta 209: 5–13

Epplen JT (1992b) The methodology of multilocus DNA fingerprinting using radioactive or nonradioactive oligonucleotide probes specific for simple repeat motifs. *In*: Chrambach A, Dunn MJ, Radola BJ (eds) Advances in Electrophoresis, VCH, Weinheim, pp 59–112

Epplen JT (1992c) On genetic components in autoimmunity. Hum Genet 90: 331–341

Epplen JT, Mathé J (1992) Multilocus DNA fingerprinting using non-radioactively labelled oligonucleotide probes specific for simple repeat elements. *In*: Kessler C (ed) Non-radioactive labelling, Springer, Berlin, pp 271–277

Epplen C, Epplen JT (1992) The human cDNA sequence homologous to the mouse MHC class I promoter-binding protein gene contains four additional codons in lymphocytes. Mamm Genome 3: 472–475

Epplen C, Epplen JT. $(cac)_n/(gtg)_n$ simple repetitive sequences are rare in mRNA of human lymphocytes. Hum Genet (submitted)

Fisher RA (ed) (1958) The genetical theory of natural selection. Ed. 2, Dover, New York

Foote S, Vollrath D, Hilton A, Page DC (1992) The human Y chromosome: overlapping DNA clones spanning the euchromatic region. Science 258: 60–66

Hundrieser J, Nürnberg P, Czeizel A, Métheneki J, Rothgänger S, Foelske C, Zischler H et al. (1992) Characterization of hypervariable, locus specific probes derived from a $(CAC)_5/(GTG)_5$ fingerprint in various Eurasian populations. Hum Genet 90: 27–33

Lubjuhn T, Curio E, Muth S, Brün J, Epplen JT. Parental care in great tits (*Parus major*) depends on true parentage. Behaviour Ecol (submitted)

Mäueler W, Muller M, Köhne AC, Epplen JT (1992a) A gel retardation assay system for studying protein binding to simple repetitive DNA sequences. Electrophoresis 13: 7–10

Mäueler W, Frank G, Siedlaczck I, Epplen JT, Melmer G (1992b) PCR amplification products are of limited use for the study of DNA/protein interaction. Electrophoresis 13: 641–643

44

Melmer G, Sood R, Rommens J, Rego D, Tsui LC, Buchwald M (1990) Isolation of clones on chromosome 7 that contain recognition sites for rare-cutting enzymes by oligonucleotide hybridization. Genomics 7: 173–181

Nakahori K, Mitani K, Yamada M, Nakagome Y (1986) A human Y-chromosome specific repeated DNA family (DYZ1). Nucleic Acids Res 14: 7569–7580

Nanda I, Deubelbeiss C, Guttenbach M, Epplen JT, Schmid M (1990a) Heterogeneities in the distribution of (GACA)$_n$ repeats in the karyotypes of primates and mouse. Hum Genet 85: 187–194

Nanda I, Feichtinger W, Schmid M, Schröder JH, Zischler H, Epplen JT (1990b) Simple repetitive sequences are associated with the differentiation of the sex chromosomes in poeciliid fish. J Molec Evol 30: 456–462

Nanda I, Schmid M, Epplen JT (1991) In situ hybridization of nonradioactive oligonucleotide probes to chromosomes. In: Adolph KW (ed) Advanced techniques in chromosome research, Dekker, New York, pp 117–134

Nanda I, Schartl M, Feichtinger W, Epplen JT, Schmid M (1992) Early stages of sex chromosome differentiation in fish as analyzed by simple repetitive DNA sequences. Chromosoma 101: 301–310

Nanda I, Schartl M, Epplen JT, Feichtinger W, Schmid M (1993) The primitive sex chromosomes in poeciliid fishes harbour simple repetitive DNA sequences. J Exp Zool 265: 301–308

Nürnberg P, Zischler H, Fuhrmann E, Thiel G, Losanova T, Kinzel D, Nisch G et al. (1991) Co-amplification of simple repetitive fingerprint fragments and the EGF receptor gene in human gliomas. Genes Chromosomes Cancer 3: 79–88

Nürnberg P, Thiel G, Weber F, Epplen JT (1993) Changes of telomere lengths in human intracranial tumours. Hum Genet 91: 190–192

Ohno S (1972) Evolutional reason for having so much junk DNA. In: Pfeiffer RA (ed) Modern aspects of cytogenetics: constitutive heterochromatin in man, FK Schattauer, Stuttgart, pp 169–180

Rieß O, Kammerbauer C, Roewer L, Steimle V, Andreas A, Albert E, Nagai T et al. (1990) Hypervariability of intronic simple (gt)$_n$(ga)$_m$ repeats in *HLA-DRB1* genes. Immunogenet 32: 110–116

Roewer L, Arnemann J, Spurr NK, Grzeschik K-H, Epplen JT (1992) Simple repeat sequences on the human Y chromosome are equally polymorphic as their autosomal counterparts. Hum Genet 89: 389–394

Santos FR dos, Pena SDJ, Epplen JT (1993) Genetic and population study of a Y-linked tetranucleotide repeat DNA polymorphism with a simple non-isotonic technique. Hum Genet 90: 655–656

Schäfer R, Böltz E, Becker A, Bartels F, Epplen JT (1986) The expression of the evolutionarily conserved GATA/GACA repeats in mouse tissues. Chromosoma 93: 496–501

Schartl M, Schlupp I, Schartl A, Meyer MK, Nanda I, Schmid M, Epplen JT et al. (1991) On the stability of dispensable constituents of the eukaryotic genome: stability of coding sequences in a clonal vertebrate, the amazon molly, *Poecilia formosa*. Proc Natl Acad Sci USA 88: 8759–8763

Schartl M, Erbelding-Denk C, Hölter S, Nanda I, Schmid M, Schröder JH, Epplen JT. Reproductive failure of the dominant males in a poeciliid fish species, *Limia perugiae*. Proc Natl Acad Sci USA (in press)

Schmid M, Guttenbach M, Nanda I, Studer R, Epplen JT (1990) Localization of the 2.1 kb repeat on the human Y chromosome. Genomics 6: 212–218

Schwaiger F-W, Buitkamp J, Weyers E, Epplen JT (1993) Typing of artiodactyl *MHC-DRB* genes with the help of intronic simple repeated DNA sequences. Mol Ecol 2: 55–59

Schwaiger W, Weyers E, Epplen C, Ruff G, Crawford A, Epplen JT. The paradox of *MHC-DRB* exon/intron evolution: α-helix and β-sheet encoding regions diverge while hypervariable intronic simple repeats co-evolve with β-sheet codons. J Mol Evol (in press)

Shelbourne P, Winqvist R, Kunert E, Davis J, Leisti J, Thiele H, Bachmann H et al. (1992) Unstable DNA may be responsible for the incomplete penetrance of the myotonic dystrophy phenotype. Hum Mol Genet 7: 467–473

Sutherland GR, Richards RI (1992) Invited editorial: Anticipation legitimized: unstable DNA to the rescue. Am J Hum Genet 51: 7–9

Weising K, Ramser J, Kaemmer D, Kahl G, Epplen JT (1991) Oligonucleotide fingerprinting in plants and fungi. In: Burke T, Dolf G, Jeffreys AJ, Wolff R (eds), DNA-fingerprinting: Approaches and applications, Birkhäuser, Basel, pp 312–329

Weising K, Kaemmer D, Weigand F, Epplen JT, Kahl G (1992) Oligonucleotide fingerprinting reveals various probe-dependent levels of informativeness in chickpea (*Cicer arietinum*).
Genome 35: 436–442

Weissenbach J, Gyapay G, Dib C, Vignal A, Morisette J, Millasseau P, Vaysseix G et al.
(1992) A second-generation linkage map of the human genome. Nature 359: 794–801

Zischler H, Nanda I, Schäfer R, Schmid M, Epplen JT (1989) Digoxigenated oligonucleotide
probes specific for simple repeats in DNA fingerprinting and hybridization *in situ*. Hum
Genet 82: 227–233

Zischler H, Kammerbauer C, Studer R, Grzeschik K-H, Epplen JT (1992) Dissecting
$(CAC)_5/(GTG)_5$ fingerprints into individual locus specific, hypervariable components.
Genomics 13: 983–990

DNA Fingerprinting: State of the Science
ed. by S. D. J. Pena, R. Chakraborty, J. T. Epplen & A. J. Jeffreys
© 1993 Birkhäuser Verlag Basel/Switzerland

Detection, cloning, and distribution of minisatellites in some mammalian genomes

G. Vergnaud, D. Gauguier[a], J.-J. Schott, D. Lepetit[b], V. Lauthier, D. Mariat[c] and J. Buard[d]

Laboratoire de Génétique Moléculaire, Centre d'Etudes du Bouchet, BP 3, F-91710 Vert le Petit, France; [a]CEPH, INSERM, U358, 27 rue Juliette Dodu, F-75010 Paris, France; [b]Laboratoire de Pharmacologie Cellulaire, 15 rue de l'Ecole de Médecine, F-75006 Paris, France; [c]Laboratoire de Génétique Moléculaire, ENVA, 7, Av. du Général de Gaulle, F-94704 Maisons-Alfort Cédex, France; [d]Laboratoire de Génétique des Tumeurs, Section Biologie, Institut Curie, 26 Rue d'Ulm, F-75231 Paris Cédex 05, France

Summary
The chromosomal distribution of minisatellites (cloned and/or detected using natural or synthetic tandem repeats) is strikingly different in man and mouse. In man, the vast majority is clustered in the terminal band of a subset of chromosome arms. Interestingly, the class of shorter tandem repeats called microsatellites is widespread along the chromosomes, suggesting that minisatellites can be created or maintained only in certain regions. In order to gain a better knowledge of these areas, we have studied a sub-telomeric cosmid from the pseudoautosomal region.

Sixty kilobases of human genomic DNA starting approximately 20 kilobases from the human sex chromosomes telomere have previously been independently isolated in two cosmid clones (locus DXYS14) (Cooke et al., 1985); Rouyer et al., 1986). We have studied in more detail one of the two cosmids from this locus and found that it contains four different minisatellite structures representing 20 kilobases of the cosmid. These structures are unrelated to each other or to the minisatellite family described by Jeffreys et al. (1985). They display different degrees of polymorphism correlated with varying amounts of inner homogeneity. Combined with the previous description of an additional minisatellite (Cooke et al., 1985; Inglehearn and Cooke, 1990) in the contiguous cosmid, our observation shows that these structures may represent an important proportion of the DNA in sub-telomeric regions.

Introduction

The discovery of minisatellites and some of the strategies developed to clone them

Minisatellites are those tandem repeats which, owing to their size-range, can be analysed using Southern blotting. They were first isolated by chance (Wyman and White, 1980) or in the vicinity of genes of interest (Bell et al., 1982). More efficient cloning procedures were developed after the observation that some tandem repeats were able to show cross-hybridisation with some others (Jeffreys et al., 1985) However, when using natural tandem repeats, libraries enriched for minisatellites (versus other shorter tandem repeats) (Wong et al., 1987; Armour et al.,

1990; Georges et al., 1991) have to be used in order to get a high efficiency of minisatellite cloning. Another strategy has involved the use of oligonucleotides. In a first instance, the oligonucleotides used were derived from the so-called 'core' sequence consensus and a total cosmid library was screened (Nakamura et al., 1987; 1988). In another instance, the oligonucleotides were selected for their ability to reveal fingerprint patterns on Southern blots (Ali et al., 1986; Schäfer et al., 1988) and an enriched library was used (Zischler et al., 1992).

In humans, where these procedures have been applied most extensively, cloning by chance has probably provided at most a few tens of minisatellites. Cloning by screening enriched libraries using natural tandem repeats has provided about 50 (Wong et al., 1987; Armour et al., 1990). Cloning by screening total libraries with oligonucleotides yielded about 60–80 published minisatellites (White et al., 1990). However, it is very difficult to have a clear estimate of the actual number of truly different human minisatellites available to date, because duplicates obtained in different laboratories are not easily detected.

In any case, minisatellites have been predominently isolated on the assumption that the amplification process is essentially sequence-dependent, and favored by recombination-prone motifs. As a consequence, existing tandem repeats should be good indicators of which sequences are amplification-prone. It is then logical to use Natural Tandem Repeats as probes for detecting other tandem repeats.

The development of Synthetic Tandem Repeats to detect minisatellites

To challenge this point of view, we have explored the efficiency of Synthetic Tandem Repeats (STRs), made by polymerisation of random units, for the detection of tandem repeats. Hybridisation signals that could be obtained on Southern blots of genomic DNAs digested with frequent cutters (such as *Hinf*I or *Hae*III) would presumably be due to detection of minisatellites, especially if polymorphisms are observed. This approach was successfully applied to human DNA (Vergnaud, 1989), and more recently to a wider panel of genomes (vertebrates, and one plant) (Mariat and Vergnaud, 1992). Approximately sixty different STRs were tested, and for each species, a selection of the most adequate STRs was provided. Although the number of species studied, as well as the number of individuals in each species, are limited, it seems that the snake and plant DNA contain a low density of minisatellites.

The use of STRs in linkage analyses

The patterns obtained are usually DNA fingerprints. Such probes can be used for genetic mapping when large pedigrees are available. Using this approach in a mouse recombinant inbred panel enables the detection and localisation by linkage analysis of more than a hundred different loci with about 20 STRs (Mariat et al., 1993). The loci detected appear to be evenly distributed along the mouse genome. This is in agreement with previous reports using human Natural Tandem Repeats as probes at low hybridisation stringency (Julier et al., 1990).

In a few cases, an STR will detect a single locus, as shown for example in sheep (Mariat and Vergnaud, 1992) or human (Vergnaud et al., 1991b; Lauthier et al., 1991b). It is then possible to localise the locus detected by linkage analysis in a set of even relatively small pedigrees, such as the CEPH panel of 40 families, established for human gene mapping purposes. Six loci detected by STRs have been localised in this way to sub-telomeric regions of the human genome (Lauthier et al., 1991a, 1991b; Vergnaud et al., 1991b).

The use of STRs for minisatellite cloning

In order to confirm that STRs are indeed detecting minisatellites, and to see whether they could give access to previously undescribed sequences, we have used them to screen total cosmid libraries. The initial results obtained were reported by Vergnaud et al. (1991a). Three different STRs were used, 14C11, 16C2, 16C4. They enabled the cloning of 9 different human minisatellites. At least one of these sequences, CEB1, is very characteristic because of its high mutation rate in male meiosis (15%), and had not been previously reported. The behaviour of the three STRs was very different with respect to the specificity of minisatellite detection (versus shorter tandem repeats). 16C2 was most efficient, with a majority of positive clones containing a minisatellite. 16C4 was the least effective, with about 10% of the positive clones containing a minisatellite. Later on, 14C21 (Lauthier et al., 1992; Lauthier and Vergnaud, 1992) and 16C27 (described in Mariat et al., 1992) were also found to be highly efficient, and about 30 minisatellites have been cloned from the human (Vergnaud et al., in preparation) or the rat genome (Gauguier et al., in preparation) following this approach of direct cosmid library screening. At the present stage, we are unable to predict and design those STRs which will have this remarkable property. However, STRs can be used for screening enriched libraries, as shown by Armour et al. (1992). In humans, four of the minisatellites obtained are hypermutable, suggesting that the use of STRs may also be of interest for the specific purpose of hypermutable locus cloning. This hypermutability can be of different kinds, with respect to the overall mutation rate as well as the male/female mutation rate ratio: CEB1 (Vergnaud et al., 1991a) and CEB15 (Lauthier et al., 1992) are hypermutable in male meiosis, CEB25 shows a weak male excess, and CEB32 no significant bias. The overall mutation rate at CEB1 is twice the mutation rate at CEB25 and ten time the mutation rate at CEB15. These observations and the results previously reported by Jeffreys et al. (1988) suggest that a wide range of mutational behaviour may exist in the genome.

The distribution of cloned minisatellites in human

Linkage analysis using the CEPH pedigree panel and the CEPH database combined with, in some cases, *in situ* hybridisation, enables the precise localisation of the polymorphic loci obtained. More than 80–90% of the loci are very telomeric (as also seen for the six loci detected directly with STRs, and previously shown for fingerprinting probes (Royle et al. 1988)), but telomeres are not equally represented: for instance, 1p36.3, the terminal band on the short arm of chromosome 1, contains a minisatellite cluster, but not the extremity of the long arm. The chromosome 1 cluster falls within a T-band as defined in Dutrillaux (1973). Telomeric regions in human demonstrate a number of other peculiar features such as an enhanced rate of recombination, and a preferential initiation of pairing, in male meiosis. As a preliminary step towards the understanding of these structural features, we are studying in some detail the most telomeric part of the human pseudoautosomal region.

The detailed molecular analysis of a subtelomeric cosmid

The pseudoautosomal region of the human sex chromosomes is well characterised from a structural point of view. Both ends have been cloned: the junction between the pseudoautosomal region and the sex specific region has been precisely described (Ellis et al., 1989), and the telomere itself has been isolated by functional complementation in yeast (Brown, 1989; Cross et al., 1989). The region has a genetic size of 50 cM in male meiosis (Rouyer et al., 1986), and a physical size of 2600 kilobases (Petit et al., 1988; Brown, 1988; Rappold and Lehrach, 1988). Physical and genetic distances are linearly related so that 1 cM corresponds to 50–60 kb (for a genome average of 1 cM every 1000 kilobases).

Two cosmid clones from the paratelomeric region of the pseudoautosomal region, 29 and 362, have been previously isolated (Cooke et al., 1985; Rouyer et al., 1986). These two clones are contiguous and correspond approximately to 50–80 kilobases of DNA beginning 20 kilobases from the telomere (see Fig. 1). Each cosmid contains one of the ends of a midisatellite (reported as 362A in Rouyer et al., 1986; also described as pDP 230 in Page et al., 1987). In addition, cosmid 29, corresponding to the telomeric side, has been shown to contain another minisatellite structure (Inglehearn and Cooke, 1990).

We have studied in more detail cosmid 362 corresponding to the centromeric side of the midisatellite. In the present work, we report the finding that this cosmid contains three additional minisatellite structures, two of which are polymorphic, and an additional tandem repeat with four units.

Materials and methods

Southern blotting and hybridisations

Southern blotting and hybridisation were as previously reported (Vergnaud, 1989; Vergnaud et al., 1991b). Genomic DNAs were obtained from the Centre d'Etudes du Polymorphisme Humain (CEPH) in Paris. Filters were prehybridized (15 minutes or more) and hybridized (overnight) at 65°C in 2% SDS, 0.45 M Na phosphate pH 7.2, 0.5% skimmed milk, 1 mM EDTA with radiolabelled DNA insert at a probe concentration of approximately 10^6 dpm/ml. DNA fragments containing repetitive sequences were annealed with total human DNA prior to hybridization, as described in Blonden et al. (1989). Washings were done in $2 \times$ SSC, 0.1% SDS (moderate stringency) or 0.1 SSC, 0.1% SDS (high stringency) at 65°C. Filters were autoradiographed at $-80°C$ for 1 to 4 days with two amplifying screens and XAR 5 Kodak film.

DNA sequencing

Sequencing was performed using the dideoxynucleotide chain termination method with the Sequenase kit (USB) after subcloning of the DNA fragment in a M13mp18 or a PUC 18 vector (in this case, double-strand DNA sequencing was performed as described by Jones and Schofield (1990).

Computer sequence handling

Sequence analyses were performed using the program package DNASIS commercialised by Pharmacia-LKB.

Results

Characterisation of cosmid 362 (Fig. 1)

Cosmid 362 was initially isolated by screening a human Y-chromosome specific cosmid library with a STIR (SubTelomeric Interspersed Repeat)

52

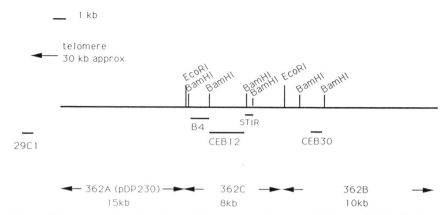

Figure 1. Location of minisatellites within cosmid 362. Cosmid 362 was initially isolated because it contains a copy of a STIR element. Tandem repeats have been found in CEB30, CEB12, B4 and 362A. The direction towards the telomere is indicated. Distances are approximate because of size variations in the VNTRs contained in 362.

element (Rouyer et al., 1990). The insert within cosmid 362 is 33 kb long with three *Eco*RI fragments of 15, 10 and 8 kb. The largest fragment called 362A detects polymorphisms that have been previously reported (Rouyer et al., 1986; Page et al., 1987). The fragment is a tandem repeat (midisatellite) structure with a unit of 61 bp spanning 20–70 kb. The telomeric extremity of that midisatellite is present in cosmid 29 independently isolated by Cooke et al. (1985) (Fig. 1). We used the 10 kb (362B) and 8 kb (362C) *Eco*RI fragments as probes after suppression of repetitive sequences with total human DNA. Both fragments detected polymorphisms when probed on unrelated individuals. The sequences responsible were further localised by testing smaller fragments.

A minisatellite in fragment 362C

A 3.4-kb *Bam*HI fragment (called CEB12) from 362C appears to detect a highly variable locus with alleles ranging in size from 1 to 4 kb when probed on a *Bam*HI genomic blot with twenty unrelated individuals under high stringency conditions. Eighteen of the 20 individuals surveyed were heterozygotes and 12 different alleles can be distinguished in this group (the heterozogosity rate in the CEPH pedigree panel is 80%). Part of the sequence data obtained is presented in Fig. 2. CEB12 contains a tandemly repeated structure with a unit motif of 26 bp spanning all but 0.9 kb of the *Bam*HI DNA fragment. There is very little sequence variations within different units. The unit is 72% G-C with a G-rich strand (13G, 6C). Within the flanking sequence, another tandem repeat of four units has been found (Fig. 2) (accession number X60004 HUMAN CEB12).

proximal
CEB30
gagttgctctctcttccacaaacactcactgtcagatgcaACCCCCANTNTNTNTAGCT
consensus 59%GC (ACCCCCACTGTCTCTAGCT) (VNTR)

AGCTCCagcacattctcatgact
CEB12 repeat 1

ggatcccaaagaaacctgaaaaacaaCTCAGGCCGTGACAGGAAGAGGGG
consensus 72%GC
(CCGCGACAGGAAGAGGGGGTCTCGGG) (VNTR)

GGAAGGAGTCTCctgtttgtagggactcatccattct

CEB12 Repeat 2   gtacaactCATGTGCATCC
                           TCCCATGTGCATCC (4 units; 56%GC)
                           TCCTCTGTGCATCC

   TCCCATGTGCATCCttgaaggggtggcctgcccctccacacct

B 4   tctctctttcttttccctagaatctgtgcataTCGATGGGGTCGA
   consensus 57%GC (GGTCATCCCTGGATGTTGGTGGGGACAA)
(monomorphic, 37 repeats)
                         GGTCATCCTGtgggtgggtgaggactgccacgtccc

pDP230 (362A)
      AAGGTTGCACAGTCTGCTCTCTATCTGTCCTCAATGAGACCTAGGCCCAAT
CAGACTCTA
50%GC   (VNTR)
(Page et al., 1987)

29C1   GGGAGGAGCGGGGTCTGGGGTGGTCCCGAG
      77%GC(VNTR)
(Inglehearn and Cooke,1990)

Telomere   TTAGGG

Figure 2. Consensus sequence of the tandem repeats. We present here partial data on the flanking sequences (lowercase letters), the first and last units, and give a consensus unit with its GC content. The sequences are presented from the most centromeric (CEB30) to the most distal one (the telomere) and read (5′-3′) proximal to distal. The complete sequence data are available under the accession number X60005 (for CEB30) and X60004 (for CEB12 and B4) in the EMBL database.

A minisatellite in fragment 362B

The polymorphism observed with the 10-kb 362B fragment is due to the 1-kb fragment called CEB30 (Fig. 1) obtained after double digestion of 362B with the restriction enzymes *Hinf*I and *Hae*III. This fragment was partially sequenced and contains a repeated unit (Fig. 2; 19 base-pair consensus unit). The sequence is 59% GC, with a G-rich strand (11G-2C). The rate of heterozygosity is 65% (accession number X60005 HUMAN CEB30).

A monomorphic tandem repeat in 362C

The 1.6-kb *Bam*HI fragment adjacent to CEB 12 (telomeric side) detects a single monomorphic band of the expected size when used as a probe on Southern blots. We have sequenced this fragment (called B4) because of its localisation between two VNTRs and found that it contains a tandem repeat of a 28-bp unit spanning approximately 900 bp (37 units). The sequence is also GC rich (57%) with a G-rich strand (11G-5C). The divergence among the different repeats is significant (accession number X60004 HUMAN CEB12).

Orientation of the tandem repeats with respect to the telomere

pDP230 (362A) has previously been described (Page et al., 1987) but its orientation had not been determined. The previous work by Inglehearn and Cooke (1990) has oriented cosmid 29 with respect to the telomere. Since 362A is found at the proximal (centromeric) side of cosmid 29, it is therefore distal to cosmid 362. We have sequenced approximately 100 nucleotides from the telomeric end of cosmid 362. As expected, the sequence obtained corresponds to the one reported for pDP230 and gives the orientation of the unit. Fragment B4 has been positioned distal to fragment CEB12 by restriction mapping. The two fragments have been independently sequenced and the sequence was then oriented by sequencing across the *Bam*HI site separating B4 and CEB12.

CEB30 is within a 2 kb *Bam*HI fragment. Restriction mapping indicates the existence of a *Pst*I fragment near the proximal *Bam*HI site (Fig. 1). Sequencing of both ends of the fragment reveals the predicted *Pst*I site 15 bp after one of the *Bam*HI sites and the start of the tandem repeat 270 bp after the *Pst*I site.

Discussion

Human telomeric regions possess different characteristics that could be related to each other: an enhanced rate of recombination towards chromosome ends, an increased density of minisatellites, a preferential initiation of pairing from the telomeres in male meiosis. The present work, combined with previous reports (Inglehearn and Cooke, 1990; Page et al., 1987) shows that some regions of the genome can be composed mostly of short unrelated tandem repeats. The subtelomeric region of the human sex chromosomes contains at least seven unrelated tandem repeats: the telomere itself, part of sequence 29C1, sequence 362A, parts of sequences B4, CEB12 (2 tandem repeats) and CEB30. These tandem repeats are unrelated to each other and represent the major part of the last 80 kb of the sex chromosome (this size estimation is very approximate because of the important size variation of the tandem repeats). In addition, all the tandem repeats described are GC rich. However, they have not been isolated by cross-hybridization with other related tandem repeats, but in the course of a systematic search for tandem repeats in a restricted area. The other systematic search of minisatellites in a restricted area around the alpha-globin genes (Jarman and Wells, 1989) has led to a similar observation, thus reinforcing the observation that minisatellite structures are predominently GC rich.

The second feature of these repeats is the existence of a G-rich strand. The G-rich strand of 29C1 runs in the same orientation as the G-rich strand from the telomere itself. However, 362A has a 50% GC content with a slightly G-rich strand in the opposite orientation. The small tandem repeat within CEB12 (14 bases unit; 6C-2G) and the VNTR from CEB30 (19 nucleotides consensus; 9C-2G) are also in the opposite direction. These two features, GC richness compared to the average 42% GC content of the human genome, and asymmetry of the two strands, found in different sequences spanning a large stretch of genomic DNA, may be related to the observation of "isochores" in the human genome (Bernardi and Bernardi, 1986): the genomes of warm-blooded vertebrates has been shown to be compartmentalised into regions with homogeneously biased GC content. It is now becoming clear that tandem repeats are of different kinds. The shortest tandem repeats, called microsatellites, are found spread along the whole genome (Weissenbach et al., 1992). Thus additional factors need to be invoked to explain the creation and conservation of minisatellites. One may speculate that this characteristic appeared recently in evolution (i.e. within vertebrates), and is active only in some parts of the genome. If activity requires GC richness with strand asymmetry, then tandem repeats created in that context are likely to be GC rich. In addition, if the high recombination rate found in telomeric regions is necessary for the maintenance of minisatellites, then these structures might progressively disappear from T-bands that have become interstitial (Dutrillaux, 1979), and as a consequence less recombination-prone, because of chromosome-ends fusions during evolution.

In the pseudoautosomal region, 1 cM corresponds to 50–60 kb in male meiosis. Within a region of approximately this size, 4 highly informative markers have been made available. Further developments should make possible the structural analysis of crossovers in humans at an unprecedented resolution within minisatellite clusters.

56

Acknowledgements
We are very grateful to the Centre d'Etudes du Polymorphisme Humain (CEPH) in Paris for the provision of DNA samples from the panel of CEPH families. We thank Monique Zoroastro and Renée Assa for technical assistance. We thank Dr Christine Pourcel for helpful discussions and important improvements of the report. The complete sequence data is available in the EMBL data base under the accession numbers X60004 HUMAN CEB12 DNA and X60005 HUMAN CEB30 DNA.

References

Ali S, Müller CR, Epplen JT (1986) DNA finger printing by oligonucleotide probes specific for simple repeats. Hum Genet 74: 239–243

Armour JAL, Povey S, Jeremiah S, Jeffreys AJ (1990) Systematic cloning of human minisatellites from ordered array charomid libraries. Genomics 8: 501–512

Armour JAL, Vergnaud G, Crosier M, Jeffreys AJ (1992) Isolation of human minisatellite loci detected by synthetic tandem repeat probes: direct comparison with cloned DNA fingerprinting probes. Human Molecular Genetics 1: 319–323

Bell GI, Serby MJ, Rutter WJ (1982) The highly polymorphic region near the human insulin gene is composed of simple tandemly repeating sequences. Nature 295: 31–35

Bernardi G, Bernardi G (1986) The human genome and its evolutionary context. Cold Spring Harbor Symp Quant Biol 51: 479–487

Blonden LAJ, den Dunnen JT, van Paassen HMB, Wapenaar MC, Grootscholten PM, Ginjaar HB, Bakker E et al. (1989) High resolution deletion breakpoint mapping in the DMD gene by whole cosmid hybridization. Nucleic Acids Res 17: 5611–5621

Brown WRA (1988) A physical map of the human pseudoautosomal region. EMBO J 7: 2377–2385

Brown WRA (1989) Molecular cloning of human telomeres in yeast. Nature 338: 774–776

Cooke HJ, Brown WRA, Rappold GA (1985) Hypervariable telomeric sequences from the human sex chromosomes are pseudoautosomal. Nature 317: 687

Cross SH, Allshire RC, McKay SJ, McGill NI, Cooke HJ (1989) Cloning of human telomeres by complementation in yeast. Nature 338: 771–774

Dutrillaux B (1973) Nouveau système de marquage chromosomique: les bandes T. Chromosoma 41: 395–402

Dutrillaux B (1979) Chromosomal evolution in primates: tentative phylogeny from Microcebus murinus (Prosimian) to man. Hum Genet 48: 251–314

Ellis NA, Goodfellow PJ, Pym B, Smith M, Palmer M, Frischauf A-M, Goodfellow PN (1989) The pseudoautosomal boundary in man is defined by an Alu repeat sequence inserted on the Y chromosome. Nature 337: 81–84

Georges M, Gunawardana A, Threadgill D, Lathrop M, Olsaker I, Mishra A, Sargeant L et al. (1991) Characterization of a set of variable number of tandem repeat markers conserved in bovidae. Genomics 11: 24–32

Inglehearn CF, Cooke HJ (1990) A VNTR immediately adjacent to the human pseudoautosomal telomere. Nucleic Acids Res 18: 471–476

Jarman AP, Wells RA (1989) Hypervariable minisatellites: recombinators or innocent bystanders. Trends Genet 5: 367–371

Jeffreys JJ, Wilson V, Thein SL (1985) Hypervariable 'minisatellite' regions in human DNA. Nature 314: 67–73

Jeffreys AJ, Royle NJ, Wilson V, Wong Z (1988) Spontaneous mutation rates to new length alleles at tandem-repetitive hypervariable loci in human DNA. Nature 332: 278–281

Jones DSC, Schofield JP (1990) A rapid method for isolating high quality plasmid DNA suitable for DNA sequencing. Nucleic Acids Res 18: 7463–7464

Julier C, de Gouyon B, Georges M, Guénet JL, Nakamura Y, Avner P, Lathrop GM (1990) Minisatellite linkage maps in the mouse by cross-hybridization with human probes containing tandem repeats. Proc Natl Acad Sci USA 87: 4585–4589

Lauthier V, Mariat D, Vergnaud G (1992) CEB15 detects a VNTR locus (Het: 92%) on chromosome 1p. Human Molecular Genetics 1: 63

Lauthier V, Mariat D, Zoroastro M, Vergnaud G (1991a) A synthetic probe STR14C19, detects a new polymorphic locus at 16pter (D16S282). Nucleic Acids Res 19: 4015

Lauthier V, Mariat D, Zoroastro M, Vergnaud G (1991b) A synthetic probe, STR14C13, detects a new polymorphic locus on chromosome arm 7q (D7S450). Nucleic Acids Res 19: 4014

Lauthier V, Vergnaud G (1992) CEB13 detects a VNTR locus (Het: 93%) on chromosome 7q. Human Molecular Genetics 1: 64

Mariat D, De Gouyon B, Julier C, Lathrop M, Vergnaud G (1993) Genetic mapping through the use of synthetic tandem repeats in the mouse genome. Mammalian Genome 4: 135–140

Mariat D, Guérin G, Bertaud M, Vergnaud G (1992) Modulation of polymorphic loci detection with synthetic tandem repeat variants. Mammalian Genome 3: 546–549

Mariat D, Vergnaud G (1992) Detection of polymorphic loci in various genomes with Synthetic Tandem Repeats. Genomics 12: 454–458

Nakamura Y, Carlson M, Krapcho K, Kanamori M, White R (1988) New approach for isolation of VNTR markers. Am J Hum Genet 43: 854–859

Nakamura Y, Leppert M, O'Connell P, Wolff R, Holm T, Culver M, Martin C et al. (1987) Variable number of tandem repeat (VNTR) markers for human gene mapping. Science 235: 1616–1622

Page DC, Bieker K, Brown LG, Hinton S, Leppert M, Lalouel JM, Lathrop M et al. (1987) Linkage, physical mapping, and DNA sequence analysis of pseudoautosomal loci on the human X and Y chromosomes. Genomics 1: 243–256

Petit C, Levilliers J, Weissenbach J (1988) Physical mapping of the human pseudo-autosomal region, comparison with genetic linkage map. EMBO J 7: 2369–2376

Rappold GA, Lehrach H (1988) A long range restriction map of the pseudoautosomal region by partial digest PFGE analysis from the telomere. Nucleic Acids Res 16: 5361–5377

Rouyer R, de la Chapelle A, Andersson M, Weissenbach J (1990) An interspersed repeated sequence specific for human subtelomeric regions. EMBO J 9: 505–514

Rouyer F, Simmler MC, Vergnaud G, Johnsson C, Levilliers J, Petit C, Weissenbach J (1986) The pseudoautosomal region of the human sex chromosomes. Cold Spring Harbor Symp Quant Biol 51: 221–228

Royle NJ, Clarkson RE, Wong Z, Jeffreys AJ (1988) Clustering of hypervariable minisatellites in the proterminal regions of human autosomes. Genomics 3: 352–360

Schäfer R, Zischler H, Birsner U, Becker A, Epplen JT (1988) Optimized oligonucleotide probes for DNA fingerprinting. Electrophoresis 9: 369–374

Vergnaud G (1989) Polymers of random short oligonucleotides detect polymorphic loci in the human genome. Nucleic Acids Res 17: 7623–7630

Vergnaud G, Mariat D, Apiou F, Aurias A, Lathrop M, Lauthier V (1991a) The use of synthetic tandem repeats to isolate new VNTR loci: cloning of a human hypermutable sequence. Genomics 11: 135–144

Vergnaud G, Mariat D, Zoroastro M, Lauthier V (1991b) Detection of single and multiple polymorphic loci by synthetic tandem repeats of short oligonucleotides. Electrophoresis 12: 134–140

Weissenbach J, Gyapay G, Dib C, Vignal A, Morissette J, Milasseau P, Vaysseix G et al. (1992) A second-generation linkage map of the human genome. Nature 359: 794–801

White R, Lalouel J-M, Lathrop M, Leppert M, Nakamura Y, O'Connell P (1990) "Linkage maps of Man (Homo Sapiens)". In: S. J. O'Brian (ed.) Genetics Maps. Locus Maps of Complex Genomes, 5th edition, Cold Spring Harbor Laboratory Press, Vol. 5, pp 134–157

Wong Z, Wilson V, Patel I, Povey S, Jeffreys AJ (1987) Characterization of a panel of highly variable minisatellites cloned from human DNA. Annu. Hum. Genet. 51: 269–288

Wyman AR, White R (1980) A highly polymorphic locus in human DNA. Proc. Natl. Acad. Sci. USA 77: 6754–6758

Zischler H, Kammerbauer C, Studer R, Grzeschik K-H, Epplen JT (1992) Dissecting $(CAC)_5/(GTG)_5$ multilocus fingerprints from man into individual locus-specific, hypervariable components. Genomics 13: 983–990

DNA Fingerprinting: State of the Science
ed. by S. D. J. Pena, R. Chakraborty, J. T. Epplen & A. J. Jeffreys
© 1993 Birkhäuser Verlag Basel/Switzerland

Frequency of restriction site polymorphisms in the region surrounding VNTR loci

I. Balazs, J. Neuweiler, L. Perlee and J. Venturini

Lifecodes Corporation, 550 West Avenue, Stamford, CT 06902, USA

Summary
Variations in allele size in loci containing tandem repeats result from changes in the number of these repeats. However, digestion of the same DNA samples with two restriction enzymes (i.e. *Pst*I and *Hae*III), that have recognition sites predominantly in the DNA region flanking the VNTR, has identified the presence of numerous site polymorphisms. Three loci (D2S44, D4S163, D17S79) were examined for the presence of restriction site polymorphisms in both North American Black and Caucasian populations. At all loci there were alleles with site polymorphisms. This type of variations were more common in the North American Black than in the Caucasian populations.

Introduction

The primary source of restriction fragment length polymorphism detected in loci composed of tandem repeats is variation in the number of these repeats. However, additional variation in length may result from mutations altering restriction sites in the flanking region or within the sequence of a VNTR locus.

The method used to identify the presence of this type of site polymorphism consisted of the digestion of the same DNA samples with two restriction enzymes (i.e. *Pst*I and *Hae*III) with recognition sites predominantly in the DNA region flanking the VNTR. The expectation was that the difference in the size of an allele between the two restriction enzymes would be the same in the absence of site polymorphisms. Three loci (D2S44, D4S163, D17S79) were examined for the presence of restriction site polymorphisms in both North American Black and Caucasian populations.

Materials and methods

DNA from random individuals were digested with *Pst*I or *Hae*III restriction endonuclease. Methods used for the fractionation of DNA, hybridization to ^{32}P-labeled probes and analysis of the size of the alleles, have been described (Balazs et al., 1989). *Pst*I-digested DNA was

60

fractionated in 28-cm-long 0.9% agarose gels. *Hae*III-digested DNA
was fractionated in 21-cm-long 1.0% agarose gels.

Results and discussion

The values obtained by subtracting the size of alleles with *Hae*III vs
*Pst*I, from the same individual, were scored and plotted against the
value of the size differences detected. The results obtained for each of
the three loci are shown in Figs 1 to 3 for D2S44, D4S163 and D17S79,
respectively. In addition to the predominant allele size difference at each
locus, there was a major secondary variant for a size difference of about
6.6 kb at D2S44 (Fig. 1) and about 3.1 kb at D4S163 (Fig. 2). Also at
all loci there were a multitude of additional variants scattered above or
below the value of the main size difference. The values of these allele
differences were determined in both the North American Caucasian and
Black populations and the frequency of these observations summarized
in Tab. 1. The differences in allele size were subdivided into 2 or 3 types
as compared to the most common size difference. One type contains all
values larger than the most abundant size difference, another the values
smaller than the most abundant and, in some loci, a third type for a
common variant. Result showed that the total frequency of this type of
variation at the D2S44 locus was approximately 40.1% of the alleles in
Blacks, with one type of variant accounting for more than 30% of the

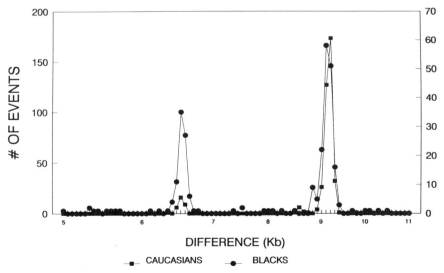

Figure 1. Size difference between *Hae*III and *Pst*I D2S44 alleles. The vertical values on the
left side are the number of events for Caucasians and the right side from Blacks.

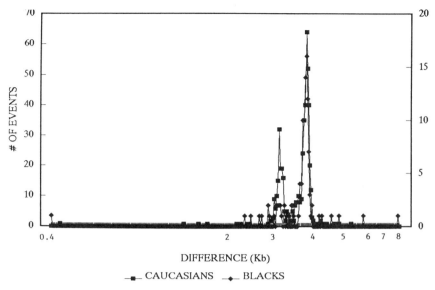

Figure 2. Size difference between *Hae*III and *Pst*I D4S163 alleles. The vertical values on the left side are the number of events for Caucasians and the right side from Blacks.

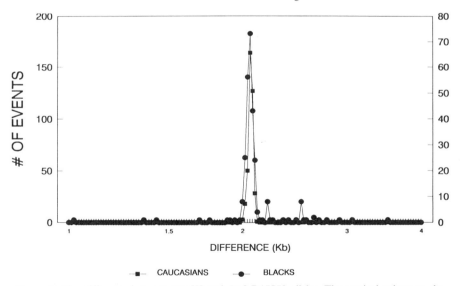

Figure 3. Size difference between *Hae*III and *Pst*I D17S79 alleles. The vertical values on the left side are the number of events for Caucasians and the right side from Blacks.

observations, and about 10.4% in Caucasians. At the D17S79 locus the frequency of variants was 13.8% in Blacks and 0.8% in Caucasians. The D4S163 locus has a major variant of about 3.1 kb and it is twice as common in Caucasian than in Blacks. However, the overall frequency

Table 1. Fraction of alleles with restriction site polymorphism

Locus	RFLP Type	Caucasian	Black
D2S44	Minor variants (large)	0.25%	1.82%
	6.6 kb variant	7.88%	31.02%
	Minor variants (small)	2.22%	7.30%
D17S79	Minor variants (large)	0.76%	10.95%
	Minor variants (small)	—	2.92%
D4S163	Minor variants (large)	1.62%	5.17%
	3.1 kb variant	27.84%	13.79%
	Minor variants (small)	2.16%	9.48%

of all variants is similar in both populations (31.6% and 28.5%, respectively).

The effect of this additional source of polymorphism is an increase in the heterogeneity or power of identification of these markers as compared with variation resulting only from changes in the number of tandem repeats.

Reference

Balazs I, Baird M, Clyne M, Meade E (1989) Human population genetic studies of five hypervariable DNA Loci. Am J Hum Genet 44: 182–190

DNA Fingerprinting: State of the Science
ed. by S. D. J. Pena, R. Chakraborty, J. T. Epplen & A. J. Jeffreys
© 1993 Birkhäuser Verlag Basel/Switzerland

Human VNTR mutation and sex

B. Olaisen, M. Bekkemoen, P. Hoff-Olsen and P. Gill[a]

Institute of Forensic Medicine, University of Oslo, Oslo, [a]Central Research and Support Establishment, The Forensic Science Service, Aldermaston, UK

Summary
Seven hypervariable VNTR loci have been studied in about 1200 parent/child pairs about equally divided between the sexes. Mutations were observed with all seven probes, the total number being 71. Fourty-four of these involved increased fragment length. Gains in fragment length were on average larger than losses. These findings indicate that mutation might be a basis for evolutionary expansion of VNTR fragment length. For five probes YNH24 (D2S44), MS31 (D7S21), g3 (D7S22), MS43A (D12S11), and CMM101 (D14S13), mutation rates were relatively low (less than 1%) with no obvious sex difference. MS1 (D1S7) mutation frequencies were substantially higher, with a tendency towards a higher paternal than maternal mutation rate (5.4% and 2.0%, respectively). The probe B6.7 (provisionally assigned to chromosome 20) exhibits about five times higher paternal than maternal mutation rates. The mutation rate of 7.6% in paternal chromosomes is among the highest reported in any VNTR locus. These findings could indicate that while low-mutant VNTRs might reflect meiotic crossover, mutation events in high-mutant loci could more often be caused by other mechanisms during cell division.

Introduction

Mutational events leading to new length alleles have been demonstrated in minisatellite fingerprints as well as in VNTR profiles. Such events may represent a number of different mechanisms including recombination events in meiosis (with or without crossover between flanking sequences), sister chromatid exchange, replication slippage, and loopout deletion. Core sequence homology to recombinational hotspots (Jeffreys et al., 1985; Steinmetz et al., 1986), may indicate that the generation of hypervariability at VNTRs could be due to a high frequency of crossover at these loci.

The object of this study was to compare VNTR mutation type and mutation rates between the sexes, in an attempt to further elucidate the mechanisms behind VNTR mutations found in blood DNA.

Materials and methods

Parent/child pairs from consecutive Norwegian paternity cases constitute the basis for this study. The kinship status was confirmed by extensive genetic marker analyses.

DNA extraction and electrophoresis were performed according to "EDNAP standards"; e.g. using *Hinf*I restriction (Schneider et al., 1991). Fragment sizes were determined using automated scanning equipment developed at the Metropolitan Police Forensic Science Laboratory.

Samples showing mutations were digested with at least two additional restriction enzymes (*Pst*I, *Hae*III, *Alu*I, or *Taq*I).

Almost all filters were hybridized consecutively with radiolabelled probes: YNH24, MS31, g3, MS43A, and CMM101. Probe MS1 was employed in 468 and probe B6.7 (Kimpton et al., 1992) in 791 consecutive parent/child pairs.

Ascertainment of mutant bands was based on independent X-ray film inspection by two trained laboratory staff members, the largest difference in band migration ordinarily accepted for a band match being about 1 mm. The power of resolution thus decreases with increasing fragment size (e.g.; 1 mm represents about 30 bp difference at fragment size 2 kb, 300 bp at 10 kb). All mutations with small band differences were confirmed in a second run on a new gel before they were accepted. The progenitor band was always chosen as the parental band most similar in size to the mutant allele (see Wolff et al., 1989).

Results and discussion

Mutations were encountered with all probes used. In Figs 1–4 are shown examples of the fragment patterns involving mutational events. The probes YNH24, MS31, g3, MS43A, and CMM101 detect low-mutant loci (range 0.000–0.009), while MS1 and B6.7 mutation rates are substantially higher (range 0.014–0.076) (Tab. 1). The observed VNTR mutation frequencies with the five low-mutant probes as well as with MS1 are in accordance with published findings (Jeffreys et al., 1988; Smith et al., 1990). This is the first report of B6.7 mutation frequencies. A male mutation rate of 7.6% is among the highest so far reported in human VNTRs.

The mutation frequency with the five low-mutation rate probes is fairly equal among the sexes. This is in good agreement with earlier reports (Jeffreys et al., 1988). These authors, however, did not encounter any obvious difference in the MS1 mutation rates between the sexes, while we observed a sperm/oocyte ratio exceeding 2:1. With probe B6.7 there is a statistically significant difference with a ratio of about 5:1. An even more pronounced sex difference in mutation rate was recently described in the hypermutable VNTR locus identified by probe CEB1 (Vergnaud et al., 1991). This tendency towards high sperm/oocyte mutation ratio in high-mutant VNTR loci might reflect the twenty-fold number of cell divisions in spermiogenesis compared to oogenesis. Our

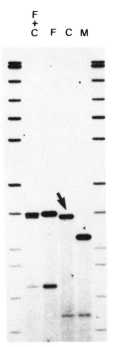

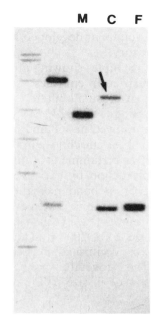

Figure 1. VNTR patterns with probe g3 (D7S22) in a family triplet with *Hinf*I digested DNA from the mother (M), child (C) and father (F) and a mixture of DNA from the child and its father (F + C). The mutant fragment in the child is marked with an arrow. The progenitor allele is probably the father's largest fragment, giving a size loss at mutation.

Figure 2. VNTR patterns with probe MS43A (D12S11) in a family triplet with *Hinf*I digested DNA from the mother (M), child (C) and father (F). The mutant fragment in the child is marked wtih an arrow. The progenitor allele is most likely the largest of the mother's very closely located fragments, giving a size gain at mutation.

Table 1. VNTR mutations – grouped by probe and sex

Probe	Paternal mutations			Maternal mutations		
	Number of mutations	Total observations	Mutation frequency	Number of mutations	Total observations	Mutation frequency
YNH24	1	577	0.002	4	649	0.006
MS31	4	581	0.007	0	656	0.000
G3	5	576	0.009	3	651	0.006
MS43A	1	580	0.002	1	654	0.002
CMM101	1	566	0.002	2	637	0.003
All five	12	2880	0.004	10	3247	0.003
MS1	11	223	0.054	5	245	0.020
B6.7	28	369	0.076	5	422	0.014

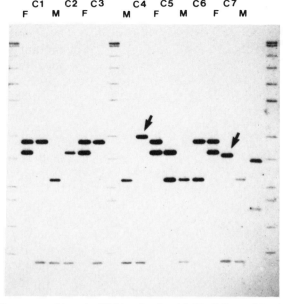

Figure 3. VNTR patterns with probe B6.7 in a family with *Hinf*I digested DNA from the mother (M), seven out of a total of 13 children (marked C1–C7) and their father (F). Paternal mutant fragments are seen in two of the children (arrows). The mutation in child 4 probably took place by a gain in the father's largest allele. In child 7, the progenitor allele most likely is the father's smallest fragment, the mutation giving rise to a small size loss.

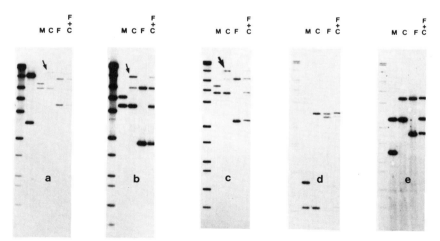

Figure 4. VNTR patterns in a family triplet with DNA from the mother (M), child (C) and father (F) and a mixture of DNA from the child and its father (F + C). In a), b), and c) are shown the patterns with probe MS43A (D12S11) and restriction enzymes *Pst*I, *Alu*I, and *Hinf*I, respectively. In d) and e) are patterns from *Hinf*I restriction and probes CMM101 (D14S13) and YNH24 (D2S44). The large, mutant fragment in the child is marked (arrow). The child has a three-band pattern with a faint paternal fragment assumed to represent the progenitor allele to a somatic mutation.

findings might therefore support the arguments given by Wolff et al. (1989) that most mutations in high-mutant VNTR loci are caused by mechanisms other than crossingover at meiosis. On the other hand, the relatively low sperm/oocyte mutation ratio in low-mutant VNTRs could reflect a significant proportion of crossovers, since the male/female crossover ratio is low (about 1:1.5).

In accordance with earlier reports (Jeffreys et al., 1988; Wolff et al., 1989), all but one of the present mutations are probably germline events. In one case (Fig. 4), the MS43A probe recognizes a relatively faint "normal" paternal band as well as an additional, mutated larger fragment. The MS43A pattern is very much like the somatic MS31 mutation described by Wolff et al. (1989) in a CEPH family lymphoblastoid cell line. Somatic mutations in MS32 have been extensively studied by single molecule analysis (Jeffreys et al., 1990), and such mutations have also been reported in a VNTR locus in mice (Kelly et al., 1989). High frequencies of somatic mutations in VNTR loci have also been described in human tumors (Armour et al., 1989).

While Jeffreys et al. (1988) found significantly larger length changes in maternal rather than paternal VNTR mutations, this tendency is weak in our material (Fig. 5).

Figure 6 shows the distribution of fragment change gain and loss at VNTR mutation. Of the 71 mutations, 44 involved fragment change gains compared to 27 losses. The tendency towards fragment size increase at mutation is statistically significantly at the 5% level. The

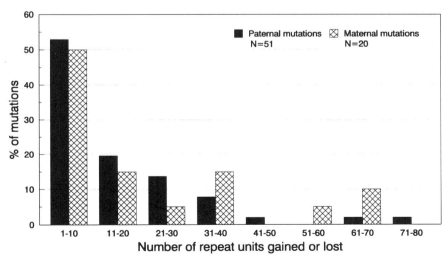

Figure 5. Relative frequency distribution, in 10 repeat unit intervals, of fragment size changes (losses or gains) in the 20 maternal and 51 paternal mutations observed. The weak tendency towards larger changes in maternal than paternal chromosomes is not statistically significant.

68

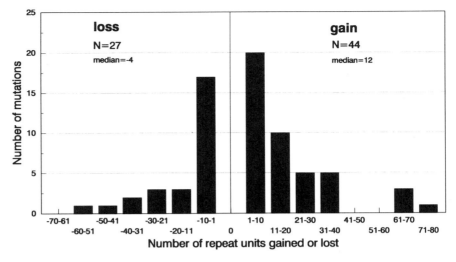

Figure 6. Frequency distribution of fragment length loss (left) and gain (right), in 10 unit intervals. There is a statistically significant surplus of gain events, and the average size of the gains is larger than that of the losses.

average fragment size difference between progenitor and mutant fragment was 19 (s.e.m. = 19) repeat units for gains, 13(14) for losses. On average there is a fragment length gain of 7 repeat units per mutation in the present material. These findings indicate that mutation might be a basis for evolutionary expansion of VNTR fragment length.

References

Schneider PM, Fimmers R, Woodroffe S, Werrett DJ, Bär W, Brinkmann B, Eriksen B, Jones S, Kloostermann AD, Mevåg B, Pascali VL, Rittner C, Schmitter H, Thomson JA, Gill P (1991) Report of a European collaborative exercise comparing DNA typing results using a single locus DNA probe. Forensic Sci Int 49: 1–15

Jeffreys AJ, Wilson V, Thein SL (1985) Hypervariable "minisatellite" regions in human DNA. Nature 314: 67–73

Jeffreys AJ, Royle NJ, Wilson V, Wong Z (1988) Spontaneous mutation rates to new length alleles at tandem-repetitive hypervariable loci in human DNA. Nature 332: 278–281

Jeffreys AJ, Neumann R, Wilson V (1990) Repeat unit sequence variation in minisatellites: A novel source of DNA polymorphism for studying variation and mutation by single molecule analysis. Cell 60: 473–485

Kelly R, Bulfield G, Collick A, Gibbs M, Jeffreys A (1989) Characterization of a highly unstable mouse minisatellite locus: evidence for somatic mutation during early development. Genomics 5: 844–856

Kimpton CP, Hopgood R, Watson SK, Gill P, Sullivan K (1992) Cloning and charcterization of novel single locus probes for forensic purposes. In: Rittner C, Schneider PM (eds) Advances in forensic haemogenetics 4, Springer-Verlag, Berlin Heidelberg, pp 129–133

Smith JC, Anwar R, Riley J, Jenner D, Markham AF, Jeffreys AJ (1990) Highly polymorphic minisatellite sequences: allele frequencies and mutation rates for five locus-specific probes in a Caucasian population. J For Sci Soc 30: 19–32

Steinmetz M, Stephan D, Lindahl KF (1986) Gene organization and recombinational hotspots in murine major histocompatibility complex. Cell 44: 895–904

Vergnaud G, Mariat D, Apiou F, Aurias A, Lathrop M, Lautier V (1991) The use of synthetic tandem repeats to isolate new VNTR loci: Cloning of a human hypermutable sequence. Genomics 11: 135–144

Wolff RK, Plaetke R, Jeffreys AJ, White R (1989) Unequal crossingover between homologous chromosomes is not the major mechanism involved in the generation of new alleles at VNTR loci. Genomics 5: 382–384

DNA Fingerprinting: State of the Science
ed. by S. D. J. Pena, R. Chakraborty, J. T. Epplen & A. J. Jeffreys

Variation of minisatellites in chemically induced mutagenesis and in gene amplification

P. Vagnarelli, E. Giulotto, P. Fattorini[a], E. Mucciolo, M. Bensi,
L. Tessera and L. De Carli

*Dipartimento di Genetica e Microbiologia, Università di Pavia, Via Abbiategrasso 207,
I-27100 Pavia, and [a]Dipartimento di Biologia animale, Università di Trieste, Trieste, Italy*

Summary
A mutation assay in cultured mammalian cells was developed based on direct analysis of
minisatellite DNA. Chinese hamster cells (V79) were mutagenized with nitrosoguanidine and
independent colonies were isolated and expanded. DNA fingerprints were then obtained after
digestion with *Hinf*I or *Hae*III and hybridization with 33.15 and 33.6 probes (Jeffreys et al.,
1985). 12 colonies from untreated cells were also analyzed. Digestion with *Hae*III and
hybridization with 33.15 probe detected the highest frequency of induced variants. The results
suggest that minisatellite sequences are hypermutable sites that can be used to monitor the
mutagenic effect of chemical agents. We have also analyzed the DNA fingerprints of 17
independent Chinese hamster (CHO) cell lines carrying amplification of the CAD gene. The
DNA fingerprint analysis showed a variation in minisatellite regions in 3 lines while no
variation was observed in independent colonies from the CHO parental cell line. The results
suggest that these sequences may be hot spots for recombination during gene amplification.

Introduction

Mutagenesis studies are in need of new tests to detect DNA sequence
alterations as opposed to phenotypic changes; when phenotypic modifications are analyzed, it is difficult to discriminate between genetic and
epigenetic events (Holliday, 1991). The distinction between point, gene
and chromosome mutations is based mainly on the detection system
used; however such a classification has little significance at the molecular level, because the extension of DNA alterations ranges within a
continuum from single base pairs to entire chromosomes. A mutagenesis test based on the analysis of modifications in DNA fingerprint band
patterns should offer two advantages. i) Minisatellite DNA repetitions
are multiple targets for mutations. The simultaneous visualization of
several possible mutable sites can reduce the sample size of orders of
magnitude. ii) Minisatellite DNA is hypervariable and it might be
hypermutable. An increased number of detectable mutation events per
site can enormously improve sensitivity of the test. A similar rationale is
followed when mutator strains are utilized in mutagenesis testing. A
selected class of mutational events could lead to modifications in a
DNA fingerprint, mainly: A) intra- or inter-locus recombination; B)

DNA slippage at replication C) alteration in the restriction sites surrounding each repetition; D) variation in copy number of DNA fragments containing minisatellites (deletions, amplifications); E) variation in chromosome number.

In mammalian cells, gene amplification is a common process that increases gene copy number. Amplification can produce over-expression of proto-oncogenes and of genes conferring drug resistance. Cell lines selected in culture for resistance to several metabolic inhibitors have been extensively used to investigate the molecular mechanisms of gene amplification. For example cells resistant to N-phosphonacetyl-L-aspartate (PALA) carry amplification of the gene encoding the multifunctional enzyme CAD, which catalyzes the first three reactions of UMP biosynthesis.

Recent studies have indicated that recombination of large chromosomal regions occurs very early during gene amplification (Smith et al., 1990; Toledo et al., 1992) and that amplified DNA is initially very unstable and can frequently recombine or be lost (Giulotto et al., 1986; Stark et al., 1986; Saito et al., 1989). Very little is known about the DNA sequences involved in these recombination processes and the observation of regularly spaced amplified units suggests that moderately repeated sequences may be preferential sites for recombination.

In the course of this work we have addressed two questions. To establish whether a mutagenesis test could be developed based on the detection of minisatellite mutations, we have analyzed DNA fingerprint alterations of Chinese hamster cells following mutagenic treatment with nitrosoguanidine. Second, to investigate the possible involvement of minisatellite sequences in the recombination events accompanying gene amplification, we have studied band pattern modifications of Chinese hamster cell lines carrying multiple copies of the CAD gene.

Materials and methods

Chemicals: Nitrosoguanidine (Sigma) and N-phosphonacetyl-L-aspartate (PALA) (Drug Synthesis & Chemistry Branch, Division of Cancer Treatment, National Cancer Institute, Bethesda) were dissolved in water and the stock solutions stored at $-20°C$.

Cell lines and culture: Chinese hamster embryonal lung fibroblasts (V79) were cultured in Eagle's Minimum Essential Medium with Dulbecco's modification (D-MEM), supplemented with 5% fetal calf serum. Chinese hamster ovary fibroblasts (CHO) were cultured in RPMI medium supplemented with 10% dialyzed fetal calf serum.

Mutagenic treatment and colony isolation: semiconfluent V79 cell cultures were treated with 3 μg/ml of nitrosoguanidine for 24 h and, after 24-h release in fresh medium, 200 cells from the treated and untreated cultures were plated in 10-cm diameter culture dishes in order to obtain clones from single cells. At 3 μg/ml nitrosoguanidine the plating efficiency of V79 cells was reduced to 0.8%. After two weeks, 15 independent colonies were isolated from both treated and untreated cells. Each clone was cultured as described above.

Selection of PALA resistant cell lines: CHO cells were plated at a density of $10^5/10$ cm plate in RPMI medium supplemented with 10% dialyzed fetal calf serum and PALA as previously described (Zieg et al. 1983). After 2–3 weeks, single visible colonies were picked, transferred to 3 cm plates and expanded in the same selective medium containing PALA. With this procedure PALA-resistant mutants P1-P6, P8-P12, were obtained using 0.1 mM PALA, A1, A3 and B5 using 0.27 mM PALA, and A2, A4 using 0.21 mM PALA. The highly resistant mutants A2-31 and A2-33 were obtained from A2 after a second step of selection in 3 mM PALA, and A3-22 was obtained from A3 with 2 mM PALA. A4-21, A4-31, A4-32 and A4-33 were obtained from A4 using 2 or 3 mM PALA as shown in Tab. 2. B5-31, B5-32, B5-33 were obtained from B5 after selection with 3 mM PALA.

Isolation of CHO clones: 200 CHO cells were plated in 10-cm diameter plates and cultured in RPMI medium. After 10–15 days culture, 24 isolated colonies from different plates were picked and expanded.

DNA extraction and electrophoresis: DNA was extracted according to standard procedures (Maniatis et al., 1982) and digested with *Hinf*I or *Hae*III. The samples were then loaded into a 0.8% agarose gel 20 cm long. Gels were electrophoresed at 2 V/cm for 24–30 h until all DNA fragments shorter than 2.0 kb had run out of the gel.

Hybridization

DNA was then transferred to Hybond-C-extra nitrocellulose membrane (Amersham). The 33.15 and 33.6 probes (Jeffreys et al., 1985) were ^{32}P labeled by random priming (Amersham). The specific activities were $> 10^9$ cpm/μg.

Membranes were prehybridized in 0.5 M Na-phosphate buffer pH 7.2, 1 mM EDTA, 7% SDS at 60°C. Hybridization was carried out in the same buffer for 12–16 h at 65°C. The membranes were then washed once in 2 × SSC, 0.1% SDS at room temperature for 10 min and then twice in 1 × SSC, 0.1% SDS at 60°C for 10 min. The membranes were kept moist and autoradiographed for 1–5 days at −70°C with intensifying screens.

Statistical analysis

The results obtained were analyzed by conventional statistical G and χ^2 test (Sokal and Rohlf, 1969).

Results and discussion

Mutagenicity testing

We have analyzed DNA fingerprint modifications of Chinese hamster cells treated with the alkylating agent nitrosoguanidine. V79 cells were treated for 24 hours with $3 \mu g/ml$ nitrosoguanidine, which reduced plating efficiency to 0.8%. After two weeks 14 independent clones were isolated and expanded. When the number of cells derived from each colony was approximately 1.6×10^7, DNA was extracted, digested with the restriction enzymes *Hae*III or *Hinf*I and hybridized with 33.15 or 33.6 probe DNA (Jeffreys et al., 1985). Control samples were prepared from independent colonies isolated from untreated cells. The DNA was digested with *Hae*III and hybridized with 33.15 probe. In Fig. 1 the band patterns of the 14 mutagenized samples and of one of the controls are shown. Several differences in the band pattern of treated colonies can be observed when compared with untreated cells. Most alterations are in the fragments of 9–20 kb; this finding suggests that the probability of detectable mutation is higher at some loci. The observation that each variant pattern is unique confirms that the mutational events that we have observed are independent.

As summarized in Tab. 1, 11 of the 14 treated samples and 3 of the 12 control samples showed band pattern variation, when 33.15 and *Hae*III enzyme were used. The difference between treated and control samples is statistically significant as demonstrated by G and χ^2 tests. No statistically significant difference was found in the other conditions.

Gene amplification

We have searched for DNA fingerprint alterations in PALA-resistant Chinese hamster cell lines carrying amplification of the CAD gene. CHO cells were plated in the presence of various selective PALA concentrations; the doses of PALA used ranged between 3 and 60 times the DR50. It is known that in this range of inhibitor concentrations, only cells with multiple copies of the CAD gene can survive. After 2–3 weeks in selective medium, independent colonies were isolated and expanded. DNA was then extracted and DNA fingerprints were obtained as described in Materials and Methods. In Tab. 2 the selection

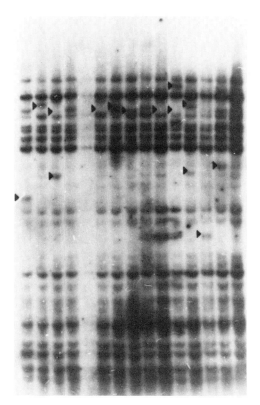

Figure 1. DNA fingerprints of 14 clones mutagenized with nitrosoguanidine. The DNA was digested with *Hae*III and hybridized with 33.15. The arrows indicate band pattern alterations.

Table 1. DNA fingerprint alterations in V79 cells after mutagenic treatment

Probe	Enzyme	Treated	Control
33.15	*Hae*III*	11/14	3/12
	*Hinf*I	2/11	1/11
33.6	*Hae*III	2/14	0/10
	*Hinf*I	2/11	2/9

*G test $0.025 < p < 0.01$.
χ^2 test $0.025 < p < 0.01$.

scheme for each clone is reported: eleven colonies (P1-6, P8-12) were isolated from the CHO line after a single step of selection with 0.1 mM PALA and one colony (A1) after selection with 0.27 mM PALA. The remaining PALA-resistant mutants belong to four different families. Each family includes one parental line, selected in one step from CHO

Table 2. DNA Fingerprint alterations in CHO cells carrying CAD gene amplification

Cell line (parental)	Dose of PALA used for selection mM	33.15		33.6	
		*Hinf*I	*Hae*III	*Hinf*I	*Hae*III
P1 (CHO)	0.10	−	−	−	−
P2 (CHO)	0.10	−	−	−	−
P3 (CHO)	0.10	−	−	−	−
P4 (CHO)	0.10	−	−	−	−
P5 (CHO)	0.10	−	−	−	−
P6 (CHO)	0.10	−	−	−	−
P8 (CHO)	0.10	−	−	−	−
P9 (CHO)	0.10	−	−	−	−
P10 (CHO)	0.10	−	−	−	−
P11 (CHO)	0.10	−	+	−	−
P12 (CHO)	0.10	−	−	−	−
A1 CHO	0.27	−	−	−	−
A2 (CHO)	0.21	+	+	+	−
A2-31 (A2)	3.00	+	+	+	−
A2-33 (A2)	3.00	+	+	+	−
A3 (CHO)	0.27	−	nt	−	nt
A3-22 (A3)	2.00	−	−	−	−
A4 (CHO)	0.21	+	+	−	−
A4-21 (A4)	2.00	+	+	−	−
Ar-31 (A4)	3.00	+	+	−	−
A4-32 (A4)	3.00	+	+	−	−
A4-33 (A4)	3.00	+	+	−	−
B5 (CHO)	0.27	−	−	−	−
B5-31 (B5)	3.00	nt	−	nt	−
B5-32 (B5)	3.00	nt	−	nt	−
B5-33 (B5)	3.00	−	−	−	−

+: Presence of a band pattern alteration compared to CHO DNA fingerprint.
−: No detectable differences.
nt: not tested.

cells (A2, A3, A4 and B5), and 1−5 clones that were obtained from the parental line after a second step of selection in a higher PALA concentration. The DNA fingerprints of the PALA-resistant cell lines were compared with that of the original CHO line (Tab. 2). After digestion of the DNA with *Hinf*I and hybridization with 33.15 probe, 8 out of 24 cell lines showed an altered band pattern; after digestion with *Hae*III, 9 out of 25 cell lines had an altered fingerprint. When 33.6 probe was used, 3 lines showed band pattern variation after digestion with *Hinf*I only. However, the PALA-resistant cell lines are not all independent and 14 of them belong to four families. We can then conclude that hybridization with 33.15 could reveal minisatellite alterations accompanying amplification of the CAD gene in three out of 16 independent cell lines when *Hae*III was used for digestion and in two lines when the DNA was digested with *Hinf*I. In contrast, 33.6 probe could detect minisatellite variation associated with gene amplification in one family only. A similar experiment was performed with DNA extracted from 24 CHO cell lines derived from unselected independent clones; no band pattern variation was observed. These results suggest that the recombination process associated with CAD gene amplification could involve minisatellite sequences. Alternatively, alterations in the DNA fingerprints could be due to secondary rearrangements occurring during the evolution of amplified DNA, which is known to be unstable.

Acknowledgements
We thank Nancita Lomax (Drug Synthesis & Chemistry Branch, Division of Cancer Treatment, National Cancer Institute, Bethesda) for kindly providing PALA. This work was funded by Associazione Italiana per la Ricerca sul Cancro (A.I.R.C.) and by Progetti Finalizzati C.N.R. "Ingegneria Genetica" e "Biotecnologie e Biostrumentazione". E.M. is supported by a fellowship from Istituto Oncologico Romagnolo.

References

Giulotto E, Saito I, Stark GR (1986) Structure of DNA formed in the first step of CAD gene amplification. EMBO J 5: 2115–2121

Holliday R (1991) Mutations and epimutations in mammalian cells. Mut Res 250: 351–363

Jeffreys AJ, Wilson V, Thein SL (1985) Hypervariable 'minisatellite' regions in human DNA. Nature 314: 67–73

Maniatis T, Fritsch EE, Sambrook J (1982) Molecular cloning: a laboratory manual. Cold Spring Harbor Laborator, Cold Spring Harbor, NY

Saito I, Groves R, Giulotto E, Rolfe M, Stark GR (1989) Evolution and stability of chromosomal DNA coamplified with the CAD gene. Mol Cell Biol 9: 2445–2452

Smith KA, Gorman PA, Stark MB, Groves RP, Stark GR (1990) Distinctive chromosomal structures are formed very early in the amplification of CAD genes in Syrian hamster cells. Cell 63: 1219–1227

Sokal RR, Rohlf FJ (1969) Introduction to biostatistics W.H. Freeman and Company, San Francisco

Stark GR, Debatisse M, Giulotto E, Wahl G (1986) Recent progress in understanding the mechanism of mammalian DNA amplification. Cell 57: 901–908

Toledo F, Smith KA, Buttin G, Debatisse M (1992) The evolution of the amplified deaminase 2 domains in Chinese hamster cells suggests the sequential operation of different mechanisms of DNA amplification. Mut Res 276: 261–274

Zieg J, Clayton CE, Ardeshir F, Giulotto E, Swyryd A, Stark GR (1983) Properties of single-step mutants of Syrian hamster cell lines resistant to N-(phosphonacetyl)-L-aspartate. Mol Cell Biol 3: 2089–2098

DNA Fingerprinting: State of the Science
ed. by S. D. J. Pena, R. Chakraborty, J. T. Epplen & A. J. Jeffreys
© 1993 Birkhäuser Verlag Basel/Switzerland

Iterons of stringently controlled plasmids and DNA fingerprinting

K. J. Huebscher, G. Dolf and J. Frey[a]

Institute of Animal Breeding, University of Berne, 3012 Berne, Switzerland, and [a]Institute of Veterinary Bacteriology, University of Berne, 3012 Berne, Switzerland

Summary
DNA probes which detect polymorphic, repetitive sequences in a variety of genomes have been developed using different approaches. Naturally occurring plasmids, with repeated units termed iterons near or within their origins (*ori*) of replication, could be of interest for the development of probes, possibly even revealing novel minisatellite families in mammals involved in replicational processes. We used the plasmids P1, pSC101 and RSF1010 or their PCR amplified *ori* regions as probes in Southern blot hybridisations with mammalian DNA. At low stringency they generated reproducible fingerprint-like patterns. A bovine genomic library was screened at the same stringency with the PCR-amplified *ori* region of P1 containing the five times repeated core sequence 5′-ATGTGTGNTGNNGGG-3′ to generate a probe for cattle DNA with higher specificity.

Introduction

DNA probes which detect polymorphic loci in a variety of genomes have been developed using different approaches (Jeffreys et al., 1985; Ali et al., 1986; Nakamura et al., 1987; Vassart et al., 1987; Vergnaud, 1989; Crawford et al., 1991). Our interest was attracted by the naturally occurring plasmids P1, pSC101 and RSF1010 with tandemly repeated units (termed iterons) near or within their origins of replication (Scott, 1984). These plasmids are found in fixed, low copy numbers and they belong to the three different incompatibility (Inc) groups IncY, pSC101 and IncQ. Their replication is precisely controlled by a mechanism involving the Inc group specific iterons (Scott, 1984; Linder et al., 1985; Persson and Nordström, 1986; Novick, 1987; Frey and Bagdasarian, 1989). They influence the rate of initiation by specifically binding the responsible RepA protein. We have used the stringently controlled plasmids P1 (pEU203), pSC101, RSF1010 or amplified parts of their *ori* regions directly as probes in low stringency Southern blot hybridisations with different mammalian DNAs. Plasmid pEU203 is the cloning vector pUC18 with incompatibility and replication genes including the iterons of P1 inserted into its polylinker. To develop a probe, which is useful for paternity testing in cattle, we screened a bovine genomic library with the amplified *ori* region of plasmid P1.

Materials and methods

Plasmid DNA was extracted according to the procedure described by Birnboim and Doly (1979). The host strains were grown in LB medium containing the appropriate antibiotic (Sambrook, 1989). Bovine DNA was extracted both from frozen semen and from blood samples by the guanidine hydrochloride procedure (Jeanpierre, 1987) with the modification of adding 2-mercaptoethanol in the case of DNA extractions from semen (Bahnak et al., 1988). A partial bovine genomic library was generated by pooling *Pst*I digested DNA of two bulls (Fig. 1). The pooled DNA was sized selected by ultracentrifugation through a salt gradient (5 to 25% NaCl). The 500-μl fractions were analysed by agarose gel electrophoresis for their size range. The 2 to 10 kb size fraction was chosen and ligated into the dephosphorylated vector pBluescript II SK – (Stratagene). The two host strains JM83 (Vieira and Messing, 1982) and SURE (Stratagene) were transformed by electroporation. The JM83 library was screened at low stringency with the 163 bp, PCR amplified *ori* region of P1 including the five repeats. The primers used were *ori*P1-L 5′-GAAGTGTATCGCGATGTG-3′ and *ori*P1-R 5′-TCCGAATTGTGTG-GATAG-3′. Positive clones were tested in Southern blot hybridisations at high stringency. The high

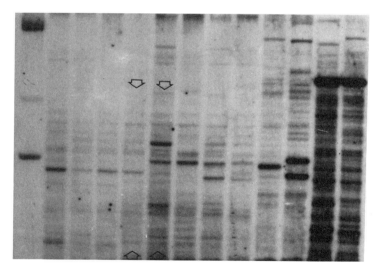

Figure 1. 0.6% agarose gel electrophoresis of 1 μg *Pst*I digested bovine, donkey and human DNAs (23 V, 63 h). Southern blot hybridisation with the PCR amplified *ori* region of P1. m: marker, lambda DNA *Hin*dIII digest. 1–4: related individuals of the Swiss Brown cattle breed. 5–8: unrelated individuals of different cattle breeds. 5: Simmental cattle. 6: Brown Swiss cattle. 7: Hereford cattle and 8: Simmental cattle. 9–10: two donkey siblings. 11–12: human dizygotic twins. The DNA fraction between the arrows in lanes 4 and 5 was used to generate a partial bovine genomic library.

stringency conditions were 60°C and 0.5 M NaCl for hybridisations and 65°C with a salt concentration of 0.2 to 0.4 M NaCl during the washes. The low stringency conditions used with the probes pEU203, pSC101 and RSF1010 and with the PCR-amplified *ori* regions were 50°C and 0.5 M NaCl during hybridisations and 54°C with 0.2 to 0.4 M NaCl during washes. The hybridisations were performed in a solution containing 7% SDS, 1 mM EDTA, 0.26 M phosphate buffer and 1% BSA which is equivalent to a 3x SSC solution (Westneat et al., 1988). The washes were performed 2 × 15 minutes in 2x SSC, 0.1% SDS and for 30 minutes in 1x SSC. Sequencing was performed according to Sanger (Sanger et al., 1977) using the Sequenase 2.0 kit (United States Biochemical Corp.).

Results

All three plasmids pEU203 (P1), pSC101 and RSF1010 generated fingerprint-like signals at low stringency hybridisations with bovine, donkey and human DNA. The strongest patterns were obtained with plasmid P1. This plasmid was used for further investigations. In order to make sure that the actual iteron repeats with the core sequence 5′-ATGT-GTGNTGNNGGG-3′ were responsible for the signals the region containing the five repeats was PCR amplified and the product pEU203-PCR163 was used as a probe (Fig. 1). Having verified this, we screened a bovine genomic library with pEU203-PCR163 and seven positive clones were selected. One clone generated strong fingerprint signals in high stringency Southern blot hybridisations with cattle and donkey DNA. It contained a 5.9-kb fragment of bovine DNA consisting of four *Eco*RI fragments. These were subcloned into the vector pUC19 and propagated in the host strains XL1-blue or SURE. The 2.3-kb *Eco*RI fragment proved to be responsible for the fingerprint signals. This segment was subcloned (pKJH7–2.3). It has been tested in cattle and donkey family material to verify Mendelian inheritance (Figs. 2 and 3). The fragment generating the fingerprint signals was finally located on a 1.2-kb *Xba*I-*Eco*RI fragment which was sequenced. Sequence analysis revealed the following compound, imperfect simple repeat sequence (Weber, 1990): a $(CT)_6$ stretch directly followed by $(CA)_n$ dinucleotide repeats (where n is 8, 3 and 2) interrupted by $(TA)_2$ repeats. Preliminary results obtained with this PCR-amplified sequence as a probe in Southern blot hybridisations with mammalian DNA are promising (data not shown).

Discussion

By screening a partial, bovine genomic library with the amplified P1 *ori* region containing the five times repeated iteron core sequence a clone

82

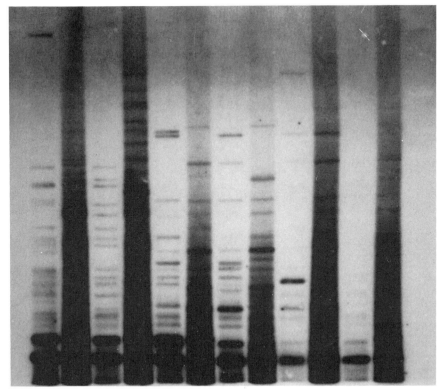

Figure 2. 0.7% agarose gel electrophoresis (21.5 V, 64 h) of *Hin*fI digested bovine DNA of three families. The probe used is pKJH7–2.3. D: dams, S: potential sires, O: offspring. DNA was extracted from blood (in the case of dams and offspring) and from frozen semen (in the case of sires). High background signals occur in the lanes of DNA extracted from frozen semen. Incomplete digestion and the interspersed C-A retroposon element found near artiodactyl microsatellites (Kaukinen and Varvio, 1992), part of which is also present near our simple repeat, have been ruled out as possible causes (data not shown).

was selected, which generates strong fingerprint signals in cattle and donkey DNA. Sequence analysis of this clone revealed a region rich in CA-dinucleotide repeats. It is a compound, imperfect simple repeat sequence (Weber, 1990). A functional reason for the hybridisation to this clone cannot be concluded. The PCR-amplified *ori* region of P1 probably hybridised to this sequence, because:

– The iteron sequence unit itself contains three uninterrupted TG-repeats and another TG-dinucleotide, in total accounting for more than 50% of the iteron sequence.
– We used low stringency conditions allowing for mismatches.

It seems that practically any oligonucelotide can be used to trace VNTRs (Vergnaud, 1989). But this does not imply that each oligonucleo-

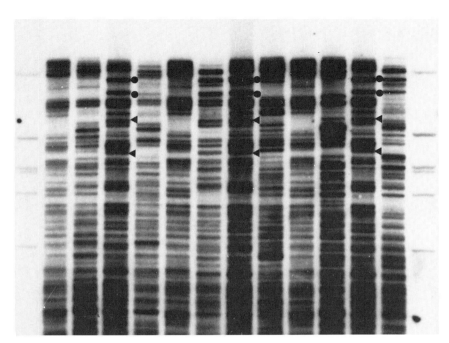

Figure 3. 0.8% agarose gel electrophoresis (65 V, 16.5 h) of *Hin*fI digested donkey DNA extracted from blood. Southern blot hybridisation with the clone pKJH7–2.3 m: *Eco*RI digested λ DNA, M: mare, O: her foal, S_1–S_6: sires 1 to 6, potential fathers. The first two bands indicated with a dot to the right of the lanes termed "O" below 21.2 kb permit exclusion of sires S_1, S_2, S_4 and S_5 as fathers. The two bands around 7.4 kb indicated with a triangle to the right of the lanes termed "O" permit the exclusion of sire S_6 as father. Sire S_3 cannot be excluded by any of these bands nor by further comparisons and therefore is identified as the true parent of offspring O. It is worth noting, that the same probe, pKHJH7–2.3, generates a greater number of bands over an equal size range in *Hin*fI digested donkey DNA than in *Hin*fI digested bovine DNA (Fig. 2).

tide constitutes its own minisatellite core sequence. A random 14 mer can consist of 0.27×10^9 different base compositions. The alignment alone of all principally possible 14 mers, however without taking into account possible overlaps, would make up the average eukaryotic genome of about 3×10^9 bp, leaving no room for the amplification to VNTRs let alone for single copy genes. Therefore we speculate, that specific minisatellites are maintained by a functional mechanism inherent in their core sequence. Most of the work done on a putative genetic function of families of minisatellite repeat units has concentrated on recombination (Steinmetz et al., 1986; Royle et al., 1988). Our interest has focused on the tandem repeats (iterons), known to have a replication control function in naturally existing plasmids, whose copy numbers are stringently controlled. The core sequences of these iterons are similar in length to previously described minisatellite core sequences,

84

that is between 11–18 bp long (Jeffreys et al., 1985; Vassart et al., 1987; Nakamura et al., 1987). The protein RepA, responsible for the initiation of replication, recognises and binds to the double-stranded iteron repeats (for a review see: Scott, 1984). Our approach was to use origins of replication of three such plasmids (P1, pSC101 and RSF1010) as a basis for detecting similar repeat units in eukaryotes by Southern blot hybridisations. At low stringency conditions they did detect polymorphic loci. Although we have not been able to isolate a sequence similar to the P1 iteron in bovine DNA yet, it remains of interest that regulating sequences, the P1 iterons, should actually contain TG-dinucleotide repeats. The P1 iterons are also most similar to the described minisatellite core sequences of the Chi-type (Jeffreys, 1985). Collick and Jeffreys (1990) have described a protein, which is specifically bound with high affinity by double-stranded DNA containing multiple repeats of the minisatellite core sequence. The finding that this protein (Msbp-1) does not seem to be involved in meiotic recombination and requires longer than normal sequences for binding specificity (Collick and Jeffreys, 1990) is reminiscent of the processes the iteron repeats of P1 are involved in. The above analogies support the idea that repeated structures might generally be used as targets for specific proteins. Their function is known in plasmids but remains obscure in eukaryotes.

Acknowledgements
We thank B. Colomb for laboratory assistance and F. Hebeisen for his photographic expertise. We should like to express our thanks to J. Scott, Emory University, Atlanta, USA for providing pEU203. K.J.H. holds a Ph.D. grant from the Central Laboratory of the Red Cross Foundation, Blood Transfusion Service SRC, Berne, Switzerland.

References

Ali S, Müller CR, Epplen JT (1986) DNA fingerprinting by oligonucleotide probes specific for simple repeats. Hum Genet 74: 239–243

Birnboim HC, Doly J (1979) A rapid akaline extraction procedure for screening recombinant plasmid DNA. Nucleic Acids Res 7: 1513–1523

Collick A, Jeffreys AJ (1990) Detection of a novel minisatellite specific DNA-binding protein. Nucleic Acids Res 18: 625–629

Crawford AM, Buchanan FC, Fraser KM, Robinson AJ, Hill DF (1991) Repeat sequences from complex ds viruses can be used as minisatellite probes for DNA fingerprinting. Animal Genetics 22: 177–181

Frey J, Bagdasarian M (1989). The molecular biology of IncQ plasmids. *In:* Thomas CM (ed) Promiscuous Plasmids of Gram-negative Bacteria. Academic Press, London: 79–94

Jeanpierre M (1987) A rapid method for the purification of DNA from blood. Nucleic Acids Res 15: 9611

Jeffreys AJ, Wilson V, Thein SL (1985) Hypervariable minisatellite regions in human DNA. Nature 314: 67–73

Kaukine J and Varvio S-L (1992) Artiodactyl retroposons: association with microsatellites and use in SINEmorph detection by PCR. Nucleic Acids Res 20: 2955–2958

Linder P, Churchward G, Guixian X, Yi-Yi Y, Caro L (1985) An essential replication gene, *rep*A, of plasmid pSC101 is autoregulated. J Mol Biol 181: 383–393

Nakamura Y, Leppert M, O'Connell P, Wolff R, Holm T, Culver M, Martin C, Fujimoto E, Hoff M, Kumlin E and White R (1987) Variable number of tandem repeat (VNTR) markers for human gene mapping. Science 235: 1616–1622

Novick RP (1987) Plasmid Incompatibility. Microbiol Rev 51: 381–395

Persson C and Nordström K (1986) Control of replication of the broad host range plasmid RSF1010: The incompatibility determinant consists of directly repeated DNA sequences. Mol Gen Genet 203: 189–192

Sambrook J, Fritsch EF, Maniatis T (1989) Molecular Cloning: A laboratory Manual. Cold Spring Harbor Laboratory Press, Cold Spring Harbor.

Sanger F, Nikeln S, Coulson AR (1977) DNA sequencing with chaintermination inhibitors. Proc Natl Acad Sci USA 74: 5463–5467

Scott J (1984) Regulation of plasmid replication. Microbiol Rev 48: 2–23

Vassart G, Georges M, Monsieur EH (1987) Hypervariable minisatellites in human and animal DNA. Science 235: 683–684

Vergnaud G (1989) Polymers or random short oligonucleotides detect polymorphic loci in the human genome. Nucleic Acids Res 19: 7623–7630

Vieira J, Messing J (1982) The pUC plasmids, an M13mp7-derived system for insertion mutagenesis and sequencing with synthetic universal primers. Gene 19: 259–268

Weber JL (1990) Informativeness of human $(dC-dA)_n \times (dG - dT)_n$ polymorphisms. Genomics 7: 524–530

Westneat DF, Noon WA, Reeve HK and Aquadro CF (1988) Improved hybridization conditions for DNA "fingerprints" probed with M13. Nucleic Acids Res NAC 16: 4161

DNA Fingerprinting: State of the Science
ed. by S. D. J. Pena, R. Chakraborty, J. T. Epplen & A. J. Jeffreys
© 1993 Birkhäuser Verlag Basel/Switzerland

Towards covering immunological genes with highly informative markers: A trans-species approach

J. Buitkamp, W. Schwaiger, C. Epplen, M. Gomolka, E. Weyers and J. T. Epplen

Molecular Human Genetics, Ruhr-University, 44780 Bochum, Germany

Summary

To establish a highly informative screening system for immunologically relevant genes ("immunoprinting") we co-amplified via polymerase chain reaction (PCR) polymorphic exons plus adjacent intronic simple repetitive dinucleotide stretches in the T-cell receptor (*Tcr*) *Vb6* and *Major Histocompatibility Complex (MHC)-DRB* loci in man and several ungulate species. In both gene families the basic structure of the simple repeat was found to be preserved for more than 70×10^6 years in all investigated species. The simple repeats exhibit extensive length variability. Distinct exon sequences are correlated with a defined repeat length and substructure. In addition, PCR and the oligonucleotides for typing were applicable to a broad range of species from different mammalian orders. Multiplex PCR of different members of the *Tcr Vb6* family and *MHC-DRB* resulted in a complex pattern similar to an oligolocus fingerprint. Hence immunoprinting can be employed for searching for associations of immunologically relevant genes with diseases even across species barriers.

Introduction

The immune system is responsible for various functions collectively called immune responses (see Klein, 1986). The genes encoding the proteins of the immune system represent a so-called reaction norm or a frame for these responses to invasions of pathogens or foreign antigens. Genes for the T lymphocyte receptor and the immunoglobulin heavy and light chain complexes, the major histocompatibility complex (*MHC*) including complement factors, for interleukins and their receptors as well as many others are distributed across different chromosomes in each vertebrate species. Allelic variations of the gene products can influence the efficiency of interactions between individual immune system components. One immunologically relevant gene family is represented by the *MHC* class I and II genes. *MHC* molecules are transmembrane glycoproteins located on the cell surfaces of every vertebrate species investigated so far. They present processed antigens to antigen receptor bearing T lymphocytes (Zinkernagel and Doherty, 1979; Bjorkman et al., 1987). These *MHC* class I and II molecules can bind vast numbers of different self and non-self antigens. Hence it is not surprising that some of these genes exhibit extreme allelic polymorphism on a population level (Bodmer, 1972; WHO Nomenclature Commitee, 1992), such that most individuals are heterozygous for these loci. Therefore the vertebrate *MHC* class I or class II genes or their gene products are used as marker systems for identification purposes, for research on disease susceptibility and quantitative trait marker associations (for review see Powis and Trowsdale, 1991). One of the most interesting disease associations was recently described for *HLA* antigens and malaria susceptibility (Hill et al., 1991).

Serological typing of the numerous allelic *MHC* products is well established in man and mouse (see Albert et al., 1984) and to some extent in cattle (Bernoco et al., 1991). Nevertheless in most domestic animals typing of *MHC* class II antigens is largely restricted and is not practicable for all the different species. A disadvantage of serological typing is that antibodies used cross react with epitopes on different *MHC* encoded molecules. Hence other systems based on molecular genetic methods have been developed. For example conventional restriction fragment length polymorphism (RFLP) systems have been described for man and several animal species using homologous and heterologous probes (see Cohen et al., 1985; Sarmiento und Storb, 1988; Jung et al., 1989; Lundén et al., 1991).

For rodents and primates numerous *MHC* class I and II sequences have been published. Based on these sequence data, polymerase chain reaction (PCR) typing systems employing polymorphisms of human and mouse *MHC* genes were established using specific oligonucleotides. In species where a large number of alleles has been sequenced this method allows efficient typing, but it is not applicable for poorly investigated species. For several domestic animal species a few cDNA sequences are available (Pratt et al., 1990; Sarmiento et al., 1990; Sarmiento und Storb, 1990). Genomic sequence data exist only for cattle (Groenen et al., 1990; Andersson et al., 1991; Ammer et al., 1992), sheep (Ballingal et al., 1992) and goat (Schwaiger et al., in press). Hence *MHC* class II typing is only poorly elaborated for artiodactyls.

T lymphocyte receptors (Tcr) play another key role in the immunological defence reaction, as they confer antigen specificity of the cellular immunological branch. As in the *MHC*, they also comprise gene families organized in the genome in three clusters: α/δ, ß and γ (Toyonaga and Mak, 1987; Jorgensen et al., 1992). The heterodimeric α/ß Tcr are exclusively expressed in T cells and recognize antigens specifically in the context of *MHC* molecules (Bjorkman et al., 1987). In order to enable recognition of the enormous variety of putative antigens efficiently, the antigen/*MHC* binding site of Tcrs is extremely variable (Chotia et al., 1988). The variability is generated by a somatic recombination mechanism involving variable (V) and joining (J) elements (for review see Davis and Bjorkman, 1988; Wilson et al., 1988). While the *MHC* genes exhibit spectacular allelic polymorphisms, varying *Tcr* alleles have rarely been described (for review see Posnett, 1990). Investigation of *Tcr* polymorphisms by serological methods is laborious since the respective antibodies have to be generated *de novo* after the definition of the polymorphisms. In man, mouse (Behlke and Loh, 1986), cattle (Tanaka et al., 1990; Takeuchi et al., 1992) and sheep (Hein and Tunnacliffe, 1990) a panel of *Tcr* gene sequences has been published. Most of the sequences were obtained from cDNA libraries of T-cell clones. Although the degree of polymorphism is low compared to the *MHC*, a few associations of *Tcr* polymorphisms with disease have been proposed in man, mainly based on RFLP data (Li et al., 1990; Posnett, 1990). Yet in cattle no polymorphisms were identified using 10 different *Tcr* probes (Tanaka et al., 1990).

Little is known about polymorphism and disease associations of other immunologically relevant loci. Immunoglobulins, interleukins, tumor necrosis factors, interferons and their respective receptors determine the vigor of the immune reaction and regulate the cell populations of the immune system. Obviously allelic variations affecting these components of the immune system could influence the individual's defence reactivity. To exploit hypervariable loci located within or near immunologically relevant loci, a procedure entitled "immunoprinting" has been suggested (Gomolka et al., 1993). This approach allows the study of different highly polymorphic loci simultaneously. It relies on the detection and correlation of allelic polymorphisms within the coding sequences combined with the variability of simple repeat loci localized within or near immunologically relevant genes. The basic method is shown for the genes of the human *Tcr Vb6* family (Fig. 1): Simultaneous amplification of the appropriate loci results in PCR products of different lengths. So far these principles have been exemplified for *MHC-DRB* class II genes in man and ungulates (Rieß et al., 1990; Ammer et al., 1992; Schwaiger et al., in press) and *Vb6 Tcr* genes in man (Gomolka et al., 1993). Can the principle of this methodology readily be introduced into a variety of additional species?

Materials and methods

PCR primers and amplification

Genomic DNA was obtained from peripheral blood leukocytes by a salting out procedure (Miller et al., 1988). The primers O-DRw11.10/O-DRBrepH were designed to amplify all human *DRB1* genes (Rieß et al., 1990) and the primers Hubo1/"GIo" (Schwaiger et al., submitted) amplify artiodactyl *DRB* genes. The sense primers are located at the intron1/exon2 boundary, the antisense primers attach in the second intron 3' to the simple repeat stretch. Using the primers Tcr-PIo and

IMMUNOPRINTING

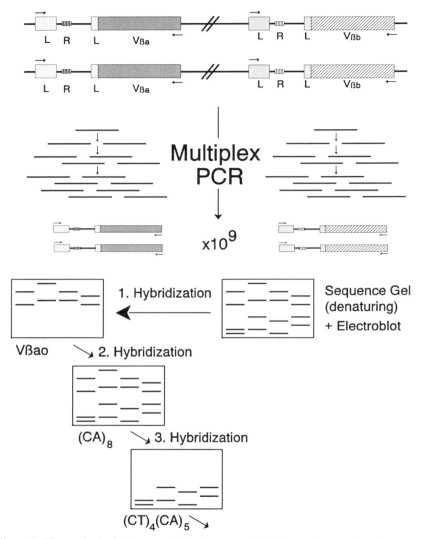

Figure 1. The method of "immunoprinting" as exemplified for the human T cell receptor *Vb6* family. Several different members (a, b) of the *Tcr Vb6* family are amplified in a PCR reaction with a single pair of primers. The PCR fragments are separated via denaturing polyacrylamide gel electrophoresis and electroblotted onto nylon membranes. Repeated hybridization steps using e.g. locus-specific (Vbao), repeat-specific ($(CA)_8$) and mixed, repeat-specific ($(CT)_4(CA)_5$) oligonucleotides enable the investigation of single specific loci. Furthermore exonic alleles can be differentiated by using polymorphic site-specific oligonucleotides.

Tcr-PIIo/Tcr-PIIIo a region from the leader to the *V* region was co-amplified spanning the first intron of different members of the *Vb6* family from genomic DNA (Fig. 1). Approximately 100 ng genomic DNA was amplified in a 50-μl PCR reaction with 2 U Taq polymerase as recommended by the manufacturer (Perkin Elmer Cetus, Norwalk, CT, USA). Amplifications were performed for 25 cycles (30-sec denaturation at 94°C, 1-min annealing at 59°C (*MHC* primers) or 61°C (*Tcr* primers), 1-min extension at 72°C followed by a 5-min extension at 72°C) in a Biometra triblock system cycler (Biometra, Heidelberg, FRG).

Electrophoresis, electroblotting and hybridizations

3 μl of PCR products were separated on a denaturing 4.5% polyacrylamide gel for 7 h at 45 W. The DNA was transferred onto a nylon membrane (Hybond N, Amersham) by electroblotting overnight. As probes the following oligonucleotides were applied for the *MHC* system: the simple repeat specific probes $(CT)_4(CA)_5$, $(CA)_8$, $(GACA)_4$, $(CT)_8$, HDß (5'-GTCCTTCTGGCTGTTCCAGTA-3') hybridizing to all known human and bovine DRB sequences. Furthermore, the oligonucleotide probes Z32H-, Z86I and Z86F [specific for the histidine codon in position 32 and isoleucine/phenylalanine residues in position 86 of artiodactyl *MHC-DRB* sequences, respectively (Schwaiger et al., in press)] were used. Specific oligonucleotide probes for the *Tcr Vb6* family (Vß6.3o, Vß6.7o, Vß6.11o, Vß6.12o, Vß6.13 + 14o) were synthesized according to the sequences of the subfamily members (Gomolka et al., 1993). Radioactive labelling of oligonucleotide probes and specific hybridizations were performed as described previously (Rieß et al., 1990).

Results and discussion

Preservation of simple repetitive DNA stretches

In the *Tcr Vb6* family as well as in the *MHC-DRB* class II loci simple repeat sequences were identified in the same intron locations in different primate and ungulate species that had separated at least 70×10^6 years ago (Schwaiger et al., submitted). This fact stands in contrast to the usually "short-lived" evolutionary history of simple sequences (Epplen et al., 1991). So far no *DRB* genes were identified harboring simple tandem repeats shorter than 44 base pairs (bp) in 97 *DRB* sequences of 13 species out of four families in three mammalian orders (Schwaiger et al., in press). Hence this simple repeat block is preserved at this position. Its persistence in various mammalian orders allows the application of the same typing method to a whole variety of species.

MHC class II typing system

The basis for typing *MHC-DRB* class II genes using the adjacent simple repeat stretch was established for humans (Rieß et al., 1990), cattle (Ammer et al., 1992), as well as sheep and goats (Schwaiger et al., in press). The second exon of the *DRB* loci (which contain practically all of the *DR* polymorphisms) were amplified including a part of the second intron with a simple repeat of the basic structure $(gt)_n(ga)_m$. Hence the *MHC-DRB* loci provide the possibility to investigate the most polymorphic exons in the eukaryotic genome (WHO Nomenclature Committee for factors of the HLA system 1992) supplemented by a hypervariable adjacent mixed simple repeat locus situated 34 bases downstream of the exon 2/intron 2 boundary in artiodactyls (Ammer et al., 1992) and about 50 bases in man (Rieß et al., 1990). This situation is so far unique and it may finally lead to a better concept about the evolution and biological meaning of these sequences. For the purpose of "immunoprinting" the simple repeat allows the separation of the amplified *DRB* sequences via gel electrophoresis. Thus many of the *DRB* haplotypes may be determined exclusively on the basis of their lengths differences (Fig. 2, 6).

In humans for example there exist several different "*HLA-DRB* supertypes" with a different number of genes. Out of the different *DRB* genes the primer O-DRw11.10/O-DRBrepH amplifies the exon 2 *DRB1* gene of DR3, DR5 or DRw6 subtypes together with the adjacent simple sequence. Furthermore, some primers were designed to amplify specific subtypes (for detail see Rieß et al., 1990). Hence different primer pairs for PCR have to be used if all subtypes are to be determined as in the conventional oligotyping systems. *HLA-DRB* was investigated by Rieß et al. (1990) to make use of simple repeats variability as an additional association marker since one and the same *DRB* allele shows variations in the (gt) units of the simple repetitive DNA stretch (Rieß et al., 1990). Comparing different *DRB* alleles the $(ga)_m$ stretch on the other hand exists in many derivatives (probably generated from $(ga)_m$ by point mutations and subsequent local multiplications). Minor variations of simple repeat length is hence mainly caused by alterations of the $(gt)_n$ units. This fact results in several different compositions of the simple repeat stretch. Surprisingly the primary composition of the repeat is group specific: for example the DRw52 supergroup repeats differ from those of the *DRB1*0101*, *DRB4*0101* and *DRB5*0101* alleles (Rieß et al., 1990). Hence each exon sequence can be characterized by the length and basic structure of its adjacent repeat.

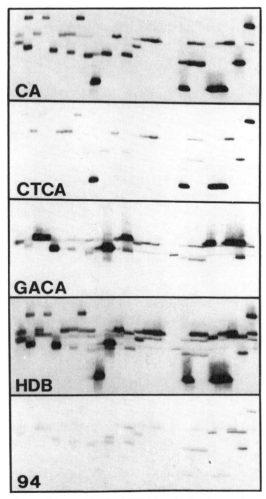

Figure 2. Length polymorphisms of *MHC-DRB* intronic simple repeat sequences. The second exon and part of the second intron were amplified via PCR, the products separated by a 4.5% polyacrylamide gel electrophoresis and subsequently electroblotted onto a nylon membrane. The membrane was hybridized sequentially with various oligonucleotides [CA = $(CA)_8$; CTCA = $(CT)_4(CA)_5$; GACA = $(GACA)_4$] and polymorphism specific oligonucleotides [HDB and 94]. Nine different length alleles can be differentiated when hybridized with the pan *DR* oligonucleotide HDB (Ammer et al., 1992). Hybridizations with the oligonucleotide bearing simple repeat motifs reveal allelic differences of the repeat composition.

In artiodactyls there is still substantial uncertainty about the number of *DRB* genes and the overall genomic organization of *MHC* (Ballingal et al., 1992). Initial studies in cattle indicate that at least three *DRB* loci exist, one of them being transcribed intensely (see Andersson and Rask, 1988; Deverson et al., 1991). On the other hand three *DRB*-like genes appear to be actively transcribed in sheep (Ballingal et al., 1992). Our primer pair Hubo1/"GIo" was designed to attach to exon and intron regions conserved between cattle and goat (Schwaiger et al., in press). *DRB* sequences were amplified from a panel of 22 cattle from different breeds, 25 goats of six different breeds (*Capra aegagrus hircus*), 25 sheep of five different breeds (*Ovis aries*), one mountain goat (*Oreamnos americanus*), one gazelle (*Gazella dorcas*) and one giraffe (*Giraffa giraffa*). As expected PCR amplifications yielded products of every ungulate species tested so far. Cloning and sequencing of the PCR products revealed a total of 67 different artiodactyl *DRB* exons 2 plus introns (22 bovine, 22 caprine, 21 ovine, 1 mountain goat, 1 gazelle and 1 giraffe; see Ammer et al., 1992; Schwaiger et al., in press). In addition we generated sequence data from gaur (*Bos gaurus*), banteng (*Bos javanicus*), bison (*Bison bison*), nyala (*Tragelaphus angasi*) and anoa (*Bubalus depressicornis*). Therefore the PCR primer employed are useful for a broad range of different artiodactyl species.

Polymorphism of *DRB* genes is thought to be maintained through evolution and surviving several speciation events (Wakeland et al., 1990; Kasahara et al., 1990). There were hints accumulating for a genetic exchange mechanism preserving once established (ancient) poly-morphisms. Shuffling of polymorphic regions in the second *DRB* exon via recombination and/or gene conversion like events results in new allelic combinations. Gene conversion like events proposed for Bovidae (Schwaiger et al., submitted) are also described for man (Gorski and Mach, 1986) and mouse (Mengle-Gaw et al., 1984). Hence sequence motives from different positions are found in variable combinations in the different alleles. For example in cattle, sheep and goat one sequence motif from amino acid (aa) position 11–13 is combined with different motifs in aa position 81–96 and vice versa. Furthermore, cassettes of polymorphic positions with the same nucleic acid sequence can be found in different species. But although the mode of evolution is not fully understood this "shuffled" motifs provide a useful scheme for efficient typing for exonic variability by hybridization with oligonucleotides specific for these motifs found in various *DRB* sequences – even across species barriers. Therefore we have to apply PSOs (polymorphic site specific oligonucleotides) and ASOs (allele specific oligonucleotides).

Hypervariability of the DRB simple repeat stretch

The simple repeat sequences are divided into two main classes, the $(gt)_n$ and the $(ga)_m$ repeat stretches. The $(gt)_n$ repeat comprises 12 (± 3.9; cattle) to 20 (± 3.7; man) copies of the dinucleotide motif. During evolution of different species the simple $(gt)_n$ repeat occurs in compara-tively stable numbers of n with only little variation. As in man also in artiodactyls the simple repeat shows a group-specific organization: *DRB* alleles with a high degree of homology in the ß-sheet region 1 are associated which simple repeat stretches of the same structure (Ammer et al., 1992; Schwaiger et al., submitted). Allelic length differences of the entire repeats can be correlated to certain exonic alleles. They are mainly due to variations of the $(ga)_m$ dinucleotide derivative structures (Schwaiger et al., in press). This fact allows a preselection of useful PSOs according to the repeat length and reduces the number of hybridization steps necessary for typing. In total we found 15 different length alleles in 22 cattle, 17 in 22 caprine and 16 in 21 ovine *DRB* sequences (Schwaiger et al., in press). Hence a few different exonic alleles have identical repeat lengths. In this case the alleles can be distinguished using different PSOs. Typing of goat *MHC-DRB* is presented in Fig. 2. Unrelated individuals are investigated and the differentiation of various simple repeat types is shown by hybridization with different repeat motif oligonucleotides. Taking into account also length variations, we are able to discriminate all investigated artiodactyl *DRB* sequences with only 14 different PSOs.

The Tcr typing system

The known allelic variations in *Tcr Vb* genes is low in comparison to that of *MHC* genes (Concannon et al., 1987). The method of *Tcr Vb6* typing in man is based on novel sequence data (Gomolka et al., 1992; 1993). In order to evaluate the extent of germline variability in the *Vb* genes a primer pair was designed to coamplify members of the *Tcr Vb6* family in man. The previously published *Vb6* sequence harbored repetitive sequences in the intron between leader and *Vb* exon (Hinkkanen et al., 1989; Posnett et al., 1990). PCR amplification using the primers TCR-PIo and TCR-PIIo/TCR-PIIIo and subsequent electroblot hybridizations shows length polymorphisms within the *Vb6.7* and *Vb6.3* sequences as well as novel *Vb6* elements (Fig. 3). In the complex electroblot hybridization patterns more *Vb6* like loci had amplified with the aforementioned primers than were originally expected. Therefore the amplification products have been cloned and sequenced. In summary four additional *Vb6* loci were identified as could also be deduced from sequence analysis. Accordingly these loci were termed *Vb6.11*, *Vb6.12*, *Vb6.13* and *Vb6.14* (Gomolka et al., 1992).

Electroblotted PCR fragments were hybridized with the oligonucleotides as follows: PII and $(CA)_8$ detected a virtually identical complex pattern including 4–6 (clusters of) bands. Thus all amplified sequences contain simple $(gt)_n$ repeats (Fig. 3). The clusters range from isolated single bands to some 3–4 evenly spaced signals which are characteristic for long stretches of perfect dinucleotide repeats after PCR (Rieß et al.,

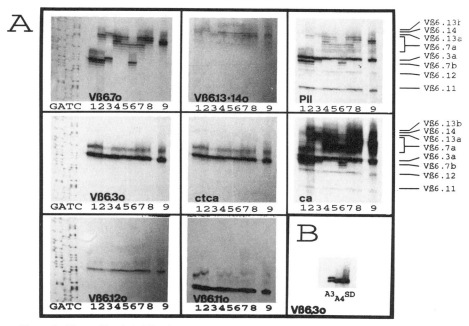

Figure 3. Electroblot hybridization detects novel polymorphic *Tcr Vb6* elements. Multilocus PCR reactions of nine (1–9) unrelated individuals were separated on a 4.5% denaturing polyacrylamide gel, electroblotted onto a Nylon membrane and sequentially hybridized with oligonucleotide probes specific for subfamilies or simple repeat sequences. A sequencing reaction was added as a size marker. Hybridization signals with the oligonucleotide probes ($CA)_8$ and PII (PCR primer) revealed an identical complex banding pattern which can not be interpreted exclusively on the basis of the polymorphisms of the expected *Vb6.3* and *Vb6.7* genes. Therefore the PCR products were cloned and sequenced. The novel exonic sequences exhibited a similarity of more than 90% to the *Vb6.3* element. All *Vb6* elements contained more or less complex organized $(ca)_n$ repeats in their introns. Highly similar sequences (introns and exons) were grouped and designated *Vb6.11*, *Vb6.12*, *Vb6.13* and *Vb6.14* (Gomolka et al., 1993). Oligonucleotide probes specific for each subfamily were hybridized to the electroblotted DNA and resolved the complex pattern into the individual *Vb6* elements. Allelic length variability is apparent for *Vb6.7*, *Vb6.14* (A) and *Vb6.3* (B).

1990). In order to resolve the complex pattern for every amplified locus the same blot was sequentially hybridized with probes specific for exonic and/or intronic target sequences in the *Vb6.7* and *Vb6.3* elements. As expected the probe Vß6.7o revealed a polymorphic banding pattern for the different homozygous or heterozygous individuals (one or two bands). The probe Vß6.3o exhibited only a small extent of polymorphism (Fig. 3). With the intronic mixed simple repeat probe $(CT)_5(CA)_4$ the same *Vb6.3* pattern was seen (Fig. 3). Mendelian inheritance and the degree of polymorphism for the *Vb6.3* and *Vb6.7* loci were analyzed in *HLA*-typed individuals (Gomolka et al., 1992). From the data of 46 unrelated caucasians a PIC (Botstein et al., 1980) of 0.75 was calculated.

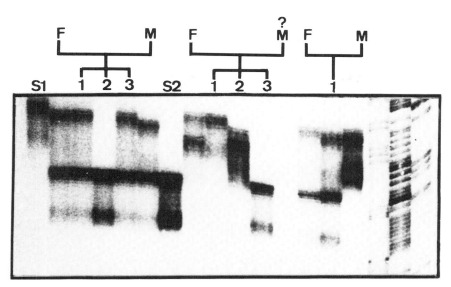

Figure 4. Mendelian inheritance of the *Tcr Vb6.7* length variations allows paternity testing. Radioactively labeled PCR products of three families were separated on a 6% denaturing polyacrylamide gel. Legal paternity for child 3 of the second family can be excluded, because the child shows none of the paternal alleles. S1, S2 represent control individuals with defined length alleles, $Vb7a(gt)_{26}$ and $Vb6.7b(gt)_{15}$, respectively.

Furthermore, Mendelian inheritance for these loci was confirmed in 22 families (Fig. 4).

Typing of immunologically relevant loci in artiodactyls

Low stringency PCR using the primer pair Tcr-PIo and Tcr-PIIIo was used to establish a PCR system in cattle, sheep and goat. PCR from genomic DNAs of all species yielded several distinct bands after agarose gel electrophoresis and ethidium bromide staining. As expected the sequence analyses show a high degree of homology to the human *Vb6* genes (data not shown). The sequence data from three unrelated Simmental cattle revealed two different silent mutations in the intraspecies comparison. Here we still have to exclude PCR artifacts. As in humans a $(gt)_n$ repeat is present in the intron between the leader and *Vb* exon. Only two different length alleles were identified in 30 unrelated cattle from three different breeds. Upon PCR and electroblot hybridization all bovine DNAs investigated showed the invariant 451 basepair fragment representing the cloned sequence. Three of them harbored an additional high molecular weight signal (Fig. 5). The longer fragment consists of the identical sequence plus a 116-bp long duplication including splice

98

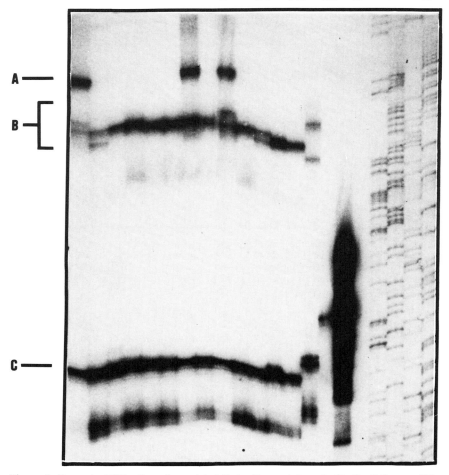

Figure 5. Genomic DNAs from 9 unrelated Swiss Simmental cattle (1–9), Galloway (10), Holstein Frisian cattle (11), Dahome (12), gaur (13), banteng (14), bison (15) and human (16) were amplified using the primers PI/PII (Gomolka et al., 1992a). The fragments were separated via denaturing polyacrylamide gel electrophoresis, electroblotted and hybridized using the probe $(CA)_8$. A: 567 base pair fragment carrying an intron with a duplicated repeat; B: co-amplified bovine satellite-like, $(CA)_8$ containing sequence. C: 451 base pair Tcr fragment (see results section).

sites and duplicated simple $(gt)_n$ repeats. Thus a dimorphic germline polymorphism is readily detectable. However in goat and sheep amplification, electroblotting and subsequent hybridization with $(CA)_8$ revealed a polymorphic multiallele system with at least six different allele lengths in each of the species (Fig. 6). The high caprine and ovine

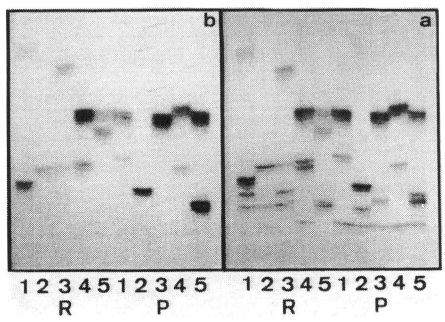

Figure 6. Amplification of *Tcr* and *MHC-DRB* sequences via multiplex PCR of unrelated individuals from two different breeds of sheep (P1–5, Perendale; R1–5, Romney). The primers developed for the human *Tcr* and for *MHC-DRB* genes were used. Hybridizing using (CA)$_8$ reveals the whole banding pattern for both amplification systems (a). HDB (b) hybridizes only with *MHC-DRB* exon 2 sequences. Note that 8 of the 10 individuals are heterozygous for the putative *Tcr* locus.

heterozygosity rates are the more remarkable in comparison to cattle. As for the *MHC-DRB* loci, this primer pair is able to amplify exon and intron sequences from a variety of different species. Surprisingly an intron simple repeat with the same basic structure is again preserved at the very same position from ungulates to primates. In other bovines such as banteng, gaur or bison, different length alleles appear by hybridization with the simple (CA)$_8$ (see Fig. 5).

Multiplex PCR and conclusions

Thus via "heterologously primed" PCR, sequencing gels, electroblotting and multiple rehybridization steps using a panel of allele-specific or simple repeat oligonucleotide probes a highly polymorphic marker system can be established on a trans-species basis. This typing system for *MHC* and *Tcr* genes in artiodactyls reveals an unprecedented degree of polymorphism information. Multiplex PCR can be performed using

PCR primers for both *MHC* and *Tcr* genes. In a first attempt genomic DNA was successfully amplified from ten unrelated individuals of two closely related sheep breeds. Figure 6 shows that there are no two identical banding patterns. All known alleles in goat, sheep and cattle can be determined for both typing systems. For this purpose less than 25 oligonucleotides are required. Only two probes are effectively necessary after preselection on the basis of the length differences of the alleles. Multiplex PCR including additional immunologically relevant loci would finally result in a complex fingerprint pattern defining individuality efficiently even only by accounting the length differences after one hybridization step with the oligonucleotide $(CA)_8$. Immunoprinting can thus also be advantageous in studies on family material when it is not necessary to determine the exact *MHC/Tcr* allele initially but only Mendelian inheritance should be proven. Furthermore, immunoprinting allows efficient investigation of several loci with the same technology. It can be applied in novel vertebrate species in contrast to the serological methods. Comparatively few oligonucleotide probes are necessary to generate a high amount of information from different chromosomal locations. In association studies for various purposes several relevant loci can be screened simultaneously in a single step. Once established large numbers of individuals can be tested efficiently using the multiplex PCR approach.

Acknowledgements
Supported by the Deutsche Forschungsgemeinschaft (Ep 7/5-2, Ep 7/6-2) and the BMFT.

References

Albert ED, Baur M-P, Mayr WR (eds) (1984) Histocompatibility testing. Springer-Verlag, New York

Ammer H, Schwaiger FW, Kammerbauer C, Gomolka M, Arriens A, Lazary S, Epplen JT (1992) Exonic polymorphism versus intronic simple repeat hypervariability in *MHC-DRB* Genes. Immunogenet 35: 332–340

Andersson L, Rask L (1988) Characterization of the MHC class II region in cattle. The number of DQ genes varies between haplotypes. Immunogenet 27: 110–120

Andersson L, Sigurdardottir S, Borsch C, Gustafsson K (1991) Evolution of MHC polymorphism: extensive sharing of polymorphic sequence motifs between human and bovine *DRB* alleles. Immunogenet 33: 188–193

Ballingall KT, Wright H, Redmond J, Dutia BM, Hopkins J, Lang J, Deverson EV, Howard JC, Puri N, Haig D (1992) Expression and characterization of ovine major histocompatibility complex class II (OLA-DR) genes. Animal Genet 23: 347–359

Behlke MA, Loh DY (1986) Alternative splicing of murine T-cell receptor β-chain transcripts. Nature 322: 379–382

Bernoco D, Lewin HA, Andersson L, Arriens MA, Byrns G, Cwik S, Davies CJ et al. (1991) Joint Report of the Fourth International Bovine Lymphocyte Antigen (BoLA) Workshop, East Lansing, Michigan, August 25, 1990. Animal Genet 22: 477–496

Bjorkman PJ, Saper MA, Samraoui B, Bennet WS, Strominger JL, Wiley DC (1987) The foreign antigen binding site and T-cell recognition regions of class I histocompatibility antigens. Nature 329: 512–518

Bodmer JG, Marsh SGE, Albert E (1990) Nomenclature for factors of the HLA system. Immunol Today 11: 3–10

Bodmer WF (1972) Evolutionary significance of the HLA system. Nature 237: 139

Botstein D, White RL, Skolnik M, Davis RW (1980) Construction of a genetic linkage map in man using restriction fragment length polymorphisms. Amer J Hum Genet 32: 314–331

Chothia C, Boswell DR, Lesk AM (1988) The outline structure of the T-cell $\alpha\beta$ receptor. EMBO J 7: 3745–3755

Cohen D, Paul P, Le Gall I, Marcadet A, Font MP, Haguenauer O, Sayagh B et al. (1985) Immunol Rev 85: 87

Concannon P, Gatti RA, Hood L (1987) Human T-cell receptor Vβ gene polymorphism. J Exp Med 165: 1130–1140

Davis MM, Bjorkman PJ (1988) T-cell antigen receptor genes and T-cell recognition. Nature 334: 395–402

Deverson EV, Wright H, Watson S, Ballingall K, Huskisson N, Diamond AG, Howard JC (1991) Class II *MHC* genes of the sheep. Anim Genet 22: 211–225

Epplen JT (1988) On simple repeated GATA/GACA sequences in animal genomes: a critical reappraisal. J Hered 79: 409–417

Epplen JT, Ammer H, Epplen C, Kammerbauer C, Roewer L, Schwaiger W, Steimle V et al. (1991) Oligonucleotide fingerprinting using simple repeat motifs: a convenient, ubiquitously applicable method to detect hypervariability for multiple purposes. *In:* Burke T, Dolf G, Jeffreys AJ, Wolff R (eds) DNA-Fingerprinting: Approaches and applications, Birkhäuser, Basel, pp 50–69

Epplen C, Epplen JT (1992) The human cDNA sequence homologous to the mouse *MHC* class I promoter-binding protein gene contains four additional codons in lymphocytes. Mamm Genome 3: 472–475

Epplen JT (1992) On genetic components in autoimmunity. Critical review based on evolutionarily orientated rationality. Hum Genet 90: 331–341

Epplen JT (1992) Diagnostic applications of repetitive DNA sequences. Clin Chim Acta 209: S5–S13

Gomolka M, Epplen C, Buitkamp J, Epplen JT (1993) Novel members and germline polymorphisms in the human T-cell receptor *Vb6* family. Immunogenet 37: 257–265

Gomolka M, Schwaiger F-W, Epplen C, Buitkamp J, Epplen JT (1992) Towards a fingerprint method covering the immunological genome. Electrophoresis 13: 623–625

Gorski J, Mach B (1986) Polymorphism of human Ia antigens: gene conversion between two DR ß loci results in a new HLA-D/DR specifity. Nature 322: 67–70

Groenen MA, Van der Poel JJ, Cijkhof RJ, Giphart MJ (1990) The nucleotide sequence of bovine *MHC* class II *DQB* and *DRB* genes. Immunogenet 31: 37–44

Hein WT, Tunnacliffe A (1990) Molecular cloning of sheep T cell receptor gamma and delta constant regions: unusual primary structure of gamma chain hinge segments. Eur J Immunol 20: 1505–1511

Hein WT, Dudler L, Beya M, Marcuz A, Grossberger D (1989) T cell receptor gene expression in sheep: differential usage of *Tcr* 1 in the periphery and thymus. Eur J Immunol 19: 2297–2301

Hill, ASV, Allsopp CEM, Kwiatkowski D, Anstey NM, Twumasi P, Rowe PA, Bennett S et al. (1991) Common West African HLA antigens are associated with protection from severe malaria. Nature 352: 595–600

Hinkkanen AE, Steimle V, Schlesier M, Peter HH, Epplen JT (1989) The antigen receptor of an autoreactive T-cell clone from human rheumatic synovia. Immunogenet 29: 131–133

Jorgensen JL, Reay PA, Ehrich EW, Davis MM (1992) Molecular components of T-cell recognition. Ann Rev Immunol 10: 835–873

Jung YC, Rothschild MF, Flanagan MP, Pollak E, Warner CM (1989) Genetic variability between two breeds based on restriction fragment length polymorphisms (RFLPs) of major histocompatibility complex class I genes in the pig. Theor Appl Genet 77: 271–274

Kasahara M, Klein D, Weimin F, Gutknecht T (1990) Evolution of the class II major histocompatibility complex alleles in higher primates. Immunol Rev 113: 65–82

Klein J (1986) Natural history of the major histocompatibility complex. Wiley, New York

Li Y, Szabo P, Robinson MA, Dong B, Posnett DN (1990) Allelic variations in the human T cell receptor Vß6.7 gene products. J Exp Med 171: 221–230

Lundén A, Sigurdardóttir S, Andersson L (1991) Restriction fragment length polymorphism of a bovine T-cell receptor β gene. Anim Genet 22: 497–502

Mengle-Gaw L, Conner S, McDevitt HO, Fathman CG (1984) Gene conversion between murine class II major histocompatibility complex loci. J Exp Med 160: 1184–1194

Miller SA, Dykes DD, Polesky HF (1988) A simple salting out procedure for extracting DNA from human nucleated cells. Nucleic Acids Res 16: 1215

Posnett DN (1990) Allelic variations of human *Tcr* V gene products. Immunol Today 11: 368–373

Powis SH, Trowsdale J (1991) HLA and disease. Br J Clin Practice 45: 116–120

Pratt K, Sachs DH, Germana ME.-gamil S, Hirsch F, Gustafsson K, LeGuern C (1990) Class II genes of miniature swine. II. Molecular identification and characterization of B (β) genes from the SLA haplotype. Immunogenet 31: 1–6

Rieß O, Kammerbauer C, Roewer L, Steimle V, Andreas A, Albert E, Nagai T, Epplen JT (1990) Hypervariability of intronic simple (gt)$_n$(ga)$_m$ repeats in *HLA-DRB*1 genes. Immunogenet 32: 110–116

Sarmiento UM, Storb RF (1988) Restriction fragment length polymorphism of the major histocompatibility complex of the dog. Immunogenet 28: 117–124

Sarmiento UM, Storb R (1990) Nucleotide sequence of a dog *DRB* cDNA clone. Immunogenet 31: 396–399

Sarmiento UM, Sarmiento JI, Storb R (1990) Allelic variation in the DR subregion of the canine major histocompatibility complex. Immunogenet 32: 13–19

Schwaiger W, Weyers E, Epplen C, Ruff G, Crawford A, Epplen JT. The paradox of *MHC-DRB* exon/intron evolution: α-helix and β-sheet encoding regions diverge while hypervariable intronic simple repeats co-evolve with β-sheet codons. J Mol Evol (in press)

Schwaiger W, Gomolka M, Geldermann H, Zischler H, Buitkamp J, Epplen JT, Ammer H (1992) Oligonucleotide fingerprinting to individualize ungulates. Appl Theor Electrophoresis 2: 193–200

Schwaiger W, Buitkamp J, Weyers E, Epplen JT (1993) Typing of artiodactyl *MHC-DRB* genes with the help of intronic simple repeated DNA sequences. Mol Ecol (in press)

Takeuchi N, Ishiguro N, Shinagawa M (1992) Molecular cloning and sequence analysis of bovine T-cell receptor delta and gamma genes. Immunogenet 35: 89–96

Tanaka A, Ishiguro N, Shimagawa M (1990) Sequence and diversity of bovine T-cell receptor ß-chain genes. Immunogenet 32: 263–271

The WHO Nomenclature Committee for factors of the HLA system (1992) Nomenclature for factors of the HLA system 1991. Immunogenet 36: 135–148

Toyonaga B, Mak TW (1987) Genes of the T-cell antigen receptor in normal and malignant T cells. Ann Rev Immunol 5: 585–620

Wakeland EK, Boehme S, She JX (1990) The generation and maintenance of MHC class II gene polymorphism in rodents. Immunol Rev 113: 39–46

Wilson RK, Lai E, Concannon P, Barth RK, Hood LE (1988) Structure, organization and polymorphism of murine and human T-cell receptor α and β chain gene families. Immunol Rev 101: 149–172

Zinkernagel RM, Doherty PC (1979) MHC-restricted T cells: studies on the biological role of the polymorphic major transplantation antigens determining T-cell restriction-specifity, function, and responsiveness. Adv Immunol 27: 221–291

DNA Fingerprinting: State of the Science
ed. by S. D. J. Pena, R. Chakraborty, J. T. Epplen & A. J. Jeffreys
© 1993 Birkhäuser Verlag Basel/Switzerland

Arbitrary primed PCR fingerprinting of RNA applied to mapping differentially expressed genes

M. McClelland, K. Chada^a, J. Welsh and D. Ralph

California Institute of Biological Research, 11099 North Torrey Pines, La Jolla, CA 92037, USA, and ^aDept. of Biochemistry, UMDNJ-Robert Wood Johnson Medical School, 675 Hoes Lane, Piscataway, NJ 08854, USA

Summary

Differential gene expression between various tissues and developmental stages or between cells *in vitro* under different growth conditions can be rapidly and efficiently compared using the RNA arbitrarily primed polymerase chain reaction (RAP) fingerprinting method (Welsh et al., 1992b; Liang and Pardee, 1992). In RAP, a primer of arbitrary sequence primes both first and second strand cDNA synthesis. The mixture of products is then PCR amplified and resolved electrophoretically, yielding highly reproducible fingerprints that are tissue-specific or growth condition-specific. Differences between fingerprints arise from differentially expressed genes, as verified by Northern blot analysis. RAP can be performed on the RNA samples using various DNA primers. Each two day experiment yields a sample of approximately twenty cDNA products per lane making the identification of differentially or developmentally regulated genes no longer rate limiting. Those PCR products representing genes that are regulated can be cloned from the gel and sequenced. Sequences can be compared to the DNA and protein sequence databases to identify homologs, motifs and members of gene families. The clones can be placed on the genetic map as Expression Tagged Sites (ETS, Adams et al., 1991a).

cDNA sequencing and the human genome project

Insight into the molecular nature of a number of diverse biological processes, such as human diseases and development, can be gained by analyzing differentially expressed mRNAs. However, methods to isolate such RNAs are cumbersome and generally require significant amounts of starting material. Thus, it has been proposed that cDNAs be sequenced at random from libraries derived from a single tissue (Adams et al., 1991a). However, the merits of this approach as a part of the human genome project has been vigorously debated since the idea of determining the complete nucleotide sequence of humans first surfaced. Proponents of cDNA sequencing have argued that because the coding sequences of genes represent the vast majority of the information content of the genome, but only 3% of the DNA, cDNA sequencing should take precedence over genomic sequencing. Conversely, proponents of genomic sequencing have emphasized the difficulty of finding every mRNA expressed in all tissues, cell types, and developmental stages. Furthermore, they have pointed out that much valuable information from cis acting regulatory domains, including control and regulatory sequences, will be missed by cDNA sequencing.

One might assume that gene coding regions, and therefore mRNA sequences, could be predicted easily after genomic cloning but this has not proven to be the case. Identification of the gene after the locus has been cloned is extremely labor intensive and time consuming without a guarantee of success (Gusella, 1983). Progress in computer predictions of coding sequences from human genomic sequences is still needed. However, technologies are being developed to identify genes within genomic DNA such as the exon trapping method (Hamaguchi et al., 1992).

Perhaps the strongest advocates for the direct sequencing and genetic mapping of expressed genes have been Venter and his colleagues (Adams et al., 1991a, b) who have generated a large number of expressed sequence tags (ESTs) from randomly selected human brain cDNA clones. cDNA characterization should facilitate the tagging of most human genes at a fraction of the cost of complete genomic sequencing, provide new genetic markers and serve as a valuable resource in diverse fields of biological research. Because sequencing is targeted to a small fraction of the genome it could be considered cost effective even with present technology. This approach of using clones picked at random from libraries derived from individual tissues does not, however, yield information concerning differential expression and is inherently redundant.

Of paramount importance for understanding development and disease is the identification of genes which are differentially and/or developmentally regulated. For example, homeodomain genes are regulatory transcription factors which are expressed in a very restricted manner (Joyner et al., 1991) and when disrupted, affect the development of the fetus. Therefore, it would be particularly relevant for large scale mapping efforts if there were high through-put methods that identify differentially expressed genes.

A standard experimental protocol for isolating a differentially regulated gene would first involve construction of a cDNA library from the relevant tissue at a single time-point in development. This library provides cloned inserts of all the genes expressed in that particular tissue. Ideally, this library might be normalized so that all genes are represented equally and can therefore be selected at random with minimal coincidence. However, normalising libraries is still at the developmental stage and requires more research before it becomes a standard methodology. Subsequent analysis must be performed in order to determine which of the inserts represent genes that are differentially expressed between the relevant tissues. This is accomplished for example by Northern blots containing RNA prepared from the various tissues or by screening tissue-specific libraries. This brute force approach has yielded valuable resources (Palazzlo et al., 1989).

Alternatively, exhaustively subtracted libraries, in theory, allow the identification of genes that are dramatically regulated (e.g. tissue specific genes). However, this is fairly sophisticated technology at which only a few laboratories have proved particularly successful (Gieser and Swaroop, 1992) and the methodology is still at a stage that the clones must be further analyzed to ensure that they are indeed tissue-specific. Also, subtractive library methods are limited in that they allow only pairwise comparisons of RNA populations.

The method we have developed is extremely simple and reveals differential gene expression immediately, in contrast to the methodologies described above. The cDNA fingerprints generated allow the pairwise comparison of the gene expression patterns for many tissues and genes simultaneously. When the technique is applied to a set of RNAs from different tissues, each standard sequencing gel-size autoradiogram generated is equivalent to a large number of Northern blots from a series of "hypothetical" normalized and subtracted cDNA libraries. Furthermore, the sampling of differentially expressed genes is unbiased to any one tissue and in this way is equivalent to the subtraction of each tissue by each other tissue in every pairwise combination. One can directly isolate from the gel, clone and sequence genes that are differentially expressed between tissues and compare the sequences with those already in the database to uncover homologs in other species or members of the same gene family. Characterized clones can be genetically mapped. The sequences could also be a resource to develop that subset of sequence tagged sites (STSs) referred to as expressed sequence tags (ESTs) by Adams et al. (1991a, b).

Arbitrary primed PCR fingerprinting of DNA

The arbitrarily primed PCR reaction uses a single arbitrarily selected primer (Welsh and McClelland, 1990; Williams et al., 1990) or two such primers (Welsh and McClelland, 1991) to produce a PCR fingerprint for DNAs ranging in complexity from bacterial to higher eukaryotic genomes. Polymorphisms that distinguish individuals can be used for genetic mapping (Williams et al., 1990; Welsh and McClelland, 1991; Welsh et al., 1991a; Welsh et al., 1991b; Michelmore et al., 1991), ecology (Smith et al., 1992), epidemiology (Welsh and McClelland, 1990; Welsh et al., 1992a) or phylogenetics (Welsh et al., 1992a).

Arbitrary primed PCR fingerprinting of RNA

Recently we (Welsh et al., 1992b), and others (Liang and Pardee, 1992) have found that arbitrarily primed PCR can be performed on total cellular RNA to identify differences between RNA populations from different sources (RAP). Fingerprinting of RNA populations uses an arbitrarily selected primer at low stringency for first and second strand cDNA synthesis, followed by conventional PCR amplification of the primer-tagged products. The method requires only a few nanograms of total RNA and is not affected by low levels of DNA contamination (Welsh et al., 1992b). A reproducible pattern of ten to twenty clearly visible PCR products is obtained from any one tissue for each arbitrary primer and the PCR fingerprint differs between various issues. Examples of differentially expressed genes detected in this manner were cloned and differential expression was confirmed for these products by Northern blot analysis. Tissue-specific differences in mRNA abundance revealed by RAP should be useful for studying differential gene expression and should be applicable to the detection of differences between RNA populations in a wide variety of situations.

Differential gene expression in the mouse

As a simple model to test the feasibility of arbitrarily primed PCR on cDNA, we compared the RNA populations of various organs from the mouse. The mouse as a model system has many persuasive advantages in order to analyze differential gene expression in the mammal. First, it's embryology and development has been thoroughly analyzed which allows the further characterization of genes that are regulated temporally. Second, the recent advent of genetic manipulation through transgenesis (Palmiter and Brinster, 1986) and ES cell knockout (Robertson, 1987) has greatly increased its utility. Third, a large body of information has accumulated over 100 years yielding thousands of mutants defining single gene variation and a genetic map which is being increasingly refined. Fourth, the mouse is often the species of choice as a model for human disease. Finally, large areas of synteny have already been correlated between the mouse and human genetic map (Nadeau et al., 1992).

In brief, total RNA was isolated from these tissues by guanadinium/CsCl ultracentrifugation (Chirgwin et al., 1979). First strand cDNA was produced by Moloney reverse transciptase using an arbitrarily selected 20 base primer. Primer extension occurs most favorably at better matches and becomes progressively less likely at worse matches. The arbitrarily primed first strand cDNA was heat denatured and subjected to arbitrarily primed second strand synthesis using Taq polymerase at low stringency. The products that result have the primer sequence at both ends and were then PCR amplified at high stringency with simultaneous radiolabelling. The products were separated by polyacrylamide gel electrophoresis and visualized by autoradiography. The resulting fingerprint patterns are highly reproducible. In Fig. 1 a portion of a gel is shown that emphasizes the kinds of differential expression that can be observed.

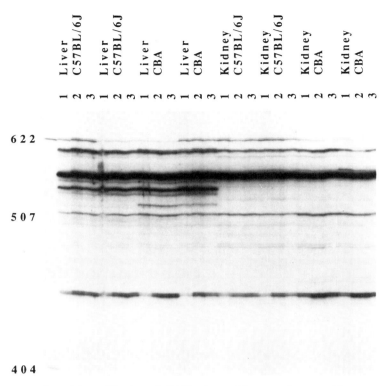

Figure 1. Differential amplification of cDNAs detected between tissues and between strains of mice. Total RNA was prepared from the livers and kidneys of the C57BL/6J and CBA inbred strains of mice and fingerprinted with the reverse sequencing primer (Welsh et al., 1992b). The resulting fingerprint was resolved on a 5% acrylamide sequencing gel and visualized by autoradiography. Molecular weights in bases are given. Differentially expressed products between the liver and kidney are visible at about 530 and 560 bases. Both products are expressed in the liver but not the kidney. In addition, the product at about 530 bases is differentially amplified between strains, presumably due to a mutation at the site of primer binding.

For each RNA sample, three concentrations were used and it can be seen that there are two liver-specific RAP products. One product in the above figure is only present in the CBA strain, reflecting a sequence polymorphism in the gene between the two inbred strains of mice. This kind of polymorphism could be useful for direct genetic mapping cDNAs using tissue from Rl strains. However, no such polymorphisms are detectable if one strain is used as a source of RNA. Subsequent experiments have confirmed these initial results and fingerprinting of RNA from mouse liver, kidney, and heart has revealed numerous differentially expressed genes, reflecting the complex gene expression pattern of these tissues (Welsh et al., 1992b).

Characterization of differentially expressed mRNAs

To unequivocally prove that differences between arbitrarily primed PCR fingerprints of RNA from different tissues reflect tissue-specific differences in the level of gene expression, the following series of experiments were performed. Several fingerprint products from differentially expressed messages in the kidney and heart were purified from the gel (Welsh et al., 1992b), reamplified and used as probes on Northern blot. One product hybridized to multiple mRNAs in both tissues, some of which were differentially expressed.

PCR products that showed evidence of differences in the level of gene expression were cloned and sequenced. No structural RNA sequences were represented in this small sample and four products contained open reading frames. The sequences were compared to the Genbank v.70 database. One is from near the middle of the reading frame for an alpha-actin mRNA that is confined to vascular smooth muscle. Its size indicated that it was from a spliced message. This mRNA is highly homologous to other members of the alpha-actin family, which explains the multiple products seen on Northern blots. The particular variant we cloned is known to have a very restricted distribution (Nakano et al., 1991). One product, present in both kidney and heart in a one to four ratio, proved to be a region of α-1-globin mRNA and spans a splice junction, indicating that it was from a spliced message. This message presumably originates from reticulocytes present in all tissues at low frequency. The sequences of the other probes were not homologous to any sequence in the database. Thus, over 50% of the products isolated from this one experiment are new differentially expressed genes.

The two sequences that were in the database allowed us to assess the match between the primer and the RNA in the reverse transcription step (first strand synthesis) and between the primer and the cDNA in the low stringency *Taq* polymerase step (second strand synthesis). In three of four cases, the primers matched the sequence in the database perfectly or almost perfectly at the seven 3′ nucelotides with a better match in the rest of the primer than would be expected by chance (Welsh et al., 1992b).

In subsequent experiments we have investigated differential gene expression in the mouse adult brain, adult liver and 10.5 day post coitum embryonic brain (unpublished). From a single gel, we have isolated cloned and sequenced eight cDNA products from the brain that are differentially expressed either in the adult or the embryo when compared to the liver. Of these eight sequences only six were found to hybridize on Northerns, although Southerns were positive, indicating relatively rare messages. Only one of the positive clones on Northerns showed any obvious homology to a known gene. This clone has over 95% DNA homology to a recently characterized message, a $Ca^{2+}/$

calmodulin-insensitive adenylyl cyclase from rat brain (Feinstein et al., 1991). This gene is known to have a very restricted distribution in only a few tissues, being present in the adult brain and lung.

RAP experiments in other model systems

A number of other laboratories are using this technique for their own specific purposes. For instance, Monica Roth (Dept. of Biochemistry, UMDNJ), has compared RNA fingerprints between non-infected and HIV infected cells in order to identify cellular genes that may increase or decrease their levels of expression after infection. She is currently investigating one differentially expressed fragment which is not a sequence present in the HIV genome. Lino Saez at the Rockefeller University has isolated and analyzed a new *per*-like (Baylies et al., 1987) circadian rhythm gene using RAP with a single *per*-specific primer.

We are studying the alterations of mRNA populations by TGF-β treatment of mink lung epithelial cells. Of five differentially expressed genes, one was the homolog of a rat extracellular matrix protein, osteonectin, known to be regulated by TGF-β (Bolander et al., 1988). Another sequence was the homolog of cyclin-A (Wang et al., 1990) and this finding further supports a possible link between cyclin and TGF-β as has been hypothesized (Aaronson, 1991). Manuel Perucho, (CIBR) has uncovered mRNAs that are differentially expressed during tumourogenesis in vitro and during the transition to malignancy in vivo in a rat model.

Development of the RAP protocol

To determine the most robust fingerprinting conditions, we tested several of the reaction parameters including magnesium concentration, input RNA and cDNA concentrations. For instance, a serial dilution of the RNA over a 500-fold range from 2.5 μg to 0.012 μg per 20 μl reaction before cDNA synthesis revaled a broad concentration optimum (Welsh et al., 1992b). Therefore, the method is reproducible over a wide range of RNA concentrations down to a few nanograms of total RNA.

Fingerprints generated in this manner are RNA-dependent and not due to contaminating genomic DNA. The pattern is insensitive to prior treatment with DNase and sensitive to RNase. In this RNA fingerprinting protocol, contaminating chromosomal DNA is double stranded during the first strand cDNA synthesis step, and therefore is not able to participate in the first low stringency step. Subsequent to first strand synthesis, only a single round of denaturation and low stringency annealing need occur (with primers >15 bases). In Welsh et al., 1992b, the presence of denatured genomic DNA almost completely eliminates the RNA-dependent pattern and results in an largely uniform background smear, presumably due to promiscuous priming in the first step under these low stringency conditions. However, when 20% of the input nucleic acid is non-denatured genomic DNA the PCR fingerprints are by and large unaffected over a wide range of concentrations. That the presence of moderate amounts of dsDNA does not adversely affect the fingerprinting of RNA suggests that the rigorous density centrifugation method used here for RNA production may not be necessary. The insensitivity to moderate dsDNA contamination combined with the observation that only a few nanograms of RNA is needed per lane could allow application to tissues or cells which are difficult to obtain the large amounts.

The PCR protocol for RAP with 18 base primers uses 37°C annealing temperature for the first cycle, 40°C for the second cycle and 60°C for subsequent cycles. We have also used ten base long primers to generate tissue-specific patterns (Welsh et al., 1992b). The protocol for use of the ten-mers was essentially the same as with the larger primers, except that a 35°C annealing step was used throughout and the ramp time for the transition to 72°C was increased to 30 sec. Short arbitrary primers may sample the RNA complexity in a manner different from longer arbitrary primers. Arbitrarily primed fingerprints produced by a ten-mer primer often give larger and fewer products compared to RAP-PCR with 18 base long primers.

Complexity sampled in RAP

The appearance of a product in RAP is a function of both the extent of the arbitrary match in the first two cycles and of the abundance of the message. RNA populations generally consist of messages that vary widely in their abundance. When the amplifications of two sequences are initiated by equally good matches, the sequence from the more abundant RNA may predominate at the end of the PCR amplification. On the other hand, the best primer matches are likely to be found among the high complexity, low abundance messages. These two factors, abundance and complexity, have opposite effects. The fingerprints are therefore only partly normalized with respect to abundance.

The issue is of importance for the detection of differentially expressed genes. Many differentially expressed genes of interest are likely to be in the low abundance class. Our initial experiments suggested partially normalized sampling, based on the homology between the primers and genes whose sequences were alrady in the database. This possibility was also supported by Northern blots: three clones for previously unknown messages gave Northern hybridization signals that ranged over an order of magnitude while giving nearly equilvalent Southern hybridization signals. We were therefore sampling over at least a ten-fold abundance range.

For the moment, it is not clear how efficiently we are sampling the low abundance, high complexity class and this issue is still a question actively under investigation. The matches between the primer and the mRNA are approximately seven bases at each end in four or five cases we examined (Welsh et al., 1992b, and unpublished data on adenylyl cyclase). Such matches would be rather rare. For example, matches of seven bases in opposite strands situated less than 1000 bases apart are calculated to occur less than once every 270,000 bases ($4^7 \times 4^7/1000$), or about 200 such matches in an RNA population with a complexity of 50,000,000 bases. Since we observe only 20 products the protocol may be only partly abundance normalized.

Nested primers

We have addressed the issue of abundance normalization by the following approach: In principle, the more extensive the match becomes between the RNA and the primer the less RNA abundance will influence the final fingerprint and the more "abundance normalized" the fingerprint pattern will be. Increasing the stringency of the arbitrary priming events in the PCR reaction would seem the easiest way of increasing the stringency of the primer match and thereby the abundance normalization. However, this has the effect of rendering irreproducible the PCR fingerprints. This observation might be related to the fact that the reaction also becomes irreproducible at very low template concentrations (Welsh et al., 1992b). Instead, we have developed a strategy to sample an arbitrarily primed fingerprint using nested primers that enhances abundance normalization. The method uses a partly nested primer for PCR at high stringency after the first low stringency PCR. This nested primer matches the original primer used in arbitrary priming but has one or more additional arbitrary bases at the 3′ end.

Arbitrarily primed PCR samples a complex RNA population by selecting the best matches between the primer and the nucleic acid (a reasonable match at both ends is presumably necessary). However, pairs of moderate matches on abundant RNAs could lead to PCR products that dominate the final fingerprint even if less abundant RNAs have a better pair of matches with the primer. Rare RNAs with good matches and abundant RNAs that had poorer matches would be represented in the mixture but at low levels. If the cDNA products in the background of an arbitrarily primed PCR fingerprint could be sampled in a high stringency PCR step then one would expect that even the rarest messages would have a chance to be sampled. This objective might be achieved if the initial arbitrarily primed PCR fingerprint was sampled with another PCR reaction performed at high stringency using a second primer that overlapped the initial primer but which had one or more extra bases at the 3′ end. One extra base would amplify 1/16 of the products in the fingerprint including products that were not visible in the initial arbitrarily primed PCR. Two extra bases would amplify 1/256. Three extra bases would amplify 1/4,096. Four extra bases would amplify 1/65,536, and so on. At some point the 3′ extension of the primer used in this second PCR reaction would be so long that a sufficiently good match would not always occur in the initial arbitrarily primed fingerprint and the pattern would become unreliable.

To achieve the objective of partly nested priming at the minimum cost a series of arbitrary primers were manufactured that overlapped each other by various numbers of bases in a circularly permuted arrangement. This allows each primer to be used in either the first PCR reaction or in the second PCR reaction with one or more arbitrarily extended bases:

```
ZF-1   AACCCCACCGGAGAGAAA
ZF-2    ACCCCACCGGAGAGAAAC
ZF-3     CCCCACCGGAGAGAAACC
ZF-4      CCCACCGGAGAGAAACCC
ZF-5       CCACCAGAGAGAAACCCA
ZF-6        CACCAGAGAGAAACCCAC
ZF-7         ACCAGAGAGAAACCCACC
ZF-8          CCAGAGAGAAACCCACCA
ZF-9           CAGAGAGAAACCCACCAG
ZF-10           AGAGAGAAACCCACCAGA
ZF-11            GAGAGAAACCCACCAGAG
ZF-12             AGAGAAACCCACCAGAGA
ZF-13              GAGAAACCCACCAGAGAG
ZF-14               AGAAACCCAGCAGAGAGA
ZF-15                GAAACCCACCAGAGAGAA
ZF-1                  AACCCCACCGGAGAGAAA etc.
```

In Fig. 2 primer ZF-1 was used in the first RAP on liver and kidney total RNAs. This was followed by PCR at higher stringency with ZF-2, or ZF-3 or ZF-4. The PCR fingerprint pattern changes almost completely between each priming event but the primer nested by three bases still yields multiple products. Nevertheless, the longer the 3′ extension in the nested step the more abundance normalized the sample should be. In future experiments this series will be continued to determine the primer extension length that no longer gives a fingerprint.

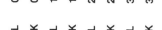

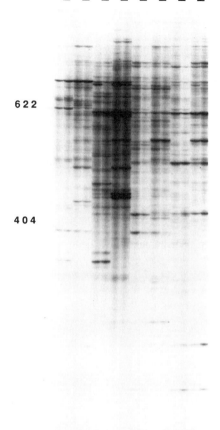

Figure 2. RAP-PCR using nested primers. Total RNA was prepared from the liver and kidney of the C57BL/6J inbred strain of mouse and fingerprinted with the primer ZF-1 followed by ZF1, ZF-2 or ZF-3. The resulting fingerprint was resolved on a 5% acrylamide sequencing gel by autoradiography. Molecular weights in bases are given. Entirely different fingerprints are given with each nested primer used in the second step.

The nested priming process was also performed on liver and brain RNAs (data not shown). Eight differentially expressed products were isolated from the gel and sequenced. Each of the products from a nested priming reaction had the sequence of the first primer and nested primers at both ends, indicating that the nested primers had sampled products made in the first RAP-PCR step. Only four sequences were found to hybridize well in Northern blot analysis although all gave good signals on Southern blots. One strongly hybridizing product, the homolog of rat brain adenylyl cyclase (type II) mRNA is known to be moderately abundant and was isolated from the first (non-nested) reaction. The four clones that do not hybridize in Northerns may be clones for less abundant messages. Seven of the eight clones have no known homolog.

Conclusion

Most of the products we have tested that are differentially amplified in RAP-PCR are also differentially expressed. To summarize data presented in these preliminary studies, fifteen clones from RAP-PCR that were differentially amplified between tissues have been tested by Northern blot analysis. The tissue distributions for mRNAs represented by all eleven clones that yielded a positive Northern blot were consistent with the distributions of the corresponding RAP-PCR fingerprint products. Four clones from nested RAP-PCR gave no signal on any tissue including the tissue from which they were isolated (while Southerns were positive) presumably because these messages are of very low abundance.

The data presented here suggest many exciting possible applications. In particular, difference between two or more RNA populations could be assessed and a sample of differentially expressed mRNAs cloned directly. These products can be sequenced and genetically mapped then correlated with other mapped phenotypes.

References

Aaronson SA (1991) Growth factors and Cancer. Science 254: 1146–1145

Adams MD, Kelley JM, Gocayne JD, Dubnick M, Polymeropoulos MH, Xiao H, Merril CR, Wu A, Olde B, Moreno RF, Kerlavage AR, McCombie WR, Venter JC (1991a) Complementary DNA sequencing: expressed sequence tags and human genome project. Science 252: 1651–1656

Adams MD, Dubnick M, Kerlavage AR, Moreno RF, Kelley JM, Utterback TR, Nagle JW, Fields C, Venter JC (1991b) Sequence identification of 2,375 human brain genes. Nature 355: 632–634

Baylies MK, Bargiello TA, Jackson FR, Young MW (1987) Changes in abundance or structure of the per gene product can alter periodicity of the Drosophila clock. Nature 326: 390–2

Bolander ME, Young MF, Fisher LW, Yamada Y, Termine JD (1988) Osteonectin cDNA sequence reveals potential binding regions for calcium and hydroxyapatite and shows homologies with both a basement membrane protein (SPARC) and a serine proteinase inhibitor (ovomucoid). Proc Natl Acad Sci USA 85: 2919–2923

Chirgwin J, Przybyla A, MacDonald R, Rutter WJ (1979) Isolation of biologically active ribonucleic acid from sources enriched in ribonuclease. Biochemistry 18: 5294–5299

Dietrich W, Katz H, Lincoln SE, Shin H-S, Friedman J, Dracopli NC, Lander ES (1992) A genetic map of the mouse suitable for typic intraspecific crosses. Genetics 131: 423–447

Feinstein PG, Schrader KA, Bakalyar HA, Tang W-J, Krupinski J, Gilman AG, Reed RR (1991) Molecular cloning and characterization of a Ca^{2+}/calmodulin-insensitive adenyl cyclase from rat brain. Proc Natl Acad Sci USA 88: 10173–10177

Gieser L, Swaroop A (1992) Expressed sequence tags and chromosomal localization of cDNA clones from a subtracted retinal pigment epithelium library. Genomics 13: 873–6

Gusella JF, Wexler NS, Conneally PM, Naylor SL, Anderson MA, Tanzi RE, Watkins PC, Ottina K, Wallace MR, Sakaguchi AY, Young AB, Shoulson I, Bonilla E, Martin JB (1983) A polymorphic DNA marker genetically linked to Huntington's disease. Nature 306: 234–238

Hamaguchi M, Sakamoto H, Tsuruta H, Sasaki H, Muto T, Sugimura T, Terada M (1992) Establishment of a highly sensitive and specific exontrapping system. Proc Natl Acad Sci USA 89: 9779–9783

Joyner AL, Herrup K, Auerbach BA, Davis CA, Rossant J (1991) Subtle cerebellar phenotype in mice homozygous for a targeted deletion of the En-2 homeobox. Science 251: 1239–1243

Ko MS (1990) An 'equalized cDNA library' by the reassociation of short double-stranded cDNAs. Nucleic Acids Res 18: 5705–5711

Liang P, Pardee A (1992). Differential display of eukaryotic messenger RNA by means of the polymerase chain reaction. Science 257: 967–971

Michelmore RW, Paran I, Kesseli RV (1991) Identification of markers linked to disease-resistance genes by bulked segregant analysis: a rapid method to detect markers in specific genomic regions by using segregating populations. Proc Natl Acad Sci USA 88: 9828–9832

Nadeau JH, Davisson MT, Doolittle DP, Grant P, Hillyard AL, Kosowsky MR, Roderick TH (1992) Comparative map for mice and humans. Mammalian Genome 3: 480–536

Nakano Y, Nishihara T, Sasayama S, Miwa T, Kamada S, Kakunaga T (1991) Transcriptional regulatory elements in the 5′ upstream and first intron regions of the human smooth muscle (aortic type) and alpha-actin-encoding gene. Gene 99: 285–289

Palmiter RD, Brinster RL (1986) Germ-line transformation of mice. Ann Rev Genet 20: 465–499

Palazzolo MJ, Hyde DR, VijayRaghavan K, Mecklenburg K, Benzer S, Meyerowitz E (1989) Use of a new strategy to isolate and characterize 436 Drosophila cDNA clones corresponding to RNAs detected in adult heads but not in early embryos. Neuron 3: 527–539

Polymeropoulos MH, Xiao H, Glodek A, Gorski M, Adams MD, Moreno RF, Fitzgerald MG, Venter JC, Merril CR (1992) Chromosomal assignment of 46 brain cDNAs. Genomics 12: 492–496

Rothstein JL, Johnson D, DeLoia JA, Skowronski J, Solter D, Knowles B (1992) Gene expression during preimplantation mouse development. Genes Dev 6: 1190–1201

Robertson, EJ (1987) Teratocarcinomas and embryonic stem cells: a practical approach (IRL Press, Oxford)

Smith ML, Bruhn JN, Anderson JB (1992) The fungus Armillaria bulbosa is among the largest and oldest living organisms. Nature 356: 428–431

Stallings RL, Ford AF, Nelson D, Torney DC, Hildebrand CE, Moyzis, RK (1991) Evolution and distribution of (GT)$_n$ repetitive sequences in mammalian genomes. Genomics 10: 807–815

Stubbs L (1992) Long-range walking techniques in positional cloning strategies. Mammalian Genome 3: 127–142

Sutcliffe JG (1988) mRNA in the central nervous system. Annu Rev NeuroSci 11: 157–198

Wang J, Chenivesse X, Henglein B, Brechot C (1990) Hepatitis B virus integration in a cyclin A gene in a hepatocellular carcinoma. Nature 343: 555–557

Welsh J, McClelland M (1990) Fingerprinting genomes using PCR with arbitrary primers. Nucleic Acids Res 18: 7213–7218

Welsh J, McClelland M (1991) Genomic fingerprinting with AP-PCR using pairwise combinations of primers: Application to genetic mapping of the mouse. Nucleic Acids Res 19: 5275–5279

Welsh J, McClelland M, Honeycutt RJ, Sobral BWS (1991a) Parentage determination in maize hybrids using arbitrarily primed PCR. Theoretical and Applied Genetics 82: 473–476

Welsh J, Petersen C, McClelland M (1991b) Polymorphisms generated by arbitrarily primed PCR in the mouse: Application to strain identification and genetic mapping. Nucleic Acids Res 19: 303–306

Welsh J, Pretzman C, Postic D, Saint Girons I, Baranton G, McClelland M (1992) Genomic fingerprinting by arbitrarily primed PCR resolves Borrelia burgdorferi into three distinct groups. Int J Systematic Bacteriol 42: 370–377

Welsh J, Chada K, Dalal SS, Ralph D, Chang R, McClelland M (1992b) Arbirarily primed PCR fingerprinting of RNA. Nucleic Acids Res 20: 4965–4970

Welsh J, Lui J-P, Efstradiatis A (1990) Cloning of PCR amplified total cDNA: Construction of a mouse oocyte cDNA library. Genetic Analysis 7: 5–17

Williams JG, Kubelik AR, Livak KJ Rafalski JA, Tingey SV (1990) DNA polymorphisms amplified by arbitrary primers are useful as genetic markers. Nucleic Acids Res 18: 6531–5

DNA Fingerprinting: State of the Science
ed. by S. D. J. Pena, R. Chakraborty, J. T. Epplen & A. J. Jeffreys
© 1993 Birkhäuser Verlag Basel/Switzerland

Rapid analysis of PCR components and products by acidic non-gel capillary electrophoresis

M. J. Pearce and N. D. Watson

Forensic Science Unit, Department of Pure and Applied Chemistry, University of Strathclyde, Glasgow, G1 1XL, UK

Summary

A capillary electrophoresis system has been developed which has the ability to rapidly analyse DNA restriction fragments, PCR products, oligonucleotides and complex deoxyribonucleoside tri-, di- and mono-phosphate mixtures in a single separating medium. Separations are performed in an internally coated capillary containing a solution of linear polymers. The separation of all DNA species is achieved through the novel use of acidic rather than alkaline pH. This has the added advantage of preserving the internal capillary coating. The use of the technique is described for rapid, high resolution separation of pBR322 and ϕX174 DNA restriction digests, quality control of dNTP and oligonucleotide primer PCR components, detection of a PCR amplified region of λ-phage DNA and detection of a PCR amplified human hypervariable region of forensic interest. The technique is termed "acidic non-gel capillary electrophoresis".

Introduction

Capillary electrophoresis (CE) has emerged as a useful technique for the separation of biomolecules (Kuhr, 1990). Analyses can be performed at high voltages due to the efficient dissipation of Joule heating from the $20-100$ μm internal diameter capillaries, resulting in rapid, ultrahigh resolution separations (Gordon et al., 1988).

CE separations of oligonucleotides and DNA restriction fragments have been described at alkaline pH in gel-filled capillaries (Kasper et al., 1988; Guttman et al., 1990) and in non-gel linear polymer solutions (Zhu et al., 1989; Heiger et al., 1990; Strege and Lagu, 1991). Non-gel polymer solutions have become the preferred media for polymerase chain reaction (PCR) product separation due to increased reproducibility and decreased capillary preparation (Heiger et al., 1990; Schwartz et al., 1991; Ulfeder et al., 1992). Both techniques require internal coating of the capillary wall to eliminate electroendosmosis. As this procedure is carried out at acidic pH (Hjerten, 1985), the coating is rapidly degraded by the use of alkaline separating media. The use of an acidic separating medium would therefore be beneficial in increasing capillary life-span.

A further advantage of acidic pH would be to allow the analysis of deoxyribonucleoside triphosphate (dNTP) mixtures. Separation of dTNP mixtures into individual components is only possible at pH < 7

(Takigiku and Schneider, 1991). In the alkaline separating media described for dsDNA and ssDNA, dNTP components are unresolved (Heiger et al., 1990) making such media unsuitable for analysis of all nucleic acid PCR components and products.

This paper describes a single non-gel polymer CE system that by operating at acidic pH, can be used for high resolution separation of DNA restriction digests, quality control of dNTP and oligonucleotide PCR components, and detection of PCR products. The technique has been applied to PCR products of the GeneAmp™ λ-phage system (Perkin-Elmer Cetus, 1989) and the human apolipoprotein B 3′ hypervariable region (ApoB HVR) (Boerwinkle et al., 1989).

Materials and methods

CE Separations: All separations were performed on a Bio-Rad HPE 100 instrument in 50 cm × 50 μm I.D. internally coated capillaries (Bio-Rad Laboratories, Richmond, CA, U.S.A.). The separation medium was 0.1 M phosphate, pH 5.7, 1.25% hydroxypropylmethylcellulose (viscosity 50 cP at 2%). Samples were loaded electrokinetically at the cathode for 6 seconds at 160 V/cm and separated at 160 V/cm. Detection was by UV absorbance at 260 nm, 47.3 cm from the cathode.

Sample preparation: 20-mer oligonucleotides (British Biotechnology, Abingdon, Oxon), ϕX174 DNA HaeIII digest and pBR322 DNA HaeIII digest (Sigma Chemical Co, Poole, Dorset) were used without further preparation. dNTP mixtures were prepared at 200 μM each of dATP, dCTP, dGTP and dTTP (I.L.S., London). Mixtures were subjected to a degradative environment of 94°C for 30 minutes.

PCR amplification of a 500 bp region of λ-phage DNA (Perkin-Elmer Cetus, 1989) and ApoB amplification from human genomic DNA (Boerwinkle et al., 1989) were as previously described. Prior to CE analysis, PCR products were purified by spin size exclusion at $650 \times g$ for 30 seconds in Bio-Spin 30 columns (Bio-Rad Laboratories, Richmond, CA, U.S.A.) preconditioned with 3 column volumes of distilled water.

Results

DNA restriction digests: Figure 1 shows the separation of pBR322 DNA HaeIII digest and ϕX174 DNA HaeIII digest by acidic non-gel CE. Analysis time is 15–35 minutes for fragment sizes in the range of 21–1353 bp. Half baseline resolution is achieved between 123 and 124 bp fragments leading to an estimate of 2 bp baseline resolution at 124 bp. Resolution decays with increased fragment size, being 150 bp at

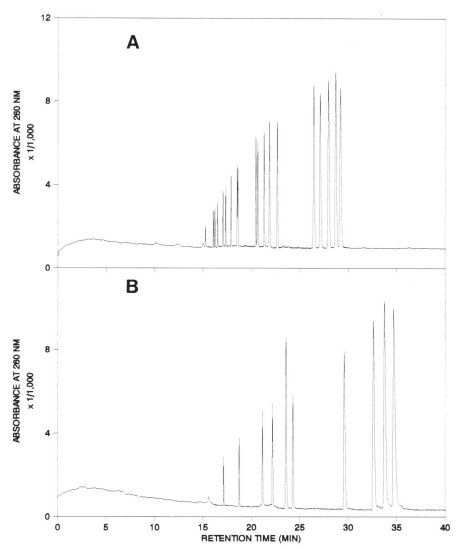

Figure 1. Separation of DNA restriction degests. A. pBR322 DNA HaeIII digest. Fragment sizes from left to right are 21, 51, 57, 64, 80, 89, 104, 123, 124, 184, 192, 213, 234, 267, 434, 458, 504, 540, and 587 base pairs. Concentration: 100 ng/µl. B. ϕX174 DNA HaeIII digest. Fragment sizes from left to right are 72, 118, 194, 234, 271/281, 310, 603, 872, 1087 and 1353 base pairs. Concentration: 100 ng/µl. Separation conditions as in Materials and Methods.

1353 bp. Column efficiency of over 1 million theoretical plates per metre is attained for fragment sizes below 140 bp.

dNTP mixtures: Figure 2 shows the separation of freshly prepared dNTP mixture and mixture subjected to a degradative environment. Freshly prepared mixture is resolved into its four components in under

120

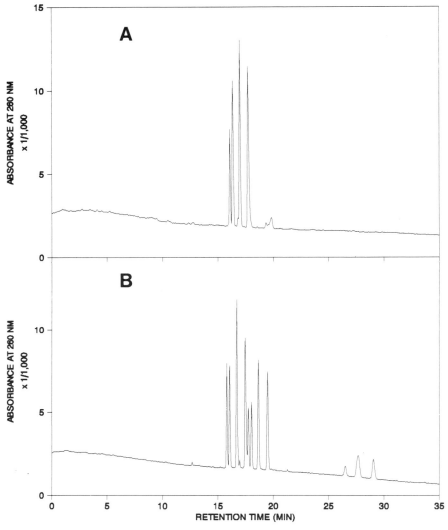

Figure 2. Separation of dNTP mixtures. A. Freshly prepared dNTP mixture. Peaks from left to right are dCTP, dTTP, dATP and dGTP. Concentration: 200 μM each. B. Degraded dNTP mixture. Peaks from left to right are dCTP, dTTP, dATP, dGTP, dCDP, dTDP, dADP, dGDP and 3 × monophosphates. Separation conditions as in Materials and Methods.

18 minutes. Degraded mixture contains seven extra peaks attributed to products of dNTP degradation.

Oligonucleotides: Figure 3 shows the separation of HPLC purified 20-mer PCR primer, unpurified 20-mer PCR primer and products of a failed oligonucleotide synthesis reaction. Analysis time is generally less than 20 minutes. HPLC purified primer displays a single major peak

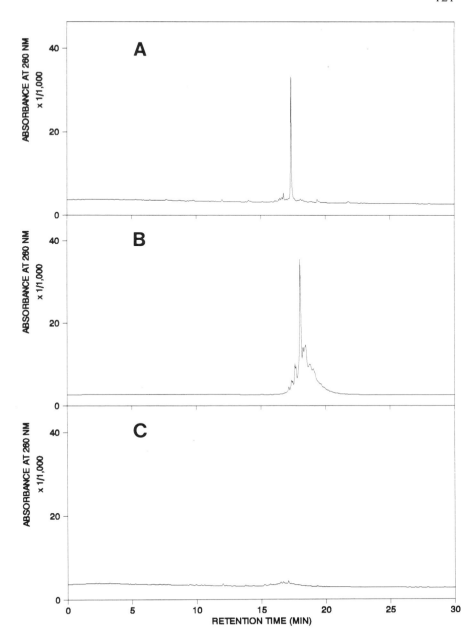

Figure 3. Separation of 20-mer oligonucleotides. A. HPLC purified. B. Unpurified. C. Products of failed synthesis. Concentration: 50 ng/μl. Separation conditions as in Materials and Methods.

whilst synthesis by-products are detected in the unpurified sample. The failed synthesis reaction is characterised by the absence of peaks.

PCR products: Figure 4 shows the separation of a PCR amplified 500 bp λ-phage DNA segment and the separation of PCR amplified ApoB HVR from two individuals. Spin-size exclusion prior to analysis

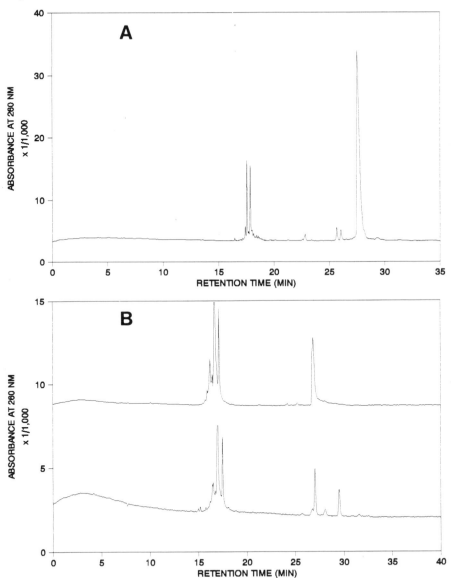

Figure 4. Separation of PCR Products. A. PCR amplified 500 bp segment of λ-phage DNA. B. PCR amplified human ApoB HVR's. Primers migrate at 15–20 minutes retention. Separation conditions as in Materials and Methods.

efficiently removes buffer salts and unincorporated dNTP's from the amplified reaction mixture. Unincorporated primers are not removed and migrate at 15–20 minutes retention. The λ-phage PCR product migrates with a retention time corresponding to the value expected from restriction digest separations. ApoB products are detected in under 35 minutes and display the expected allelic differences between individuals.

Discussion

Acidic non-gel capillary electrophoresis enables rapid, high resolution analysis of nucleotides, oligonucleotides and double stranded DNA using a single separating medium. The system is therefore ideal for both quality control of nucleic acid PCR components and the detection of PCR products.

The integrity of dNTP and PCR primer components can be confirmed in under 20 minutes. In our laboratory, this has allowed use of dNTP mixtures beyond the manufacturers control date and has identified a failed primer synthesis reaction as the cause of a failed PCR amplification.

Separations of DNA restriction digests and PCR products are achieved with resolution comparable to polyacrylamide gel electrophoresis. However, preparation and analysis times are significantly less for small sample numbers and the amount of sample consumed is negligible (less than 1%), allowing further analysis if required. The technique has enabled rapid DNA typing of the human ApoB HVR. Work is currently in progress to detect other PCR amplified HVR's of forensic interest including the widely dispersed CA repeat VNTR's (Weber and May, 1989) which have previously required radiolabelling for detection and separation on high resolution sequencing gels.

Acknowledgements
We thank Anne Coxon and Patricia Flanigan for blood donations. This work was supported by the Science and Engineering Research Council. The conference presentation was funded in part by Bio-Rad Laboratories Ltd.

References

Boerwinkle E, Xiong W, Fourest E, Chan L (1989) Rapid typing of tandemly repeated hypervariable loci by the polymerase chain reaction: Application to the apolipoprotein B 3′ hypervariable region. Proc Natl Acad Sci USA 86: 212–216

Gordon MJ, Huang X, Pentoney Jr SL, Zare RN (1988) Capillary electrophoresis. Science 242: 224–228

Guttman A, Cohen AS, Heiger DN, Karger BL (1990) Analytical and micropreparitive ultrahigh resolution of oligonucleotides by polyacrylamide gel high-performance capillary electrophoresis. Anal Chem 62: 137–141

Heiger DN, Cohen AS, Karger BL (1990) Separation af DNA restriction fragments by high performance capillary electrophoresis with low and zero crosslinked polyacrylamide using continuous and pulsed electric fields. J Chromatogr 516: 33–48

Hjerten S (1985) High performance electrophoresis: Elimination of electroendosmosis and solute adsorption. J Chromatogr 347: 191–198

Kasper TJ, Melera M, Gozel P, Brownlee RG (1988) Separation and detection of DNA by capillary electrophoresis. J Chromatogr 458: 303–312

Kuhr WG (1990) Capillary electrophoresis. Anal Chem 62: 403R–414R

Perkin-Elmer Cetus (1989) GeneAmp™ DNA amplification reagent kit. Protocol 55635-2/89, Perkin-Elmer Cetus, Norwalk, CT.

Schwartz HE, Ulfelder K, Sunzeri FJ, Busch MP, Brownlee RG (1991) analysis of DNA restriction fragments and polymerase chain reaction products towards detection of the AIDS (HIV-I) virus in blood. J Chromatogr 559: 267–283

Strege M, Lagu A (1991) Separation of DNA restriction fragments by capillary electrophoresis using coated fused silica capillaries. Anal Chem 63: 1233–1236

Ulfelder KJ, Schwartz HE, Hall JM, Sunzeri FJ (1992) Restriction fragment polymorphism analysis of ERBB2 oncogene by capillary electrophoresis. Anal Biochem 200: 260–267

Weber JL, May PE (1989) Abundant class of human DNA polymorphisms which can be typed using the polymerase chain reaction. Am J Hum Genet 44: 388–396

Zhu M, Hansen DL, Burd S, Gannon F (1989) Factors affecting free zone electrophoresis and isoelectric focusing in capillary electrophoresis. J Chromatogr 480: 311–319

DNA Fingerprinting: State of the Science
ed. by S. D. J. Pena, R. Chakraborty, J. T. Epplen & A. J. Jeffreys
© 1993 Birkhäuser Verlag Basel/Switzerland

Minisatellite variant repeat mapping:
Application to DNA typing and mutation analysis

A. J. Jeffreys, D. G. Monckton, K. Tamaki, D. L. Neil,
J. A. L. Armour, A. MacLeod, A. Collick, M. Allen and M. Jobling

*Department of Genetics, University of Leicester, Adrian Building, University Road,
Leicester, LE1 7RH, England*

Summary

Most DNA typing systems assay allele length variation at tandemly repeated loci such as minisatellites and microsatellites. Allele length measurements are approximate, which impedes the use of such loci in forensic analysis and in studies of allelic variability at hypervariable loci. We now review progress in the development of alternative DNA typing systems based on allelic variation in the interspersion patterns of variant repeat units along minisatellite alleles. Minisatellite variant repeat mapping by PCR (MVR-PCR) not only provides a powerful new digital approach to DNA typing, but also for the first time allows investigation of the true level of allelic variability at minisatellite loci and of the mutational mechanisms that generate ultravariability.

Introduction

"Classical" DNA typing systems based on genomic DNA hybridization with multilocus minisatellite probes (DNA fingerprinting) or single locus minisatellites (DNA profiling) are now used routinely in criminal and civil investigations (see Jeffreys et al., 1991a). While these systems are powerful, the nature of the information recovered (band position on an autoradiograph, converted to estimated DNA fragment length by comparison with a reference marker ladder) is at best an approximation of the true level of variation. Measurement errors in quasi-continuous allele length frequency distributions make it impossible to identify alleles with precision, and for DNA fingerprints to relate bands to loci. They also provide ammunition for defence lawyers to undermine the validity of DNA typing, as well as impeding the construction of unambiguous DNA profile data bases and investigations of the population genetic behaviour of the hypervariable loci that provide the basis of these DNA typing systems.

More recently, there has been considerable interest in the development of extremely sensitive DNA typing systems based on the amplification of repeat loci such as minisatellites (AMP-FLPs; Jeffreys et al., 1988; Budowle et al., 1991), microsatellites and simple tandem repeat loci (Litt and Luty, 1989; Weber and May, 1989; Edwards et al., 1991), and loci that show extensive base substitutional polymorphism such as HLA-DQα and the control region of mitochondrial DNA (see Sensabaugh and von Beroldingen, 1991). Of necessity, only relatively short repeat loci can be amplified and typed in their entirety, with a substantial loss of variability and thus power of discrimination compared with the most variable minisatellites. Also, information is recovered as estimated allele length which can introduce measurement errors, particularly for larger alleles.

We have therefore sought to develop an alternative approach to DNA typing which combines the extreme variability of large minisatellites with the speed and sensitivity of PCR, and further to eliminate DNA fragment length measurement from the procedure.

Minisatellite repeat variation

Owerbach and Aagaard (1984) were the first to show, by sequence analysis of a cloned hypervariable locus near the insulin gene, that minisatellites are not composed of identical repeat units but instead contain intermingled arrays of different types of repeats that differ subtly from the consensus repeat sequence. Subsequent analysis of other minisatellite loci, including loci near the c-Ha-ras oncogene (Capon et al., 1983), α-globin gene cluster (Jarman et al., 1986) and those isolated by cross-hybridization with multilocus DNA fingerprint probes (Jeffreys et al., 1985; Wong et al., 1987) has shown in every case repeat unit sequence heterogeneity. There is evidence that heterogeneity decreases with increasing allele length variability (and thus allele length mutation rate), as expected from the interplay between base substitutional mutation, which will create novel repeat sequences in a tandem array, and allele length change (repeat copy number change) mutation, which will lead to the diffusion of variants along arrays or extinction of variants from the array. Repeat unit heterogeneity is not restricted to minisatellites, but has been extensively documented in satellite DNA (see for example Willard and Waye, 1987), midisatellites (Nakamura et al., 1987), telomere repeat arrays (Allshire et al., 1989), microsatellites (Weber, 1990) and retroposon poly(dA)-based tails (Epstein et al., 1990). For minisatellites, it has proved possible to map the location of minisatellite variant repeats (MVRs) along the tandem array, to provide a second dimension to studies of minisatellite variability.

MVR mapping – early approaches

Initial sequence surveys of cloned human minisatellites (Wong et al., 1987) revealed MS32 (locus D1S8) as a prime candidate for MVR mapping. This locus, located at 1q42–q43, is highly variable with at least 50 different alleles distinguishable by length. Sequencing of cloned MS32 identified two sites of base substitutional variation in the 29 bp repeat unit, one of which affected a *Hae*III site to create a repeat unit RFLP (Fig. 1). There was no evidence for any abnormal length repeat units, and all repeats contained a single site for *Hin*fI.

Our first attempt at MVR mapping was therefore based on charting the position of *Hae*III-cleavable repeat units along MS32 (Jeffreys et al., 1990). This was achieved by amplifying MS32 alleles in their

A

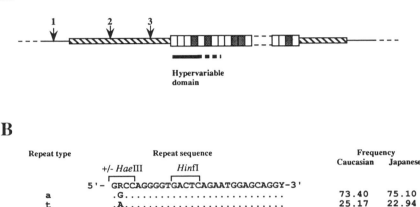

B

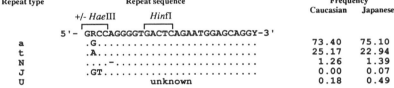

C

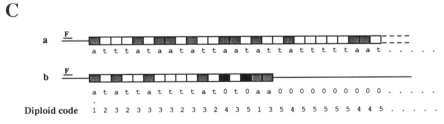

Figure 1. Digital coding at the human minisatellite MS32. A, structure of MS32, showing the two major classes of repeat unit (grey and white boxes) and the sites of three flanking polymorphisms (1–3) used for knockout MVR-PCR. MS32 has amplified from within a retroviral LTR (hatched). B, variants of the 29 bp MS32 repeat unit discovered to date, and their frequencies in Caucasians and Japanese alleles. C, principle of digital coding by MVR-PCR, using an amplimer F at a fixed site in the flanking DNA plus either **a**-type or **t**-type repeat specific amplimers. a, binary code of a typical long MS32 allele comprised of **a**- and **t**-type repeats only. b, **O**-type coding created by unamplifiable "null" repeats (black boxes) and by non-existent repeats beyond the end of a short allele. The diploid digital code of an individual containing alleles a and b is also shown, with codes 1 (**a/a**), 2 (**t/t**), 3 (**a/t**), 4 (**a/O**), 5 (**t/O**), [and 6 (**O/O**)].

entirety, followed by radiolabelling one or other end of the amplified allele and partial digestion with HinfI or HaeIII. Electrophoresis yielded a continuous ladder of end-labelled digest products extending to the HinfI site in each repeat unit, from which repeat unit copy number could be counted, and a discontinuous ladder of HaeIII partials from which each repeat unit could be classified in a binary fashion according to whether or not it contained a HaeIII site.

MS32 allele binary codes generated by this approach showed substantial levels of allelic variation in both allele length *and* internal distribution of HaeIII$^+$ and HaeIII$^-$ repeats. Most significantly, identical length alleles shared by unrelated individuals frequently showed totally different internal maps, indicating allele length convergence rather than true isoallelism. Similarly, apparent homozygotes could sometimes be shown, via allele separation by single molecule dilution and PCR recovery, to contain alleles of indistinguishable length but different internal maps (Monckton and Jeffreys, 1991), again indicating that MS32 allele length measurement significantly underestimates the true level of allelic variability at this locus. MVR codes also showed that different length alleles could nevertheless share regions of MVR map similarity or identity. Curiously, there was a strong polarity in variability, with the 3′ ends of alleles showing limited variation in Caucasian populations, compared with the 5′ end which showed extreme polymorphism in both repeat copy number and MVR map. This polarity of variation implies the existence of a hotspot for mutation at the 5′ end of MS32.

MS32 binary coding by PCR amplification and digestion, as described above, is unfortunately extremely tedious and limited to the minority of alleles short enough (<6 kb) to amplify efficiently by PCR. Also, it can only be applied to minisatellite loci which contain MVRs which create or destroy restriction sites. To generalize MVR mapping, we have therefore devised a strictly PCR-based strategy which can map *any* suitable MVR, irrespective of allele length. We term this approach MVR-PCR (minisatellite variant repeat mapping by PCR).

MVR-PCR

The basis of this approach, fully described elsewhere (Jeffreys et al., 1991b; Tamaki et al., 1992), is the use of MS32 MVR-specific amplimers which prime specifically either off HaeIII$^+$ repeats (termed **a**-type repeats) or HaeIII$^-$ repeats (**t**-type repeats) (Fig. 1C). Amplification with an **a**-type primer plus a primer in the flanking DNA 5′ to MS32 will create, from a single allele, a set of PCR products extending from the flanking site to each **a**-type repeat. The complementary set extending to each **t**-type repeat will be generated using the **t**-specific amplimer. By electrophoresing the two sets of products, two complementary "ladders" will be generated, from which the allele binary code can be read. This approach unfortunately leads to fade-out of the code after the first few repeats, due to internal priming by MVR amplimers within PCR

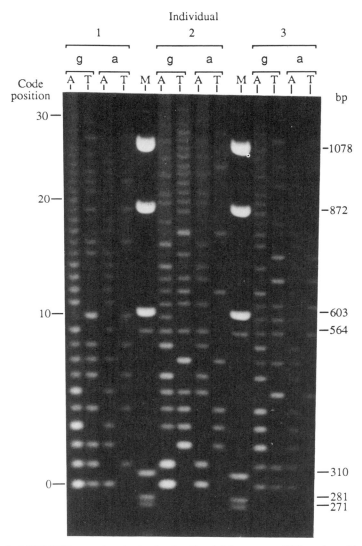

Figure 2. MVR-PCR mapping to levels directly visible on an ethidium bromide stained agarose gel. MS32 MVR-PCR was performed on three individuals (1, 2 and 3) using an **a**-type (A) or **t**-type (T) MVR primer plus a universal flanking primer (g) to produce a standard diploid code, or an allele-specific flanking primer (a) in knockout MVR-PCR. All three individuals are heterozygous for this flanking polymorphism and therefore have one allele knocked out, producing code from only one allele. Marker DNA (M) is also shown (λ DNA $\times$ *Hind*III and ϕX174 DNA $\times$ *Hae*III).

products, causing progressive shortening at each PCR cycle. To overcome this problem, the processes of MVR detection and subsequent amplification are effectively uncoupled by providing a 5' extension to each MVR primer and driving subsequent amplification by using the extension itself as a driver primer. By this strategy, it is possible to generate binary codes extending 50–70 or more repeat units into MS32 and spanning the ultravariable end of this locus. By altering the ratio of MVR primer to driver primer, it is possible to manipulate at will the size distribution of PCR products in the MVR ladder.

This approach can also be applied to total genomic DNA to generate a digital code derived from both alleles superimposed (Figs 1C, 2). For a locus containing two MVRs, this generates a ternary code. Using Southern blot hybridization of PCR products, it is possible to generate digital codes extending for 70 or more repeats. Alternatively, MVR-PCR can be performed for additional cycles and the products visualized on ethidium bromide stained agarose gels to give codes extending for approximately 30 repeats (Fig. 2). Alternative detection strategies being investigated include silver staining following polyacrylamide gel electrophoresis and the use of fluorescent labelled amplimers followed by in-gel detection.

To date, the digital codes from over 500 unrelated individuals have been determined and databased. The great advantage of digital typing is that all subsequent data manipulations such as comparisons can be carried out by computer. Pairwise analysis of all 500 codes (124,750 pairwise comparisons in total) has shown that no two people share even similar codes (the closest match shows 4 definitive points of dissimilarity over the first 50 repeats). Note that the theoretical maximum number of ternary codes over the first 50 repeats is $3^{50} = 7 \times 10^{23}$, close to Avogadro's Number! Each position in the code shows a uniform probability of 0.60 of identifying a mismatch between two unrelated individuals. Strong linkage disequilibrium effects between these extremely closely linked repeats means, however, that match probabilities at each position cannot be treated as independent. Also, while MS32 digital code variability between unrelated individuals is enormous, this is not true for siblings who have a $\sim 25\%$ chance of sharing the same parental alleles and therefore the same digital code.

Forensic considerations

Our experience to date indicates that MVR-PCR is sufficiently simple, sensitive and robust to be of potentially great use in forensic analysis. Digital codes appear to be highly reproducible and contain considerable informational redundancy which assists in checking code authenticity. Any uncertain code positions can be entered into the database as "?"

and ignored in subsequent database searches. Correct phasing of the code is ensured by reading from the first detectable repeat and double-checked by running a standard individual on all gels. Coding requires no length measurements and is not affected by problems of band shift and gel distortion. Diploid codes can be obtained reliably down to 1–10 ng genomic DNA. Below this level, stochastic loss of PCR products and the occasional mispriming off the wrong repeat type can introduce code uncertainties. However, replicate runs on the same sample can produce consensus codes that are reliable, even down to 100 pg DNA (17 diploid genomes). MVR-PCR can also be applied to partially degraded DNA, since the technique does not require intact minisatellite alleles. Such DNA samples yield truncated codes due to disappearance of longer PCR products; these codes are nevertheless fully compatible with database searches, though with less discriminatory power. MVR-PCR is currently being evaluated on forensic DNA samples rather than pristine DNA, with encouraging results. For example, an unknown individual has been successfully typed from saliva traces recovered from the back of a postage stamp and the individual correctly and uniquely identified by interrogation of our current code database (B. Hopkins, N.J. Williams, M.B.T. Webb, P.G. Debenham and A.J.J., unpublished data).

MVR-PCR can also be applied to mixed DNA samples frequently encountered in forensic casework, for example, mixed semen and vaginal stains from rape victims. Mixed samples can be analysed according to whether or not the MVR code of the victim is known. If the code is known, then the profile of the presumptive mixed DNA sample can be checked to see whether it is consistent with admixture of the victim's DNA with the DNA from other individual(s). If it is, then partial information concerning the code of the assailant may be deduced. For example, if at a given repeat position the victim is code 1 (**a**/**a**) and the mixture contains bands in both the **a**- and **t**-tracks, then a (single) assailant must contain **t**-type repeat(s) at this position and therefore be code 2(**t**/**t**) or 3(**a**/**t**). Conversely, if the victim is code 1(**a**/**a**) and the mixture contains only a band in the **a**-track, then *any* individual of code 2(**t**/**t**) or 3(**a**/**t**) is excluded from the mixture (at the current sensitivity limit for detecting admixtures, approximately 10%). Computer analysis shows that on average 99.9993% of false suspects would be excluded using such information from mixed DNA samples. Similar logic applies even if no victim information is available. Thus, any code 2(**t**/**t**) or code 3(**a**/**t**) individual cannot be a contributor (at the sensitivity limit) to a DNA sample which shows a band only in the **a**-track. The only difference is with mixtures that contain bands in both the **a**- and **t**-tracks: if, for example, the victim is code 1(**a**/**a**), then the (single) assailant cannot be code 1; if the victim is unknown, then *anyone* could be a contributor to the DNA sample. These above considerations apply to conventional MVR-PCR; as discussed below, an alternative approach (knockout MVR-PCR) has been developed which can also be used to dissect mixed DNA samples.

The forensic prospects for MVR-PCR are very encouraging, to provide a means for defining objectively matches between crime-scene samples and criminal suspects, to enable the construction of enormous investigative and reference computer databases, and to simplify statistical estimation of profile population frequencies by counting the number of matching individuals (probably zero) in such large databases.

MVR-PCR in paternity testing

Digital typing can also be used in principle to analyse parentage, by using the simple Mendelian rules operating at each repeat code position to search for positions which would exclude parentage. For example, if the mother is code 1(**a**/**a**) and the child 3(**a**/**t**), then the true father must have contributed a **t**-type repeat and be code 2(**t**/**t**) or 3(**a**/**t**) but not 1(**a**/**a**). The mean power of exclusion of non-fathers (assuming correct maternity, rarely an issue in paternity disputes) is 99.8%, a remarkably high figure for a single locus although the actual power of exclusion varies substantially depending on the diploid codes of the mother and child. Paternity testing is however limited by the relatively high mutation rate at MS32 (see below) and by the presence of unamplifiable "null" repeats in some alleles which can arise from additional repeat variants and from non-existent repeats beyond the end of short alleles (Fig. 1C). Incorrect scoring of heterozygous null positions in diploid codes (e.g. **a**/**a** for **a**/**O**) does not affect identity testing but does lead to incorrect genotypes and can introduce false parental exclusions. However, such positions can be identified with ~90% reliability from band intensity (dosage). Also, sequence analysis has shown that 85% of null repeats share the same variant ("N-type" repeats, Fig. 1B) which can be diagnosed precisely using an N-type specific MVR-PCR primer. The remaining nulls are a heterogeneous variety of additional variant repeats, many of which appear to have arisen by recent base substitutional mutation; one of these has been defined by sequence analysis ("**J**-type" repeats, Fig. 1B).

Additional digitised loci

The requirements for diploid coding of minisatellite loci are stringent. First, allele length heterozygosity must be high (>95%), otherwise high-frequency alleles will limit the power of individual discrimination. Second, the tandem repeat array must be dominated by relatively few (preferably two) MVRs. Third, abnormal length MVRs must be rare or non-existent, otherwise the MVR-PCR ladders of each constituent allele in an individual will be thrown out of register, making the diploid code ladder uninterpretable. Most minisatellites studied fail one or more of these criteria (unpublished data). We have, however, identified a second locus comprised of 20 bp repeats which has been successfully developed for MVR-PCR, with code variability at least as high as at MS32. Furthermore, it has proved possible to amplify both loci simultaneously by duplex MVR-PCR, to increase discrimination power, particularly between close relatives, and to increase the amount of information recoverable from degraded DNA.

We are also investigating a Y chromosome specific minisatellite as a candidate for MVR-PCR (M. Jobling, unpublished data). If successful, this could provide a novel single-allele typing system of interest for typing forensic semen samples, even in the presence of contaminating female DNA, and for studying patrilineal genealogy (in males of most populations, the family name should be "co-inherited" with the Y chromosome).

Allelic variability at MS32

Approximately 50 alleles at MS32 can be distinguished on the basis of allele length. To determine the true level of variability at this locus, we have determined the binary codes of alleles sampled from various populations. Individual alleles can be mapped by three approaches. First, different length alleles in heterozygotes can be electrophoretically separated prior to MVR-PCR. Second, and much more efficiently, parental allele codes can be extracted from the diploid codes of a father, mother and offspring. A single child will yield some ambiguities in the four parental haplotypes (wherever all three individuals are code 3 [a/t]). Two children sharing just one parental allele in common are the minimal resource required to solve completely all parental haplotypes in the absence of mutation. The third approach is to make use of three common base substitutional polymorphisms now discovered in the DNA flanking MS32 (Fig. 1A) to design allele-specific flanking primers to selectively amplify by MVR-PCR one or other allele in flanking heterozygotes (Fig. 2). 70% of individuals are heterozygous at one or more of the flanking loci and can therefore be subjected to this efficient approach to single allele mapping, which we term "knockout MVR-PCR". This approach can also be combined with pedigrees to extract single allele data; for example, the single allele codes determined by knockout from a flanking-heterozygous child can be used to determine codes from a flanking-homozygous parent by allele subtraction from the parent's diploid code. Knockout MVR-PCR also has forensic applications for mixed DNA samples, by selectively amplifying single alleles or groups of alleles from mixtures of two or more individuals. This approach, which can be used for example to ablate the victim's alleles prior to typing in some mixtures (dependent on the genotype of individuals in the mixture), can be used to type remarkably small amounts of DNA in mixtures (down to 1% admixture).

The allelic variability in Caucasians uncovered by these mapping approaches is enormous (Tab. 1); there are no common alleles and nearly all alleles so far mapped have been seen only once in our survey. A parallel survey of Japanese has revealed equally vast levels of variability. It is also possible to obtain a minimal estimate of MS32 allele diversity in the global human population; the 5×10^9 individuals now alive have arisen from 10^{10} gametes, of which 10^8 will contain new mutants (see below). Since most mutations will create alleles with codes not present in the world, then we can estimate the minimal number of different alleles at MS32 at 10^8, an astonishingly huge figure vastly greater than allele diversity defined on the basis of allele length.

From the sampling distributions of different alleles, and assuming selective neutrality and panmictic populations, it is possible to extract θ values and thence estimates of effective population size, N_e, and homozygosity. The N_e estimates tend to be higher (70,000–150,000) than those estimated for more conventional loci (10,000–50,000), as expected since most alleles are young and variability is thus controlled by recent relatively large demographic population sizes. Homozygosity estimates (0.02–0.04%) are also very low; it is interesting that several Caucasian and Japanese homozygotes have already been seen, at a level indicating clear departure from Hardy Weinberg equilibrium and thus probable evidence for inbreeding/consanguinity in some or all of these homozygotes. The absolute degree of homozygote excess is however very

Table 1. Allelic variability at MS32 revealed by MVR-PCR

	Caucasian	Japanese
No. alleles mapped	395	148
No. alleles seen: 1x	372	140
2x	10	4
3x	1	0
No. different alleles	383	144
Max allele frequency	0.007	0.014
θ^+	5800	2600
N_e	150,000	65,000
H^+	0.00017	0.00038

$^\dagger\theta(=4N_e u)$ was determined from the number of different alleles n_a seen in a sample of i individuals; under the infinite allele model and assuming selective neutrality, $n_a = \Sigma_1^{2i}(\theta/\theta + i - 1)$ (Ewens, 1972).
$^+$Homozygosity, H, was estimated as $1/1 + \theta$.

small, and can only be detected by MVR-PCR studies of allelic diversity, and not by conventional minisatellite allele length analysis.

Related alleles

While almost all MS32 alleles so far mapped are different, segments of MVR code similarity can frequently be found between non-identical alleles. Heuristic dot-matrix algorithms have been developed to identify significant allele alignments and have shown that 70% of the current set of mapped alleles (Tab. 1) can be grouped into 60 sets of alignable alleles each containing 2–63 alleles. The two very large groups each contain a diverse set of alleles, indicating relatively ancient groups of related alleles present in diverse population groups. The smaller groups of alleles show a strong tendency to be population-specific (e.g. Japanese-specific), consistent with recent divergence from a common ancestral allele. In most groups, the 5′ ends of the aligned MVR maps show most variability, confirming the existence of a variability hotspot at the 5′ end of MS32.

Many of these aligned alleles have also been typed for the 5′ flanking polymorphisms (Fig. 1A). Significantly, groups of closely-related alleles sometimes show changes in the flanking haplotype, indicating that MS32 alleles are not evolving along strictly haploid lineages, but instead are engaging in recombination/gene conversion events which disrupt linkage disequilibrium between the flanking DNA and the minisatellite. Detailed analysis suggests that recombination/conversion over the 5′ end of MS32 must be elevated several hundred fold over the mean rate of recombination in the genome to give the observed level of haplotype switching, and suggests that the hypervariable domain in MS32 may be a recombination/conversion hotspot.

Mutation rate at MS32

Almost all allele length change events at MS32 will create diploid code mismatches between an offspring and its parents, including changes of a single repeat unit which cannot be detected by allele length analysis. Screening of the CEPH panel of large families, plus additional large kindreds, has identified 7 germline mutants, giving a mutation rate of 0.9% per gamete to new length alleles. We have recently developed a more efficient approach to detecting germline mutants by PCR analysis of small pools of sperm DNA (10–100 sperm per pool); PCR is sufficiently faithful to allow abnormal length alleles to be detected and counted in each pool. Using this approach, it is possible to screen tens of thousands of sperm for new mutants; the mutation rate so deter-

136

mined is similar to that estimated by pedigree analysis. A third approach to detecting mutation is to electrophoretically fractionate sperm DNA to enrich for fractions containing abnormal length alleles which can then be recovered and quantitated by single molecule PCR. Application of this approach to large deletions in MS32 has shown that extremely rare events ($< 10^{-6}$ per sperm) can be detected (Jeffreys et al., 1990). These single molecule approaches can be used to gain information on mutation load in an *individual* and can be applied to somatic as well as germline DNA.

Mutation processes at MS32

Since the first discovery of the minisatellite core sequence, there has been much speculation over the role if any of recombination in the minisatellite mutation process (see Jeffreys et al., 1991b). Some circumstantial evidence suggests recombinogenicity, for example, the preferential hybridization of minisatellites to chiasmata, the enhanced recombination seen in minisatellite-containing plasmids transfected into mammalian cells, and the presence of minisatellite-like sequences near some known meiotic recombination hotspots. Other more direct but low resolution evidence from studies of markers flanking minisatellites has failed to show any major association between minisatellite mutation and recombination detected by exchange of flanking DNA markers. Structural analysis of new mutant alleles offers the most direct approach to distinguish recombination-based mutation events from other processes such as replication slippage.

MVR mapping of new mutant alleles and comparison with the progenitor alleles is still ongoing, but data already available are providing important clues concerning the mutation process. First, most but not all events are small (change in 1–7 repeat units), with a major (75%) bias towards gains in repeats rather than losses. Second, most mutation events are confined to the 5′ end of MS32 alleles, often involving the very first repeat unit and proving directly the existence of a mutation hotspot at the beginning of the array. Analysis of two other minisatellites has shown a very similar phenomenon, suggesting that variation and mutation polarity, and thus the existence of localised hotspots, may be the rule rather than the exception at minisatellites. Third, at least some mutant alleles contain MVR map segments from *both* parental alleles, and must therefore have arisen by interallelic exchange and not slippage; the frequency of such exchanges implies that the mutation hotspot is a recombination/conversion hotspot, consistent with population genetic evidence for recombinogenicity. Fourth, recombinant alleles have not so far shown exchange of flanking markers, implying that the major mutation process may be gene conversion involving the non-reciprocal transfer of repeat units from a donor allele into the 5′ end of a recipient allele. Our current working hypothesis is that minisatellite mutation is largely driven by gene conversion initiated perhaps at double strand breaks in the 5′ region of minisatellite alleles which are then restored by gap repair (see Sun et al., 1991) using either the sister chromatid or homologous allele as donor. If so, then the recombinational proficiency of MS32 would not only be a property of the tandem repeat array itself, but also of some as-yet unidentified cis-acting element responsible for initiating recombination/conversion, perhaps by directing breaks into the beginning of the tandem array. Under this model, minisatellites are not recombinators *per se*, but instead "reporters" of neighbouring initiators of recombination.

Minisatellite binding proteins

There have been several reports of minisatellite-specific DNA binding proteins (Msbp's), though no studies yet of DNA binding proteins that interact with the 5′ flanking DNA and which may play a crucial role in initiating conversion/recombination. Four Msbp's have now been identified and partially purified (Collick and Jeffreys, 1990; Collick et al., 1991; Wahls et al., 1991; Yamazaki et al., 1992). Msbp-I is a single-stranded DNA binding protein found widely in somatic and germline tissues which binds specifically to the G-rich strand of a variety of minisatellites, provided that the repeat contains a sequence reasonably similar to the minisatellite core sequence. Mouse Msbp-4 binds specifically to the C-rich strand but is only detectable in testis and tumours. It is plausible that these single-stranded DNA binding proteins may serve to lock minisatellites in a recombinogenic single-stranded state, perhaps facilitating strand invasion into the homologous minisatellite. There is, however, no direct evidence as yet for the involvement of any of these proteins in the minisatellite mutation process.

Transminisatellitic mice

Clearly, identification of the elements that initiate minisatellite recombination/conversion will be essential to unravelling the mutation process and to dissecting the possible relationship between minisatellite mutation, recombination and chromosomal processes such as homologue recognition. To this end, we have, in collaboration with A. Surani and colleagues (Cambridge), initiated a study of human MS32 alleles plus flanking DNA introduced into mice by pronuclear microinjection. To date, 13 founder mice have yielded 8 different transgenes, 3 of which are multicopy (creating novel loci composed of tandem repeats of the entire

MS32 locus) and 5 single-copy, either complete or variably truncated. Almost all transgenes have abnormal MVR maps, suggesting major minisatellite instability during the transgenesis process. Also, several instances of minisatellite instability have already been detected on transmission of the transgenes to progeny. These mice can now be used to determine whether both instability and, more important, mutational polarity have been transferred with the transgene. If so, then deletion analysis of the flanking DNA should enable us to identify elements that control polarity. More generally, these transgenic mice will also provide a valuable model for analysing effects of genotype and environment (e.g. radiation) on minisatellite mutation load.

Acknowledgements
This work was supported by grants from the Medical Research Council, Wellcome Trust and the Royal Society. MVR-PCR is the subject of patent applications.

References

Allshire RC, Dempster M, Hastie ND (1989) Human telomeres contain at least three types of G-rich repeat distributed non-randomly. Nucleic Acids Res 17: 4611–4627

Budowle B, Chakraborty R, Giusti AM, Eisenberg AJ, Allen RC (1991) Analysis of the VNTR locus D1S80 by the PCR followed by high-resolution PAGE. Am J Hum Genet 48: 137–144

Capon DJ, Chen EY, Levinson AD, Seeburg PH, Goeddel DV (1983) Complete nucleotide sequence of the T24 human bladder carcinoma oncogene and its normal homologue. Nature 302: 33–37

Collick A, Dunn MG, Jeffreys AJ (1991) Minisatellite binding protein Mspb-I is a sequence-specific single-stranded DNA-binding protein. Nucleic Acids Res 19: 6399–6404

Collick A, Jeffreys AJ (1990) Detection of a novel minisatellite-specific DNA-binding protein. Nucleic Acids Res 18: 625–629

Edwards A, Civitello A, Hammond HA, Caskey CT (1991) DNA typing and genetic mapping with trimeric and tetrameric tandem repeats. Am J Hum Genet 49: 746–756

Epstein N, Nahor O, Silver J (1990) The 3′ ends of *alu* repeats are highly polymorphic. Nucleic Acids Res 18: 4634

Ewens WJ (1972) The sampling theory of selectively neutral alleles. Theor Popul Biol 3: 87–112

Jarman A, Nicholls RD, Weatherall DJ, Clegg JB, Higgs DR (1986) Molecular characterization of a hypervariable region downstream of the human α-globin gene cluster. EMBO J 5: 1857–1863

Jeffreys AJ, Wilson V, Thein SL (1985) Hypervariable 'minisatellite' regions in human DNA. Nature 314: 67–73

Jeffreys AJ, Wilson V, Neumann R, Keyte J (1988a) Amplification of human minisatellites by the polymerase chain reaction: towards DNA fingerprinting of single cells. Nucleic Acids Res 16: 10953–10971

Jeffreys AJ, Neumann R, Wilson V (1990) Repeat unit sequence variation in minisatellites: a novel source of DNA polymorphism for studying variation and mutation by single molecule analysis. Cell 60: 473–485

Jeffreys AJ, Royle NJ, Patel I, Armour JAL, MacLeod A, Collick A, Gray IC, Neumann R, Gibbs M, Crosier M, Hill M, Signer E, Monckton D (1991a) Principles and recent advances in human DNA fingerprinting. *In:* DNA fingerprinting: approaches and applications (eds T. Burke, G. Dolf, A.J. Jeffreys and R. Wolff; Birkhäuser Verlag, Basel) pp 1–19

Jeffreys AJ, Macleod A, Tamaki K, Neil DL, Monckton DG (1991b) Minisatellite repeat coding as a digital approach to DNA typing. Nature 354: 204–209

Litt M, Luty JA (1989) A hypervariable microsatellite revealed by in vitro amplification of a dinucleotide repeat within the cardiac muscle actin gene. Am J Hum Genet 44: 397–401

Monckton DG, Jeffreys AJ (1991) Minisatellite "isoallele" discrimination in pseudohomozygotes by single molecule PCR and variant repeat mapping. Genomics 11: 465–467

Nakamura Y, Julier C, Wolff R, Holm T, O'Connell P, Leppert M, White R (1987) Characterization of a human 'midisatellite' sequence. Nucleic Acids Res 15: 2537–2547

Owerbach D, Aagaard L (1984) Analysis of a 1963-bp polymorphic region flanking the human insulin gene. Gene 32: 475–479

Sensabaugh GF, von Beroldingen C (1991) The polymerase chain reaction: application to the analysis of biological evidence. *In:* Forensic DNA Technology (eds M.A. Farley and J.J. Harrington; Lewis, Chelsea) pp 63–82

Tamaki K, Monckton DG, MacLeod A, Neil DL, Allen M, Jeffreys AJ (1992) Minisatellite variant repeat (MVR) mapping: analysis of 'null' repeat units at D1S8. Human Mol Genet 1: 401–406

Wahls WP, Swenson G, Moore PD (1991) Two hypervariable minisatellite DNA binding proteins. Nucleic Acids Res 19: 3269–3274

Weber JL (1990) Informativeness of human $(dC-dA)_n \cdot (dG-dT)_n$ polymorphisms. Genomics 7: 524–530

Weber JL, May PE (1989) Abundant class of human DNA polymorphisms which can be typed using the polymerase chain reaction. Am J Hum Genet 44: 388–396

Willard HF, Waye JS (1987) Hierarchical order in chromosome-specific alpha satellite DNA. Trends Genet 3: 192–198

Wong Z, Wilson V, Patel I, Povey S, Jeffreys AJ (1987) Characterization of a panel of highly variable minisatellites cloned from human DNA. Ann Hum Genet 51: 269–288

Yamazaki H, Nomoto S, Mishima Y, Kominami R (1992) A 35-kDa protein binding of a cytosine-rich strand of hypervariable minisatellite DNA. J Biol Chem 267: 12311–12316

DNA Fingerprinting: State of the Science
ed. by S. D. J. Pena, R. Chakraborty, J. T. Epplen & A. J. Jeffreys
© 1993 Birkhäuser Verlag Basel/Switzerland

Microsatellites and disease: A new paradigm

K. Wrogemann, V. Biancalana, D. Devys, G. Imbert, Y. Trottier
and J.-L. Mandel

*LGME/CNRS and INSERM U184, Institut de Chimie Biologique, Faculté de Médecine,
Strasbourg, France*

Introduction

Disease-causing mutations are generally stable within the span of a few
generations during which we can follow them by DNA analyses. This is
not true for three diseases, uncovered during a span of less than a year,
which are caused by mutations in microsatellites, by trinucleotide repeat
expansions. These mutations are unstable. They vary between different
members in a kindred, between sibs, and even between tissues and cells
of the same individual. This new type of unstable or dynamic mutation
is responsible for the fragile X syndrome, myotonic dystrophy and
X-linked spinal and bulbar muscular atrophy (SBMA) also called
Kennedy disease. While at the root of these diseases, variable triplet
repeat expansion also offers an explanation for some unusual genetic
features of at least two of these diseases, the phenomenon of anticipation and that of variable expression and incomplete penetrance. Several
recent reviews and editorials have discussed the unusual features and
characteristics of this new type of mutation (Mandel and Heitz, 1992;
Caskey et al., 1992; Rousseau et al., 1992a; Richards and Sutherland,
1992; Rousseau et al., 1992b; Harper et al., 1992; Sutherland and
Richards, 1992).

The fragile X syndrome

The fragile X syndrome is one of the most common genetic diseases and
after Down syndrome the most common cause of mental retardation. It
affects approximately 1 in 1500 males and, less severely, 1 in 2500
females. It is often associated with some facial dysmorphism (elongated
face, prominent lower jaw, large everted ears), macroorchidism in
postpubertal males, loose joints, and mitral valve prolapse. It thus is a
multisystem disorder affecting many tissues.

The disease is associated with a fragile site on the long arm of the X-chromosome at Xq27.3, which was only discovered in 1969 (Lubs, 1969) and gave the syndrome its name. This site is inducible in cells in culture under conditions that interfere with thymidine or deoxycytidine supply and is believed to be the result of local underreplication of DNA. Induction of the fragile site has been used for diagnosis, but its use has limitations. While affected males almost always express the site in 2–60% of cells, it can be detected at best in only about 50% of obligate females carrying the mutation.

The fragile X syndrome has some very unusual genetic characteristics (Sherman et al., 1985) for an X-linked disease: from segregation analyses of fragile X families it was found that 20% of males who carry a fragile X mutation do not express the clinical and cytogenetic phenotype. They are termed normal transmitting males (NTMs) and often appear as grandfathers of affected children. Penetrance varies between families and even within families. It is low in brothers of NTMs and high in brothers of affected patients. The proportion of individuals with mental impairment in fragile X families increases in successive generations: typically, in families with NTMs sibs of a NTM have a low risk of expressing the disease. His daugthers who inherit his X-chromosome virtually have no risk, while children of these carrier daughters have a high risk of expressing the disease (Sherman et al., 1985). This form of anticipation has become known as the Sherman paradox.

The mutation underlying the fragile X syndrome was identified by a positional cloning approach. The first marker linked to the disease locus was Factor IX (Camerino et al., 1983). By linkage analysis the locus was mapped close to or at the fragile site. Somatic cell hybrids were constructed with X chromosomes carrying the fragile site and induced to break in culture (Warren et al., 1990). Closer and closer markers were found. Eventually YACs were isolated which spanned the fragile site, and the fragile X syndrome became the first disease uncovered with the aid of large cloned inserts in these vectors. The first indication for detecting the mutation was obtained by pulsed field gel electrophoresis (PFGE) which allowed the detection of abnormally methylated restriction sites which segregated with fragile X patients, but not with NTMs (Vincent et al., 1991). The region was cloned by several groups and found to contain a CpG island with the observed abnormal methylation, and an unstable fragment consisting of a tandem trinucleotide CGG repeat. In situ hybridization with flanking probes showed that the fragile site itself contains the repeat.

The gene belonging to this CpG island has been identified as the FMR-1 gene. Its cDNA corresponds to a 4.8-kb transcript that contains the CGG repeat in the first exon. The repeat is not translated. The gene is expressed in brain and other tissues. Its sequence shows no similarities to known proteins in the data banks, except that it has a nuclear localization domain and may thus be a nuclear protein (Verkerk et al., 1991). In patients with the full fragile X mutation the gene is not expressed (Pieretti et al., 1991).

With probes adjacent to the mutation target, e.g. StB12.3 (Fig. 1), it is possible to determine in a single test the size of the triplet repeat and the methylation status of the adjacent CpG island of the FMR-1 gene (Rousseau et al., 1991). In a Southern blot of genomic DNA digested with EcoRI and the methylation sensitive enzyme EagI normal active X-chromosomes will give a band of 2.8 kb, while the inactive normal X of females will give a band of 5.2 kb, as EagI will not cut. Chromosomes with expansion of the repeat will show correspondingly larger fragments, and those with very large expansion to the full mutation will show correspondingly larger bands. These often appear as a smear as an indication of somatic heterogeneity. Associated with the large expansion is abnormal methylation of the CpG island so that EagI cannot cut. The small 2.8-kb fragment is therefore not seen on chromosomes with the full mutation.

Analysis of the CGG repeat in normal individuals and in large numbers of patients has revealed very unusual features and provided explanations for the unusual inheritance pattern of this disease (Tab. 1).

In the normal population the CGG repeat is highly polymorphic and numbers up to approximately 50 repeats are found; 29 repeats are carried by the most commonly found allele (Heitz et al., 1992). Oberlé et al. (1991) were the first to describe the existence of two types of mutations in fragile X families: premutations and full mutations with abnormal methylation. A moderate expansion of the repeat, up to 200, is termed a "premutation". Premutations do not produce an altered phenotype. They are found in NTMs and in carrier females with no risk for mental deficits. Premutations are stable in the individual, but carry

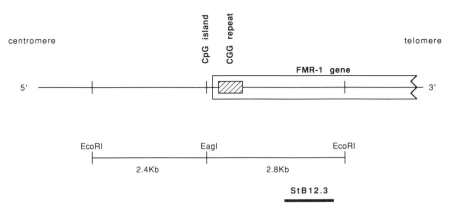

Figure 1. Map of the fragile X locus with position of the diagnostic probe StB12.3.

Table 1. Molecular genetics of the fragile X syndrome

Genotype	Phenotype	No. of CGG repeats (approx.)	Methylation of CpG Island	Stability
Normal	Normal	6–50	Only on inactive X	Stable in family, polymorphic in population
Premutation	Normal	50–100	Only on inactive X	Unstable: risk of transition to full mutation
		100–200	Only on inactive X	100% risk of transition to full mutation
Full mutation	Ment. Ret. in 100% males and 50% females	>230	Active and inactive X	Unstable, often includes somatic heterogeneity

the risk of further expansion when transmitted through a female. This risk for expansion increase with the size of the premutation, reaching 100% at the longer end of the spectrum of premutations (Heitz et al., 1992).

Full mutations show a further massive expansion of the repeat up to several kilobases and, associated with it, abnormal methylation of the adjacent CpG island (Tab. 1). The methylation of the CpG island shuts down expression of the FMR-1 gene (Sutcliffe et al., 1992).

The full mutation is unstable both in meiosis and mitosis. It thus shows also somatic variation in the individual, visible on Southern blots as multiple bands and/or a smear. Some 15% of individuals carrying a full mutation show, in addition to the large-size methylated full mutation band or smear an additional non-methylated band of premutation size. Such individuals have been termed "mosaics" (Oberlé et al., 1991). In such individuals one can observe some expression of the FMR-1 gene (Pieretti et al., 1991). Overall there is a correlation between size of repeat expression and severity of phenotype both clinically and cytogenetically at the fragile site. In large kindreds the proportion of members with mental impairments increases in successive generations as the triplet repeats tend to expand when passing through female meioses.

The spectrum of full mutations together with somatic heterogeneity explains the wide variety of phenotypes seen in fragile X families. The existence of premutations and full mutations provides the basis for the unusual segregation pattern of this X-linked disease, including the phenomenon of anticipation.

Thus, the fragile syndrome became the first disease with a new type of mutation, an unstable trinucelotide repeat expansion. It has also aptly been named "dynamic mutation" (Richards and Sutherland, 1992). It

has been postulated (Sutherland et al., 1991) that other diseases known
to have unusual genetic features, like anticipation (Harper et al., 1992)
might be caused by heritable unstable DNA sequences, and within a few
months this was proved for myotonic dystrophy.

Myotonic dystrophy

Myotonic dystrophy (DM) is the most common adult muscular dystrophy
affecting 1 in 8000 persons. Its mode of inheritance is autosomal dominant.
The disease is characterized by the typical myotonia, the difficulty to relax
a firm contraction, by muscle wasting, cardiac conduction defects,
cataracts, premature balding and hypogonadism. Thus, it is again a
multisystem disorder.

The putative genetic defect was again identified by positional cloning
strategies and the isolation of YAC clones (Harley et al., 1992; Aslanidis
et al., 1992; Buxton et al., 1992). One group actually screened GC-rich
triplet sequences to scan for unstable genetic sequences in cosmids
subcloned from YACs of the critical region and identified the unstable
CTG-triplet repeat in this way (Fu et al., 1992). The CTG-repeat was
found in the 3′ untranslated transcript of a gene, which, from sequence
similarities appears to be a protein kinase (Brook et al., 1992). It is
expressed in tissues affected by myotonic dystrophy.

Similar to fragile X syndrome, the repeat is highly polymorphic in the
normal population with 5–37 repeats (Suthers et al., 1992), 5 copies being
the most common one (Brook et al., 1992). In patients the repeat is
amplified up to 200 times (Fig. 2).

The repeat length tends to increase in successive generations as does
the severity and age at onset of the disease (Mahadevan et al., 1992), and
this provides a sound explanation and proof for the phenomenon of anticipation in DM (Harper et al., 1992). Expansion of the CTG repeat occurs
in both female and male meioses. In this respect the observation differs
from fragile X syndrome, where expansion is only observed through female meiosis. On the other hand, the most severe form of DM, congenital
DM, is only observed when the mother carries the disease gene, and these
cases show the largest triplet repeat expansions (Tsilfidis et al., 1992).

A third triplet expansion, again involving CTG, but as a CAG-repeat
of the opposite (coding) strand, has been discovered in Kennedy disease.

X-Linked Spinal and Bulbar Muscular Atrophy (SBMA) or
Kennedy disease

SBMA is a rare X-linked recessive disorder of adult onset characterized
by progressive weakness of proximal and bulbar muscles. The clinical

FMR-1 - Fragile X Syndrome

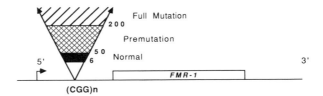

(CGG)n

DM-1 - Myotonic Dystrophy

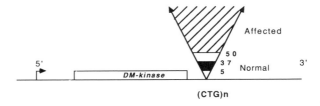

(CTG)n

AR - Kennedy Disease

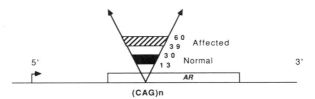

(CAG)n

Figure 2. Location of the trinucleotide repeat expansions in the genes for fragile X syndrome, myotonic dystrophy (DM) and X-linked spinal and bulbar muscular atrophy. The 5′ start sites of transcription are indicated and the translated portions are boxed. AR = androgen receptor. Modified after (Richards, Sutherland, 1992).

features of X-linked SBMA frequently include gynaecomastia, often the earliest manifestation of the disease. When thoroughly examined some patients have also been noted to have testicular atrophy and azoospermia (Harding et al., 1982; Arbizu et al., 1983). The latter findings are considered the mildest form of androgen insensitivity due to androgen receptor mutations. Fischbeck et al. (1986) found linkage between *SBMA* and *DXYS*1 on the proximal long arm of the X-chromosome, the same region to which the androgen receptor had been mapped (Brown et al., 1989). Thus, the androgen receptor became a candidate gene.

La Spada et al. (1991) studied all 8 exons of the androgen receptor and found as the only alteration in SBMA patients an increase in the number of CAG repeats in exon 1 at the N-terminus of the androgen receptor gene. The triplet repeat expanded to approximately twice the normal repeat size, and this has been confirmed by others (Belsham et al., 1992; La Spada et al., 1992). The CAG-repeat is highly polymorphic in the normal population with an average of 21 repeats in the normal population, ranging from 13–30. Repeats in patients range from 40–62, with no overlap between the groups detected so far (La Spada et al., 1992). However, intermediate sizes have been observed by others (Biancalana et al., 1992; Wrogemann et al., unpublished), although their correlation to phenotype has not been pursued yet.

Very large triplet repeat expansions have not (yet) been observed for the androgen receptor. Considering that the triplet repeat in this case is translated as a polyglutamine tract in the protein, very large expansion may not be compatible with a functional protein. However, there is also moderate meiotic instability (Biancalana et al., 1992; La Spada et al., 1992) and a positive correlation between disease severity and CAG-repeat length (La Spada et al., 1992).

The intriguing aspect of the CAG-repeat expansion in the androgen receptor gene is that it leads to SBMA, a disease totally different from other more common forms of androgen receptor mutations which lead to the wide spectrum of androgen insensitivity syndrome (Trifiro et al., 1991b; Griffin, 1992; Pinsky et al., 1992; Prior et al., 1992). In the complete form, patients with a male (XY) genotype present with a female phenotype, but no symptoms of SBMA.

Pathogenetics of trinucleotide repeat expansions

The question on pathogenesis requires answers both on how the pathogenic triplet repeat expansions arise and how the expanded microsatellites cause the disease phenotype.

Linkage analysis with closely linked flanking markers in fragile X chromosomes indicates that amplification does not result from meiotic recombination (Yu et al., 1992). From studies of microsatellites we know that the polymorphisms increase with the number of the tandem repeats (Weber, 1990). It is possible that instability only occurs after subtle increase in repeat number, e.g. by slippage synthesis (Schlötterer and Tautz, 1992), until the repeat reaches a critical number after which instability sets in. It would be this event that could then be considered the "new" mutation. New mutations have not been found in either DM or fragile X syndrome, and nobody has reported a full mutation in fragile X syndrome that did arise directly from a normal sequence rather than through the obligatory premutation (Rousseau et al., 1992a).

For myotonic dystrophy there is strong evidence that most cases date back to a single ancestral founder chromosome (Brook et al., 1992;

Yamagata et al., 1992). There is good evidence for the existence of rather few founder chromosomes for the fragile X syndrome as well (Richards et al., 1992; Oudet et al., 1993; Chakravarti, 1992).

The pathogenetic effects of the fragile X mutation are becoming clear. They are caused by suppressing the expression of the FMR-1 gene (Pieretti et al., 1991). This in turn appears to be the result of methylation of its CpG island presumably effected by the triplet-repeat expansion (Sutcliffe et al., 1992), although the cause and effect relationship between repeat expansion and methylation remains to be established. A recent observation of the fragile X syndrome in a patient without CGG amplification due to an FMR-1 gene deletion indicates that lack of FMR-1 expression causes the phenotype and that other genes are not required (Gedeon et al., 1992).

How the CTG-triplet expansion in myotonic dystrophy causes the disease is not at all clear, especially since one has to explain an autosomal dominant mode of inheritance. A simple suppression of expression of the protein kinase gene, as in the FMR-1 gene of the fragile X syndrome is unlikely to be sufficient explanation, unless the extent of gene expression is very critical and thus very tightly controlled. A gain of function caused by the mutation in form of an abnormal allele is another possible explanation. Abnormal splicing has been found for the protein kinase gene. If it plays a physiological role, it is conceivable that the abnormal triplet repeat expression leads to disturbances of the alternative splicing scheme (Jansen et al., 1992). One also should not exclude the possibility that the triplet expansion in the 3'-untranslated region of the protein kinase gene affects the expression of other nearby genes as well. One such gene, termed *DMR-N9*, has been found. It is mainly expressed in brain and testis (Jansen et al., 1992). Imprinting may also be involved in the pathogenesis, especially, since the congential form of DM occurs if the mother carries the mutation and the clinical phenotype.

To date there are no data available on the quantitative expression of the DM protein kinases (Roses, 1992). However, it is noteworthy that almost 20 years ago phosphorylation of membrane proteins was ascribed to changes in endogenous protein kinase activities (Roses and Appel, 1973; Roses and Appel, 1974).

The CAG-repeat expansion found in the androgen receptor gene of patients with SBMA is the same as that for DM, but from the opposite strand. It differs from the fragile X and DM mutation in that the expansion occurs in exon 1 of the translated region of the gene, the repeat coding for a polymorphic poly-glutamine stretch in the N-terminal region of the androgen receptor (Fig. 2).

It is puzzling that mutations, mainly point mutations, are found all over the 8 exons of the androgen receptor gene, but they cause the unrelated syndrome of androgen insensitivity with a wide spectrum from very mild forms to the complete form, formerly called testicular feminization, a syndrome where in a genetic 46XY male a female phenotype may result from as little as a point mutation in critical regions of the androgen receptor (Griffin, 1992; Pinsky et al., 1992). Interestingly these patients, at least as we know so far, exhibit no signs of spinal muscular atrophy. Furthermore, patients with a complete deletion of the androgen receptor gene express the syndrome of complete androgen insensitivity, but with no signs of spinal muscular atrophy (Trifiro et al., 1991a). This would suggest that the triplet-repeat expansion causes a gain of functions, rather than a loss. One should also consider the possibility that the altered androgen receptor protein affects domains that interact with other transcription factors, e.g. tissue-specific ones necessary for the expression of the androgen receptor in motoneurons. Another possibility is that the androgen receptor is a multifunctional protein and that its function with respect to the cause of SBMA is distinct from what we generally see as those for a typical steroid receptor.

Expansions of the CAG-repeat in the androgen receptor only reach approximately twice the normal size. Very large expansions have not been observed (yet). Since the repeat is translated and very large expansions should seriously disrupt the function of any androgen receptor molecule, one wonders whether these, if they exist, would lead to the syndrome of complete androgen insensitivity.

Conclusions

Microsatellite mutations in the form of trinucleotide repeat expansions have been found as the cause of three diseases, the fragile X syndrome, myotonic dystrophy and X-linked spinal and bulbar muscular atrophy. The hallmark of this new form of mutation is the instability of the repeat. In normal sizes the instability is moderate and results in polymorphisms in the population; when expanded in disease causing mutations, the instability increases and results in variable expansions in the same kindred and even in different cells and tissues of an individual. In addition, the repeats have the tendency to increase in successive generations, explaining the phenomenon of anticipation. In general the severity and time at onset of the disease correlate with the size of expansion.

These unstable mutations provide a molecular explanation for the unusual genetics especially of the fragile X syndrome and myotonic dystrophy, which include incomplete penetrance, variable expression and the phenomenon of anticipation. These diseases apparently have originated from very few founder chromosomes. It is highly likely that other diseases with such unusual genetics are caused by unstable dynamic mutations of microsatellites (Sutherland et al., 1992).

Acknowledgements
We gratefully acknowledge the support by the Association Française contre les Myopathies (AFM) and the Muscular Dystrophy Association of Canada.

References

Arbizu T, Santamaria J, Gomez JM, Quilez A, Serra JP (1983) A family with adult spinal and bulbar muscular atrophy, X-linked inheritance and associated testicular failure. J Neurol Sci 59: 371–382

Aslanidis C, Jansen G, Amemiya C, Shutler G, Mahadevan M, Tsilfidis C, Chen C, Alleman J, Wormskamp NGM, Vooijs M, Buxton J, Johnson K, Smeets HJM, Lennon G, Carrano AV, Korneluk RG, Wieringa B, de Jong PJ (1992) Cloning of the essential myotonic dystrophy region and mapping of the putative defect. Nature 355: 548–551

Belsham DD, Yee WC, Greenberg CR, Wrogemann K (1992) Analysis of the CAG repeat region of the androgen receptor gene in a kindred with X-linked spinal and bulbar muscular atrophy. J Neurol Sci 112: 133–138

Biancalana V, Serville F, Pommier F, Julien J, Hanauer A, Mandel JL (1992) Moderate instability of the trinucleotide repeat in spino bulbar muscular atrophy. Hum Mol Genet 1: 255–258

Brook JD, McCurrach ME, Harley HG, Buckler AJ, Curch D, Aburatani H, Hunter K, Stanton VP, Thirion J-P, Hudson T, Sohn R, Zemelman B, Snell RG, Rundle SA, Crow S, Davies J, Shelbourne P, Buxton J, Jones C, Juvonnen V, Johnson K, Harper PS, Shaw DS, Housman DE (1992) Molecular basis of myotonic dystrophy: expansion of a trinucleotide (CTG) repeat at the 3′ end of a transcript encoding a protein kinase family member. Cell 68: 799–808

Brown CJ, Goss SG, Lubahn DB, Joseph DR, Wilson EM, French FS, Willard HF (1989) Androgen receptor locus on the human X Chromosome: Regional localization to Xq11–12 and description of a DNA polymorphism. Am J Hum Genet 44: 264–269

Buxton J, Shelbourne P, Davies J, Jones C, Van Tongeren T, Aslanidis C, de Jong P, Jansen G, Anvret M, Riley B, Williamson R, Johnson K (1992) Detection of an unstable fragment of DNA specific to individuals with myotonic dystrophy. Nature 355: 547–548

Camerino G, Mattei MG, Mattei JF, Jaye M, Mandel JL (1983) Close linkage of fragile X-mental retardation syndrome to haemophilia B and transmission through a normal male. Nature 306: 701–704

Caskey CT, Pizzuti A, Fu Y-H, Fenwick J, Nelson DL (1992) Triplet repeat mutations in human disease. Science 256: 784–788

Chakravarti A (1992) Fragile X founder effect? Nature Genet 1: 237–238

Fischbeck KH, Ionasescu V, Ritter AW, Ionasescu R, Davies K, Ball S, Bosch P, Burns T, Hausmanowa Petrusewicz I, Borkowska J, et al. (1986) Localization of the gene for X-linked spinal muscular atrophy. Neurology 36: 1595–1598

Fu Y-H, Pizzuti A, Fenwick RG, Jr., King J, Raynarayan S, Dunne PW, Dubel J, Nasser GA, Ashizawa T, DeJong P, Wieringa B, Korneluk R, Perryman MB, Epstein HF, Caskey CT (1992) An unstable triplet repeat in a gene related to myotonic dystrophy. Science 255: 1256–1258

Gedeon AK, Baker E, Robinson H, Partington MW, Gross B, Manca A, Korn B, Poustka A, Yu S, Sutherland GR, Mulley JC (1992) Fragile X syndrome without CCG amplification has an FMR1 deletion. Nature Genet 1: 341–344

Griffin JE (1992) Androgen resistance – the clinical and molecular spectrum. N Engl J Med 326: 611–617

Harding AE, Thomas PK, Baraitser M, Bradbury PG, Morgan-Hughes JA, Ponsford JR (1982) X-linked recessive bulbospinal neuronopathy: a report of ten cases. J Neurol Neurosurg Psychiatry 45: 1012–1019

Harley HG, Brook JD, Rundle SA, Crow S, Reardon W, Buckler AJ, Harper PS, Housman DE, Shaw DJ (1992) Expansion of an unstable DNA region and phenotypic variation in myotonic dystrophy. Nature 355: 545–546

Harper PS, Harley HG, Reardon W, Shaw DS (1992) Anticipation in myotonic dystrophy: New light on an old problem. Am J Hum Genet 51: 10–16

Heitz D, Devys D, Imbert G, Kretz C, Mandel JL (1992) Inheritance of the fragile X syndrome: size of the fragile X premutation is a major determinant to full mutation. J Med Genet 29: 794–801

Jansen G, Mahadevan M, Amemiya C, Wormskamp N, Segers B, Hendriks W, O'Hoy K, Baird S, Sabourin L, Lennon G, Jap PL, Iles D, Coerwinkel M, Hofker M, Carrano AV, de Jong PJ, Korneluk RG, Wieringa B (1992) Characterization of the myotonic dystrophy region predicts multiple protein isoform-encoding mRNAs. Nature Genet 1: 261–266

La Spada AR, Wilson EM, Lubahn DB, Harding AE, Fischbeck KH (1991) Androgen receptor gene mutations in X-linked spinal and bulbar muscular atrophy. Nature 352: 77–79

La Spada AR, Roling D, Harding AE, Warner CL, Spiegel R, Hausmanowa Petrusewicz I, Yee WC, Fischbeck KH (1992) Meiotic stability and genotype-phenotype correlation of the trinucleotide repeat in X-linked signal and bulbar muscular atrophy. Nature Genet 2: 301–304

Lubs HA (1969) A marker X-chromosome. Am J Hum Genet 21: 231–244

Mahadevan M, Tsilfidis C, Sabourin L, Shutler G, Amemiya C, Jansen G, Neville C, Narang M, Barcelo J, O'Hoy K, Lebond S, Earle-MacDonald J, De Jong P, Wieringa B, Korneluk RG (1992) Myotonic dystrophy mutation: an unstable CTG repeat in the 3′ untranslated region of the gene. Science 255: 1253–1255

Mandel JL, Hetiz D (1992) Molecular genetics of the fragile-X syndrome: a novel type of unstable mutation. Curr Opin Genet Dev 2: 422–430

Oberlé I, Rousseau F, Heitz D, Kretz C, Devys D, Hanauer A, Boue J, Bertheas MF, Mandel JL (1991) Instability of a 550-base pair DNA segment and abnormal methylation in fragile X syndrome. Science 252: 1079–1102

Oudet C, Mornet E, Serre JL, Thomas F, Lentes-Zingerling S, Kretz C, Deluchat C, Tejada I, Boué A, Mandel JL (1993) Linkage disequilibrium between the fragile X mutation and two closely linked CA repeats suggests that fragile X chromosomes are derived from a small number of founder chromosomes. Am J Hum Genet 52: 297–304

Pieretti M, Zhang F, Fu Y-H, Warren ST, Oostra BA, Caskey CT, Nelson DL (1991) Absence of expression of the FMR-1 gene in fragile X syndrome. Cell 66: 817–822

Pinsky L, Trifiro M, Prior L, Sabbaghian N, Bouchard J, Bordet S, Mhatre A, Lumbruso R, Kaufman M, Gottlieb B (1992) The molecular genetics of androgen insensitivity syndrome in man. In: Wachtel SS, Simpson JL (eds) Molecular Genetics of Sex Determination, Blackwell Scientific Publications, Oxford

Prior L, Bordet S, Trifiro MA, Mhatre A, Kaufman M, Pinsky L, Wrogemann K, Belsham DD, Pereira FA, Greenberg CR, Trapman J, Brinkmann AO, Chang C, Liao S (1992) Replacement of arginine 773 by cysteine or histidine causes complete androgen insensitivity with different androgen receptor phenotypes. Am J Hum Genet 51: 143–155

Richards RI, Holman K, Friend K, Kremer E, Hillen D, Staples A, Brown WT, Goonewardena P, Tarleton J, Schwartz C, Sunderland GR (1992) Evidence of founder chromosomes in fragile X syndrome. Nature Genet 1: 257–260

Richards RI, Sutherland GR (1992) Dynamic mutations: a new class of mutations causing human disease. Cell 70: 709–712

Roses AD (1992) Myotonic dystrophy. Trends Genet 8: 254–255

Roses AD, Appel SH (1973) Protein kinases activity in erythrocyte ghosts of patients with myotonic muscular dystrophy. Proc Natl Acad Sci USA 70: 1855–1859

Roses AD, Appel SH (1974) Muscle membrane protein kinase in myotonic muscular dystrophy. Nature 250: 245–257

Rousseau F, Heitz D, Biancalana V, Blumenfeld S, Kretz C, Boué J, Tommerup N, Van der Hagen C, DeLozier-Blanchet C, Croquette M-F, Gilgenkrantz S, Jalbert P, Voelckel MA, Oberlé I, Mandel JL (1991) Direct diagnosis by DNA analysis of the fragile X syndrome of mental retardation. N Engl J Med 325: 1673–1681

Rousseau F, Heitz D, Mandel JL (1992a) The unstable and methylatable mutations causing the fragile X syndrome. Hum Mut 1: 91–96

Rousseau F, Heitz D, Mandel JL (1992b) Les mutations instables: Une nouvelle cause de maladies héréditaires. La Recherche 23: 934–936

Schlötterer C, Tautz D (1992) Slippage synthesis of simple sequence DNA. Nucleic Acids Res 20: 211–215

Sherman SL, Jacobs PA, Morton NE, Froster-Iskenius U, Howard-Pebbles PN, Brondum-Nielsen K, Partington MW, Sutherland GR, Turner G, Watson M (1985) Further segregation analysis of the fragile X syndrome with special reference to transmitting males. Hum Genet 69: 289–299

Sutcliffe JS, Nelson DL, Zhang F, Pieretti M, Caskey CT, Saxe D, Warren ST (1992) DNA methylation represses FMR-1 transcription in fragile X syndrome. Hum Mol Genet 1: 397–400

Sutherland GR, Haan EA, Kremer E, Lynch M, Pritchard M, Yu S, Richards RI (1991) Hereditary unstable DNA: a new explanation for some old genetic questions? Lancet 338: 289–292

Sutherland GR, Richards RI (1992) Invited editorial: Anticipation legitimized: Unstable DNA to the rescue. Am J Hum Genet 51: 7–9

Suthers GK, Huson SM, Davies KE (1992) Instability versus predictability: the molecular diagnosis of myotonic dystrophy. J Med Genet 29: 761–765

Trifiro M, Gottlieb B, Pinksy L, Kaufman M, Prior L, Belsham DD, Wrogemann K, Brown CJ, Willard HF, Trapman J, Brinkman AO, Chang C, Liao S, Sergovich F, Jung J (1991a) The 56/58 kDa androgen-binding protein in male genital skin fibroblasts with a deleted androgen receptor gene. Mol Cell Endocrinol 75: 37–47

Trifiro M, Prior L, Sabbaghian N, Pinsky L, Kaufman M, Nylen E, Belsham DD, Greenberg CR, Wrogemann K (1991b) Amber mutation creates a diagnostic *Mae*I site in the androgen receptor gene of a family with complete androgen insensitivity. Am J Med Genet 40: 493–499

Tsilfidis C, MacKenzie AE, Mettler G, Barcelo J, Korneluk RG (1992) Correlation between CTG trinucleotide repeat length and frequency of severe congenital myotonic dystrophy. Nature Genet 1: 192–195

Verkerk AJMH, Pieretti M, Sutcliffe JS, Fu Y-H, Kuhl DPA, Pizzuti A, Reiner O, Richards S, Victoria MF, Zhang F, Eussen BE, van Ommen GJB, Blonden LAJ, Riggins GJ, Chastain JL, Caskey CT, Nelson DL, Oostra BA, Warren ST (1991) Identification of a gene (FMR-1) containing a CGG repeat coincident with a breakpoint cluster region exhibiting length variation in fragile X syndrome. Cell 65: 905–914

Vincent A, Heitz D, Petit C, Kretz C, Oberlé I, Mandel JL (1991) Abnormal pattern detected in fragile-X patients by pulsed-field gel electrophoresis. Nature 349: 624–626

Warren ST, Knight SL, Peters JF, Stayton CL, Gonsalez GG, Zhang F (1990) Isolation of the human chromosome band Xq28 with somatic cell hybrids by fragile X breakage. Proc Natl Acad Sci USA 87: 3856–3860

Weber JL (1990) Informativeness of human $(dC-dA)_n \cdot (dG-dT)_n$ polymorphisms. Genomics 7: 524–530

Yamagata H, Miki T, Ogihara T, Nakagawa M, Higuchi I, Osami M, Shelbourne P, Davies J, Johnson K (1992) Expansion of unstable DNA region in Japanese myotonic dystrophy patients. Lancet 339: 692

Yu S, Mulley J, Loesch D, Turner G, Donnelly A, Gedeon A, Hillen D, Kremer E, Lynch M, Pritchard M, Sutherland GR, Richards RI (1992) Fragile-X syndrome: Unique genetics of the heritable unstable element. Am J Hum Genet 50: 968–980

DNA Fingerprinting: State of the Science
ed. by S. D. J. Pena, R. Chakraborty, J. T. Epplen & A. J. Jeffreys
© 1993 Birkhäuser Verlag Basel/Switzerland

A unified approach to study hypervariable polymorphisms: Statistical considerations of determining relatedness and population distances

R. Chakraborty and L. Jin

Genetics Centers, Graduate School of Biomedical Sciences, University of Texas Health Science Center at Houston, P.O. Box 20334, Houston, Texas 77225, USA

Summary

Relatedness between individuals as well as evolutionary relationships between populations can be studied by comparing genotypic similarities between individuals. When hypervariable loci are used to describe genotypes, it is shown that both of these problems can be approached with a unified theory based on allele sharing between individuals. The distributions of the number of shared alleles between individuals indicate their kin relationships. Extending this, we obtain statistics for genetic distances between populations based on average number of alleles shared between individuals within and between two different populations.

Traditional statistical inferential procedure can be used to establish specific kinship relationships between individuals. We derive estimates of the number of hypervariable loci needed for a specified reliability of such an inference. Evolutionary dynamics of genetic distance statistics based on allele sharing is also studied. It shows that such measures of genetic distances remain linear with the time of divergence for a period comparable to that of the gene frequency-based measures of genetic distances.

Statistical properties of measures based on allele sharing establish that for using such summary statistics it is not necessary to know the full characteristics of all loci used. It is enough to know the degree of heterozygosity per locus and the number of loci. Therefore, in principle, this approach can also be used for DNA fingerprinting data in the studies of relatedness between individuals as well as between populations. The possible compromising features of multilocus DNA fingerprinting data are also discussed.

Introduction

The utility of genetic markers has been enhanced tremendously with the discovery of hypervariable polymorphisms (Wyman and White, 1980; Jeffreys et al., 1985, 1986; Nakamura et al., 1987). While the classical serological and biochemical genetic markers have played important roles in various types of human population genetic studies, one of the problems that limited their practical utility results from the limited number of possible genotypes at each of such loci. The discovery of hypervariable DNA loci offers the opportunity to ameliorate this problem.

This is mainly due to the fact that all hypervariable loci are characterized by their large number of alleles, and consequently high heterozygosity per locus. As a result, such loci, commonly called the

154

Variable Number of Tandem Repeat (VNTR) loci, have been shown to be efficient markers for gene mapping (Nakamura et al., 1987; Weissenbach et al., 1992); they are also useful for forensic identification of individuals (Budowle et al., 1991a; Chakraborty and Kidd, 1991); they can be used for determining relatedness between individuals (Jeffreys et al., 1988, 1991); and they can be used for studying evolutionary relationships of genetically close populations or species (Gilbert et al., 1990, 1991).

In this presentation, our purpose is to provide a brief review of the recent work on the utility of such markers for studying relatedness between individuals and populations. In this process we intend to demonstrate that the use of hypervariable loci in studying relatedness between individuals as well as that between populations can be approached under a unified theory, without compromising the extensive degree of polymorphism at such loci. Furthermore, we shall illustrate that such a unified approach can also utilize the DNA fingerprinting data obtained by using multilocus hypervariable probes even when a complete characterization of the underlying loci governing the genetic variation of DNA fingerprint patterns is not available. While the validity of the proposed methods will be illustrated with data, we shall also indicate possible effects of some of the technical limitations of using multilocus probes in such studies.

Some implications of relatedness studies at individual and population levels

The examination of relatedness between individuals is important in pedigree analysis of genetic traits, studying inbreeding and its effects, establishing claims of inheritance, and resolving relationships. Relatedness studies at the individual level are also important to conservation biologists since breeding strategies in captive populations require the determination of biological relationships between individuals so that intense inbreeding may be avoided in pairing individuals for breeding purposes. Biologists interested in studying mating and parental care behaviors in animals and birds also have been using hypervariable loci to know how they breed and care for offspring (Burke et al., 1990).

Relatedness studies at the population level are mainly important for evolutionary investigations. While the classic serological and biochemical markers have contributed a great deal in this area (see e.g. Nei, 1975, 1987), and the introduction of DNA sequences in evolutionary studies has facilitated the study of long-term evolution, one problem remained common for these types of data. This is the case where short-term evolutionary relationships between populations or taxa are of interest. Because of low variability, the classical genetic markers indicate very little genetic divergence between populations (Nei and Roychoudhury, 1982), while because of the low rate of substitution rate at the DNA sequence level, very large segments of nuclear DNA sequences are necessary to know the precise evolutionary relationships between closely related populations or species (Saitou and Nei, 1986). The characteristic higher rate of mutational change at hypervariable loci (Jeffreys et al., 1988) should ameliorate this problem to some extent, since more mutations can accumulate between populations within a short period of divergence.

Our goal is to present a general statistical treatment of the problems of identifying relationships at individual as well as population level from DNA typing data using a single-locus DNA probe (SLP), from which a generalization to data on DNA fingerprinting using a multi-locus probe (MLP) can also be derived considering summary statistics that are observed from DNA fingerprinting profiles.

Features of genetic data with hypervariable loci

Unlike the classical markers, where the allelic distinctions are due to alterations in the coding sequence that lead to either different antigentic specificity, or differences in electrophoretic mobility of the proteins, hypervariable probes detect copy number variations of repeat sequences present usually in non-coding DNA. Therefore, alleles are distinguished by length of a DNA fragment that contains different numbers of copies of the repeat unit at that region of the genome. For a single-locus probe, through the use of the PCR technique, the alleles may be classified by their copy numbers, so that allelic types represent the copy numbers (or the total length) of the repeat units of the tandemly repeated DNA sequence.

When a single-locus probe (SLP) is used, an individual's genotype would then be represented by one or at most two bands of a possible allelic ladder. In contrast, when a multi-locus probe (MLP) is used, a DNA fingerprint results in a profile which shows multiple bands, corresponding to copy number variations of similar sequences at an unknown number of loci at different regions of the genome. Therefore, the DNA profile, called DNA fingerprint (Jeffreys et al., 1985a), from a single MLP represents a composite multi-locus genotype, generally without giving any further information regarding the number of loci underlying the genotype, nor providing the allelic relationships between the various individual fragments represented within the pattern observed.

Therefore, there are two contrasting features of DNA typing data obtained through the single-locus probes (SLPs) versus the multi-locus probes (MLPs). First, data from each SLP may be treated as a standard multiallelic codominant locus, although depending on the resolution of electrophoresis, sometimes alleles of nearly equal sizes may not be totally distinguished. Furthermore, if some alleles give DNA fragments of very small (or large) length as compared to others, they may not be resolved either, giving pseudo-homozygosity for actual heterozygotes carrying one such allele. When multi-locus data are needed, several SLPs may be used either separately, or by simultaneous PCR amplification, and scoring protocol, called multiplexing (Edwards et al., 1991). In contrast, use of MLPs is comparatively more efficient and cost-effective, since many loci are simultaneously typed even with a single MLP. Of course, population genetic charcterization of the individual underlying loci is unknown, since allele frequencies and number of loci remain unknown.

However, the above-mentioned limitations do not hinder the use of MLP or SLP data for population genetic purposes. For example, Devlin et al. (1990) and Chakraborty et al. (1992) have shown that the standard population genetic methods of data analysis of SLP data can easily be modified to take into account the problems of coalescence of similar size alleles, as well as nondetectability of alleles. Similarly, Stephens et al. (1992) discussed a method of analyzing MLP data whereby information with regard to allele frequencies, number of loci, as well as average heterozygosity may be obtained from DNA fingerprint data.

Statistical formulation of the general problem of relatedness

Geometric representation of genotypes of pairs of individuals. For any sets of polymorphic loci, data on genotypes of two individuals may be summarized by noting whether the two individuals' genotypes share no, one, or two alleles identical by descent. Therefore, a pair of genotypes is equivalent to a single realization of three probabilities, k_0, k_1, and k_2, which represent the probabilities for the number of alleles identical by descent being 0, 1, and 2, respectively.

Some examples of such coefficients for several common biological relationships between two individuals are shown in Tab. 1. Any given

Table 1. Co-efficients for common relationships

Relationship		k_0	k_1	k_2
Identical (monozygous twin)	MZ	0	0	1
Parent-offspring	PO	0	1	0
Full sib	S	1/4	1/2	1/4
Half sib, uncle-niece	H	1/2	1/2	0
First cousin	1C	3/4	1/4	0
Second cousin	2C	15/16	1/16	0
Unrelated	U	1	0	0

specified biological relationship between two individuals becomes mathematically equivalent to a trio of probabilities (k_0, k_1, k_2) where the three coefficients are related by $k_0 + k_1 + k_2 = 1$. Although there may be some kinship relationships that may yield the same trio of coefficients, they will belong to the same equivalence class of kinships that will always be impossible to distinguish from genotype data alone. This implies that in general the genotypic data of a pair of individuals may be represented through a triangular co-ordinate representation, where the proportions of alleles sharing are calculated by the identity-by-descent (IBD) method, or by Li and Sack's (1954) *I-T-O* matrix method. A pair of genotypes would represent a point within an equilateral triangle, since each point is uniquely specified by $(k_0, k_1,$ and $k_2)$, its vertical distances from the sides of the triangle, representing the probabilities that the individuals would share no allele, one allele, or two alleles with each-other. This is shown in Fig. 1, where the points within the parabolic (infeasible) region are not possible to obtain for any biologically related pairs, since for any biological relationship between

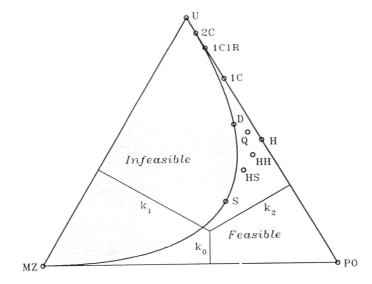

TRIANGULAR CO−ORDINATE REPRESENTATION

OF RELATENESS

Figure 1. Triangular co-ordinate representation of kinship relationships in terms of the probabilities of allele sharing through identity by descent. U = Unrelated; MZ = Monozygotic twins; PO = Parent-offspring; S = Fullsib; H = Half-sib, uncle-niece, grandparent-grandchild; HS = Halfsibs whose unshared parents are sibs; HH = Halfsibs whose unshared parents are halfsibs; 1C = First cousin; D = Double first cousin; Q = Quadruple half first cousin; 1C1R = First cousin once removed; 2C = Second cousin.

individuals $k_1^2 \geq 4k_0k_2$ (Thompson, 1991). Figure 1 also shows the expected positions of several common relationships through the translation of their genotype data into corresponding probabilities.

Several observations may be made from such representation of genotype data. First, while it is clear that some of the relationships are quite closely situated within the triangle, the point corresponding to two identical genotypes (represented by MZ, monozygotic twin) is quite far from all others. Therefore, if the question is to assert whether or not the genotypes obtained from two samples represent the same individual (the problem of forensic identification of individuals), the discriminatory power of such data reduction is still quite good. Second, the points representing the parent-offspring pair (PO) and unrelated pairs (U) are also quite distant from each other, suggesting that paternity identification is also not difficult even if the genotype data of the mother of a disputed child is not available.

Likelihood approach with genotype data. Using the (k_0, k_1, k_2) coefficients the likelihood function for any genotype combinations at L loci, $\{(G_{Xl}, G_{Yl}), l = 1, 2, \ldots, L\}$ for any relationship $R = (k_0, k_1, k_2)$ may be written as

$$L_R = P[\{(G_{Xl}, G_{Yl}), l = 1, 2, \ldots, L\}; R]$$

$$= \prod_{l=1}^{L} P[(G_{Xl}, G_{Yl}); R]$$

$$= \prod_{l=1}^{L} P[G_{Yl}; R \mid G_{Xl}] \cdot P(G_{Xl})$$

$$= \prod_{l=1}^{L} (k_0 O_{XY} + k_1 T_{XY} + k_2 I_{XY}) \cdot P(G_{Xl}), \tag{1}$$

where I_{XY}, T_{XY}, and O_{XY} are the corresponding elements of Li and Sack's I, T, O matrices for the genotypes (G_{Xl}, G_{Yl}) for the l-th locus.

For a multi-allelic autosomal locus, the elements of the I, T, O matrices are obtained by simple extensions of Li and Sack's (1954) work, shown in Tab. 2.

Substituting these elements of the I-T-O matrices in equation (1), the likelihood for any specified relationships between individuals X and Y may be determined. The absolute numerical values of such likelihood computations, however, will be always small, and with an increasing number of loci such likelihoods will decrease, as expected. When two specified relationships are contrasted, in the tradition of a likelihood ratio test, one may draw inference regarding relationships depending on which likelihood is relatively larger. This is analogous to the resolution of paternity disputes using the concept of paternity index (Essen-Möller, 1938).

Table 2. Elements of *ITO* matrices for a multiallelic locus

G_X and (n_X)		G_Y and (n_Y, n_{XY})			
		A_iA_i (1, 1)	A_iA_j (2, 1)	A_iA_j (1, 0)	A_jA_k (2, 0)
$A_iA_i(1)$	I	1	0	0	0
	T	p_i	p_j	0	0
	O	p_i^2	$2p_ip_j$	p_j^2	$2p_jp_k$

G_X and (n_X)		G_Y and (n_Y, n_{XY})						
		A_iA_i (1, 1)	A_jA_j (1, 1)	A_iA_j (2, 2)	A_iA_k (2, 1)	A_jA_k (2, 1)	A_kA_k (1, 0)	A_kA_r (2, 0)
$A_iA_j(2)$	I	0	0	1	0	0	0	0
	T	$\frac{1}{2}p_i$	$\frac{1}{2}p_j$	$\frac{1}{2}(p_i + p_j)$	$\frac{1}{2}p_k$	$\frac{1}{2}p_k$	0	0
	O	p_i^2	p_j^2	$2p_ip_j$	$2p_ip_k$	$2p_jp_k$	p_k^2	$2p_kp_r$

The problem of this approach is that it is difficult to ascertain what likelihood ratio is acceptable for reliable determination of relatedness. This is so, since the exact distributional theory of such likelihood functions is complicated because of the large numbers of possible multi-locus genotype combinations, each of which individually has a small probability of occurrence.

I-T-O approach and number of shared alleles. This problem may be ameliorated with some data summarization. For example, instead of the actual genotypes, we may summarize the data in terms of number of different alleles in an individual's genotype (n_X and n_Y) and numbers of different alleles shared between individuals (n_{XY}).

Summing over all allelic possibilities, we get the joint distribution of the number of bands and bands shared between two individuals X and Y shows in Tab. 3, in which the quantity a_t represents the summation of the t-th power of all alleles segregating at a locus. This indicates that a full characterization of the joint distributions of number of distinct and shared alleles (bands) between two individuals (n_X, n_Y, and n_{XY}, respectively) is available from sum of squares, cubes, and the fourth-power of allele frequencies at a locus.

When data on L single-locus probes are simultaneously used, we obtain the joint distribution for n_X, n_Y, and n_{XY} by taking convolutions over L loci. Although closed form solution of such distributions is not available, an iterative solution is possible, following an algorithm originally suggested by Chakraborty and Schull (1976).

Table 3. Joint distribution of number of bands and number of shared bands between individuals X and Y at a multi-allelic locus

n_X	n_Y	n_{XY}	Probability when X and Y are		
			Identical	Parent-Offspring	Unrelated
1	1	0	0	0	$a_2^2 - a_4$
1	1	1	a_2	a_3	a_4
1	2	0	0	0	$a_2 - 2a_3 + 2a_4 - a_2^2$
1	2	1	0	$a_2 - a_3$	$2a_3 - 2a_4$
2	1	0	0	0	$a_2 - 2a_3 + 2a_4 - a_2^2$
2	1	1	0	$a_2 - a_3$	$2a_3 - 2a_4$
2	2	0	0	0	$1 - 6a_2 + 8a_3 - 6a_4 + 3a_2^2$
2	2	1	0	$1 - 3a_2 + 2a_3$	$4a_2 - 8a_3 + 8a_4 - 4a_2^2$
2	2	2	$1 - a_2$	$a_2 - a_3$	$2a_2^2 - 2a_4$

a_t = sum of the t-th power of allele frequencies at the locus.

For example, the distribution of n_X for any individual X over L loci may be computed using the recurrence relationship

$$Q_r^{(l)} = Q_{r-2}^{(l-1)} \cdot P_2(l) + Q_{r-1}^{(l-1)} \cdot P_1(l), \tag{2}$$

where $Q_r^{(l)}$ is the probability that with the first l of the L loci the individual's genotype has r distinct alleles; $P_1(l)$ and $P_2(l)$ being the number of distinct alleles for the l-th locus. The boundary conditions for the recurrence equation (2) are

$$Q_l^{(l)} = \prod_{j=1}^{l} P_1(j), \tag{3a}$$

and

$$Q_{2l}^{(l)} = \prod_{j=1}^{l} P_2(j). \tag{3b}$$

Similarly, the exact distribution of n_{XY} over L loci may be computed using the recurrence relationship

$$Q_r^{(l)} = Q_{r-2}^{(l-1)} \cdot P_2(l) + Q_{r-1}^{(l-1)} \cdot P_1(l) + Q_r^{(l-1)} \cdot P_0(l), \tag{4}$$

where $Q_r^{(l)}$ is the probability that in the first l of the L loci the two individuals share r alleles, and $P_0(l)$, $P_1(l)$, $P_2(l)$ being the allele sharing probabilities for the l-th locus. As in equation (2), this recurrence relationship has also several boundary conditions, given by

$$Q_0^{(l)} = \prod_{j=1}^{l} P_0(j), \tag{5a}$$

$$Q_1^{(l)} = Q_0^{(l)} \cdot \sum_{j=1}^{l} P_1(j)/P_0(j), \tag{5b}$$

and

$$Q^{(l)}_{2l} = \prod_{j=1}^{l} P_2(j). \qquad (5c)$$

Inferential procedure and properties of the distribution of the number of shared alleles between pairs of relatives. Once the distribution of n_{XY} is evaluated, the discrimination of two specific relationships between X and Y may be done following the classical Neyman-Pearson theory of statistical inference. For example, Fig. 2 shows a schematic diagram of how two stated relationships between a specified pair of individuals (parent-offspring versus unrelated) may be discriminated using data on the number of shared alleles (bands). The probabilities of two types of errors, required for any cut-off point, C, can be determined from the probability distributions of the number of shared bands (n_{XY}) under each of the two hypotheses, as long as the characteristics of the individual loci underlying the composite DNA profiles are known (Tab. 3 and equation 4).

Although the computations of the probability distributions of n_X and n_{XY} for any stated relationship R requires knowing allele frequencies at all loci, it has been shown (Chakraborty and Jin, 1993) that under some assumptions, we can approximate such distributions simply from the knowledge of average heterozygosity per locus and number of loci. For example, Fig. 3 shows the comparisons of distributions of shared bands

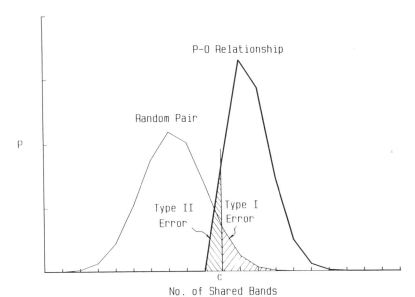

Figure 2. Schematic diagram for discriminating a parent-offspring relationship from random pairing of individuals from the data on band sharing between individuals.

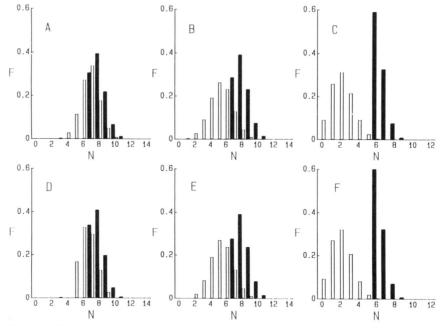

Figure 3. The distribution of band (allele) sharing between parent-offspring (dark histograms) and random pairs (blank histograms) using three different types of loci. Panels A and D are for seven protein loci, B and E for seven STR loci, and C and F for six VNTR loci. Panels A, B, and C are based on computations using the actual allele frequencies (heterozygosities for the six VNTR loci), while panels D, E, and F are based on the mutation-drift expectations of the moments of allele frequencies. See Chakraborty and Jin (1993) for details of the loci and the methods of computations used.

for seven classical serological markers used in paternity testing in the USA (panels A and D), seven STR markers (panels B and E) and six VNTR markers (panels C and F) used in forensic DNA typing. The panels A, B and C are with allele frequency data known for each locus, while panels C, D, and F are simply from the knowledge of number of loci and average heterozygosities per locus, assuming that the population is at mutation-drift equilibrium under the infinite allele model. The blank histograms are for unrelated pairs, and the solid histograms are for parent-offspring relationships.

Clearly, it shows that the approximation based on the number of loci (*L*) and average heterozygosity (*H*) per locus is quite reasonable. Therefore, we may determine for what values of average heterozygosity and number of loci such distributions become almost non-overlapping so that from the number of shared alleles between individuals a reliable inference regarding relationships may be inferred, as done in Chakraborty and Jin (1993).

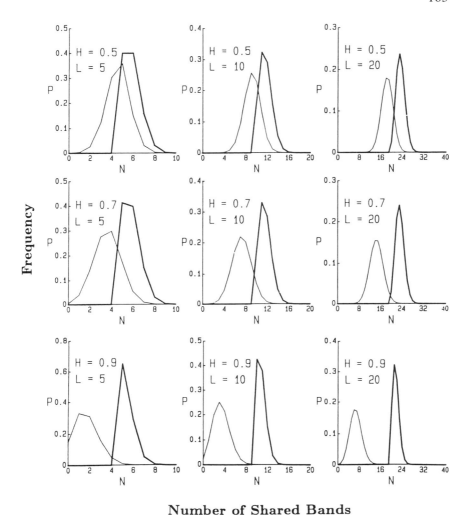

Number of Shared Bands

Figure 4. The probability distribution of band sharing between parent offspring (distributions at right) and random pairs (distributions at left) as a function of heterozygosity per locus (*H*) and number of loci (*L*).

Figure 4 shows such results, again for P-O versus unrelated pairs. This shows that the degree of non-overlap increases with *H* as well as *L*. For *H* = 70% (which is the case with STR loci), somewhere between 15 to 20 loci may be needed to distinguish between P-O and unrelated pairs, while for *H* = 80%, even with half-a-dozen markers such relationships may be discriminated. Most VNTR markers have heterozygosities above 80%, indicating that the prospect of reliable inference regarding P-O relationship is possible even with 6 such markers.

Table 4. The number of loci (L) needed to determine parent-offspring relationship

Heterozygosity (H)	Number of Loci (L)	Critical Value (C)	Probabilities of errors of	
			Type I	Type II
0.90	6	5	0.027	0.000
0.80	11	10	0.040	0.000
0.70	18	18	0.031	0.042
0.60	26	27	0.041	0.048
0.50	48	48	0.028	0.045

How many loci are needed? Table 4 presents some more detailed computations in this regard. It clearly shows that while for classical markers, a reliable inference regarding P-O relationships may require over 50 loci (since the average heterozygosity at such loci rarely exceeds 50%), with VNTR loci the prospect of such inference is quite good even with a limited number of loci.

Using the logic developed in Tab. 3, and using the distributions obtained from equations (3) and (4), the discriminatory power of this approach may be evaluated for a larger set of possible relationships. Tab. 5 shows some summary statistics of this nature, where the distributions of the number of shared bands for different types of related individuals are summarized here by their means and standard deviations. The four groups of relationships (unrelated, PO and FS, HS, and Identical) can be discriminated when hypervariable loci are used. For example, if we decide to employ the short tandem repeat loci ($H \approx 70\%$), we would need 15–20 loci to discriminate these four types of relationships, while if minisatellite VNTR loci ($H \geq 90\%$) are used,

Table 5. Mean and (s.d.) of n_{XY}

L	Identical	PO	FS	HS	Unrelated
			$H = 0.5$		
10	15.0(1.6)	11.7(1.2)	11.9(1.5)	10.4(1.4)	9.2(1.6)
20	30.0(2.2)	23.3(1.7)	23.3(2.2)	20.8(2.0)	18.3(2.2)
50	75.0(3.5)	58.3(2.6)	59.4(3.4)	52.1(3.2)	45.8(3.5)
			$H = 0.7$		
10	17.0(1.4)	11.6(1.2)	11.9(1.8)	9.4(1.7)	7.2(1.8)
20	34.0(2.0)	23.2(1.6)	23.7(2.5)	18.9(2.3)	14.5(2.5)
50	85.0(3.2)	58.1(2.6)	59.3(4.0)	47.1(3.7)	36.2(4.0)
			$H = 0.9$		
10	19.0(0.9)	10.8(0.8)	11.0(2.1)	7.1(1.7)	3.3(1.6)
20	38.0(1.3)	21.6(1.2)	22.0(2.9)	14.1(2.5)	6.6(2.2)
50	95.0(2.1)	54.1(1.9)	54.9(4.6)	35.3(3.9)	16.6(3.5)

even 6 would be enough. Of course, the discrimination between PO and FS relationships is troublesome, which is the case with complete genotyping information as well.

Since such a theory depends only upon the observed number of shared bands between individuals, and the knowledge of average heterozygosity and number of loci, we may even use this approach for DNA fingerprinting data scored by using a multi-locus probe, once suitable methods are developed for estimating the average heterozygosity H and number of loci from DNA fingerprinting data. Stephens et al. (1992) and Chakraborty and Jin (1993) explored such problems, neglecting the technical limitations of co-migration and resolution of similar size fragments in the MLP data. While each of these technical limitations would potentially compromise the reliability of inference regarding the discrimination of contrasting relationships, further investigation is needed to determine to what extent such inferences are affected.

Study of population distances

The study of genetic differentiation between populations can be similarly formulated, since the extent of allele sharing between members of two populations is dictated by the degree of genetic isolation between populations. Of course, because of hypervariability, adjustments for within population differences between individuals have to be made in such formulations.

Distance based on allele sharing. Genetic distances between populations may be obtained by defining the number of shared alleles when two individuals are drawn from a single population (within-population allele sharing) and when they are drawn from two different populations (between-population allele sharing). The averages of these two quantities, defined by n_w and n_b, over all possible combinations of individuals sampled, would define the genetic distances between populations. The alternative distance functions may be defined, given by

$$D(t) = \frac{n_{w1} + n_{w2}}{2} - n_b(t), \qquad (6a)$$

and

$$D_i(t) = 1 - \frac{2n_b(t)}{n_{w1} + n_{w2}}, \qquad (6b)$$

where n_{w1} and n_{w2} represent the average numbers of alleles (bands) shared between individuals within populations 1 and 2, and $n_b(t)$ is the average number of alleles shared between two individuals each drawn from different populations that diverged t generations ago from each other. Both definitions of genetic distances adjust for within population variation; the first one is mathematically quite analogous to Nei's minimum genetic distance function (Nei, 1972) while the second one resembles the complement of the similarity index suggested earlier (Nei and Li, 1979; Lynch, 1988).

Evolutionary dynamics. In order to examine the adequacy of such distance functions for evolutionary studies, the evolutionary dynamics of these quantities under a specific mutation-drift model have to be evaluated. Jin and Chakraborty (1993) make an attempt of this type, using the infinite allele model (Kimura and Crow, 1964) of mutations.

For example, when the expectations of each of the above two distance statistics are approximated by the ratio of expectations of the quantities appearing in the right hand side of equations (6a) and (6b), the question of how $E[D(t)]$ and $E[D_i(t)]$ depend upon the time of divergence reduces to determining $E[n_{w1}]$, $E[n_{w2}]$, and $E[n_b(t)]$. Within any population, the random variable n_w had a distribution given by

$$n_w = \begin{cases} 0 \text{ with probability } 1 - 4a_2 + 4a_3 - 3a_4 + 2a_2^2, \\ 1 \text{ with probability } 4a_2 - 4a_3 + 5a_4 - 4a_2^2, \\ 2 \text{ with probability } 2a_2^2 - 2a_4, \end{cases} \quad (7)$$

where $a_m = \Sigma \, x_i^m(l)$, in which $x_i(l)$ is the frequency of the i-th allele at the l-th locus. The mutation-drift expectation of n_w then becomes

$$E[n_w] = 4E[a_2] - 4E[a_3] + E[a_4]. \quad (8)$$

Li and Nei (1975) derived such quantities, which show that under a mutation-drift balance, when mutations follow the infinite allele model, $E[n_w]$ reaches an equilibrium value, so that for two populations each of which is at mutation-drift balance with the same effective size, $E[n_{w1}] = E[n_{w2}]$, and the resultant quantity depends only upon $M = 4Nv$, the product of effective population size (N) and the mutation rate per locus per generation (v).

In contrast, the distribution of $n_b(t)$ is given by

$$n_b(t) = \begin{cases} 0 \text{ with probability } 1 - 4b_{11} + 2b_{12} + 2b_{21} - 3b_{22} + 2b_{11}^2, \\ 1 \text{ with probability } 4b_{11} - 2b_{12} - 2b_{21} + 5b_{22} - 4b_{11}^2, \\ 2 \text{ with probability } 2b_{11}^2 - 2b_{22}, \end{cases} \quad (9)$$

where $b_{mn} = \Sigma \, x_i^m(l)y_i^n(l)$, in which $x_i(l)$ and $y_i(l)$ are the frequencies of the i-th allele at the l-th locus in two populations. The mutation-drift expectation of n_w then becomes

$$E[n_b(t)] = 4E[b_{11}] - 2E[b_{12}] - 2E[b_{21}] + E[b_{22}], \quad (10)$$

which depends upon the time of divergence (t) as well as on the composite parameter $M = 4Nv$ (Jin and Chakraborty, 1993).

Algebraic simplifications yield the following equations for the expectations of the above two genetic distance measures

$$E[D(t)] = \frac{2M}{(M+1)(M+2)^2(M+3)}[1 - e^{-2(M+1)T}]$$

$$+ \frac{4(M+1)}{(M+2)^2}[1 - e^{-MT}], \tag{11}$$

and

$$E[D_i(t)] = \frac{M}{(2M^2 + 6M + 3)(M+2)}[1 - e^{-2(M+1)T}]$$

$$+ \frac{2(M+1)^2(M+3)}{(M+2)(2M^2 + 6M + 3)}[1 - e^{-MT}], \tag{12}$$

where $M = 4nV$, and $T = t/2N$. Clearly, the expected genetic distance for each definition depends upon only two composite parameters, M, and the time of divergence between populations measured in units of $2N$ generations. Therefore, numerical evaluations of these two equations should reveal up to what level of population divergence these definitions of genetic distance have a well-defined relationship with the time of divergence between populations. Since the parameter $M = 4Nv$ is related to the average heterozygosity (H) by the relationship $H = M/(M+1)$, the parameter $M = H/(1-H)$ can also be translated in terms of the average heterozygosity within populations (Kimura and Crow, 1964). In other words, this establishes that, like the gene frequency-based measures of genetic distances (Li and Nei, 1975), the above two definitions of genetic distance based on allele (band) sharing data as well are dependent on the two quantities, the average heterozygosity within populations and their time of divergence.

Comparison with Nei's distance and relationship with time of divergence. Figure 5 shows some numerical computations on the expected distance between populations as functions of their time of divergence, for different levels of average heterozygosity values within populations. The solid lines in these diagrams are the relationships for the distance functions defined in equations (6a) and (6b), while the dotted lines are for Nei's minimum (compared with our D) and standard (compared with our D_i) distance statistics.

These computations indicate several important features of the proposed distance functions. First, both measures of genetic distances are not completely proportional to the time of divergence. However, the deviation from linearity with the time of divergence starts approximately at a point of time when Nei's distance statistics also fall off from the linear time-dependence. Second, the proportionality with time of divergence holds for a time period that depends on the degree of heterozygosity (H). When H is larger, the linearly holds for a shorter

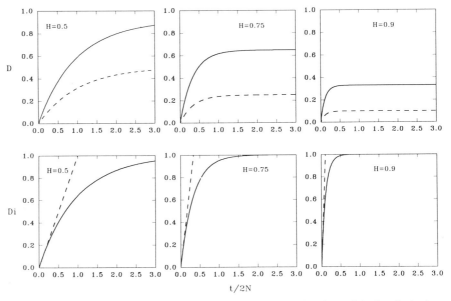

Figure 5. Relationship of genetic distance measures (D and D_i) based on allele (band) sharing data with time of divergence ($t/2N$), measured in units of $2N$ generations. Solid lines are for expectations of allele sharing-based distance statistics (equations 11 and 12) while the dotted lines are for Nei's minimum (panels on top row) and standard (panels on bottom row) genetic distances based on allele frequency data. H represents average heterozygosities within each population.

time of divergence. Third, the distance function (D_i) based on the similarity-index continues to be linearly related to the time of divergence for a comparatively longer period of time. For $H \leq 90\%$ (as in the case of many STR and VNTR loci), $D_i(t)$ appears to hold the linear relationship quite adequately for $t \leq N$ generations.

While each of the two equations relating distance with evolutionary time of separation between populations has two components (see equations 11 and 12), a closer examination of these equations indicates that the two terms do not contribute equally. In fact, the predominant component is the second one, so that for the above two definitions of genetic distances, their approximate relationship with the time of divergence can be studied keeping only the second terms, giving the relationships

$$E[D(t)] \approx \frac{4(M+1)}{(M+2)^2}[1 - e^{-MT}], \qquad (13)$$

and

$$E[D_i(t)] \approx \frac{2(M+1)^2(M+3)}{(M+2)(2M^2+6M+3)}[1 - e^{-MT}]. \qquad (14)$$

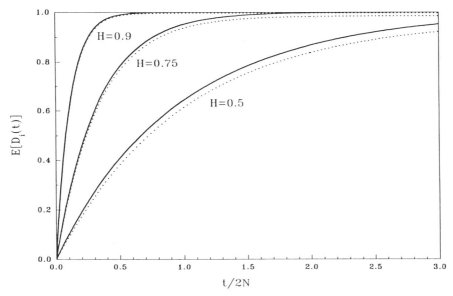

Figure 6. Effects of approximations (equation 12 versus equation 14) on the relationship of expected genetic distance based on similarity index, $E[D_i(t)]$, and time of divergence ($t/2N$) of populations, measured in units of $2N$ generations. H represents the average heterozygosity within populations.

Figure 6 shows the effect of such approximations for different levels of average heterozygosity per locus, where the solid line is the exact relationship (equation 12), while the dotted lines are using the approximation of equation (14). Although these computations are done for the similarity-index-based definition of genetic distance alone (equation 6b), the qualitative conclusions hold for $D(t)$ as well, namely, the simpler equations (13) and (14) are fairly accurate for describing the evolutionary dynamics of allele sharing based measures of genetic distances between populations.

An example. Recently Edwards et al. (1992) described several short tandem repeat (STR) loci, each of which demonstrate considerable degrees of polymorphism within populations. The population genetic characteristics of these loci are previously described (Edwards et al., 1992). Two more such STR loci have not been typed in Caucasians (200 individuals), American Blacks (200 individuals), and Orientals (80 individuals) of Houston, Texas.

Using 7-locus genotype data we computed the pairwise numbers of shared alleles (based on 7 loci) among all pairs of individuals. Figure 7 shows the distribution of the number of shared alleles between individuals within each of these populations. While the average number of shared alleles between Afro-American individuals is somewhat lower

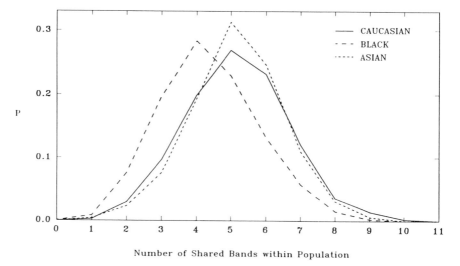

Figure 7. Distributions of allele sharing at seven STR loci between individuals within three human population groups. See Chakraborty and Jin (1993) for details of the characteristics of the loci used in these computations.

than that within the other two samples, these distributions of number of shared alleles between Caucasians and that between the Asians are not significantly distinguishable from each other. This is consistent with the notion that the Afro-Americans are genetically more diverse than the other two major racial groups, as seen also from other molecular data. However, all three distributions are in accordance with the predictions of the mutation-drift equilibrium model.

The distributions of between-population allele sharing computed from all pairwise comparisons of individuals when the contrasted individuals are selected from two different populations for the same data are shown in Fig. 8. The degree of allele sharing between the Asians and Caucasians is somewhat higher than the other two comparisons, indicating a smaller degree of genetic divergence between them.

Based on these computations the numerical values of the genetic distance based on the measure of similarity index (D_i) are presented in Tab. 6. For comparison, the allele frequencies from each locus are also used to compute Nei's minimum and standard genetic distances, using the estimation procedure suggested by Nei (1978). These computations show that even though the measures of genetic distances based on allele sharing data consider only a summary measure of genotype data (number of alleles shared between individuals), such data summarization does not compromise the evaluations of evolutionary distances between populations, since the computed distance values are virtually identical to the ones obtained by Nei's method of estimation of genetic distances.

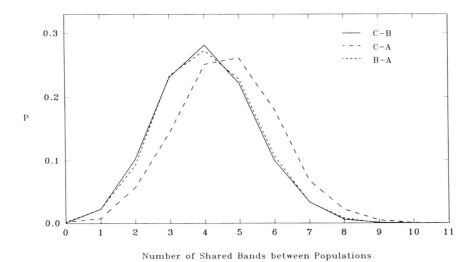

Number of Shared Bands between Populations

Figure 8. Distributions of allele sharing at seven STR loci between individuals; individuals are drawn one each from two different populations.

Table 6. Comparison of D_i with Nei's distances by using 7-loci STR data

	D_i	D_s	D_m
C–B	0.15027	0.14957	0.14622
C–A	0.09765	0.11355	0.10844
B–A	0.14299	0.14139	0.14579

D_s: Nei's standard distance.
D_m: Nei's minimum distance/average homozygosity.

Discussion and conclusions

The theory discussed above exhibits several important features of analysis of DNA typing data with regard to the determination of relatedness at the individual as well as population level. First, it is quite evident from Tables 4 and 5 that the data on hypervariable polymorphic loci offer an opportunity to discriminate between even closely related individuals with a precision much above the classical markers. Second, even in the presence of inter-locus allele frequency differences, the distribution of shared alleles between individuals may be approximated accurately from the knowledge of the number of loci (*L*) and average heterozygosity per locus (*H*). Third, for hypervariable loci where the heterozygosity per locus is above 90% (as in the case of the VNTR loci used in the forensic context), the number of loci required for reliable determination of relatedness is quite reasonable. For example, a parent-offspring relationship may be asserted with even six such loci. Fourth, when estimation of L and H is possible for DNA fingerprinting data using a multi-locus probe, such theory is also applicable to MLP data to determine relatedness between individuals. Of course, the effects of comigration of fragments produced by different alleles and resolution of fragments of nearly equal size should be examined in greater detail.

Along the same line, the examination of the evolutionary dynamics of allele sharing data indicates that suitable measures of genetic distances between populations can be defined based on allele sharing data alone. No significant loss of information occurs in such data summarization, nor are the allele sharing-based measures of genetic distances any poorer as an indicator of the degree of genetic divergence between populations as compared to allele frequency-based measures of genetic distances (Fig. 6). Computations shown in Tab. 6 indicate that for the same set of data, the allele frequency-based estimates of genetic distances are virtually identical to those based on allele sharing within and between populations.

The advantages of allele (band) sharing based statistics are mainly two-fold. First, as shown above, the same set of statistics may be used for determining relatedness between individuals as well as between populations. Second, since allele sharing data may be simply pooled over loci, we may not even need to know the exact allelic relationships between different DNA fragments (bands), so that multi-locus DNA fingerprint data may also be used for carrying out the same analysis.

Two possible criticisms may be raised with regard to the above conclusions. First, the theory discussed above heavily rests on the assumption of the infinite allele model of mutations. While the molecular basis of the mechanism of production of new variation at tandemly repeated loci is not yet precisely known, there are several indirect lines of evidence that the infinite allele model may not be a bad approximation for VNTRs that have a large or more complex repeat motif (Jeffreys et al., 1988; Flint et al., 1989; Clark, 1987; Chakraborty et al., 1991; Budowle et al., 1991b). Of course, recent data on simpler repeat motif loci (such as the short tandem repeat, STR, loci) indicates that instead of the infinite allele model, a forward-backward stepwise mutation model may be more appropriate for some of the hypervariable loci. While a thorough examination of the evolutionary dynamics of the stepwise mutation model is needed for a level of heterozygosity at a level of 70% or higher, two intuitive conclusions may be reached based on the present theory. First, a stepwise mutation model would bring the saturation of $D(t)$ quicker, so that the linear relationship of expected distance with time of divergence would fall off should the stepwise mutation model be the mode of mutations. On the other hand, since stepwise mutation model seems to hold better for STR loci which have a smaller heterozygosity (Edwards et al., 1992; Deka et al., 1992) compared with the more complex VNTRs for which the infinite allele model is a better descriptor of the mode of mutations (Chakraborty et al., 1991; Budowle et al., 1991b), our results of Fig. 6 indicate that the general conclusion that $D_i(t)$ or $D(t)$ is proportional to t for $t \leq N$ may also hold for all classes of VNTR loci irrespective of the mutation model.

Second, in extending the allele sharing analysis to MLP data, we have effectively neglected the problems of comigration of alleles of different loci, and incomplete resolution of alleles. We contend that while the comigration of alleles of different loci can be a valid technical limitation of MLP data, incomplete resolution of alleles may not affect the above analysis to any appreciable degree, since the definition of alleles is always a technology-based operational one. For instance, when alleles are defined by copy number variation alone, it is shown in several instances that a large fraction of underlying molecular variation remains undetected (see e.g., Boerwinkle et al., 1989). Indeed, internal-mapping of VNTR alleles has shown that only a small fraction of true alleles are identified as distinct ones when allelic classes are defined by copy numbers of repeat units (Jeffreys et al., 1991). When a full resolution of alleles is done by internal mapping, almost all new variations are unique, so that irrespective of the molecular mechanism of production of new variation, the infinite allele model is the only descriptor that would fit the data on genetic variation. The problem of comigration, of course, deserves a more careful study, but the analysis of MLP data to relatedness and evolutionary studies (Jeffreys et al., 1991; Gilbert et al., 1991) indicate that unless a large fraction of alleles at different loci comigrate to the same or similar position on a gel, this technical limitation also should not be a hindering factor in using the present theory for band sharing data obtained from MLPs.

Acknowledgements

This research was supported by US Public Health Service research grants GM 41399 and GM 45816 from the US National Institutes of Health and grant 92-IJ-CX-K024 from the US National Institute of Justice. We thank Drs. B. Budowle, A. Jeffreys, and S. D. J. Pena for their helpful comments on the work. However, the opinions expressed in this document are those of the authors, and they do not represent endorsements by the granting agencies or the reviewers.

References

Boerwinkle E, Xiong W, Fourest E, Chan L (1989) Rapid typing of tandemly repeated hypervariable loci by the polymerase chain reaction: Application to the apolipoprotein B 3' hypervariable region. Proc Natl Acad Sci USA 86: 212–216

Burke T, Hanotte O, Bruford MW, Cairns E (1991) Multilocus and single locus minisatellite analysis in population biological studies. *In:* Burke T, Dolf G, Jeffreys AJ, Wolff R (eds) DNA Fingerprinting: Approaches and Applications. Birkhäuser Verlag, Basel, pp 154–168

174

Budowle B, Giusti AM, Waye JS, Baechtel FS, Fourney RM, Adams DE, Presley LA, Deadman HA, Monson KL (1991a) Fixed-bin analysis for statistical evaluation of continuous distributions of allelic data from VNTR loci, for use in forensic comparisons. Am J Hum Genet 48: 841–855

Budowle B, Chakraborty R, Giusti AM, Eisenberg AE, Allen RC (1991b) Analysis of the VNTR locus D1S80 by the PCR followed by high-resolution PAGE. Am J Hum Genet 48: 137–144

Chakraborty R, de Andrade M, Daiger SP, Budowle B (1992) Apparent heterozygote deficiencies observed in DNA typing data and their implications in forensic applications. Ann Hum Genet 56: 45–59

Chakraborty R, Fornage M, Gueguen R, Boerwinkle E (1991) Population genetics of hypervariable loci: analysis of PCR based VNTR polymorphism within a population. In: Burke T, Dolf G, Jeffreys AJ, Wolff R (eds) DNA Fingerprinting: Approaches and Applications. Birkhäuser, Basel, pp 127–143

Chakraborty R, Jin L (1993) Determination of relatedness between individuals by DNA fingerprinting. Hum Biol (in press)

Chakraborty R, Kidd KK (1991) The utility of DNA typing in forensic work. Science 254: 1735–1739

Chakraborty R, Schull WJ (1976) A note on the distribution of the number of exclusions to be expected in paternity testing. Am J Hum Genet 28: 615–618

Clark AG (1987) Neutrality tests of highly polymorphic restriction-fragment-length polymorphisms. Am J Hum Genet 41: 948–956

Deka R, Chakraborty R, DeCroo S, Rothhammer, F, Barton SA, Farrell RE (1992) Characteristics of polymorphism at a variable number of tandem repeat (VNTR) locus 3′ to the apolipoprotein B gene in five human populations. Am J Hum Genet 51: 1325–1333

Devlin B, Risch N, Roeder K (1990) No excess of homozygosity at loci used for DNA fingerprinting. Science 249: 1416–1420

Edwards A, Civitello A, Hammond HA, Caskey CT (1991) DNA typing and genetic mapping with trimeric and tetrameric tandem repeats. Am J Hum Genet 49: 746–756

Edwards A, Hammond HA, Jin L, Caskey CT, Chakraborty R (1992) Genetic variation of five trimeric and tetrameric tandem repeat loci in four human population groups. Genomics 12: 241–253

Essen-Möller E (1938) Die Beweiskraft der Ähnlichkeit im Vaterschaftsnachweis; theoretische Grundlagen. Mitt Anthrop Ges 68: 9–53

Flint J, Boyce AJ, Martinson JJ, Clegg JB (1989) Population bottlenecks in Polynesia revealed by minisatellite. Hum Genet 83: 257–263

Gilbert DA, Lehman N, O'Brien SJ, Wayne RK (1990) Genetic fingerprinting reflects population differentiation in the California Channel Island fox. Nature 344: 764–767

Gilbert DA, Packer C, Pusey AE, Stephens JC, O'Brien SJ (1991) Analytical DNA fingerprinting in lions: parentage, genetic diversity, and kinship. J Hered 82: 378–386

Jeffreys AJ, Brookfield JFY, Semenoff R (1985a) Positive identification of an immigration test-case using human DNA fingerprints. Nature 317: 818–819

Jeffreys AJ, MacLeod A, Tamaki K, Neil DL, Monckton DG (1991) Minisatellite repeat coding as a digital approach to DNA typing. Nature 354: 204–209

Jeffreys AJ, Neumann R, Wilson V, Wong Z (1988) Spontaneous mutation rates to new length alleles at tandem-repetitive hypervariable loci in human DNA. Nature 332: 278–281

Jeffreys AJ, Turner M, Debenham P (1991) The efficiency of multilocus DNA fingerprint probes for individualization and establishment of family relationships, determined from extensive case-work. Am J Hum Genet 48: 824–840

Jeffreys AJ, Wilson V, Thein SL (1985) Hypervariable 'minisatellite' regions in the human DNA. Nature 314: 67–73

Jeffreys AJ, Wilson V, Thein SL, Weatherall DJ, Ponder BAJ (1986) DNA 'fingerprints' and segregation analysis of multiple markers in human pedigrees. Am J Hum Genet 39: 11–24

Jin L, Chakraborty R (1993) Population dynamics of DNA fingerprinting patterns within and between populations. Genet Res (in press)

Kimura M, Crow JF (1964) The number of alleles that can be maintained in a finite population. Genetic 49: 725–738

Li CC, Sacks L (1954) The derivation of joint distribution and correlation between relatives by the use of stochastic matrices. Biometrics 10: 347–360

Li WH, Nei M (1975) Drift variances of heterozygosity and genetic distance in transient states. Genet Res 25: 229–248

Lynch M (1988) Estimation of relatedness by DNA fingerprinting. Mol Biol Evol 5: 584–599

Nakamura Y, Leppert M, O'Connell P, Wolff R, Holm T, Culver M, Martin C, Fujimoto E, Hoff M, Kumlin E, White R (1987) Variable number of tandem repeat (VNTR) markers for human gene mapping. Science 235: 1616–1622

Nei M (1972) Genetic distance between populations. Amer Nature 106: 283–292

Nei M (1975) Molecular Population Genetics and Evolution. North-Holland, Amsterdam New York

Nei M (1987) Molecular Evolutionary Genetics. Columbia University Press, New York

Nei M, Li WH (1979) Mathematical model for studying genetic variation in terms of restriction endonucleases. Proc Natl Acad Sci USA 76: 5269–5273

Nei M, Roychoudhury AK (1982) Genetic relationship and evolution of human races. Evol Biol 14: 1–59

Saitou N, Nei M (1986) The number of nucleotides required to determine the branching order of three species with special reference to the human-chimpanzee-gorilla divergence. J Mol Evol 24: 189–204

Stephens JC, Gilbert DA, Yuhki N, O'Brien SJ (1992) Estimation of heterozygosity for single-probe multilocus DNA fingerprints. Mol Biol Evol 9: 729–743

Thompson EA (1991) Estimation of relationship from genetic data. In: Rao CR, Chakraborty R (eds) Handbook of Statistics 8. North-Holland. Amsterdam London New York Tokyo

Weissenbach J, Gyapay G, Dib C, Vignal A, Morissette J, Milasseau P, Vaysseix G, Lathrop M (1992) A second-generation linkage map of the human genome. Nature 359: 794–801

Wyman AR, White R (1980) A highly polymorphic locus in human DNA. Proc Natl Acad Sci USA 77: 6754–6758

DNA Fingerprinting: State of the Science
ed. by S. D. J. Pena, R. Chakraborty, J. T. Epplen & A. J. Jeffreys
© 1993 Birkhäuser Verlag Basel/Switzerland

The forensic significance of various reference population databases for estimating the rarity of variable number of tandem repeat (VNTR) loci profiles

B. Budowle and K. L. Monson

Forensic Science Research and Training Center, FBI Academy, Quantico, Virginia 22135, USA

Summary
The likelihood of occurence of 1,964-HaeIII-generated target DNA profiles was estimated using fixed bin VNTR frequencies from various Caucasian, Black, and Hispanic databases and the product rule. The data in this study demonstrate that for forensic purposes there are smaller differences in statistical estimates of DNA profile frequencies among subgroup databases than among estimates across major population databases. This observation does not support the premise asserted by the NCR Report (1992) that the differences among subgroups within a race would be greater than between races (at least for forensic purposes). Therefore, the data do not support the need for alternative procedures, such as the ceiling principle approach (NRC Reports, 1992), for deriving statistical estimates of DNA profile frequencies. Comparisons across major population groups provide reasonable, reliable, and meaningful estimates of DNA profile frequencies without forensically significant consequences.

Introduction

Variable number of tandem repeat (VNTR) loci are highly polymorphic and, therefore, quite useful for identity testing. When there is a failure to exclude a suspect as a potential contributor of a sample by DNA typing of VNTR loci, it is desirable to convey the statistical significance of the match. The weight of the match often is estimated as the product of the frequencies of each VNTR locus profile. General population reference groups, such as American Blacks, Caucasians, southeastern Hispanics, and southwestern Hispanics, are used for estimating allele frequencies.

Lewontin and Hartl (1991) have claimed that, because subgroups within major population categories have genetic differences that are maintained by endogamy, the multiplication approach advocated by the forensic community (Budowle et al., 1991; Evett and Gill, 1991; Evett and Pinchin, 1991) and others (Brookfield, 1992; Chakraborty and Jin, 1992; Chakraborty and Kidd, 1991; Chakraborty et al., 1992, 1992a, 1993, in press; Devlin and Risch, 1992 and 1992a; Devlin et al., 1992; Risch and Devlin, 1992; Weir, 1992) can lead to potentially *serious* errors in estimates of DNA profile frequencies. Lewontin and Hartl (1991) specifically address Caucasian, American Black, and Hispanic population groups, and assert that these general population categories can not be used reliably due to ancestral ethnic differences and/or racial admixture differences among regional subgroups.

It is universally accepted that substructure exists within major population groups. However, the important issue for forensic DNA typing purposes is whether or not general population group databases, in lieu of more defined subpopulation groups, will yield probability estimates that would convey reliable and/or meaningful results in the forensic context. Differences in statistical estimates are deemed "forensically significant" when the likelihood of occurrences of the DNA profile would be meaningfully different (Chakraborty and Kidd, 1991). Comparisons of various reference population data should provide insight as to whether or not statistical estimates based on general population groups would produce forensically significant differences from other databases from regions of the United States, and from databases around the world. Moreover, comparisons of regional United States populations would be the most meaningful for determining forensic significance of statistical estimates for DNA profiles derived from evidence from crimes committed in the United States, because they would provide a valid reflection of the population of potential perpetrators. This paper makes use of VNTR population data generated by the forensic community using the restriction endonuclease HaeIII to evaluate the forensic significance of subpopulations on statistical inferences drawn from general population databases.

Materials and Methods

RFLP population data on several VNTR loci were kindly provided by the contributors displayed in Tab. 1. The data consisted of fragment lengths generated by digestion with the restriction endonuclease HaeIII. The loci analyzed also are shown in Tab. 1.

In this study, several conventions were followed to facilitate comparisons of populations. The conventions were generally those used by the FBI in casework analyses (Budowle et al., 1991; Monson and Budowle, 1992). All fragment lengths in each population sample were sorted into 31 fixed bin categories as previously described (Budowle et al., 1991). The number of DNA fragments which fell into each bin was divided by the total number of alleles (i.e., twice the number of individuals) in the sample population to determine the frequency of each bin. Additionally, frequencies were derived by a process termed "rebinning" whereby bins with fewer than five counts were merged with contiguous bins. After the bin tables were thus established, the frequency of a target allele was

Table 1. Reference databases and loci analyzed[a]

Laboratory	D1S7	D2S44	D4S139	D10S28
CA Caucasians[b]	212	215	217	215
FBI Caucasians[c]	595	792	594	429
FBI Israelis[c]	97	116	115	124
FL Caucasians[d]	239	241	215	204
GA Caucasians[e]	287	292	289	281
MN Caucasians[f]	251	255	242	242
OR Caucasians[g]	272	273	272	273
VT Caucasians[h]	219	227	216	233
Montreal Caucasians[i]	658	457	611	749
RCMP Caucasians[j]	326	458	461	413
French Caucasians[k]	156	128	203	116
Swiss Caucasians[l]	405	412	409	411
CA Blacks[b]	213	213	220	222
FBI Blacks[c]	359	475	448	288
FBI Haitians[c]	98	98	97	89
FL Blacks[d]	148	153	140	128
GA Blacks[e]	508	488	455	494
MI Blacks[m]	451	486	503	507
MN Blacks[f]	213	213	211	210
SC Blacks[n]	230	245	241	245
CA Hispanics[b]	258	259	245	256
FBI SE Hispanics[c]	305	300	311	230
FBI SW Hispanics[c]	216	215	211	210
MI Hispanics[g]	87	91	87	91

[a]The numbers in locus column represent the number of individuals typed.
[b]Orange County Sheriff's Coroner Department, Santa Ana, CA
[c]FBI
[d]Broward County Sheriff's Office Crime Laboratory, Fort Lauderdale, FL
[e]Georgia Bureau of Investigation, Decatur, GA
[f]Minnesota Bureau of Criminal Apprehension, St. Paul, MN
[g]Oregon State Police, Portland, OR
[h]Vermont State Police, Waterbury, VT
[i]Laboratoire de Police Scientifique, Montréal, Canada
[j]Royal Canadian Mounted Police (RCMP) Central Forensic Laboratory, Ottawa, Ontario, Canada
[k]Laboratoire de Génétique Moléculaire, Nantes, France
[l]Institut für Rechtsmedizin, Bern, Switzerland
[m]Michigan State Police, East Lansing, MI
[n]South Carolina State Police, SLED, Columbia, SC

estimated by determining in which bin(s) the fragment could reside, using a $\pm 2.5\%$ measurement error window (Budowle et al., 1991). Although measurement error can vary among laboratories, the $\pm 2.5\%$ was used to facilitate this study. If the size range spanned a bin boundary, the frequency of the higher frequency bin was assigned to the allele (Budowle et al., 1991). The single-locus frequency of a two-band pattern was calculated using $2pq$, where p and q are the estimated binned allele frequencies for each VNTR band, while the frequency of occurence of a single-band pattern was estimated using $2p$ (Budowle et al., 1991). The frequency of occurrence of a profile composed of multiple single-locus profiles was calculated as the product of the single-locus frequencies. Since measurement error for the FBI RFLP system can be greater than $\pm 2.5\%$ for fragments above 10,000 base pairs (bp), any profile at a particular locus that contained an allele greater than 10,090 bp was assigned a locus frequency of 1.00. Additionally, since the size of fragments less than 640 bp can not be ascertained for the FBI RFLP system, any single-locus profile containing such a fragment was assigned a frequency of 1.00.

To determine forensic significance when using HaeIII population data, target profiles of 1,964 individuals from the FBI's Caucasian ($N = 808$), Black ($N = 517$), and Hispanic ($N = 639$) databases were used. The likelihood of occurrence of each profile, using the loci D1S7, D2S44, D4S139, and D10S28, was calculated in every available database using primarily rebinned formats. To visualize comparisons of databases, the inverse of the frequency estimated for the composite profile was plotted on a logarithmic (base 10) scale (i.e., a scatter plot) for evaluation of forensic significance between/among various reference populations.

Some scatter plots were generated using population data sorted into the original 31 bins. When this was done, a minimum frequency of $1/n$ (where $n = $ the total number of alleles at a locus for a particular database), or a minimum bin frequency of 0.001, was used to enable multiplication of a bin containing no observed alleles.

An alternative approach involving random sampling of the larger database was performed to evaluate forensic significance when a large database is compared with a much smaller database. The number of individuals sampled from the larger database was defined by the number of samples in the smaller database at each locus. Five random samplings were performed, the 31 bin data resulting from each sampling were averaged, and then the averaged 31 bin tables were rebinned. Averaged rebinned data of the FBI Caucasian database were compared with the rebinned French and Israeli databases by scatter plot analysis. Additionally, the averaged rebinned data of the Black database were compared with the rebinned Haitian database, and the averaged rebinned southeastern Hispanic database was compared with the rebinned Michigan Hispanic database by scatter plot analysis.

It should be noted that some of the 1,964 profiles contain information from fewer loci than others in the scatter plots. Additionally, because of the conventions described above, some operational constraints were placed on the data. Single-locus profiles that contain alleles whose sizes fall outside the 640–10,090 bp range are not considered when deriving a multiple locus frequency estimate. Therefore, while data for four loci may be available for an individual sample, fewer loci might be involved in the final estimate; such values should not be construed as reflecting the relative rarity of four locus profiles.

Results and Discussion

The VNTR loci studied were highly polymorphic in all databases described in Tab. 1. As an example, Fig. 1 displays 31 bin frequency histograms for the locus D1S7 in various reference populations. In accordance with previous studies (Chakraborty and Kidd, 1991; Devlin et al., 1992; Monson and Budowle, 1992; Weir, 1992) the data strongly support that multiple locus VNTR DNA profiles are rare events in any relevant database. The greatest contribution to human diversity (approximately 85%) at blood group and protein loci is due to variation among individuals; only a small contribution is due to racial and ethnic differences (Lewontin, 1972). The observation of the rarity of multiple locus highly polymorphic VNTR profiles in all relevant databases further supports the position that most variation is due to differences among individuals. Therefore, the contribution that different reference population groups might have on the estimate of the likelihood of occurrence of a DNA profile was considered.

The concern for the forensic community is not *statistical* significance but rather the *forensic* significance of estimates of the likelihood of occurrence of DNA profiles when using various DNA databases. Scatter plots comparing the likelihood of occurrence of DNA profiles in various reference populations are more useful for evaluating forensic significance of DNA statistical estimates using a database which may not precisely represent the demographics of the region where the crime was committed (Monson and Budowle, 1992). Therefore, the FBI Caucasian, Black, and Hispanic databases, which represent composite databases, were compared with several regional and ethnic databases. This scatter plot approach presents a worst case scenario, particularly since the allele frequencies in each database are subject to sampling variances, and there can be measurement biases in the methods used by the various laboratories that have generated the population data. Although it would be more appropriate for forensic significance to consider the ratio of the DNA profile estimate in a particular database to the mean value, the scatter plot approach was utilized to show extreme examples.

For the HaeIII data each point represents a probability comparison for a DNA profile of each of the 1,964 individuals (defined as either Black, Caucasian, southeastern Hispanic or southwestern Hispanic) in the FBI population databases. Thus, real DNA profiles were used to evaluate the forensic significance of estimating the likelihood of occurrence of each DNA profile in different databases. The diagonal on each scatter plot indicates the theoretical line where both reference databases would produce the same estimate (actual scatter plots not shown; for more data see Compendium in preparation). Generally, when the data points fall close to the diagonal line, the databases would yield similar results.

182

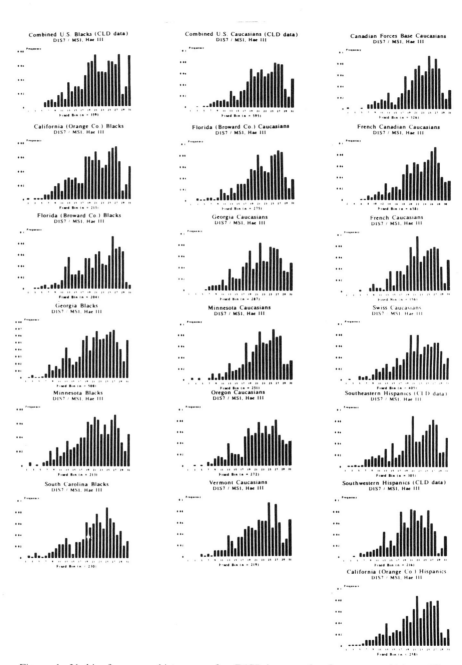

Figure 1. 31 bin frequency histograms for D1S7 in several reference populations. The displayed sample populations contain at least 150 individuals.

Furthermore, points which fall closer to the origin tend to represent a single-locus profile, while those furthest from the origin tend to represent four single-locus profiles. Scatter plots that contain incomplete sample profiles can be informative in depicting forensic significance for situations encountered in casework: even though a four- or five-probe battery may be available to the forensic scientist for analyses, the quality and/or quantity of the DNA derived from the forensic specimen may preclude typing of all available loci.

Due to an intentionally designed characteristic of the fixed bin method, under certain conditions cross-group comparisons may not fall on the diagonal even if the population databases are similar. Bins with fewer than five counts are merged with contiguous bins; therefore, smaller databases generally will have fewer bins and larger databases will have more bins. The intent of merging bins is to yield more conservative estimates when smaller databases are used (Budowle et al., 1991; Monson and Budowle, 1992). Thus, when comparing databases via scatter plots, the data points may cluster above or below the diagonal depending on which database has the greater number of samples (e.g. FBI Caucasian vs. Israelis, Monson and Budowle, 1992).

Therefore, when comparing statistical estimates with different sized databases using the fixed bin method, it may be meaningful to evaluate the breadth of the data point cluster by scatter plots of probability estimates calculated using population data sorted into the original 31 bins rather than rebinned categories. The additional conservative bias placed on smaller-sized databases by rebinning for use in forensic casework analyses for frequency estimations then would not confound the interpretation of the data with respect to differences which might be ascribable to subgroups. Alternatively, the random sampling approach of the larger database can be used to evaluate forensic significance.

The variation in breadth of the scatter plots is different for within major population group comparisons (e.g. FBI Caucasian vs. Swiss) and between group comparisons (e.g. FBI Black vs. FBI Caucasian). For HaeIII Caucasian population sample databases, FBI Caucasian frequencies were compared with several United States regional Caucasian databases (Oregon, California, Florida, Georgia, Minnesota and Vermont), a French and an English Canadian database, one Swiss database, and an Israeli database (Tab. 2). There do not appear to be forensically significant differences among statistical estimates using different Caucasian databases. The breadth of the scatter plots is narrow. Using the rebinned data formats, 95.7%–99.9% of the 1,964 target DNA profile frequency estimates from the FBI Caucasian sample population, when compared with regional/ethnic Caucasian databases, were within an order of magnitude (excluding the French and Israeli samples). For those scatter plot Caucasian population comparisons with databases of more similar size (i.e., FBI Caucasian vs. either English

Table 2. Distribution (percentages) of ratios of frequency estimates calculated in various pairs of Caucasian reference populations

Reference Population Comparison	Bin Fmt[b]	Ratio Interval[a]					
		1	>1–2	>2–5	>5–10	>10–100	>100
FBI[c] v. California[d]	R	0.8	69.9	21.3	5.7	2.2	0.1
	31	1.0	77.3	19.5	1.8	0.4	0
FBI[c] v. Florida[e]	R	0.9	73.8	20.4	3.1	1.9	0
	31	0.9	78.6	18.6	1.7	0.3	0
FBI[c] v. Georgia[f]	R	1.3	77.9	19.5	1.3	0.1	0
	31	1.2	79.7	18.2	0.8	0.1	0
FBI[c] v. Minnesota[g]	R	0.7	73.1	21.1	3.6	1.6	0
	31	0.8	78.1	19.3	1.6	0.2	0
FBI[c] v. Oregon[h]	R	0.7	74.1	21.1	2.9	1.2	0.1
	31	0.7	76.8	20.6	1.7	0.2	0
FBI[c] v. Vermont[i]	R	0.8	70.7	19.5	4.7	4.3	0
	31	0.8	75.8	19.8	3.4	0.2	0
FBI[c] v. English Canadian[j]	R	1.1	74.3	21.4	2.2	1.0	0
	31	0.6	74.3	21.2	2.6	1.3	0
FBI[c] v. French Canadian[k]	R	0.9	86.3	12.2	0.6	0.1	0
	31	0.9	81.0	15.1	2.2	0.8	0
FBI[c] v. Swiss[l]	R	1.7	77.3	16.6	3.1	1.2	0
	31	1.5	77.5	16.6	3.2	1.2	0
FBI[c] v. French[m]	R	1.2	52.8	30.2	9.1	6.2	0.5
	31	1.1	58.1	31.1	7.7	2.0	0
	RS/R	0.7	67.6	28.3	3.3	0.2	0
FBI[c] v. Israeli[n]	R	0.5	38.6	33.2	13.0	13.4	1.3
	31	0.5	48.3	35.4	10.7	5.1	0
	RS/R	0.5	53.1	34.4	9.0	3.1	0

[a]Ratios were determined by dividing the more common frequency by the less common frequency in the designated reference databases for each of the 1,964 target profiles. Each ratio interval represents the magnitude of the ratio for each target profile. The percentages are the portion of target profiles falling within each ratio interval.
[b]Bin Formats (Fmt) are: R = rebinned data; 31 = 31 bin data; and RS/R = rebinned random sampling data of the larger size reference population compared with rebinned data of the smaller sized reference population.
[c]Reference population from the FBI.
[d]Reference population from Orange County Sheriff's Coroner Department, Santa Ana, CA.
[e]Reference population from Broward Sheriff's Office Laboratory, Fort Lauderdale, FL.
[f]Reference population from Georgia Bureau of Investigation, Decatur, GA.
[g]Reference population from Minnesota Bureau of Criminal Apprehension, St. Paul, MN.
[h]Reference population from Oregon State Police, Portland, OR.
[i]Reference population from Vermont State Police, Waterbury, VT.
[j]Reference population from RCMP Central Forensic Laboratory, Ottawa, Ontario, Canada.
[k]Reference population from Laboratoire de Police Scientifique, Montréal, Canada.
[l]Reference population from Institut für Rechtsmedizin, Bern, Switzerland.
[m]Reference population from Laboratoire de Génétique Moléculaire, Nantes, France.
[n]Reference population from the FBI.

Canadian or French Canadian or Swiss), 98.8%–99.9% of the frequency estimate comparisons, with rebinned format data, were within an order of magnitude. Only one target DNA profile of the comparisons, among the larger data bases (FBI Caucasian vs. English Canadians) had an estimate that exceeded an order of magnitude and a frequency more common than 1/1,000,000; however, it was not a Caucasian target profile.

When comparing within major group databases of different size, the sorting of data into 31 bin categories can reduce the variation in statistical estimates between the two sample populations, compared with using rebinned data (Tab. 2). The slightly greater differences observed with rebinned data comparisons are the result of the intentional conservative bias placed on smaller-sized databases by rebinning. Compared with the FBI Caucasian sample population, California, Florida, Georgia, Minnesota, Oregon, Vermont, French, and Israeli Caucasian databases have considerably smaller sample sizes. Therefore, to determine whether or not any forensically significant effects would be encountered using these various databases either 31 bin data or the random sampling of the larger database in the comparison should be evaluated. As shown in Tab. 2, 99.6%–99.9% of the regional U.S. comparisons are within an order of magnitude when 31 bin data are used. Of these regional U.S. 31 bin Caucasian data comparisons only one target profile, that had one order of magnitude difference in the estimate and had a frequency more common than 1/1,000,000, was from a Caucasian individual (FBI Caucasian vs. Minnesota with an 11.4 fold difference). If within-major group databases are more equivalent in size, the 31 bin format and rebinned data generally yield a more similar range of estimates (if anything, the 31 bin formatted data should increase the range of differences slightly, particularly for rare events, and these differences would not be considered forensically significant) (see FBI Caucasians vs. English Canadians; FBI Caucasians vs. Swiss; FBI Caucasians vs. French Canadians; Tab. 2). Because deviations based on ratios are going to show a large variance due to sampling, the very few observed differences are extreme examples. Therefore, there are no real differences for forensic purposes among these databases.

The French and Israeli (as well as the Swiss and Canadian, above) databases should not be considered as relevant databases for the population of potential perpetrators in the United States. However, under the highly unlikely assumption of no gene flow among subgroups in the United States, these population groups can be used to gain insight into the effects of subgroups on forensic DNA statistical estimates. Obviously, any differences observed would be less in the United States, if there is even a small amount of gene flow between or among subgroups of a particular major-population group. Due to the much smaller size of the French Caucasian database, the random sampling approach was employed. When sample size was taken into consideration in this way, 99.8% of the comparisons with the FBI Caucasian database were within an order of magnitude. There were only two target DNA profiles that had frequency estimate differences exceeding an order of magnitude and also were more common than 1/1,000,000; only one of the two target profiles was from a Caucasian and the difference was 10.9-fold. The slightly wider breadth of the scatter plot in the FBI Caucasian vs. Israeli comparison was anticipated due to the genetic differences between the two groups; however, the estimates still did not produce forensically significant differences. 94.9% of the comparisons between the FBI Caucasian and Israeli estimates were less than an order of magnitude different from each other, using 31 bin data, and 96.9% of these comparisons were within an order of magnitude when using the random sampled FBI Caucasian database (Tab. 2). With the random sampling approach, 16 target DNA profiles exceeded an order of magnitude difference, while having a frequency more common than 1/1,000,000. Only four of these target profiles were from Caucasians, ranging in differences of 10.9–45.1-fold, with the most common frequency being 1/163,000 (still a rare event). Since a degree of gene flow among groups in the United States reasonably can be anticipated, these very few differences will be even more diminished when considering the United States population of potential perpetrators.

The same trends hold for the rest of the HaeIII data comparisons. The FBI Black database yields estimates similar to those for regional Black databases (Tab. 3); and intra-Hispanic (Tab. 4) database comparisons rarely produce forensically significant differences in the estimated likelihood of occurrence of a particular DNA profile.

The data from comparisons of regional U.S. Black population samples are very telling of the absence of effects of population substructure on the estimate of the likelihood of occurrence of a DNA profile in the general population (Tab. 3). Previous studies (Chakraborty et al., 1992a; Reed, 1969) have shown that there are differences in the degree of Caucasian admixture for Southern versus Northern or Western Blacks. Although Caucasian admixture has been estimated to be as little as 4–10% in the South and as much as 30% in the North, there were no forensically significant differences in the likelihood of occurrence of the 1,964 target DNA profiles among regional Black population samples (Tab. 3). 99.5%–99.9% of the estimates of the target DNA profiles from the FBI Black database, compared with regional U.S. Black sample populations using a rebinned format, were within an order of magnitude. Out of all the regional Black sample population comparisons only three target profiles had differences exceeding an order of magnitude and frequencies more common than 1/1,000,000; none of these target profiles were from Black individuals. The Michigan Black vs. South Carolina Black data comparisons yielded very similar results,

Table 3. Distribution (percentages) of frequency estimates calculated in various pairs of Black reference populations

Reference Population Comparison	Bin Fmt[b]	Ratio Interval[a]					
		1	>1–2	>2–5	>5–10	>10–100	>100
FBI[c] v.	R	0.5	75.9	21.4	2.2	0.1	0
California[d]	31	0.6	76.0	21.3	2.0	0.2	0
FBI[c] v.	R	0.9	70.4	24.6	3.6	0.5	0
Florida[e]	31	1.0	70.5	24.6	3.5	0.5	0
FBI[c] v.	R	0.9	83.9	14.5	0.7	0.1	0
Georgia[f]	31	1.1	83.0	15.1	0.7	0.1	0
FBI[c] v.	R	0.6	78.1	19.7	1.5	0.1	0
Minnesota[g]	31	0.6	77.6	18.8	2.3	0.6	0
FBI[c] v.	R	1.3	87.8	10.5	0.3	0.1	0
Michigan[h]	31	1.3	87.4	10.4	0.9	0.1	0
Michigan[h] v.	R	0.8	70.1	27.1	1.9	0.1	0
South Carolina[i]	31	0.9	68.4	28.0	2.4	0.4	0
FBI[c] v.	R	0.7	66.8	24.7	5.6	2.2	0
Haitian[j]	31	1.0	74.5	20.8	2.9	0.8	0
	RS/R	0.9	72.4	24.7	1.9	0.2	0

[a]Ratios were determined by dividing the more common frequency by the less common frequency in the designated reference databases for each of the 1,964 target profiles. Each ratio interval represents the magnitude of the ratio for each target profile. The percentages are the portion of target profiles falling within each ratio interval.
[b]Bin Formats (Fmt) are: R = rebinned data; 31 = 31 bin data; and RS/R = rebinned random sampling data of the larger size reference population compared with rebinned data of the smaller sized reference population.
[c]Reference population from the FBI.
[d]Reference population from Orange County Sheriff's Coroner Department, Santa Ana, CA.
[e]Reference population from Broward Sheriff's Office Crime Laboratory, Fort Lauderdale, FL.
[f]Reference population from Georgia Bureau of Investigation, Decatur, GA.
[g]Reference population from Minnesota Bureau of Criminal Apprehension, St. Paul, MN.
[h]Reference population from Michigan State Police, East Lansing, MI.
[i]Reference population from South Carolina State Police, SLED, Columbia, SC.
[j]Reference population from the FBI.

with no forensically significant differences, i.e., no Black target DNA profiles with frequencies more common than 1/1,000,000 had estimate differences exceeding an order of magnitude (Tab. 3). Additionally, with the random sampling approach 99.8% of the FBI Black vs. Haitian comparisons were within an order of magnitude. There was only one target DNA profile in the FBI Black vs. Haitian comparisons that exceeded an order of magnitude and had a frequency more common than 1/1,000,000; it was a Black target profile (two loci) with a 12.0-fold difference and the more common frequency was 1/9,150. Therefore, finding forensically significant differences even between U.S. Blacks and Haitians is an unlikely occurrence. These observations were expected since the frequencies of VNTR alleles in general are more rare in Black

Table 4. Distribution (percentages) of ratios of frequency estimates calculated in various pairs of Hispanic reference populations

Reference Population Comparison	Bin Fmt[b]	Ratio Interval[a]					
		1	>1–2	>2–5	>5–10	>10–100	>100
FBI Southeast[c] v.	R	0.8	58.5	33.9	5.5	1.4	0
FBI Southwest[c]	31	0.6	53.3	35.8	7.8	2.6	0
FBI Southwest[c] v.	R	0.8	69.0	27.3	2.8	0.1	0
California[d]	31	0.7	67.6	28.6	2.8	0.4	0
FBI Southwest[c] v.	R	0.5	46.6	33.0	12.0	7.7	0.2
Michigan[e]	31	0.9	60.4	31.1	5.5	2.1	0
FBI Southeast[c] v.	R	0.6	42.7	34.0	12.8	9.7	0.3
Michigan[e]	31	0.6	51.8	34.2	9.1	4.4	0
	RS/R	0.6	60.1	31.0	6.3	2.1	0

[a]Ratios were determined by dividing the more common frequency by the less common frequency in the designated reference databases for each of the 1,964 target profiles. Each ratio interval represents the magnitude of the ratio for each target profile. The percentages are the portion of target profiles falling within each ratio interval.
[b]Bin Formats (Fmt) are: R = rebinned data; 31 = 31 bin data; and RS/R = rebinned random sampling data of the larger size reference population compared with rebinned data of the smaller sized reference population.
[c]Reference population from the FBI.
[d]Reference population from Orange County Sheriff's Coroner Department, Santa Ana, CA.
[e]Reference population from Michigan State Police, East Lansing, MI.

populations studied than in other major population groups (Balazs et al., 1989; Chakraborty and Kidd, 1991; Devlin and Risch, 1992a; Weir, 1992), and the differences among allele frequencies in different population samples are diminished when the collections of alleles comprising a multiple locus DNA profile is used (Weir, 1992).

Even though southeastern and southwestern Hispanic populations have different racial admixture (Cerda-Flores et al., 1991, 1992), there were very few differences for frequency estimates of the 1,964 target profiles among the Hispanic sample population comparisons (Tab. 4). The increase in the ratios with Michigan Hispanics is due to the smaller sample size in that database (Tab. 1). As an example, the random sampling approach was applied to the larger FBI southeastern Hispanic database and compared with rebinned data from Michigan Hispanics. Using this approach, 2.1% of the target DNA profiles had differences in estimates greater than one order of magnitude between FBI southeastern Hispanics and Michigan Hispanics (Tab. 4). However, only 0.7% of the total target profiles (i.e, 14 profiles) had frequency differences greater than one order of magnitude (ranging from 10.2–20.4-fold) where estimates were more common than 1/1,000,000.

An across-major group comparison of FBI Caucasian and FBI Black reference populations yielded a broader scatter plot than any of the within-group comparisons. Using the rebinned data format, 8.7% of the target profiles had ratios exceeding one order of magnitude. This portion of the ratios of target profiles that exceeded one order of magnitude was greater than in any of the within Caucasian or within Black reference population comparisons. Although the databases were not tested specifically for genetic differences or similarities, it would be expected that reference data bases from genetically more similar groups would yield estimates that are more similar than those drawn from different groups. However, when databases are not genetically similar, such as would be anticipated with across-major group comparisons (e.g. FBI Caucasian vs. FBI Black), a 31 bin format generally increases the range of estimates between the two sample populations. For the FBI Caucasian vs. FBI Black comparison, there were 10.9% of the target profiles that exceeded one order of magnitude using the 31 bin data format. In contrast, the smoothing effect of rebinning on allele frequencies decreases DNA profile frequency estimate differences across major population group databases (8.7% of the ratios of the target profiles for the FBI Caucasian vs. Black comparisons exceeded one order of magnitude using rebinned data).

The assertion of Lewontin and Hartl (1991) and the National Research Council (NCR) report (1992), that differences between major population groups cannot be used to provide a meaningful bound on the variation of DNA profile frequency estimates for forensic purposes, because the genetic diversity between subgroups within a major-population group is greater than the genetic variation between major-population groups, is not supported by the data. The scatter plots of within-group comparisons tend to cluster far more than between-group comparisons. Differences greater than two orders of magnitude in DNA profile frequency estimates from different U.S. databases are unlikely events and usually occur when frequencies are less common than 1/1,000,000. Such differences in this frequency estimate range would not be forensically significant.

Conclusions

Subdivision, either by ethnic group or by U.S. geographic region, within a major population group does not substantially affect forensic estimates of the likelihood of occurrence of a DNA profile. One should not construe that 1/1,000,00 (or for that matter 1/100,000) is a dividing line for what should be considered as an acceptable likelihood of occurrence for a DNA profile; the values simply provide an operational point where differences among less common occurrences would have no forensic significance. Therefore, estimated frequencies among regional groups and several subgroups of a major population category are forensically similar. Estimates of the likelihood of occurrence of a DNA profile using major population group databases (e.g., Caucasian, Black, and Hispanic) provide a greater range of frequencies than would estimates from subgroups of a major population category. Furthermore, Chakraborty et al. (1993) recently calculated the confidence intervals for DNA profile estimates using FBI general population databases. The range of the confidence intervals was narrower than the range of estimates observed in the across-major group scatter plot. The most appropriate approach, therefore, is to estimate the likelihood of occurrence of a particular DNA profile in each major group. Since the greatest variation in statistical estimates occurs in across-major population groups, in most cases, there will be no unfair bias applying the general population database approach. Additionally, the significance of the magnitude of the very few differences that were observed wanes when it is taken into consideration that the binning procedure used yields conservative estimates. On average, each allele frequency is over-estimated at least two-fold (Chakraborty et al., in press). Furthermore, these very few differences also are exaggerated due to sampling fluctuations for each database and measurement biases that exist in the methods used by the various laboratories that have generated the population data. Therefore, based on empirical data, there is no demonstrable need for employing alternative approaches, such as the ceiling approach (NRC report 1992), to derive statistical estimates. VNTR frequency data from major population groups provide reasonable, reliable, and meaningful estimates for DNA profile frequencies without significant consequences for forensic inferences.

Acknowledgements

We express our thanks and gratitude to TWGDAM members and others who contributed their population data. Without their generosity this study could not have been undertaken. This is publication number 93-03 of the Laboratory Division of the Federal Bureau of Investigation. Names of commercial manufacturers are provided for identification only and inclusion does not imply endorsement by the Federal Bureau of Investigation.

References

Balazs I, Baird M, Clyne M, Meade E (1992) Human population genetic studies of five hypervariable DNA loci. American Journal of Human Genetics 44: 182–190

Brookfield J (1992) Brookfield replies. Nature 358: 483

Budowle B, Giusti AM, Waye JS, Baechtel FS, Fourney RM, Adams DE, Presley LA, Deadman HA, Monson KL (1991) Fixed-Bin analysis for statistical evaluation of continuous distributions of allelic data from VNTR loci, for use in forensic comparisons. Am J Hum Genet 48: 841–855

Cerda-Flores RM, Kshatriya GK, Barton SA, Leal-Garza CH, Garza-Chapa R, Schull WJ, Chakraborty, R (1991) Genetic structure of the populations migrating from San Luis Potosi and Zacatecas to Nuevo Leon in Mexico. Human Biology 63: 309–327

Creda-Flores RM, Kshatriya GK, Bertin TK, Hewett-Emmett D, Hanis CL, Chakraborty R (1992) Genetic diversity and estimation of genetic admixture among Mexican-Americans of Starr County, Texas. Ann Hum Biol 19: 347–360

Chakraborty R, Jin L (1992) Heterozygote deficiency, population substructure and their implications in DNA fingerprinting. Hum Genet 88: 267–272

Chakraborty R, Kidd KK (1991) The utility of DNA typing in forensic work. Science 254: 1735–1739

Chakraborty R, DeAndrade M, Daiger SP, Budowle B (1992) Apparent heterozygote deficiencies observed in DNA typing data and their implications in forensic applications. Annals of Hum Genet 56: 45–57

Chakraborty R, Jin L, Zhong Y, Srinivasan MR, Budowle B (1993) On allele frequency computation from DNA typing data. Int J Leg Med (in press)

Chakraborty R, Kamboh MI, Nwankwo M, Ferrell RE (1992a) Caucasian genes in American blacks. Am J Hum Genet 50: 145–155

Chakraborty R, Srinivasan MR, Daiger SP (1993) Evaluation of standard error and confidence interval of estimated multilocus genotype probabilities and their implications in DNA forensics. Am J Hum Genet 52: 60–70

Devlin B, Risch N (1992) A note on Hardy-Weinberg equilibrium of VNTR data using the FBI's fixed bin method. Am J Hum Genet 51: 549–553

Devlin B, Risch N (1992a) Ethnic differentiation at VNTR loci, with special reference to forensic applications. Am J Hum Genet 51: 534–548

Devlin B, Risch N, Roeder K (1992) Forensic inference from DNA fingerprints. J Am Statist Ass 87: 337–350

Evett IW, Gill P (1991) A discussion of the robustness of methods for assessing the evidental value of DNA single locus profiles in crime investigation. Electrophoresis 12: 226–230

Evett IW, Pinchin R (1991) DNA single locus profiles: tests for the robustness of statistical procedures within the context of forensic science. Int J Legal Medicine 104: 267–272

Lewontin RC (1972) The apportionment of human diversity. Evol Biol 6: 381–398

Lewontin RC, Hartl DL (1991) Population genetics in forensic DNA typing. Science 254: 1745–1750

Monson KL, Budowle B (1993) VNTR population frequency estimation for forensics: effects of reference population and calculation method. J Forens Sci (in press)

National Research Council (1992) DNA typing: statistical bases for interpretation. *In*: DNA Technology in Forensic Science, Chapter 3, Washington, D.C., National Academy Press, pp 74–96

Reed TE (1969) Caucasian genes in American Negroes. Science 165: 762–768

Risch N, Devlin B (1992) On the probability of matching DNA fingerprints. Science 255: 717–720

Weir BS (1992) Independence of VNTR alleles defined by fixed bins. Genetics 130: 873–887

DNA Fingerprinting: State of the Science
ed. by S. D. J. Pena, R. Chakraborty, J. T. Epplen & A. J. Jeffreys
© 1993 Birkhäuser Verlag Basel/Switzerland

Population genetics of 14 ethnic groups using phenotypic data from VNTR loci

I. Balazs

Lifecodes Corp., Stamford, CT 06902, USA

Summary

Population genetic studies were performed using five VNTR loci (D2S44, D4S163, D14S13, D17S79, D18S27). The populations examined were Caucasian (Australia, Brazil and U.S.A.), Australian aborigine, Chinese, Amerindian (Cheyenne, Maya, Navajo, Pima, Tobas/Wicnis), North American Black, North American Hispanic (California, Miami, New York, Texas). The overall size range of the alleles for these loci, in PstI-digested DNA, was the same in all populations. The major difference among populations was the relative frequency of particular groups of alleles. These differences were small among similar ethnic groups, while sometimes varying several fold among some of the more distinct populations. However, groups of alleles that were rare in the major ethnic groups (Caucasian, Black, Chinese) were also rare in the other populations.

The frequency databases generated by typing individuals for 4 loci were used to compare the random DNA profile frequencies among populations. The results show that the estimated frequency of any 4 locus profile is very low in all populations examined (e.g. median value $<10^{-8}$). Analysis of relative genetic similarity among populations was used to create the most likely clustering of these ethnic groups. Results show an uncanny similarity between the clusters generated and genetic distance measurements obtained with traditional calculations of conventional genetic markers.

Introduction

The identification of large number of DNA polymorphism has greatly expanded the number of markers available for population genetics studies and human evolution. DNA sequence variations among individuals in different populations have been examined either with loci showing restriction fragment length polymorphism (RFLP) (Cavalli-Sforza et al., 1986; Bowcock et al., 1991; Kidd et al., 1991) or with loci having alleles containing variable number of tandem repeats (VNTR) (Balazs et al., 1989; Flint et al., 1989; Deka et al., 1991; Kidd et al., 1991; Balazs et al., 1992). Some of these studies compared the frequency distribution of alleles among different populations and/or used these markers to perform evolutionary studies.

The high level of polymorphism of VNTR loci could make them useful markers for population genetic studies. However, traditional methods used to estimate genetic distance or to examine the similarities among populations rely on the use of allele frequencies for their calculations. This can be easily performed when the number of alleles is small and the difference in size between alleles is large enough to be resolved by current fractionation procedures (Bowcock et al., 1991; Deka et al., 1991; Edwards et al., 1992). Highly polymorphic VNTR loci have a large number of alleles and current methodologies for DNA fractionation do not allow every allele to be separated and identified (Baird et al., 1986; Balazs et al., 1989; Devlin and Risch, 1992). Therefore, most studies estimate allele frequencies by grouping the observations into discrete size ranges (bins). These bins become the operational definitions of alleles and are used to perform population genetic studies. More recently, nonparametric methods of statistical analysis have been developed to estimate the frequency of alleles and to test for independence within and between loci (Devlin et al., 1991; Devlin and Risch, 1992; Weir, 1992; Chakraborty et al., 1993). This study compares the data of 5 VNTR loci from 14 populations. The comparisons between populations were done in terms of allele size, relative frequency of alleles, apparent heterozygosity, multilocus phenotype profiles, and a measure of genetic similarity or affinity.

Populations and methods

The origin of the samples used for the study of North American Black, Caucasian, Chinese and Australian populations has been described elsewhere (Balazs et al., 1989; Balazs et al., 1992). Caucasian individuals from Brazil represent unrelated individuals received for paternity testing. Hispanic populations from New York, Texas and California represent unrelated individuals from paternity testing cases. Hispanic individuals from Miami were collected by the American Red Cross from unrelated individuals living in the Miami area of Florida. An anonymous questionnaire asking for the country of origin of their parents indicated more than 90% of individuals' parents were from Cuba. Samples of Cheyenne individuals were collected at the Lame Dear Reservation in Montana and kindly provided by C. Lantz (Lame Dear Reservation, MT). Navajo and Pima individuals were collected in Arizona and provided by B. Williams (Arizona State Univ., AZ). Pima individuals are from the Gila River Indian Community of Arizona (Williams et al., 1992). Maya individuals were collected from individuals living in the Yucatan peninsula, in Mexico (Kidd et al., 1991). Tobas and Wicnis were collected from Native americans living in the North Western region of Argentina and kindly provided by E. Raimondi (PRICAI, Buenos Aires, Argentina).

The general procedures used in the analysis of these loci were those described by Balazs et al. (1989, 1992). Briefly, DNA was isolated from peripheral blood cells and digested with PstI restriction endonuclease. Fractionation of DNA fragments was performed by agarose gel electrophoresis. DNA was transferred to nylon membranes, hybridized to P^{32}-labeled DNA probes and the position of the alleles detected by autoradiography. The size of the DNA fragments was measured relative to that of a series of DNA standards using a digitizing tablet connected to a computer (Baird et al., 1986) or a video based digitizing instrument (BioImage Corp.)

Statistical methods

Estimates for the frequency of randomly generated four-locus VNTR profiles (D2S44, D14S13, D17S79, D18S27) were obtained for pairs of populations using the method described by Weir (1992). Frequencies were estimated as the products of the phenotype frequency of individual loci.

Calculations for population similarities, in the sense of affinities rather than strict identity by descent relations, were performed using an index similar to that developed by Nei (1972, 1987). Nei's measure of similarity is simply the probability of a random match of alleles, when drawn from different populations, divided by the geometric mean of the probabilities of randomly drawing matching alleles within each of the pair of populations. This measure uses the same basic formulation. Because alleles at the loci examined are not discrete, or easily classified. the definition of matching alleles was different than Nei's, whose measure relies on discrete alleles. Instead, the definition of a match was based on whether two randomly-chosen fragments could in fact be two measurements of the same allele, by using the measurement error distributions of the alleles (Balazs et al., manuscript in preparation).

Pairwise affinities among populations are presented as a symmetric square of similarities. While this matrix is in itself rather informative, other type of analyses are also being presented to make the information more intuitive. Thus the matrix of affinities is summarized using principal component analysis, with a plot of the leading two eigenvectors providing an illustration of the affinities to each other. The data was also summarized using standard clustering algorithms such as "unweighted pair group method of analysis" (UPGMA) and complete linkage (Sokal and Sneath, 1963).

Results and discussion

Heterozygosity. A general discussion on the measurement of heterozygosity of VNTR loci has been presented in a previous publication (Balazs et al., 1992). Suffice to say that this value represents the fraction of individuals with two visually identifiable DNA fragments and this underestimates the true heterozygosity. The extent of underestimation will be determined by the choice of restriction enzyme, the size of the polymorphic DNA fragments and the resolution provided by the method used for their fractionation and detection (Devlin et al., 1991).

A simple analysis of the relative genetic heterogeneity of these 14 populations was performed by measuring their heterozygosity at several loci. A summary of the values obtained for each population and locus is shown in Tab. 1. A comparison of the average heterozygosity of VNTR loci shows that the American Black population has the highest value (92%) followed by Caucasian populations (USA and Brazil). Next comes the group of Hispanic populations that range from 82% to 91%. The ethnic origins of individuals composing the Hispanic populations are expected to differ in different regions of the USA. However, as shown below, their average heterozygosity is similar to the Caucasian population. Only the Hispanic population from California has an average heterozygosity more than 5% below those of the other Hispanic or Caucasian populations. The Chinese population has an average heterozygosity of 83%. This value is the lowest of the three large world populations examined (i.e. Black, Caucasian, Oriental). It is worthwhile to note that even relatively small populations, such as Amerindian and Australian aborigine populations have high average heterozygosity (i.e.: 74% to 85%); however, the values are lower than in almost all the other populations.

Pairwise comparisons were performed to test whether the difference between heterozygosity values for two populations were statistically significant. This comparison between populations was done individually for the loci D2S44, D14S13, D17S79, D18S27. The number of loci with statistically significant difference in heterozygosity among pairs of popu-

Table 1. Heterozygosity of 14 populations

	D2S44	D17S79	D18S27	D14S13	D4S163	Average
Black USA	0.92 (831)	0.91 (827)	0.89 (411)	0.94 (542)	0.92 (318)	0.92
Cauc. USA	0.86 (2349)	0.85 (2285)	0.87 (1085)	0.93 (1555)	0.94 (530)	0.89
Cauc. Brazil	0.96 (94)	0.83 (93)	0.80 (90)	0.95 (60)	0.97 (57)	0.90
Hisp. Calif.	0.79 (180)	0.86 (185)	0.78 (100)	0.86 (117)		0.82
Hisp. Miami	0.86 (215)	0.92 (211)	0.91 (196)	0.94 (199)		0.91
Hisp. Texas	0.84 (197)	0.86 (192)	0.81 (148)	0.97 (126)		0.87
Hisp. New York	0.91 (79)	0.89 (74)	0.82 (60)	0.93 (59)		0.89
Chinese	0.75 (153)	0.76 (172)	0.76 (166)	0.92 (166)	0.94 (179)	0.83
Tobas	0.72 (214)	0.65 (214)	0.65 (212)	0.94 (205)	0.89 (215)	0.77
Maya	0.73 (70)	0.83 (65)	0.63 (57)	0.80 (35)		0.75
Pima	0.83 (138)	0.79 (138)	0.32 (132)	0.98 (129)	0.76 (130)	0.74
Cheyenne	0.85 (93)	0.84 (79)	0.71 (92)	0.96 (91)	0.87 (87)	0.85
Navajo	0.87 (83)	0.70 (83)	0.72 (83)	0.95 (83)	0.81 (59)	0.81
Aust. Aborig.	0.68 (90)	0.72 (87)	0.76 (76)	0.80 (59)	0.94 (70)	0.78

Number of individuals examined is shown in parentheses

Table 2. Number of loci with statistically significant difference in heterozygosity for D2S44, D14S13, D17S79, D18S27

	(2)	(3)	(4)	(5)	(6)	(7)	(8)	(9)	(10)	(11)	(12)	(13)	(14)
(1) Black USA	2	2	3	1	3	0	3	3	3	3	2	2	4
(2) Cauc. USA		1	3	1	1	0	3	3	2	2	1	2	4
(3) Cauc. Brazil			1	3	1	0	1	3	3	2	1	2	2
(4) Hisp. Calif.				2	1	1	1	2	1	2	1	2	1
(5) Hisp. Miami					1	0	3	3	3	2	1	2	4
(6) Hisp. Texas						0	2	3	2	1	0	1	3
(7) Hisp. New York							2	3	2	2	0	0	3
(8) Chinese								2	0	2	1	1	1
(9) Tobas									2	3	1	1	1
(10) Maya										2	1	2	0
(11) Pima											0	3	
(12) Cheyenne												1	2
(13) Navajo													2
(14) Aust. Aborig.													

lations is shown in Tab. 2 (strictly speaking these comparisons are presented as a descriptive tool, because the significance of any particular comparison is not simple to infer from the large number of comparisons). For a 95% confidence interval almost all populations showed statistically significant differences in heterozygosity at one to four loci. However, the New York hispanic population did not show statistically significant difference in heterozygosity at any locus with more than half of the populations compared.

Allele frequency distribution. The size distributions of the DNA fragments, at a given locus, in the 14 populations described in this and previous studies (Balazs et al., 1989, 1992) have several features in common: a) in all populations the allele size range is essentially the same; b) in general, the most common alleles were found at very similar size ranges; c) the main difference among populations was the frequency of particular size range of alleles.

One way to present the frequency distribution of alleles for a VNTR locus is a histogram representing the frequency of DNA fragments observed at small increments of DNA fragment size. An example of this type of presentation is shown for the D2S44 locus in Figs 1 and 2. The frequency values in these figures were calculated at increments of 0.5% of fragment size. This type of graphic representation does not provide the real frequency of an allele, rather an overview of the relative abundance of the DNA fragments detected at very small intervals. Under the experimental conditions used for this study, this interval is smaller than the resolution of the gels or the accuracy of the size determinations. Therefore, in this type of VNTR locus the actual frequency of an allele is strictly functional. It results from summing up

198

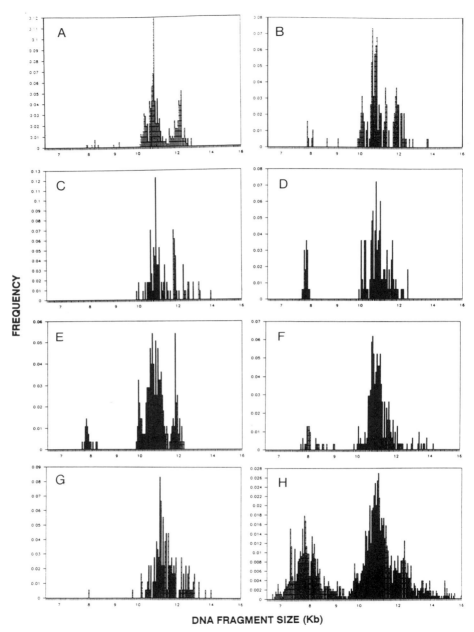

Figure 1. Frequency distribution of PstI-DNA fragments in individuals at the D2S44 locus; (A) Tobas, (B) Cheyenne, (C) Maya, (D) Navajo, (E) Pima, (F) Chinese, (G) Australian aborigine, (H) North American Black. The number of individuals tested are indicated in Tab. 1.

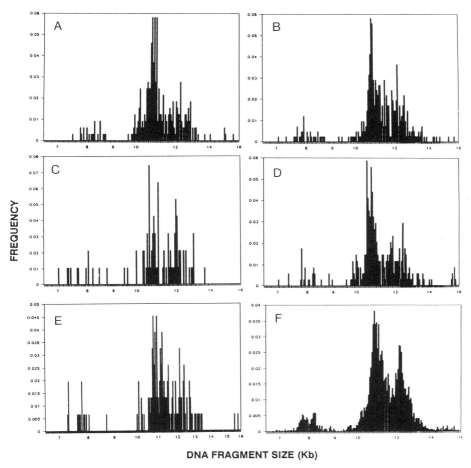

Figure 2. Frequency distribution of PstI-DNA fragments in individuals at the D2S44locus; (A) Hispanic-California, (B) Hispanic-Miami, (C) Hispanic-New York, (D) Hispanic-Texas, (E) Caucasoid-Brazil, (F) Caucasoid-North America. The number of individuals tested are indicated in Tab. 1.

the observations for a specific size range of DNA fragments. This size range can be defined in practical terms as a window or running average delimited by the size measurement error. Under our conditions of fractionation this error is about 0.6% of the fragment size. Therefore, the frequency of an allele was expressed as the frequency of events within ±3 times the standard error or ±1.8% of the fragment size. The result of this type of calculation for the frequency distribution of D2S44 alleles in each population is shown in Figs 3 and 4. The frequency estimate obtained by this type of calculation may vary due to sampling

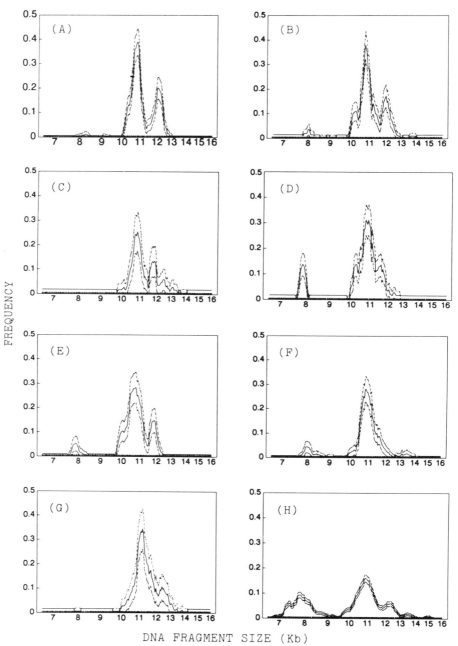

Figure 3. Running average for the frequency distribution of PstI-DNA fragments at the D2S44 locus. The size range of the window was equal to ±1.8% of the DNA fragment size. (A) Tobas, (B) Cheyenne, (C) Maya, (D) Navajo, (E) Pima, (F) Chinese, (G) Australian aborigine, (H) North American Black.

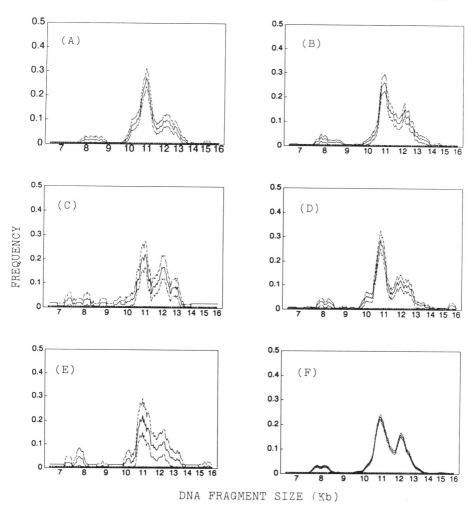

DNA FRAGMENT SIZE (Kb)

Figure 4. Running average for the frequency distribution of PstI-DNA fragments at the D2S44 locus. The size range of the window was equal to ±1.8% of the DNA fragment size. (A) Hispanic-California, (B) Hispanic-Miami, (C) Hispanic-New York, (D) Hispanic-Texas, (E) Caucasoid-Brazil, (F) Caucasoid-North America.

error. Therefore, a 95% confidence interval for the frequency values was also included in these figures.

The common feature of all these D2S44 distributions is that, in each population, the majority of DNA fragments are found between 10 Kb and 13 Kb. However, there are some differences in the frequency values among the various populations. One method used in the past to determine whether two distributions were the same was the Kolmogorov-Smirnov test (Balazs et al., 1989). Even if two distributions have statistically significant differences, the effect of these differences in calculations of phenotype frequency or in the chances of two random DNA profiles matching can not be assessed from these results. Instead, it would be more informative to compare the frequencies of random DNA profiles, across several loci, in one population versus the frequencies in other populations.

A curious intellectual exercise was proposed by a committee from the National Research Council on "DNA technology in forensic science" (National Research Council, 1992). In the chapter entitled "DNA typing: technical considerations" it was suggested that a conservative estimate of the frequency of an allele should be obtained by testing "samples from 100 randomly selected persons in each of 15–20 relatively homogenous populations" and using "the highest allele frequency found in any of the 15–20 populations or 5% (whichever is larger)". Several of the conceptual and mathematical errors present in the report have been addressed by Weir (1993). However, it is worth emphasizing that there is a lack of scientific basis for the recommended sampling strategy and it is unclear what would be gained from such exercise. The large sampling errors associated with databases containing 100 individuals would magnify nonexistent differences and probably hide many real ones. As an example, the results representing the frequency distributions obtained for two random samplings of the Caucasian database (100 individuals per sampling) for the D2S44 locus are shown in Figs 5A and 5B. These results were compared with the equivalent frequency values obtained from a large Caucasian database (Fig. 5C). As expected from sampling error, the differences in allele frequency between the two small databases vary by as much as two fold at several regions of the distribution curve. The sampling error will artificially inflate the frequency values derived from a collection of small size databases.

Another problem with the NCR recommendations is the lack of definition of what are "relatively homogeneous populations". Like most natural populations of humans, the 14 populations examined in our study are an admixture of populations. Even the Chinese population is composed of people from different regions of the country. However, in terms of estimating the frequency of a DNA profile, these populations are clearly more relevant than an arbitrary collection of allele frequencies pooled haphazardly from 15 to 20 different populations. In particular, in a forensic setting, the use of these combined databases would produce the absurd situation that the frequency of the DNA profile from, let us say, a Caucasian suspect would be obtained by multiplying the allele frequencies from 8 or 10 different populations (e.g. one Chinese, one Australian aborigine, one Tobas, one American Black, one Maori, one Caucasian, one Pima, etc.). What is the scientific significance of such calculation? It would make more sense to enact a law that sets a limit on

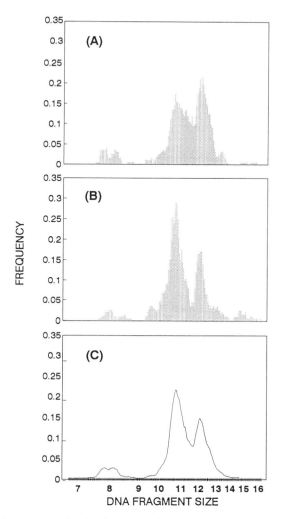

Figure 5. Running average for the frequency distribution of PstI-DNA fragments at the D2S44 locus in Caucasoid databases consisting of 100 individuals (A and B) and 2349 individuals (C).

the power of DNA profiling than to propose poorly thought out experiments as the basis of such calculation.

Frequency of heterozygote DNA profiles at 4 loci

Frequencies for 500 random DNA profiles, across 4 loci, were calculated for different combinations of population pairs. There were very few examples of DNA profiles with frequencies $< 10^{-5}$ and the median

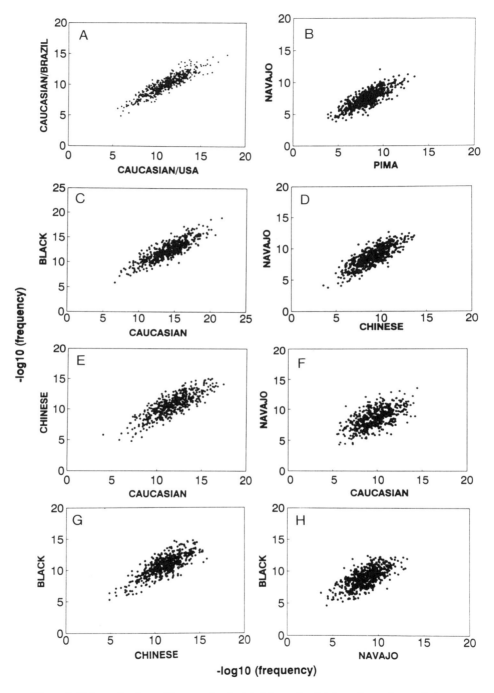

Figure 6. Values of $-\log_{10}$ (frequency) calculated from the database for each population.

values were $< 10^{-8}$ in all the populations compared. Examples of some of the comparisons between population pairs are shown as scatterplots in Figs 6(A–F). A relatively narrow distribution of values could be explained partly due to the fact that the differences in individual allele frequencies have canceled each other or that there is significant genetic similarity between the two populations for these loci. A broader scattering of the frequency values may indicate greater genetic difference between the two populations being compared. However, since most of the populations used in these comparisons contain less than 150 individuals a large fraction of the differences observed might be the result of error in the frequency estimates for individual alleles. Still, the tightest distribution was obtained between two Caucasian populations (USA vs Brazil) (Fig. 6A). The frequency values generated by comparing Caucasian, Chinese and Black populations (Figs 5C, 5E, 6G), were not as scattered as those between Caucasian and any of the native American populations (Fig. 6F). The values obtained by comparing Amerindian populations between themselves resulted in more narrowly distributed frequency estimates (e.g., Navajo vs Pima; Fig. 6B) than with other populations (Figs 6D, 6F, 6H). Overall, these results suggest a qualitative relationship between the degree of scattering of the frequency values and the known phylogenetic similarity between populations. There is less scatter between related or similar populations than more distant ones.

One major caveat with the study of genetic similarities, is that the results will be affected by population admixture. Most of the populations, with the exception of Chinese, are a composite of a native population and Caucasian populations. For example, the propoption of Caucasian genes has been estimated to be 3% to 17% in Australian aborigine (Balazs et al., 1992), about 25% in North American Black (Chakrabouty et al., 1992), and 5.4% in Pima (Williams et al., 1992). In this study the maximum proportion of Caucasian genes in some of the native American populations was estimated using data from two VNTR loci. These calculations were performed assuming that the alleles in a particular size range were present only in Caucasians (or absent in the ancestor populations for native Americans). The most informative loci were D18S27 and D17S79. The frequency of D18S27 alleles, from 5.5 to 6 Kb, and D17S79, from 2.5 to 3.3 Kb was used to calculate the proportion of Caucasian genes. In the Pima population the value of about 6% admixture is consistent with the 5.4% value reported by Williams et al. (1992). The admixture in Cheyenne was about 26%. This value is consistent with the proportion of indian heritage (72%) calculated from stated-admixture values reported by individuals in that population. It is also consistent with the genetic similarity studies, described below, indicating a preferential clustering of this population with the Caucasian population. The results obtained with the Tobas and

Navajo populations show that these populations may contain 4% and 5% of Caucasian genes respectively. The Hispanic populations are composed mostly of Caucasian individuals, probably mixed with individuals from American populations.

Genetic similarity between populations. A clustering study

Defining similarity as the ratio of between-population and average within-population allele match probabilities, the matrix of pairwise similarities of populations, shows predictable affinities among populations (Tab. 3) and the values are quite high even between the most dissimilar populations. This is consistent with the observation that overall, alleles that are rare in one population remain so in all populations and alleles that are relatively common in one population are also common in the others. For instance, the plotting of the two leading eigenvectors (Fig. 7) shows that Hispanic populations tend to group together and so do the native American populations. This same pattern is also evident in the plotted UPGMA and complete linkage clustering trees (Figs 8 and 9). (The UPGMA clustering algorithm is based on average similarities among clusters and the complete linkage algorithm is based on maximal differences among clusters.) The negative log transformation is an arbitrary scale that was taken only to simplify presentation and can not be interpreted in terms of a degree of similarity or divergency among populations. Although the values for the match probabilities are very small, the ratio of match

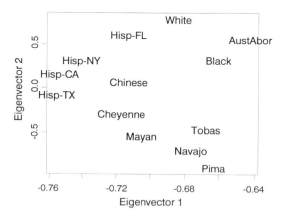

Figure 7. Plot of the leading two eigenvectors of the similarity matrix from Table 3 for the 13 populations. The intersection point for each population corresponds to the center of each name.

Table 3. Similarities among populations (unbiased) using VNTR loci (D2S44, D14S13, D17S79, D18S27)

	(2)	(3)	(4)	(5)	(6)	(7)	(8)	(9)	(10)	(11)	(12)	(13)
(1) Aust. Aborig.	0.834	0.820	0.832	0.797	0.861	0.622	0.629	0.714	0.840	0.754	0.694	0.720
(2) Cauc. USA		0.965	0.993	0.900	0.926	0.677	0.582	0.784	0.832	0.818	0.690	0.732
(3) Hisp. New York			0.986	0.976	0.988	0.824	0.782	0.891	0.884	0.865	0.800	0.859
(4) Hisp. Miami				0.935	0.948	0.741	0.650	0.844	0.893	0.834	0.747	0.783
(5) Hisp. Texas					0.988	0.888	0.885	0.956	0.890	0.844	0.876	0.948
(6) Hisp. Calif.						0.835	0.833	0.939	0.901	0.875	0.852	0.904
(7) Navajo							0.951	0.855	0.809	0.746	0.784	0.911
(8) Pima								0.847	0.821	0.709	0.830	0.923
(9) Cheyenne									0.855	0.765	0.880	0.898
(10) Chinese										0.789	0.853	0.797
(11) Black											0.654	0.746
(12) Tobas												0.857
(13) Maya												

Clustering of Ethnic Groups

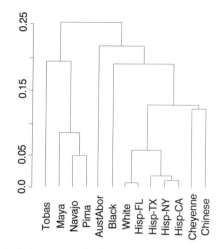

Figure 8. Clustering of ethnic groups using UPMGA. Vertical axis represents the −log of the average similarity between two clusters from the matrix data (Tab. 3). (The negative log transformation was taken to simplify presentation; these figures cannot be interpreted in terms of genetic distance.)

Clustering of Ethnic Groups

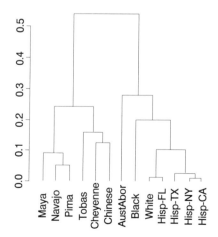

Figure 9. Clustering of ethnic groups by complete linkage. Vertical axis represents the −log of the maximum difference between two clusters from the matrix data (Tab. 3).

probabilities between these values are substantially different from 1 (Devlin and Risch, 1992). In addition, the mutation rate of this type of locus is orders of magnitude higher than those of protein markers traditionally used for studying similarity among populations. Therefore, these figures can not be interpreted in terms of genetic distance.

These trees show a high degree of similarity in the relative placement of the populations with the exception of the Cheyenne population. The complete linkage method (Fig. 9) emphasizes the affinities of the Cheyenne population to the other Amerindian groups. The UPGMA clustering method (Fig. 8), however, is most influenced by the Cheyenne's high Caucasian admixture rate, which naturally increases the average similarity between the Cheyenne, Caucasian, and Hispanic populations (which besides having a high proportion of Caucasian genes, in some populations, they also have substantial Amerindian admixture).

Overall, it is interesting to note that the relative affinity between populations obtained through the analysis of these VNTR loci resembles the genetic similarities deduced using conventional type of protein and RFLP polymorphic markers.

In conclusion, the results obtained by the analysis of DNA profiles, obtained with several VNTR loci, show that there is a high degree of similarity even among very different populations and that regardless of the population studied these loci are a powerful and highly discriminating tool for human identification.

Acknowledgements
I thank B. Devlin for useful discussion and for the development of the statistical methods and computer programs used to study the affinity between populations and B. Weir for providing the computer programs used for random DNA profile comparisons. Also I thank, J. Kidd, J. Kuhl, C. Lantz, M. Liu, L. Mattos, E. Raimondi, B. Williams, for contributing the samples for several of the populations used in this study.

References

Baeid M, Balazs I, Giusti A, Miyasaki GL, Nicholas L, Wexler K, Kanter E, Glassberg J, Allen F, Rubinstein P, Sussman L (1986) Allele frequency distribution of two highly polymorphic DNA sequences in three ethnic groups and its application to the determination of paternity. Am J Hum Genet 39: 489–501

Balazs I, Baird M, Clyne M, Meade E (1989) Human population genetic studies of five hypervariable DNA loci. Am J Hum Genet 44: 182–190

Balazs I, Neuweiler J, Gunn P, Kidd J, Kidd KK, Kuhl J, Liu M (1992) Human population studies using hypervariable loci. I. Analysis of Asamese, Australian, Cambodian, Caucasian, Chinese and Melanesian populations. Genetics 131: 191–198

Bowcock AM, Kidd JR, Mountain JL, Hebert JM, Carotenuto L, Kidd KK, Cavalli-Sforza LL (1991) Drift, admixture, and selection in human evolution: A study with DNA polymorphisms. Proc Natl Acad Sci USA 88: 839–843

Cavalli-Sforza LL, Kidd JR, Kidd KK, Bucci C, Bowcock AM, Hewlett BS, Friedlander JS (1986) DNA markers and genetic variation in human species. Cold Spring Harbor Symp Quant Biol 51: 411–417

210

Cavalli-Sforza L, Piazza A, Menozzi P, Mountain J (1988) Reconstruction of human evolution: Bringing together genetic, archaeological, and linguistic data. Proc Natl Acad Sci USA 85: 6002–6006

Chakraborty R, Kamboh MI, Nwankwo M, Ferrell RE (1992) Caucasian genes in American Blacks: New data. Am Soc Hum Genet 50: 145–155

Chakraborty R, Srinivasan MR, Andrade M de (1993) Intraclass and interclass correlations of allele sizes within and between loci in DNA typing data. Genetics 133: 411–419

Deka R, Chakraborty R, Ferrell RE (1991) A population genetic study of six VNTR loci in three ethnically defined populations. Genomics 11: 83–92

Devlin B, Risch N, Roeder K (1991) Estimation of allele frequencies for VNTR loci. Am J Hum Genet 48: 662–676

Devlin B, Risch N (1992) Ethnic differentiation at VNTR loci, with special reference to forensic applications. Am J Hum Genet 51: 534–548

Edwards A, Hammond H, Jin L, Caskey CT, Chakraborty R (1992) Genetic variation at five trimeric and tetrameric tandem repeat loci in four human population groups. Genomics 12: 241–253

Flint J, Boyce A, Martinson J, Clegg J (1989) Population bottlenecks in Polynesia revealed by minisatellites. Hum Genet 83: 257–263

Kidd J, Black F, Weiss K, Balazs I, Kidd K (1991) Studies of three amerindian populations using nuclear DNA polymorphisms. Human Biology 63: 775–794

Long J, Williams R, McAuley J (1991) Genetic variation in Arizona Mexican Americans: Estimation and interpretation of admixture proportions. American Journal of Physical Anthropology 84: 141–157

National Research Council (1992) DNA technology in forensic science. National Academy Press, Washington, DC

Nei M (1972) Genetic distance between populations. Am Nat 106: 283–292

Nei M (1987) Molecular evolutionary genetics. Columbia University press, New York

Nei M, Livshits G (1989) Genetic relationships of Europeans, Asians and Africans and the origin of Modern Homo sapiens. Hum Hered 39: 276–281

Risch N, Devlin B (1992) On the probability of matching DNA fingerprints. Science 255: 717–720

Sokal RR, Sneath PHA (1963) Principles of numerical taxonomy. W.H. Freeman, San Francisco

Weir BS (1992) Independence of VNTR alleles defined as floating bins. Am J Hum Genet 51: 992–997

Weir BS (1993) Forensic population genetics and the NRC. Am J Hum genet 52: 437–442

Williams RC, Knowler WC, Pettitt DJ, Long JC, Rokala DA, Polesky HF, Hackenberg RA, Steinberg AG, Bennett PH (1992) The magnitude and origin of European–American admixture in the Gila river community of Arizona: A union of genetics and demography. Am J Hum Genet 51: 101–110

DNA Fingerprinting: State of the Science
ed. by S. D. J. Pena, R. Chakraborty, J. T. Epplen & A. J. Jeffreys
© 1993 Birkhäuser Verlag Basel/Switzerland

Genetic variation among the Mapuche Indians from the Patagonian region of Argentina: Mitochondrial DNA sequence variation and allele frequencies of several nuclear genes

C. Ginther[a], D. Corach[b], G. A. Penacino[b], J. A. Rey[c], F. R. Carnese[d], M. H. Hutz[e], A. Anderson[a], J. Just[a], F. M. Salzano[e] and M.-C. King[a]

[a]*Department of Molecular & Cell Biology and School of Public Health, University of California, Berkeley, CA 94720, USA;* [b]*Department of Genetics and Molecular Biology, School of Pharmacy and Biochemistry, University of Buenos Aires, Argentina;* [c]*Service of Hematology and Immunohematology, School of Medicine, University of Buenos Aires, Argentina;* [d]*Juan B. Ambrosetti Museum of Ethnography, Buenos Aires, Argentina;* [e]*Department of Genetics, Institute of Biosciences, Federal University of Rio Grande del Sur, Porto Alegre, Brazil*

Summary

DNA samples from 60 Mapuche Indians, representing 39 maternal lineages, were genetically characterized for (1) nucleotide sequences of the mtDNA control region; (2) presence or absence of a nine base duplication in mtDNA region V; (3) HLA loci DRB1 and DQA1; (4) variation at three nuclear genes with short tandem repeats; and (5) variation at the polymorphic marker D2S44. The genetic profile of the Mapuche population was compared to other Amerinds and to worldwide populations.

Two highly polymorphic portions of the mtDNA control region, comprising 650 nucleotides, were amplified by the polymerase chain reaction (PCR) and directly sequenced. The 39 maternal lineages were defined by two or three generation families identified by the Mapuches. These 39 lineages included 19 different mtDNA sequences that could be grouped into four classes. The same classes of sequences appear in other Amerinds from North, Central, and South American populations separated by thousands of miles, suggesting that the origin of the mtDNA patterns predates the migration to the Americas. The mtDNA sequence similarity between Amerind populations suggests that the migration throughout the Americas occurred rapidly relative to the mtDNA mutation rate.

HLA DRB1 alleles 1602 and 1402 were frequent among the Mapuches. These alleles also occur at high frequency among other Amerinds in North and South America, but not among Spanish, Chinese or African-American populations. The high frequency of these alleles throughout the Americas, and their specificity to the Americas, supports the hypothesis that Mapuches and other Amerind groups are closely related. Frequencies of alleles of the nuclear genes encoding renin, tyrosine hydroxylase, D2S44 and CD4 in the Mapuche population did not significantly differ from the frequencies found in Caucasian, African-American, Mexican-American, or Asian populations.

Introduction

Knowledge of the amount and nature of genetic diversity in modern humans would provide insight into our evolutionary history (Cavalli-Sforza et al., 1991). Much of this diversity exists in genetically isolated populations with genetic characteristics that reflect their unique evolutionary past, and that are only rarely found in the general population. However, many isolated, genetically unique population groups are disappearing as their cultures are integrated into the general society where their genetic profiles become indistinguishable in the general gene pool. In the worst cases, isolated peoples may completely disappear, with permanent loss of their unique genetic characteristics. As a result, there is presently great interest in preserving genetic information of populations that are in danger of disappearing (Cavalli-Sforza et al., 1991).

Genetic analysis of Amerind populations can reveal the time(s) of their origin in the Americas, the rate at which the Americas were populated, and the genetic relationships between modern Amerinds in North, South and Central America. Mapuches are of particular interest because they inhabit a large portion of southern Chile and Argentina extending from Patagonia to the northeastern pampas. Thus Mapuches represent a southern geographical extreme of Amerind migration. In this study, DNA samples from 60 Mapuches were characterized for mitochondrial sequences and several nuclear genes.

The mtDNA control region sequence was examined because it is the most polymorphic region of mtDNA (Vigilant, 1986; Horai and Hayasaka, 1990; DiRienzo and Wilson, 1991; Stoneking et al., 1991; Ward et al., 1991). mtDNA is also maternally inherited, making it possible to follow mutational changes in mtDNA sequences more easily than those at nuclear genes. In addition, a sequence of non-coding region V of mtDNA was examined because it contains a length polymorphism of 9 nucleotides in East Asian populations (Horai and Matsunaga, 1986; Hertzberg et al., 1989; Harihara et al., 1992), and Amerind populations (Schurr et al., 1990; Ward et al., 1991; Wallace and Torroni, 1992; C. Orrego, personal communication).

Several nuclear polymorphic markers were examined. HLA DRB1 and DQA1 were selected because they are highly polymorphic, and are among the most well-studied genetic markers in human populations, including Amerinds (Fernandez-Vina et al., 1991; Black et al., 1991). In addition, tetranucleotide and pentanucleotide repeat polymorphisms at tyrosine hydroxylase (THO1), renin (REN), and CD4 were genotyped (Edwards et al., 1991a, b, 1992). These and other polymorphisms based on tandem repeats of 3 to 5 nucleotides may become especially useful for genetic analysis of populations, because they are sufficiently polymorphic to distinguish closely related populations (Black, 1991) and may be typable by automated systems (Edwards et al., 1991a). Finally, D2S44 was examined, because it has proven highly polymorphic in all populations.

Population and methods

The Mapuche population

This study includes Mapuches from the community of Anecon Grande in the Department of 25 de Mayo, Province of Rio Negro, Argentina ($69°30'W$; $41°30'S$). Anthropological studies indicate that this community comprises 76 individuals (37 males, 39 females) from 22 families (the demographics of this population will be described by Carnese and Caratini, Runa XXI, in press). DNA was obtained from 60 individuals who represented 39 maternal lineages.

DNA Extraction and polymerase chain reaction

Blood (10 ml) was drawn into tubes with anticoagulant, and DNA extracted by standard methods (Sambrook et al., 1982). The DNA regions of interest were PCR amplified using conditions that have been described: symmetrical and asymmetrical amplification of the mtDNA control region (Vigilant, 1986; Ginther et al., 1992); amplification of region V (Wrischnik et al., 1987); amplification of polymorphic genomic marker pentamer CD-4 (Edwards et al., 1991b), and trimeric or tetrameric tandem repeats HUMTHO1 and HUMREN (Edwards et al., 1991a, 1992); and HLA alleles (Lahammar et al., 1982; Tsuji et al., 1992). PCR amplifications of region V, CD-4, HUMTHO1 and HUMREN incorporated [α-^{32}P]-ATP for labeling of the product.

Analysis of PCR products

The method used for directly sequencing regions 1 and 2 of the mtDNA control region has been described (Vigilant, 1986; Ginther et al., 1992). PCR amplification of the mtDNA control region was conducted in two stages. Initially, the entire mtDNA control region was symmetrically amplified using primers L15926 and H580. The symmetrical DNA product was used for subsequent asymmetrical PCR amplifications of variable regions 1 (using primers L15996 and H16498) and 2 (using primers L29 and H408) to produce single-stranded DNA for sequencing. Nucleotide sequences of the single-stranded DNA were determined using the dideoxynucleotide method (Sequenase 2.0 reagent kit, U.S. Biochemical) with α-^{35}S ATP as the labeling nucleotide. Reaction products were separated by electrophoresis on 6% polyacrylamide/7 M urea gels and detected by exposure to film (Kodak XAR-5) for 1–2 days. Approximately 350 nucleotides were determined in region 1 (nucleotides

16050–16400 in the Anderson system) and 300 in region 2 (nucleotides 70–370) for a total of 650 nucleotides.

The length variations in radioactively labeled region V and the minisatellite alleles were analyzed by electrophoresis on 6% polyacrylamide/7 M urea gels and detected by exposure to film (Kodak XAR-5) for 1 day. The sizes of the alleles were determined by comparison with a labeled M13 phage sequence ladder. Data reported are only for individuals thought to be unrelated.

HLA DQA1 alleles were detected by hybridizing amplified sequences with P32-labeled sequence-specific oligonucleotides (Gyllensten and Erlich, 1988). HLA DRB1 was genotyped by digestion of DNA with *Taq* I followed by Southern blot hybridization with probe pRTV1 (Bidwell and Jarrold, 1986). Some DRB1 genotypes based on southern blot were defined more specifically by hybridizing amplified DRB1 with sequence specific oligonucleotides (Tsuji et al., 1992).

D2S44 alleles were identified by probing *Hinf* I restricted Mapuche DNA with radioactively labeled probe YNH-24 using standard Southern hybridization methods (Sambrook et al., 1989).

Results

Mitochondrial DNA variation

Variation in the mtDNA sequences of the 39 Mapuche lineages is shown in Tab. 1. There were 19 different sequences, each falling into one of four patterns defined by shared nucleotides (in the boxed columns of Tab. 1). The sequences in Group 1 share the following characteristics: C at position 16217, C at position 16189, and a nine base deletion in region V. There was no exception to the association between the presence of the region V deletion and the Group I sequence pattern in the control region. Unlike the other patterns, these sequences contain a C at 16223. Group I contained 15 (38%) of the maternal lineages with 6 different sequences. Group II sequences all have a double deletion of two adenosine residues at positions 286–291, and one of the two adenosine residues at positions 248–249. They also share common sequence variations of a C at 16298, C at 16325 and T at 16327. Group II contained 8 (21%) maternal lineages with 5 different sequences. Group III sequences all share the pattern variation: T at 16223, T at 16290, A at 16319, C at 16362, C at 146, T at 150, and G at 153. Group III contained 6 (15%) of the maternal lineages with 2 different sequences. Group IV is a more diverse group sharing the following: T at 16223; C at 16362, and often C at 16325 and/or 16304, and T at 16187. This group contained 10 (26%) of the maternal lineages and 8 unique sequences.

Table 1. Mapuche mtDNA Sequences[a]

Number of lineages	Region 1 (16000+) 051	092	124	187	189	207	217	223	242	245	249	270	290	291	294	298	311	319	325	327	362	390	Region 2 073	143	146	150	152	153	189	195	207	249	258	263	290	291	309	316	316
Pattern 1																																							
2	.	.	.	.	C	G	C	.	.	.	.	.	.	T	.	.	.	.	.	.	.	.	G	.	.	.	C	.	.	.	.	.	.	G	.	.	C	C	C
2	.	.	.	.	C	.	C	.	.	.	.	.	.	.	T	.	.	.	.	.	.	.	G	.	.	.	.	.	.	.	A	.	.	G	.	.	C	–	C
5	.	.	.	.	C	.	C	.	.	.	.	.	.	.	.	.	.	C	.	.	.	.	G	.	.	.	.	.	.	.	A	.	.	G	.	.	C	–	C
1	.	.	.	.	C	.	C	.	.	.	.	.	.	.	.	.	.	C	.	.	.	.	G	.	.	.	.	.	.	.	A	.	.	G	.	.	C	C	C
4	.	.	C	.	C	.	C	.	.	.	C	.	.	.	.	.	.	.	.	.	.	.	G	.	.	.	.	G	C	.	A	.	.	G	.	.	C	–	C
1	.	.	.	.	C	.	C	.	.	.	C	.	.	.	.	.	.	.	.	.	.	.	G	.	.	.	.	G	.	.	A	.	.	G	.	.	C	–	C
All pattern 1 sequences have 9 nucleotide deletion in region V																																							
Pattern 2																																							
3	.	.	.	.	.	.	.	T	.	.	.	.	.	.	.	C	.	.	C	T	.	.	G	.	.	.	.	.	.	.	.	–	T	G	–	–	C	–	C
2	.	.	.	.	.	.	.	T	.	.	.	.	.	.	.	C	.	.	C	T	.	.	G	.	.	.	.	.	.	.	.	–	T	G	–	–	C	C	C
1	.	.	.	.	C	.	.	T	.	.	.	.	.	.	.	C	.	.	C	T	.	.	G	.	.	.	.	.	.	.	.	–	.	G	–	–	C	C	C
1	G	.	.	.	.	.	.	T	.	.	.	.	.	.	.	C	.	.	C	T	.	.	G	.	.	.	.	.	.	.	.	–	T	G	–	–	C	C	C
1	.	.	.	.	.	.	.	T	.	.	.	.	.	.	.	C	.	.	C	T	.	.	G	.	.	.	.	.	.	.	.	–	T	G	–	–	C	–	–
Pattern 3																																							
4	.	.	.	.	.	.	.	T	T	.	.	.	.	.	.	.	C	.	C	.	C	.	G	.	.	.	C	.	.	.	.	.	.	G	.	.	C	–	–
2	.	.	.	T	.	.	.	T	.	.	.	.	.	.	.	.	.	.	C	.	C	.	G	.	.	.	.	.	.	.	.	.	.	G	.	.	C	–	C
1	.	.	.	T	.	.	.	T	.	.	.	.	.	.	.	.	.	.	C	.	C	.	G	.	.	.	C	.	.	.	.	.	.	G	.	.	C	–	C
1	.	.	.	T	.	.	.	T	.	.	.	.	.	.	.	.	.	.	C	.	?	A	G	.	C	.	C	.	.	.	.	.	.	G	.	.	C	–	C
1	.	.	.	T	.	.	.	T	.	T	.	T	.	.	.	.	.	.	C	.	C	A	G	.	C	.	C	.	.	.	.	.	.	G	.	.	C	–	–
1	.	C	.	T	C	.	.	T	.	.	.	.	.	.	.	.	.	.	.	.	C	.	G	A	.	.	.	.	.	.	.	.	.	G	.	.	C	–	–
Pattern 4																																							
4	.	.	.	.	.	.	.	T	.	.	.	.	T	.	.	.	.	A	.	.	C	.	G	.	C	T	.	G	.	.	.	.	.	G	.	.	C	–	–
2	.	.	.	.	.	.	.	T	.	.	.	.	T	.	.	.	.	A	.	.	C	.	G	.	C	T	.	G	G	.	.	.	.	G	.	.	C	–	–

[a]Nucleotides are numbered according to Anderson et al. (1981)

Table 2. Frequencies of DRB1-DQA1 haplotypes among Mapuches (N = 56 chromosomes)

DRB1	DQA1	Frequency
01	0101	0.02
04	0301	0.23
0701	0201	0.02
08	0401	0.16
1001	0101	0.02
11	0501	0.02
1302	0102	0.07
1401	0101	0.03
1402	0501	0.30
1602	0501	0.11
0301	0501	0.02

Table 3. Allele frequencies at nuclear loci among Mapuches

Marker	N^a	Allele	Frequency
CD4	79	A3[b]	0.38
		A4	0.06
		A5	0.00
		A6	0.03
		A7	0.10
		A8	0.43
THO1	77	6[c]	0.45
		7	0.17
		8	0.00
		9	0.03
		10	0.35
REN	72	8[c]	0.79
		9	0.00
		10	0.19
		11	0.02
D2S44	40	5080[d]	0.025
		4600	0.050
		4420	0.025
		4072	0.025
		3909	0.125
		3753	0.075
		3402	0.025
		3279	0.050
		2947	0.025
		2798	0.025
		2431	0.075
		2142	0.300
		1711	0.050
		1681	0.050

[a]N = number of chromosomes. Data from parents within families and individuals with no family designation (theoretically 40 people with 80 alleles). In several cases, alleles of missing parents were deduced from those of the children. Some parental alleles could not be deduced.
[b]Alleles as described in Edwards et al. (1991b)
[c]Number of repeats
[d]Fragment size by comparison to 1 kb ladder; 20 Mapuche examined

Frequencies of HLA DRB1-DQA1 haplotypes among 28 unrelated Mapuches are presented in Tab. 2. The Mapuche population included 11 different DRB1-DQA1 haplotypes, but 80% were the four types 04-0301 (23%); 08-0401 (16%); 1402-0501 (30%); and 1602-0501 (11%). DRB1 alleles 1602 and 1402, which are rare in Spanish, Chinese, and African-American populations, but common in other Amerind populations (Tsuji et al., 1992), were also common among Mapuches, with frequencies 0.11 and 0.30. Allele frequencies at CD-4, tyrosine hydroxylase, renin, and D2S44 loci among the Mapuches are shown in Tab. 3.

Discussion

Genetic studies of Amerind mtDNA sequences suggest common origins for the Amerind populations of North, Central, and South America (Wallace and Torroni, 1982). These groups appear to be descended from four mtDNA lineages. All four sequence pattern types occurred in the Mapuche community that we examined. These patterns are also characteristic of the Nuu-Chah-Nulth (Ward et al., 1991), the Xavante (Salzano, unpublished), the Aymara, the Toba, and the Quechua (Ginther et al., unpublished), and a wide variety of other North, South and Central Amerinds (Torrino et al., unpublished), suggesting that the four basic patterns predate the arrival of the Amerind maternal ancestors in the New World. Variations within each pattern may reflect mutations that occurred after migration into the Americas. The relatively small amount of variation within each pattern indicates that the original mtDNA patterns spread throughout the Americas rapidly relative to the mtDNA mutation rate.

The sequence variations that exist within the mtDNA pattern types may be useful for tracing Amerind migrations and relationships. As more Amerind sequences become available, it may be possible to follow the appearance and flow of specific subsets of each pattern during the development of different Amerind groups. There are nucleotide variations within the Mapuche sequences that have not been observed in the small number of published Amerind sequences. It will be interesting to discover if these variations are found in other South Amerinds or are unique to the Mapuche.

The HLA types of Toba, Toba-Pilaga, and Mataco-Wichi populations from Gran Chaco in Argentina, and of Mapuche from the reservation of Ruca Choroi in the Provincia de Neuquen, Argentina have been determined (Cerna et al., 1992; Haas et al., 1985). In the Amerind populations from Gran Chaco, 90% of DRB1 alleles were DRB1*04, 14, and 0802, and in the previously studied Mapuche of Ruca Choroi, the most common alleles were DR4 (DRB1*04; 0.61), and DR2 (DRB1*1601, 1602; 0.15). The Mapuches examined in this study have high frequencies of DRB1*04 (0.23), 0802 (0.16) 14 (0.30 of DRB1*1402), and DRB1*1602 (0.11), sharing the most frequent alleles of both previously examined Argentine Amerind groups. Differences in allele frequencies may reflect as-yet-unidentified selective pressure or genetic drift. The shared alleles among South Amerind populations suggest a relatively recent common genetic past.

The other genomic markers (THO1, REN, CD4, and D2S44) in the Mapuches did not have unusual allele frequencies relative to other populations worldwide.

Our mtDNA data are consistent with an early and rapid spread of Amerind populations through the Americas. It is possible that the Pacific coastline provided an efficient route of transport along the west coast of the Americas, allowing rapid migration to widely separated geographic portions of the New World. As other Amerind groups are examined, it will be interesting to discover if there are especially close similarities between Amerinds of the west coast of the Americas compared to areas such as northeastern South America and the Caribbean Islands.

Acknowledgements
This work was supported in part by NIH grant HG00263 to MCK and CG and grants from CONICET (PID:3148500/88) and the Antorchas Foundation to DC.

References

Anderson S, Baker AT, Barrell BG, de Bruijn MHL, Coulson AR, Drouin J, Eperon IC, Nierlich DP, Roe BA, Sanger F, Schreier PH, Smith AJH, Staden R, Young IG (1981) Sequence and organization of the human mitochondrial genome. Nature 290: 457–465

Bidwell JL, Jarrold EA (1986) HLA-DR allogenotyping using exon-specific cDNA probes and application of rapid minigel methods. Molec Immunol 23: 1111–1116

Cavalli-Sforza LL, Wilson AC, Cantor CR, Cook-Deegan R, King MC (1991) Editorial. Call for a worldwide survey of human genetic diversity: A vanishing opportunity for the human genome project. Genomics 11: 490–491

Cerna M, Falco M, Friedman H, Raimondi E, Fernandez-Vina MA, Stastny P (1992) HLA class II alleles in South American Indians reflect their ancient migratory movements. Human Immunol 34: 19

DiRienzo A, Wilson AC (1991) Branching pattern in the evolutionary tree for human mitochondrial DNA. Proc Natl Acad Sci USA 88: 1597–1601

Edwards A, Civitello A, Hammond HA, Caskey CT (1991a) DNA typing and genetic mapping with trimeric and tetrameric tandem repeats. Am J Hum Genet 49: 746–756

Edwards A, Hammond HA, Jin L, Caskey CT, Chakraborty R (1992) Genetic variation at trimeric and tetrameric tandem repeat loci in four human population groups. Genomics 12: 241–253

Edwards ML, Clemens PR, Tristan M, Pizzuti A, Gibbs RA (1991b) Pentanucleotide repeat length polymorphism at the human CD4 locus. Nucleic Acids Res 19: 4791

Fernandez-Vina M, Moraes JR, Moraes ME, Miller S, Stastny P (1991) HLA class II haplotypes in Amerinds and in black North and South Americans. Tissue Antigens 38: 234–237

Ginther C, Issel-Tarver L, King M-C (1992) Identifying individuals by sequencing mitochondrial DNA from teeth. Nature Genet 2: 135–138

Gyllensten UB, Ehrlich HA (1988) Generation of single-stranded DNA by the polymerase chain reaction and its application to direct sequencing of the HLA-DQα locus. Proc Natl Acad Sci USA 85: 7652–7656

Haas EJC, Salzano FM, Araujo HS, Grossman F, Baretti A, Weimer TA, Franco M, Verruno I, Nasif O, Morales VII, Arienti R (1985) HLA antigens and other genetic markers in the Mapuche Indians of Argentina. Hum Hered 35: 306–313

Harihara S, Hirai M, Suutou Y, Shimizu K, Omoto K (1992) Frequency of a 9-bp deletion in the mitochondrial DNA among Asian populations. Hum Genet 64: 161–166

Hertzberg M, Mickleson KNP, Serjeantson SW, Prio JF, Trent RJ (1989) An Asian specific 9 bp deletion of mitochondrial DNA is frequently found in Polynesians. Amer J Hum Genet 44: 504–510

Horai S, Hayasaka K (1991) Intraspecific nucleotide sequence differences in the major noncoding region of mitochondrial DNA. Amer J Hum Genet 46: 828–842

Horai S, Matsunaga E (1986) Mitochondrial DNA polymorphism in Japanese. II. Analysis with restriction enzymes of four or five base pair recognition. Hum Genet 72: 105–117

Larhammar C, Schenning L, Gustafsson K, et al. (1992) Complete amino acid sequence of an HLA-DR antigen-like beta chain as predicted from nucleotide sequence: Similarities with immunoglobin and HLA-A, -B and -C antigens. Proc Natl Acad Sci USA 79: 3678–3691

Sambrook J, Fritsch HF, Maniatis T (1989) Molecular Cloning: A Laboratory Manual. 2nd ed. Cold Spring Harbor Laboratory Press, New York.

Schurr TG, Hallinger SW, Gan YY, Hodge JA, Merriwether DA, Lawrence DA, Knowler WC, Weiss KM, Wallace DC (1990) Amerindian mitochondrial DNAs have rare Asian mutations at high frequencies, suggesting they derived from four primary maternal lineages. Amer J Hum Genet 46: 613–623

Stoneking M, Hedgecock D, Higuchi RG, Vigilant L, Erlich HA (1991) Population variation of human mtDNA control region sequences detected by enzymatic amplification and sequence-specific oligonucleotide probes. Amer J Hum Genet 48: 370–382

Stoneking M, Wilson AC (1988) In: Hill A, Serjeantson S (eds) The Colonization of the Pacific: A Genetic Trail. Oxford University Press, Oxford

Tsuji K, Aizawa M, Sasazuki T, eds. (1992) Proceedings of the 11th Histocompatibility Workshop and Conference, November 1991. Oxford Press, Oxford

Vigilant LA (1986) Control region sequences from African populations and the evolution of human mitochondrial DNA. PhD dissertation, Univ California, Berkeley

Wallace DC, Torroni A (1992) American Indian prehistory as written in the mitochondrial DNA: A review. Human Biology 64: 403–416

Ward RH, Frazier BL, Dew-Jager K, Paabo S (1991) Extensive mitochondrial diversity within a single Amerind tribe. Proc Natl Acad Sci USA 88: 8720–8724

Wrischnik LA, Higuchi RG, Stoneking M, Erlich HA, Arnheim N, Wilson AC (1987) Length mutations in human mitochondrial DNA: direct sequencing of enzymatically amplified DNA. Nucleic Acids Res 15: 529–542

DNA Fingerprinting: State of the Science
ed. by S. D. J. Pena, R. Chakraborty, J. T. Epplen & A. J. Jeffreys
© 1993 Birkhäuser Verlag Basel/Switzerland

Microsatellite and HLA class II oligonucleotide typing in a population of Yanomami Indians

L. Roewer, M. Nagy, P. Schmidt[a], J. T. Epplen[a] and
G. Herzog-Schröder[b]

Institut für Gerichtliche Medizin, Humboldt-Universität, Hannoversche Str. 6, 10115 Berlin, Germany; [a]*Molekulare Humangenetik, MA, Ruhr-Universität, Universitätsstr. 150, 44780 Bochum, Germany;* [b]*Forschungsstelle für Humanethologie, Max-Planck-Gesellschaft, Von-der Tann-Strasse 3–5, 82346 Andechs, Germany*

Summary
We have used three different microsatellites (on chromosome 12 and Y) together with HLA class II oligonucleotide typing (*DQA* and *DQB*) to analyze families of Yanomami indians settling in villages in Southern Venezuela. There exist complex networks of biological relationship between villages as a result of wife exchange, village fissioning and changing patterns of alliances associated with inter-village warfare. Social status in this society is largely determined by the kinship system. Polygyny is common, especially among headmen, with additional wives, frequently being chosen among the sisters of the first wife. Our preliminary results mainly obtained from inhabitants of the village HAP show the expected allele distribution in populations with a high degree of consanguinity: (i) deficiency of observed heterozygotes at the autosomal loci and (ii) almost all men carry the same Y chromosomal allele. Nevertheless in the Yanomami village two thirds of the described autosomal microsatellite alleles were identified. Several paternities were clarified.

Introduction

One of the few peoples of the Amazon lowland who stayed in relative isolation until recent times are the Yanomami indians. Traditionally the Yanomami settled around small rivulets in the headwaters of the Orinoco, Rio Negro and Rio Branco. The Yanomami live in self-contained communities of 40 to 200 inhabitants and subsist by simple agriculture, hunting and gathering. The number of Yanomami living in Venezuela is estimated at 10,000 (Herzog-Schröder, in press).

The kinship system of the Yanomami is a classificatory one according to the Iroqouis type (i.e. siblings and parallel cousins are terminologically equivalent but distinguished from cross-cousins) and the bilateral cross-cousin is the prescriptive marriage-partner. Husbands or wives are found within or without the local group. Due to an imbalanced sex-ratio and polygyny, women are in short supply, so that many men are forced to obtain women from other villages. Within a village 95% of the inhabitants are cognative relatives. 50% of a village population stands in an in-law relationship to an ego. The other 50% are "cultural relatives", i.e. the group among which a spouse can not be chosen.

222

Figure 1. Territory inhabited by the Yanomami in Southern Venezuela and Northern Brazil.

These proportions warrant that each individual can marry his or her ideal partner according to the cross-cousin marriage rule (Chagnon, 1980).

The band-society of Yanomami indians has been studied with respect to their blood groups, serum proteins and erythrocyte enzyme systems (Gershowitz et al., 1972; Weitkamp et al., 1972; Weitkamp and Neel, 1972; Tanis et al., 1973; Ward et al., 1975). A few studies have been carried out involving DNA analysis in Amerindian populations (Wallace et al., 1985; Schurr et al., 1990; Kidd et al., 1991; Guerreiro et al., 1992).

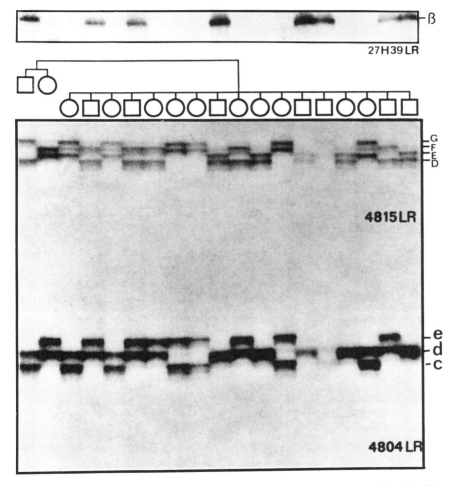

Figure 2. DNA samples of a large German family typed at 3 microsatellite loci. For methodological details see the materials and methods section. The autosomal loci 4804LR and 4815LR were PCR-amplified simultaneously, the Y-chromosomal 27H39LR locus was amplified separately. The lengths of the alleles c, d, e (4804LR) are 159 bp, 163 bp and 167 bp, respectively; the allele lengths of D, E, F, G are 246 bp, 250 bp, 254 bp and 258 bp, respectively; the allele β (27H39LR) is 190 bp long.

Table 1. Characteristics of autosomal and Y-chromosomal polymorphic loci in Germans and Yanomami indians from the village of HAP

Locus (chromosomal localization)	Allele	Allele frequencies [Heterozygosity rates: observed/expected]	
		Germans	Yanomami
		no. of chromosomes 208	no. of chromosomes 44[a]
4804 LR (12)	a	12	0
	b	12	3
	c	121	35
	d	37	4
	e	22	2
	f	4	0
		[0.612/0.611]	[0.364/0.353]
		no. of chromosomes 188	no. of chromosomes 32[a]
4815 LR (12)	A	6	0
	B	6	0
	C	18	1
	D	47	4
	E	47	13
	F	35	13
	G	21	2
	H	8	0
		[0.846/0.815]	[0.687/0.670]
		no. of chromosomes 48	no. of chromosomes 11[a]
27H39 LR (Y)	α	8	10
	β	21	1
	γ	11	0
	δ	8	0
	[gene diversity:	0.706	0.165]
		no. of chromosomes 350	
HLA-DQA	03	54	–
	04	9	–
		no. of chromosomes 622	
HLA-DQB	0402	16	–

[a]For the calculations of allele frequencies and heterozygosity rates in the Yanomami sample only largely unrelated individuals were included.

The microsatellite DNA markers used in this study are of the GATA type located on chromosome 12 (4804 LR and 4815 LR) and Y (27H39 LR) (Roewer et al., 1992). 6 alleles are described for 4804LR, 8 for 4815LR and 4 for the 27H39LR locus in a number of caucasoids (Roewer et al., 1992; and Tab. 1). Because of the shortness of the PCR amplified length variable alleles informative typing of old and degraded DNA is possible. The sensitivity of PCR allows the collection of hairs instead of blood for discriminative DNA analysis. HLA class II genes are analyzed by the PCR-based oligotyping method.

Materials and methods

Genomic DNA was extracted from 3–10 hairs by an "in-one-tube extraction" method (Kawasaki, 1990). Repeat flanking oligonucleotide primers for the $(GATA)_n$ microsatellite loci were used as described previously (Roewer et al., 1992). Approximately 100–250 ng DNA was used for a 25-μl PCR sample with 2 U Taq polymerase in the buffer recommended by the suppliers (Promega). The $MgCl_2$ concentration was 2.5 mM. Amplifications were performed for 30 cycles with 30 sec denaturation at 94°C, 30 sec primer annealing at 51°C and 90 sec extension at 72°C in a PCR thermocycler (Biomed). Simultaneous multilocus PCR using the 3 primer pairs was carried out under identical conditions. Gel purification of the repeat-containing fragments, radioactive labelling of the fragments, PAGE and X-ray exposure were performed as previously described (Roewer et al., 1991). A standard ladder of the known alleles was used for sizing the bands.

HLA class II oligotyping (*DQA1* and *DQB1* loci) was done following the protocols of the 11th International Histocompatibility Workshop in Yokohama (1991).

Results

89 individuals were analyzed at the $(GATA)_n$ microsatellite loci 4804LR, 4815LR (both linked on chromosome 12) and 27H39LR (chromosome Y). 75 individuals originate from the village HAP, the remaining ones stem from the surrounding villages WAW, SHI, ARI, MAH and MAA (Tab. 2).

In HAP 33 males and 42 females live in 3 generations. We found several polygyneous families and 2 polyandreous families. 23 individuals of the ancestral generation, who are possibly also more or less related, were chosen for the calculation of observed allele frequencies, heterozygosity rates and gene diversities (Nei, 1973) (see Tab. 1). The

Table 2. Microsatellite typing of 89 Yanomami indians from 6 villages (*F* father; *M* mother; *C* child; *m* male; *f* female; *04* locus 4804LR; *15* locus 4815LR; *Y* locus 27H39LR); closely related individuals are put to groups if possible

HAP		Sex	04/15	/Y
1	F	m	cc/EF	/α
2	M	f	cd/DF	/−
3	C1	m	cd/DE	/α
4	C2	m	cd/DE	/α
5	C3	f	cd/DF	/−
6	C4	f	cd/DE	/−
7	F	m	cc/DF	/α
8	M	f	bc/EF	/−
9	C1	m	cc/DF	/α
10	C2	m	bc/ED	/α
11	F	m	cc/EE	/α
12	M	f	cc/EF	/−
13	C1	f	cc/EF	/−
14	C2	m	cc/EE	/α
15	C3/M	f	cc/EG	/−
16	F	m	cc/FF	/α
17	C1/F	m	cc/FG	/α
18	M	f	cc/EG	/−
19	C	f	cc/GG	/−
20	M	f	cd/EE	/−
21	C1	f	cc/	/−
22	C2	f	cc/EF	/−
23	C3	f	cd/	/−
24	C4	m	/	/α
25	C5/M	f	cd/EF	/−
26	C1	m	cc/	/α
27	C2	f	cc/EF	/−
28	C3	m	cd/EF	/β
56		f	cd/DF	/−
29	F	m	cc/	D/α
30	M	f	ce/	/−
31	C1	m	ce/	/
32	C2	f	cc/	/−
33	C3/M	f	cc/EF	/−
34	F	m	cc/	/α
35	C1	m	cc/EF	/α
36	C2	f	cc/	/−
37	C3	m	cc/	/α
38	C4	f	cc/	/−
39	C5	f	cc/	/−
40	C6	m	cc/EF	/
41	F	m	be/CE	/α
42	C1	f	bc/EG	/−
43	C2	m	ce/CG	/α

HAP		Sex	04/15	/Y
44	F	m	cc/EF	/α
45	M	f	bc/ F	/−
46	C1	f	bc/DF	/−
47	C2	f	cc/FF	/−
48	C3	m	cc/DF	/α
49	C4		cc/FF	/−
50	M	f	cc/EE	/−
51	C1	f	cc/EE	/−
52	C2	m	cc/	/α
53		m	cc/FF	/α
54		m	cc/FG	/α
55		m	bc/EF	/α
57	M	f	cc/FF	/−
58	C1	m	cc/	/α
59	C2	f	bc/	/−
60		f	cc/	/−
61		m	cd/DF	/α
62		f	bc/	/−
63	F	m	cc/	/α
64	M	f	cc/	/−
65	C	m	/	/α
66		f	cc/EG	/−
67		f	cd/	/−
68		f	cc/	/−
69		f	cc/EF	/−
70		m	/	/
71		f	cc/	/−
72		m	cc/	/α
73		f	/	/−
74		f	cc/	/−
75		f	cc/	/−

WAW

		Sex	04/15	/Y
1		m	/	/α
4		m	/	/β
7	F	m	cc/EF	/α
8	M	f	cc/DE	/−
9	C1	f	cc/DF	/−
10	C2	f	cc/DE	/−
13		m	/	/α

MAH

		Sex	04/15	/Y
1		m	/	/β
4		m	/	/α
11		m	/	/α
19		m	/	/α

MAA

		Sex	04/15	/Y
1		m	/	/β

ARI

		Sex	04/15	/Y
1		m	/	/α

SHI

		Sex	04/15	/Y
1		m	/	/α

alleles found in the Yanomami are not different from those observed in a German control sample. Both populations were tested for different allele frequencies using Fisher's exact test (SAS Institute Inc., 1991). For each locus allele-wise comparisons were evaluated allowing for multiple testing. Appropriate thresholds for the error probability P, calculated by division of 0.050 by the number of alleles, were 0.008 (4804LR), 0.006 (4815LR), and 0.012 (27H39LR), respectively. Significant differences were found for 4804LR, with allele c being significantly more frequent in the Yanomami sample ($P = 0.005$), and for 27H39LR, with allele α being dramatically overrepresented among Yanomami males ($P = 6.52 \times 10^{-6}$). For locus 4815LR, the deficiency of allele G (2/33 vs 21/188) respresents a borderline result ($P = 0.0098$). According to the test the allele distribution at the autosomal loci appears to be not substantially different from that in caucasoids. Rare alleles are lacking in the investigated Yanomami most probably because of the small sample size. As expected the observed heterozygosity rates differ markedly between the populations. In contrast to the diversity at the chromosome 12 loci we see in HAP at the Y chromosomal locus 27H39LR always the α allele with only one exception. In this case the allele β was typed, a man (HAP 28) whose father is dead and whose descent is unknown due to a strong taboo of mentioning deceased relatives. Also WAW 4, MAA 1 and MAH 1 carry the allele β (MAA 1 is the father of MAH 1, and WAW 4 is the son-in-law of MAA 1). Historically the villages ARI and WAW are relatively isolated, whereas the village MAA is a split of MAA and SHI. All the investigated villages are located within walking distance. Other Y chromosomal alleles are lacking in the investigated population.

Sequence analysis confirmed identity between α alleles in Germans and Yanomami (data not shown).

Several families were additionally typed at the MHC loci *DQA1* and *DQB1*. Due to the limited amount of DNA extracted from hairs the sample size was too small to calculate *HLA-DQ* allele frequencies for Yanomami indians. Despite the comparatively homogeneous Yanomami population two exclusions from paternity were found: a) HAP 49 is not the son of HAP 3 but probably of HAP 44: b) Hap 41 is not the son of HAP 57. Further details concerning family relationships are shown in figures. In the pedigree depicted in Fig. 3 the "strange" woman HAP 18, brought by HAP 17 from another village, is probably his true cross-cousin. Neither of the parents of HAP 17 has direct siblings so he probably chose to look back at least two generations to keep the idea of the cross-cousin marriage rule. Figure 4 shows the situation of two possible fathers for the deceased woman HAP X. The typing at the locus 4815LR increases the probability that HAP 54 is her father rather than HAP 1.

228

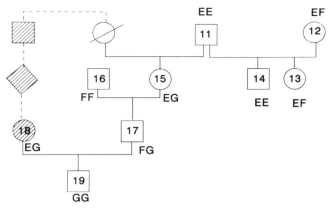

Figure 3. Pedigree of a HAP Yanomami family. Capitals symbolize the typed 4815LR alleles. Hatched symbols mark putative relatives of the mother of HAP 15 who transmit the rare allele G. The family of HAP 18 lives in another village. Symbolized is the hypothetic inheritance of the allele G typed in the "stranger", HAP 18. HAP 17 and HAP 18 are probably marriage partners corresponding to the preferential cross-cousin marriage rule. Additionally typed HLA class II alleles: *DQA*: HAP 15: *03, 04*; HAP 16, 17: *03*. *DQB*: HAP 15, 16, 17: *0402*.

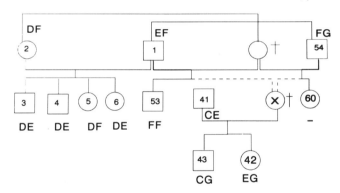

Figure 4. Pedigree of a Yanomami family of HAP. Capitals symbolize the typed 4815LR alleles. HAP 1 and HAP 54 represent two putative fathers of the deceased woman HAP X. The rare allele G identified in the children of HAP X increases the paternity probability of HAP 54.

Discussion

Anthropological field observations, especially the ethological research, is generally dependent upon more or less reliable information by the observed people themselves. DNA microsatellite typing via PCR is a promising method for more objectivity in anthropology. One can individualize minimal amounts of DNA e.g. in hairs which are easier to collect from people and are easy to preserve for months than blood. Microsatellites based on tetranucleotide repeats yield short PCR-amplifiable alleles with a simpler profile (less slippage artifacts) than seen at the frequently used CA repeat loci (Roewer et al., 1992; Edwards et al., 1992).

Microsatellite polymorphisms are in the informative range of some serological markers, but the information increases by typing two or more loci consecutively or even better simultaneously. In a multiplex PCR one hair root is enough to type the 3 above-mentioned markers. The MHC class II oligotyping requires more DNA but delivers more higher information. The Y chromosomal microsatellite is essential to yield information about male descendence lineages in the investigated populations. The village HAP seems to be founded by close male relatives after fissioning of a larger community. Probably females contribute mainly to the considerable variability checked at the autosomal loci. These women were either captured or came from other villages to which exist alliances. The preferential cross-cousin marriage rule (ccm) was additionally confirmed in some cases with the help of microsatellite typing. In all cases one has to have the ethnological field research data in mind contributing to the probability of paternity.

The similar allele distribution in unrelated Germans and Yanomami reflects the origin of the polymorphisms by slippage mutation events without influence of selection pressure.

Acknowledgements
We are indebted to the friendly cooperating people of the Yanomami. We would like to thank Dr. Michael Krawczak for valuable comments. This work was supported by the VW-Stiftung.

References

Chagnon NA (1980) Kin selection theory, kinship, marriage and fitness among the Yanomama indians. *In:* Barlow GW, Silverberg J (eds) Sociobiology: Beyond Nature/Nurture. Reports, Definitions, Debate. American Anthropol Association 35: 545–571

Edwards A, Hammond HA, Jin L, Caskey CT, Chakraborty R (1992) Genetic variation at five trimeric and tetrameric tandem repeat loci in four human population groups. Genomics 12: 241–253

Gershowitz H, Layrisse M, Layrisse Z, Neel JV, Chagnon NA, Ayres M (1972) The genetic structure of a tribal population, the Yanomama Indians. II. Eleven blood group systems and the ABH-Le secretor traits. Ann Hum Genet 35: 261–269

Guerreiro JF, Figueiredo MS, Santos SEB, Zago MA (1992) β-Globin gene cluster haplotypes in Yanomama Indians from the Amazon region of Brazil. Human Genet 89: 629–631

Herzog-Schröder G (1993) Yanomami. *In:* The illustrated Encyclopedia of Humankind, Vol. 5 (in press)

Kawasaki ES (1990) Sample preparation from blood, cells and other fluids. *In:* Innis MA, Gelfand DH, Sninsky JJ, White TJ (eds) PCR protocols. A guide to methods and applications. Academic Press Inc., pp 146–152

Kidd JR, Black FL, Weiss KM, Balazs I, Kidd KK (1991) Studies of three Amerindian populations using nuclear DNA polymorphisms. Hum Biol 63: 775–794

Nei M (1973) Analysis of gene diversity in subdivided populations. Proc Natl Acad Sci USA 70: 3321–3323

230

Roewer L, Rieß O, Prokop O (1991) Hybridization and polymerase chain reaction amplification of simple repeated DNA sequences for the analysis of forensic stains. Electrophoresis 12: 181–186

Roewer L. Arnemann J, Spurr NK, Grzeschik K-H, Epplen JT (1992) Simple repeat sequences on the human Y chromosome are equally polymorphic as their autosomal counterparts. Hum Genet 89: 389–394

SAS Institute Inc. (1991) SAS/STAT user's guide, release 6.03 edition. SAS Institute Inc., Cary NC, pp 283–357

Schurr TG, Ballinger SW, Gan Y-Y, Hodge JA, Merriwether DA, Lawrence DN, Knowler WC, Weiss KM, Wallace DC (1990) Amerindian mitochondrial DNAs have rare Asian mutations at high frequencies, suggesting they derived from four primary maternal lineages. Am J Hum Genet 46: 613–623

Tanis RJ, Neel JV, Dovey H, Morrow M (1973) The genetic structure of a tribal population, the Yanomama Indians. IX. Gene frequencies for 18 serum protein and erythrocyte enzyme systems in the Yanomama and five neighboring tribes: nine new variants. Am J Hum Genet 25: 655–676

Wallace DC, Garrison F, Knowler WC (1985) Dramatic founder effects in Amerindian mitochondrial DNAs. Am J Phys Anthropol 68: 149–155

Ward RH, Gershowitz H, Layrisse M, Neel JV (1975) The genetic structure of a tribal population, the Yanomama Indians. IX. Gene frequencies for 10 blood groups and the ABH-Le secretor traits in the Yanomama and their neighbors: the uniqueness of the tribe. Am J Hum Genet 27: 1–30

Weitkamp LR, Neel JV (1972) The genetic structure of a tribal population, the Yanomama Indians. IV. Eleven erythrocyte enzymes and a summary of protein variants. Ann Hum Genet 35: 443–444

Weitkamp LR, Arends T, Gallango ML, Neel JV, Schultz J, Shreffler DC (1972) The genetic structure of a tribal population, the Yanomama Indians. III. Seven serum protein systems. Ann Hum Genet 35: 271–279

DNA Fingerprinting: State of the Science
ed. by S. D. J. Pena, R. Chakraborty, J. T. Epplen & A. J. Jeffreys
© 1993 Birkhäuser Verlag Basel/Switzerland

Isérables: A Bedouin village in Switzerland?

C. Brandt-Casadevall, N. Dimo-Simonin, A. Sutter and H.-R. Gujer

Institut de Médecine légale, Bugnon 21, 1005 Lausanne, Switzerland

Summary
Isérables is an alpine village – about 1000 inhabitants – which remained isolated till these recent years because of its particular geographical situation. The Isérables inhabitants call themselves "Bedjuis" (Bedouin in local dialect) and regard themselves as descendants of the Sarrazins who invaded the Alps during the VIII–X centuries.

Our goal, in studying several DNA-VNTR polymorphims, in addition to some blood groups, within the Isérables community, was to see if there was any evidence supporting this popular belief.

As a preliminary phase of this project, the allelic frequencies for six VNTR loci analysed for 102 individuals of the village (all descendants of nine original families) are presented. The results are compared with those reported for Swiss and white populations.

Introduction

Isérables is a Swiss alpine village of about 1000 inhabitants that has remained isolated until recent years due to its particular geographic location. Until 1942, the date of construction of a cable-car, the village was difficult to access and was even completely isolated during the winter season. This geographical isolation has contributed to an isolation of the population. In the civil register, it was found that 11 family names existed in the village at the start of the century and that some family names have since disappeared. In our study, only 9 family names have been found. The history of these families is nearly as old as that of Isérables. Roman relics indicate an ancient occupation of the site, whereas the first written document concerning Isérables dates back to 1227. The oldest document in this respect concerns the Sauthier family (1295), while the more "recent" one dates back to 1482 (Gillioz family).

The inhabitants of Isérables call themselves "Bedjuis" (Bedouin in local dialect) and regard themselves as descendants of the Sarrazins who invaded the Alps during the VIII–X centuries. According to the history of Valais (the Canton where Isérables is located), the Sarrazins came from the South of France and were originally warriors who plundered the region and blocked the passes demanding tolls and ransoms from travelers. But some of them may have settled in the region, marrying local women and cultivating the land. It is from these people that the inhabitants of Isérables claim to have descended (Boccard, 1844; Favre, 1984).

The purpose of establishing the polymorphism of several DNA-VNTR loci, in addition to some blood groups, was to determine if there was any evidence to support a Sarrazin ancestry of the Isérables inhabitants. In this preliminary study, the allelic frequencies for six VNTR loci are reported for a sample of the village's population. The results are compared with those from Swiss and white populations.

Materials and methods

Blood samples (on EDTA) were taken from 102 individuals. Demands were made to people over 40 years of age who were originally from the village. For the present study, all of the samples were considered despite the fact that part of the group was composed of closely related individuals.

Six different loci were studied (D7S21, D12S11, D2S44, D7S22, D5S43, D1S7) using the probes MS31, MS43a, YNH24, g3, MS8 and MS1 and the technique described by Dimo-Simonin et al. (1992).

Results

Allele frequency distribution within the Isérables community for the D7S21, D12S11, D2S44, D7S22 loci were compared to those of the general Swiss population (Bär, personal communication). The allelic frequencies for the D5S43 and D1S7 loci were compared with those from a general white population (Smith et al., 1989). It is important to note that the experimental conditions, measurement technique and interpretation criteria in our laboratory are identical to those of the reference Swiss laboratory.

The histograms corresponding to the D7S21, D12S11 and D2S44 loci in the Isérables and reference populations are shown in Fig. 1. For the D7S21 locus only one cluster is present in the two populations, with a more restricted size distribution for the Isérables community. For the D12S11 locus, the two clusters observed in the Swiss population are found in the Isérables sample; their relative importance appears similar within the two populations. Concerning the D2S44 locus, aside from the presence of two bands in the high kb range, the only cluster present in the Isérable population corresponds to that observed in the Swiss population.

The histograms corresponding to the D7S22, D5S43 and D1S7 loci are shown in Fig. 2. For the first one, the three principal clusters detected in the Swiss population were found in the Isérables sample; however, it was noted that the more common alleles were not the same in the two populations (see alleles at 1.6 and 6.8 kb). With respect to the D5S43

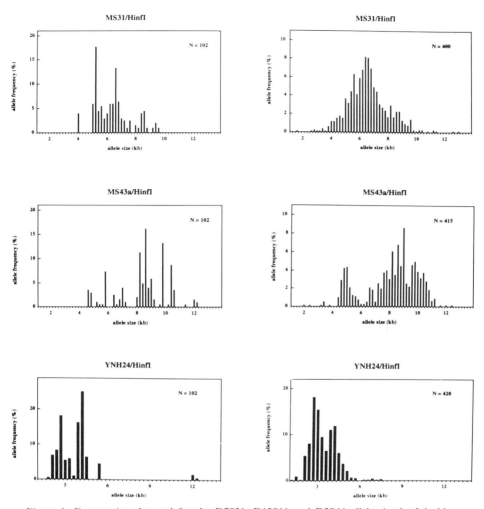

Figure 1. Frequencies observed for the D7S21, D12S11 and D2S44 alleles in the Isérables population (left) and Swiss population (right), using the probes MS31, MS43a and YNH24, respectively.

locus three clusters are found in the two populations (general white population and the Isérables sample). For the D1S7 locus the allele distribution in the Isérables population is nearly as large as in the general white population, but the center of gravity is offset towards the high molecular weights in the Isérables community.

The MS8 probe gave the highest level of apparent homozygosity with 15.7%, which is very close to that reported in the white population (Smith et al., 1989). For the remaining probes, the extreme levels ranged from 10.8% (MS43a) to 7.8% (YNH24); these values are higher than

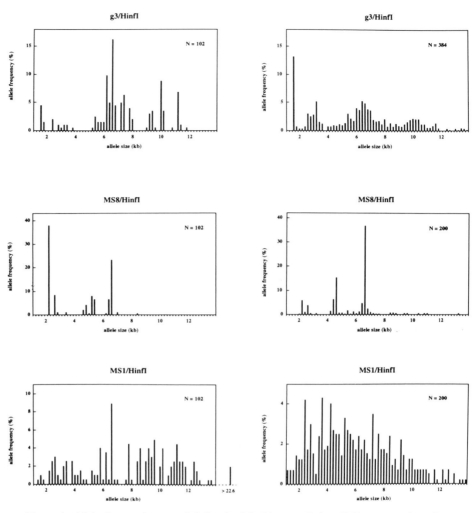

Figure 2. Allele frequencies recorded for the Isérables population (left) compared to those reported for the Swiss (D7S22) and Caucasian populations (D5S43 and D1S7) (right) using the probes g3, MS8 and MS1, respectively.

for the chosen reference populations (Bär, personal communication; Smith et al., 1989).

The only eccentricities, that is to say the presence of alleles not seen in the reference populations, were found for the D1S7 and D2S44 loci. Family trees were established for the 8 individuals concerned in order to detect any family ties between them. For the D1S7 locus, four persons showed a band higher than 22.6 kb (two of these persons were sisters, and the other two were first cousins). In addition, going back three generations, it was found that all four individuals had the same great-grandparent. It therefore indicates a common family characteristic.

For the D2S44 locus, three persons showed a band at 12.0 kb and one person a band at 12.3 kb. The three persons with a band at 12.0 kb proved to be two sisters and their mother, while the fourth person was not directly related. Going back five generations, it was not possible to locate any ancestor common to all four individuals. It was therefore concluded that the 12.3 kb band was probably different and unrelated to the 12.0 kb band.

Discussion and conclusions

The study of a village community, constituting practically an isolated ethnic group, has been undertaken with the aid of six genetic markers concerning six independent VNTR loci: D7S21, D12S11, D2S44, D7S22, D5S43, D1S7.

This study, which must be considered as a preliminary phase of a project aimed at searching evidence for a Sarrazin ancestry in the Isérables community, reports observed allele frequencies and compares them with those from Swiss and Caucasian populations.

The general aspect of the histograms obtained for the Isérables population is, for each locus, very similar to that of the reference population. It was also noted that: a) The more common alleles were not necessarily the same in the two populations; and that b) certain alleles found in the reference populations were not found in the Isér-ables sample.

A more detailed analysis of the data should allow us to establish if the Isérables community may be considered as genetically isolated. In particular, the study must be revised in order to remove any closely related individuals from the sample population.

Acknowledgements
The authors would like to thank Mrs C. Besançon and A. Grini for technical assistance.

References

Boccard F (1844) Histoire du Vallais, avant et sous l'ère chrétienne. Berthiers-Guers (Ed) Genève
Favre M (1984) Essai d'histoire de la commune d'Isérables. Commune d'Isérables (Ed)
Dimo-Simonin N, Brandt-Casadevall C, Gujer H-R (1992) Chemiluminescent DNA probes: evaluation and usefulness in forensic cases. Forensic Sci Int 57: 119–127
Smith JC, Anwar R, Riley J, Jenner D, Markham AF, Jeffreys A (1989) Highly polymorphic minisatellite sequences: allele frequencies and mutation rates for five-locus specific probes in a Caucasian population. J Forensic Sci Soc 30: 19–32

DNA Fingerprinting: State of the Science
ed. by S. D. J. Pena, R. Chakraborty, J. T. Epplen & A. J. Jeffreys
© 1993 Birkhäuser Verlag Basel/Switzerland

Paternity testing with the F10 multilocus DNA fingerprinting probe

S. D. J. Pena[a,b], P. C. Santos[b], M. C. B. N. Campos[a] and
A. M. Macedo[a,b]

[a]Núcleo de Genética Médica de Minas Gerais (GENE/MG), Av. Afonso Pena 3111/9,
30130-909 Belo Horizonte, Brazil, and
[b]Department of Biochemistry, Universidade Federal de Minas Gerais, C.P. 2486,
30161 Belo Horizonte, Brazil

Summary
Empirical analysis of 200 paternity cases by multilocus DNA fingerprinting with the F10 probe
showed that it was capable of distinguishing fathers from non-fathers in every case. The average
exclusion probability was 0.99998. A very effective discrimination parameter was the proportion
of non-maternal (test) bands which cannot be detected in the alleged father (unassignable
bands) almong all test bands. Values below 0.2 were seen in true fathers while in all cases of
non-fathers the values were above 0.35. Minisatellite mutations occurred at a rate of 0.004 per
band per child. The distribution of band-sharing among first degree relatives and unrelated
individuals showed only a small overlap. Thus, band-sharing of the F10 fingerprints should
provide a useful statistic for testing genetic relationships in deficiency cases.

Introduction

Jeffreys et al. (1985a) were the first to show that minisatellite probes
derived from the human myoglobin gene were capable of recognizing
simultaneously several variable number of tandem repeat (VNTR)
regions in the human genome. These multilocus probes generated on
Southern blots highly complex and individual-specific banding patterns
that were called "DNA fingerprints" (Jeffreys et al., 1985b). Application of DNA fingerprints with two largely non-overlapping multilocus
probes (33.6 and 33.15) to over one thousand of paternity cases showed
the method to be extremely efficient, being capable of distinguishing
fathers from non-fathers in virtually every case (Jeffreys et al., 1991).
Besides, both empirical observations and theoretical considerations
demonstrated that the method was quite robust and unlikely to be
affected by population substructuring. Multilocus DNA fingerprinting
has been considered statistically reliable for paternity testing even by
some critics of the medico-legal applications of DNA methodology
(Lander, 1991).

F10, the gene encoding the major eggshell protein of the parasitic
trematode *Schistosoma mansoni* has recently been cloned and sequenced
(Rodrigues et al., 1989). The nucleotide sequence predicted a protein

with 160 amino acids, 48.7% being glycines. Most of the glycine residues were in a stretch extending from amino acid 25 to 112, corresponding to nucleotides 329 to 593 in the gene sequence. We aligned this stretch trying to maximize its internal homology and were able to deduct a 12 bp consensus repeat motif TATGGTGGTGGT. This motif was clearly homologous to the CHI sequence of *Escherichia coli* and to the consensus sequence of Jeffreys 33.6 and 33.15 fingerprinting probes (Jeffreys et al., 1985a, 1987). On this basis we tested if F10 was also able to recognize multiple minisatellites in the human genome. As predicted, F10 cloned in M13mp10 and labeled non-isotopically with biotin-11-dUTP (Macedo et al., 1989) hybridized to human genomic DNA digested with *Bsp*RI generating on Southern blots a complex and highly variable DNA fingerprinting pattern (Pena et al., 1990).

We present here a review of 200 paternity cases analyzed in Brazil with the F10 multilocus DNA fingerprinting probe. This analysis has the purpose of investigating its efficiency in paternity testing and of ascertaining some of the population characteristics of this probe.

Materials and methods

Population studied

The patients were paternity cases studied in the Núcleo de Genética Médica de Minas Gerais (GENE/MG) in Belo Horizonte, Brazil. In addition to the F10 probe analysis, the mother/child/putative father trios had also been tested with the multilocus probe (CAC)₅ (Schafer et al., 1988; Pena et al., 1991) and/or studied by PCR amplification of the following VNTR loci: D1S80 (Budowle et al., 1991), D17S30 (Horn et al., 1989), Apolipoprotein B 3′ hypervariable region (Boerwinkle et al., 1989) and two VNTRs in intron 40 of the von Willebrand factor gene (Peake et al., 1990; Ploos van Amstel and Reitsma, 1991; S. D. J. Pena, K. Souza, M. Andrade and R. Chakraborty, submitted for publication). All mother/putative father pairs studied were unrelated Caucasian, representing an apparently random sample of Brazilian upper middle class, predominantly with European ancestry, although with some Black, Amerindian and Middle Eastern contributions (Salzano and Freire-Maia, 1970).

DNA fingerprinting with the F10 probe labeled with biotin

Human genomic DNA was prepared from peripheral blood, digested with *Bsp*RI (an isoschizomer of *Hae*III), run on agarose gel electrophoresis and Southern blotted onto nylon membranes (Pall Biodyne

B) exactly as described elsewhere (Pena et al., 1991). The F10 probe was prepared and labeled by PCR amplification in the presence of biotin-11-dUTP. The primers used were designed from the known sequence of F10 in order to amplify a 305 bp fragment containing the 21 imperfect repeats of the reiterated motif, thus being suitable as a multilocal DNA fingerprinting probe. The primers were: 5'-TACACCACATC-ACATGAC-3' and 5'-AGGGAAGGGCTCATCGAA-3'. For PCR, each probe amplification mix (total reaction volume 200 μl) contained 50 ng of template F10 cloned in M13mp10, 10 units of *Thermus aquaticus* DNA polymerase (Promega), 250 μM each of dATP, dCTP, dGTP and TTP, 200 μM bio-11-dUTP (Sigma Chemical Co.) and 520 nM of each primer in the buffer provided with the enzyme by the manufacturer. The PCR was carried out in a Biometra TRIO-thermoblock (Goettingen, Germany) thermal cycler for 30 cycles. Following an incubation for 10 minutes at 94°C, cycles consisted of 2 min at 55°C for primer annealing, 3 min at 72°C for extension and 2 minute at 94°C for denaturation. The last cycle ended in a prolonged extension at 72°C for 7 min. After amplification the probes were generally purified in a spin column of Sephadex G50, although they could also be used without purification at the cost of a slightly higher background.

Southern hybridizations were done exactly as previously described (Pena et al., 1991). The membrane (Biodyne B, BRL, USA) was hybridized with the biotinylated F10 probe (200 ng/ml) for 24 h and after the appropriate washes was incubated with a streptavidin-alkaline phosphatase conjugate (BRL). The membrane was then developed in a solution containing 5-bromo-4-chloro-3-indolyl phosphate and nitro-blue tetrazolium, dried and photographed. On each membrane were included size markers which were the *Hind*III fragments of bacteriophage λ, labeled with biotin by the Photoprobe (BRL) procedure.

Chemiluminescent DNA fingerprinting with an F10 oligonucleotide probe conjugated with alkaline phosphatase

From the sequence of the repeat motif of the F10 gene, a 24-mer oligonucleotide was designed. This was custom synthesized and conjugated to alkaline phosphatase by Lifecodes Corporation (Stamford, Conn., USA). Hybridization was performed as follows. After Southern blotting, the nylon membrane was washed with $1 \times$ SSC (0.15 M Na citrate, 0.15 M NaCl, pH 7.0) containing 1% SDS and incubated for 30 min at 37°C in a "Hyb Buffer" containing $20 \times$ SSC, 1% SDS and $5 \times$ modified Denhardt's solution (0.02% respectively of polyvinylpirrolidone, Ficoll 400 (Pharmacia) and calf skin gelatin). Hybridization was for 30 min at 37°C with 2 nM probe conjugate in Hyb buffer. The membranes were then washed four times with $1 \times$ SSC containing 1%

SDS at 37°C and blocked with $1 \times$ SSC, 1% BSA, 1% triton X-100 for 15 min. This was followed by four washes in 0.1 M Tris-HCl pH 9.1, 0.1 M NaCl, 5 mM MgCl$_2$ (Stain Buffer), spraying with AMPPD solution and autoluminograph exposure to Kodak X-Omat film for 5–8 hours at room temperature.

Data analysis

For analysis, gel photographs were enlarged to an 18×24 cm size and scored by eye. We studied only bands larger than the 4.4 kb *Hind*III fragment of lambda phage. The total number of bands in the mother, child and alleged father were scored, as well as the partial numbers in the size ranges 4.4–6.6, 6.6–9.4, 9.4–23.1 and >23.1 kb. The data from mother, child and alleged father were entered by hand, in this order, in the computer programs DNA-POP and PATER (Pena and Nunes, 1990). Both programs use as a basic feature a vertical division of the gels in mobility levels. A level was defined by the presence of at least one band in one of the three persons. Thus, vertically, the gel is composed of infinite theoretical stacked levels. In practice, the maximum number of levels depends at least in part on the thickness of bands. In this sense, non-isotopic gels stained with chromogenic substrates have an advantage, because the bands are much sharper than those seen with autoradiography or chemiluminescence. The gel was scanned from top to bottom with a ruler and as soon as a band was seen in a lane (thus defining a level), the number of the lanes containing a band in that level were entered in the keyboard. If two or more bands were present in a level, they were considered to be comigrating ("shared") even if they were slightly misaligned or differed in intensity. The output of the programs included, for the whole gel and each of the molecular size ranges indicated above, the proportion of bands shared between the three pairs mother-child, child-alleged father and mother-alleged father, the total number of "test" bands (i.e. child's bands not shared with mother and consequently inherited from the biological father) and number of "test" bands not present in the alleged father (unassigned bands).

Results

We used the F10 multilocal DNA fingerprint probe to analyze 200 Caucasian mother-child-alleged father trios referred to the Núcleo de Genética Médica de Minas Gerais (GENE/MG) for paternity testing. Typical results are shown in Fig. 1. Only bands above 4.4 kb, corresponding to the well resolved region of the gel, were scored. Paternity

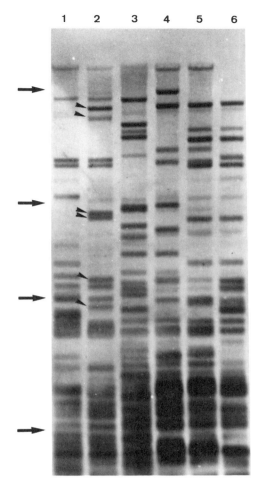

Figure 1. F10 BIOPRINTS – Non-isotopic DNA fingerprints of two mother/child/alleged father trios, lanes 1–3 and 4–6 respectively, obtained by hybridization with the F10 probe labeled with biotin. In one case (lanes 1–3) there is clear exclusion of the paternity and the unassigned bands are indicated by arrowheads. On the left, arrows indicate the migration of the HindIII digestion fragments of lambda phage, with molecular sizes, from top to bottom, 23.1 Kb, 9.4 Kb, 6.6 Kb and 4.4 Kb.

was established in 156 cases (78%) and excluded in the remaining 44 cases (22%) (see below). In all cases the results obtained with F10 matched those obtained with another multilocal probe [$(CAC)_5$] and/or a set of VNTR loci studied by PCR. The basic DNA fingerprint parameters are band numbers and band-sharing. There are given in Tab. 1 for each of the molecular size ranges. The distribution of the proportion of bands shared between mother and alleged father (unrelated individuals) and between mother and child are shown in Fig. 2.

Table 1. Summary of DNA fingerprint data from the mother and alleged father in 200 paternity cases studied with the F10 probe

Size range	Number bands (n)	Band-sharing (x)	Mean allele frequency (q)	Proportion of maternal bands (P_{MB})	Expected number of test bands $n \cdot (1 - P_{MB})$
> 23.1 kb	0.7	0.03	0.013	0.51	0.3
$23.1 > n > 9.4$ kb	4.3	0.15	0.079	0.56	1.9
$9.4 > n > 6.5$ kb	4.6	0.22	0.115	0.59	1.9
$6.5 > n > 4.4$ kb	8.2	0.36	0.197	0.64	2.9
Total	17.6	0.26	0.141	0.60	7.0

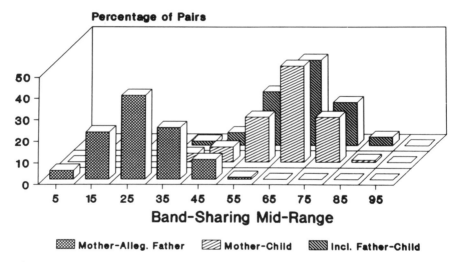

Figure 2. Distribution of band-sharing among mother-alleged father, mother-child and child-included father pairs.

The distributions show little overlap. As expected, the distribution of the proportion of bands shared between child and "included" alleged father parallels closely the mother-child distribution (Fig. 2).

Among the 156 cases in which there was inclusion of paternity, in eleven there was an unassigned band in the child which was attributed to mutation. In the 156 cases we had a total of 2739 child bands, giving a mutation frequency of $11/2739 = 0.004$ per band per child which is very near to the observed mutation rate for the 33.6 and 33.15 probes (Jeffreys et al., 1991). One of these mutant bands had a molecular size larger than 23.1, four were in the range 9.4–23.1 and six were in the range 6.5–9.4. No mutant bands were seen in the range 4.4–6.5.

To be able to analyze population data of multilocal DNA fingerprints we used a model with three basic simplifying assumptions (Jeffreys et al., 1991): 1) the bands observed in the fingerprint gel are a random sample of a much larger number of hypervariable loci and consequently the bands behave independently, not being linked or allelic; 2) in each hypervariable locus the allelic frequencies are approximately uniformly distributed and 3) comigrating bands are the same allele at the same locus. Jeffreys et al. (1986, 1991) have shown for the 33.6 and 33.15 probes that assumption 1 holds well, that is, allelism and linkage are not common in fingerprints. Assumption 2 has been shown to be true for some hypervariable loci such as MS1 (Wong et al., 1987) but not for several other ones (Balazs et al., 1989). Assumption 3 makes paternity analysis more conservative and thus it is generally still used although it is probably largely incorrect (Jeffreys, 1990). Using this model, we can calculate the probability that two non-related individuals have an identical band pattern as $0.03^{0.7} \times 0.15^{4.3} \times 0.22^{4.6} \times 0.36^{8.2} = 6.7 \times 10^{-12}$, which is several orders of magnitude lower than the reciprocal of the world population. Thus, DNA fingerprints obtained with the F10 probe appear to be truly individual-specific and can be explored as an useful tool in forensic medicine. Also, from the average total proportion of shared bands (x) we can calculate the average allelic frequency by the relation $x = 2q - q^2$ (Tab. 1).

Paternity disputes are most simply investigated by counting the number of bands in a child that cannot be assigned to the mother (test bands) and determining how many of these test bands can be detected in the alleged father. The expected band-sharing between mother and child is given by $P_{MB} = (1 + q - q^2)/(2 - q)$ (Honma and Ishiyama, 1990) and the expected number of test bands, i.e. non-maternal bands, can be calculated as $n(1 - P_{MB})$, where n is the number of bands. Table 1 gives the expected number of test bands for each of the molecular size ranges. The expected probability that a non-father will have by chance all the test bands in a paternity case is given by $0.03^{0.3} \times 0.15^{1.9} \times 0.22^{1.9} \times 0.36^{2.9} = 2.5 \times 10^{-5}$. Thus the average probability of excluding a non-father is 0.99998. In a theoretical average case with seven test bands, all present in the alleged father, we would have an expected Paternity Index (L) of 39858 and, given prior probabilities of paternity of 0.5, an expected Probability of Paternity (W) of 0.99998 (Honma and Ishiyama, 1990).

If we plot the number of unassigned bands in a large of paternity cases there will inevitably be a very small amount of overlap between cases with true paternity and false paternity because of the occurrence of mutations in the former and the chance occurrence of very few unassigned bands among rare cases of the latter. However, these cases

244

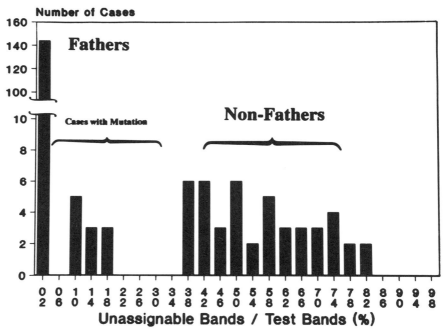

Figure 3. Distribution of the ratio unassigned bands/test bands expressed as a percentage among all 200 paternity cases studied.

with chance occurrence of only one or two unassigned bands are expected to occur mainly among cases with few tests bands and thus the *proportion* of unassigned bands among test bands should remain at a high level in contrast to cases with mutation in which this *proportion* should remain low (Jeffreys et al., 1991). This prediction held true when we plotted unassigned bands among test bands in all paternity cases (Fig. 3). Two groups clearly separated could be seen with no overlap: all cases with true fathers had proportions below 20% while all caes with non-fathers had proportions above 35%. These figures are very similar to those obtained by Jeffreys et al. (1991).

The results with the F10 oligonucleotide-alkaline phosphatase conjugate and chemiluminescence were excellent (Fig. 4). With the increased sensitivity, the amount of genomic DNA loaded in the gel was decreased to 3 μg and the total time involved in hybridization was much diminished. Switch from hybridization with the complete F10 probe labeled with biotin to the F10 oligonucelotide conjugated to alkaline phosphatase led to changes in less than 10% of the bands in the fingerprints. Thus, for the purposes of calculation of the likelihood ratios, one can probably safely apply the same parameters obtained above.

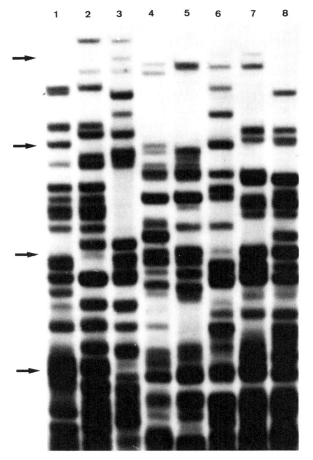

Figure 4. DNA fingerprints of two mother/child/alleged father trios (lanes 1–3 and 6–8), and one child/alleged father pair (lanes 4–5) obtained by chemiluminescence with an F10 oligonucleotide probe conjugated with alkaline phosphatase. In the left, arrows indicate the migration of the *Hind*III digestion fragments of lambda phage, with molecular sizes, from top to bottom, 23.1 Kb, 9.4 Kb, 6.6 Kb and 4.4 Kb.

Discussion

Empirical analysis of 200 paternity cases with the F10 multilocus DNA fingerprinting probe showed that it was capable of distinguishing fathers from non-fathers in every case. The average exclusion probability was 0.99998. A very effective discrimination parameter was the proportion of non-maternal (test) bands which cannot be detected in the alleged father (unassignable bands) among all test bands. Values below 0.2 were seen in true fathers while in all cases of non-fathers the values were above 0.35. The distribution of band-sharing among first degree relatives and unrelated individuals showed only a small overlap. Thus, band-sharing of the F10 Bioprints should provide a useful statistic for testing genetic relationships in deficiency cases. These data are very similar to those reported by Jeffreys et al. (1991) for the 33.6 and 33.15 probes.

Minisatellite mutation occurred at a rate of 0.004 per band per child. Since a person has on average 17.6 bands scored, the probability of observing one mutation in a given child is 0.07 and two mutations 0.005. On the other hand, since the expected number of test bands is seven and the probability of band sharing is 0.26, the probability of observing only two unassignable (exclusion) bands in a child when compared to a non-father is 0.014 and a single one is 0.0016. Thus, for two unassignable bands the likelihood ratio would be 0.36. In this situation, further testing would be necessary. In fact, in our paternity service (GENE/MG) all cases with any unassignable band are tested sequentially with a battery of minisatellites and microsatellites amplified by PCR in an independently prepared second DNA sample. In this fashion we confirm all exclusion cases independently, thus completely ruling out the possibility of diagnostic mistakes due to mutation, partial digestion, sample switches and other sources of error.

In conclusion, DNA fingerprinting with the F10 multilocus probe is an extremely useful technique for paternity testing.

Acknowledgements
This work was supported by grants-in-aid of the Conselho Nacional de Pesquisas (CNPq) of Brazil and the Fundação de Amparo à Pesquisa do Estado de Minas Gerais (FAPEMIG).

References

Balazs I, Baird M, Clyne M, Meade E (1989) Human population genetic studies of five hypervariable DNA loci. Am J Hum Genet 44: 182–190

Boerwinkle E, Xiong W, Fourest E, Chan L (1989) Rapid typing of tandemly repeated hypervariable loci by the polymerase chain reacton: application to the apolipoprotein B 3′ hypervariable region. Proc Nat Acad Sci USA 86: 212–216

Budowle B, Chakraborty R, Giusti AM, Eisenberg AJ, Allen RC (1991) Analysis of the VNTR locus D1S80 by the PCR followed by high-resolution PAGE. Am J Hum Genet 48: 137–144

Honma M, Ishiyama I (1990) Application of DNA fingerprinting to parentage and extended family relationship testing. Hum Hered 40: 356–362

Horn GT, Richards B, Klinger KW (1989) Amplification of a highly polymorphic VNTR segment by the polymerase chain reaction. Nucl Acids Res 17: 2140

Jeffreys AJ (1987) Hypervariable minisatellites and DNA fingerprints. Biochem Soc Trans 15: 309–317

Jeffreys AJ, Wilson V, Thein SL (1985a) Hypervariable "minisatellite" regions in human DNA. Nature 314: 67–73

Jeffreys AJ, Wilson V, Thein SL (1985b) Individual-specific "fingerprints" of human DNA. Nature 316: 76–79

Jeffreys AJ, Wilson V, Thein SL, Weatherall DJ, Ponder BAJ (1986) DNA "fingerprints" and segregation analysis of multiple markers in human pedigrees. Am J Hum Genet 39: 11–24

Jeffreys AJ, Neumann R, Wilson V (1990) Repeat unit sequence variation in minisatellites: a novel source of DNA polymorphisms for studying variation and mutation by single molecule analysis. Cell 60: 473–485

Jeffreys AJ, Turner M, Debenham P (1991) The efficiency of multilocus DNA fingerprint probes for individualization, establishment of family relationships, determined from extensive casework. Am J Hum Genet 48: 824–840

Lander E (1991) Research on DNA typing catching up with courtroom application. Am J Hum Genet 48: 819–823

Macedo AM, Medeiros AC, Pena SDJ (1989) A general method for efficient non-isotopic labeling of DNA probes cloned in M13 vectors: application to DNA fingerprinting. Nucleic Acids Res 16: 10394

Peake IR, Bowen D, Bignell P, Liddell MB, Sadler JE, Standen G, Bloom AL (1990) Family studies and prenatal diagnosis in severe von Willebrand disease by polymerase chain reaction amplification of a variable number tandem repeat region of the von Willebrand factor gene. Blood 76: 555–561

Pena SDJ, Macedo AM, Braga VMM, Rumjanek FD, Simpson AJG (1990) F10, the gene for the glycine-rich major eggshell protein of Schistosoma mansoni recognizes a family of hypervariable minisatellites in the human genome. Nucl Acids Res 18: 7466

Pena SDJ, Macedo AM, Gontijo NF, Medeiros AC, Ribeiro JCC (1991) DNA BIOPRINTS: simple non-isotopic DNA fingerprints with biotinylated probes. Electrophoresis 12: 146–152

Pena SDJ, Nunes AC (1990) DNA-POP and PATER: two simple computer programs for population studies and paternity analyses with DNA fingerprints, Fingerp News 2(3): 7–8

Ploos van Amstel HK & Reitsma P (1991) Tetranucleotide repeat polymorphism in the vWF gene. Nucleic Acids Res 18: 4957

Rodrigues V, Chaudhri M, Knight M, Meadows H, Chambers AE, Taylor WR, Kelly C, Simpson AJG (1989) Predicted structure of a major Schistosoma mansoni eggshell protein. Mol Biochem Parasitol 32: 7–14

Salzano FM, Freire-Maia N (1970) "Problems in Human Biology: A study of Brazilian Populations," pp 174–180, Wayne State University Press, Detroit, MI

Schafer R, Zischler H, Birsner U, Becker A, Epplen JT (1988) Optimized oligonucleotide probes for DNA fingerprints. Electrophoresis 9: 369–374

Wong Z, Wilson V, Patel I, Povey S, Jeffreys AJ (1989) Characterization of a panel of highly variable minisatellites cloned from human DNA. Ann Hum Genet 51: 269–288

DNA Fingerprinting: State of the Science
ed. by S. D. J. Pena, R. Chakraborty, J. T. Epplen & A. J. Jeffreys
© 1993 Birkhäuser Verlag Basel/Switzerland

The formal analysis of multilocus DNA fingerprints

M. Krawczak[a] and B. Bockel[b]

[a]*Abteilung Humangenetik, Medizinische Hochschule, Konstanty-Gutschow-Str. 8, 30623 Hannover, Germany, and* [b]*Institut für Humangenetik, Universität Göttingen, 37073 Göttingen, Germany*

Summary
A description is given of a novel method for the formal analysis of multilocus DNA fingerprints, the so-called 'genetic factor model'. Using this model, multilocus DNA fingerprints can be shown to be a robust means for both paternity testing and pedigree reconstruction.

Introduction

While DNA typing results obtained with single locus probes formally represent codominant traits, analysis of multilocus DNA fingerprints is more difficult. This is due to some peculiarities intrinsic to the method itself: Hidden allelism, comigration of non-allelic fragments, partial homozygosity, and the effect of genetic linkage. This notwithstanding, multilocus probes allow one to extract genetic information very efficiently, and several approaches to the computational analysis of multilocus DNA fingerprints have been reported in the context of paternity testing (see Krawczak and Bockel, 1992, for references). We have recently proposed an analysis model in which a band at a particular gel position was attributed to a variable number, F, of position-specific 'genetic factors' (Krawczak and Bockel, 1992). The term 'genetic factor' was introduced only to facilitate mathematical treatment, and under the assumption of complete heterozygosity at all contributing loci, corresponds to 'DNA fragment'.

The genetic factor model

At a given gel position, the number of genetic factors is assumed to follow a Poisson distribution with parameter λ_F. If x denotes the probability of presence of a band at a specified position, then

$$x = P(F > 0) = 1 - e^{-\lambda_F},$$

and therefore $\lambda_F = -\ln(1 - x)$. A small number, M, of genetic factors results from *de novo* mutations. M is assumed to follow a Poisson distribution, too. If w denotes the probability of a band present for an offspring, given that it is lacking for both parents, then

$$w = P(M > 0) = 1 - e^{-\lambda_M},$$

and thus $\lambda_M = -\ln(1 - w)$. By backward mutations, factors get lost with probability say v, and when mutation equilibrium is assumed, it follows that $v = \lambda_M / \lambda_F$. If an individual is 'heterozygous for a factor', i.e. only one allele produces a band at a particular gel position, then this factor is transmitted to an offspring with probability $(1 - v)/2$. If the individual is 'homozygous for the factor', i.e. both alleles produce the same band, then the factor is transmitted with probability $1 - v$. Let h denote the proportion of 'homozygous' factors in an individual's genome. The final probability of a factor being transmitted to an offspring is, on average,

$$(1 - h) \cdot \frac{1 - v}{2} + h \cdot (1 - v).$$

From the genetic factor model, position-wise likelihood formulae can be derived for the DNA fingerprints of mother-father-child trios. For example, $\text{Prob}(-_c +_m +_f) = x^2(1 - z)^2$ with

$$z = \frac{x - e^{(1 + h) \cdot \frac{\lambda_M - \lambda_F}{2} - \frac{\lambda_M}{2}} + e^{-\lambda_F - \frac{\lambda_M}{2}}}{x}$$

The likelihoods of all eight possible hybridization patterns have been published elsewhere (Krawczak and Bockel, 1992).

Independence of bands

For the formal analysis, phenotypes at different gel positions are usually regarded as stochastically independent, although this has been shown to be not always the case (Cohen, 1990; Jeffreys et al., 1991). Nevertheless, the assumption of independence receives theoretical justification from the fact that only a fraction of the DNA fragments contributing to a multilocus DNA fingerprint is actually scored: The distribution of bands over gel positions can be thought of as drawing (to completeness) balls *without replacement* from a box containing a large number of black (band) and white (no band) balls. However, a basic theorem in probability theory tells us that this model is equivalent to that of drawing the balls *independently* and *with replacement* if

- the analyzed window of a DNA fingerprint is comparatively small, i.e. drawing is not to completeness,
- the level of heterozygosity at the analyzed loci is high, and
- the degree of allelic association between the loci is small.

Simulation

In order to assess the possible effects of partial homozygosity, allelism, linkage, and of imprecise estimates of the bandsharing probability, x, on the power of discrimination between fathers and non-fathers via DNA fingerprints, we performed simulations. Effects were measured by changes in the distributions of the log-likelihood ratios (LR) of paternity vs. non-paternity, caused by varying parameters or deviations of the underlying model from the ideal one. For any trio, the likelihood under the assumption of non-paternity was taken as the likelihood of the mother-child duo alone. In the simulations, the 'mutation probability', w, was set to 10^{-3} while the band sharing probability x was taken as 0.25 on 60 *independent* positions (Nürnberg et al., 1989). The total number of trios simulated in each run was 20,000.

- Increasing h from 0.0 to 0.1 results in a larger distance between the distributions of LR-values for fathers and non-fathers (Fig. 1). The distribution for fathers is shifted upwards, that for non-fathers is shifted downwards. However, an increased proportion of homozygous factors does not appear to have any practical consequences. The distributions are fairly similar for LR-values between -3 and $+3$, i.e. the region that is relevant for decision making (Krawczak and Schmidtke, 1992).
- x was varied to 0.5 and 1.5 times the original average value, respectively, and subsequent likelihood calculations were carried out assuming the original x. Again, no practical impact on decision making is to be expected (Fig. 2).
- In order to study the effects of allelism and linkage, transmission of factors was simulated for *pairs* of gel positions as follows: If a parent carried at least one factor at *both* positions, then exactly one of these two (allelism, linkage in *trans*) or either both or none (linkage in *cis*) were transmitted with probability $1 - v$, respectively. All remaining factors were transmitted with probability $(1 - v)/2$ each. Although this model is conservative as far as independence is concerned, the LR distributions exhibited even less pronounced effects than before.

Likelihoods in extended families

An obvious application of the genetic factor model of multilocus DNA fingerprints consists in its combination with published algorithms for the analysis of complex pedigree data (Elston and Stewart, 1971). To this end, founders in a pedigree (i.e. individuals, the ancestors of which were not tested) are assumed to be selected at random from the general population, assuming that the number of genetic factors at each gel

Fathers

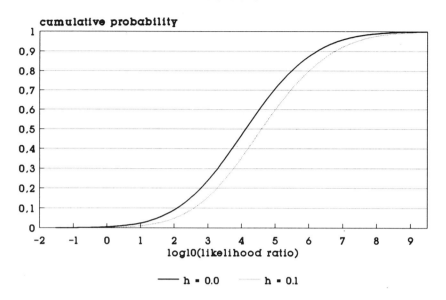

Non-Fathers

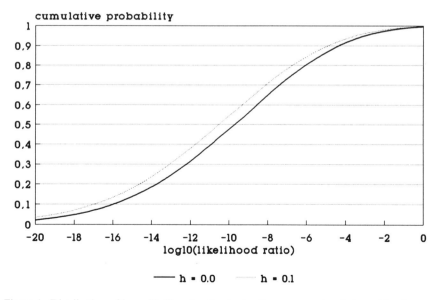

Figure 1. Distribution of $\log_{10}$-likelihood ratios (paternity vs. non-paternity) resulting from a simulation of 20,000 trios. h: proportion of homozygous factors.

Fathers

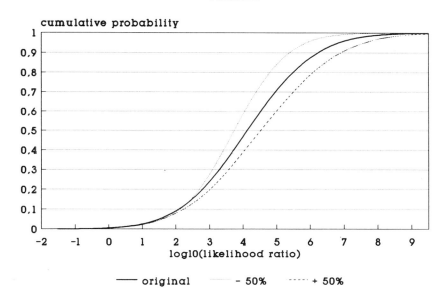

Non-Fathers

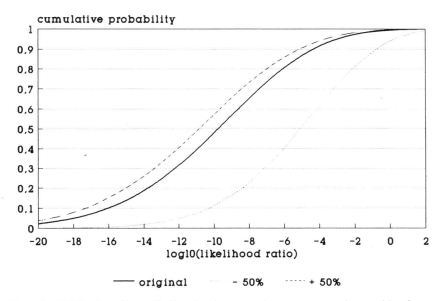

Figure 2. Distribution of $\log_{10}$-likelihood ratios (paternity vs. non-paternity) resulting from a simulation of 20,000 trios. Parameter x was varied $\pm 50\%$ around its original value of 0.25.

position follows a Poisson distribution in these individuals. Analysis of transmission follows the genetic factor model which allows calculation of the conditional probability for a particular number of factors in the offspring, given the number of factors carried by each parent (see Bockel et al., 1992, for a detailed description). This combined approach will be useful in many aspects since any attempt to make inferences on familial relationships on the basis of inherited characters involves the comparison of phenotype likelihoods obtained for alternative pedigree structures.

Applying the methods described above, it has been demonstrated (Bockel et al., 1992) that approximately 90% of paternity disputes can be solved if mother, child and *paternal grandparents*, instead of the putative father, are tested. If phenotype information on a *single paternal sib* is available, true paternity will still be detected in up to 64% of cases. Exclusion of false paternity remains possible in 40% of cases.

Discussion

Comparison with other analytical models shows that, when realistic parameters are used in the calculations, substantially different results are not obtained with our model. It does, for example, coincide with that given by Yassouridis and Epplen (1991) as long as mutations are neglected (i.e. $w = 0$). On the basis of theoretical considerations and extensive simulation applying the genetic factor model, we conclude that substantial objections cannot reasonably be put forward against the use of DNA fingerprints in paternity testing.

The feasibility of 'pedigree reconstruction' from phenotype data on distant relatives has several legal and scientific implications. The major benefit is, of course, a higher proportion of paternity cases that can be solved correctly. This improvement, however, may be achievable only at the expense of further restrictions on individual rights. For example, a positive proof of paternity might well be against the legitimate interests of some relatives. Scientific applications of pedigree reconstruction are manifold and need not be restricted to humans alone. Detailed studies of kinship among animals promise to provide new insight into behavioural and medical science as, for example, by correlating social ranking and reproductive success, by potentiating linkage analysis, or in breeding programmes.

References

Bockel B, Nürnberg P, Krawczak M (1992) Likelihoods of multilocus DNA fingerprints in extended families. Am J Hum Genet 51: 554–561

Cohen JE (1990) DNA fingerprinting for forensic identification: Potential effects on data interpretation of subpopulation heterogeneity and band number variability. Am J Hum Genet 46: 358–368

Elston RC, Stewart J (1971) A general model for the genetic analysis of pedigree data. Hum Hered 21: 523–542

Jeffreys AJ, Turner M, Debenham P (1991) The efficiency of multilocus DNA fingerprint probes for individualization and establishment of family relationships, determined from extensive casework. Am J Hum Genet 48: 824–840

Krawczak M, Bockel B (1992) A genetic factor model for the statistical analysis of multilocus DNA fingerprints. Electrophoresis 13: 10–17

Krawczak M, Schmidtke J (1992) The decision theory of paternity disputes: Optimization considerations applied to multilocus DNA fingerprinting. J Forens Sci 37: 1525–1533

Nürnberg P, Roewer L, Neitzel H, Sperling K, Pöpperl A, Hundrieser J, Pöche H, Epplen C, Zischler H, Epplen JT (1989) DNA fingerprinting with the oligonucleotide probe $(CAC)_5/(GTG)_5$: Somatic stability and germline mutations. Hum Genet 84: 75–78

Yassouridis A, Epplen JT (1991) On paternity determination from multilocus DNA profiles. Electrophoresis 12: 221–226

DNA Fingerprinting: State of the Science
ed. by S. D. J. Pena, R. Chakraborty, J. T. Epplen & A. J. Jeffreys
© 1993 Birkhäuser Verlag Basel/Switzerland

Oligonucleotide DNA fingerprinting: Results of a multi-center study on reliability and validity

I. Böhm[a], M. Krawczak[b], P. Nürnberg[c], J. Hampe[c], J. Hundrieser[b1], H. Pöche[d], C. Peters[d], R. Slomski[d2], J. Kwiatkowska[d2], M. Nagy[f], A. Pöpperl[g], J. T. Epplen[h], and J. Schmidtke[b]

[a]*Labor für Genetische Diagnostik, Dr. C. Waldenmaier, 81545 München, Germany;* [b]*Medizinische Hochschule, Abt. Humangenetik, Konstanty-Gutschow-Str. 8, 30623 Hannover, Germany;* [c]*Institut für Medizinische Genetik, Charité/Humboldt-Universität, 10117 Berlin, Germany;* [d]*Institut für Humangenetik, 37073 Göttingen, Germany;* [f]*Institut für gerichtliche Medizin, Charité/Humboldt-Universität, 10115 Berlin, Germany;* [g]*Institut für Humangenetik, Freie Universität Berlin, 14059 Berlin, Germany; and* [h]*Ruhr-Universität, Molekulare Humangenetik, 44780 Bochum, Germany (present addresses:* [1]*Medizinische Hochschule, Transplantationslabor, Hannover;* [2]*Laboratory of Molecular Genetics, Poznan, Poland)*

Summary

We report the results of an empirical study of 256 paternity cases referred to 7 different German laboratories for DNA fingerprinting with oligonucleotide probe $(CAC)_5/(GTG)_5$. All parameters characteristic of such multilocus DNA fingerprints were found to differ significantly between the contributing centres. Despite these differences, clear-cut decisions between paternity and non-paternity could be made in all but one case. Furthermore, we found no systematic deviation of the gel-phenotype distribution among trios from random expectation as derived from commonly adopted analytical models. Thus, we conclude that oligonucleotide DNA fingerprinting is a robust and reliable means for the resolution of paternity cases.

Introduction

Due to their theoretical complexity, multilocus DNA fingerprints have sometimes been questioned as a reliable means for paternity testing (e.g. Cohen, 1990). This notwithstanding, several approaches have been published which allow an accurate formal analysis of cases and the computation of paternity probabilities (see Krawczak and Bockel, 1992, for references). In order to demonstrate that the impact of technical and interpretative variations on the accuracy and discriminative power of multilocus DNA fingerprints is small, we will present the results of an empirical study of 256 paternity cases, referred to seven different laboratories in Germany for paternity testing with oligonucleotide probe $(CAC)_5/(GTG)_5$. It follows that even if a particular multilocus DNA fingerprint might be difficult to reproduce in another laboratory, the conclusions drawn from it would remain largely unchanged.

Material and methods

In all cases, DNA was digested to completion by restriction endonuclease *Hinf* I. Experimental conditions were as described by Schäfer et al. (1988), with minor variations concerning (i) gel concentrations: between 0.8% and 0.95%; (ii) running buffers: TRIS-acetate or TRIS-borate buffer; (iii) gel running time: between 48 and 52 hours at 2 V/cm, resulting in separation distances of 16 to 20 cm for 4-kb fragments. Autoradiographs were scored by eye in all laboratories (for a description of phenotype evaluation see, for example, Yassouridis and Epplen, 1991). The entirety of positions that could potentially be occupied by a band was determined by superimposing a grid upon the analyzed window, ranging from the band corresponding to the highest molecular weight to the lowest scorable band in the 4-kb region. Line spacing of the grid corresponded to the average extension of clearly resolvable bands, ranging from 1.2 mm to the most conservative value of 2.0 mm. Only fragments longer than 3.5 kb were recorded, and bands less than 0.5 mm apart were usually regarded as 'matching' or being 'shared' by different individuals.

The following parameters characteristic of multilocus DNA fingerprints were evaluated either for an individual or for each possible pair of individuals: (i) the number of analyzed gel positions (Np); (ii) the number of bands scored per individual (Nb); (iii) the number of bands shared by two individuals (Ns); (iv) the number of 'unassigned bands' exhibited by the child (Na), i.e. of bands that could not be attributed to either mother or putative father; (v) the band-sharing probability of a pair of individuals (β); (vi) the probability of occurrence of a band at a particular gel position (x); and (vii) the proportion of 'unassigned' bands among the non-maternal bands of the child (α). Data were analyzed statistically using the SAS software package.

Results and discussion

When compared by a Wilcoxon rank sum test, all parameters described above differed significantly between the contributing laboratories. Parameter x, as estimated from both mothers and fathers, varied between 0.145 and 0.329. The most plausible explanation for this finding was that x was calculated on the basis of different values of Np (with mean values ranging from 50.0 to 109.7, depending on line spacing) and Nb (mean: 11.6 to 20.4). As considerable standard deviations of x were observed in all laboratories, it is therefore advisable to estimate x from a large number of multilocus fingerprints worked out in the same laboratory. Band-sharing probabilities were found to range from 0.164 to 0.309 (mother and putative father), and from 0.580 to 0.684 (mother and child).

The study revealed that fathers and non-fathers can already be distinguished efficiently on the basis of two parameters: α and β (for putative father and child), irrespective of any variations between laboratories. Parameters α and β, being significantly correlated, divide the set of paternity cases into two distinct groups (Fig. 1). This ultimate partitioning, confirmed by all clustering procedures of the SAS package, links those 213 cases with $\alpha < 0.50$ together in one group (I), and the 43 cases with $\alpha > 0.50$ in another (II).

The above mentioned parameter variations are also reflected in laboratory differences with respect to the case-wise $\log_{10}$-likelihood ratios (LR) of paternity vs. non-paternity. However, as suggested by the findings for α and β, no overlap of LR-distributions was documented for the two generated groups. All LR-values were either smaller than -3.929 (group II; corresponding to a paternity probability of $P = 0.0002$), or larger than 1.943 (group I; $P = 0.9887$). Only one case yielded $P = 0.8931$. Since two unassigned bands were observed here, this case could be attributed either to two independent mutations or to paternity of a close relative of the alleged father.

In some laboratories the normalized number of bands scored per individual failed to fit a Standard Normal distribution. A Normal

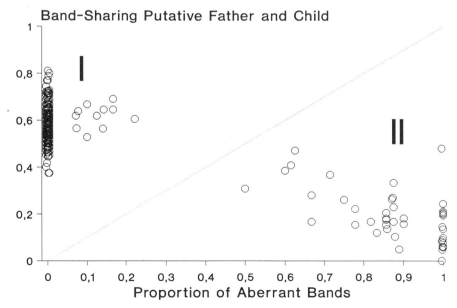

Figure 1. Proportion of unassigned bands (aberrant bands) (α) and band-sharing of putative father and child (β). Each circle represents a single case. Note: For better resolution, some cases without any unassigned bands are displayed slightly dislocated.

distribution would have been expected if bands (as well as the positions they potentially occupy) were statistically independent from each other along the gel. In fact, systematic deviations from a model of bands resulting from independent Bernoulli experiments could be excluded. Furthermore, observed frequencies of phenotype patterns of trios were found to be not notably different from their theoretical expectations (Krawczak and Bockel, 1992).

In summary, we conclude that oligonucleotide DNA fingerprinting is a robust technique for obtaining reliable information about paternity, even under varying laboratory protocols. Nevertheless, standardization of protocols is in progress in Germany.

References

Cohen JE (1990) DNA fingerprinting for forensic identification: Potential effects on data interpretation of subpopulation heterogeneity and band number variability. Am J Hum Genet 46: 358–368

Krawczak M, Bockel B (1992) A genetic factor model for the statistical analysis of multilocus DNA fingerprints. Electrophoresis 13: 10–17

Schäfer R, Zischler H, Birsner U, Becker A, Epplen JT (1988) Optimized oligonucleotide probes for DNA fingerprinting. Electrophoresis 9: 369–374

Yassouridis A, Epplen JT (1991) On paternity determination from multilocus DNA profiles. Electrophoresis 12: 221–226

Oligonucleotides $(CAC)_5/(GTG)_5$ are under license of Fresenius AG, Oberursel, Germany

DNA Fingerprinting: State of the Science
ed. by S. D. J. Pena, R. Chakraborty, J. T. Epplen & A. J. Jeffreys
© 1993 Birkhäuser Verlag Basel/Switzerland

Testing deficiency paternity cases with a Y-linked tetranucleotide repeat polymorphism

F. R. Santos[a], J. T. Epplen[b] and S. D. J. Pena[a,c]

[a]*Department of Biochemistry, Universidade Federal de Minas Gerais, C.P. 2486, 30161 Belo Horizonte, Brazil;* [b]*Molekulare Humangenetik der Ruhr-Universität, 44780 Bochum, Germany; and* [c]*Núcleo de Genética Médica de Minas Gerais (GENE/MG), Av. Afonso Pena 3111/9, 30130-909 Belo Horizonte, Brazil*

Summary
Because a son's genotype at a Y-linked locus uniquely specifies his father's genotype at that locus irrespective of the maternal contribution, Y-linked polymorphisms show increased exclusion power over autosomal polymorphisms in paternity cases involving a male child. This advantage is even more obvious when the alleged father is deceased or otherwise unavailable for testing. In this situation, any individual connected by patrilineage to the alleged father may be tested in his place.
The usefulness of the Y-linked tetranucleotide repeat locus Y-27H39 in deficiency cases was evaluated in a set of 41 families that had a deceased alleged father and that had been tested at GENE/MG with multilocal and unilocal DNA fingerprinting probes. In sixteen of these cases the proband (child tested) was male and there were male relatives. In the thirteen cases in which paternity was included, Y-27H39 would contribute significantly to the paternity index. In one of three cases in which there was exclusion by fingerprinting probes there was also exclusion by Y-27H39. Thus, Y-27H39 is useful in deficiency paternity cases and will be specially valuable in situations where autosomal polymorphisms have limited power, such as when there is only one male living relative of the deceased father. However, our experience is that Y-linked probes can only be applied in approximately 40% of cases.

Introduction

The efficiency of a genetic system in paternity testing is measured by the average exclusion probability, which in turn depends on its degree of polymorphism. Because of their peculiar holandric inheritance, Y-linked polymorphic traits have a much higher exclusion power than equally variable autosomal loci (Chakraborty, 1985). They have however the disadvantage of being limited in use to the 50% of cases in which the child being tested is a male. Besides, with the advent of multilocal and single-locus probes and PCR approaches to the study of hypervariable minisatellites, the exclusion power of test batteries is no longer a limiting factor, since it has approximated very closely the theoretical ideal of 100%. There is, however, one situation in which Y-linked polymorphisms may be uniquely suited for paternity testing, namely, when the alleged father is deceased and relatives are tested in his place. Any male relative in patrilineal line with the deceased alleged father will provide complete information on his Y-chromosome molecular constitution, thus permitting a stringent test of paternity in those cases in which the possible child is a male.

Recently a polymorphic microsatellite (Y-27H39) based on a (GATA)$_n$ repeat was discovered on the short arm of the human Y chromosome (Roewer et al., 1992). We have used a simple technique based on PCR amplification and native polyacrylamide gel electrophoresis followed by highly sensitive silver staining, to study the inheritance, the genetic stability and the allele frequency distribution of this polymorphism in the Brazilian population (Santos et al., 1992). We analyzed 100 randomly chosen Caucasian Brazilian father-son pairs with proven paternity. Five alleles, four base-pairs apart, were easily distinguishable. Their frequencies were: A (186 bp): 0.19, B (190 bp): 0.49, C (194 bp): 0.24, D (198 bp): 0.07 and E (202 bp): 0.01. In all father-son pairs there was complete allelic concordance. Calculated from these data, the average probability of exclusion for paternity cases (Chakraborty, 1985) was 0.66.

In the present study we evaluated the potential usefulness of the Y-27H39 polymorphism in 41 deficiency paternity cases. For that, we identified all deficiency cases in which the alleged father was dead in a series of close to 1,000 paternity tests done in the Núcleo de Genética Médica de Minas Gerais (GENE/MG) in Belo Horizonte. We then ascertained in which of these cases tests of a Y-linked polymorphism would be applicable and restudied these with Y-27H39.

Materials and methods

The patients were randomly drawn from paternity cases studied in the Núcleo de Genética Médica de Minas Gerais (GENE/MG) in Belo Horizonte, Brazil. In all cases paternity had been previously established by DNA fingerprinting with the multilocal probes F10 (Pena et al., 1990, 1991) and/or (CAC)$_5$ (Schafer et al., 1988; Pena et al., 1991) and with a battery of PCR polymorphisms that included Apo B (Boerwinkle et al., 1989), D17S30 (Horn et al., 1989), D1S80 (Budowle et al., 1991) and VWF1 and VWF2 (Pena et al., 1993). DNA was prepared from peripheral blood as described elsewhere (Pena et al., 1991).

The primers used for PCR of Y-27H39 were those designed by Roewer et al. (1992) namely: 5'-CTACTGAGTTTCTGTTATAGT-3' and 5'-ATGGCATGTAGTGAGGACA-3'. As a positive control, we amplified simultaneously (in the same PCR tubes) an autosomal polymorphic region from chromosome 12 (4815LR = D12S67) which is also based on a (GATA)$_n$ repeat (Roewer et al., 1992). For PCR, each sample contained 100 ng DNA template, 1 unit Taq DNA Polymerase (Promega), buffer provided by manufacturer, 1.5 mM MgCl$_2$, 1 μM of each primer and 250 μM of each dNTP. The total reaction volume was

25 μl and each sample was overlaid with 25 μl of mineral oil. The PCR was carried out in a MJ Research PTC-100 Thermal Cycler or a Biometra TrioBlock for 25 cycles. Each cycle consisted of 30 s at 94°C for denaturation, 30 s at 51°C for primer annealing and 90 s at 72°C for primer extension. After amplification the samples were stored at −20°C until run on electrophoresis. The samples were resolved in 16 cm 10% native polyacrylamide gels (9.67% acrylamide, 0.33% bisacrylamide) in TBE buffer for 4 h at 150 V. Following electrophoresis the fragments were visualized by a simple and highly sensitive silver staining, extensively modified from Herring et al. (1982) as follows: the gels were fixed for 20 min at room temperature with 300 ml of an aqueous solution of 10% (v/v) ethanol and 0.5% (v/v) acetic acid, after which they were incubated with 300 ml of 0.17% (w/v) silver nitrate for 20 min with agitation. The gels were then rinsed in 300 ml of deionized water for 3 min and developed in 300 ml of an aqueous solution of 3% (w/v) sodium hydroxide/0.1% (w/v) formaldehyde until the bands were well visualized, at which point the staining reaction was stopped with fixative solution.

Results and discussion

As reported previously (Santos et al., 1992), in males Y-27H39 amplified as a single band with a variable size of around 190 bp. No amplification product was seen in females (Fig. 1).

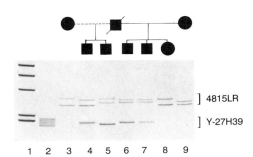

Figure 1. The silver-stained gel shows coamplification of the Y-27H39 region and the autosomal 4815LR (D12S67) in a paternity case where the alleged father was deceased. This case was studied previously by single and multilocus DNA fingerprinting at the GENE/MG, where the probands (lanes 4 and 5) were respectively included and excluded. This result was confirmed in our study comparing the alleles from the probands with those from the legal sons. The alleles seen from the Y-27H39 region were: C (lanes 4, 6 and 7) and B (lane 5). In lane 2 a ladder is shown of the five alleles from the Y-27H39 region. No amplification products of the Y-27H39 region are seen in females (lanes 3, 8 and 9) and the amplification products of the 4815LR autosomal region are seen in males and females. In lane 1: 1 kb ladder (BRL) with sizes: 396, 344, 298, 220 and 201 bp.

Of the 41 deficency cases ascertained with the deceased alleged father, study of a Y-linked polymorphism was applicable (families with male probands and living male relatives of the deceased alleged father) in 16 families (39%) with a total of 22 tested children. With the complete battery of multilocal DNA fingerprinting probes and autosomal PCR-VNTRs an unambiguous result was obtained for these children, with an exclusion being observed in only three of them. The results of Y-27H39 agreed with the others in all inclusion cases; paternity indices varied between 2.0 and 5.1. Y-27H39 provided a clear exclusion in one of the three instances of non-paternity (Fig. 1) but failed to exclude the other two. Overall the performance of Y-27H39 in these deficiency cases was good and it has been included in our test battery for future cases.

One can easily envisage several situations in which paternities can be resolved by application of a Y-linked polymorphism but not by autosomal hypervariable loci. Examples of these would be families in which only one patrilineal relative of the deceased alleged father (however distant) was available for testing. These cases may now be tested with Y-27H39. We did not have in the 41 cases any one that matched that profile but we were working with a sample that was biased by having been already selected for being amenable to regular testing. An even more attractive situation would occur if we had a set of polymorphisms that permitted identification of a Y-chromosomal patrilineal specific pattern. The development of such a set should be achievable shortly with the intensive molecular studies of the Y-chromosome that are being pursued by several groups including our own.

Acknowledgements
This work was supported by grants-in-aid of the Conselho Nacional de Pesquisas (CNPq) of Brazil and the Fundação de Amparo à Pesquisa do Estado de Minas Gerais (FAPEMIG).

References

Boerwinkle E, Xiong W, Fourest E, Chan L (1989) Rapid typing of tandemly repeated hypervariable loci by the polymerase chain reaction: application to the apolipoprotein B 3′ hypervariable region. Proc Natl Acad Sci USA 86: 212–216

Budowle B, Chakraborty R, Giusti AM, Eisenberg AJ, Allen RC (1991) Analysis of the VNTR locus D1S80 by the PCR followed by high-resolution PAGE. Am J Hum Genet 48: 137–144

Chakraborty R (1985) Paternity testing with genetics markers: Are Y-linked genes more efficient than autosomal ones? Am J Hum Genet 21: 297–305

Herring AJ, Inglis NF, Ojeh CK, Snodgrasse DR, Rumjes JD (1982) Rapid diagnosis of rotavirus infection by direct detection of viral nucleic acid in silver stained polyacrylamide gels. J Clin Microbiol 16: 473–477

Horn GT, Richards B, Klinger KW (1989) Amplification of a highly polymorphic VNTR segment by the polymerase chain reaction. Nucl Acids Res 17: 2140

Pena SDJ, Macedo AM, Braga VMM, Rumjanek FD, Simpson AJG (1990) F10, the gene for the glycine-rich major eggshell protein of Schistosoma mansoni recognizes a family of hypervariable minisatellites in the human genome. Nucl Acids Res 18: 7466

Pena SDJ, Macedo AM, Gontijo NF, Medeiros AC, Ribeiro JCC (1991) DNA BIOPRINTS: simple non-isotopic DNA fingerprints with biotinylated probes. Electrophoresis 12: 146–152

Pena SDJ, Souza KT, Andrade M, Chakraborty R (1993) Allelic associations of two polymorphic microsatellites in intron 40 of the human von Willebrand factor gene. Proc Natl Acad Sci USA (in press)

Roewer L, Arnemann J, Spurr Grzeschik K-H, Epplen JT (1992) Simple repeat sequences on the human Y chromosome are equally polymorphic as their autosomal counterparts. Hum Genet 89: 389–394

Santos FR, Pena SDJ, Epplen JT (1993) Genetic and population study of a Y-linked tetranucleotide repeat DNA polymorphism with a simple non-isotopic technique. Hum Genet 90: 655–656

Schafer R, Zischler H, Birnser U, Becker A, Epplen JT (1988) Optimized oligonucleotide probes for DNA fingerprinting. Electrophoresis 9: 369–374

DNA Fingerprinting: State of the Science
ed. by S. D. J. Pena, R. Chakraborty, J. T. Epplen & A. J. Jeffreys
© 1993 Birkhäuser Verlag Basel/Switzerland

Short tandem repeat loci: Application to forensic and human remains identification

M. M. Holland, D. L. Fisher, D. A. Lee, C. K. Bryson and
V. W. Weedn

*The Armed Forces DNA Identification Laboratory, The Armed Forces Institute of Pathology,
14th and Alaska Streets, Washington, DC 20306-6000, USA*

Summary
The short tandem repeat (STR) locus ACTBP2 (common name SE33) was analyzed for its
potential use in forensic and human remains identification. PCR amplification conditions were
determined, and an allele-specific ladder was generated so that discrete alleles could be scored.
The allele frequency distributions were determined for both Caucasian and Black populations.
The frequency data meets Hardy-Weinberg expectations, and the allele distributions were
similar from one racial group to another and between ethnic groups. SE33 analysis was
subsequently used to confirm the identification of human remains for the Office of the Armed
Forces Medical Examiners.

Introduction

The majority of forensic cases requiring DNA analysis can be
completed using RFLP (*r*estriction *f*ragment *l*ength *p*olymorphism)
methodologies. RFLP analysis includes agarose gel electrophoresis,
Southern transfer (Southern 1975) to a nylon membrane, and detection
of specific DNA fragments using isotopically labeled oligonucleotides.
A typical RFLP profile takes six weeks to complete. Consequently,
RFLP analysis is labor intensive, time consuming, and requires the use
of radioactive materials.

There are a significant number of forensic cases (approximately 20%)
which cannot be analyzed using RFLP methods. The success of RFLP
analysis is dependent on the quality and quantity of DNA extracted
from evidentiary material. DNA degradation, insufficient quantities of
DNA (less than 100 ng), or both could result in an incomplete RFLP
profile.

With the advent of PCR (*p*olymerase *c*hain *r*eaction) (Saiki et al.,
1985), the analysis of minute quantities of DNA has become available.
The amplification of specific genomic sequences allows for forensic
analysis of DNA quantities as low as 100 picograms (Saiki et al., 1988).
Given an elevated level of sensitivity, the analysis of DNA from a stamp
that has been licked by an embezzler, or the DNA from a cigarette butt

left at the scene of the crime by a thief, can be routinely analyzed using PCR-based DNA typing methods (Hochmeister et al., 1991; Walsh et al., 1992).

Minisatellite VNTR (*v*ariable *n*umber of *t*andem *r*epeats) loci are being analyzed and validated to address the problems associated with DNA degradation. Combined with the PCR, AmpFLP (*amp*lified *f*ragment *l*ength *p*olymorphism) alleles, some as large as 1500 base pairs in length (Boerwinkle et al., 1989; Horn et al., 1989; Kasai et al., 1990), can be selectively amplified from limited quantities of highly degraded DNA. AmpFLP analysis has been used successfully in both paternity and criminal cases around the world.

Microsatellites, or STRs (*s*hort *t*andem *r*epeats), are AmpFLP loci which have repeat units of 2–5 base pairs (Weber and May, 1989; Litt and Luty, 1989; Peake et al., 1990; Edwards et al., 1991, 1992). There is growing interest in the forensic community towards the use of STR loci for DNA typing. The advantages of STRs are that they are easy to amplify, have relatively small allele sizes, and can be separated into discrete alleles using conventional polyacrylamide gel electrophoresis (PAGE) methods (both slab gel and capillary formats are being analyzed). In addition, allelic dropout due to severe degradation, and preferential amplification due to large allele size differences, are not common problems associated with STR analysis.

Following PAGE, detection of DNA fragments can be achieved using non-isotopic methods, without the need for a hybridization step. The FBI has developed a horizontal, discontinuous PAGE system to resolve AmpFLP and STR alleles, and a silver stain method for detection of the amplification product (Budowle et al., 1990, 1991). Discontinuous vertical PAGE, using the SA32 apparatus from Bethesda Research Laboratory, and silver stain detection is being used routinely. Using either system, the entire process, from extraction to data analysis, can be performed in one to two days.

The development of fluorescence based methods for detecting DNA fragments has progressed rapidly in the past few years. The Applied Biosystems 362 Fluorescent Fragment Analyzer (Gene Scanner) is being evaluated by a number of laboratories to analyze STR loci for casework (Sullivan et al., 1992). The Gene Scanner is an attractive alternative to conventional methods for many reasons. Both agarose and acrylamide formats are available depending on the resolution needs of the user. Multiple fluorophors allow for internal lane standards and for multiplexing many AmpFLP or STR systems together in the same lane. Fluorescently labeled DNA fragments are detected in real time using laser technologies so that no further steps are required following electrophoresis to visualize the alleles. Finally, data analysis and manipulation is computerized, eliminating the need for additional imaging systems.

The STR locus ACTBP2 (SE33) on chromosome 6, contains a highly polymorphic tetranucleotide repeat (AAAG). SE33 was first discovered and analyzed by Moos and Polymeropoulos, respectively (Moos et al., 1983; Polymeropoulos et al., 1992). The potential use of SE33 for forensic and human remains identification was subsequently evaluated (Holland et al., 1993). This manuscript briefly describes some of the data generated by Holland et al., the application of SE33 analysis to human remains identification, and discusses some of the advantages of STR analysis performed on the ABI Gene Scanner.

Materials and methods

PCR amplification was carried out on a Perkin Elmer GeneAmp PCR System 9600 thermal cycler. A 50-μl PCR reaction contained 10 mM Tris, pH 8.3, 50 mM KCl, 1.5 mM MgCl$_2$, 0.2 mM dATP, dTTP, dCTP, dGTP, 2.5 units of DNA Taq Polymerase (Cetus), approximately 5 ng of target DNA, 0.01% gelatine, and 0.4 μM primers 5'-AAT CTG GGC GAC AAG AGT GA-3' and 5'-ACA TCT CCC CTA CCG CTA TA-3' (Polymeropoulos et al., 1992). The cycling parameters were 94°C for 10 seconds, 66°C for 10 seconds, and 72°C for 10 seconds for 10 cycles (this step has subsequently been reduced to 7 cycles), and then the same denaturing and extension conditions, but an annealing temperature of 64°C for an additional 20 cycles.

Approximately 5–7 μl of PCR product was loaded onto a 7% acrylamide, 3.3% piperazine diacrylamide gel and the electrophoresis was carried out at 600 V, 15 W, and 20 mA of continuous current for 17 cm according to the method of Budowle et al. (Budowle et al., 1991). Following electrophoresis, the gel was stained with silver to detect the alleles.

The allele specific ladder was generated by pooling together single alleles isolated from an acrylamide gel. The pooled alleles were reamplified using the same PCR parameters as above. The allelic ladder is available to all laboratories interested by contacting Dr. Mitchell M. Holland, AFDIL, 14th and Alaska Streets, Washington, DC 20306-6000. (An allele-specific ladder is also available for the D21S11 locus.)

The amplification of SE33 for the ABI Gene Scanner analysis was performed using the same PCR conditions with the exception that 5 pmol of each primer was used and the TTTC-strand was labeled at the 5'-end with the fluorodye FAM. One microliter of PCR product was added to 4 fmol of ROX labeled GS-2500 (a *Pst*I digest of lambda DNA) internal molecular weight standard and the electrophoresis was carried out according to the ABI protocol.

Results and discussion

Using PCR and the horizontal, discontinuous PAGE system developed by the FBI, SE33 has been analyzed for its application to forensic and human remains identification (Holland et al., 1993). More than 21 alleles have been observed at the SE33 locus. A preliminary allele-specific ladder has been generated consisting of 10 alleles, approximately every other repeat unit (Fig. 1). The spacing of alleles in the ladder, however, is not the expected eight base pair differences. There is a dinucleotide repeat in proximity to the tetranucleotide repeat which may contribute additional polymorphic character to the system. The effect of the dinucleotide repeat is being addressed through DNA sequence analysis of individual alleles.

Three different racial or ethnic populations (at least 100 unrelated U.S. Caucasians, U.S. Blacks, and Barbados Blacks) have been analyzed for allele frequency distributions and compared for potential statistical differences (Fig. 2). SE33 alleles are evenly distributed, meet Hardy-Weinberg equilibrium, and show minimal differences between populations. A heterozygosity value of 95%, the number and distribution of alleles, and the lack of significant ethnic disparity makes SE33 an excellent candidate for forensic and human remains identification.

The Armed Forces DNA Identification Laboratory (AFDIL) has successfully used SE33 analysis for human remains identification and re-association in a number of cases for the Office of the Armed Forces Medical Examiner (OAFME). All case samples analyzed to date (as of 1 January, 1993) have resulted in two banded patterns (heterozygous genotypes), including references. In a case performed for the OAFME,

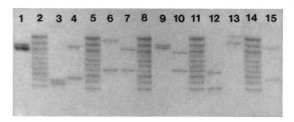

Figure 1. Discontinuous PAGE (7% acrylamide, 3.3% PDA) of SE33 ladder and representative population samples. Lane 1 is the K562 human control. Lanes 2, 5, 8, 11, and 14 are allelic ladder, and lanes 3, 4, 6, 7, 9, 10, 12, 13, and 15 are unrelated individuals.

SE33 Allele Frequency Data

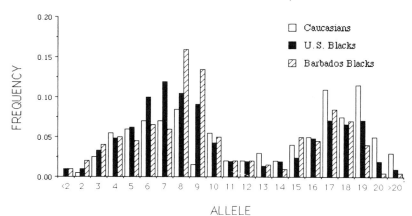

Figure 2. SE33 allele frequency data for 100 unrelated U.S. Caucasians, 105 U.S. Blacks, and 100 Barbados Blacks.

six military personnel were killed in a high speed airplane crash. The six sets of remains were fragmented and severely burned. DNA extraction was performed using the Chelex method (Walsh et al., 1992). SE33 analysis was able to differentiate all six sets of remains, identify the remains by paternity analysis, and to re-associate fragmented material. The discrimination power of SE33 has been a useful tool for the AFDIL in making identifications.

In addition to SE33, AFDIL has been analyzing the STR locus D21S11. The tetranucleotide repeat at the D21S11 locus was first described by Sharma and Litt (Sharma and Litt, 1992). Once again, a preliminary ladder, consisting of 8 alleles, has been constructed to analyze two ethnic groups for allele frequency distribution, and for comparison of ethnic differences (Fig. 3). At least 12 alleles have been observed, with adequate allele distribution. The allele distributions, for one Caucasian and one Black population, determined by AFDIL were consistent with the data reported by Sharma and Litt, for European Caucasians. The heterozygosity of D21S11 is approximately 85%, due to the high frequency of alleles 3, 4, and 5. AFDIL is in the process of optimizing D21S11 for use in human remains identification.

Manual methods of STR analysis are adequate for present day needs, however the future is moving towards fluorescence automation. Amplified STR alleles can be compared to either internal allele-specific ladders or molecular weight standards. The SE33 ladder has been successfully amplified and analyzed on the Gene Scanner (Fig. 4). Only nine of the ten original alleles were detected when amplified together. In general, amplification of allelic ladders has been difficult due to the

272

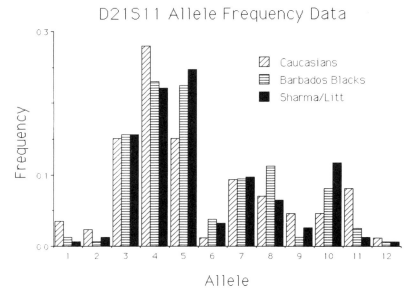

Figure 3. D21S11 allele frequency data for 75 unrelated U.S. Caucasians, 50 Barbados Blacks, and 72 European Caucasians (Sharma and Litt, 1992).

dynamics of fluorescence based methodologies. Amplification of larger alleles is generally less efficient than smaller alleles. Unlike silver stain or hybridization methods of detection, fluorescent label is not incorporated into alleles uniformly during the PCR process. Smaller alleles tend to receive more label than larger alleles. Recent advances in labeling techniques, using labeled dNTPs or intercolaters, should compensate for these problems (personal communication). In the interim, amplification of individual alleles, or small groups of alleles, and pooling of the products can be used to generate fluorescently labeled allelic ladders.

Regardless of the labeling method used, allele specific ladders may not be necessary in the future. Currently available internal standards are able to accurately size alleles. Preliminary studies in our laboratory to determine the precision of sizing alleles using internal molecular weight standards resulted in minor variances. When comparing the size of individual SE33 alleles (ranging in size from approximately 230 to 320 base pairs), lane-to-lane variation does not exceed 1–2 base pairs (0.3–0.9%), and generally the difference is less than a single base pair. Recent data, however, suggests that with the agarose format, gel-to-gel variation of sizing or defining alleles is greater when using an internal molecular weight standard than when using an allele-specific ladder (Sullivan et al., 1992). AFDIL is currently addressing these and other issues in an effort to multiplex STR systems on the Gene Scanner to

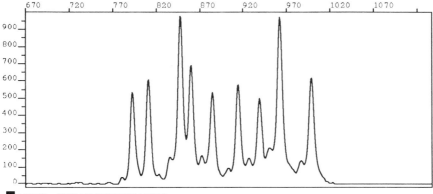

Lane 21: SE33 Allele Specific Ladder

Peak/Lane	Min.	Size	Peak Height	Peak Area	Scan #
1Y, 21	79	240.78	566	4010	793
2Y, 21	81	246.40	667	4731	811
3Y, 21	84	258.20	1057	7762	848
4Y, 21	86	262.09	742	4704	860
5Y, 21	88	270.38	533	4396	885
6Y, 21	91	280.76	628	4552	915
7Y, 21	94	289.43	502	4126	940
8Y, 21	96	297.28	1007	8594	963
9Y, 21	99	309.44	654	5402	999

Figure 4. SE33 allele specific ladder analyzed on the ABI 362 Fluorescent Fragment Analyzer. Allele sizes were determined using the ABI GS 2500 internal lane standard. The SE33 locus contains a polymorphic dinucleotide repeat which may account for the unequal distribution of allele sizes.

increase both throughput and discrimination capabilities for future casework.

Acknowledgement
The authors wish to thank the Federal Bureau of Investigation, specifically Dr. Bruce Budowle and Mark Wilson of the Forensic Science Research and Training Center, for their contributions to the evaluation of the SE33 locus.

References

Boerwinkle E, Xiong W, Fourest E, Chan L (1989) Rapid typing of tandemly repeated hypervariable loci by the polymerase chain reaction: application to the apolipoprotein B 3′ hypervariable region. Proc Nat Acad Sci USA 86: 212–216

Budowle B, Allen RC (1990) Discontinuous polyacrylamide gel electrophoresis of DNA fragments. *In:* Mathew C (ed.) Methods in Molecular Biology–Molecular Biology in Medicine, Vol. 7. Humana, London

Budowle B, Chakraborty R, Giusti AM, Eisenberg AJ, Allen RC (1991) Analysis of the VNTR locus D1S80 by the PCR followed by high-resolution PAGE. Am J Hum Genet 48: 137–144

Edwards A, Civitello A, Hammond HA, Caskey CT (1991) DNA typing and genetic mapping with trimeric and tetrameric tandem repeats. Am J Hum Genet 49: 746–756

274

Edwards A, Hammond HA, Jin L, Caskey CT, Chakraborty R (1992) Genetic variation at five trimeric and tetrameric tandem repeat loci in four human population groups. Genomics 12: 241–253

Hochmeister MN, Budowle B, Jung J, Borer UV, Comey CT, Dirnhofer R (1991) PCR-based typing of DNA extracted from cigarette butts. Internat J Leg Med 104: 229–233

Horn GT, Richards B, Klinger KW (1989) Amplification of a highly polymorphic VNTR segment by the polymerase chain reaction. Nuc Acids Res 17: 2140

Kasai K, Nakamura Y, White R (1990) Amplification of a variable number tandem repeat (VNTR) locus (pMCT118) by the polymerase chain reaction (PCR) and its application to forensic science. J For Sci 35: 1196–1200

Holland MM, Wilson M, Prenger VL, Polymeropoulos MH, Lee DA, Weedn VW, Budowle B (1993) Analysis of the STR locus ACTBP2 (SE33) for forensic and human remains identification. Am J Hum Genet, will be submitted for publication in 1993

Litt M, Luty JA (1989) A hypervariable microsatellite revealed by in vitro amplification of a dinucleotide repeat within the cardiac muscle actin gene. Am J Hum Genet 44: 397–401

Moos M, Gallwitz D (1983) Structure of two human beta-actin-related processed genes one of which is located next to a simple repetitive sequence. The EMBO J 2: 757–761

Peake IR, Bowen D, Bignell P, Liddell MB, Sadler JE, Standen G, Bloom AL (1990) Family studies and parental diagnosis in severe von Villebrand disease by polymerase chain reaction amplification of a variable number tandem repeat region of the von Villebrand factor gene. Blood 76: 555–561

Polymeropoulos MH, Rath DS, Xiao H, Merril CR (1992) Tetranucleotide repeat polymorphism at the human beta-actin-related pseudogene H-beta-Ac-psi-2 (ÅCTBP2). Nuc Acids Res 20: 1432

Saiki RK, Scharf S, Faloona F, Mullis KB, Horn GT, Erlich HA, Arnheim N (1985) Enzymatic amplification of beta-globin sequences and restriction analysis for diagnosis of sickle cell anemia. Science 230: 1350–1354

Saiki RK, Walsh PS, Levenson CH, Erlich HA (1988) Genetic analysis of amplified DNA with immobilized sequence-specific oligonucleotide probes. Proc Nat Acad Sci USA 86: 6230–6234

Sharma V, Litt M (1992) Tetranucleotide repeat polymorphism at the D21S11 locus. Hum Mol Genet 1: 67

Southern EM (1975) Detection of specific sequence among DNA fragments separated by gel electrophoresis. J Mol Biol 98: 503–517

Sullivan KM, Pope S, Gill P, Robertson JM (1992) Automated DNA profiling by fluorescent labeling of PCR products. PCR Methods and Applications, Cold Spring Harbor Laboratory 2: 34–40

Walsh DJ, Corey AC, Cotton RW, Forman L, Herrin GL, Jr, Word CJ, Garner DD (1992) Isolation of deoxyribonucleic acid (DNA) from saliva and forensic science samples containing saliva. J For Sci JFSCA 37: 387–395

Walsh PS, Metzger DA, Higuchi R (1991) Chelex 100 as a medium for simple extraction of DNA for PCR-based typing from forensic material. BioTechniques 10: 506–513

Weber JL, May PE (1989) Abundant class of human DNA polymorphisms which can be typed using the polymerase chain reaction. Am J Hum Genet 44: 388–396

DNA Fingerprinting: State of the Science
ed. by S. D. J. Pena, R. Chakraborty, J. T. Epplen & A. J. Jeffreys

Forensic DNA typing by the solid-phase minisequencing method

A.-C. Syvänen[a], A. Sajantila[a] and M. Lukka[b]

[a]*Department of Human Molecular Genetics and* [b]*Department of Immunobiology,
National Public Health Institute, Helsinki, Finland*

Summary
We describe a method for DNA-typing, in which a panel of biallelic markers are detected by
the solid-phase minisequencing method (Syvänen et al., 1990). This method identifies single
nucleotide variations in DNA fragments amplified by the PCR. Determination of the panel of
12 markers selected in this study proved to be an efficient and reliable method for forensic
identification of individuals. We also introduce a novel approach for rapid determination of
allele frequencies by quantitative analysis of pooled DNA samples.

Introduction

The amplification of DNA fragments containing polymorphic regions
of the human genome by the PCR technique (Mullis and Faloona,
1987) has proved to be particularly useful in forensic medicine because
minute amounts of DNA can be amplified from virtually any type of
biological material. Amplification of minisatellite regions (Jeffreys et al.,
1988) followed by size separation of the alleles by gel electrophoresis is
a widely used strategy in forensic analysis (Kasai et al., 1990; Budowle
et al., 1991). Detection of multiple single nucleotide variations at the
HLADQα locus by the "reversed dot blot" method (Saiki et al., 1989)
is also at present used in forensic typing. Single nucleotide variations,
which give rise to biallelic sequence polymorphism, can also be used for
identification purposes. Here we describe the development of a method
for forensic DNA typing, in which a panel of 12 biallelic markers
located on different chromosomes are detected by the solid-phase
minisequencing method (Syvänen et al., 1990).

Materials and methods

DNA samples

The individual samples had been sent for analysis to the National Public
Health Institute (Helsinki, Finland). A rapid cell lysis procedure was

applied to prepare the blood and stain samples (3 mm^3 on fabric) for the PCR (Higuchi, 1989). Batches of leukocytes originating from 90 or 180 Finnish individuals were obtained from the Finnish Red Cross Blood Transfusion Service. DNA was purified from an aliquot of each batch and combined into three pools containing an equal amount of DNA from about 1000 individuals each.

Primers

The primers were designed as described in Syvänen et al. (1993). They were synthesized on an Applied Biosystems 392 DNA/RNA synthesizer. One of each PCR primer were biotinylated at their 5′-end as previously described (Bengtström et al., 1990) or during the synthesis using a biotinyl phosphoramidite reagent (Misiura et al., 1990) (Amersham, RPN 2012).

PCR

Five μl of cell lysate (approximately 2×10^4 DNA molecules), $25-50$ ng of purified DNA, or 1/20 of stain sample was amplified using 10 pmoles of biotinylated primer and 50 pmoles of unbiotinylated primer and 1.25 units of *Thermus aquaticus* (Taq) DNA polymerase (Promega Biotech) at standard PCR conditions (Syvänen et al., 1993). "Multiplex" PCR with four primer pairs in one reaction (ADH3, ARSB, METH and LDLR; APOB, PROS1, PRP and D21S13E; and 3BHSD, LPL, IGF, and BCL2, respectively) was carried out with 10 pmoles of each biotinylated primer and 50 pmoles of each unbiotinylated primer, and using 2.5 units of Taq DNA polymerase.

Solid-phase minisequencing

Figure 1 shows the principle of the method. One tenth of each single PCR product or 1/20 of the "multiplex" PCR products were analyzed in each solid-phase minisequencing reaction as described in detail by Syvänen et al. (1993).

Statistical evaluations

The power of discrimination of the panel of 12 markers and the probability of a random match for the individual samples were calculated as described by Jones (1972). The average probability of exclusion

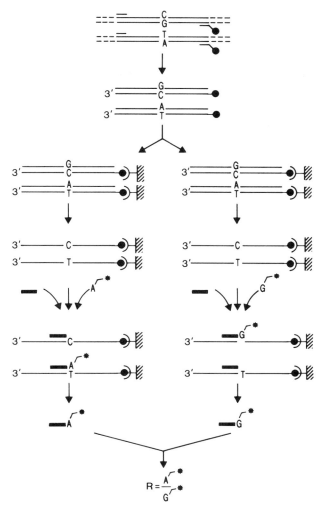

Figure 1. Solid-phase minisequencing. A DNA-fragment spanning the polymorphic site is amplified using a biotinylated and an unbiotinylated PCR primer. The biotinylated PCR product is captured in a streptavidin-coated microtiter well in 50 μl of buffer for 1.5 hours at 37 , the wells are washed, and the unbiotinylated DNA strand is removed by denaturation with 50 mM NaOH. The nucleotides at the polymorphic site are identified in the immobilized DNA strand by two separate minisequencing reactions. A detection step primer annealing immediately adjacent to the mutation (10 pmoles per reaction), is elongated by Taq DNA polymerase (0.05 unit) with one single [3]H[dNTP] (0.1 μCi) complementary to the nucleotide at the polymorphic site in 50 μl of PCR-buffer for 10 min at 50 C. After washing the well the detection step primer is released with 50 mM NaOH, and the incorporated label is measured in a scintillation counter. The result of the test is expressed as the ratio between the labels incorporated in the two reaction. (Figure from Syvänen et al., 1993.)

in paternity analyses, the percentage of potential fathers and paternity indexes in the individual cases were calculated according to Gürtler (1956).

Analysis of VNTR-loci and conventional markers

The case samples were typed by amplified fragment length polymorphism (AmpFLP) analysis (Budowle et al., 1991) of three VNTR loci as previously described (Sajantila et al., 1992; Helminen et al., 1992). In addition, the paternity case samples were typed using the conventional markers.

Results

Allele frequencies of the markers

Fourteen polymorphic biallelic markers located on different chromosomes with reported allele frequencies close to 0.5 were initially selected for the solid-phase minisequencing test (Tab. 1). The distribution of the genotypes and alleles of the markers in the Finnish population were first determined by analyzing individual DNA samples (Tab. 1). For most of the markers the Finnish allele frequencies were similar to those reported from other Caucasian populations, but for the ARSB, VWF and TP53 markers significant differences in the allele frequencies were observed. For all markers the observed genotypes conform to Hardy-Weinberg expectations. The result of the solid-phase minisequencing method is expressed as the ratio between the two incorporated ^{3}H[dNTPs] corresponding to the nucleotide at the polymorphic site (the R-value). The R-values fall into three distinct categories, which unequivocally define the genotype of the individuals (Tab. 2). In all samples the R-value obtained in samples from heterozygous individuals differs by at least a factor of 10 from those obtained in samples from homozygous individuals.

The ratio between the two labelled dNTPs incorporated in the minisequencing reaction directly reflects the proportion of the two sequences in the sample also when the sequences are present in other than the predefined 1:1 (heterozygote) or 2:0 (homozygote) ratios. Taking advantage of this quantitative feature of the minisequencing method, we determined the allele frequencies of each marker by analyzing three pooled DNA samples, each of which represented about 1000 individuals. The ratio between the two sequences in the pooled DNA samples is equivalent to the allele frequencies in the population sample. The allelic frequencies determined from the pooled samles were in good agreement

Table 1. Genotype and allele frequencies of the markers

Marker[a] Location	Number of chromosomes analyzed	Genotype frequency	Allele frequency	
			Individual samples	Pooled[b] samples
ADH3 4q21–23	152	AA 0.28 AG 0.47 GG 0.25	A 0.51 G 0.49	A 0.58 G 0.42
ARSB 5q13–14	128	AA 0.36 AG 0.55 GG 0.09	A 0.63 G 0.37	A 0.67 G 0.33
METH 7q21–31	106	AA 0.30 AG 0.47 GG 0.23	A 0.54 G 0.46	A 0.58 G 0.42
LDLR 19p13.3–31.1	140	AA 0.19 AG 0.48 GG 0.33	A 0.43 G 0.57	A 0.45 G 0.55
APOB 2p24–23	174	CC 0.31 CT 0.49 TT 0.20	C 0.56 T 0.44	C 0.55 T 0.45
PROS1 3p11.1–q11.2	104	AA 0.46 AG 0.29 GG 0.25	A 0.61 G 0.39	A 0.58 G 0.42
PRP 20p12-pter	100	AA 0.53 AG 0.43 GG 0.04	A 0.74 G 0.26	A 0.66 G 0.34
D21S13E 21q11.2	130	TT 0.46 TG 0.35 GG 0.19	T 0.64 G 0.36	T 0.72 G 0.28
3BHSD 1p13	100	AA 0.68 AC 0.28 CC 0.04	A 0.82 C 0.18	A 0.77 G 0.23
LPL 8p22	96	AA 0.25 AG 0.54 GG 0.21	A 0.52 G 0.48	A 0.52 G 0.48
IGF2 11p15.5	108	AA 0.04 AG 0.57 GG 0.39	A 0.32 G 0.68	A 0.20 G 0.80
BCL2 18q21	118	AA 0.32 AG 0.54 GG 0.14	A 0.59 G 0.41	A 0.56 G 0.44
VWF 12pter–p12	92	AA 0 AG 0.20 GG 0.80	A 0.10 G 0.90	A 0.14 G 0.86
TP53 17p13	42	AA 0 AG 0.14 GG 0.86	A 0.07 G 0.93	A 0.08 G 0.98

[a]ADH3, alcohol dehydrogenase; ARSB, arylsulphatase B; METH, met proto-oncogene; LDLR, low density lipoprotein receptor; APOB, apolipoprotein B; PROS1, protein S; PRP, prion protein; 3BHSD, 3-hydroxysteroid dehydrogenase; LPL, lipoprotein lipase; IGF2, insulin like growth factor II; BCL2, B-cell lymphomas/leukemia protein 2; VWF, von Willebrand factor; TP53, transformation related protein p53.
[b]The allele frequencies are mean values of five parallel assays of three pools representing about 1000 individuals each.

280

Table 2. Genotyping of three samples at the ADH3 locus by solid-phase minisequencing

| Genotype of sample | ^{3}H[dNTP] incorporated (cpm)[a] | | R-value A_{cpm}/G_{cpm} |
	A-allele	G-allele	
AA	5430	43	129
AG	3300	1770	1.86
GG	170	5170	0.034

[a]The specific activities of the ^{3}H[dATP] and ^{3}H[dGTP] were 62 Ci/mmol and 31 Ci/mmol, respectively.

with those observed by analyzing individual samples (Tab. 1). The 12 most informative markers were selected for further study. The power of discrimination between individuals using the selected marker panel was calculated to be 0.99996 in the Finnish population, and the average probability of exclusion of the marker panel in paternity testing is 0.90.

Application to paternity and forensic cases

The solid-phase minisequencing method was used to solve two cases of disputed paternity, which both incuded two putative fathers. In the first paternity case the result obtained with the marker BCL2 excluded Man 1 as the father, and in the second case exclusion of Man 1 was obtained with the markers ADH3, LDLR, APOB and D21S13E. The average probability of exclusion was 0.89 and 0.94, respectively. The calculated paternity index for Man 2 was 11.4 in the first case and 16.9 in the second case. The method was also applied to a homicide case, which included reference blood samples from two victims and two suspects and three stain samples. The genotype of Stain 1 matched with the genotype determined from the blood sample of Suspect 2, and the genotypes of Stain 2 and Stain 3 matched with those of Victim 2 and Victim 1, respectively. Each of the three other reference samples were excluded as the source of the stain. In the Finnish population the probability of a random match for individuals of the genotypes determined from the stain samples were 1/85,000, 1/50,000 and 1/2,100,000, respectively. In all three cases the result obtained with the solid-phase minisequencing test was consistent with that obtained with three VNTR-markers and ten additional conventional markers in the paternity cases.

Discussion

We have developed a new method for identification of individuals, in which a panel of 12 biallelic nucleotides, are detected by the solid-phase minisequencing method (Syvänen et al., 1990). The method is particularly suitable for the simultaneous detection of multiple nucleotide variations in a large number of samples. First, the method is generally applicable for detection of any variable nucleotide and the hybridization conditions employed for annealing of the minisequencing detection step primer are non-stringent. Therefore the same reaction conditions can, contrary to hybridization with allele specific probes, be applied for analysis of all sites. Second, the solid-phase reactions in a microtiter well format make the test suitable for automatization. Non-radioactive detection methods are also applicable (Syvänen et al., 1990). Third, the result of our test is obtained as numeric values unequivocally define the genotype of the individuals. This facilitates computer-assisted interpretation and handling of the data.

The panel of 12 markers selected for the solid-phase minisequencing test yielded a similar power of discrimination and exclusion as the three VNTR-markers routinely used in forensic identification at our institute. The method was applied to type samples from two paternity cases and one homicide case. In all three cases the result was consistent with that obtained by the routine methods. Since biallelic polymorphisms are very frequent in the human genome, and detection of the polymorphic nucleotide is technically simple, the power of the minisequencing test can easily be further improved by including additional markers.

When detecting sequence polymorphisms in forensic testing the typing of samples containing DNA from more than one individual is more difficult than when length polymorphisms are analyzed. However, the R-value obtained in our test directly reflects the ratio of the alleles initially present in the sample. If the R-value in a sample falls outside the normal range of R-values, this indicates that it contains DNA from more than one individual. The quantitative nature of the solid-phase minisequencing method also allowed us to determine the allele frequencies of each marker in the Finnish population in a few reactions by quantitative analysis of pooled DNA samples representing 3000 individuals.

In conclusion, the solid-phase minisequencing method is a promising alternative for DNA-based identification in paternity testing and forensic case work. Obviously it can also be applied for analyzing biallelic markers and haplotypes in genetic linkage analysis and population studies.

Acknowledgements
We thank Hanna-Leena Kauppinen at the Finnish Red Cross Blood Transfusion Service for giving us access to the leukocyte pools.

References

Bengtström M, Jungell-Nortamo A, Syvänen A-C (1990) Biotinylation of oligonucleotides using a water soluble biotin ester. Nucleosides Nucleotides 9: 123–127

Budowle B, Chakraborty R, Giusti AM, Eisenberg AJ, Allen R (1991) Analysis of the VNTR locus D1S80 by the PCR followed by high resolution PAGE. Am J Hum Genet 48: 137–144

Gürtler H (1956) Principles of blood group statistical evaluations of paternity cases at the University of Forensic Medicine, Copenhagen. Acta Medicine Legalis et Socialis (Liege) 9: 83–93

Helminen P, Sajantila A, Johnsson V, Lukka M, Ehnholm C, Peltonen L (1992) Amplification of three hypervariable DNA regions by polymerase chain reaction for paternity determinations: comparison with conventional methods and DNA fingerprinting. Mol Cell Probes 6: 21–26

Higuchi R (1989) Simple and rapid preparation of samples for PCR. *In:* Erlich HA (ed) PCR technology – Principles and applications for DNA amplification. Stockton press, New York, 1989, pp 31–39

Jeffreys AJ, Wilson V, Neumann R, Keyte J (1988) Amplification of human minisatellites by the polymerase chain reaction: towards DNA fingerprinting of single cells. Nucleic Acids Res 16: 10953–10971

Jones DA (1972) Blood samples: Probability of discrimination. J Forens Sci Soc 12: 355–359

Kasai K, Nakamura Y, White R (1990) Amplification of a variable number of tandem repeats (VNTR) locus (pMCT118) by the polymerase chain reaction (PCR) and its application to forensic science. J Forensic Sci 35: 1196–1200

Misiura K, Durrant I, Evans MR, Gait MJ (1990) Biotinyl and phosphotyrosinyl phosphoramidite derivates useful in the incorporation of multiple reporter groups on synthetic oligonucleotides. Nucleic Acids Res 18: 4345–4354

Mullis KB, Faloona F (1987) Specific synthesis of DNA in vitro via a polymerase-catalyzed chain reaction. *In:* Wu R (ed) Recombinant DNA, part F. Vol. 155, Colowick SP, Kaplan NO (eds) Methods Enzymol. Academic Press, New York, pp 335–350

Saiki RK, Walsh PS, Lewenson CH, Erlich HA (1989) Genetic analysis of amplified DNA with immobilized sequence-specific oligonucleotide probes. Proc Natl Acad Sci USA 86: 6230–6234

Sajantila A, Puomilahti S, Johnsson V, Ehnholm C (1992) Amplification of reproducible allele markers for amplified fragment length polymorphism analysis. BioTechniques 12: 16–22

Syvänen A-C, Aalto-Setälä K, Harju L, Kontula K, Söderlund H (1990) A primer-guided nucleotide incoporation assay in the genotyping of apolipoprotein E. Genomics 8: 684–692

Syvänen A-C, Sajantila A, Lukka M (1993) Identification of individuals by analysis of biallelic DNA markers using PCR and solid-phase minisequencing. Am J Hum Genet 52: 46–59

DNA Fingerprinting: State of the Science
ed. by S. D. J. Pena, R. Chakraborty, J. T. Epplen & A. J. Jeffreys
© 1993 Birkhäuser Verlag Basel/Switzerland

The use of polymorphic *Alu* insertions in human DNA fingerprinting

G. E. Novick[a], T. Gonzalez[a], J. Garrison[a], C. C. Novick[a], M. A. Batzer[b], P. L. Deininger[c] and R. J. Herrera[a]

[a]*Department of Biological Sciences, Florida International University, University Park Campus, Miami, Florida 33199, USA;* [b]*Human Genome Center, L-452, Biology and Biotechnology Research Program, Lawrence Livermore National Laboratory, P.O. Box 808, Livermore, California 94551, USA; and* [c]*Department of Biochemistry and Molecular Biology, Louisiana State University Medical Center, 1901 Perdido Street, New Orleans, Louisiana 70112, USA*

Summary
We have characterized several Human Specific (HS) *Alu* insertions as either dimorphic (TPA25, PV92, APO), slightly dimorphic (C2N4 and C4N4) or monomorphic (C3N1, C4N6, C4N2, C4N5, C4N8) based on studies of Caucasian, Asian, American Black and African Black populations. Our approach is based upon: 1) PCR amplification using primers complementary to the unique DNA sequences that flank the site of insertion of the different *Alu* elements studied; 2) gel electrophoresis and scoring according to the presence or absence of an *Alu* insertion in one or both homologous chromosomes; 3) allele frequencies determined by gene counting and compared to Hardy-Weinberg expectations. Our DNA fingerprinting procedure using PCR amplification of diallelic polymorphic (dimorphic) Human Specific *Alu* insertions, may be used as a tool for genetic mapping, to characterize populations, study human migrational patterns, and track the inheritance of human genetic disorders.

Introduction

Finding patterns to identify, differentiate, classify and group individuals is probably one of the earliest and most intriguing puzzles in the history of science, starting centuries ago with simple observations of gross morphological traits. Early studies on blood types in humans represent the first attempt to classify individuals and populations based upon variation at the molecular level. Later, the discovery of restriction fragment length polymorphisms or RFLPs (Kan and Dozy, 1978) and hypervariable minisatellite regions (Jeffreys et al., 1985) marked the beginning of the DNA fingerprinting era. Currently, multiple approaches are being used for molecular identification and successfully applied to a broad range of disciplines, from medical diagnosis to human evolution and from forensic sciences to pedigree analysis.

Data generated by the more widely used DNA typing procedures, VNTR and RFLP analyses, is today being complemented by a whole new series of strategies (for review see Herrera and Tracey, 1992). These technologies include the use of monoclonal antibodies for the identification of body fluids (Martin and Parking, 1988), protein polymorphisms (Hobart, 1979), HLA typing (Ishitani and Hirota, 1988), short tandem repeats PCR polymorphism (STRs-PCR) (Edwards, 1991), amplified fragment length polymorphism (AMPFLP) (Eisenberg and Maha, 1991) and minisatellite variant repeat-PCR (MVR-PCR) also called tandem repeat internal mapping (TRIM) (Jeffreys et al., 1991). However, not all of these techniques can be used to answer the same type of questions. The degree of variability observed by the different procedures will limit their optimum range of usage. For example, ABO typing may not be a conclusive method to differentiate between individuals because different individuals may share the same blood group. VNTRs, on the other hand, would not be ideal to study population differences because the same allelic variant can arise in parallel multiple times in different populations.

Alu sequences represent the largest family of short interspersed repetitive elements (SINEs) in humans (Singer, 1982) with an excess of 500,000 copies per haploid genome (Rinehart et al., 1981). Each member being about 300 bp long, *Alu* elements are distributed throughout the genomes of primates. For reviews on SINEs and LINEs see Deininger (1989), Hutchinson III et al. (1989), von Sternberg et al. (1992), and Novick and Herrera (submitted). Recently, one *Alu* subfamily was found to be relatively human specific (HS) (Batzer et al., 1990; Batzer and Deininger, 1991). Members of this subfamily have not only recently inserted into the human genome (within the last 200,000 to 6 million years) (Batzer and Deininger, 1991; Batzer et al., 1991), but they are also transcriptionally active (Matera et al., 1990). These data and the finding of a *de novo* HS *Alu* insertion (Wallace et al., 1991), demonstrates that this subfamily is actively undergoing amplification into other genomic locations. In addition, the presence of an *Alu* insertion has been correlated with a high risk factor for myocardial infarction (Tiret et al., 1992; Cambien et al., 1992). These insertions represent a distinct, easy to measure genetic change which results from an event that occurred one time within the human lineage. In addition, it is very improbable that the same insertion occurs independently in two different individuals. These characteristics make the HS *Alu* insertions valuable tools for DNA typing that may provide information for the window of genetic variability left by highly variable sequences on one hand and more conserved single and multiple copy genes on the other.

We present a DNA typing method based upon PCR amplification of HS *Alu* insertions that, although showing dimorphism, are stable enough to characterize populations, study migrational patterns and follow the inheritance of human genetic disorders.

Materials and methods

DNA samples: A total of four populations were studied: Caucasians, Asians, American Blacks and African Blacks (Batzer et al., 1991).

We have also begun to study different Amerindian populations (Novick et al., in preparation).

DNA isolation: DNA from peripheral blood mononuclear cells was isolated as previously described (Ausabel et al., 1987).

Oligonucleotide primers: Six different pairs of primers, each complementary to different *Alu* insertion loci were used: TPA25, C2N4, C4N6, C4N2, C4N5, C4N8 (Batzer et al., 1991; Batzer and Deininger, 1991). Each pair is directed to the 3′ and 5′ single copy flanking sequences of six different *Alu* insertions. These *Alu* family members were isolated from a randomly sheared human genomic library based upon hybridization to an oligonucleotide which is complementary to 2 of 5 unique mutations that define the subset of recently inserted *Alu* family members (Batzer et al., 1990; Matera et al., 1990; Batzer and Deininger, 1991). In each case the HS *Alu* elements reported here have in fact been shown to be unique to the human lineage and absent from orthologous positions within the great ape and other primate genomes (Batzer and Deininger, 1991; Batzer et al., 1991).

The Amerindian populations were characterized with three dimorphic primer pairs TPA25, APO and PV92 (Novick et al., in preparation). The TPA locus is located on chromosome 8 (p12–q11.2) (Yang-Feng et al., 1986), and the APO *Alu* is near the Apolipoprotein AI-CIII-AIV gene cluster on the long arm of chromosome 11 (Bruns et al., 1984; Karathanasis, 1985). The location of the PV92 *Alu* family member is unknown (Matera et al., 1990). The sequences of the APO and PV92 primers will be published elsewhere (Batzer et al., unpublished data).

PCR amplification: PCR amplification was carried out in a final total volume of 100 μl as previously described (Batzer et al., 1991; Batzer and Deininger, 1991).

Gel Electrophoresis: 4 μl of PCR products dissolved in TE were electrophoresed in 3% TAE agarose gel with 0.5 μg of Hae III digested phiX 174 DNA as molecular weight marker. DNA fragments were visualized with ethidium bromide using a Cybertech CS1 Imaging System and scored according to the following criteria. Homozygous individuals for the insertion exhibit one band approximately 400 bp long. In other words, the *Alu* insertion is present at that locus in both homologous chromosomes. Homozygous individuals for the lack of insertion allele are represented by one band approximately 120 bp long. In these individuals the element is not present in either of the two homologues. Heterozygous individuals exhibit both bands, one of each of the two fragment lengths.

286

Data analysis: Allele frequencies were calculated using the gene counting method and tested for Hardy-Weinberg equilibrium using the Chi-square test for goodness of fit.

Results and discussion

Figure 1 represents a typical electrophoretic separation of PCR products from TPA25, one of the three dimorphic loci. Allelic frequencies derived from the four populations studied are shown in Tab. 1.

Alu elements first appeared in the primate genome about 65 million years ago (Deininger and Daniels, 1986). They have undergone amplification from what is called and *Alu* "source" or "master gene" (Deininger and Slagel, 1988; Deininger et al., 1992) at a rate of approx-

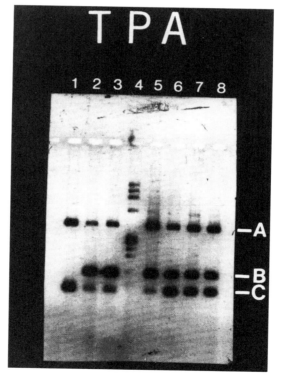

Figure 1. Agarose gel electrophoresis of PCR products using TPA25 primers. TPA25 primers amplify a dimorphic HS *Alu* insertion. The gel shows a homozygous individual for the insertion in lane 1 represented by a band about 400 bp (band A). Lanes 2, 3, 5, 6, 7 and 8 are PCR products of heterozygous individuals exhibiting two bands: one about 400 bp and the other about 120 bp (band B). The molecular weight marker used was Hae III digested phiX 174 (lane 4). Band C represents primer dimer amplification products.

imately 8×10^{-3} *Alu* elements per year (Zuckerkandl et al., 1989) with a calculated number of substitutions of 5×10^{-7} per element, per year (Zuckerkandl et al., 1989). The *Alu* family of repetitive elements is known to retropose to different parts of the genome by way of an RNA intermediate that is then reverse transcribed into a cDNA copy which is inserted into the genome. A 3' oligo dA tail and short direct repeats are structural characteristics that point to this retroposition mode of dispersion. Although there may be some insertional preferences at A + T rich regions (Daniels and Deininger, 1985; Batzer et al., 1991), *Alu* insertions are distributed fairly randomly, so the possibility of having two elements inserted independently within the same locus by chance are minimal.

The HS *Alu* subfamily has an additional feature that makes it unique: some members are currently being amplified. For example, one may find populations in which an HS *Alu* insertion took place earlier in the human lineage and is present in homozygous form in all individuals tested (HASTS, Human *Alu* Sequence Tagged Site; see locus C4N6 in Tab. 1). On the other hand, very recent insertions are expected to be dimorphic in some of the populations (DASTS, Dimorphic *Alu* Sequence Tagged Sites; see TPA25 in Tab. 1). The frequency and distribution of the insertion allele for any given locus would depend on how recent the insertions is, in which population it originated, how much gene flow has occurred between the populations, and whether or not selection has been acting on it. In addition, we found two other categories of HS *Alu* insertions. One exhibits very low frequencies for the lack of insertion allele and most likely represents events that occurred very early in the direct lineage to man, after their divergence from great apes. The other type is rather unusual in that every individual tested appears to be heterozygous. The mechanism responsible for the generation of heterozygous banding patterns in all individuals in all populations is not clear but the fact that at least one pre integration site shares nucleotide identity with L1 elements, provides some insight to this phenomenon. It is possible that these loci represent insertions into other repetitive sequences like L1 family members. In theory, this type of insertion would produce a large, approximately 400 bp, DNA fragment while the vast majority of repetitive loci lacking the *Alu* insertion would amplify small, approximately 118 bp, DNA fragments. Thus, an *Alu* element has in fact retroposed into another sequence which was originally dispersed throughout the genome (the L1 family) and later experienced an HS *Alu* insertion in only one copy. In addition to the "insertion–lack of insertion" type of dimorphic variability described in this study, sequencing studies of the oligo dA track at the 3' end of most *Alu* elements, shows variability (PASTS, Polymorphic *Alu* Sequence Tagged Sites). These polymorphisms involve the number of As and the number and position of the other three nucleotides within the adenosine-rich region (Novick et al., unpublished data; Economou et al., 1990). All the characteristics of HS

Table 1. Distribution of human-specific *Alu* elements[1,2]

Group		TPA25	HS C2N4	HS C4N6	HS C4N2	HS C4N5	HS C4N8
Asians	+ +	10 [0.66]	19 [1.0]	19 [1.0]	0 [0.5]	0 [0.5]	0 [0.5]
	+ −	5	0	0	19	19	19
	− −	4 [0.34]	0 [0]	0 [0]	0 [0.5]	0 [0.5]	0 [0.5]
Caucasians	+ +	10 [0.63]	22 [1.0]	22 [1.0]	0 [0.5]	0 [0.5]	0 [0.5]
	+ −	9	0	0	22	22	22
	− −	4 [0.37]	0 [0]	0 [0]	0 [0.5]	0 [0.5]	0 [0.5]
American Blacks	+ +	4 [0.38]	23 [0.98]	24 [1.0]	0 [0.5]	0 [0.5]	0 [0.5]
	+ −	11	1	0	24	24	24
	− −	10 [0.62]	0 [0.02]	0 [0]	0 [0.5]	0 [0.5]	0 [0.5]
African Blacks	+ +	1 [0.42]	NT	NT	NT	NT	NT
	+ −	8					
	− −	3 [0.58]					

[1]Genotypes, followed by allele frequency in [ ]; [2]NT = Not Tested.

Alu elements described thus far (mechanism of retroposition, nonspecific site of insertion, rate of amplification, variability of the oligo dA track) suggest that the possibility of two populations of unrelated origin having the same insertional pattern for a HS *Alu* insertion is remote and make HS *Alu* elements ideal markers for population studies due to their stability, their dimorphic distribution and their degree of variability.

When typing biological evidence, although multiple approaches are currently being used to discriminate between individuals, not a single method seems to be conclusive in differentiating populations. A number of morphologically distinct populations may generate indistinguishable databases, due to extensive or minimal variations. Hypervariability could generate populations with few alleles in common and therefore no basis for comparison. On the other hand, hypovariability would provide little allelic difference for comparison. In addition, our work with American Indians (Novick et al., in preparation) reveals the need for creating population-specific databases for these closely related groups. Considering the less dynamic nature of HS *Alu* insertions compared to VNTRs and RFLPs, it is significant that all 13 Amerindian populations studied are genotypically distinct with regards to the dimorphic TPA25, APO and PV92 loci. Since these related populations exhibit unique allele frequencies for these three insertions which are more conserved than the currently used highly variable genetic markers (e.g. VNTRs), independent databases for hypervariable loci is clearly justified. In light of our data and using these three dimorphic loci, it would be informative to ascertain the genetic similarity of different populations or subpopulations within Caucasians, Blacks, Hispanic, Orientals, etc. This data may establish the need for independent databases to be used in forensic studies. The evidence presented clearly supports the use of DASTS not only as a valuable alternative for DNA fingerprinting and genetic analysis at the population level, but also as a means of ascertaining the genetic uniqueness of gene pools and populations when designing forensic databases.

Acknowledgements
This research was supported by U.S. Public Health Service (USPHS) Grant RR08205 to RJH and USPHS Grant RO1 HG00340 to PLD. Work by MAB was performed at LLNL under the auspices of U.S. Department of Energy contract No. W-7405-ENG-48.

References

Ausabel FM, Brent R, Kingston UE, Moore DD, Seldman JG, Smith JA, Struhl K (eds) (1987) Current Protocols in Molecular Biology. John Wiley and Sons, NY, NY
Batzer MA, Deininger PL (1991) A Human-specific subfamily of *Alu* sequences. Genomics 9: 481–487
Batzer MA, Gudi VA, Mena JC, Foltz DW, Herrera RJ, Deininger PL (1991) Amplification dynamics of Human-specific (HS) *Alu* family members. Nucleic Acids Res 19: 3619–3623

Batzer MA, Kilroy GE, Richard PE, Shaikh TH, Desselle TD, Hoppens CL, Deininger PL (1990) Structure and variability of recently inserted *Alu* family members. Nucleic Acids Res 18: 6793–6998

Bruns GAP, Karathanasis DK, Bresiow JL (1984) Human apolipoprotein AI-CIII gene complex is located on chromosome 11. Arteriosclerosis 4: 97–102

Cambien F, Poirier O, Laure L, Evans A, Cambou JP, Arveiler D, Luc G, Bard J-M, Bara L, Ricard S, Tiret L, Amouyel P, Alhenc-Gelas F, Soubrier F (1992) Deletion polymorphism in the gene for angiotensin-converting enzyme is a potent risk factor for myocardial infarction. Nature 359: 641–644

Daniels GR, Deininger PL (1985) Integration site preferences of the *Alu* family and similar repetitive DNA sequences. Nucleic Acids Res 13: 8939–8954

Deininger PL, Daniels GR (1986) The recent evolution of mammalian repetitive elements. Trends Genet 2: 76–80

Deininger PL, Slagel VK (1988) Recently amplified *Alu* family members share a common parental *Alu* sequence. Mol Cell Biol 8: 4566–4569

Deininger PL (1989) SINEs: short interspersed repeated DNA elements in higher eucaryotes. *In:* Howe M and Berg D (eds) Mobile DNA. ASM Press, Washington, DC, pp 619–636

Deininger PL, Batzer MA, Hutchinson III C, Edgell MH (1992) Master genes in mammalian repetitive DNA amplification. Trends Genet 8: 307–312

Economou EP, Bergen AW, Warren AL, Antonarakis SE (1990) The polydeoxyadenylate tract of *Alu* repetitive elements is polymorphic in the human genome. Proc Natl Acad Sci USA 87: 2951–2954

Edwards A (1991) DNA typing with trimeric and tetrameric tandem repeats: polymorphic loci, detection systems and population genetics. *In:* Promega (ed.) Proceedings from the Second International Symposium of Human Identification, pp 31–52

Eisenberg M, Maha G (1991) AMPFLP analysis in parentage testing. *In:* Promega (ed) Proceedings from the Second International Symposium of Human Identification, pp 129–154

Herrera RJ, Tracey ML (1992) DNA fingerprinting: basic techniques, problems and solutions. J Criminal Justice 20: 237–248

Hobart MJ (1979) Genetic polymorphism of human plasminogen. Ann Hum Genet 42: 419–423

Hutchinson III CA, Hardies SC, Loeb DD, Shehee WR, Edgell MH (1989) LINEs and related retroposons: long interspersed repeated sequences in the eucaryotic genome. *In:* Howe M and Berg D (eds) Mobile DNA, ASM Press, Washington, DC, pp 593–617

Ishitani A, Hirota T (1988) Personal identification by HLA typing of cultured fibroblast derived from caderveric tissues. *In:* Mayr WR (ed.) Advances in Forensic Haemogenetics 2, pp 59–63

Jeffreys AJ, Wilson V, Thein SL (1985) Hypervariable "minisatellite" regions in human DNA. Nature 314: 67–73

Jeffreys AJ, Mac Leod A, Tamaki K, Neil D, Monckton DG (1991) Minisatellite repeat coding as a digital approach to DNA typing. Nature 354: 204–209

Kan YW, Dozy A (1978) Polymorphism of DNA sequences adjacent to human β-globin structural gene: relationship to the sickle mutation. Proc Natl Acad Sci 75: 5631–5635

Karathanasis SK (1985) Apolipoprotein multigene family: tandem organization of human apolipoprotein AI, CIII, AIV genes. Proc Natl Acad Sci USA 82: 6374–6378

Martin PD, Parkin BH (1988) The use of monoclonal antibodies in forensic sciences. *In:* Mayr WR (ed) Advances in Forensic Haemogenetics 2, pp 284–297

Matera AG, Hellmann U, Hintz MF, Schmid CW (1990) Recently transposed *Alu* repeats result from multiple source genes. Nucleic Acids Res 18: 6019–6023

Novick GE, Gonzales T, Garrison J, Novick CC, Batzer MA, Deininger PL, Herrera RJ. Study of Amerindian evolution using Human-specific *Alu* insertions (in preparation)

Novick GE, Herrera RJ. Transposons in the human genome. *In:* VCH Verlagsgesellschaft mbH (ed.) The Encyclopedia of Molecular Biology. VCH Publishers Inc., New York. (submitted)

Rinehart FP, Ritch TG, Deininger PL, Schmid CW (1981) Renaturation rate studies of a single family of interpersed repeated sequences in human deoxyribonucleic acid. Biochemistry 20: 3003–3010

Sambrook J, Fritsch EF, Maniatis T (1989) *In:* Molecular Cloning: A Laboratory Manual (2nd edition) Cold Spring Harbor Laboratory Press

Singer MF (1982) SINEs and LINEs: highly repeated short and long interpersed sequences in mammalian genomes. Cell 28: 433–434

Tiret L, Rigat B, Visvikis S, Breda C, Corvol P, Cambien F, Soubrier F (1992) Evidence, from combined segregation and linkage analysis, that a variant of the angiotensin I-converting enzyme (ACE) gene controls plasma ACE levels. Am J Hum Genet 51: 197–205

von Sternberg RM, Novick GE, Gao GP, Herrera RJ (1992) Genome canalization: the coevolution of transposable and interspersed repetitive elements with single copy DNA. Genetica 86: 215–246

Wallace MR, Andersen LB, Saulino AM, Gregory PE, Glover TW, Collins FS (1991) A *de novo Alu* insertion results in neurofibromatosis type 1. Nature 353: 854–866

Yang-Feng TL, Opdenakker G, Volckaert G, Franke U (1986) Human tissue-type plasmino-gen activator gene located near chromosomal breakpoint in myeloproliferative disorder. Am J Hum Genet 39: 79–87

Zuckerkandl E, Latter G, Jurka J (1989) Maintenance of function without selection: *Alu* sequences as "cheap genes". J Mol Evol 29: 504–512

DNA Fingerprinting: State of the Science
ed. by S. D. J. Pena, R. Chakraborty, J. T. Epplen & A. J. Jeffreys

Applications of DNA fingerprinting in plant population studies

H. Nybom

Balsgård – Department of Horticultural Plant Breeding, Swedish University of Agricultural Sciences, Fjälkestadsvägen 123-1, S-291 94 Kristianstad, Sweden

Summary

Many plant species are characterized by a large variability in breeding system and the frequent occurrence of one or several means of vegetative propagation, resulting in complicated population structures. Multi-locus DNA fingerprinting with probes specific for minisatellite and simple repetitive sequences has proven to be a very sensitive method for detecting genetic variation. Thus clones consisting of genetically identical plants can be distinguished and their spatial distribution analyzed. Similarly, offspring resulting from apomictic processes (asexual seed set) can be told apart from those resulting from sexual recombination. Genetic related-ness between different individuals can be estimated, albeit crudely, from band-sharing values obtained by pairwise comparison of different DNA fragment profiles. These estimates appear to be associated with breeding system, with selfing species and/or populations showing considerably less intrapopulational variation than their outcrossing counterparts. In species or species groups with relatively low levels of genetic variation due to e.g. apomixis, DNA fingerprinting may prove valuable even in taxonomy.

Introduction

Studies of plant speciation and evolution frequently emphasize modes of reproduction and propagation, an area in which plants exhibit a large number of varying strategies. Most plant species reproduce mainly by seed, but a considerable number are also capable of vegetative propagation.

Genetic variability in the produced seed depends mainly on the breeding system, which may vary even between closely related species. Thus some species are strictly outcrossing due to some kind of self-in-compatibility system whereas other species are obligate selfers. Often seed set is instead achieved by a combination of cross-pollination and selfing due to mechanisms that promote one or the other but do not completely exclude the alternative. Finally, seed set may also occur by apomixis, i.e. embryo development without prior fertilization of the egg cell. Whereas genetic recombination results in individual-specific geno-types in the offspring of obligately outcrossing species, the situation is quite different in species that are mainly self-pollinated. Several subse-quent generations of selfing lead to a decrease in genetic variation, eventually resulting in genetically identical plants. Apomictic seed set, on the other hand, may result in instantaneous formation of a new clone. Moreover, most apomicts are facultatively apomictic and thus retain the ability to set seed sexually as well. Thus some seed may result from genetic recombination whereas other entail the perpetuation of the maternal genotype only.

Vegetative propagation is widespread in the plant kingdom, encompassing several different means of enlarging the distributional area via e.g. the production of bulbils (a small bulb or bulblike organ often produced on above ground organs), root suckers (new shoots arising from the root system of an older plant) or runners (plants produced on above ground outgrowths, so called stolons, from the mother plant). Thus a successful genotype may attain great size, eventually consisting of a large number of ramets (plants having an identical genotype due to descent of origin).

There is also a time dimension; whereas individual plants die after a certain time span, clonal genotypes can become extremely long-lived and go on to produce new ramets as long as the habitat remains suitable. Thus species with apomictic seed production and/or vegetative propagation may contain genotypes that are thousands of years old occurring side-by-side with recently evolved ones.

Accurate estimates of the occurrence and distribution of genetic variation are of prime importance for many areas of research like plant taxonomy, ecology, population genetics and conservation biology. When acquiring and evaluating these estimates, we must however take into account the facts of reproduction and propagation. In species that are strictly outcrossing and totally lacking vegetative propagation, each individual plant is the result of a recombinational event. Studies of species that instead have a clonal population structure, benefit greatly if individual clones are first identified and their spatial distribution analyzed. Unfortunately, vegetative propagation is often difficult to investigate in the field and we may not be able to ascertain the origin of individual ramets. Similarly, apomictically derived seeds and seedlings are usually impossible to distinguish from sexually derived ones. We thus need a methodology that allows us to identify individual genotypes in the field with a high level of certainty. Multi-locus DNA fingerprinting using probes specific for minisatellite and simple repetitive sequences is a very sensitive method for detecting genetic variation. Moreover, it has also proven a worthwhile addition to commonly applied methods of assessing genetic relatedness. Here some studies will be reviewed that involve the utilization of DNA fingerprinting in wild plant species.

Methodology and evaluation

Various methods have been utilized for DNA extraction, digestion, electrophoresis, blotting and hybridization (see Weising et al., 1991;

Bierwerth et al., 1992; and also review in Nybom, 1991). In plant studies primarily multi-locus minisatellite DNA probes like the Jeffreys 33.5 and 33.16 (Jeffreys et al., 1985), and the hypervariable M13 sequence (Vassart et al., 1987) have been used. Recently, promising results have been obtained with various oligonucleotide probes complementary to simple repetitive sequences (Weising et al., 1991; Beyermann et al., 1992; Bierwerth et al., 1992; Lönn et al., 1992; Nybom et al., 1992). Single-locus minisatellite DNA probes have so far not been developed for plant materials in spite of having proved to be very useful in studies of genetic variation in humans and many animal species (Bruford et al., 1992).

Detection of the hybridizing DNA fragments is usually achieved with ^{32}P-labeling of the probe, though some investigations have instead made use of non-isotopic methods (Weising et al., 1991; Bierwerth et al., 1992). Evaluation of the resulting autoradiographs is usually done by eye, comparing position and intensity of the signal bands. Normally only those bands are included in the evaluation of which presence or absence can be scored in all samples on a gel. Differences between individual DNA fragment profiles can then be quantified with the two commonly utilized similarity indices (alternatively termed 'band-sharing coefficients'):

$$D \text{ (sometimes denoted as 's')} = 2N_{AB}/(N_A + N_B)$$

and

$$x = [(N_{AB}/N_A) + (N_{AB}/N_B)]/2$$

where N_{AB} is the number of scorable bands common to DNA profiles A and B, N_A is the number of scorable bands in A, and N_B is the number of scorable bands in B. The band-sharing values D and x yield rather similar results though D is biased slightly downward (Bruford et al., 1992). In plants band-sharing values obtained with minisatellite probes tend to be relatively high as compared to e.g. 0.2 in humans (Jeffreys et al., 1985). Typical values are 0.30–0.50 for presumably unrelated con-specific individuals (Nybom, 1991), and with averages reaching as high as 0.80 for comparisons among siblings and between parent and off-spring (Nybom, 1990a). When oligonucleotide probes complementary to simple repetitive sequences are used, the average band-sharing values usually differ considerably according to the sequence motif utilized. Band-sharing values derived from oligonucleotide fingerprints are generally comparable with those obtained from the use of minisatellite probes or even higher. However, they provide a broader range of informativeness, e.g. in chickpea (*Cicer arietinum*) between almost zero [for (GATA)$_4$] and one [for (GTG)$_5$] (Weising et al., 1992).

Individual band-sharing values do not allow a conventional interpretation from the standpoint of population genetics since the individual

DNA fragments cannot be assigned to specific loci. However, over a broad spectrum of DNA fragment frequency distributions, the mean band-sharing value or similarity index does approximate the average identity-in-state-of pairs of individuals (Lynch, 1990). Estimated chances of finding the same DNA fingerprint in two different samples can then be calculated as D^n where n equals the average number of scored fragments per sample. For unrelated con-specific plant individuals values of 10^{-3}–10^{-5} are commonly encountered (Nybom, 1991).

Interpretation of the similarity index and its utilization in various formulas for assessing the degree of genetic relatedness, rely on the assumption that the DNA fragments analyzed are derived from many independent loci. Ideally, for each new material studied, possible co-segregation of fragments due to linkage or internal cleavage of the minisatellite sequences, should be determined. This can be done either by a pedigree analysis or by checking band-sharing values for known relatives and non-relatives (Bruford et al., 1992). Whereas this has been achieved in some cultivated plants (Dallas, 1988; Nybom, 1990a; Nybom & Schaal, 1990a; Lavi et al., 1991; Nybom & Hall, 1991; Tzuri et al., 1991), similar studies are as yet lacking for wild populations or have been carried out on a very limited number of loci (van Houten et al., 1991).

Vegetative propagation

Ideally DNA fingerprint identity versus non-identity can be determined unambiguously, but occasionally fragment profiles differ in only one or two bands. These differences may be due to mutation and typically occur in the order of 10^{-3} per DNA fingerprint fragment per gamete depending on the organism/probe/enzyme combination utilized (Bruford et al., 1992). For plants few estimates have been made, however pointing to relatively low ratios like $<1/900$ in carnation, genus *Dianthus* (Tzuri et al., 1991). Accordingly, high levels of fingerprint stability have been found in vegetatively propagated material of e.g. apples, *Malus × domestica* (Nybom, 1990b) and raspberries, *Rubus idaeus* (Hoepfner et al., 1993). Thus, DNA fingerprinting appears to be a very useful method to distinguish and delimit clones, as suggested also by the following examples.

A species that is well-known for its vigorous vegetative propagation by root suckering is the North American quaking aspen, *Populus tremuloides*. This wind-pollinated tree species covers large areas in the North American midwest. In one study plants were collected from (1) several different locations in Colorado, (2) along a 4-km footpath at one of these locations, and (3) in two dense stands about 1 km apart from each other at one of these locations (Rogstad et al., 1991a). A surprisingly high number of different genotypes were encountered, with all plants sampled in the first two parts of the study exhibiting different DNA fragment profiles (Fig. 1). Average band sharing values of 0.35–0.49 were encountered following digestion with one of the enzymes *Dra* I, *Hae* III or *Hin*f I and hybridization to the M13 probe (Rogstad et al., 1991a, and unpublished results). The material collected in two dense stands comprised two and three clones, respectively, with the three different enzymes yielding consistent results.

Hazel, *Corylus avellana*, instead has rather limited vegetative propagation. In Sweden this small, wind-pollinated tree occurs in large, more or less continuous populations in the south and middle parts, and in small isolated populations to the north. These northern populations are relicts from a much larger distribution area during the relatively warm bronze age. In a study of the effects of population size and gene flow for genotypic diversity and distribution, plants from a large southern population and from a very small northern population were analyzed with DNA fingerprinting (Fig. 2). Following digestion with *Rsa* I and hybridization to the M13 probe, seven plants in the southern population

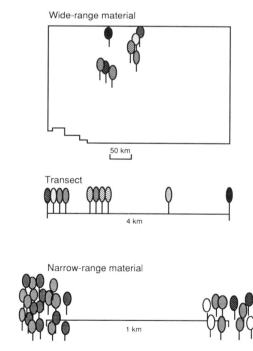

Figure 1. Genotype distribution in American quaking aspen (*Populus tremuloides*), as determined from DNA fingerprints obtained by digestion of the DNA with each of the enzymes *Dra* I, *Hae* III and *Hin*f I, and hybridization to the M13 minisatellite probe.

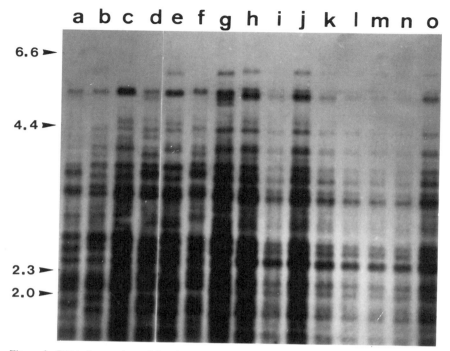

Figure 2. DNA fingerprints of hazel plants (*Corylus avellana*), obtained by digestion of the DNA with *Rsa* I and hybridization to the M13 minisatellite probe. a–g 7 plants from the population Södra Tvet in S Sweden; h–o 8 plants from the population Skuleberget in N Sweden. Size standards were derived from digestion of λ DNA with *Hin*d III.

exhibited individual-specific DNA fingerprints, with an average similarity index of 0.52. On the other hand, all eight plants analyzed in the northern population were identical, presumably due to vegetative propagation. Present investigations (Persson & Nybom, manuscript in prep.) aim to analyze genetic variation in several additional populations, and to assess to what extent reduction in genetic variability is due to restricted gene flow, and to vegetative propagation, respectively.

In DNA samples of the North American paw-paw, *Asimina triloba*, hybridized to the M13 probe, surprisingly low levels of fragment profile diversity were encountered (Rogstad et al., 1991b). Thus a wide range sample of trees collected from northwestern USA, yielded an average similarity index of 0.68. Even higher *D*-values were obtained for narrow-range samples collected within the state of Missouri. At one plot of $100 \, m^2$ all 20 plants investigated even exhibited identical DNA fingerprints. Probably these plants were derived by vegetative propagation. Moreover, nine offspring plants proved to be identical with the tree from where the seeds had been collected. This may be due to high levels of selfing. However, apomixis, albeit not described previously for this genus, cannot be ruled out.

Substantial intrapopulation variation was found in DNA finger-prints obtained by hybridization to a (TG)$_n$ probe in a recently intro-duced population of the leguminous shrub, *Coronilla emerus*, in Central Sweden. In contrast, no variation was detected within or be-tween three relict and highly-isolated populations in Southern Norway (Lönn et al., 1992). Further, more extensive, investigations show low levels of within-population variation in native *C. emerus* in both Nor-way and Sweden but there is a high degree of differentiation between regional populations. This pattern of variation probably reflects the species' history of population disjunction (Lönn, Tegelström & Pren-tice, pers. comm.).

Breeding systems

In some cases DNA fingerprinting has been used to analyze levels of genetic variability resulting from different breeding systems. Thus within and among population variation in three different plantain species, genus *Plantago*, was investigated (Wolff et al., manuscript submitted). The levels and patterns of variation detected by the M13 probe were in good accordance with those expected from the different breeding sys-tems of the species. The highly selfing *P. major* had relatively low variability within populations but high differentiation among popula-tions, whereas the obligately outcrossing *P. lanceolata* exhibited higher variability within populations and moderate differentiation among pop-ulations. *P. coronopus*, with a mixed breeding system, had levels of variation intermediate between *P. major* and *P. lanceolata*. Moreover, the levels of variation within and among populations corresponded, in general, to the levels of allozyme variation measured in an earlier study (Wolff, 1991).

Box elder, *Acer negundo*, is dioecious, i.e. female and male flowers occur on separate trees. Thus all seeds are produced by cross fertiliza-tion. Moreover, there is no vegetative propagation, and so each tree should be the result of genetic recombination. DNA samples from 21 plants collected in Missouri, USA, were hybridized to the M13 probe (Nybom & Rogstad, 1990). Each plant was found to have a unique hybridization pattern as postulated, with an average similarity index of 0.55. Since this species is insect-pollinated, gene flow can be expected to decrease with increasing distance between plants. This was also sug-gested by the DNA fingerprint results, since closely occurring plants had higher band-sharing values than more distant ones (Nybom & Rogstad, 1990). However, even though band-sharing values for pairwise compari-sons show a maximum for plants growing closely together, there is great

300

overlapping as well as an unexplicable second maximum for comparisons among the most distant plants (Fig. 3).

DNA fingerprinting may be especially valuable for analysis of species with unusually low levels of genetic variation, like the Chilean annual *Microseris pygmaea*, thought to have arisen by dispersal from North America of only one seed (van Houten et al., 1991). Whereas isozymes and other molecular markers yield low levels of variability in this predominantly inbreeding species, hybridization of DNA samples with a $(GATA)_n$ probe resulted in fragment patterns that differed considerably among various inbred strains (van Houten et al., 1991). Most field-collected plants from one and the same population also proved to have different fragment patterns, as did their offspring.

Initial results show higher levels of band-sharing with the $(TG)_n$ probe for comparisons within populations of the insect-pollinated herbaceous species *Silene uniflora* than for comparisons between individuals in England and in Sweden, respectively (Lönn et al., 1992). Few DNA fingerprint studies exist as yet for gymnosperms. However, DNA samples of some trees of Norway spruce, *Picea abies*, have been hybridized to the M13 probe (Kvarnheden & Engström, 1992). Suitable levels of fingerprint variation were encountered, and the method might thus become useful for studies of population genetics also in conifers.

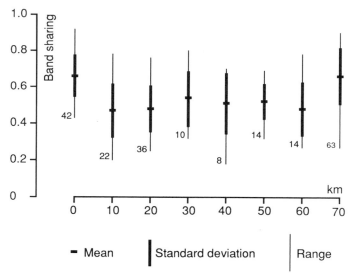

Figure 3. Band-sharing values obtained from pairwise comparisons of DNA fingerprints in box elder (*Acer negundo*), obtained from digestion of the DNA with *Hin*f I and hybridization to the M13 minisatellite probe. Number of pairwise comparisons is given for each of 8 different collection site distances, as also the mean band-sharing value, one standard deviation and the range.

Apomixis

Taxonomy in apomictic plant species is often quite problematic, with numerous microspecies described on morphological grounds only. Common dandelions, genus *Taraxacum*, comprise obligately apomictic triploids as well as some sexual diploids. Some of the apomictic microspecies appear to be uni-clonal whereas others are clearly multi-clonal as determined with isozyme studies (van Oostrum et al., 1985). To further investigate clonality in *Taraxacum*, DNA fingerprints were obtained with the (GATA)$_4$ probe for some North and Central European species (van Heusden et al., 1991). One of these, *T. hollandicum*, appears to be represented by the same clone in Czechoslovakia and France as suggested by identical DNA fingerprints in the four populations sampled, whereas a slightly deviating fragment profile was encountered in a Dutch population. On the other hand, one and the same DNA fragment pattern was found in Dutch populations of *T. gelricum*, *T. maritimum* and in two slightly dissimilar morphotypes of *T. palustre*, thereby suggesting that these three microspecies must be derived from the same clone! Two other morphotypes of *T. palustre* exhibited slightly deviating fingerprints, most likely due to either somatic mutations or to genetic recombination. This investigation suggests that a taxonomic revision of the species complex would be appropriate, especially if a future application of several different probes yielded consistent results.

Many apomictic plant species also propagate vegetatively. Thus clones can evolve either from apomictically derived seeds or by some means of vegetative propagation. Whereas seedlings and root suckers of e.g. blackberries are easily distinguished on habitus the first one or two years in the field, it is virtually impossible to ascertain the origin of an older plant (Nybom, 1987a). Sometimes DNA fingerprinting can, however, be helpful in analyzing the occurrence of apomixis versus vegetative propagation. Thus genotypic distribution was investigated in two North American *Rubus* species utilizing the M13 probe (Nybom & Schaal, 1990b). Both species exhibit vigorous vegetative propagation but seed production is different. The black raspberry, *R. occidentalis*, reproduces sexually whereas the highbush blackberry, *Rubus pensilvanicus*, appears to be facultatively apomictic. Among the 20 shoots sampled from each species, 15 genotypes were found in *R. occidentalis* as opposed to only five in *R. pensilvanicus*. Moreover, *R. occidentalis* shoots with an identical genotype grew only 2–4 m from each other, whereas *R. pensilvanicus* shoots with an identical genotype occurred up to 500 m apart. Most likely, the drastic increase in distance between plants of identical genotype in *R. pensilvanicus* is due to dispersal of apomictically produced seed. Plotting frequencies of pairwise band-sharing values for the two species separately illustrate the differences in genetic composition (Figs 4 and 5).

302

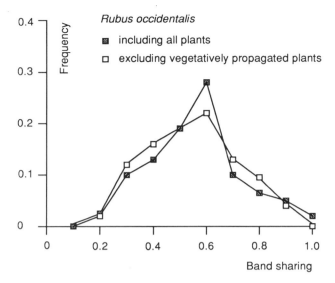

Figure 4. Frequency of band-sharing values in a stand of black raspberry (*Rubus occidentalis*), obtained by pairwise comparisons of DNA fingerprints resulting from digestion of the DNA with *Hin*f I and hybridization to the M13 minisatellite probe.

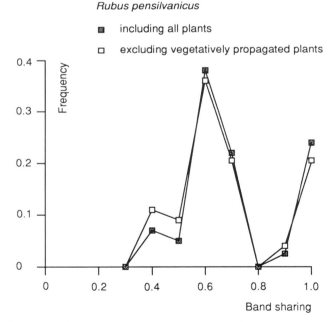

Figure 5. Frequency of band-sharing values in a stand of high-bush blackberry (*Rubus pensilvanicus*), obtained by pairwise comparisons of DNA fingerprints resulting from digestion of the DNA with *Hin*f I and hybridization to the M13 minisatellite probe.

In order to investigate variation between apomictic microspecies in Swedish *Rubus* species, DNA samples from one plant each of several species were hybridized to the M13 probe, yielding completely different DNA fingerprints (Fig. 6). Intraspecific variation was studied in *R. nessensis*, which had already been utilized in previous investigations on reproduction and propagation. Thus four populations (3–18 km apart) of *R. nessensis* were analyzed in a demographic study (Nybom, 1987a, b). These populations, and to some extent also neighboring stands within a population, differed greatly as to average shoot height and density, seed and root sucker production, as well as life expectancy of individual plants. However, the 4–6 plants randomly sampled from each population, quite surprisingly exhibited completely identical DNA fingerprints (Fig. 7).

High levels of M13 and $(TG)_n$ DNA fingerprinting homogeneity were encountered also in a recent study of some Swedish and German *Rubus* species (Kraft & Nybom, manuscript in prep.). Thus no intraspecific variation could be found in Swedish populations of *R. fuscus*, *R. hartmanni*, *R. pedemontanus*, *R scheutzii*, and *R. grabowskii*, and only minor variation within *R. insularis*, where a geographically isolated population on the Swedish West coast deviated somewhat from the standard type. When

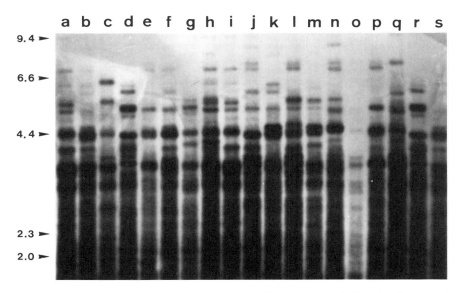

Figure 6. DNA fingerprints of various Swedish blackberry species, obtained by digestion of the DNA with *Hae* III and hybridization to the M13 minisatellite probe. a and i *Rubus vigorosus*; b and s *R. laciniatus*; c *R. divaricatus*; d and r *R. pedemontanus*; e *R. hartmanni*; f *R. insularis*; g *R. lindebergii*; h *R. polyanthemus*; j *R. pyramidalis*; k *R. radula*; l *R. axillaris*; m *R. infestus*; n *R. discolor*; o *R. grabowskii*; p *R. vestitus*; q *R. wahlbergii*. Size standards were derived from digestion of λ DNA with *Hin*d III.

304

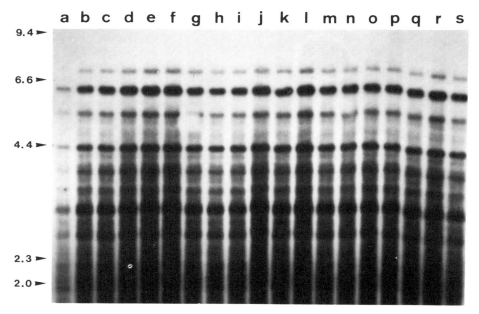

Figure 7. DNA fingerprints of *Rubus nessensis* plants collected in four different populations (one of these represented by two adjacent stands), obtained by digestion of the DNA with *Hae* III and hybridization to the M13 minisatellite probe. a–c and s Bjävröd stand 1; d–f Bjävröd stand 2; g–j Ludvigsborg; k–n Syrkhult; o–r Toftaröd. Size standards were derived from digestion of λ DNA with *Hin*d III.

Swedish and German populations were compared, only minor band differences were encountered in *R. fuscus* and none at all in *R. polyan-themus*. Moreover, identical DNA fingerprints were sometimes found when closely related species pairs were compared, e.g. the Swedish *R. scheutzii* with the German *R. muenterii*, and the Swedish *R. insularis* (standard type) with the German *R. gracilis*. In conclusion, these results suggest that most of these microspecies have been derived from one recombinational event only, and that the resulting genotype, more or less unaltered, has subsequently spread over a large area.

Frequently population studies are insufficient to analyze breeding systems, and must be complemented with pollination experiments. Like many other polyploid species groups, different *Rubus* species usually produce fertile offspring upon interspecific hybridization. However, it has been suggested that the ability to reproduce by facultative apomixis in *Rubus* may be lost in the hybrids due to genetic recombination (Gustafsson, 1943). In an attempt to study this further, interspecific cross-pollinations involving various Swedish blackberry species were performed (Nybom, 1988). The resulting offspring were then tentatively classified on morphological grounds as to being derived by apomixis or by sexual reproduction. Some of the resulting hybrid plants, as well as some apomictically derived ones, were cross-pollinated and a second generation of plants obtained. Analysis of this second generation should establish the reproductive behavior of first-generation hybrids. However, morphologic characters were not always adequate for determining whether a seedling was purely maternal or also incorporated some traits of the pollen parent. This was true especially for crosses involving a group of closely related species in the sect. *Suberecti.* Thus a total of 69 second-generation plants, emanating from pollinations between *Suberecti* species, were analyzed with DNA fingerprinting (Nybom, manuscript in prep.) Some of these, resulting from digestion of the DNA samples with *Hae* III and subsequent hybridization to the M13 probe, are shown in Fig. 8.

Two different plants resulting from the initial pollination of *R. nessensis* with *R. scissus* had been pollinated with *R. sulcatus.* One of these plants was apparently a hybrid, and, in its turn, gave rise sexually to a second-generation plant (lane b in Fig. 8) since the banding pattern of this plant suggests that all three putatively parental species contributed to the genotype. The other plant had instead been derived by apomixis, and also reproduced apomictically. Thus all of its seven seedlings (lanes c–f and k–m in Fig. 8) had fragment profiles identical to *R. nessensis.* In a third combination, a hybrid between *R. scissus* and

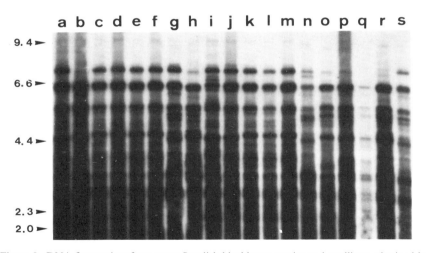

Figure 8. DNA fingerprints from some Swedish blackberry species and seedlings, obtained by digestion of the DNA with *Hae* III and hybridization to the M13 minisatellite probe. a and j *Rubus nessensis*; b seedling S1; c–f and k–m seedlings T1–T7; g and s *R. sulcatus*; h *R. scissus*; i *R. nessensis scissus* deviating form; n–r seedlings R1–R5. Seedling populations S and T were derived from two different series of cross-pollinations (*R. nessensis* × *R. scissus*) × *R. sulcatus*, and seedling population R from (*R. scissus* × *R. nessensis*) × *R. sulcatus*. Size standards were derived from digestion of λ DNA with *Hin*d III.

R. nessensis had been pollinated with *R. sulcatus*, giving rise to five plants with individual-specific fingerprints (lanes n–r).

In yet another case (not shown) a plant emanating from a pollination of *R. scissus* with *R. sulcatus*, yielded four identical offspring following pollination with a *R. scissus × plicatus* hybrid. These four plants incorporated some bands found exclusively in *R. scissus* and some found in *R. sulcatus*, and must have been derived from hybridization between these two species. However, the first-generation hybrid obviously then proceeded to set seed apomictically since (1) its offspring were identical, and (2) no evidence of any exclusive *R. plicatus* bands were found.

In total, 59 of the analyzed plants were obtained from pollination of a non-hybridogenous plant. Of these offspring plants, 54 exhibited a DNA fragment pattern identical to that of the seed parent and were thus produced by apomixis, whereas the remaining 8% contained additional bands derived from the pollen parent. Finally, there were also three hybrid plants that were pollinated. Of these, one yielded one sexually derived offspring, another yielded five sexually derived offspring, and the last one yielded four apomictically derived offspring. Obviously some, but not all, *Rubus* hybrids reproduce sexually.

Determination of paternity

DNA fingerprinting has become a major tool for paternity determination in humans. Similarly, fingerprint-aided paternity studies now play a major role in gene flow studies in animals. On the contrary, few applications have yet been presented in wild plants. This is probably to a considerable extent due to the high band-sharing values commonly encountered with minisatellite probes in plant material as well as technical difficulties in obtaining high-quality autoradiographs. Experimental studies of cultivated rice, genus *Oryza* (Dallas, 1988), apples (Nybom & Schaal, 1990a), avocados, genus *Persea* (Lavi et al., 1991), and carnations (Tzuri et al., 1991), have shown that inheritance is Mendelian and that linkage occurs comparatively seldom. However, distribution of fragments in a parent-offspring study in *Microseris pygmaea* yielded some non-Mendelian results, pointing perhaps to unusually high mutation levels (van Houten et al., 1991). A major problem with paternity studies on wild material is, however, the fitting of offspring to be investigated as well as all putative candidates into the same electrophoresis gel. The alternative, i.e. to make band-sharing comparisons across gels, is not completely reliable when utilizing multilocus probes due to the technical difficulties mentioned above. Probably this field of work will have to await the introduction of single-locus probes, that are more suitable for detailed genetic analyses.

Genetic relatedness and taxonomy

Whereas DNA fingerprinting may quite adequately describe genotypic distribution within a population, interpopulation and interspecific levels of variation are much more difficult to analyze. At least in most animal species, levels of variation are so high already within populations, that a quantification at higher levels may be meaningless except for some cases with much reduced genetic variability (Bruford et al., 1992). Up till now, few studies in plants have involved interspecific comparisons. In fungi, DNA fingerprinting using simple repeat probes however appears to be quite useful for classification of closely related strains or species (Meyer et al., 1992). Similarly, it might prove valuable also in higher plants for certain species groups like apomictic dandelions (van Heusden et al., 1991).

Choice of probe is very important, since different probes can be used to gain information at different levels. Thus oligonucleotide probes have yielded promising results in a set of chick pea species (Weising et al., 1992), cultivated banana, genus *Musa* (Kaemmer et al., 1992) as well as in carnations (Tzuri et al., 1991). Studies of cultivated *Rubus* (blackberries and raspberries) comprising several species as well as interspecific hybrids, similarly point to a direct relationship between taxonomic distance and band-sharing values also with the M13 probe (Nybom et al., 1989; Nybom & Hall, 1991). Similarly, the geographic origin of various avocado accessions was clearly associated with band-sharing values obtained from hybridization of DNA samples with several different multi-locus probes (Lavi et al., 1991).

Conclusions

The full potential of DNA fingerprinting for plant population studies has yet to be realized but some very promising work has been initiated. Multi-locus DNA fingerprint patterns thus appear to have become a convenient and sensitive means of identifying genetic differences at the level of individuals, clones and inbred lines. For more distantly related individuals, faster, cheaper and less sensitive methods like isozymes and RAPDs may prove more feasible. However, in some plant groups with reduced genetic recombination due to apomixis, selfing and/or vegetative propagation, multi-locus DNA fingerprinting may contribute to taxonomical research also on the species level. Potentially, DNA profiling with single-locus probes may become an extremely useful additional tool for e.g. gene flow studies.

Acknowledgements
Valuable comments on the manuscript have been given by J. T. Epplen, M. Lönn, H. Prentice and K. Weising. Financial assistance has been provided by the Swedish Natural Science Research Council.

308

References

Beyermann B, Nürnberg P, Weihe A, Meixner M, Epplen JT, Börner T (1992) Fingerprinting plant genomes with oligonucleotide probes specific for simple repetitive DNA sequences. Theor Appl Genet 83: 691–694

Bierwerth S, Kahl G, Weigand F, Weising K (1992) Oligonucleotide fingerprinting of plant and fungal genomes: a comparison of radioactive, colorigenic and chemiluminescent detection methods. Electrophoresis 13: 115–120

Bruford MW, Hanotte O, Brookfield JFY, Burke T (1992) Single-locus and multilocus DNA fingerprinting. In: Hoelzel AR (ed) Molecular genetic analysis of populations. A practical approach, pp 225–269. IRL Press, Oxford

Dallas JF (1988) Detection of DNA "fingerprints" of cultivated rice by hybridization with a human minisatellite probe. Proc Natl Acad Sci USA 85: 6831–6835

Gustafsson Å (1943) The genesis of the European blackberry flora. Lunds Univ Årsskrift 39(6): 1–200

Hoepfner A-S, Nybom H, Carlsson U, Franzén R (1993) DNA fingerprinting useful for monitoring cell line identity in micropropagated raspberries. Acta Agricult Scand, Sect B 43: 53–57

Jeffreys AJ, Wilson V, Thein SL (1985) Individual-specific 'fingerprints' of human DNA. Nature 316: 76–79

Kaemmer D, Afza R, Weising K, Kahl G, Novak FJ (1992) Oligonucleotide and amplification fingerprinting of wild species and cultivars of banana (*Musa* spp.). Bio/Technology 10: 1030–1035

Kvarnheden A, Engström P (1992) Genetically stable, individual-specific differences in hypervariable DNA in Norway spruce, detected by hybridization to a phage M13 probe. Can J Forest Res 22: 117–123

Lavi U, Hillel J, Vainstein A, Lahav E, Sharon D (1991) Application of DNA fingerprints for identification and genetic analysis of avocado. J Amer Soc Hort Sci 116: 1078–1081

Lynch M (1990) The similarity index and DNA fingerprinting. Mol Biol Evol 7: 478–484

Lönn M, Tegelström H, Prentice HC (1992) The synthetic $(TG)_n$ polydinucleotide: a probe for gene flow and paternity studies in wild plant populations? Nucleic Acids Res 20: 1153

Meyer W, Morawetz R, Börner T, Kubicek CP (1992) The use of DNA fingerprint analysis in classification of some species of the *Trichoderma* aggregate. Curr Genet 21: 27–30

Nybom H (1987a) A demographic study of the apomictic blackberry, *Rubus nessensis* (Rosaceae). Nord J Bot 7: 365–372

Nybom H (1987b) Flowering and fruiting phenology in the apomictic blackberry, *Rubus nessensis* (Rosaceae). Nord J Bot 7: 373–381

Nybom H (1988) Apomixis versus sexuality in blackberries (*Rubus* subgen. *Rubus*, Rosaceae). Plant Syst Evol 160: 207–218

Nybom H (1990a) Genetic variation in ornamental apple trees and their seedlings (*Malus*, Rosaceae) revealed by DNA 'fingerprinting'. Hereditas 113: 17–28

Nybom H (1990b) DNA fingerprints in sports of 'Red Delicious' apples. Hort Science 25: 1641–1642

Nybom H (1991) Applications of DNA fingerprinting in plant breeding. In: Burke T, Dolf G, Jeffreys AJ, Wolff R (eds) DNA fingerprinting: approaches and applications, pp 294–311. Birkhäuser, Basel

Nybom H, Hall HK (1991) Minisatellite DNA "fingerprints" can distinguish *Rubus* cultivars and estimate their degree of relatedness. Euphytica 53: 107–114

Nybom H, Ramser J, Kaemmer D, Kahl G, Weising K (1992) Oligonucleotide DNA fingerprinting detects a multiallelic locus in box elder. Molecular Ecology 1: 65–67

Nybom H, Rogstad SH (1990) DNA "fingerprints" detect genetic variation in *Acer negundo*. Plant Syst 173: 49–56

Nybom H, Schaal BA, Rogstad SH (1989) DNA "fingerprints" can distinguish cultivars of blackberries and raspberries. 5th International Symposium on *Rubus & Ribes*, Acta Hortic 262: 305–310

Nybom H, Schaal BA (1990a) DNA "fingerprints" applied to paternity analysis in apples (*Malus × domestica*). Theor Appl Genet 79: 763–768

Nybom H, Schaal BA (1990b) DNA "fingerprints" reveal genotypic distributions in natural populations of blackberries and raspberries (*Rubus*, Rosaceae). Amer J Bot 77: 883–888

Rogstad SH, Nybom H, Schaal BA (1991a) The tetrapod DNA fingerprinting M13 repeat probe reveals genetic diversity and clonal growth in quaking aspen (*Populus tremuloides*, Salicaceae). Plant Syst Evol 175: 115–123

Rogstad SH, Wolff K, Schaal BA (1991b) Geographical variation in *Asimina triloba* Dunal (Annonaceae) revealed by the M13 "DNA fingerprinting" probe. Amer J Bot 78: 1391–1396

Tzuri G, Hillel J, Lavi U, Haberfeld A, Vainstein A (1991) DNA fingerprint analysis of ornamental plants. Plant Science 76: 91–98

van Heusden AW, Rouppe van der Voort J, Bachmann K (1991) Oligo-(GATA) fingerprints identify clones in asexual dandelions (*Taraxacum*, Asteraceae). Fingerprint News 3(2): 5–10

van Houten WHJ, van Heusden AW, van der Woort JR, Raijmann L, Bachmann K (1991) Hypervariable DNA fingerprint loci in *Microseris pygmaea* (Asteraceae, Lactuceae). Botanica Acta 104: 252–255

van Oostrum H, Sterk AA, Wijsman HJW (1985) Genetic variation in agamospermous microspecies of *Taraxacum* sect. *Erythrosperma* and sect. *Obliqua*. Heredity 55: 223–228

Vassart G, Georges M, Monsieur R, Brocas H, Lequarré A-S, Cristophe D (1987) A sequence in M13 phage detects hypervariable minisatellites in human and animal DNA. Science 235: 683–684

Weising K, Beyermann B, Ramser J, Kahl G (1991) Plant DNA fingerprinting with radio-active and digoxigenated oligonucleotide probes complementary to simple repetitive DNA sequences. Electrophoresis 12: 159–169

Weising K, Kaemmer D, Weigand F, Epplen JT, Kahl G (1992) Oligonucleotide fingerprinting reveals various probe-dependent levels of informativeness in chickpea (*Cicer arietinum*). Genome 35: 436–442

Wolff K (1991) Analysis of allozyme variability in three *Plantago* species and a comparison to morphological variability. Theor Appl Genet 81: 119–126

Wolff K, Rogstad SH, Schaal BA. Population structure of three *Plantago* species revealed by minisatellite DNA analysis (submitted)

DNA Fingerprinting: State of the Science
ed. by S. D. J. Pena, R. Chakraborty, J. T. Epplen & A. J. Jeffreys

DNA- and PCR-fingerprinting in fungi

W. Meyer[a], E. Lieckfeldt, K. Kuhls, E. Z. Freedman[a], T. Börner and T. G. Mitchell[a]

[a]*Duke University Medical Center, Department of Microbiology, P.O. Box 3803, Durham, NC 27710, USA; and Humboldt University of Berlin, Department of Biology, Institute of Genetics, Microbiology and Biochemistry, 10117 Berlin, Germany*

Summary
DNA-fingerprinting has been successfully used to detect hypervariable, repetitive DNA sequences (minisatellites and microsatellites) in fungi. Combined with methods used to identify random amplified polymorphic DNA (RAPD), conventional DNA-fingerprinting hybridization probes can also be used as single primers to detect DNA polymorphisms among fungal species and strains. The oligonucleotides $(CA)_8$, $(CT)_8$, $(CAC)_5$, $(GTG)_5$, $(GACA)_4$ and $(GATA)_4$, as well as the phage M13 and its core sequence, have been used as specific probes in hybridization experiments and as primers for PCR analysis. Both methods have enabled the differentiation of all the fungal species and strains that were examined, including species of *Penicillium*, *Trichoderma*, *Leptosphaeria*, *Saccharomyces*, *Candida* and *Cryptococcus*. These methods have been used 1) to clarify the taxonomic relationships among relevant species of the *Trichoderma* aggregate, 2) to discriminate between aggressive and non-aggressive isolates of the rape seed phytopathogen, *Leptosphaeria maculans*, and 3) to identify strains of the pathogenic yeasts, *Cryptococcus neoformans* and *Candida albicans*. PCR-fingerprinting allowed serotypes of *C. neoformans* to be distinguished. The application of DNA- and PCR-fingerprinting to fungal DNA should aid in clarification of their taxonomy and improved diagnosis of mycotic disease.

Introduction

Filamentous fungi and yeast are becoming increasingly important for a variety of industrial purposes, and many are serious plant and human pathogens. The identification, differentiation and classification of species or strains of lower eukaryotes, including filamentous fungi, has often been very difficult when based solely on morphological traits or cultural characteristics. Additional biochemical (e.g., isoenzymes), antigenic and molecular markers (e.g., DNA hybridization, RFLP analysis, pulsed field gel electrophoresis) have been used successfully to overcome these problems (e.g., Wöstemeyer, 1985; Vilgalys and Johnson, 1987; Perfect et al., 1989). However, the utility of these markers is limited, and the methods are time-consuming and laborious. Therefore, they are not easily applied to routine identification for diagnostic or epidemiological purposes. As fungal infections have become increasingly prevalent and serious in plants, domestic animals, and humans, especially for patients with AIDS or organ transplants, the need for simple, rapid methods to identify species and strains has intensified. Molecular approaches appear to be increasingly promising for genetic identification of fungal strains and species.

In the last few years, two methods have manifested considerable potential for the genetic identification of individual strains. DNA-fingerprinting, which was described in 1985 (Jeffreys et al., 1985), is based on the detection of hypervariable repetitive sequences (mini-satellite and microsatellite or simple repetitive DNAs). DNA-fingerprinting is able to detect genetic variability among even closely related individuals of humans, animals, plants and fungi (Jeffreys et al., 1985; Ali et al., 1986; Epplen, 1988; Nybom et al., 1990; Meyer et al., 1991, 1992a, b). The other method employs single primers of arbitrary nucleotide sequences to randomly amplify polymorphic DNA (RAPD) fragments from different individuals (RAPD, Williams et al., 1990; AP-PCR, Welsh and McClelland, 1990). Because each of these methods is capable of detecting variation among individuals, we reasoned that a combination of both methods might yield a rapid, sensitive and more reliable method that would be applicable to large scale experiments. We have found that probes useful for conventional DNA-fingerprinting hybridization may also be used as specific single primers for the amplification of hypervariable DNA sequences in fungi. This report describes the successful use of DNA-fingerprinting and PCR-fingerprinting to 1) clarify the taxonomic relationships of relevant species of the *Trichoderma* aggregate, 2) discriminate between aggressive and non-aggressive isolates of the rape seed phytopathogen, *L. maculans*, and 3) distinguish serotypes and identify strains of the pathogenic yeast *C. neoformans*.

Material and methods

Fungi and DNA isolation

Strains (Tab. 1) were obtained from the following culture collections: *Trichoderma*, ATCC (Rockville, MD, USA), CBS (Baarn, The Netherlands) and TU-Wien (Vienna, Austria); *Leptosphaeria*, IGF (Berlin, Germany); *Cryptococcus*, DUMC (Durham, NC, USA) and UCLA (Los Angeles, CA, USA); and all other fungi, HUB-Microbiology (Berlin, Germany) and IFZ (Berlin, Germany). Fungi were cultivated, harvested and genomic DNA was isolated from liquid nitrogen frozen cells as previously described (Meyer et al., 1991, 1993; Gruber, 1990).

Table 1. Fungal genera analyzed by DNA- and PCR-fingerprinting; indication of probes and primers used

Division	Genera	Probe* or primer°
Zygomycotina	Absidia	(CT)*$_8$, (GTG)*$_5$, (GACA)*$_4$, M13*
	Mucor	(CT)*$_8$, (GTG)*$_5$, M13*
	Parasitella	(CT)*$_8$, (GTG)*$_5$, (GACA)$_4$, M13*
Ascomycotina	Chaetomium	(CT)*$_8$, (GTG)$_5$, (GACA)$_4$, M13*
	Emericella	(CT)*$_8$, (GTG)$_5$, (GACA)$_4$, M13*
	Eurotium	(CT)*$_8$, (GTG)$_5$, M13*
	Eupenicillium	(CA)*$_8$, (CT)$_8$, (GTG)°$_5$, (GACA)*$_4$, (GATA)$_4$, M13*°
	Gibberella	(CT)$_8$, (GTG)$_5$, (GACA)$_4$, M13*
	Leptoshaeria	(CT)$_8$, (GTG)$_5$, (GACA)$_4$, M13*
	Klyveromyces	(CT)$_8$, (GTG)*°$_5$, (GACA)*$_4$, (GATA)$_4$, M13*°
	Saccharomyces	(CT)*$_8$, (GTG)$_5$, (GACA)*$_4$, (GATA)$_4$, M13*°
Deuteromycotina	Arxula	(GTG)*$_5$, M13*
	Aspergillus	(CT)°$_8$, (CAC)°$_5$, (GTG)$_5$, (GACA)*°$_4$, (GATA)*$_4$, M13*°
	Candida	(CT)°$_8$, (GTG)°$_5$, (GACA)*$_4$, (GATA)$_4$, M13*°
	Cryptococcus	(GTG)*°$_5$, (GACA)*$_4$, (GATA)*$_4$, M13*°
	Fusarium	(CT)*$_8$, (CAC)°$_5$, (GTG)*°$_4$, M13*°
	Geosmithia	(CA)$_8$, (CT)$_8$, (CAC)°$_5$, (GTG)$_5$, (GACA)$_4$, (GATA)°$_4$, M13*°
	Penicillium	(CA)*$_8$, (CT)*$_8$, (CAC)°$_5$, (GTG)$_5$, (GACA)°$_4$, (GATA)*°$_4$, M13*°
	Stachybotrys	(CT)*$_8$, (GTG)*$_5$, M13*
	Trichoderma	(CA)$_8$, (CT)*$_8$, (CAC)°$_5$, (GTG)$_5$, (GACA)*$_4$, (GATA)*°$_4$, M13*°
	Trichothecium	(CT)$_8$, (GTG)$_5$, (GACA)$_4$, M13*
	Ulocladium	(CT)*$_8$, (GTG)$_5$, M13*
	Verticillium	(CT)*$_8$, (GTG)$_5$, (GACA)*$_4$, M13*

DNA-fingerprinting

3 μg of genomic DNA were digested with restriction enzymes according to the conditions recommended by the manufacturers (Amersham, Braunschweig, Germany, or Boehringer Mannheim, Germany). DNA fragments were separated in 0.8% agarose gels run in TAE buffer (Maniatis et al., 1982) and vacuum blotted on Hybond N membrane (Amersham, Braunschweig, Germany). DNA of the phage M13 and its core sequence (GAGGGTGGXGGXTCT) and the oligonucleotides (CA)$_8$, (CT)$_8$, (GTG)$_5$, (GACA)$_4$ and (GATA)$_4$, were used for hybridization, which was carried out as previously described (Meyer et al., 1991).

PCR-fingerprinting

Amplification reactions were performed in volumes of 50 μl containing 10 to 25 ng genomic DNA, 3 mM magnesium acetate, 0.2 mM of each dNTP (USB, Cleveland, OH, USA), 20 to 30 ng primer [(CA)$_8$, (CT)$_8$, (CAC)$_5$, (GTG)$_5$, (GACA)$_4$, (GATA)$_4$ or the phage M13 core sequence (GAGGGTGGXGGXTCT)], and 2.5 U Amplitaq DNA polymerase (Perkin Elmer Cetus, Norwalk, CT, USA). The PCR was performed using buffer conditions recommended by the manufacturer for 40 cycles in a Perkin Elmer Cetus DNA Thermal Cycler (Model 480), using the following parameters: 20 s denaturation at 93°C; 60 s annealing at 50°C and 20 s primer extension at 72°C, followed by a final extension cycle for 6 min at 72°C. Amplification products were analyzed by electrophoresis in 1.4% agarose gels run in 1 × TBE buffer (Maniatis et al., 1982) and detected by staining with ethidium bromide under UV light.

Results

Application of DNA-fingerprinting and PCR-fingerprinting to several genera of filamentous fungi

Over 70 species representing 18 genera of filamentous fungi and 5 genera of yeasts were investigated by DNA-fingerprinting studies (Tab. 1). The amount of information of the resulting DNA-fingerprint patterns was strongly dependent on the optimal combination of enzyme, hybridization probe and species (Meyer et al., 1991). Highly informative DNA fingerprint patterns were obtained using restriction enzymes with a recognition site of 6 base pairs in combination with (GTG)$_5$, (GACA)$_4$ or the phage M13 sequence as hybridization probes. The complexity and variability of patterns obtained showed a strong dependence on the repeated sequence motif used for hybridization in the species under investigation. The optimal combination of probe and species must be determined empirically for each taxon. Individual patterns could be detected in all species and strains investigated (Meyer et al., 1992b; Meyer et al., 1991).

In PCR-fingerprint analysis, the same oligonucleotides, which were designed as hybridization probes for DNA-fingerprinting, were used as single PCR primers to amplify hypervariable DNA fragments. The resulting electrophoretic profiles varied even among individual strains and are useful for identification. PCR-fingerprints have been used recently to analyze genetic variation within the genera *Penicillium*, *Trichoderma*, *Leptosphaeria*, *Saccharomyces*, *Candida* and *Cryptococcus* (Lieckfeldt et al., 1993; Meyer et al., 1993).

Re-classification of some species of the Trichoderma aggregate

Both DNA- and PCR-fingerprinting were used to clarify the taxonomic relationships of nine species of the genus *Trichoderma*, including three mutant strains of *T. reesei*. (*T. reesei* is important in biotechnology as a producer of cellulase.) Based on morphological studies, *T. reesei* was assumed to be derived from *T. longibrachiatum* (Rifai, 1969). However, DNA-fingerprints obtained with the oligonucleotides $(CT)_8$, $(GTG)_5$, $(GACA)_4$ and the phage M13 core sequence clearly demonstrated that *T. reesei* is quite different from *T. longibrachiatum* (Fig. 1A). The mutants of *T. reesei* were not distinguished by this method, and striking similarity was also observed between fingerprints of *T. reesei* and *T. todica* (Fig. 1A). In general these results agree with traditional taxonomic classification in the *Trichoderma* aggregate, which is based on morphological characters.

The results of DNA-fingerprinting by PCR were similar and supported these conclusions about the identity of *Trichoderma* strains (Fig. 1B). By means of DNA and PCR-fingerprinting, a re-classification of the *Trichoderma* aggregate should now be possible (Meyer et al., 1992b).

Differentiation of pathotypes of the phytopathogen,
Leptosphaeria maculans

L. maculans, the teleomorph of *Phoma lingam*, causes systemic infections of the oilseed rape *Brassica napus* L. var. *oleifera*, affecting its growth and causing devastation of the crop (Hassan et al., 1991). Genomic DNA from sixteen different isolates of *L. maculans* was investigated by DNA-fingerprinting following digestion with BamHI

316

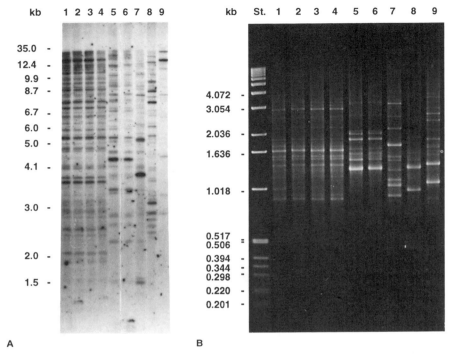

Figure 1. DNA-fingerprinting patterns of genomic DNA from *Trichoderma* isolates, with BamHI and hybridized with the ^{32}P-labelled oligonucleotide $(CA)_8$ (A) and PCR-fingerprinting patterns obtained by amplification of genomic DNA from the *Trichoderma* isolates using $(GTG)_5$ as a single primer in the PCR analysis (B). Lane 1, T. todica (ATCC # 36396); 2, T. reesei QM6a (ATCC # 13631); 3, T. reesei QM9414 (ATCC # 26921); 4, T. reesei QM9123 (ATCC # 24449); 5, T. longibrachiatum (CBS # 816.68); 6, T. longibrachiatum (Tu-Wien); 7, T. pseudokoningii (ATCC # 24961); 8, T. saturnisporum (ATCC # 18903); 9, T. harzianum (ATCC # 36042); St., 1 kb ladder (GIBCO-BRL).

and hybridization with the oligonucleotides, $(GTG)_5$, $(GACA)_4$ (Fig. 2), $(CT)_8$, or the M13 sequence. These probes revealed extensive DNA polymorphism within this species. All of the investigated isolates could be clearly and unequivocally distinguished by their DNA-fingerprints. Genetic differences among the aggressive and non-aggressive strains were also apparent, based on the similarity of their multi-locus phenotypes. Both appeared as consistent groups with high degrees of similarity. Striking differences in DNA-fingerprints were particularly evident by the absence of bands in the high molecular weight region of the non-aggressive isolates when MspI is used as restriction enzyme and $(GTG)_5$ as hybridization probe (data not shown). DNA-fingerprinting has been demonstrated to be an appropriate tool for molecular diagnosis of this important plant pathogen (Meyer et al., 1992a).

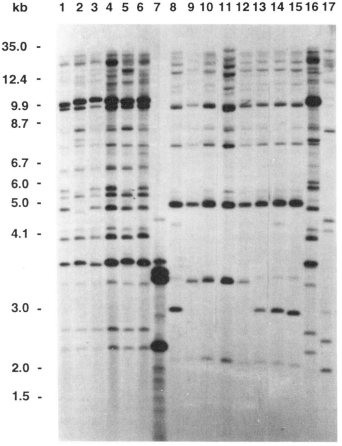

Figure 2. DNA-fingerprinting patterns of genomic DNA from *Leptosphaeria maculans* restricted with BamHI and hybridized with ^{32}P-labelled oligonucleotide (GACA)$_4$. Lanes 1–6, *L. maculans* isolates belonging to the aggressive pathotype group (IIa1, V2, MIX7, IX2, IV2, IX4); lane 7, human marker DNA digested with HinfI; lanes 8–15, *L. maculans* isolates belonging to the non-aggressive pathotype group (VI, VII3, VIII3, NV6, NXI10, S18, SIII2, SV1); lane 16, aggressive strain BBA no. 63698; lane 17, strain IMI147195.

Identification of strains of Cryptococcus neoformans and differentiation of their serotypes

Hypervariable multi-fragment profiles from different isolates of *C. neoformans* from patients were obtained through PCR-fingerprinting using single oligonucleotide primers (CA)$_8$, (CT)$_8$, (GTG)$_5$, (GACA)$_4$ and the phage M13 core sequence (GAGGGTGGXGGXTCT). *C. neoformans* is an encapsulated yeast species and an important human pathogen. Approximately 5 to 15% of AIDS patients acquire cryptococcal menin-

318

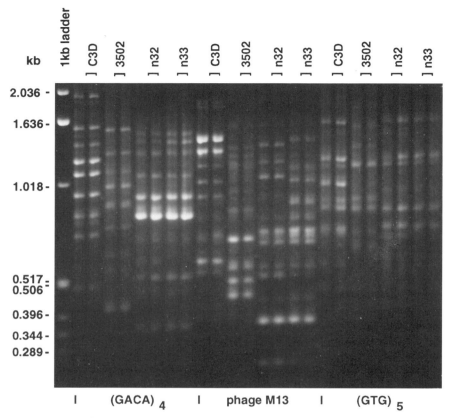

Figure 3. PCR-fingerprinting patterns obtained after amplification of genomic DNA from *Cryptococcus neoformans* with the primers (GACA)$_4$, phage M13 core sequence (GAGGGTGGXGGXTCT) and (GTG)$_5$. Strains: C3D, *C. neoformans* var. *neoformans*, serotype A; 3502, *C. neoformans* var. *neoformans*, serotype D; n32, *C. neoformans* var. *gattii*, serotype B; n33, *C. neoformans* var. *gattii*, serotype C; St., 1 kb ladder (GIBCO-BRL).

gitis, the leading cause of life-threatening fungal infection associated with AIDS (Diamond, 1991; Clark et al., 1990; Mitchell, 1992). All 42 investigated strains of *C. neoformans* could be distinguished using this method. Using the primers (GTG)$_5$, (GACA)$_4$ and M13 sequence, specific PCR-fingerprint patterns were also obtained, which made it possible to differentiate between the two varieties: *C. neoformans* var. *neoformans*, represented by serotypes A and D, and *C. neoformans* var. *gattii*, serotypes B and C (Fig. 3). These primers have also been successfully applied to the amplification of hypervariable PCR sequences in other *Cryptococcus* species and pathogenic fungi (e.g, species of *Candida*) and provide a convenient method for identifying species (Meyer et al., 1993).

Discussion

Both conventional DNA-fingerprinting and PCR-fingerprinting seem to be generally applicable to fungi. Both techniques were highly reproducible and useful for identification and differentiation of fungal species, strains, pathotypes and serotypes. The ability to detect multilocus profiles in a variety of species suggests that many fungi contain highly variable repetitive DNA sequences.

Amplification of polymorphic DNA by PCR using the minisatellite and microsatellite primers offers several advantages over conventional DNA-fingerprinting techniques. It is rapid, simple, sensitive, more easily applicable to large scale experiments and appears to be more reliable than other PCR based methods for detecting polymorphic DNA (e.g., RAPD). Although the intensity of some bands obtained by PCR-fingerprinting varied in duplicate experiments, their positions were always the same for a given strain.

DNA- and PCR-fingerprinting both promise to be useful for addressing a variety of questions regarding the biology of fungi. The greatest potential of both methods appears to be as an aid to the identification of plant and human pathogens and for typing of biotechnologically important microorganisms. When appropriately combined with morphological and biochemical data, these methods could also be useful for many evolutionary and taxonomical questions.

Acknowledgements
We wish to thank U. Stegert (Microbiology, Humboldt Universität zu Berlin, Berlin, Germany), P. Liebs, E. Winsel, and H. Toussaint (IFZ Forschungs- und Entwicklungs GmbH, Berlin, Germany), C. P. Kubicek (TU-Wien, Vienna, Austria), J. Wöstemeyer (IGF, Berlin, Germany), J. R. Perfect and W. Schell (Duke University Medical Center, Durham, NC, USA) and D. Howard (University of California at Los Angeles, USA) for providing fungal isolates. We thank J. Epplen (Ruhr Universität, Bochum, Germany) and P. Nürnberg (Humboldt Universität, Institut für Humangenetik, Berlin, Germany) for providing oligonucleotides and offering critical comments. The oligonucleotide probes are subject to patent applications. Commercial enquiries should be directed to Fresenius AG, Oberursel, Germany. We also thank R. J. Vilgalys (Duke University, Department of Botany, Durham, NC, USA) for helpful comments and critical reading of the manuscript.

This work was supported by grants from the Bundesministerium für Forschung und Technologie, Germany, to Th. Börner (No. 30K008708), from the Verband der Chemischen Industrie, Germany, to H. Toussaint (No. 0310178A), and from the U.S. Public Health Service, National Institutes of Health to T. G. Mitchell (Nos. AI 28836 and AI 25783).

References

Ali S, Müller CR, Epplen JT (1986) DNA fingerprinting by oligonucleotide probes specific for simple repeats. Hum Genet 74: 239–243

Clark RA, Greer D, Atkinson W, Valainis GT, Hyslop N (1990) Spectrum of *Cryptococcus neoformans* infection in 68 patients infected with human immunodeficiency virus. Rev Infect Dis 12: 768–777

320

Diamond RD (1991) The growing problem of mycoses in patients infected with the human immunodeficiency virus. Rev Infect Dis 13: 480–486

Epplen JT (1988) On simple repeated GATA/GACA sequences in animal genomes: a critical reappraisal. J Heredity 79: 409–417

Gruber, F (1990) Homologe und heterologe Transformation von Trichoderma reesei mit den Ortidin-5′-Phosphat-Decarboxylase Genen als Selektionsmarker. Ph.D. Thesis, Vienna: TU-Wien

Hassan AK, Schulz C, Sacristan MD, Wöstemeyer J (1991) Biochemical and molecular tools for the differentiation of aggressive and non-aggressive isolates of the oilseed rape pathogen, *Phoma lingam*. J Phytopathol 131: 120–136

Jeffreys AJ, Wilson V, Thein S (1985) Hypervariable 'minisatellite' regions in human DNA. Nature 314: 67–73

Lieckfeldt E, Meyer W, Börner T (1993) Rapid identification and differentiation of yeast by DNA and PCR fingerprinting. J Basic Microbiol

Maniatis T, Fritsch EF, Sambrook J (1982) Molecular cloning: a laboratory manual, Cold Spring Harbor, NY, USA

Meyer W, Koch A, Neimann C, Beyermann B, Epplen JT, Börner T (1991) Differentiation of species and strains among filamentous fungi by DNA fingerprinting. Curr Genet 19: 239–242

Meyer W, Lieckfeldt E, Wöstemeyer J, Börner T (1992a) DNA fingerprinting for differentiating aggressivity groups of the rape seed pathogen *Leptosphaeria maculans*. Mycol Res 96: 651–657

Meyer W, Morawetz R, Börner T, Kubicek CP (1992b) The use of DNA-fingerprint analysis in the classification of some species of the *Trichoderma* aggregate. Curr Genet 21: 27–30

Meyer W, Mitchell TG, Freedman EZ, Vilgalys RJ (1993) Hybridization probes for conventional DNA fingerprinting can be used as single primers in the PCR to distinguish strains of *Cryptococcus neoformans*. J Clin Microbiol 31(9) (in press)

Mitchell TG (1992) Opportunistic mycoses. *In*: Joklik WK, Willett HP, Amos DB, Wilfert CM (eds) Zinsser microbiology, Appleton & Lange, Norwalk, pp. 1135–1157

Nybom H, Rogstad SH, Schall BA (1990) Genetic variation detected by the use of the M13 "DNA fingerprint" probe in *Malus*, *Prunus* and *Rubus* (*Rosaceae*). Theor Appl Genet 79: 153–156

Perfect JR, Magee BB, Magee PT (1989) Separation of chromosomes of *Cryptococcus neoformans* by pulsed field gel electrophoresis. Infect Immun 57: 2624–2627

Rifai MA (1969) A revision of the genus *Trichoderma*. Mycol Papers 116: 1–56

Vilgalys RJ, Johnson JL (1987) Extensive genetic divergence associated with speciation in filamentous fungi. Proc Natl Acad Sci USA 84: 2355–2358

Welsh J, McClelland M (1990) Fingerprinting genomes using PCR with arbitrary primers. Nucleic Acids Res 18: 7213–7218

Williams JGK, Kubelik AR, Livak KJ, Rafalski JA, Tingey SV (1990) DNA polymorphisms amplified by arbitrary primers are useful as genetic markers. Nucleic Acids Res 18: 6531–6535

Wöstemeyer J (1985) Strain-dependent variation in ribosomal DNA arrangement in *Absidia glauca*. Eur J Biochem 146: 443–448

DNA Fingerprinting: State of the Science
ed. by S. D. J. Pena, R. Chakraborty, J. T. Epplen & A. J. Jeffreys
© 1993 Birkhäuser Verlag Basel/Switzerland

DNA fingerprinting reveals relationships between strains of *Trypanosoma rangeli* and *Trypanosoma cruzi*

A. M. Macedo[a], G. A. Vallejo, E. Chiari and S. D. J. Pena[a]

[a]*Departamento de Bioquímica e Imunologia, and Departamento de Parasitologia, Instituto de Ciências Biológicas, UFMG, Caixa Postal 2486, Belo Horizonte, MG. Brazil*

Summary
Very little is known about the structure and sequence of the genomic DNA and kDNA of *T. rangeli* and no highly polymorphic markers are known. In this paper, we show that the Jeffreys' multilocal probe 33.15 produces characteristic DNA fingerprints with these trypanosomes. The multiband patterns can be used to differentiate *T. cruzi* from *T. rangeli* and for recognizing relationships between strains of the latter from widely different geographic areas and different hosts. The topology of a UPGMA phenetic tree constructed from band-sharing data suggests the existence of two groups of *T. rangeli*: one encompassing parasites from Central America and the northern part of South America and another with the parasites from southern Brazil. This splitting was confirmed by the use of both nuclear and kinetoplast unique sequence probes. Among strains of *T. rangeli*, band sharing was generally negatively correlated with geographical distance. This work confirms the usefulness of DNA fingerprints as a potent technique for the analysis of relationships in trypanosomatid populations.

Introduction

DNA fingerprinting is a powerful technique for detecting simultaneously differences at a large number of hypervariable loci by using multilocal probes (Jeffreys, 1987). The most explored applications of this technique have been in identity and parentage testing (Jeffreys et al., 1985; Burke and Brufford, 1987; Wetton et al., 1987; Medeiros et al., 1989). Its use in comparisons of populations has been limited by the high mutation rate of minisatellites, which leads to a fast evolution of fingerprint profiles. However, Kuhnlein et al. (1989) were able to show that DNA fingerprinting can characterize genetic relationships between different breeding populations of poultry, reflecting their evolution history. Similar results were obtained by Gilbert et al. (1990) who demonstrated that DNA fingerprinting could be used to study differentiation of populations of foxes in the California Channel Islands. More recently, we showed that the multilocus fingerprinting probe 33.15 is capable of producing complex and hypervariable multiband profiles in species and strains of *Leishmania* and *Trypanosoma cruzi* (Macedo et al., 1992a, b). In *Leishmania*, a quantitative treatment of DNA fingerprint data permitted the construction of phenetic trees which mirrored well the population history and the geographical distance of different species and strains. In the present work we wish to confirm the usefulness of DNA fingerprinting as a valuable technique for the determination of relationships between different populations of a parasite about which little genetic information is available: *Trypanosoma rangeli*.

Trypanosoma rangeli is a mammalian trypanosome whose geographical occurrence coincides in various Latin American countries with the pathogenic protozoan *Trypanosoma cruzi*, the causative agent of Chagas' disease. Both parasites can infect man and indeed they can produce mixed simultaneous infections in both the vertebrate hosts and triatomine vectors. This frequently confuses the diagnostic and epidemiological studies of these parasites (Hoare, 1972; D'Alessandro, 1976). *T. rangeli* is apparently not pathogenic for man nor for a variety of wild and domestic animals (Añez, 1982) but causes disease in the insect vectors (Grewal, 1957; Marinkelle, 1968). In contrast to *T. cruzi*, the transmission of *T. rangeli* to the vertebrate host occurs by the bite of reduviids and subsequent inoculation of the metacyclic trypomastigotes formed in the salivary glands. The capacity to invade salvary glands is one of the most useful diagnostic features of *T. rangeli*.

Very little is known about the biology of *T. rangeli*. Until recently, efforts for biochemical characterization were restricted to analysis of isoenzyme patterns, producing a limited and controversial literature. Several groups (Miles et al., 1983; Holguín et al., 1987; Acosta et al., 1991) observed little or no polymorphism of the enzyme patterns in *T. rangeli* strains from the Brazilian Amazon basin, Colombia and Honduras. On the other hand, Kreutzer & Souza (1981) and Ebert (1986) found a high polymorphism between *T. rangeli* strains from Colombia and Venezuela. More recently, Steindel et al. (1991), showed that strains of *T. rangeli* isolated in southern Brazil present isoenzyme patterns that resemble *T. cruzi* strains rather than other Latin-American strains of *T. rangeli*.

Materials and methods

Parasites. We used 9 strains of *T. rangeli* isolated from Central and South America. The geographic distribution is shown in Fig. 1. The strains H8, H9, H14 were obtained from human patients from two different states of Honduras (H8 and H9 from Choluteca and H14 from La Paz). The San Agustín (human origin) and Choachí (triatomine origin) strains were isolated from the same district of Cundinamarca, a central state of Colombia. P19 (triatomine origin) was also isolated from Colombia, but from Norte de Santander, an eastern state. The strain Macias was isolated from human patient from Venezuela and the

Figure 1. Geographic distribution of *T. rangeli* strains. The parasites were isolated from Honduras (strains H8, H9 and H14), Colombia (strains San Agustín and P19), Venezuela (strain MAcias) and Santa Catarina, Brazil (strains SC58 and SC61). The shadowed areas represent the distribution of Chagas' disease. The clear area on the northern part of South America corresponds to the Amazon basin.

strains SC58 and SC61 were isolated from wild rodents from Santa Catarina, a state in southern Brazil. For comparative purposes we used two *T. cruzi* reference strains: Y isolated from a patient in São Paulo (southern Brazil; Silva & Nussensweig, 1963) and CL isolated from triatomine of Rio Grande do Sul (southern Brazil, Brener & Chiari, 1963).

DNA extraction, endonuclease digestion and gel electrophoresis. For DNA extraction the parasites were grown in liver infusion tryptose (LIT) medium (Camargo, 1964), spun down, washed in Krebs-Ringer/ Tris (KRT) buffer and the pellets were stored at -70°C until processed. The total DNA extraction of the frozen parasites was done as described previously (Macedo et al., 1992b). For the kDNA extraction, 5×10^9

cells were processed as described by Gonçalves et al. (1984). Samples containing 5 μg of total DNA (nuclear and kDNA) or 1 μg of kDNA were digested with *Bsp*RI (an isoschizomer of *Hae*III, Fundação Oswaldo Cruz, Brazil) as described previously (Macedo et al., 1992b). One μg of completely digested DNA was then electrophoresed in a 15 cm long 0.8% agarose gel in TBE (89 mM Tris-Borate/2 mM EDTA, pH 8.0) at 1.5 V cm^{-1} for 18–20 h until the bromophenol blue marker had migrated out of the gel. The electrophoresed DNA was transfered to nitrocellulose filter paper according to Southern (1975).

Preparation and labeling of DNA probes. The 33.15 fingerprinting probe cloned in M13mp8 (Jeffreys et al., 1985) was a kind gift from Prof. A.J. Jeffreys, University of Leicester, England. The biotin-labeling of the recombinant M13 phage was done by primer extension as described earlier (Macedo et al., 1989). The nuclear (NP1) and kDNA (KP1) unique sequence probes had been cloned in pUC18 vector. For the biotin-labeling of these probes, we added 6 nmol of bio-11-dUTP (Sigma) to a typical 100 μl PCR reaction mixture containing 25 nmol of each dNTP, 100 ng of purified recombinant vector and 20 pmoles of each of universal M13 primers (Sigma). PCR was carried out in a MJ Research PTC-100 Thermal Cycler for 35 cycles. Each cycle consisted of 2 min at 94°C for denaturation, 2 min at 50°C for primer annealing and 5 min at 72°C for primer extension. After amplification the samples were purified in Sephadex G-50 according to Maniatis et al. (1981).

Hybridization. The hybridization was done as described earlier (Pena et al., 1991). The stringency of hybridization was 45% formamide and 42°C for both multilocal and unilocal probes and the stringency of washing was 1 × SSC and 52°C for multilocal probe and 0.1 × SSC and 65°C for unilocal probes.

Results

DNA fingerprinting. When total DNA from *T. cruzi* and *T. rangeli* was digested with *Bsp*RI and hybridized in Southern blots with Jeffreys' 33.15 multilocal probe under low stringency, there emerged a complex banding pattern typical of DNA fingerprints (Fig. 2). The pattern showed on average 29 ± 1.4 bands (mean ± s.d.) for strains CL and Y of *T. cruzi* and a simpler pattern with 20 ± 2.5 bands for *T. rangeli* strains, ranging from 17 to 23 bands above 350 bp. With the exception of H8, H9, SC58 and SC61, all strains presented different patterns. On average we detected 49% of shared bands (32% above 4.4 kb, 47% between 4.4 to 2.0 kb, 63% below 2.0 kb) between any two strains. Although there was clear individuality between the strains of *T. rangeli*, there was more similarity between the strains isolated from closer geographic areas. This can be seen by visual inspection of the profile of the strains from

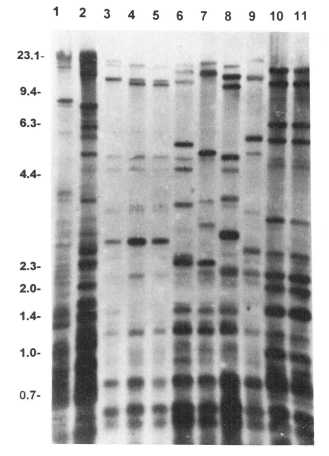

Figure 2. Non-isotopic DNA fingerprint of *T. cruzi* (lanes 1–2) and *T. rangeli* (lanes 3–11). The lanes from 1 to 11 refer respectively to strains CI, Y, H14, H8, H9, SA, P19, CH, MA, SC58, SC61. On the left is shown the migration of lambda *Hind*III fragments plus *Bsp*RI digestion fragments of *T. cruzi* minicircle kDNA.

Honduras (Fig. 2, lanes 3–5), Colombia (Fig. 2, lanes 6–8) and Brazil (Fig. 2, lanes 10–11). We detected two cases of identical profiles: the H8 and H9 strains isolated from the same district of Choluteca state in Honduras and the SC58 and SC61 strains from the same district in Santa Catarina in Brazil.

Phenogram building. We used the parameter $D = 1 - S$ [where $S = 2n_{XY}/(n_X + n_Y)$, n_X and n_Y being the number of bands in strain X and Y, and n_{XY} the number of shared bands between strains X and Y] as a distance metric for building a phenetic tree by the unweighted pair group method with arithmetic mean (UPGMA) whose topology is shown in Fig. 3. This tree showed several interesting features. First,

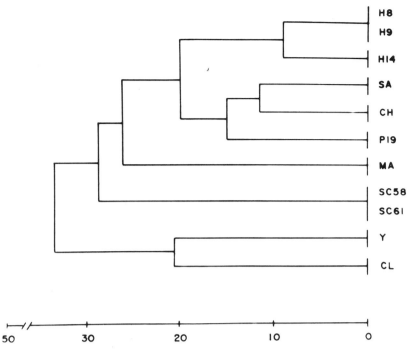

Figure 3. Phenetic tree obtained by UPGMA. The scale refers to the *D* values among the taxa. CI and Y are strains of *T. cruzi*; H14, H8, H9, SA, P19, CH and MA are strains of *T. rangeli* from northern South America and Central America; SC58, SC61 are strains of *T. rangeli* from southern Brazil.

there was clustering of the strains of *T. rangeli* and *T. cruzi* in different major branches. Second, in the *T. rangeli* branch, the strains isolated from southern Brazil (which presented identical fingerprints; Fig. 2, lanes 10–11), were grouped together in a sub-branch apart from the others. The *T. rangeli* strains isolated from Central America and the north of South America were sub-clustered according to their geographic distances. For example, the strains from Honduras (H8, H9, H14) were set in a different sub-branch from that containing the Colombian strains (SA, CH, P19). In the Honduras branch (upper branch), H8 and H9 isolated from the same district in Choluteca, presented identical profiles (Fig. 2, lanes 4–5) and were placed together with H14, which had been isolated from a different state of the same country. Similar behavior was detected among the Colombian strains. SA and CH, close together in a sub-branch, were both isolated from the state of Cundinamarca in the central region of Colombia, while P19 (set apart) was isolated from a different state in the eastern region of the same country. The MA strain isolated from Venezuela was set in a specific sub-branch grouped together to the other of Central America origin.

Comparison of the T. rangeli strains by using unique sequence probes. The great dissimilarity detected between the *T. rangeli* strains isolated from the southern part of Brazil and Central and northern part of South America led us to search for specific probes that could be used for a better characterization of these strains. Two probes, one from nuclear DNA (NP1) and other from minicircle kDNA origin (KP1), showed to be very useful for this purpose. Fig. 4 shows the pattern of *T. cruzi* (lanes 1, 2) and *T. rangeli* (lanes 3–7) hybridized with NP1 (right side) and KP1 (left side). No clear bands could be detected with either probe in *T. cruzi* DNA while all *T. rangeli* strains, except SC58, gave similar profiles with both. The strain SC58 isolated from Santa Catarina presented a smaller band (0.9 kb) compared with the other *T. rangeli* when hybridized with NP1 (Fig. 4, lane 7 – right side) and no bands with the KP1 probe (Fig. 4, lane 7). Similar results were obtained with 8 other *T. rangeli* strains analyzed (data not shown).

Discussion

Hybridization of total DNA from *Trypanosoma rangeli* with the 33.15 multilocal probe revealed a complex banding pattern characteristic

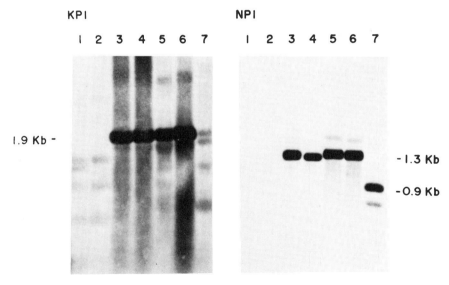

Figure 4. Hybridization patterns obtained with the unique sequence probes NP1 (right side) and KP1 (left side) with strains of *T. cruzi* (lane 1 – Y; lane 2 – CI) and of *T. rangeli* (lane 3 – H14, lane 4 – H8, lane 5 – CH, lane 6 – MA, lane 7 – SC58).

of DNA fingerprinting as demonstrated previously for *Leishmania* (Macedo et al., 1992a) and *T. cruzi* (Macedo et al., 1992b). Although our data are limited, the patterns obtained with *T. rangeli* seem to be simpler and less hypervariable than those obtained with other trypanosomatids. This can be seen by the lower number of bands detected with *T. rangeli* and the existence of several well-resolved monomorphic bands that are absent in *T. cruzi* or *Leishmania* profiles (data not shown; Macedo et al., 1992a and b).

The use of the DNA fingerprinting data to build the phenogram by UPGMA showed a great divergence between the *T. rangeli* strains isolated from Santa Catarina, in southern Brazil and the others isolated from Central America and the northern part of South America (Fig. 3). On the other hand, great homogeneity was detected among the parasites isolated from Central America and the northern part of South America. Similar results were obtained by using the NP1 and KP1 unique sequence probes (Fig. 4) and had also been demonstrated by zymodem analysis, where the strains isolated from Santa Catarina showed to be more related to *T. cruzi* than to the other *T. rangeli* strains (Steindel et al., 1991). All these results together suggest the existence of two groups of *T. rangeli* strains whose divergence can be correlated with the geographic distribution and may reflect a process of speciation of these parasites. It is interesting to point out that between the two groups is the Amazon basin (Fig. 1). This basin has been cited as a border line characterizing two great regions of different clinical forms of Chagas' disease (Prata, 1985) and may represent an important natural barrier blocking southward and northward spread of trypanosome strains. The absence of sexual recombination in these trypanosomatids certainly helps maintain the observed divergence. Our results demonstrate that when appropriately used, DNA fingerprinting may be a useful tool for the study of populations of parasites and other animals.

Acknowledgements

This work was supported by grants from Conselho Nacional de Pesquisas (CNPq), Fundação de Amparo à Pesquisa do Estado de Minas Gerais (FAPEMIG), Conselho de Aperfeiçoamento de Pessoal a nível Superior (CAPES) and World Health Organization (WHO). We are grateful to Prof. Alec Jeffreys from the University of Leicester, who gave us the 33.25 fingerprinting probe and to Dr. Urdaneta Morales, Venezuela; Dr. Lucila Acosta, Honduras; Dr. Felipe Guhl, Colombia; Dr. Mario Steindel, Brazil, who kindly provided the parasites.

References

Anez N (1982) Studies on *Trypanosoma rangeli* Tejera, 1920. IV – A reconsideration of its systematic position. Mem Inst Oswaldo Cruz R J 77(4): 405–415

Burke T, Bruford MW (1987) DNA fingerprinting in birds. Nature 327: 149–152

Acosta L, Romanha AJ, Cosenza H, Krettli AU (1991) Trypanosomatid isolates from Honduras: Differentiation between *Trypanosoma cruzi* and *Trypanosoma rangeli*. Am J Trop Med Hyg 44: 676–683

Camargo EP (1964) Growth and differentiation in *Trypanosoma cruzi*. I. Origin of metacyclic trypomastigotes in liquid media. Rev Inst Med Trop Säo Paulo 6: 93–100

Brener Z, Chiari E (1963) Variaçöes morfológicas observadas em diferentes amostras de *Trypanosoma cruzi*. Rev Inst Med Trop Säo Paulo 5: 220–224

D'Alessandro A (1976) Biology of *Trypanosoma* (*Herpetosoma*) *rangeli* Tejera, 1920. *In*: Biology of Kinetoplastida. Vol. I., Lumsden, WHR and Evans, DA (eds), London, New York and San Francisco: Academic Press, pp 327–493

Ebert F (1986) Isoenzymes of *Trypanosoma rangeli* stocks and their relation to other trypanosomes transmitted by triatomine bugs. Trop Med Parasit 37: 251–254

Gilbert DA, Lehman N, O'Brien SJ, Wayne RK (1990) Genetic fingerprinting reflects population differentiation in the California Channel Island fox. Nature 344: 764–766

Gonçalves AM, Nehme NE, Morel CM (1984) Trypanosomatid characterization by schizodeme analysis. *In*: Genes and Antigenes of Parasites: A Laboratory Manual. Morel CM (ed), Second Ed. Fund. Oswaldo Cruz, Rio de Janeiro. pp 96–109

Grewal MS (1957) Pathogenicity of *Trypanosoma rangeli* Tejera, in the invertebrate host. Experimental Parasitology 6: 123–130

Hoare CA (1972) The Trypanosomes of Mammals. A Zoological Monograph. Blackwell, Oxford. 749 pp

Holguin AF, Saravia NC, D'Alessandro A (1987) Lack of isoenzyme polymorphism in *Trypanosoma rangeli* stocks from sylvatic and domiciliary transmission cycle in Colombia. Am J Trop Med Hyg 36: 56–58

Jeffreys AJ, Wilson V, Thein SL (1985) Individual specific fingerprints of human DNA. Nature 316: 76–79

Kreutzer RD, Souza OE (1981) Biochemical characterization of *Trypanosoma* spp. by isoenzyme electrophoresis. Am J Trop Med Hyg 30: 308–317

Macedo AM, Medeiros AC, Pena SDJ (1989) A general method for efficient non-isotopic labeling of DNA probes in M13 vectors: application to DNA fingerprinting. Nucl Acids Res 17: 4414

Macedo AM, Melo MN, Gomes RF, Pena SDJ (1992) DNA fingerprints: a tool for identification and determination of the relationships between species and strains of *Leishmania*. Mol Biochem Par 53: 63–70

Macedo AM, Martins MS, Chiari E, Pena SDJ (1992) DNA fingerprinting of *Trypanosoma cruzi*: A new tool for characterization of strains and clones. Mol Bioch Par 55: 147–154

Medeiros AC, Macedo AM, Pena SDJ (1989) M13 Bioprints: Non-isotopic detection of individual specific human DNA fingerprints with biotinylated M13 bacteriophage. Forensic Science International 43: 275–280

Maniatis T, Fritsch EF, Sambrook J (1982) Molecular Cloning: A Laboratory Manual. Cold Spring Harbor Laboratory Press, Cold Spring Harbor/NY

Marinkelle CJ (1968) Pathogenicity of *Trypanosoma rangeli* in *Rhodnius prolixus* Stal in nature. J Med Ent 5(4): 497–499

Miles ME, Arias JE, Valente SAS, Naiff RD, Souza AA, Povoa MM, Lima JAN, Cedillos EA (1983) Vertebrate hosts and vectors of *Trypanosoma rangeli* in the Amazon Basin of Brazil. Am J Trop Med Hyg 32: 1251–1258

Pena SDJ, Macedo AM, Gontijo NF, Medeiros AM, Ribeiro JCC (1991) DNA bioprints: simple non-isotopic DNA fingerprints with biotinylated probes. Electrophoresis 12: 146–152

Prata A (1985) Significance of *Trypanosoma cruzi* differentiation and selection, relationship with clinical and epidemiological varieties. Rev Soc Bras Med Trop 18: 9–16

Southern EM (1975) Detection of specific sequences among DNA fragments separated by gel electrophoresis. J Mol Biol 98: 508–517

Silva LHP, Nussensweig V (1963) Sobre uma cepa de *Trypanosoma cruzi* altamente virulenta para o camundongo branco. Folia Clin Biol 20: 191–203

Steindel M, Carvalho-Pinto JC, Toma HK, Mangia HR, Ribeiro-Rodrigues R, Romanha AJ (1991) *Trypanosoma rangeli* (Tejera, 1920) isolated from sylvatic *Echimiys dasythrix* in Santa Catarina island, Santa Catarina state: first report of this trypanosome in southern Brazil. Memorias do Instituto Oswaldo Cruz R J 86: 73–79

Wetton JH, Carter RE, Parken DT, Walters D (1987) Demographic study of a wild house sparrow population by DNA fingerprinting. Nature 327: 147–149

DNA Fingerprinting: State of the Science
ed. by S. D. J. Pena, R. Chakraborty, J. T. Epplen & A. J. Jeffreys

The use of RAPDs for the analysis of parasites

A. J. G. Simpson, E. Dias Neto, M. Steindel, O. L. S. D. Caballero,
L. K. J. Passos and S. D. J. Pena[a]

*Laboratório de Bioquímica e Biologia Molecular, Centro de Pesquisas "René Rachou",
Avenida Augusto de Lima, 1715, 30190-002 Belo Horizonte, 31.090-002, Minas Gerais,
Brazil; and [a]Dept. Bioquímica e Imunologia, Universidade Federal de Minas Gerais,
30161 Belo Horizonte, Minas Gerais, Brazil*

Summary
There is a lack of sequence information concerning polymorphic loci in parasite genomes.
Thus, the use of arbitrary PCR primers under low temperature annealing conditions to
generate random amplified polymorphic DNAs (RAPDs) represents an important approach
to the study of the structure of parasite populations, their genetic variation as well as
improved diagnosis of the diseases they cause. Following the examination of all variables and
their effect on the reproducibility of the reaction, we have established a protocol for the
analysis of RAPDs that involves amplification at two separate DNA concentrations followed
by polyacrylamide gel electrophoresis and silver staining. We find the technique to be
sensitive, reproducible, simple and relatively cheap. It has already provided insight into the
genetic variation in populations of schistosomes and trypanosomes and is being used to study
various other endemic infections. We also use specific primers under low stringency conditions
in situations where the objective of the amplification is the detection of a particular sequence
and where normal high stringency conditions give a positive/negative answer such as sex
determination or diagnosis of blood born infections. Under low stringency conditions, specific
amplification products persist but products of low stringency priming are also apparent and
serve as a perfect internal control for negative samples.

Introduction

Fundamental questions remain to be answered concerning the structure
of populations of parasites and other infectious organisms as well as the
influence of genetic variation on the clinical outcome of infection. In
addition, the challenge of developing sensitive and rapid methods of
identifying infectious organisms and their variants has yet to be fully
answered. The polymerase chain reaction (PCR) has a central role to
play in these areas but as yet its full usefulness has not been exploited
principally due to the lack of sequence information concerning suitable
polymorphic loci. The advent of techniques in which arbitrary primers
are used to amplify genomic DNA creating complex banding patterns
that include polymorphic markers (Williams et al., 1990; Welsh and
McClelland, 1990) offers a promising new approach.

This paper reviews the methodological approach that we have
adopted for the use of random amplified polymorphic DNA (RAPD)

analysis in our laboratory where high throughput, low cost and simplified protocols are of the essence.

We also report a novel use of the RAPD protocol with specific primers, which we have termed low stringency-PCR (LS-PCR), that has resolved the problem of adequately controlling PCR DNA detection in the context of, for example, sex determination and diagnosis, which we here illustrate with studies of sex determination in the schistosome.

Materials and methods

Amplifications were undertaken in a final volume of $10 \mu l$ containing 0.8 unit of Taq polymerase (Cenbiot RS, Brazil), $200 \mu M$ of each dNTP, 1.5 mM $MgCl_2$, 50 mM KCl, 10 mM Tris-HCl, pH 8.5 together with 6.4 pmoles of primer and either 0.1 or 1.0 ng of template DNA. This mixture was overlaid with mineral oil and, following an initial denaturation at 95°C for 5 min, was subjected to two cycles through the following temperature profile: 30°C for 2 min for annealing, 72°C for 1 min for extension and 30 sec at 95°C for denaturation followed by 33 cycles where the annealing step was altered to 40°C. In the final cycle, the extension step was continued for 5 min. Following amplification, $3 \mu l$ of the mixture was applied to a 4% polyacrylamide gel in TBE. Following electrophoresis, gels were fixed with 10% ethanol/0.5% acetic acid for 20 min and the DNA bands revealed by staining with silver nitrate for 30 min and reduction with 0.75 M NaOH/0.1 M formaldehyde for 10 min as previously described (Santos et al., 1992).

For LS-PCR the same conditions were used as described above for RAPD analysis except that a pair of specific primers were used.

For specific amplifications, the same reaction conditions were used except that the amplification profile was shortened to 25 cycles and the annealing step to between 50 and 60°C depending on the primer.

Results

We used DNA extracted from *Trypanosoma cruzi* which has a genome size of approximately 10^7 bp and which is the causative agent of Chagas' disease (Steindel et al., 1992) and *Schistosoma mansoni* which has a genome size of approximately 10^8 bp and which causes schistosomiasis (Dias Neto et al., 1993), for undertaking the basic studies required to standardize the protocol shown above. Some details of the analytical results obtained with these parasites are shown in the accompanying paper by Dias Neto et al. (1993).

Our initial concern in the adaptation of RAPD analysis to a research laboratory with relatively limited resources was to establish a simple, high throughput and reproducible technology that we could apply to a range of endemic biological problems. In our preliminary experiments we found two variables to be particularly important: the quantity of the template DNA and the number of reaction cycles. Use of less than 100 pg of template of either organism resulted in the absence of some of the amplification products while the use of more than 10 ng often did not result in detectable amplification as shown in Fig. 1. We attribute this to the copurification of inhibitors of Taq polymerase with the template DNA.

The amplification of contaminating DNA is an important technical consideration. Despite taking every recommended precaution to reduce contamination, very high cycle numbers were found to frequently result in the amplification of non-parasite DNA bands in control tubes, although the same bands were not apparent in tubes containing parasite DNA presumably due to competition. Thirty-five cycles of amplification, however, have been found to result in controls being negative in all amplifications undertaken to date while preserving the full complement of RAPD products, and we have adopted this cycle number as standard.

In order to achieve reproducible results, we found it to be essential that DNA extractions be undertaken with highest quality reagents and that the DNA be treated with RNase. In a number of instances, DNA which failed to produce clear RAPD profiles was re-extracted and subsequently found to be capable of acting as a high quality template. To reduce costs and thus allow extensive repetition of the amplifications

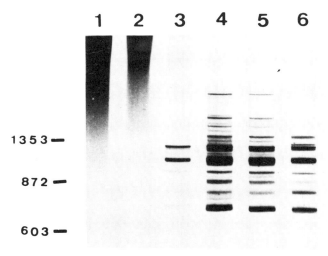

Figure 1. Varying concentrations of *T. cruzi* DNA were amplified as described in Materials and Methods using the primer 5′-TCACGATGCA-3′. 1 = 500 ng, 2 = 100 ng, 3 = 10 ng, 4 = 1 ng, 5 = 0.1 ng, 6 = 0.01 ng.

334

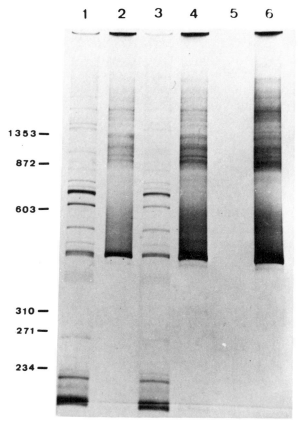

1 2 3 4 5 6

1353 —
872 —
603 —
310 —
271 —
234 —

Figure 2. Schistosome DNA prepared from male (1, 3, and 5) and female DNA (2, 4 and 6) cercariae was amplified using the primers 5′-GTGAAATTCTTCCTTCACAC-3′ and 5′-GACATTCAACTCAATGTTCG-3′ specific for the amplification of the repetitive female-specific sequence W1 (Webster et al., 1989). In lanes 5 and 6 specific amplification conditions were used, in lanes 1 to 4, LS-PCR conditions were used.

to check reproducibility, we used small reaction volumes, 10 μl, of which 3 μl is sufficient to visualize the products using polyacrylamide gels and silver staining.

We undertook all amplifications at two concentrations of template, 100 pg and 1.0 ng. At these two concentrations, the RAPD profiles only differ in terms of the intensity of some bands when reaction conditions are optimized, the enzyme is of high specific activity and the DNA is of high quality, as shown in Fig. 1. When this result was achieved we found the bands to be reproducible in separate amplifications and could thus be scored with confidence. However, there are pronounced differences when the conditions are sub-optimal and particularly when the DNA is of poor quality, and it is thus clear that bands produced cannot be used for genetic analysis.

We have used this protocol in projects involving not only the parasites listed above but also with the snail host of the schistosome, *Biomphalaria*, hookworm parasites and the spirochete Leptospira. We found that the results match well with conclusions drawn from experiments using isozymes where available and to be reproducible irrespective of the biological system.

In our work with parasite genetics and diagnosis we have been confronted with a number of situations where specific PCR amplifications are used to obtain an all-or-none response such as the detection of an infectious agent or in sex determination. In these cases an internal control is required for negative samples. This can be achieved by the use of the specific primers under low stringency conditions, a method that we term low stringency PCR (LS-PCR). We have found in all cases tested that under low stringency conditions the specific product is still readily detectable but additional arbitrarily primed products are also apparent that can serve as a control for the reaction. This approach is illustrated here with an experiment involving sex determination of cercariae of *Schistosoma mansoni*. In schistosomes it is the female that is heterogametic (ZW as opposed to the male ZZ). The primers used amplify a highly reiterated set of tandem repeats on the W chromosome (Webster et al., 1989) so that under high stringency conditions an intense band of 450 bp together with a series of higher molecular weight products that presumably result form degenerate regions in the repeats. There are no detectable PCR products when male DNA is used under high stringency conditions. Alteration to LS-PCR conditions does not result in a significant alteration in the amplification pattern obtained with female DNA, probably due to the highly repetitive nature of the target sequence which effectively competes with potential arbitrarily primed products. The specific primers produce a relatively complex pattern of amplification products using male DNA which contrasts significantly with that obtained with female DNA. We use these contrasting patterns for the purposes of routine parasite sex determination in the laboratory.

We have also used this approach for sex determination with human DNA where in addition to the amplification of the Y-specific locus ZFY, under LS-PCR conditions the appropriate specific primers also amplify a background of arbitrarily primed products present in both male and female DNA serving as a control for the reaction. A further application is in diagnosis where we have shown the applicability of the technique using Leptospira present in serum samples as a model situation. Here again we find that the diagnosis is improved because of the presence of the background bands in all tubes, whether positive or negative, and the presence of a strong specific band only in positive samples.

Discussion

Random amplified polymorphic DNA analysis is undoubtedly a powerful approach for analysis of genetic variation and the identification of genetic markers. It is of particular value in the study of parasites because of the scarcity of sequence information for the majority of organisms that would allow the design of specific primers for genome analysis. The major limitation of the technique, in terms of the study of parasites which by definition are found intimately associated with other organisms, is the fact that there is no *a priori* basis for distinguishing amplification products derived from host and parasite DNA. Thus, the direct application of the technique to diagnosis is complicated. Nevertheless, for studies where the organisms are first cultured in vitro or where the organisms are large and numerous enough to be physically separated from host material, RAPD represents a powerful and efficient means of genome comparison.

Once useful polymorphic markers have been identified by RAPD analysis, their sequencing should yield the information required for the construction of specific primers which can then be used for specific amplification from parasite DNA isolated from blood or other tissues. In this situation, the ability of the primer to amplify host DNA as well, under low stringency conditions, becomes a positive advantage since the presence or absence of the specific product is thus internally controlled. The advantage of this approach over multiplex PCR, for example, is that the control products are produced by the same primer pair as used for the specific amplification. We believe that the simultaneous amplification of specific and arbitrarily primed products by LS-PCR has many applications in situations of "all or none" amplifications for the purposes of specific DNA detection.

Acknowledgements
The work involving RAPD analysis of schistosome DNA received financial assistance from the UNDP/World Bank/WHO Special Programme for Research and Training in Tropical Diseases.

References

Dias Neto E, Pereira de Souza C, Rollinson D, Katz N, Pena SDJ, Simpson AJG (1993) The random amplification of polymorphic DNA allows the identification of strains and species of schistosome. Mol Biochem Parasitol 57: 83–88

Santos FR, Pena SDJ, Epplen JT (1993) Genetic and population study of a Y-linked tetranucleotide repeat DNA polymorphism. Hum Genet 90: 655–656

Steindel M, Dias Neto E, Menezes CLP, Romanha AJ, Simpson AJG (1993) Random amplified DNA analysis of *Trypanosoma cruzi* strains. Mol Biochem Parasitol (in press)

Webster P, Mansour TE, Bieber D (1989) Isolation of a female-specific, highly repeated *Schistosoma mansoni* DNA probe and its use in an assay of cercarial sex. Mol Biochem Parasitol 36: 217–222

Welsh J, McClelland M (1990) Fingerprinting genomes using PCR with arbitrary primers. Nucleic Acids Res 18: 7213–7218

Williams JGK, Kubelik AR, Livak KJ, Rafalski JA, Tingey SV (1990) DNA polymorphisms amplified by arbitrary primers are useful as genetic markers. Nucleic Acids Res 18: 6531–6535

DNA Fingerprinting: State of the Science
ed. by S. D. J. Pena, R. Chakraborty, J. T. Epplen & A. J. Jeffreys

The use of RAPDs for the study of the genetic diversity of *Schistosoma mansoni* and *Trypanosoma cruzi*

E. Dias Neto[a], M. Steindel[a,b], L. K. F. Passos[a], C. Pereira de Souza[a], D. Rollinson[c], N. Katz[a], A. J. Romanha[a], S. D. J. Pena[d] and A. J. G. Simpson[a]

[a]*Centro de Pesquisas "René Rachou", Avenida Augusto de Lima, 1715, 30190-002 Belo Horizonte, Minas Gerais, Brazil;* [b]*Universidade Federal de Santa Catarina, Florianopolis, 88040-900, Santa Catarina, Brazil;* [c]*The Natural History Museum, Cromwell Road, London, SW7 5BD, U.K.; and* [d]*Núcleo de Genética Médica de Minas Gerais (GENE/MG), Av. Afonso Pena 3111/9, 30130-909 Belo Horizonte, Brazil*

Summary
Arbitrary primers have been used for the production of complex, PCR generated DNA profiles in order to undertake a preliminary random amplified polymorphic DNA (RAPD) analysis of strains (and related species) of two parasitic organisms that are responsible for important diseases endemic in Brazil: *Schistosoma mansoni* that causes schistosomiasis, and *Trypanosoma cruzi* that causes Chagas' disease. A relatively low level of polymorphism was found in *S. mansoni* when strains isolated from different regions of Brazil were compared, with less than 10% of bands exhibiting polymorphism. Comparison of different schistosome species, on the other hand, showed them to be distantly related with very few bands shared by even the more closely related species. Trypanosome strains were found to be much more variable. When strains were compared between zymodemes (groups of parasite strains with the same isoenzyme profiles), a maximum of 7% of bands were found to be common whereas among strains in the same zymodeme a clear characteristic pattern was observed. In the zymodeme most thoroughly studied, it was found that 59% of bands were shared. Band sharing analysis showed that the relationships of strains within a zymodeme correlate with their geographical origin and that the relationship between zymodemes correlates closely with that previously determined by isoenzyme analysis. These preliminary data indicate the ready applicability of RAPD analysis to the study of parasites where largely unexplored genetic variations may have an important bearing on the complexity and diversity of diseases.

Introduction

The analysis of genetic diversity of populations of parasites is central to the understanding of host parasite relationships and the variety of clinical forms of the diseases that they cause. We have been investigating two parasites that cause serious and widespread diseases in Brazil, *Schistosoma mansoni*, a digenetic trematode that causes schistosomiasis, and the protozoa *Trypanosoma cruzi*, the etiological agent of Chagas' disease.

In Brazil there are 8–10 million people infected or at risk of infection by *S. mansoni* which is contracted by contact with water infested with infected water snails. The clinical symptoms range from being essentially undetectable to advanced and life threatening liver pathology.

Chagas' disease is a zoonosis that affects about 5 million people in Brazil, with 25 million being at risk of infection. The parasite is transmitted via faeces of hematophagous triatomid bugs. However, alternative routes such as blood transfusion, organ transplantation and congenital transmission are also common. The disease in man is extremely diverse, varying from the relatively benign indeterminate form to the fatal cardiac form.

There has been relatively little previous investigation into the extent and significance of genetic diversity in schistosomes. However, the data available from isoenzyme analysis (Fletcher et al., 1981) and variation in ribosomal RNA gene structure (McCutchan et al., 1984; Walker et al., 1989) indicate that there is relatively restricted diversity in these species and strains with no distinct genetic constitutions have been identified. In contrasts, *T. cruzi* has been the subject of extensive genetic analysis using isoenzymes (Ready and Miles, 1980), variation in kDNA (Morel et al., 1980) and multilocal DNA fingerprinting probes (Macedo et al., 1992). These data have proved that the *T. cruzi* population is clonal and extremely diverse (Tibayrenc et al., 1986). It remains to be established, however, whether variation is continuous or whether distinct genetic grouping exist. In addition, linkage between defined genetic polymorphisms and the biological and clinical characteristics of the organism have not, as yet, been established.

We here report a summary of preliminary investigations into the variation between different strains and species of schistosomes and trypanosomes using DNA profiles consisting of RAPD markers, more complete accounts of which are published elsewhere (Dias Neto et al., 1992; Steindel et al., 1992). The data obtained correlate with those previously obtained with these parasites using isoenzymes and confirm the applicability of RAPD analysis to further detailed investigations into the extent and significance of parasite genetic diversity.

Materials and methods

Five *S. mansoni* strains were obtained from different regions of Brazil (strains of *S. mansoni*) and 8 different species from Africa. Adult schistosomes were perfused from mice or hamsters after 45 days of infection for DNA preparation. The 32 *T. cruzi* strains used were from different regions of Central and South America. All were maintained in *in vitro* prior to harvesting and DNA preparation from the culture epimastigote form.

Parasite DNA was digested with Proteinase K and RNAse, phenol-chlorophorm extracted, ethanol precipitated and used for arbitrary primed PCR amplifications at 0.1 or 1.0 ng per tube. Each amplification was done in a final volume of $10\,\mu$l containing 0.8 units of Taq polymerase (Cenbiot RS, Brazil), $200\,\mu$M of each dNTP, 1.5 mM MgCl$_2$, 50 mM KCl, 10 mM Tris-HCl pH 8.5, together with 6.4 pmoles of primer. This reaction mixture was overlaid with $20\,\mu$l of mineral oil and, following an initial denaturation at 95°C for 5 minutes, was subjected to two cycles through the following temperature profile: 30°C for 2 min for annealing, 72°C for 1 min for extension and 30 sec at 95°C for denaturation followed by 33 cycles where the annealing step was altered to 40°C. In the final cycle the extension step was for 5 min. After amplification, $3\,\mu$l of the reaction was mixed with DNA sample buffer, subjected to electrophoresis through a 4% polyacrylamide gel, and stained by silver (Santos et al., 1992).

Band-sharing analysis of the data obtained with *T. cruzi* was undertaken using the Dice's Similarity Coefficient. Phenetic trees derived from the resulting similarity matrix were constructed by Unweighted Pair Group Method Analysis (UPGMA).

Results

The RAPD profiles obtained with pooled DNA of different *S. mansoni* strains were very similar (Fig. 1). Nevertheless a small number of

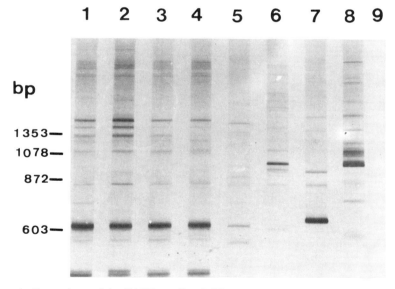

Figure 1. Comparison of the RAPD profile of different strains of *S. mansoni* and different species of schistosomes obtained with primer 3303 (5′ TCACGATGCA 3′). Lane 1 – AL strain; Lane 2 – BAR strain; Lane 3 – JNA strain; Lane 4 – LE strain; Lane 5 – *S. rhodaini*; Lane 6 – *S. matthei*; Lane 7 – *S. haematobium*; Lane 8 – *S. intercalatum*; Lane 9 – negative control (no DNA added).

342

polymorphic loci were identified. When taking into account all the bands obtained with three different primers and DNA prepared from five strains from different geographical regions, 4 of the 57 amplified bands were found to be polymorphic. Three of these polymorphisms were detected in the same strain. When individual organisms of a single strain were studied, polymorphisms were evident that were not apparent when strains were compared. In a preliminary analysis, the number of such intra-strain polymorphisms was greater than that of inter-strain polymorphisms. Species of schistosomes presented quite distinct DNA amplification patterns in that almost all bands were found to be species-specific even when the more closely related species were compared. Of the species shown in Fig. 1, *S. rhodaini* is closely related to *S. mansoni* and *S. haematobium* and *S. intercalatum* are closely related as judged by their biological characteristics.

The analysis of strains of *T. cruzi* was based on strains defined by isoenzyme analysis which divided them into four zymodemes, Z1, Z2, ZB and ZC, within each one of which the isoenzyme profiles of the individual strains were the same. We found there to be a high degree of similarity in the RAPD profiles of strains in the same zymodeme whereas quite destinct patterns were obtained with strains from different zymodemes. These results are illustrated in Fig. 2 where RAPD profiles

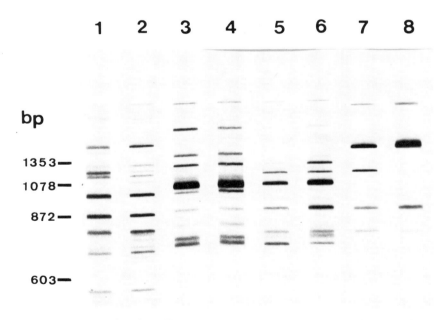

Figure 2. RAPD profile of 2 different strains of 4 *T. cruzi* zymodemes obtained using the primer 3303. Lane 1 – SC-14 (Z1; Lane 2 – A-99 (Z1); Lane 3 – 229 (Z2); Lane 4 – SC-56 (Z2); Lane 5 – 147 (ZB); Lane 6 – CL (ZB); Lane 7 – 231 (ZC); Lane 8 – 254 (ZC).

obtained with two randomly selected strains from each of the four zymodemes studied are shown. Within a single zymodeme the degree of similarity varied from 59.0 to 86.0% as calculated by band sharing analysis. In the most thoroughly studied zymodeme, Z1, 21 strains were examined from diverse regions of South and Central America. A clear zymodeme-specific pattern was maintained despite the wide geographical divergence of the strains with 59% of bands shared by all strains. A phenetic analysis based on band sharing, however, indicated that the interrelationships of their strains reflected the geographical origin, with strains from nearby localities being more closely related than strains from widely separated regions. When strains from different zymodemes were compared the average level of band sharing was 34.5%. A phenetic tree of the zymodemes was constructed, and it was found that the similarities of the four zymodemes correlated closely with the genetic distances calculated from isoenzyme analysis. Thus, ZB and ZC were found to be the most closely related and to form a group separated from either Z1 or Z2.

Comparison of *T. cruzi* with 10 *T. rangeli strains*, which also infects man but produces no detectable pathology, has shown that the RAPD profiles of the two species share a low number of bands (16%).

Discussion

The two parasite populations studied differ greatly in their genetic structure. *S. mansoni*, a sexually reproducing organism, exhibits a relatively homogeneous pattern of RAPD products irrespective of the geographic origin of the strain examined. To date, we have found more variation within a strain than between strains considered as a whole. Further work is being undertaken to establish a larger panel of polymorphisms and to attempt to correlate these with biological characteristics. Nevertheless, the data obtained thus far are consistent with isoenzyme analysis that suggests that the species *S. mansoni* is relatively homogeneous with little strain-specific variation (Fletcher et al., 1981). The differences in the RAPD profiles between species of schistosome vary to the extent that it has not been possible to yet undertake analysis of their relatedness. Again, further analysis is required to identify primers that amplify sufficient bands shared by the species to permit a quantitative analysis. At present, however, RAPD profiles adequately serve to differentiate even the most closely related species. This has not been previoulsy achieved with rRNA probes (Walker et al., 1989) and will be of use in the identification of parasites in, for example, surveys of potential endemic areas and for precise determination of host specificity.

The data obtained with the *T. cruzi* strains, an organism that does not apparently undergo recombination and thus has a clonal population

344

structure, shows clear linkage disequilibrium when strains of different zymodemes are compared. The data that we have generated to date are consistent with the species being composed of groups of closely related organisms that correspond to the originally described zymodemes (Miles et al., 1977; Romanha, 1982). The phenetic tree obtained suggests a close relationship between zymodemes B and C with zymodemes 1 and 2 being more distantly related. The phenon line (average similarity between all the groups studied) shows that within the strains studied there are 3 groups that comprise ZB and ZC, Z1 and Z2. It is of interest to note the extent of the difference between the different zymodemes which is more characteristic of the difference between species than strains of sexually reproducing organisms. Again the clear differences between the two trypanosome species studied permit their rapid identification even in mixed infections.

Our preliminary data indicate the potential value of RAPD analysis in the context of the study of parasite populations. We are encouraged by the consistency of data with earlier isoenzyme data with both parasites. The next stages of investigation will require the use of many more primers and parasite isolates to begin the task of attempting to identify polymorphisms linked to important characteristics such as drug resistance, pathogenicity and virulence.

Acknowledgements
The work involving RAPD analysis received financial assistance from the UNDP-World Bank-WHO Special programme for Research and Training in Tropical Diseases and from the FIOCRUZ.

References

Dias Neto E, Pereira de Souza C, Rollinson D, Katz N, Pena SDJ, Simpson AJG (1993) The random amplification of polymorphic DNA allows the identification of strains and species of schistosome. Mol Biochem Parasitol 57: 83–88

Fletcher M, LoVerde PT, Woodruff DS (1981) Genetic variation in *Schistosoma mansoni*: Enzyme polymorphisms in populations from Africa, Southwest Asia, South America, and West Indies. Am J Trop Med Hyg 30: 406–421

Macedo AM, Martins MS, Chiari E, Pena SDJ (1992) DNA fingerprinting of *Trypanosoma cruzi*: A new tool for characterization of strains and clones. Mol Biochem Parasitol (in press)

McCutchan TF, Simpson AJG, Mullins JA, Sher A, Nash TE, Lewis F, Richards C (1984) Differentiation of schistosomes species, strain and sex using cloned DNA markers. Proc Natl Acad Sci USA 81: 889–893

Miles MA, Toye PJ, Oswald SC, Godfrey DG (1977) The identification by isoenzyme patterns of two distinct strain-groups of *Trypanosoma cruzi*, circulating independently in a rural area of Brazil. Trans Roy Soc Trop Med Hyg 71: 217–225

Morel CM, Chiari E, Plessmann Camargo E, Mattei DM, Romanha AJ, Simpson L (1980) Strains and clones of *Trypanosoma cruzi* can be characterized by pattern of restriction endonuclease products of kinetoplast DNA minicircles. Proc Natl Acad Sci USA 77: 6810–6814

Ready PD, Miles MA (1980) Delimination of *Trypanosoma cruzi* zymodemes by numerical taxonomy. Trans Roy Soc Trop Med Hyg 74: 238–242

Romanha AJ (1982) Heterogeneidade isoenzimatica do *Trypanosoma cruzi.* Doctoral thesis. Universidade Federal de Minas Gerais, 106pp

Santos FR, Pena SDJ, Epplen JT (1993) Genetic and population study of a Y-linked tetranucleotide repeat DNA polymorphism. Hum Genet 90: 655–656

Steindel M, Dias Neto E, Menezes CLP, Romanha AJ, Simpson AJG (1993) Random amplified polymorhhic DNA analysis of *Trypanosoma cruzi.* Mol Biochem Parasitol (in press)

Tibayrenc M, Ward P, Moya A, Ayala F (1986) Natural populations of *Trypanosoma cruzi,* the agent of Chagas' disease, have a complex multiclonal structure. Proc Natl Acad Sci USA 83: 115–119

Walker T, Simpson AJG, Rollinson D (1989) Differentiation of *Schistosoma mansoni* from *Schistosoma rhodaini* using cloned DNA probes. Parasitology 98: 75–80

DNA Fingerprinting: State of the Science
ed. by S. D. J. Pena, R. Chakraborty, J. T. Epplen & A. J. Jeffreys
© 1993 Birkhäuser Verlag Basel/Switzerland

Variability and intra nest genetic relationships in Hymenoptera: DNA fingerprinting applied to the solitary bee *Megachille rotundata*

A. Blanchetot

Department of Biochemistry, University of Saskatchewan, Saskatoon, Saskatchewan S7N OWO, Canada

Summary
It is commonly known that Hymenoptera has a low level of genetic variability compared to other insects. DNA fingerprinting (DNAfp) has been used to detect genetic variation and assess nest mate relationships in the solitary bee species *M. rotundata*. The M13 sequence and a synthetic oligonucleotide sequence homologous to the 3′ hypervariable region of the α globin gene (3′HVR-α Glo) were used as probes. Therefore, both probes reveal different set of loci and the DNAfp profiles are individual specific. DNAfp profile comparisons among offspring were used to establish the genealogical structure in *M. rotundata*. The results indicate that the phenomenon of polyandry by a large number of males is not the general rule, it is concluded that in the solitary bee species *M. rotundata*, the broods raised in single nests are mostly the offspring of singly mated females.

Introduction

Behavioural patterns such as cooperative care of the brood by the adults, overlapping of generation and reproductive division of labour are characteristic of eusocial insects. Insects without these attributes are called solitary. Hamilton in 1964, was the first to propose a genetic interpretation for the evolution of insect sociality and explain the importance of haplodiploidy in Hymenoptera. He argued that intra-group relatedness between interacting individuals is a determinant factor for the understanding of the kinship theory. In Hymenoptera, male are haploid and they transmit 100% of their genes to the next generation, therefore offspring female raised from a mother and the same father share 75% of their genes. These full sisters only have 50% of their genes in common with their mother and their putative daughters. From a genetic point of view, it is better for a female to care for a sister than to produce its own offspring. The general concept of single matings is not always the rule in Hymenoptera and this is particularly the case for social insects such as honey bees. For example, if a queen mates with several males, the nest mate relationship between sisters will decrease below 50% and therefore, the genetic advantage of caring for sisters rather that your own offspring is no longer a valid argument. Multiple matings by genetically similar or identical males that increase relatedness between sisters has been proposed as a justification to the observed behaviour in social insects (Hamilton, 1964; Wilson, 1975).

Evaluation of genetic variability at the population level and estimation of intra-group relatedness have been traditionally obtained by electrophoresis of allozymes. It is known that Hymenoptera have a low level of genetic variability compared to other insect species, therefore estimation of relatedness coefficients based on observed polymorphism could lead to large standard errors (Graur, 1985).

Megachille rotundata, known as the alfalfa leaf-cutting bee, is classified as a solitary bee species. Interest in studying this bee species is mainly due to its economical return as a pollinator agent of alfalfa rather than for its specific behavioural attributes.

The development of DNA fingerprinting (DNAfp) has recently offered a wide range of applications in the analysis of family relationships in natural population (Burke, 1989). My general interest has been mainly focused on applying DNAfp to insect species (Blanchetot, 1991a, b). This paper describes the application of DNAfp to study genetic variability and genealogical structure in *M. rotundata* bee species.

Material and methods

In nature, *M. rotundata* females make their nests in tunnels. The nest consists of cells provisioned with food and eggs are laid in each of them. Each female can produce up to 10 offspring in a single nest. It is commonly accepted that the eggs found in a tunnel are the progeny of one female. In addition, *M. rotundata* can be domesticated and mass reared in individual tunnels made from straws; this feature makes leaf-cutting bees a very practical model to study in laboratory conditions. The leaf-cutting bees *M. rotundata* were collected around Saskatoon, Sask., Canada and were kindly provided by Dr. J. Rank from the Department of Biology, University of Saskatchewan.

The M13 sequence (Vassart et al., 1987) and the tandem array of sequence found at the 3′ end of the α-globin gene (Fowler et al., 1990) were used as DNAfp probes. The latter probe, termed 3′HVR-α Glo, was constructed from synthetic oligonucleotide sequences (Collick and Jeffreys, 1990). The experimental conditions to perform DNAfp from individual bees were exactly as previously described (Blanchetot, 1991a).

Results

DNAfp variability from unrelated leaf-cutting bees

DNA isolated from a population sample of 30 unrelated male and female leaf-cutting bees were hybridised consecutively with the M13 and

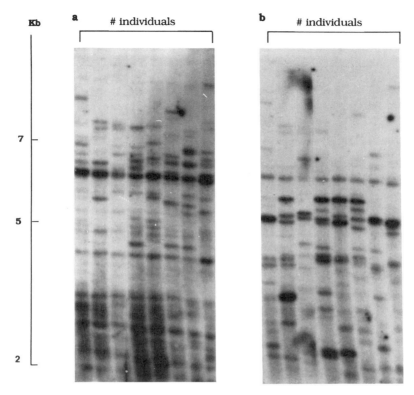

Figure 1. Hybridisation of DNA from unrelated *M. rotundata* leaf-cutting bees. a) DNAfp profiles obtained using the M13 sequence as a probe; b) DNAfp profiles from the same individuals probed with the 3′HVR-α Glo sequence.

the 3′HRV-α Glo sequences as probes (see Fig. 1a, 1b). Each probe detects complex DNAfp profiles of multiple components and in the individual patterns a few bands are revealed by both probes. It is clear that the M13 and the 3′HVR-α Glo probes detect mostly different sets of dispersed loci in the *M. rotundata* genome. Statistical data analysed from profile comparisons between individuals, are summarised in Tab. 1. The data were calculated and compiled for each probe separately and the combination of the two. In addition, comparisons were made within and between sexes. The different profiles were compared on the same gel and a band was scored as shared only if it had the same mobility and the same intensity. Incomplete resolution of bands on the gels was ignored in the statistical analysis. Band sharing estimates, x, defined as the mean number of bands shared between individuals were used to quantify genetic variability at the population level. The overall band-sharing estimates, x, between unrelated male-male, female-female and male-female average 0.29 (M13) and 0.16 (3′HVR-α Glo). The genetic

Table 1. Estimates between unrelated and nest mate siblings

Probe	Unrelated leafcutting bees			Related leafcutting bees		
	M13	α Glo	Average	M13	α Glo	Average
Size range (kb)		2–10	2–10	2–10	2–10	2–10
1. Male-male						
Mean no fragments (±SD)	17.5 (±6.8)	11 (±2.1)				
n = pairwise comparisons	21	21	42	73	56	129
Band Sharing x^a (±SD)	0.33 (±0.11)	0.18 (±0.11)	0.26 (±0.14)	0.62 (±0.11)	0.53 (±0.08)	0.59 (±0.1)
Mean allele frequency q^b	0.33	0.18	0.26			
Probability of identity Pf^d	1.4×10^{-6}	1.1×10^{-7}				
2. Female-female						
Mean no fragments (±SD)	23.4 (±6.5)	12.8 (±2.4)				
n = pairwise comparisons	47	70	117	32	39	71
Band Sharing x^a (±SD)	0.28 (±0.09)	0.16 (±0.10)	0.19 (±0.11)	0.75 (±0.12)	0.68 (±0.07)	0.71 (±0.1)
Mean allele frequency q^c	0.15	0.08	0.1			
Probability of identity Pf^d	4.2×10^{-11}	1.8×10^{-9}				
3. Male-female						
n = pairwise comparisons	66	63	129	91	44	135
Band Sharing x^a (±SD)	0.26 (±0.11)	0.15 (±0.08)	0.21 (±0.11)	0.59 (±0.13)	0.62 (±0.09)	0.6 (±0.12)

$x^a = [(N_{AB}/N_A) + (N_{AB}/N_B)]/2$: N_A and N_B are the number of bands in individuals A and B, N_{AB} is the number of bands shared in both.
$q^b = x$ for haploid males.
$q^c = 1 - (1 - x)^{0.5}$ for diploid females.
$Pf^d = (1 - 2 + 2x^2)^{N_A}$. N represents the average number of bands in an individual.
Offspring in certain nests have been analysed with only one probe.

variability detected by these two probes and compiled within and between sexes, is comparable with that observed in other animal species (Georges et al., 1988). The results in Tab. 1 also indicate that 3'HVR-α Glo is more informative to detect variation at the population level than the M13 sequence. It is clear that the application of DNA probes such as hypervariable sequences offers powerful means of measuring population genetic variations in the solitary bees *M. rotundata*. In addition, these probes could provide useful markers especially in insect species such as Hymenoptera showing a low level of genetic variability at the protein level. Within a 2–10 kb range, the M13 sequence detects an average of 24 bands in diploid females and 16 bands in haploid males, whereas an average of 12 fragments in females and 10 in males are revealed by the 3'HVR-α Glo probe. The probability of two unrelated leaf-cutting bee males or females having identical DNAfp is the order of magnitude of 10^{-8}. This result indicates that DNAfp profiles in *M. rotundata* are individual specific and suggest that the two probes M13 and 3'HVR-α Glo can be used for determining nest mate genetic relationships. The mean allele frequency of bands, q, detected by the probes can be related to the mean probability of band-sharing between individuals (see Tab. 1). It is found that q for both probes averages 0.26 in males and 0.1 in females. The asymmetrical value of mean allele frequencies of bands in males and females represents a consequence of haplodiploidy in *M. rotundata*.

Intra-nest relationships

One particular feature of the *M. rotundata* model is that neither the females (as mothers) nor her mating male(s) are available in the analyses. Therefore, no direct segregation of bands in the DNAfp patterns can be followed from the parents to the offspring. The analysis of nest mate relationships only relies on profile comparisons between individuals found in the same tunnel. It is commonly assumed that bees found in one tunnel are raised from the same mother. Examples of DNAfp profiles established from *M. rotundata* offspring probed with the M13 and the 3'HVR-α Glo sequences are presented in Fig. 2a, b. Genetic variation between nest mates from different and same sex was calculated using band-sharing estimates for each separate and the combined probes. The results were analysed by plotting the frequencies of distribution of band-sharing estimates from relatives and compared with the background frequency of distribution of band-sharing estimates from unrelated individuals. Figure 3 represents the different histograms that have been combined for the M13 and the 3'HVR-α Glo probes. Frequency of distribution of band-sharing between pairs of unrelated leaf-cutting bees having the same or different sex are largely overlapping, but these profiles do not overlap with their counterpart established from related offspring. The histograms from nest males and nest male-females overlap and pairs of sibling share on average 60% of bands, whereas nest mate females appear to belong to a separate group with an average band-sharing estimate of 71%, the unimodal frequency of distribution of band sharing between relatives implies a simple under-laying in the *M. rotundata* bee species. It appears that the DNAfp profiles can be used to discriminate pairs of related leaf-cutting bees from unrelated ones.

DNAfp has been employed for parentage analysis primarily in assessment of paternity and maternity within the brood (Burke, 1989; Westneat, 1990). It has also been shown that depending upon the proportion of bands shared between non relatives the use of DNAfp to estimate relatedness may lead to problems (Lynch, 1988). When no genealogical data are available a method using a calibration curve has been applied in an attempt to correlate band sharing and relatedness and quantify nest mate relationships in *M. rotundata*. A linear relationship, $X = x + r(1 - x)$, correlates the observed band-sharing between relatives, X, the degree of relatedness, r, and the proportion of band sharing x between non relatives (Jones et al., 1991). In the present study, it has been assumed that the haploid nest mate males collected from the same tunnel are the brood of the same female. Thus, these individuals are considered as brothers and have a relatedness, r, equal

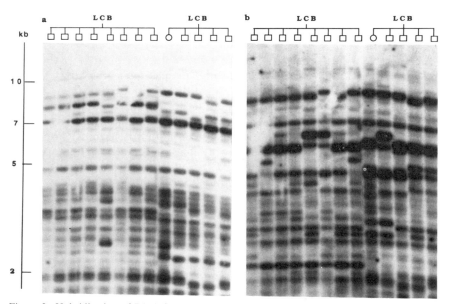

Figure 2. Hybridisation of DNA from siblings collected from the different tunnels. a) M13 as a probe; b) 3′HVR-α Glo sequence as a probe.

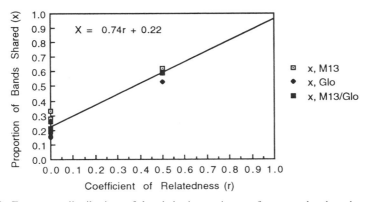

Figure 3. Frequency distribution of band-sharing estimates from unrelated and related leaf-cutting bees. The profiles correspond to data obtained from the combined M13 and 3'HVR-α Glo probes.

to 0.05. Figure 4 represents the empirical calibration plot from the data in Tab. 1 using the mean band-sharing between unrelated males, females and male-females ($r = 0$) and the mean band sharing estimate between nest mate males ($r = 0.5$). The linear equation correlating observed band-sharing estimates and the degree of relatedness coefficients is equal to $0.74r + 0.22$. A mean relatedness coefficient of 0.65 (range 0.62–0.71) is calculated between pairs of nest mate females whereas a mean relatedness estimate of 0.51 (range 0.50–0.54) has been found between pairs of nest mate male-females. If the female parent has only mated once, 75% of genes are expected to be shared between nest mate females and 50% of genes are expected to be shared between nest mate male-females. The relatedness coefficient of 0.51 between nest mate male-females is a good indication that these offspring have inherited their genes from a single paternal origin. The relatedness coefficients between nest mate females ranging from 0.62–0.71 deviate from the theoretical value of 0.75 for single matings. Different explanations can be proposed to justify such a result: i) the calibration curve is incorrect since the preexisting genealogical structure of the leaf-cutting bee in the tunnels is unknown, ii) two females have contributed to the offspring found from the same tunnel, iii) the offspring found in certain tunnels are the result of a mating of a single female with two males having an uneven genetic contribution. In conclusion, one can rule out that leaf-cutting nest mates are the progeny of multiple matings by a large number of males. The results support that single matings are most likely to occur in the solitary bee species *M. rotundata*. However, if it is commonly accepted that nest usurpation is a rare phenomenon, one cannot preclude that in a few tunnels more than one male has contributed to the progeny.

354

Unrelated

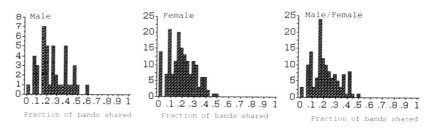

Related

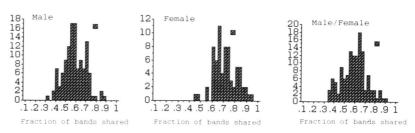

Figure 4. Calibration plot of band-sharing estimates in relation to nest mate relatedness. The data include band-sharing estimates from unrelated leaf-cutting bees ($r = 0$) and related nest mate males ($r = 0.5$).

Acknowledgements
The author thanks Dr. J. Rank, Department of Biology, University of Saskatchewan, for the leaf-cutting bees. The author also thanks V. Catinot for technical assistance. This work was supported by a Development Grant from the Medical Research Council of Canada.

References

Blanchetot A (1991a) Genetic relatedness in honey bees as established by DNA fingerprinting. J Hered 82: 391–396

Blanchetot A (1991b) A *Musca domestica* satellite sequence detects individual polymorphic regions in insect genomes. Nucleic Acids Res 19: 929–932

Burke T (1989) DNA fingerprinting and other methods for the study of mating success. Trends Evol Ecol 4: 139–144

Georges M, Lequarré AS, Castelli M, Hanset R, Vassart G (1988) DNA fingerprinting in domestic animals using four different minisatellite probes. Cytogenet Cell Genet 47: 127–131

Graur D (1985) Gene diversity in Hymenoptera. Evolution 39: 190–199

Hamilton WD (1964) The genetical evolution of social behaviour I and II. J Theor Biol 7: 1–52

Jones CS, Lessells CM, Krebs JR (1991) Helpers at the nest in European bee-eaters (*Merops apiaster*): a genetic analysis. *In*: Burke T, Dolf G, Jeffreys A.J. and Wolff R. (eds) DNA Fingerprinting: Approaches and Applications. Birkhäuser, Basel, pp 169–192

Lynch M (1988) Estimation of relatedness by DNA fingerprinting. Mol Biol Evol 5: 584–599

Westneat DF (1990) Genetic parentage in the indigo bunting: a study using DNA fingerprinting. Behav Ecol Sociobiol 27: 67–76

Wilson EO (1975) A theory of group selection. Proc Natl Acad Sci USA 72: 143–146

DNA Fingerprinting: State of the Science
ed. by S. D. J. Pena, R. Chakraborty, J. T. Epplen & A. J. Jeffreys

Sperm utilization in honeybees as detected by M13 DNA fingerprints

J. Corley[a], M. Rabinovich[a], M. Seigelchifer[b], J. Zorzópulos[c] and E. Corley[b]

[a]*Departamento de Tecnología, Universidad Nacional de Luján, 5700 Luján, Argentina;* [b]*Genargen SRL, Pringles 10, 1183 Buenos Aires, Argentina; and* [c]*Fundación CIMAE, Luis Viale 2831, Buenos Aires, Argentina*

Summary
Sperm utilization by multiply inseminated females, such as honeybee queens, is of key importance because of its relationship to kin selection theory and the evolution of eusociality. We have used M13 phage DNA fingerprinting analysis to study the number of drones that contribute patrilines to an *Apis mellifera ligustica* colony in Argentina. Ten different paternal patterns were clearly distinguished in a 28 worker offspring of this naturally inseminated queen. Relative paternal contributions ranged from 3.5% to 25%. These results do not seem to adjust to random sperm use nor do they support sperm clumping. M13 phage DNA fingerprinting has proven to be an adequate tool for sperm use studies in this species.

Introduction

Sperm utilization by multiply inseminated females, such as honeybee (*Apis mellifera ligustica*) queens, is of key importance because of its relationship to kin selection theory and the evolution of eusociality (Laidlaw et al., 1984). Sperm utilization patterns can affect the genetic relationships within broods. This may alter the likelihood and the rate at which kin selection can occur affecting in turn the genetic component of the evolution of sterile castes and hence eusociality.

Honeybees are extremely polyandrous. Queens mate with an estimated average of 10–12 males, establishing a colony. A colony is a matriarchal family consisting of a queen mother, her female progeny of workers and her male progeny of drones. All worker bees, around 95% of the 30,000 or so members of a typical colony, are females and perform all tasks except the production of eggs, as they never mate or lay eggs as long as their mother is alive. Workers develop from fertilized eggs and in consequence are diploid. In contrast, male reproductives i.e. drones, accounting for 5% of the colonies' members, develop from unfertilized eggs and are haploid (Seeley, 1985).

Although all members of a colony share the same mother, the female members may not share the same father constituting different patrilineal groups. Workers from the same patriline are termed "supersisters" as they have a coefficient of relatedness (r) of 0.75. Half-sisters belonging to different patrilines will have an $r = 0.25$. The actual number of drones contributing to the worker progeny affect the average relatedness within a colony.

In spite of the importance of the knowledge of sperm use in this group there have been no reports of number of patrilines and their relative frequencies in naturally inseminated queens. This could result from the paucity of genetic markers due to the low genetic variation characteristic of the social hymenopterans (Hall, 1991). Patterns of sperm use have been determined for instrumentally inseminated queens using visible phenotypic mutants or allozymic markers. These experiments have several drawbacks, mainly the unknown effect of artificial insemination on sperm mixing and the limited number of drones with recognizable genetic traits that can be used in an experiment. Morever different authors have obtained contradictory results. Though there is no evidence for long-term sperm precedence it is not clear whether there may be short-term nonrandom sperm use (Page, 1986).

Recently, DNA fingerprinting techniques have been used with success in honeybees to discriminate patrilines (Blanchetot, 1991; Moritz et al., 1991; Corley et al., 1992) allowing the possibility of addressing this problem in natural conditions.

In this paper we have studied bees from a single colony derived from a naturally inseminated queen using M13-HaeIII DNA fingerprinting (Vassart et al., 1987) and have determined the number of patrilines and the relative representation of each one. We also present data of band-sharing in presumably unrelated individuals.

Materials and methods

Sample collection

Honeybee pupae were obtained from a single colony of the Universidad de Luján, Buenos Aires, Argentina. All individual insects were collected on the same day in Eppendorff tubes and were kept in a dry ice/ethanol bath until they reached the laboratory where they were stored at $-20°C$ until use.

DNA extraction

Each individual sample was homogenized with a sterile toothpick, in the tube in which it had been stored, after the addition of 300 μl of

100 mM Tris-ClH pH 8, 50 mM EDTA, 50 mM NaCl. The buffer was made 1% in SDS and 10 μl of proteinase K (10 mg/ml) were added. The homogenate was incubated 3 h at 55°C and left at 37°C overnight. Tubes were centrifuged in a microfuge for 10 min and the supernate was transferred to another tube. A half volume of 7.5 M ammonium acetate pH 7.5 and 2 volumes of ethanol were added and the tube was left to stand at room temperature for 15 min. The DNA was collected with a sterile toothpick and resuspended in 300 μl of sterile water. Ammonium acetate (150 μl 7.5 M, pH 7.5) was added and the tube was left to stand 15 min at room temperature. After this incubation, DNA was precipitated by the addition of 1 ml of ethanol, 10 min room temperature incubation and 30 min of centrifugation in a microfuge. The ethanol precipitation step was repeated once more. The DNA pellet was allowed to dry thoroughly and was redissolved in 300 μl of sterile water.

DNA restriction and electrophoresis

100 μl of these DNAs (approx. 5 μg) were digested with 50 units of HaeIII (Gibco BRL) overnight at 37°C in a final volume of 200 μl. 1/20th volume of each sample was electrophoresed in an 0.7% agarose gel to verify restriction and to adjust DNA quantity between samples. The restrictions were precipitated with 7.5 M ammonium acetate pH 7.5 and ethanol, resuspended in 40 μl of sterile water; 5 μl of loading buffer were added and the samples were electrophoresed in 20 cm long 0.6% agarose gels at 16 V for 40 h.

Hybridization

Gels were denatured in 1 N OHNa, 1.5 M NaCl; neutralized in 1 M ammonium acetate; transferred using 1 M ammonium acetate to Ze-taprobe (BioRad) membranes and fixed by baking 2 h at 80°C. Membranes were prehybridized at 55°C in 7% SDS, 1 mM EDTA pH 8, 0.263 M Na_2HPO_4 and 1% BSA (Westneat et al., 1988). Hybridization was performed at the same temperature in the same buffer containing 30 ng/ml of single strand M13mp18 DNA for 18 h (Weihe et al., 1990). Filters were washed in 2 × SSC, 0.1% SDS (1 × SSC = 0.15 M NaCl, 0.015 M sodium citrate) at 55°C and prehybridized again as described. After prehybridization 10 ng/ml of double-strand M13mp18 DNA labelled by the random priming method (Feinberg et al., 1983) were added and the filters were autoradiographed from 1 to 5 days with intensifying screens.

358

Results

Bandsharing

As preliminary results of bandsharing within our apiary were very high, around 70% (not shown), we thought colonies could be related because of the apicultural practice applied. In order to elude this possible drawback we studied bandsharing in 6 bees obtained from different apiaries of the Luján area in which different origins of their mother queens could be ascertained.

As can be observed in Tab. 1, bandsharing in honeybees is extremely high ($x = 0.74$) with a standard deviation of 0.07. However of the approximately 17 bands obtained in a typical fingerprint, 10 bands appear invariantly in all bees studied. When these apparently monomorphic "bee bands" are excluded from the bandsharing analysis, bandsharing falls to $x = 0.35$ with a standard deviation of 0.16.

Patrilines

In spite of the unusually high bandsharing it was possible to distinguish patrilines within a colony and determine their relative frequency. To this end, 28 worker bee pupae collected from a single colony, were analyzed in comparison to their queen mother considering any extra bands appearing in the workers as of paternal origin as exemplified in Fig. 1. In general 1 or 2 paternal bands were found per worker. In 3 workers no extra bands were found and these were considered developed from unfertilized eggs. This observation is consistent with the fact that up to 7% of unfertilized eggs laid by the queen develop into workers (Tucker, 1958). The analysis revealed the simultaneous presence of 10 different patrilines which are schematically represented in Fig. 2.

Table 1. Bandsharing data from all pairwise comparisons between individuals A and B calculated as $2V_{AB}/(N_A + N_B)$ where V_{AB} is the total number of common bands and N_A and N_B are the total number of bands in A and B. The upper triangle presents data from comparisons including "bee bands" whereas the lower triangle presents data from comparisons excluding "bee bands"

	1	2	3	4	5	6
1	—	0.72	0.70	0.74	0.77	0.75
2	0.37	—	0.80	0.71	0.69	0.73
3	0.28	0.40	—	0.76	0.87	0.61
4	0.40	0.18	0.22	—	0.84	0.81
5	0.50	0.17	0.60	0.54	—	0.68
6	0.47	0.31	0	0.50	0.31	—

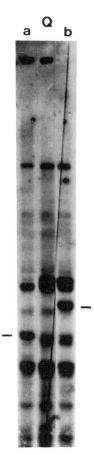

Figure 1. DNA fingerprint profiles from the mother-queen (Q) and two different patrilines labeled a and b. Extra bands of paternal origin are indicated.

All workers presenting the same extra bands were considered belonging to the same patriline and the relative frequencies were calculated. As can be seen in Fig. 3, patriline representation ranged from 25% to 3.5%.

Discussion

M13 HaeIII DNA fingerprints in the honeybee, *Apis mellifera ligustica*, reveal patterns with unusually high bandsharing. This is not surprising as eusocial hymenopteran species have reportedly low genetic variation (Hall, 1990). However the bandsharing probability we have determined is greater than the one reported by Blanchetot in the same species

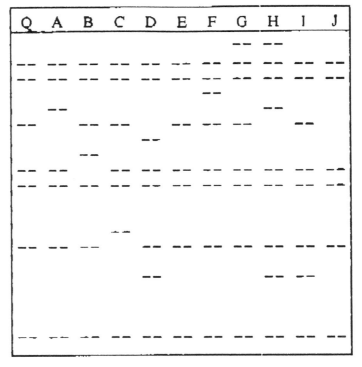

Figure 2. Schematic representation of patrilines labeled A through J in comparison with the mother queen profile labeled Q.

(Blanchetot, 1991). This discrepancy could reflect differences in the bee populations analyzed, or could simply reflect sampling error (in both papers the number of individuals analyzed is small) or different electrophoretic resolution. It would be interesting to explore this subject further as such low variation in fingerprints as reflected in the "bee bands" is intriguing given the high mutation rate of minisatellites (Jeffreys et al., 1991).

Regarding the number of patrilines detected, the results we have obtained in a colony from an apiary coincide with the number of patrilines determined by Blanchetot (11 patrilines) in a feral colony. These data are consistent with observational information indicating a queen mates with an average of 10–12 drones (Seeley, 1985) and contradict hypotheses sustaining that at any given time only one or two drones are represented within a colony (Page, 1986).

However the number of patrilines must be considered a minimum for two reasons. High bandsharing could be masking other patrilines as two

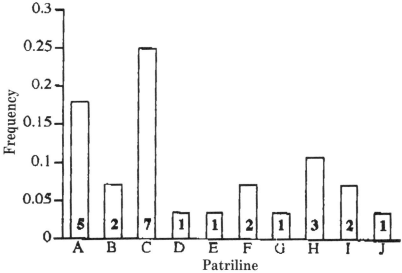

Figure 3. Histogram representing frequency of each patriline identified A through J. The number within each column represents the number of bees in the respective patriline.

drones could present the same pattern. The other reason is that because of the small sample size we could have missed one or more patrilines.

When the relative frequency of patrilines was observed, differences of 7 times in frequency were found between the most represented and least represented patriline. Blanchetot found a 6.5 times difference between the most represented and the least represented patriline and Laidlaw has found nonrandom sperm use within samples studied (Laidlaw et al., 1984). To see if the sperm use we have determined was random or nonrandom, we ran a Montecarlo simulation extracting samples of 28 individuals from a colony with 10 equally represented patrilines. In several runs of 100 iterations each, the probability of finding a sample in which at least one patriline was represented in 25% of the individuals was less than 10%.

To our knowledge, this is the first report of honeybee sperm use in a naturally inseminated queen. The results obtained may indicate nonrandom sperm use at a given time point in colony life, though complete elucidation of this question will require further work analyzing larger samples.

Acknowledgements
This research was funded by PRONINTEC grant number 22MJ19090. We wish to thank Juan Carlos Reboreda for critical reading of the manuscript.

362

References

Blanchetot A (1991) Genetic relatedness in honeybees as established by DNA fingerprinting. J Hered 82: 391–396

Corley J, Rabinovich M, Seigelchifer M, Zorzopulos J, Corley E (1992) DNA fingerprinting in honeybees. Fingerprint News 4(2): 8–11

Feinberg AP, Vogelstein BA (1983) Technique for radiolabelling DNA restriction endonuclease fragments to high specific activity. Anal Biochem 132: 6–13

Hall G (1991) Genetic characterization of honeybees through DNA analysis. *In*: Spivak M, Fletcher DJC, Breed MD (eds) The "African" Honeybee. Westview press, Boulder, Colorado, pp 45–73

Jeffreys AJ, Turner M, Debenham P (1991) The efficiency of multilocus DNA fingerprint probes for individualization and establishment of family relationships, determined from extensive casework. Am J Hum Genet 48: 824–840

Laidlaw HH, Page RE (1984) Polyandry in honey bees (*Apis mellifera L.*): Sperm utilization and intracolony genetic relationships. Genetics 108: 985–997

Moritz RFA, Meusel MS, Harberl M (1991) Oligonucleotide DNA fingerprinting discriminates super- and half-sisters in honeybee colonies (*Apis mellifera L.*). Naturwissenschaften 78: 422–424

Page RE (1986) Sperm utilization in social insects. Ann Rev Entomol 31: 297–320

Seeley TD (1985) Honeybee ecology. Princeton University press, Princeton, New Jersey

Tucker K (1958) Automictic parthogenesis in the honey bee. Genetics 43: 299–316

Vassart G, Georges M, Monsieur R, Brocas H, Lequarré AS, Christophe DA (1987) Sequence in M13 phage detects hypervariable minisatellites in human and animal DNA. Science 235: 683–684

Weihe A, Niemann C, Lieckfield D, Meyer W, Borner T (1990) An improved hybridization procedure for DNA fingerprinting with bacteriophage M13 as a probe. Fingerprint News 2(4): 9–10

Westneat DF, Noon WA, Reeve HK, Aquadro CF (1988) Improved hybridization conditions for DNA fingerprints probed with M13. Nucleic Acids Res 16: 4161

DNA Fingerprinting: State of the Science
ed. by S. D. J. Pena, R. Chakraborty, J. T. Epplen & A. J. Jeffreys
© 1993 Birkhäuser Verlag Basel/Switzerland

High mating success of low rank males in *Limia perugiae* (Pisces: Poeciliidae) as determined by DNA fingerprinting

M. Schartl[a], C. Erbelding-Denk[b], S. Hölter[a], I. Nanda[c], M. Schmid[c], J. H. Schröder[b] and J. T. Epplen[d]

[a]*Physiologische Chemie I, Theodor-Boveri-Institut für Biowissenschaften am Biozentrum der Universität, Am Hubland, 97074 Würzburg, Germany;* [b]*Institut für Säugetiergenetik, GSF Forschungszentrum, Ingolstädter Landstraße 1, 85764 Neuherberg, Germany;* [c]*Institut für Humangenetik am Biozentrum der Universität, Am Hubland, 97074 Würzburg, Germany; and* [d]*Molekulare Humangenetik, Ruhr-Universität, 44780 Bochum, Germany*

Summary
Hierarchical structures among male individuals in a population are frequently reflected in differences in aggressive and reproductive behaviour and access to the females. In general social dominance requires large investments which in turn may have to be compensated for by high reproductive success. However, this hypothesis has so far only been sufficiently tested in small mating groups due to the difficulties of determining paternity by classical methods using non-molecular markers. DNA fingerprinting overcomes these problems offering the possibility to determine genetic relationships and mating patterns within larger groups. Using this approach we have recently shown (Schartl et al., 1993) that in the poeciliid fish *Limia perugiae* in small mating groups the dominant male has 100% mating success, while in larger groups its contribution to the offspring unexpectedly drops to zero. The reproductive failure under such social conditions is explained by the inability of the α-male to protect all the females simultaneously against mating attempts of his numerous subordinate competitors.

Introduction

In many species of poeciliids males are polymorphic for body size (Constantz, 1975; Kallman, 1984; Hughes, 1985). Large males outcompete smaller ones and become dominant in the social structure of a given group (see Farr, 1989). In at least one genus it has been conclusively shown that differences in body size result primarily from allelic variation of a single polymorphic Y chromosome linked locus (known as the *P*-locus, Kallman and Schreibman, 1973; Kallman, 1984; Borowsky, 1987; Kallman, 1989). The different size classes differ with respect to their sexual behaviour. Large males display a pronounced courtship behaviour that precedes copulation attempts while small males show simple "sneaking" behaviour (Constantz, 1975; Ryan, 1988; Zimmerer and Kallman, 1989). This is in agreement with considerations that in the natural environment alternate mating tactics exist as an evolutionarily stable strategy (Maynard Smith, 1976, 1981). Large males reach sexual maturity at a much later age than smaller ones imposing costs in form of an increased risk of pre-reproductive mortality (Hughes, 1985) due to predation, etc. Additional costs of a courting male include a higher risk of becoming predated because of its garishness due to the more brilliant coloration of the α-animal (Farr, 1975; Endler, 1980) and the energy input required to defend the hierarchy and protect females from the mating attempts of subordinate males. In female choice tests large males are preferred (Ryan and Wagner, 1987; Zimmerer and Kallman, 1989; Hughes, 1985). The large, spectacularly pigmented male morphs are the result of sexual selection. Behavioural polymorphisms as well as the accompanying phenotypic polymorphisms are maintained or balanced by natural selection.

Using phenotypic markers in progeny tests of two females with one large and one small male the dominant large male was found to be rewarded by a greater reproductive success (Zimmerer and Kallman, 1989). In the guppy dominant males were more successful even when the females showed preference for the subordinate male (Kodric-Brown, 1992). All these observations are in agreement with the expected increased fitness for the α-animal.

We have used *Limia perugiae*, a poeciliid fish endemic to the southeast of the Caribbean island Hispaniola, to study mating patterns in relation to male polymorphism and mating group size by DNA fingerprinting. These fish inhabit freshwater biotopes, clear springs as well as muddy creeks and polluted man-made ditches. Males are polymorphic for adult size ranging from 20 up to sometimes 60 mm total length. The onset of sexual maturation which results in cessation of growth is determined by a genetic system comparable to the *P*-locus of *Xiphophorus* with Y-chromosomal alleles for large and small size. However, additionally at least one autosomal modifier locus interacts with *P*, thus allowing intermediate size males to appear (Erbelding-Denk et al., submitted). Of course environmental factors modulate to a certain extent the final size of each genotype. Females constitute a single size class with a mean adult size of 40 mm. Like all other poeciliid fish species they are livebearing and do not provide parental care. Males are not territorial. The sex ratio is on average one to one. The highest rank males are marked by a very intensive coloration: blue body contrasted by a black dorsal fin and a bright yellow caudal fin with black margin.

Simple repeat oligonucleotides are useful tools to study genetic relationships within all species tested at all levels of eukaryotic organismic evolution (Epplen et al., 1991). This approach seemed especially advantageous to determine paternity in large social groups (Burke, 1989).

Materials and methods

For details on the experimental animals see Schartl et al. (1993). DNA was prepared from pooled organs of individual fish and processed for restriction enzyme digest and agarose gel electrophoresis essentially as described (see Schartl, 1988). For DNA fingerprinting the gel was dried and hybridized to ^{32}P-end labelled oligonucleotides. For details on the hybridization and washing conditions see Nanda et al. (1990). Paternity was determined after 3–4 oligonucleotide hybridization steps by comparing all multilocus fingerprint patterns of each child with those of the mother defining the paternally inherited bands. The latter were compared to the patterns of the putative fathers thus sequentially excluding each of the non-fathers.

Results

In a first series of mating experiments one large and one small male were tested with two females. Offspring from two different broods in two independent experiments were analysed for paternity. In the first experiment 13 of 14 animals were attributable to the large dominant male and one was of uncertain paternity. In the second case all 12 F_1 fish tested were unequivocally offspring of the α-male. These observations are in accordance with findings using similar sized mating groups in the pygmy swordtail, *Xiphophorus nigrensis* (Zimmerer and Kallmann, 1989) and the guppy, *Poecilia reticulata* (Kodric-Brown, 1992). The reproductive success of the large male in this kind of competition experiment can be attributed to the selective advantage gained by its dominance and the pronounced courtship behaviour. It is in perfect agreement with the expectation that a high commitment of energy and cost into sexual and social behaviour leads to high fitness. If the aforementioned test situation relates to anything determining the evolutionary history of *L. perugiae* in feral populations, this, however, would predict that the small phenotype which is invariably connected to subordinateness is prone to disappearance by negative selection.

In the second set of experiments four males ranging in size from 25 mm to 49 mm were assembled with four or five juvenile, virgin females. Within few days the male fish established size-dependent ranking that remained stable throughout the duration of the experiment. Neonates were taken out of the aquarium immediately after birth and raised separately. DNA fingerprinting of a representative number of offspring ($n = 155$) revealed that most females had contributed to the offspring generation and that generally individual broods were of mixed paternity. After experiments 2 and 3 full fertility of the α males was confirmed by mating them without competition to virgin females.

366

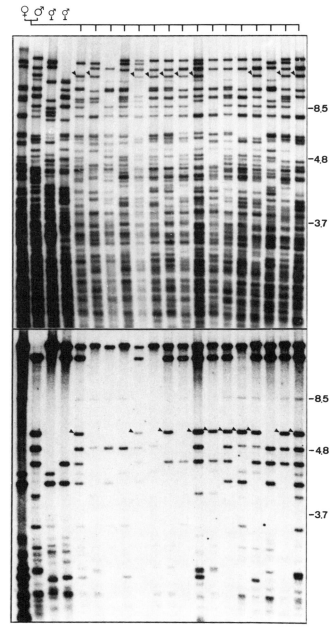

Figure 1. Determination of paternity in large mating groups of *L. perugiae* by DNA fingerprinting showing three possible fathers (♂; lanes 2–4 from left: β-, γ- and ω-males), the mother (♀; lane 1) as well as their offspring as obtained with the probes (GGAT)₄ (top) and (CA)₈ (bottom). Representative diagnostic bands could only be transmitted by one of the possible fathers (arrows). Fragment length markers are indicated in kilobase pairs on the right.

In the first mating group all offspring tested were from the subordinate β-male (see Fig. 1). In the second and third group paternity was assigned to the β and γ males. In all cases the smallest and most subordinate male never had offspring. This is in agreement with its exclusively defensive behaviour. Surprisingly, we could not identify progeny of the dominant male (see Tab. 1). This observation is in direct contradiction to the expected results and the behavioural data on fish reported so far. However, the only component of fitness that has been possible to monitor before is the number of observed matings or mating attempts by each male, but even this may be misleading as the number of successful fertilizations can be substantially different. After analysing the genetic relationships of the progeny with the males it became apparent that intermediate size males, that exhibit only little courtship but simple "sneaking" behaviour are more effective reproductively than the more extreme social and size classes (represented by the α and ω males), who are practically excluded from reproduction. The size of the group used in the second set of experiments is more similar to the situation found in nature (Lechner and Radda, 1980; Lechner and Meyer, pers. commun.) and may help to explain the result obtained. As population size increases the dominant male must spend more time fighting and less time pursuing females. Futhermore, attacks on non-aggressive subordinates decrease as aggressive males devote proportionally more time fighting each other allowing lower rank males a greater opportunity to successfully mate. To test this hypothesis the behaviour of the males was quantified (according to Parzefall, 1969). It was revealed that indeed the dominant male spent most of his time with agonistic behaviour and also courtship display (Schartl et al., 1993). Under such social conditions the highest rank male is heavily engaged in defending the hierarchy and protecting females from mating attempts of his competitors. As he spends a lot of time with courtship display, the dominant male is obviously not able

Table 1. Paternity of offspring in large mating groups of *Limia perugiae*

Trial	α	β	γ	ω	uncertain
I	0	29	0	0	1*
II	0	53	15	0	8**
III	0	24	12	0	3**
IV [#]	12	8	7	5	0

*not unequivocally ascribable to one of the four possible fathers because of too few paternal bands transmitted. **attributable either to β or γ. [#] social hierarchy less clearly established, see text.

to prevent the subordinates from successful mating after simple "sneaking" behaviour.

In a fourth independent large mating group males were assembled that did not establish a pronounced hierarchy although size differences allowed some ranking. The lowest rank male did not exhibit hiding, and the α-male was far less aggressive than in the three other mating groups. In this experiment all four males produced offspring.

Discussion

The question arises as to how in the mating system identified for larger social groups with a pronounced hierarchy a size polymorphism in males can be maintained if the genes of the extreme size class males are only rarely transmitted to the progeny. If size is determined by polygenic systems and/or environmental conditions the maintenance of polymorphisms is readily explained. However, if a single locus, such as the *P*-locus of *Xiphophorus* (Kallman, 1984), is of major importance in determining the onset of maturation and therefore adult size, only a balanced system of different modifier alleles for *P* present in males and females will guarantee the reappearance of all size classes in the off-spring generations.

Our findings in *L. perugiae* are not compatible with the current understanding that social dominance increases reproductive success. We cannot exclude that the mating system that we observed in *L. perugiae* will be unstable in the long run. A possible explanation for the observed phenomenon, however, would be "inclusive fitness" (Hamilton, 1964). Populations of *L. perugiae* like most poeciliid fish live in limited habitats. Therefore the chance that a subordinate male is a close relative to the dominant male is high. It should also be taken into consideration that *L. perugiae* like most teleosts produce a large surplus of offspring of which only a minute number reaches maturity due to heavy predative pressure. This may counteract or bias the gene pool of the survivors as compared to the newborn population. In any of the possible explanations the biological significance of aggressiveness, social hierarchy and courtship behaviour remains obscure.

The difference observed in reproductive success of the dominant *L. perugiae* male in small and large groups documents the need to apply efficient molecular biology methods to study also in other species mating success in groups larger than the 3–4 individuals that can be studied by conventional methods. DNA fingerprinting provides the powerful tool to extend such analyses even to the genetic relationships in natural populations. Such data will provide the most relevant basis for sociobiological considerations.

Acknowledgements
We thank B. Wilde for technical assistance and M. Meyer (Bad Nauheim) for helpful information on the biology of *L. perugiae* in its natural habitats and for supplying founder fish for our stocks. Supported by grants to Ma. S. (DFG), J. T. E. (VW-Stiftung) and Mi. S. (DFG).

References

Borowsky RL (1987) Genetic polymorphism in adult male size in *Xiphophorus variatus* (Atheriniformes: Poeciliidae). Copeia 1987: 782–787

Burke T (1989) DNA fingerprinting and other methods for the study of mating success. Trends Ecol Evol 4: 139–144

Constantz GD (1975) Behavioural ecology of mating in the male Gila topminnow, *Poeciliopsis occidentalis* (Cypridontiformes: Poeciliidae). Ecology 36: 966–973

Endler JA (1980) Natural selection on color patterns in *Poecilia reticulata*. Evolution 34: 76–91

Epplen JT, Ammer H, Epplen C, Kammerbauer C, Mitreiter R, Roewer L, Schwaiger W et al. (1991) Oligonucleotide fingerprinting using simple repeat motifs: a convenient, ubiquitously applicable method to detect hypervariability for multiple purposes. *In*: Burke T, Dolf G, Jeffreys AJ, Wolff R (eds) DNA Fingerprinting: Approaches and Applications. Birkhäuser Verlag, Basel, pp 50–69

Erbelding-Denk C, Schröder JH, Schartl M, Nanda I, Schmid M, Epplen JT. Male polymorphism in *Limia perugiae* (Pisces: Poeciliidae) (submitted)

Farr JA (1975) The role of predation in the evolution of social behavior of natural populations of the Guppy, *Poecilia reticulata* (Pisces: poeciliidae). Evolution 29: 151–158

Farr JA (1989) Sexual selection and secondary sexual differentiation in Poeciliids: determinants of male mating success and the evolution of female choice. *In*: Meffe GK, Snelson FF Jr (eds) Ecology and Evolution of Livebearing Fishes (Poeciliidae). Prentice Hall, Englewoods Cliffs, New Jersey, pp 91–123

Hamilton WD (1964) The genetical evolution of social behaviour. J Theor Biol 7: 1–16

Hughes AL (1985) Male size, mating success, and mating strategy in the mosquitofish *Gambusia affinis* (Poeciliidae). Behav Ecol Sociobiol 17: 271–278

Kallman KD (1984) A new look at sex determination in Poeciliid Fishes. *In*: Turner BJ (ed) Evolutionary Genetics of Fishes. Virginia Polytechnic Institute and State University, Blacksburg, Virginia. Plenum Press, New York, pp 95–171

Kallman KD (1989) Genetic control of size at maturity in Xiphophorus. *In*: Meffe GK, Snelson FF Jr (eds) Ecology and Evolution of Livebearing Fishes (Poeciliidae). Prentice Hall, Englewood Cliffs, New Jeresy, pp 163–184

Kallman KD, Schreibman MP (1973) A sex-linked gene controlling gonadotrop differentiation and its significance in determining the age of sexual maturation and size of the platyfish, *Xiphophorus maculatus*. Gen Comp Endocrinol 21: 287–304

Kodric-Brown A (1992) Male dominance can enhance mating success in guppies. Anim Behav 44: 165–167

Lechner P, Radda AC (1980) Poeciliiden-Studien in der Dominikanischen Republik. Aquaria 27: 1–13

Maynard Smith J (1976) Evolution and the theory of games. Amer Sci 64: 41–45

Maynard Smith J (1981) Will a sexual population evolve to an ESS? Amer Natur 117: 1015–1018

Nanda I, Feichtinger W, Schmid M, Schröder JH, Zischler H, Epplen JT (1990) Simple repetitive sequences are associated with differentiation of the sex chromosomes in the Guppy fish. J Mol Evol 30: 456–462

Parzefall J (1969) Zur vergleichenden Ethologie verschiedener *Mollienesia* Arten einschließlich einer Höhlenform von *M. sphenops*. Behaviour 33: 1–37

Ryan MJ (1988) Phenotype, genotype, swimming endurance and sexual selection in a swordtail (*Xiphophorus nigrensis*). Copeia 1988: 484–487

Ryan MJ, Wagner WE (1987) Asymmetries in mating preferences between species: Female swordtails prefer heterospecific males. Science 236: 595–597

Schartl M (1988) A sex chromosomal restriction-fragment-length marker linked to melanoma-determining *Tu* loci in Xiphophorus. Genetics 119: 679–685

Schartl M, Erbelding-Denk C, Hölter S, Nanda I, Schmid M, Schröder JH, Epplen JT (1993) Reproductive failure of dominant males in the poeciliid fish *Limia perugiae* determined by DNA-fingerprinting. Proc Natl Acad Sci USA (in press)

Zimmerer EJ, Kallman KD (1989) Genetic basis for alternative reproductive tactics in the pygmy swordtail, *Xiphophorus nigrensis*. Evolution 43: 1298–1307

DNA Fingerprinting: State of the Science
ed. by S. D. J. Pena, R. Chakraborty, J. T. Epplen & A. J. Jeffreys
© 1993 Birkhäuser Verlag Basel/Switzerland

Quantitative traits in chicken associated with DNA fingerprint bands

G. Dolf[a], J. Schläpfer[a], C. Hagger[b], G. Stranzinger[b] and C. Gaillard[a]

[a]Institute of Animal breeding, University of Berne, 3012 Berne, Switzerland; and
[b]Institute of Technology, 8092 Zurich, Switzerland

Summary

In an unselected control line of a selection experiment in chicken the following traits were evaluated: number of eggs, average egg weight, egg mass, age at first egg, body weight at 20 weeks, body weight at 40 weeks, feed consumption and feed efficiency (feed consumption/egg mass). Data and blood samples of 143 females of the same age were available for analysis. The animals were ranked for each trait according to the phenotypic performance adjusted for hatch and laying house effect rather than the breeding value. DNA mixes of the top 5 and the bottom 5 hens were compared to each other by DNA fingerprinting. The most striking differences could be observed with the probe pV47 in the mixes for body weight at 20 weeks and the feed efficiency. In the following the study focused on feed efficiency. Five groups of 10 hens each, around quantiles 0%, 25%, 50%, 75% and 100%, were analyzed with respect to the occurrence of 7 particular DNA fingerprint bands. The association of the groups' mean feed efficiency with the groups' band frequencies was assessed by linear regression. For 2 bands significant regression coefficients ($P < 0.005$) were found.

Introduction

In farm animals economically important traits primarily concern production, e.g. milk yield in cattle or number of eggs in chicken. Such traits have in common that their variation is continuous and that they can therefore be quantified, hence the name quantitative traits. The expression of quantitative traits is controlled by many genes and considerably modified by the environment. The loci concerned are called quantitative trait loci (QTL) (Geldermann, 1975). Up to very recently, lacking even rudimentary marker maps, it was the exception to find genetic linkage to QTL (Sax, 1923; Rasmusson, 1933; Thoday, 1961; Tanksley et al., 1982). Only the exploitation of restriction fragment length polymorphism (Botstein et al., 1980) and various repetitive DNA elements (Vogt, 1990) now provides the opportunity to systematically hunt for QTL markers. But animal breeding did not have to wait for analyses on the molecular level. Quantitative genetics provided the means to continuously ensure selection response in breeding programs. Based on the assumption that an infinite number of loci contribute equally to a quantitative trait, statistical procedures have been developed to assess the genotype using data on the phenotype, e.g. Best

Linear Unbiased Prediction (Henderson, 1973) together with the Animal Model (Quaas and Pollak, 1980). Now the mapping of QTL (Geldermann, 1975; Soller et al., 1976; Soller and Beckmann, 1990) offers the possibility of marker assisted selection (MAS) (Soller, 1978; Smith and Simpson, 1986; Soller, 1990; Dekkers and Dentine, 1991) which recently moved into the range of possibility with the finding of first markers for QTL (Paterson et al., 1988; Georges et al., 1990; Cowan et al., 1990). But quantitative genetics have also dealt with the mapping of quantitative traits and the potential benefits of MAS (Soller et al., 1976; Soller, 1978; Smith and Simpson, 1986; Kennedy et al., 1990). Of the various strategies to find markers DNA fingerprinting (Jeffreys et al., 1985, 1986) seems to be especially suitable (Haley, 1991). Most efforts so far have been restricted to chicken (Plotsky et al., 1990; Kuhnlein et al., 1991; Lamont et al., 1992) due to their availability and low cost.

Material and methods

Blood samples and data on performance were available for 143 hens of the control line in the 7th generation of a selection experiment (Hagger, 1990). A true F1 cross of Rhode Island Red males and White Plymouth Rock females served as base population. In each generation 80 females and 20 males were chosen as parents in a scheme that minimized inbreeding. The following traits were recorded: age at first egg (AFE), body weight at 20 weeks (BW20) and at 40 weeks number of eggs (NE40), average egg weight (EW40), egg mass (EM40), body weight (BW40), feed consumption (FC40) and feed efficiency (FE40) i.e. the ratio FC40/EM40. All traits were adjusted for hatch and laying house effects. BLUPs of Animal Model breeding values were estimated for each trait.

For each animal DNA was extracted from 0.1 ml blood basically following the protocol by Jeanpierre (1987). DNA digestion, gel electrophoresis (0.8% agarose, 2.17 V/cm for 16 h 30 min), blotting and hybridization with the probes pV47 (Longmire et al., 1990) and pKJH-7 (unpublished) followed our standard procedures (Dolf et al., 1991).

Hens were ordered for each trait according to their phenotypic values. DNA mixes of the top 5 hens were compared to the corresponding DNA mixes of the bottom 5 hens for each trait. Based on these comparisons groups of 10 hens each around quantiles 0%, 25%, 50%, 75% and 100% of the total of 143 birds were analyzed with respect to the FE40. The presence of bands was judged by eye. Bands of similar intensity were considered present and weaker bands absent. Associations between the FE40 and 7 DNA fingerprint bands generated with the probe pV47 were characterized by linear regression.

Results and discussion

For all traits the DNA fingerprint patterns showed differences between the DNA mixes of the top 5 and the bottom 5 hens with both, pV47 (Fig. 1) and with pKJH-7. In the following the study focused on the FE40 the economically most important trait of those investigated. For each of the 7 DNA fingerprint bands (Fig. 2) generated with the probe pV47 a linear regression was calculated using the frequencies and the mean FE40 at each quantile (Tab. 1). The regression coefficient was significant for bands I and V (Tab. 2) meaning that the FE40 is dependent on the occurrence of those bands. At a closer look it becomes apparent that this dependence is caused by the group at quantile 100% at the bottom end. The standard deviation of 0.743 can be reduced to 0.377 if the group is reduced to 8 hens by excluding the 2 animals with the highest FE40, without substantially changing the regression coefficient or its level of significance. Since only clinically healthy animals were included in the study other reasons must be sought for the high standard

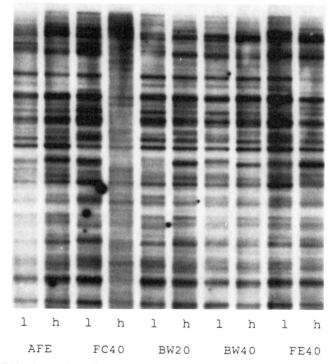

```
  l   h     l   h     l   h     l   h     l   h

   AFE       FC40      BW20      BW40      FE40
```

Figure 1. DNA fingerprints of DNA mixes of the 5 hens showing the highest values (h) and the lowest values (l) for the traits age at first egg (AFE), feed consumption at 40 weeks (FC40), body weight at 20 weeks (BW20), body weight at 40 weeks (BW40) and feed efficiency at 40 weeks (FE40).

Table 1. Band frequencies

Quantiles %	0	25	50	75	100
Number of hens	10	10	10	10	10
FE40	2.098	2.328	2.459	2.602	3.889
SD	0.068	0.010	0.012	0.032	0.743
I	0.5	0.5	0.5	0.4	0.1
II	0.3	0.3	0.6	0.6	0.4
III	0.2	0.4	0.1	0.3	0.2
IV	0.4	0.2	0.4	0.5	0.5
V	0.8	0.7	0.7	0.7	0.5
VI	0.6	0.6	0.5	0.3	0.5
VII	0.7	0.4	1.0	0.7	0.3

Table 2. Dependence of band frequencies on the FE40 as estimated by linear regression

Band	b	SE	P
I	−0.242	0.026	0.003
II	−0.088	0.183	0.663
III	−0.021	0.095	0.839
IV	0.093	0.085	0.355
V	−0.152	0.016	0.002
VI	−0.040	0.098	0.711
VII	−0.226	0.186	0.311

deviation. By plotting the regressions it can be seen that the distribution of the mean FE40's is skewed, with the groups at quantiles 0% to 75% lying close together and the corresponding frequencies being almost equal. A possible explanation could be that one or more major genes influencing the FE40 are fixed in a large part of this population and therefore contribute very little to the variation. This would not surprise as the source of this population was a F1 cross between Rhode Island Red and White Plymouth Rock. Thus the high standard error of the FE40 in the group at quantile 100% would be due to a medley of unfavourable alleles at the loci concerned.

The estimated breeding value for a trait should describe the additive genetic background of an animal better than the phenotypic value as it includes information about relatives. But for this kind of study phenotypic values adjusted for environmental effects seem to be advantageous compared to breeding values. Since breeding values tend to lean towards the middle they obscure the actual phenotypic differences. Also, methods commonly used to estimate breeding values do not allow for unknown major genes and therefore reduce their effects. In the present study breeding values were estimated with the Animal Model which considers all additive information on relatives. The breeding values for

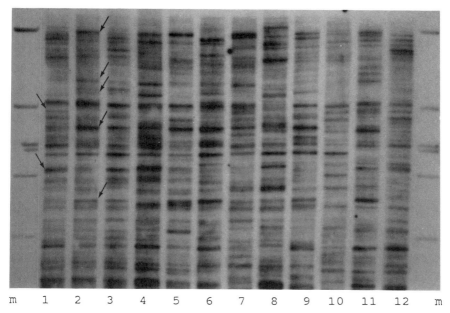

Figure 2. Individual DNA fingerprints of the 10 hens around quantile 0% as ordered by feed efficiency (FE40) (lanes 3 to 12). DNA fingerprints of the DNA mixes of the 5 hens showing the highest values (lane 1) and the lowest values (lane 2) for FE40. The arrows indicate the bands I through VII, beginning at the top, that were investigated for an association with FE40 by linear regression. m: lambda digested with *Eco*RI.

the FE40 then were ordered and again groups of 10 hens were formed around the quantiles concerned. Of these 50 animals only 20 were the same as in the phenotypically ordered groups and of these 20 animals only 13 belonged to the corresponding group. Of the remaining 7 animals 5 changed to a neighbouring group and 2 skipped a group. A possible explanation can be demonstrated using the following example: A sire is heterozygous at a major gene showing the favourable allele A and allele B with little effect. Closely associated with this major gene is a DNA fingerprint band (+). Assuming no recombination one offspring will show allele A and the band (+), and another offspring will show allele B and no band (−). Ordering these offspring by phenotype adjusted for environment will place offspring (A/+) far apart from offspring (B/−). Ordering these offspring by breeding values places (A/+) much closer to (B/−) because among others one component of the breeding value of (A/+) is the information on (B/−) and vice versa.

This study focused on a single population rather than two divergent selection lines, accepting smaller differences in the extreme values for traits. This loss of variation does not seem to be critical since only very

376

close associations between traits and DNA fingerprint bands are of interest. Further, and maybe more important, this approach reduces the problem of drift, provided the population does not show substructures.

Acknowledgements
The authors wish to thank D. Steiger-Stafl for collecting blood samples, B. Colomb and M. Holub for their excellent lab work, F. Hebeisen for the art work and J.L. Longmire, Los Alamos National Laboratory, for providing the probe pV47-2.

References

Botstein D, White RL, Skolnick M, Davies RW (1980) Construction of a genetic linkage map in man using restriction fragment length polymorphisms. Am J Hum Genet 32: 314–331

Cowan CM, Dentine MR, Ax RL, Schuler LA (1990) Structural variation around prolactin gene linked to quantitative traits in an elite Holstein sire family. Theor Appl Genet 79: 577–582

Dekkers JCM, Dentine MR (1991) Quantitative genetic variance associated with chromosomal markers in segregating populations. Theor Appl Genet 81: 212–220

Dolf G, Glowatzki M-L, Gaillard C (1991) Searching for genetic markers for hereditary diseases in cattle by means of DNA fingerprinting. Electrophoresis 12: 109–112

Geldermann H (1975) Investigations on inheritance of quantitative characters in animals by gene markers 1. Methods. Theor Appl Genet 46: 319–330

Georges M, Lathrop M, Hilbert P, Marcotte A, Schwers A, Swillens S, Vassart G, Hanset R (1990) On the use of DNA fingerprints for linkage studies in cattle. Genomics 6: 461–474

Hagger C (1990) Response from selection for income minus food cost in laying hens, estimated via the animal model. Br Poult Sci 31: 701–713

Haley CS (1991) Use of DNA fingerprints for the detection of major genes for quantitative traits in domestic species. Anim Genet 22: 259–277

Henderson CR (1973) Sire evaluation and genetic trends. Proceedings of the Animal Breeding and Genetics Symposium in Honor of JL Lush, ASAS and ADSA, Champaign, Illinois

Jeanpierre M (1987) A rapid method for the purification of DNA from blood. Nucleic Acids Res 15: 9611

Jeffreys AJ, Wilson V, Thein SL (1985) Hypervariable 'minisatellite' regions in human DNA. Nature 314: 67–73

Jeffreys AJ, Wilson V, Thein SL, Weatherall DJ, Ponder BAJ (1986) DNA "fingerprints" and segregation analysis of multiple markers in human pedigrees. Am J Hum Genet 39: 11–24

Kennedy BW, Verrinder Gebbins AM, Gibson JP, Smith C (1990) Coalescence of molecular and quantitative genetics for livestock improvement. J Dairy Sci 73: 2619–2627

Kuhnlein U, Zadworny D, Gavora JS, Fairfull RW (1991) Identification of markers associated with quantitative trait loci in chickens by DNA fingerprinting. *In*: Burke T, Dolf G, Jeffreys AJ, Wolff R (eds) DNA fingerprinting: approaches and applications. Birkhäuser, Basel, Switzerland, pp 274–282

Lammont SJ, Plotzky Y, Kaiser MG, Arthur JA, Beck NJ (1992) Identification of quantitative trait loci markers in commercial egg-laying chicken lines by using DNA fingerprinting. Procdings of the 19th World's Poultry Congress, Amsterdam, vol 1: 518–522

Longmire JL, Kraemer PM, Brown NC, Hardekopf LC, Deaven LL (1990) A new multi-locus DNA fingerprinting probe: pV47-2. Nucleic Acids Res 18: 1658

Paterson AH, Lander ES, Hewitt JD, Peterson S, Lincoln SE, Tanksley SD (1988) Resolution of quantitative traits into Mendelian factors by using a complete linkage map of restriction fragment length polymorphisms. Nature 335: 721–726

Plotzky Y, Cahaner A, Haberfeld A, Lavi U, Hillel J (1990) Analysis of genetic association between DNA fingerprint bands and quantitative traits using DNA mixes. Proceedings of the 4th World Congress on Genetics Applied to Livestock Production, Edinburgh, vol XIII: 133–136

Quaas RL, Pollak EJ (1980) Mixed model methodology for farm and ranch beef cattle testing programs. J Anim Sci 51: 1277–1287

Rasmusson JM (1933) A contribution to the theory of quantitative character inheritance. Hereditas 18: 245–261

Sax K (1923) The association of size differences with seed-coat pattern and pigmentation in Phaseolus vulgaris. Genetics 8: 552–560

Smith C, Simpson SP (1986) The use of genetic polymorphisms in livestock improvement. J Anim Breed Genet 103: 205–217

Soller M (1978) The use of loci associated with quantitative traits in dairy cattle improvement. Anim Prod 27: 133–139

Soller M (1990) Genetic mapping of the bovine genome using deoxyribonucleic acid-level markers to identify loci affecting quantitative traits of economic importance. J Dairy Sci 73: 2628–2646

Soller M, Beckmann JS (1990) Marker-based mapping of quantitative trait loci using replicated progenies. Theor Appl Genet 80: 205–208

Soller M, Brody T, Genizi A (1976) On the power of experimental designs for the detection of linkage between marker loci and quantitative loci in crosses between inbred lines. Theor Appl Genet 47: 35–39

Tanksley SD, Medina-Filho H, Rick CM (1982) Use of naturally-occurring enzyme variation to detect and map genes controlling quantitative traits in an interspecific backcross of tomato. Heredity 49: 11–25

Thoday JM (1961) Location of polygenes. Nature 191: 368–370

Vogt P (1990) Potential genetic functions of tandem repeated DNA sequence blocks in the human genome are based on a highly conserved "chromatin folding code". Hum Genet 84: 301–336

DNA Fingerprinting: State of the Science
ed. by S. D. J. Pena, R. Chakraborty, J. T. Epplen & A. J. Jeffreys
© 1993 Birkhäuser Verlag Basel/Switzerland

Influence of extra-pair paternity on parental care in great tits (*Parus major*)

T. Lubjuhn, E. Curio, S. C. Muth, J. Brün and J. T. Epplen[a]

Arbeitsgruppe für Verhaltensforschung/Fakultät für Biologie and [a]Molecular Human Genetics, Ruhr-Universität Bochum, 44780 Bochum, Germany

Summary
The extent of parental care should usually increase with the benefits expected in terms of reproductive success. In monogamous birds, parental care should therefore increase with brood size. Some recent studies failed to show such a relationship, and we wondered if this may be due to phenomena like extra-pair copulations and/or intraspecific brood parasitism, that could lead to nestlings which are unrelated to one or both putative parents. Thus, measuring the expected benefits by counting the nestlings may be misleading. In our study on parental care in the great tit (*Parus major*) we determine parentage via multilocus DNA fingerprinting and show that parental care (measured as anti-predator nest defence) seems to be adjusted to the number of offspring fathered by the resident male rather than to the total number of nestlings.

Introduction

Alternative reproductive strategies like extra-pair copulations (EPCs) and intraspecific brood parasitism (IBP) are widespread in monogamous avian species (for review see Birkhead and Møller, 1992). Thus the number of nestlings may often not correspond to the reproductive success of an individual. This fact may also help to explain why in some recent studies an expected increase of parental care with increasing brood size (e.g. Lazarus and Inglis, 1986; Montgomerie and Weatherhead, 1988) was not found (e.g. Regelmann and Curio, 1983; Wiklund and Stigh, 1983; Bjerke et al., 1985): The theory on the evolution of parental care suggests that animals should invest according to the benefits expected in terms of reproductive success (e.g. Dawkins and Carlisle, 1976). But if there are young that are due to EPCs or IBP, the benefits expected are related to the number of true offspring rather than to the total number of nestlings. With the development of the DNA fingerprinting technique (Jeffreys et al., 1985; Ali et al., 1986) there is now a useful tool to investigate such problems. One study that failed to show the predicted relationship between parental care and brood size has been performed in great tits (*Parus major*) (Reglemann and Curio, 1983). Consequently, we wondered if there is an influence of alternative reproductive strategies on parental care in great tits by measuring anti-predator nest defence while simultaneously determining parentage via multilocus DNA fingerprinting.

Material and methods

Great tits are small passerine birds that are common in Europe. They are monogamous and territorial hole breeders and both parents guard their nest from potential predators and feed nestlings and fledglings. Our study was performed during spring 1990 and 1992 in two different locations in Germany.

Parentage analyses via multilocus DNA fingerprinting

To determine parentage DNA was isolated from the blood samples of 17 (1990) and 15 (1992) complete families. After Hae III digestion, DNA was separated by agarose gel electrophoresis (0.8%, 40 cm, 2 V/cm). Gels were dried followed by in-gel hybridization with ^{32}P-labeled oligonucleotide $(CA)_8$. A more detailed description of the general procedures has been given elsewhere (Epplen, 1992).

For statistical analyses of the band patterns we used the program "patern" that was kindly provided by M. Krawczak. Individuals were excluded from parentage if the probability was below 0.005%. For a detailed description of the statistics used in this program see Krawczak and Bockel (1992).

Measuring the extent of parental care

Anti-predator nest defence was measured to estimate the extent of parental care. A stuffed tawny owl (*Strix aluco*) was presented near the nestbox with a simultaneous playback of a mixed-species mobbing chorus. The test lasts 8 min. For further details of the test procedure see Curio (1980), Regelmann and Curio (1983), Windt and Curio (1986). From the behavioural data an index of predation-risk (*R*) was calculated as follows:

$$R = \sum_{i=1}^{n} \frac{t_i}{d_i}$$

Thereby the increased predation-risk each individual runs with shrinking distance (d_i) from the owl and with increasing time (t_i) at a given distance was taken into account for each change of perches (i). The usefulness of this index of risk has been established in several independent studies (e.g. Windt and Curio, 1986; Onnebrink and Curio, 1991).

Results and discussion

Occurrence of alternative reproductive strategies

There was no compelling evidence for IBP in both years, but appr. 50% of broods contained at least one nestling that was due to EPC of the female (Tab. 1; Fig. 1).

Cuckoldry and paternal care

In 1990 there was a significant correlation between the resident male's level of nest defence and the number of nestlings fathered by himself (Fig. 2; $r = 0.59$, $p_{2\text{-tailed}} = 0.012$). As in previous studies (e.g. Regelmann and Curio, 1983), a correlation with the total number of nestlings was not found ($r = 0.44$, $p_{2\text{-tailed}} > 0.05$). In the second study in 1992, a correlation between brood size and the male's nest defence as measured by the index of risk ($r = -0.17$, $p_{1\text{-tailed}} = 0.27$) as well as between the number of "true" offspring and the male's nest defence ($r = -0.04$, $p_{1\text{-tailed}} = 0.45$), was not found. But there was a lowered male nest defence in broods containing extra-pair young (EPY) compared to those without EPY (Fig. 3a; $p_{1\text{-tailed}} = 0.05$). This difference is more plausibly explained by differences in the number of "true" offspring (Fig. 3b; $p_{1\text{-tailed}} = 0.18$) than by differences in brood size (Fig. 3c; $p_{1\text{-tailed}} = 0.12$); whereas the difference in brood size was in the opposite direction than would be expected by the data on nest defence, the difference in the number of "true" offspring corresponds to the difference in nest defence. Combining the two-tailed probabilities of both years (Sokal and Rohlf, 1981) there is a significant influence of cuckoldry on the extent of paternal care ($p < 0.01$). Thus we conclude that males adjust their effort to the benefits expected in terms of reproductive success.

Table 1. Distribution of extra-pair young per brood from spring 1990 and 1992

Number of extra-pair young per brood	0	1	2	3	4	5
Number of broods (1990)	9	—	5	—	1	2
Number of broods (1992)	7	2	1	3	—	2

47.1% of broods in 1990 and 53.3% of broods in 1992 contained at least one nestling that was due to EPC. Overall 16.6% of nestlings in 1990 and 20.2% in 1992 were due to EPCs of the females.

382

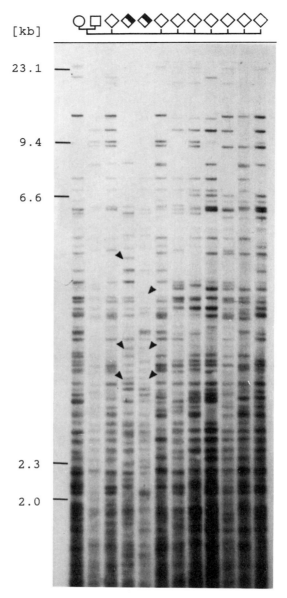

Figure 1. Oligonucleotide fingerprints of a "family" of great tits (*Parus major*) after Hae III digestion and in-gel hybridization with the ^{32}P-labeled oligonucleotide $(CA)_8$. There are two chicks in this family (◆) that could be attributed to the female (○) but not the male (□) territory owner. They are due to EPC of the female. Arrows indicated some diagnostic bands. Length markers of 23.1, 9.4, 6.6, 2.3 and 2.0 kilobases are indicated on the left.

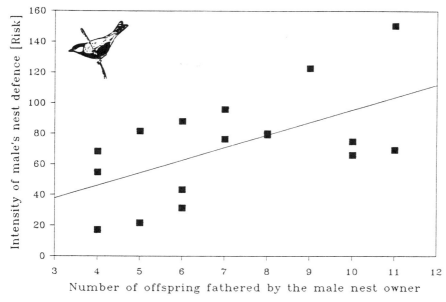

Figure 2. Intensity of males' nest defence in relation to the number of offspring fathered by themselves. There is a significant increase of nest defence intensity (for the term risk see text) with increasing number of "true" offspring ($r = 0.59$, $p_{2\text{-tailed}} = 0.012$). Nest defence intensity was not correlated with the total number of offspring ($r = 0.44$, $p_{2\text{-tailed}} > 0.05$) as has been found in previous studies (e.g. Regelmann and Curio, 1983).

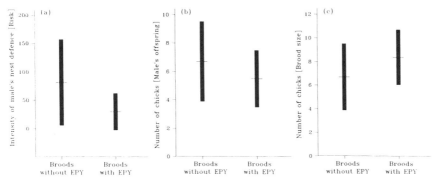

Figure 3. Comparison of intensities of males' nest defence (a), number of "true" offspring (b) and brood size (c) comparing broods with ($n = 8$) and without extra-pair young ($n = 7$). Given values represent means $\pm$ SD. There is a lowered intensity of nest defence in broods containing extra-pair young (Fig. 3a; $p_{1\text{-tailed}} = 0.05$). Because of the direction of the differences, the nest defence difference is more plausibly due to differences in the number of "true" offspring (Fig. 3b; $p_{1\text{-tailed}} = 0.18$) than to differences in brood size (Fig. 3c; $p_{1\text{-tailed}} = 0.12$).

Alternative explanations

In principle there is also an alternative, constraint-based explanation for the findings of this study: Males which are not able to ensure their paternity may be also of lower "overall quality" and therefore may not be able to reach a higher level of anti-predator nest defence. But several arguments contradict this reasoning: (i) Males selected at random *increase* their defence effort with 1) age of nestlings (Regelmann and Curio, 1983) and 2) if their survival chances are experimentally lowered (Windt, 1991). This could not be expected if each individual was constrained in nest defence ability. (ii) Males of higher quality tend to have larger broods than inferior males (e.g. Perrins, 1979; Pettifor et al., 1988). Thus, if inferior males can not guard their paternity as well as high quality males there should be an inverse correlation between brood size and the extent of cuckoldry. In both years investigated there was neither a correlation between the extent of cuckoldry (measured as the proportion of EPY per brood) and brood size (1990: $r = -0.037$, $p_{2\text{-tailed}} = 0.89$; 1992: $r = 0.287$, $p_{2\text{-tailed}} = 0.3$), nor was there a difference in brood size comparing broods with and without EPY (1990: $p_{2\text{-tailed}} = 0.75$; 1992: $p_{2\text{-tailed}} = 0.23$). Therefore a constraint-free, adaptive interpretation of the data is more likely.

Potential mechanisms

The mechanisms that enable male great tits to recognize the extent of cuckoldry by their mates remain unknown. In principle two possibilities have to be considered: (i) Male great tits might be able to distinguish eggs and/or young fathered by themselves from those due to EPCs of the female. But until now there is no compelling evidence that birds are able to do so (Birkhead and Møller, 1992). (ii) Males may actually observe EPCs or they may recognize some other indicators related to the EPC-rate of their mates. Møller (1988) suggested for barn swallows (*Hirundo rustica*) that males estimate the extent of cuckoldry from the interest other males take in their mates (but see Wright, 1992, for criticism). An assessment mechanism has also been found for polyandrous dunnocks (*Prunella modularis*): Burke et al. (1989) showed that each male invests into the brood according to his access to the female during her fertile period. These studies show that a direct recognition mechanism is not necessary for adaptive behaviour to occur, as has been shown here for the great tit.

Acknowledgements
This work was supported by the Deutsche Forschungsgemeinschaft (Cu 4/31-2 and Cu 4/28-4), the VW-Stiftung and the Ruth und Gerd Massenberg-Stiftung. In addition we would

like to thank J. Ehrhardt and J. Kretzschmar for help in the field and Dr. W. Winkel for letting us work in his study area.

References

Ali S, Müller CR, Epplen JT (1986) DNA fingerprinting by oligonucleotide probes specific for simple repeats. Hum Genet 74: 239–243

Birkhead TR, Møller AP (1992) Sperm competition in birds; Evolutionary causes and consequences. Academic Press, London

Bjerke T, Espmark Y, Fonstad T (1985) Nest defense and parental investment in the redwing *Turdus iliacus*. Ornis scand 16: 14–19

Burke T, Davies NB, Bruford MW, Hatchwell BJ (1989) Parental care and mating behaviour of polyandrous dunnocks *Prunella modularis* related to paternity by DNA fingerprinting. Nature 338: 249–251

Curio E (1980) An unknown determinant of a sex-specific altruism. Z Tierpsychol 53: 139–152

Dawkins R, Carlisle TR (1976) Parental investment, mate desertion and a fallacy. Nature 262: 131–133

Epplen JT (1992) The methodology of multilocus DNA fingerprinting using radioactive or nonradioactive oligonucleotide probes specific for simple repeat motifs. *In*: Chrambach A, Dunn MJ, Radola BJ (eds) Advances in electrophoresis, Vol 5, VCH, Weinheim, pp 59–112

Jeffreys AJ, Wilson V, Thein SL (1985) Hypervariable 'minisatellite' regions in human DNA. Nature 314: 67–73

Krawczak M, Bockel B (1992) A genetic factor model for the statistical analysis of multilocus DNA fingerprints. Electrophoresis 13: 10–17

Lazarus J, Inglis IR (1986) Shared and unshared parental investment, parent-offspring conflict and brood size. Anim Behav 34: 1791–1804

Møller AP (1988) Paternity and parental care in the swallow, *Hirundo rustica*. Anim Behav 36: 996–1005

Montgomerie RD, Weatherhead PJ (1988) Risks and rewards of nest defence by parent birds. Q Rev Biol 63: 167–187

Onnebrink H, Curio E (1991) Brood defense and age of young: a test of the vulnerability hypothesis. Behav Ecol Sociobiol 29: 61–68

Perrins CM (1979) British tits. Collins, London

Pettifor RA, Perrins CM, McCleery RH (1988) Individual optimization of clutch size in great tits. Nature 336: 160–162

Regelmann K, Curio E (1983) Determinants of brood defence in the great tit *Parus major* L. Behav Ecol Sociobiol 13: 131–145

Sokal RR, Rohlf FJ (1981) Biometry, 2nd ed. Freeman and Company, New York

Wiklund CG, Stigh J (1983) Nest defence and evolution of reversed sexual size dimorphism in snowy owls *Nyctea scandiaca*. Ornis Scand 14: 58–62

Windt W (1991) Die Brutverteidigung von Kohlmeisen (*Parus major*) und der Concorde-Fehler. PhD thesis, Ruhr-Universität, Bochum, Germany

Windt W, Curio E (1986) Clutch defence in great tit (*Parus major*) pairs and the Concorde Fallacy. Ethology 72: 236–242

Wright J (1992) Certainty of paternity and parental care. Anim Behav 44: 380–381

DNA Fingerprinting: State of the Science
ed. by S. D. J. Pena, R. Chakraborty, J. T. Epplen & A. J. Jeffreys
© 1993 Birkhäuser Verlag Basel/Switzerland

Paternity testing of endangered species of birds by DNA fingerprinting with non-radioactive labelled oligonucleotide probes

J. Máthé, C. Eisenmann and A. Seitz

Institute of Zoology, University of Mainz, Saarstr. 21, 55122 Mainz, Germany

Summary
In the last years, DNA fingerprinting became the most powerful tool for identification and paternity testing in man. The success of this method encouraged the German Federal Ministry of Environment, Natural Protection and Reactor Safety to apply DNA fingerprinting in the field of protection of endangered species of birds, such as birds of prey or parrots. In the last three years, we received more than 400 blood and tissue samples of 23 species of birds of prey or parrots, most of them obtained by confiscation, to establish paternity and legal breeding success. We used digoxigenated oligonucleotide probes, mainly $(GGAT)_4$ and $(GACA)_4$ for hybridization. In most cases of confiscated families of birds, paternity testing showed exclusions of nestlings.

Introduction

The discovery of DNA fingerprinting rendered possible a great tool for applications such as paternity disputes (Jeffreys et al., 1986), positive identification in immigration cases (Jeffreys et al., 1985a, b) or pedigree analysis (Hill, 1987a). DNA fingerprinting also finds application in zoological problems. Jeffery's probes 33.15 and 33.6 were successfully tested in DNA of dogs and cats (Jeffreys & Morton, 1987), non-human primates (Weiss, 1989) and especially birds (Burke & Bruford, 1987; Wetton et al., 1987; Quinn et al., 1987; Arctander, 1988; Gyllenstein et al., 1989; Longmire et al., 1991). Epplen et al. (1989) used oligonucleotide probes of different sequences to compare their features in the hybridization to DNA of some groups of vertebrates, such as fish, amphibians, snakes, chicken, mice and man. Since DNA fingerprinting was acknowledged as evidence in paternity testing in man (Jeffreys et al., 1986; Nürnberg et al., 1989) it was interesting to prove its application in threatened animal species. The German Federal Ministry of Environment, Natural Protection and Reactor Safety subsidizes a project to apply DNA fingerprinting when it comes to the protection of endangered species, such as birds of prey or parrots (Wolfes et al., 1991; Máthé et al., 1991)

The Washington Convention on International Trade in Endangered Species of Fauna and Flora (Cities) only allows the sale of rare species bred in captivity. However, many rare species hardly breed in captivity. Therefore dealers often obtain eggs or nestlings illegally and sell them with high profit margins. These dealers can now be convicted by DNA fingerprinting (Wolfes et al., 1991).

Material and methods

We got more than 400 blood and tissue samples of 23 species of birds of prey and parrots (Tab. 1).

Peripheral blood (0.5–1 ml per sample) was diluted in 2 volumes of anticoagulant preservative solution (APS) buffer (Arctander, 1988). DNA was extracted by the salting out method of Miller (Miller et al., 1988). 10 micrograms DNA were digested with Hin$f$I and electophoretically fractionated in 0.6% agarose gels in $1 \times$ TBE for 1 or 2 days. After denaturation in alkaline buffer (NaOH 0.5 mol/l, NaCl 1.5 mol/l) gels were blotted and DNA was transferred to nylon membranes for at least 6 h. Nylon membranes (Amersham, Hybond N$^+$) were baked for two hours at 80°C or crosslinked (Stratagene, Stratalinker). Nylon

Table 1. All proved species of birds with number of families and cases of exclusion

Species of bird	Total number of families	Fam. with exclusions	Fam. with related siblings
Peregrine falcon (*Falco peregrinus*)	19	8	11
Lanner falcon (*Falco biarmicus*)	5	2	3
Laggar falcon (*Falco subniger*)	1		1
Saker falcon (*Falco cherrug*)	10	4	6
Gyrfalcon (*Falco rusticolus*)	6	3	3
Prairie falcon (*Falco mexicanus*)	1		1
Kestrel (*Falco tinnunculus*)	2	2	
Common buzzard (*Buteo buteo*)	1		1
Long-legged buzzard (*Buteo ruficus*)	1	1	
Sparrow hawk (*Accipiter nisus*)	1	1	
Goshawk (*Accipiter gentilis*)	5	5	
Kite (*Milvus milvus*)	1	1	
Snowy owl (*Nyctea scandiaca*)	1		1
Eagle owl (*Bubo bubo*)	2		2
Griffon vulture (*Gyps fulvus*)	1		1
Bonelli's eagle (*Hieraaetus fasciatus*)	1	1	
Golden eagle (*Aquila chrysaetos*)	3	3	
Scarlet macao (*Ara macao*)	1	1	
Cuban amazon (*Amazona leucocephala*)	2	2	
Yellow-shouldered amazon (*Amazona barbadensis*)	1		1
Yellow-and-green lorikeet (*Trichoglossus flavoviridis*)	1		1
Grey-parrot (*Psittacus erithacus*)	2		2
Yellow-crested cackatoo (*Cacatua galerita triton*)	1		1

membranes were prehybridized at 38°C for at least one hour and then hybridized at the same temperature for at least three hours or over night with Dig-labelled oligonucleotide probes of Fresenius AG, mainly (GGAT)$_4$ and (GACA)$_4$. Hybridization buffer consisted of 50% formamide, $5 \times$ SSC, blocking reagent (2% w/v), N-Lauroylsarcosine (0.2% w/v), SDS (0.02% w/v). After hybridization, blots were washed three times with $6 \times$ SSC for 20 minutes, then for 5 minutes with washing buffer (malic acid, 0.1 mol/l, NaCl 0.15 mol/l, 0.5% (v/v) Polyoxyethylenesorbitan monolaurate (Tween 20), pH 7.5). Blots were blocked for at least 30 minutes with blocking buffer (malic acid, 0.1 mol/l, NaCl 0.15 mol/l, blocking reagent (1% w/v)), then incubated for 45 minutes with Dig-AP conjugate (Boehringer, Mannheim) and washed two times for 15 minutes with washing buffer. Before color reaction, blots were incubated 2×5 minutes in alkaline buffer (Tris-HCl 0.1 mol/l, NaCl 0.1 mol/l, MgCl$_2$ 50 mmol/l, pH 9.5). Color substrates, nitroblue tetrazolium salt (NBT) and 5-bromo-4-chloro-3-indolyl phosphate (BCIP) or chemoluminescent substrates 3-(2′-Spiroadamantane)-4-methoxy-4-(3″-phosphoryloxy)-phenyl-1,2-dioxetane (AMPPD) or disodium 3-(4-methoxyspiro-(1,2-dioxetane-3,2′-(5′-chloro)tricyclo-(3.3.1.1.^{3,7})-decan-4-yl)phenyl-phosphate (CSPD), were given in the alkaline buffer. In the case of AMPPD and CSPD it took five minutes. The blots were exposed with X-ray films for a few minutes up to one hour.

Results

In our project, we tested 69 families of birds with 1 to 16 siblings for paternity. There were exclusions in 33 families (Tab. 1). An example of exclusion is shown in Fig. 1. The detection of the probe (GGAT)$_4$ was carried out with AMPPD at different time points. In spite of short exposure times, the detection shows high sensitivity and small clear banding patterns. Figure 2 presents the same falcon family, but the detection was carried out with NBT and BCIP. All bands which led to exclusion are indicated. Compared to Fig. 1 the signal to noise ratio is worse. In Fig. 3 a yellow-shouldered amazon family is presented; detection was carried out with CSPD. All siblings are related to the parents. The comparison with Fig. 1 shows background (Figs 1–3).

The fingerprints were mostly analyzed by hand. The patterns of nestlings were compared with the patterns of putative parents. The bandsharing frequency was calculated in accordance with the formula bsf(%) = $2n/(a + b)$, where n is the number of common bands and a, b the total number of bands per lane (Jeffreys et al., 1985b). Normally about 20% of bands agree even with non-related individuals. This

390

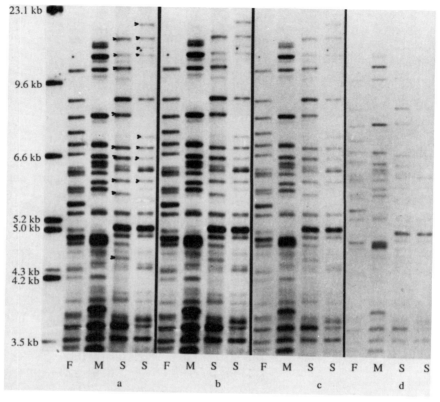

Figure 1. A family of peregrine falcons is presented (F = father, M = mother, S = sibling). The two siblings are excluded, the bands which led to exclusion are marked. The oligonucleotide probe was (GGAT)$_4$, the detection was carried out with AMPPD. The exposure time was 10 minutes 2 hours after incubation (a), 5 minutes 6 hours after incubation (b), 3 minutes 6 hours after incubation (c) and 1 minute 6 hours after incubation (d). Even with this short exposure time clear bands can be seen and the signal to noise ratio is very good.

conformity can be affected either by chance or by sex or typical for population or species. Therefore, particular conformity of bands does not demonstrate a relationship. The analysis of fragment patterns is based on the principle of exclusion; this means that only non-corresponding bands of nestlings in comparison with their putative parents were searched for. In all cases of exclusioned paternity we calculated a bandsharing frequency of 10% up to 25%, which is in agreement with the frequency of about 20% as calculated for men (Schacker et al., 1990) whereas related individuals had a bandsharing frequency of 55% up to 85%.

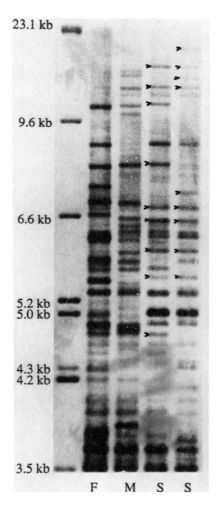

Figure 2. The same falcon family as in Fig. 1 is presented (F = father, M = mother, S = sibling). The hybridization was carried out with the oligonucleotide probe (GGAT)$_4$ at 38°C, colour substrates were NBT/BCIP. The signal to noise ratio is much worse than with AMPPD.

Discussion

The advantage of the chemoluminescent substrates is given by the short exposure time, high sensitivity and low background. Furthermore, within one day several exposures at many different time points with X-ray films could be carried out to determine the best signal to noise ratio. This contrast with the detection using NBT/BCIP, where only one time point of detection could be obtained. The reprobing of the

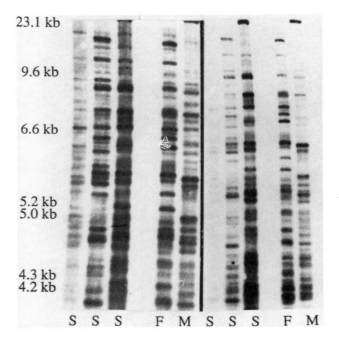

Figure 3. A family of yellow-shouldered amazons is presented (F = father, M = mother, S = sibling). All nestlings are related to the putative parents. The hybridization was carried out with $(GACA)_4$ at 38°C and CSPD was used as chemoluminescent substrate. The exposure time was one hour after incubation (a) and 30 minutes after incubation (b). In this case the signal to noise ratio was worse than with AMPPD, but normally the quality of CSPD is equal to AMPPD.

membranes in the case of the chemoluminescent substrates is much easier: the substrates are washed out with water, whereas for NBT/ BCIP-detected membranes dimethyl-formamide must be used. The latter reduces the quality of membranes and DNA. Furthermore, within this short detection time of one day only one exposition with radioactive probes could be done. Therefore non-radioactive oligonucleotide fingerprinting is a fast and simple procedure with high quality of bands.

All the bird species we tested, showed polymorphic fragment patterns, especially with the probes $(GGAT)_4$ and $(GACA)_4$. In every case of paternity testing we were able to get a clear result, so that dealers which had obtained eggs by robbery or smuggling could be convicted on trial. As a result of our success in paternity testing, a significant reduction in "breeding success" of some dealers occurred. Some dealers actually send us blood probes to prove their legal breeding success by DNA fingerprinting to get CITES papers for selling.

Acknowledgements
We thank the Federal Minister of Environment, Natural Protection and Reactor Safety for supporting of this work.

References

Arctander P (1988) Comparative studies of avian DNA by restriction fragment length polymorphisms analysis: convenient procedures on blood samples from live birds. J Orn 129: 205–216

Burke T, Bruford MW (1987) DNA fingerprinting in birds. Nature 327: 149–152

Epplen JT, Kammerbauer D, Steimle V, Zischler H, Alber E, Andreas A, Hala K, Nanda I, Schmid M, Rieß O, Weising K (1989) Methodology and application of oligonucleotide fingerprinting including characterization of individual hypervariable loci. *In*: Radola BJ (ed) Electrophoresis Forum 89, Technische Universität München, pp 175–186

Gyllenstein UB, Jakobsson S, Temrin H, Wilson AC (1989) Nucleotide sequence and genomic organization of bird minisatellites. Nucleic Acids Res 17: 2203–2214

Hill WG (1987) DNA fingerprints applied to animal and bird populations. Nature 327: 98–99

Jeffreys AJ, Wilson V, Thein SL (1985a) Hypervariable 'minisatellite' regions in human DNA. Nature 314: 67–73

Jeffreys AJ, Wilson V, Thein SL (1985b) Individual-specific 'fingerprints' of human DNA. Nature 316: 76–79

Jeffreys AJ, Wilson V, Thein SL, Weatherall DJ, Ponder BAJ (1986) DNA 'fingerprints' and segregation analysis of multiple markers in human pedigrees. Am J Hum Genet 39: 11–24

Jeffreys AJ, Morton DB (1987) DNA fingerprints of dogs and cats. Anim Genet 18: 1–5

Longmire JL, Ambrose RE, Brown NC, Cade TJ, Maechtle TL, Seegar WS, Ward FP, White CM (1991) Use of sex-linked minisatellite fragments to investigate genetic differentiation and migration of North American populations of the peregrine falcon (*Falco peregrinus*). *In*: Burke T, Dolf G, Jeffreys AJ, Wolff R (eds) DNA fingerprinting: approaches and applications, 1st ed. Birkhäuser Verlag, Basel Boston Berlin, pp 217–229

Máthé J, Wolfes R, Seitz A (1991) DNA fingerprinting for the protection of endangered species. *In*: Berghaus G, Brinkmann B, Rittner C, Staak M (eds) DNA-technology and its forensic application, 1st ed. Springer Verlag, Berlin, pp 170–171

Miller SA, Dykes DO, Polesky HT (1988) A simple salting out procedure for extracting DNA from human nucleated cells. Nucleic Acids Res 16: 1215

Quinn TW, Quinn JS, Cooke F, White BN (1987) DNA marker analysis detects multiple maternity and paternity in single broods of the lesser snow goose. Nature 326: 392–394

Schacker U, Schneider PM, Holtkamp B, Bohnke E, Fimmers R, Sonneborn HH, Ritter C (1990) Isolation of the DNA minisatellite probe MZ1.3 and its application to DNA fingerprinting analysis. Forensic Sci Int 44: 209–224

Weiss ML (1989) DNA fingerprints in physical anthropology. Am J Hum Biol 1: 567–579

Wetton JH, Carter RE, Parkin DT, Walters D (1987) Demographic study of a wild house sparrow population by DNA fingerprinting. Nature 327: 147–149

Wolfes R, Máthé J, Seitz A (1991) Forensics of birds of prey by DNA fingerprinting with ^{32}P-labeled oligonucleotide probes. Electrophoresis 12: 175–180

DNA Fingerprinting: State of the Science
ed. by S. D. J. Pena, R. Chakraborty, J. T. Epplen & A. J. Jeffreys
© 1993 Birkhäuser Verlag Basel/Switzerland

Characterization and applications of multilocus DNA fingerprints in Brazilian endangered macaws

C. Y. Miyaki[a,b], O. Hanotte[b], A. Wajntal[a] and T. Burke[b]

[a]*Departamento de Biologia, Instituto de Biociências, USP, Rua do Matão n°277, CEP 05508, São Paulo, Brazil; and* [b]*Department of Zoology, University of Leicester, University Road, Leicester, LE1 7RH, England*

Summary
This is the first attempt to study wild Brazilian endangered macaws with human multilocus minisatellite probes 33.6 and 33.15. Twenty individuals belonging to four species (*Ara araruna, A. chloroptera, A. macao, A. nobilis*) were studied. The band sharing values observed between unrelated individuals vary from 0.16 to 0.25 using the minisatellite probe 33.6. The number of bands detected with 33.15 is low, with possibly one or more intense W chromosome-specific fragments detected in all species. The application of multilocus fingerprints in the genetic management of captive and wild populations of macaw is discussed in the light of these results.

Introduction

The destruction of natural habitats and the illegal trading of wild parrots are causing a decrease in many populations, even putting them in danger of extinction (Forshaw, 1978). Even though Amazonia harbours one-third of the neotropical parrot species, the endangered groups are mainly found in other areas. This is probably due to smaller influence of man in the rain forest compared to other regions. There are many such endangered Brazilian species, including the big macaws (*Anodorhyncus leari, A. hyacinthinus, Cyanopsita spixii, Ara araruna, A. macao, A. chloroptera*), conures (*Aratinga guarouba, A. auricapilla*). parakeets (*Brotogeris versicolorus*), parrotlets (*Touit melanonota*), parrots (*Pionopsitta pileata*) and amazons (*Amazona pretei, A. brasiliensis, A. rhodocorytha, A. vinacea*) (Ridgely, 1981).

The official bodies for the protection of wild animals in Brazil have little experience in breeding parrots. Nevertheless, there are breeders who have achieved successful reproduction of different species in captivity. Their work is important to the constitution of breeding stocks of these endangered parrots in a safe environment and for further eventual reintroduction of individuals to the wild. However, there is so far no control of the birds maintained in captivity. Little is known about the origin of the birds (place and condition of capture) and of their relatedness. Also, in order to be able to accredit the reputable breeders it is important to have a method for confirming the identity and the parentage of the birds bred in captivity (Mathé and Seitz, 1992). Finally, maintenance of genetic variability is essential for the health of captive populations and for the preservation or eventual increase of genetic diversity of wild populations by the reintroduction of captive-bred birds and a method is needed for measuring the genetic relationship among individuals.

In birds, the DNA fingerprinting technique has mainly been used in studies of reproductive behaviour (see Burke et al., this book for a review). Brock and White (1991) analysed in detail the multilocus DNA fingerprints of the Hispanolian parrot, *Amazona ventralis*. They reported the detection of a large haplotype using the multilocus minisatellite probe 33.15 in combination with the restriction enzyme *Alu*I. More recently, it was shown that the human 33.15 multilocus minisatellite probe detects two more intense bands that are female-specific in *Aratinga* parrots (Miyaki et al., 1992).

In this study, the application of multilocus DNA fingerprints was investigated in four different species of macaws as a potential tool for the management of captive and wild populations. More particularly, we determined the band sharing coefficients of wild caught macaws as a preliminary step to an evaluation of the level of inbreeding in the captive populations.

Material and methods

The blood samples were provided by two collections in São Paulo, Brazil: three *Ara ararauna* (Parque Ecológico do Tietê), four *Ara chloroptera* (Parque Ecológico do Tietê), four *Ara macao* (Parque Ecológico do Tietê) and nine *Ara nobilis* (Parque Ecológico do Tietê and Sorocaba Zoo). The Parque Ecológico do Tietê is a public organisation in São Paulo where all the illegally-held wild animals which are confiscated are taken and quarantined until their subsequent destination is determined. The samples collected in both places were believed to be from unrelated birds recently caught from the wild. The sex of the birds was unknown.

The protocols used to obtain multilocus fingerprints have been described in detail elsewhere (Bruford et al., 1992). 5 μg of genomic DNA from each bird was digested with the restriction enzyme *Hae* III. The fragments were separated by electrophoresis through a 30 cm long 1% horizontal agarose gel. Electrophoresis was stopped when the 2 kilobase (kb) marker band had migrated to the bottom of the gel. The fractionated DNA fragments were transferred onto a nylon membrane (Hybond Nfp, Amersham) by standard capillary Southern blotting (Sambrook et al., 1989).

Multilocus minisatellite RNA probe was prepared from 33.6 (Jeffreys et al., 1985) using the plasmid prepared by Carter et al. (1989). The 33.6 probe was [α-^{32}P]rCTP labelled according to the instructions of the labelling kit supplier (Riboprobe, Promega). The membrane was pre-hybridized in 1 × SSC, 1% SDS, 1% BSA, 0.002% sodium azide, 50 μl DEPC at 65°C. After 4 hours, the probe was added to the solution and left overnight at the same temperature. The membrane was washed in 2 × SSC, 0.1% SDS and in 1 × SSC, 0.1% SDS at 65°C. The filter was then autoradiographed for three days at $-70°C$ using Fuji RX film and two intensifying screens.

The membrane was stripped and reprobed with minisatellite 33.15 (Jeffreys et al., 1985) PCR product which was oligolabelled with [α-^{32}P] dCTP producing a DNA probe. The pre-hybridization in 0.263 M Na_2HPO_4, 1 mM EDTA, 7% SDS, 1% BSA at 65°C lasted for 4 hours and the probe was added and left overnight at 65°C. The washing and exposure conditions were as described above.

The 23 to 3.2 kb bands were scored. The coefficient of band sharing (index of similarity) between individuals was calculated following the formula: $x = 2N_{AB}/(N_A + N_B)$; where N_A and N_B are the number of bands present in individuals A and B, respectively, and N_{AB} is the number of bands shared by A and B (Wetton et al., 1987; Bruford et al., 1992).

Assuming that the bands scored are independent markers, we can estimate the mean probability that all n bands in an individual's fingerprint are present in a second random individual as $<x^n$ (Bruford et al., 1992).

Results

The multilocus fingerprint patterns observed after the hybridization using probe 33.6 are characterized by a large number of bands in all individuals of the four species studied (the mean number of bands per individual ranged from 21 to 28 depending on the species, Fig. 1a; Tab. 1). The index of similarity ranged from 0.16 to 0.25. The pattern

Table 1. Results of hybridization with human minisatellite multilocus probes

Probe	Species	N	$n \pm$ sd	$x \pm$ sd	x^n
	Ara ararauna	3	28.33 ± 4.16	0.21 ± 0.06	6.3×10^{-20}
33.6	Ara chloroptera	4	27.75 ± 3.59	0.19 ± 0.07	9.7×10^{-21}
	Ara macao	4	25.2 ± 4.5	0.25 ± 0.06	6.7×10^{-16}
	Ara nobilis	9	21.55 ± 2.96	0.16 ± 0.07	7×10^{-18}

N – number of individuals; n – mean number of bands; x – mean band sharing coefficient; sd – standard deviation; x^n – probability of two unrelated individuals sharing the same pattern.

398

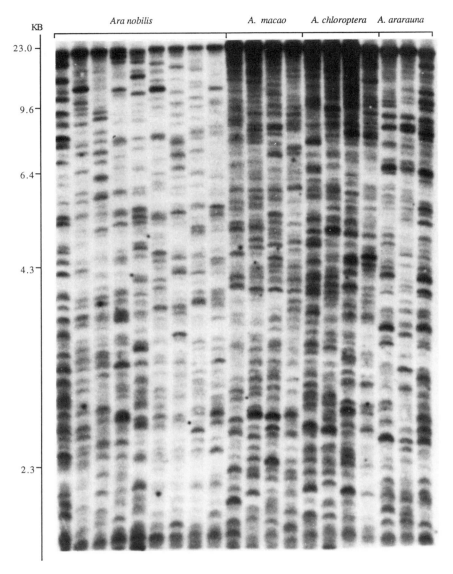

Figure 1a. Multilocus DNA fingerprints of 20 individuals of 4 *Ara* species (A. *Ara nobilis*; B. *Ara macao*; C. *Ara chloroptera*; D. *Ara ararauna*) obtained with human minisatellite multi-locus probe 33.6.

observed was highly variable between individuals. Assuming that the bands are unlinked, the probability that two unrelated birds will show identical patterns is expected to be very low ($< 10^{-15}$).

In contrast, the pattern obtained with the multilocus probe 33.15 was less complex (Fig. 1b). In some individuals, belonging to all

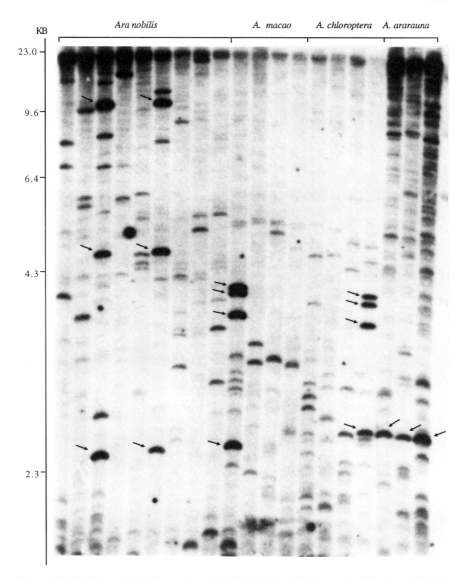

Figure 1b. Multilocus DNA fingerprints of 20 individuals of 4 *Ara* species (A. *Ara nobilis*; B. *Ara macao*; C. *Ara chloroptera*; D. *Ara ararauna*) obtained with human minisatellite multi-locus probe 33.15.

the four species of *Ara* studied, the multilocus probe 33.15 hybridized strongly to one or several bands (Fig. 1b). Given the low number of bands detected here, the index of similarity and the probability of two individuals showing the same multilocus pattern were not calculated.

Discussion

In this study, we have obtained preliminary data on the utility of the human minisatellite probes 33.15 and 33.6 for population studies of four different species of endangered macaws. Band sharing coefficients and expected probabilities of identity were calculated using the multilocus probe 33.6 for wild birds belonging to four different species of *Ara* (Tab. 1). The values obtained are in accordance with data obtained in other wild birds (Burke and Bruford, 1987). Values for captive populations of the species studied are unknown but they can be expected to be similar or higher for inbred populations. In the future, it should be possible to monitor the genetic variability of the endangered macaws and to be able to advise the breeders in order to minimize the loss of genetic variability. The expected low values calculated for the probability of identity between random individuals emphasize the potential utility of probe 33.6 for individual identification and parentage analysis. This appears to be of particular importance in the context of illegal trade where definitive proof of birds' identities is required. The values obtained are in accordance with data obtained in other wild population of birds (Burke and Bruford, 1987). However, these values should be treated with caution in the absence of any pedigree analysis to allow us to assess the independence of the bands detected. Indeed, in some species, in particular, in different species of Galliforms (Hanotte et al., 1992) and in Puerto Rican parrots (Brock and White, 1991) it has been shown that some of the fragments scored in a multilocus fingerprint are linked.

The multilocus probe 33.15 in combination with the restriction enzyme *Hae* III does not give highly informative results in the species studied. The number of bands detected is small and the intensity of most of the fragments is generally weak. This could be due to the fact that DNA probes hybridize less intensively than RNA probes (Carter et al., 1989). However, in some individuals few strong bands are present (Fig. 1b). This result is similar to that obtained in two species of conures (*Aratinga guarouba* and *A. aurea*). In these two species, we were able to demonstrate that the intense fragments detected in some individuals were W-chromosome specific (Miyaki et al., 1992). The genera *Aratinga* and *Ara* are closely related (Forshaw, 1978). It is tempting, therefore, to postulate that the birds presenting these intense bands are females. Further studies using macaws of known sex are required to resolve this question. There is no morphological dimorphism between macaws of each sex. If confirmed, sexing via DNA fingerprinting will thus be particularly useful to the management of breeding programs for these endangered species.

Acknowledgements
C. Y. M. has a CNPq scholarship and a Fundo BUNKA/90 prize and thanks C. F. Menck for his constant support. A. W. received Conference funds from FAPESP. We thank SERC

and the Royal Society for financial support; R. E. Carter for probe pSPT18.15 and pSPT19.6; L. A. Labruna and I. Biasia (Parque Ecológico do Tietê, SP) and A. L. V. Nunes (Sorocaba Zoo) for parrot blood samples and M. Gibbs for invaluable comments. The Jeffreys probes 33.6 and 33.15 and pSPT derivatives are the subject of patent n° GBA 2166445 and worldwide patents (pending) for commercial diagnostic use.

References

Brock MK, White BN (1991) Multifragment alleles in DNA fingerprints of the parrots *Amazona ventralis*. J Hered 82: 209–212

Bruford MW, Hanotte O, Brookfield JFY, Burke T (1992) Single-locus and multilocus DNA fingerprinting. *In*: Hoelzel AR (ed) Molecular genetic analysis of populations – a practical approach. Oxford University Press, New York, pp 225–269

Burke T, Bruford MW (1987) DNA fingerprinting in birds. Nature 327: 149–152

Burke T, Davies NB, Bruford MW, Hatchwell BJ (1989) Parental care and mating behaviour of polyandrous dunnocks *Prunella modularis* related to paternity by DNA fingerprinting. Nature 338: 249–251

Carter RE, Wetton JH, Parkin DT (1989) Improved genetic fingerprinting using RNA probes. Nucleic Acids Res 17: 5867

Forshaw J (1978) The parrots of the world, 2nd ed., Landsdowne Editions, Melbourne

Hanotte O, Bruford MW, Burke T (1992) Multilocus DNA fingerprints in gallinaceous birds: general approach and problems. Heredity 68: 481–494

Jeffreys AJ, Wilson V, Thein SL (1985) Hypervariable minisatellite regions in human DNA. Nature 314: 67–73

Mathé J, Seitz A (1992) Paternity testing of endangered species of birds by DNA fingerprinting with non-radioactive labelled oligonucleotide probes. Second International Conference on DNA Fingerprinting, Belo Horizonte, Brazil, November 9–12, Poster Abstract P59

Miyaki CY, Hanotte O, Wajntal A, Burke T (1992) Sex typing of *Aratinga* parrots using the human minisatellite probe 33.15. Nucleic Acids Res 20: 5235–5236

Ridgely RS (1981) The current distribution and status of mainland neotropical parrots. *In*: Pasquier RF (ed) Conservation of New World parrots – Proceedings of the ICBP Parrot Working Group Meeting, Smithsonian Institution Press, Washington, pp 233–384

Sambrook J, Fritsch EF, Maniatis T (1989) Molecular cloning – a laboratory manual, Cold Spring Harbor Laboratory Press, New York

Wetton JH, Carter RE, Parkin DT, Walters D (1987) Demographic study of a wild house sparrow population by DNA "fingerprinting". Nature 327: 147–149

DNA Fingerprinting: State of the Science
ed. by S. D. J. Pena, R. Chakraborty, J. T. Epplen & A. J. Jeffreys
© 1993 Birkhäuser Verlag Basel/Switzerland

DNA fingerprinting of trait-selected mouse lines and linkage analysis in reference families

G. Brockmann[a], J. Buitkamp, L. Bünger[a], J. T. Epplen and M. Schwerin[a]

[a]Research Institute for Biology of Farm Animals, Department of Molecular Biology, Wilhelm-Stahl-Allee 2, 18196 Dummerstorf, Germany; and Department of Molecular Human Genetics, MA5, Ruhr University, 44780 Bochum, Germany

Summary
The first aim of the study was the molecular genetic characterization of long-term trait-selected (growth, adaptability and fertility) lines of mice using multilocus DNA fingerprinting with the simple tandem repetitive oligonucleotide probes $(GAA)_6$ and $(GACA)_4$. Secondly polymorphic markers were screened for association with growth performance based on DNA fingerprint analysis in reference families.

Pooled DNA samples of ten unrelated mice of trait-selected mouse lines (over 40 generations) and the unselected control lines were analyzed. Resulting differences in band patterns were reanalyzed comparing individual fingerprints of the animals included in the pooled DNA samples of the different lines. Between the mouse lines about 30% of analyzed fingerprint bands were polymorphic. Individuals of long-term selected mouse lines show only a few individual-specific bands. Most polymorphic bands observed in DNA mixes appear in all animals included in the DNA mix of the corresponding line.

Line-specific DNA fingerprint bands were analyzed for their inheritance and linkage with growth performance in reference families using animals with extreme growth performance of the first backcross after crossing of growth-selected with unselected mice. Scanning the distribution of line-specific bands in the reference panel few bands were identified which are associated with growth performance. They appear as useful markers for growth selection. Nevertheless most line-specific bands result from genetic drift rather than from selection.

Introduction

In animal breeding the ability to identify different genetic variants of single genes offers new strategies for selection (Soller, 1990; Georges et al., 1990, 1991). However most traits of economic importance are of a quantitative nature, resulting from the cumulative effect of so-called quantitative trait loci (QTL). Quantitative traits are characterized by a continuous variation in phenotype within populations and sometimes by a low heritability index. Thus it is difficult to identify the molecular basis for differentiated trait performances.

The identification of polmorphic allelic markers associated with such breeding traits may be a first step in investigations into the nature of a QTL. Such markers for trait-involved DNA loci can be detected by multilocus DNA fingerprint probes which scan simultaneously several multiallelic, hypervariable minisatellite or simple repeat regions (Jeffreys et al., 1987; Epplen et al., 1991). For chicken and quail, multilocus DNA fingerprint probes for linkage analysis with QTLs have already proved powerful (Kuhnlein et al., 1991; Hillel et al., 1991).

Here we examine the polymorphisms of DNA fingerprint band patterns of long-term trait-selected mouse lines to identify line-specific bands as candidates for trait-linked markers. The inheritance of line-specific bands of the growth-selected mouse lines and their linkage to the examined trait were analyzed in the first backcross after crossing animals of the selected growth lines with the unselected control. The analysis was carried out based on the assumption that most allelic loci that participate in the phenotypic trait differences are homozygous in these lines because of long-term selection.

Material and methods

Animals

The analysis was carried out with long-term trait-selected mice which were developed in the Research Institute for Biology of Farm Animals, Dummerstorf, Germany. The selected lines differ in their performances from the unselected control group by over 100% in body weight, up to 180% in adaptability and about 65% in fertility traits (Bünger et al., 1990a, b; Renne et al., 1990). The selected lines had progressed far beyond the range of the original outbred population and some of them are near the selection limit. The breeding aims of the different mouse lines are summarized in Tab. 1. The three different control lines differ only in the number of breeding pairs and they were kept in different breeding rooms.

For reference family analysis, the first backcross was produced after crossing animals of each of the three growth selected lines with the unselected control line 1 (G1 × C1, G2 × C1, G3 × C1). It is assumed

Table 1. Breeding aims of long term trait-selected mouse lines

Line		Selection trait	Number of generations
Growth	G1	body weight at day 42 of life	60
	G2	body weight at day 42 of life, high carcass protein amount	60
	G3	body weight at day 42 of life, high treadmill performance	60
Adaptability	A1	high open field activity	40
	A2	high treadmill performance	40
	A3	low treadmill performance	40
Fertility	F1	high number of offspring	80
	F2	high number of offspring, partially with superovulation	80

that F1 is heterozygous in most trait-involved alleles. Parents and individuals with extreme high or low body weight within a backcross generation were analyzed and used for linkage studies. In each family panel 40 animals were examined by DNA fingerprinting.

DNA isolation, restriction, probes and hybridization

DNA was isolated from 10 unrelated male and female individuals from each line. 1–2 cm pieces of tail tissue were minced, digested overnight with proteinase K (0.5 mg/ml), followed by phenol extraction and DNA precipitation (Sambrook et al., 1989). For the analysis of genetic variability between the different lines, pools of DNA were used, as previously analyzed for lines in chicken and quail (Plotsky et al., 1990; Dunnington et al., 1990). As a first step the DNA fingerprint patterns of each 10 male and 10 female mice of all lines were compared in one gel. 6 μg DNA per sample was digested with 30 U of either *Hinf*I or *Hae*III and separated in 0.8% agarose gel at 0.8 V/cm for 42 or 66 h. Gels were dried and hybridized with simple tandem repeated oligonucleotide probes $(GAA)_6$ and $(GACA)_4$ according to the standard protocol (Epplen et al., 1989). In a second step polymorphic bands of the growth-selected lines were studied in individual mice to analyze if they were line or individual specific.

Results

Characterization of long-term trait-selected mouse lines with multilocus probes

Polymorphic bands in the DNA fingerprints of DNA pools of the long-term selected and unselected mouse lines were demonstrated after digestion of the DNA with *Hinf*I or *Hae*III and hybridization with $(GAA)_6$ and $(GACA)_4$ probes. Figure 1a shows the DNA fingerprint patterns of the mouse lines obtained in *Hae*III-digested DNA mixes after hybridization with $(GACA)_4$. The distribution of hybridizing fragments (Fig. 1b) shows that some polymorphic bands were observed within both sexes, whereas others appear only in male or female pools and seem to be sex specific. Similar results were obtained after hybridization with $(GAA)_6$ probe (data not shown).

Examining DNA fingerprints of unrelated individual male mice of the growth lines indicated uniform distribution of most bands within the lines as shown in Fig. 2 for *Hinf*I-digested DNA after hybridization with $(GAA)_6$. Polymorphic bands detected in DNA pools of the selected lines and in more than 50% of individuals were considered to be typical

406

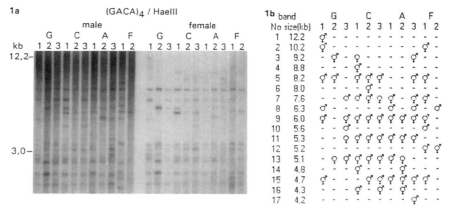

Figure 1. DNA fingerprint patterns of long-term trait-selected (G – growth, A – adaptability, F – fertility) and unselected (C) mouse lines (Tab. 1) obtained in *Hae*III-digested DNA pools of 10 male and female individuals per line after hybridization with the simple tandem repeat oligonucleotide probe (GACA)$_4$ (Fig. 1a). Size markers are given in kb. Figure 1b summarizes the appearance of bands in male (♂) or female (♀) DNA pools or in both sexes (♂/♀) for the different lines.

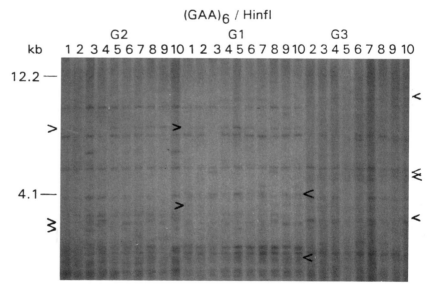

Figure 2. DNA fingerprint pattern of each individual involved in the DNA pool of the growth selected lines (Tab. 1) after restriction with *Hinf*I and hybridization with the oligonucleotide (GAA)$_6$. Bands which appear in more than 50% of all individuals were defined as typical for the line and bands in 90% of individuals were defined as line specific. Line typical (>) and line specific (<) bands are labeled. Size marker is given in kb.

for the line, and those bands which were detected in 90% of individuals were defined as line specific. Depending upon the combination of restriction enzyme and probes used, 2 to 6 line-specific bands were identified. Few bands proved to be specific for the individuals, less than 17% for the probe $(GAA)_6$ and less than 20% for $(GACA)_4$.

Linkage analysis in reference families

The segregation of polymorphic bands was used to analyze the nature of the correlation between the growth trait and the respective bands. Thus, DNA fingerprint patterns of R1 offspring revealing extremely high or low growth performances were compared to their parents. Within all families three trait-linked bands were identified. In the family of the cross-breed G1 × C1 a band of 7.1 kb was identified after *Hinf*I digestion and hybridization with $(GACA)_4$ for most R1 mice of low body weight after backcross of F1 to the unselected control (Fig. 3a). This band is missing in animals of high body weight after backcrossing the F1 to the selected line. For the family of the cross-breed G2 × C1 *Hae*III-digested DNA showed after hybridization with $(GACA)_4$ a characteristic band distribution between 9.2 and 8.8 kb which is inherited from the high or low body weight parent, respectively (Fig. 3b). Linkage can be established between high body weight and the 9.2 kb band, low body weight is correlated with the 8.8 kb hybridizing fragment.

   Linkage of the described fingerprint bands with high or low body weight was proven by variance analysis. The 2 × 2 contingency table with the two random variables, 1) the presence or absence of the fingerprint band and 2) the body weight smaller or greater than the mean value of backcross individuals, was analyzed by the χ^2-test. The χ^2-values, which are greater than 26 for $\alpha = 0.001$, indicate dependence between the presence of the band and body weight. To check the distance between marker and growth associated locus the whole backcross panel has to be investigated.

   In the family of crossbreed G3 × C1 no trait linked fragment was identified by the enzymes and probes used.

Discussion

The DNA fingerprint patterns of DNA pools of different trait-selected mouse lines are characterized by a limited number of polymorphic bands. Some of them differ between the sexes and seem to be sex specific. This was expected using the $(GACA)_4$ and $(GAA)_6$ probes which are known to demonstrate sex specificity (Epplen et al., 1988, 1989). For the growth selected lines it could be shown that more than

408

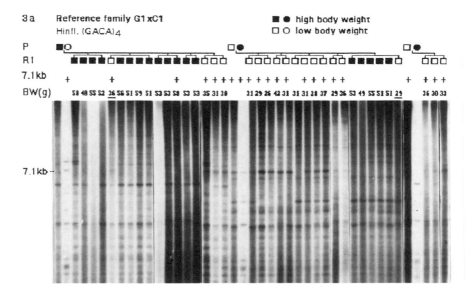

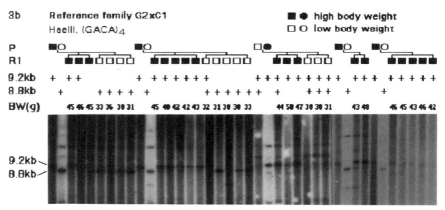

Figure 3. Distribution of polymorphic DNA fingerprint bands of individual mice in the reference families G1 × C1 (Fig. 3a) and G2 × C1 (Fig. 3b). The family structure includes first backcross (R1) male animals with an extremely high or low body weight (BW) on day 42, and the parental (P) generation that was crossed. Trait-linked bands are specified by the size marker in kb.

70% of the bands are uniformly distributed within the males of each line. The high number of uniform bands between unrelated individuals in each line indicates a decrease of genetic variability during selection.

Line-specfic bands may result from three major evolutionary forces: selection, genetic drift and mutation. Genetic drift is the result of a limited number of animals maintained per line during selection, resembling inbreeding for 60 generations in growth-selected lines. The inbreeding level in these lines reached about 40% (Dietl et al., 1992). According to Dietl et al. (1992) the highest loss of genetic variability in connection with accumulation of alleles related to trait performance occurred within the first 10 generations of selection, thereafter selection favors the most effective allele combinations for performance. As deduced from the experiments in quail, selection is expected to generate line-specific bands only if there is linkage disequilibrium between DNA fingerprint loci and QTLs controlling body weight (Hillel et al., 1991).

The number of line-specific bands is well in excess of the number of bands which could be associated with the growth trait in the reference animal panel. This indicates that genetic drift is the cause for line-specific bands rather than selection. Despite this fact, the examination of reference families with multilocus DNA fingerprinting indicated that the simultaneous analysis of different loci of the genome with only two tandem repetitive probes allows the identification of bands which are linked to a trait. Cloning of these bands offers the possibility to localize the marker site and to design site-tagged primers for PCR analysis.

Acknowledgements
Technical assistance was provided by K. Zorn for the production of reference families and by H. Keil for help in DNA preparation and hybridization. The simple repeated oligonucleotides are subject to patent applications (Fresenius AG, Oberursel, Germany). This work was supported by the German Research Foundation, Grant No BR 1285/1-1 and the VW-Stiftung.

References

Büger L, Herrendörfer G, Renne U (1990a) Results of long-term selection for growth traits in laboratory mice. Proc. 4th World Congr. Genet. Appl. Livestock Prod., Edinburgh, Vol XIII, pp 321–324

Büger L, Herrendörfer G, Renne U (1990b) Long-term selection – demonstration of a model of analysis using 3 examples. Paper presented at the 7. Leipziger Tierzuchtsymp., Universität Leipzig, Germany, December 12–13, Vortragssammelband, pp 102–117

Dietl G, Bünger L, Rinne U (1992) Partial inbreeding and identity coefficients for controling of breeding populations. Paper presented at the 66. Sitzung des Genetisch-Statistischen Ausschusses der DGfZ, Malente, Germany, October 5–7

Dunnington EA, Gal O, Plotzky Y, Haberfeld A, Kirk T, Goldberg A, Lavi U, Cahaner A, Siegel PB, Hillel J (1991) DNA fingerprints of chickens selected for high and low body weight for 31 generations. Anim Genet 21: 221–231

Epplen JT, Studer R, McLaren A (1988) Heterogeneity in the Sxr (sex reversal) locus of the mouse as revealed by synthetic GATA/GACA probes. Genet Res 51: 239–246

Epplen JT, Kammerbauer C, Steimle V, Zischler H, Albert E, Andreas A, Hala K, et al. (1989) Methodology and application of oligonucleotide fingerprinting including characterization of individual hypervariable loci. *In*: Radola BJ (ed.) Electrophoresis Forum '89. Bode-Verlag München, pp 175–186

Epplen JT, Ammer H, Epplen C, Kammerbauer C, Mitreiter R, Roewer L, Schweiger W, et al. (1991) Oligonucleotide fingerprinting using simple repeat motifs: A convenient, ubiquitously applicable method to detect hypervariability for multiple purposes. *In*: Burke T, Dolf G, Jeffreys AJ, and Wolff R (eds) DNA Fingerprinting: Approaches and Applications. Birkhäuser, Basel, pp 50–69

Georges M, Lathrop M, Hilbert P, Marcotte A, Schwers A, Swillens S, Vassard G, Hanset R (1990) On the use of DNA fingerprinting for linkage studies in cattle. Genomics 6: 461–474

410

Georges M (1991) Perspectives for marker-assisted selection and velogenetics in animal breeding. *In*: Pedersen RA, McLaren A, and First NL (eds) Animal Applications of Research in Mammalian Development. Cold Spring Harbor Laboratory Press, pp 285–325

Hillel J, Gal O, Schaap T, Haberfield A, Plotzky Y, Marks H, Siegel PB, Dunnington EA, Cahaner A (1991) Genetic factors accountable for line-specific DNA fingerprint bands in quail. *In*: Burke T, Dolf G, Jeffreys AJ, and Wolff R (eds) DNA Fingerprinting: Approaches and Applications. Birkhäuser, Basel, pp 263–273

Jeffreys AJ, Wilson V, Thein SL, Weatherall DJ, Ponder BAJ (1986) DNA 'fingerprints' and segregation analysis of multiple markers in human pedigrees. Am J Hum Genet 39: 11–24

Kuhnlein U, Zadworny D, Gavora JS, Fairfull RW (1991) Identification of markers associated with quantitative trait loci in chickens by DNA fingerprinting. *In*: Burke T, Dolf G, Jeffreys AJ, Wolff R (eds) DNA Fingerprinting: Approaches and Applications. Birkhäuser, Basel, pp 274–282

Plotzky Y, Cahaner A, Haberfeld A, Lavi U, Hillel J (1990) Analysis of genetic association between DNA fingerprint bands and quantitative traits using DNA mixes. Proc. 4th World Congr. Genet. Appl. Livestock Prod., Edinburgh, Vol XIII, pp 133–136

Renne U, Bünger L, Herrendörfer G (1990) Results of endurance fitness trait model analysis with laboratory mice. Paper presented at the 7. Leipziger Tierzuchtsymp., Universität Leipzig, Germany, December 12–13, Vortragssammelband, pp 118–129

Sambrook J, Fritsch EF, Maniatis T (1989) Molecular Cloning. A Laboratory Manual. Cold Spring Harbor Laboratory Press, pp 9.16

Soller M (1990) Genetic mapping of the bovine genome using DNA-level markers with particular attention to loci affecting quantitative traits of economic importance. J Dairy Sci 73: 2628–2646

DNA Fingerprinting: State of the Science
ed. by S. D. J. Pena, R. Chakraborty, J. T. Epplen & A. J. Jeffreys
© 1993 Birkhäuser Verlag Basel/Switzerland

Dog genetic polymorphism revealed by synthetic tandem repeats

D. Mariat and L. Robert

*URA-INRA de Génétique Moléculaire, Ecole Nationale Vétérinaire de Maisons-Alfort,
Maisons-Alfort, France*

Summary
We are studying the genetic polymorphism associated with Variable Number of Tandem
Repeat (VNTR) loci in 13 breeds of dogs, namely: Alaskan Malamute, Barzoi, Beagle,
Belgian Shepherd, Fox Terrier, Griffon, Labrador, Irish Setter, Spaniel, Dachshund, Irish
Terrier, Shar Pei and Poodle.
   Our approach is based upon synthetic tandem repeats (STRs). Using a panel of these
arbitrary unit polymers to detect minisatellites, we are attempting to develop paternity testing
systems on pure bred dog pedigrees. We are evaluating the potential importance of STRs as
a tool for the isolation of minisatellites in dogs, as well as for the characterization of dog
genetic markers.

Introduction

Since their characterization (Jeffreys et al., 1985a) minisatellites have
become a preferred tool for the establishment of relationships between
individuals and for genetic linkage studies. Because they are often
associated with highly variable number of tandem repeats (VNTRs)
(Bell et al., 1982; Stoker et al., 1985) minisatellites enable individual
typing and provide genetic markers. Applications of variable minisatellites were rapidly developed in various domains of human and animal
genetics, including DNA fingerprinting (Jeffreys et al., 1985b), forensic
medicine (Gill et al., 1985), paternity testing (Jeffreys et al., 1991), and
genetic mapping (Nakamura et al., 1987).

   The development of such a wide range of applications requires the
isolation of VNTRs. This was first performed through sequence similarities with consensus motifs of already known minisatellites (Nakamura
et al., 1987). Taking advantage of the frequent occurrence of minisatellites in the human genome, synthetic tandem repeats (STRs) were also
developed (Vergnaud, 1989); it has been shown that random polymers
of overlapping oligonucleotides are able to detect polymorphic loci
(Vergnaud et al., 1991a) and allow the isolation of VNTRs (Vergnaud
et al., 1991b).

   We previously reported the use of STRs on complex genomes from
mammals, birds and fish, where a subset of STRs was selected as

appropriate to probe each species considered (Mariat et al., 1992a). We now report the results obtained with a single STR from the "dog STRs subset" on two Beagle pedigrees, and present the study planned for other purebred dog pedigrees.

Materials and methods

Synthetic tandem repeats (STRs)

The 2 complementary oligonucleotides 5′-ACCTCTACAGTCCAGA-3′ and 3′-TCAGGTCTTGGAGATG-5′ were purified, phosphorylated, ligated and size selected as already described (Vergnaud et al., 1991a).

Dog DNA extraction and probing

DNA was extracted from lymphocytes following usual procedures as described (Mariat et al., 1992a). STR labeling, Southern blotting and hybridization were performed as previously described (Vergnaud et al., 1991a).

Results

We used a synthetic probe, named STR 16C2, obtained by polymerization of a tandem array of 16 bases motifs with the sequence (ACCTCTACAGTCCAGA)$_n$ (Vergnaud et al., 1991a). The polymer was synthesized starting from two oligonucleotides overlapping 8 bases to generate sticky ends which were annealed, ligated and size selected for lengths greater than 400 bp. Subsequent artificial minisatellites obtained from random or arbitrary synthetic motifs are called Synthetic Tandem Repeats (STRs) (Vergnaud, 1989).

Figure 1 shows the pattern obtained when a Southern blot carrying HaeIII genomic DNA digests from two Beagle families is hybridized with STR 16C2 as a probe. Under low stringency conditions the probe detects several polymorphic loci, and the segregation of the bands can be analyzed. Despite similarities between the two pedigree patterns, the STR detects polymorphic fragments present in one pedigree and absent in the other as exemplified by the arrows. These variable fragments cannot correspond to new loci carried by one individual but not by the other. They instead suggest extensive size variation associated with different alleles at either a single or several loci, which are either detected or not in the well-resolved molecular weight range.

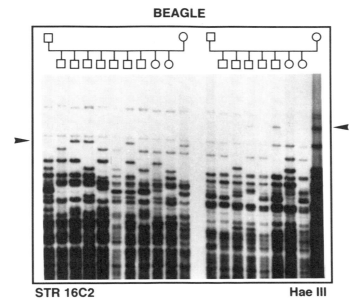

BEAGLE

STR 16C2   **Hae III**

Figure 1. Hybridization of STR 16C2 to two beagle pedigrees. The size range is 0.5 kb to 9 kb.

This hybridization pattern is consistent with a multi-locus probe detecting simultaneously several variable loci and opens the route towards the development of DNA fingerprints in dog using STRs as molecular probes.

Discussion

In this report, a single STR was used to probe samples of a dog breed for the detection of polymorphic loci. This STR has been selected from a general study where several STRs have been tested for their ability to detect polymorphic loci on two unrelated DNA samples from different animal species (Mariat et al., 1992a). The results reported here, performed on a larger dog pedigree, confirm that STR 16C2 is appropriate for the detection of variable loci in dogs.

STR 16C2 was synthesized from a random 16-mer oligonucleotide. It has been used to study the variability of the human genome. It also provides a human genetic marker under high stringency hybridization conditions (Vergnaud et al., 1991a), and allowed the isolation of four different polymorphic loci (Vergnaud et al., 1991b). We are testing whether this particular STR will allow the isolation of polymorphic loci in the genome of dogs by screening a dog genomic library with STR 16C2 as a probe.

Concurrently, we are completing our STR panel by testing other purebred dog pedigrees for the development of suitable paternity testing systems (which are difficult to achieve because of the high inbreeding coefficient in purebred dogs), and by selecting for the most informative STRs.

The motif of the STR used here is 16 bases long. We are also testing an STR with a motif of 14 bases, since we have shown previously that length and sequence variations of the polymerized motif lead to variations in the detection of a given locus (Mariat et al., 1992b). We are also investigating the effect of STR variants when probing a dog sample panel. Such an approach could provide locus-specific STRs which could then be regarded directly as cloned dog genetic markers, or lead to markers associated with quantitative trait loci (QTL).

Acknowledgements
This work is supported by, the INRA, the Société Centrale Canine and the Ministère di l'Agriculture et de la Forêt. We are grateful to Dr Gilles Vergnaud for kindly providing the STR probes. We thank Pr Jean-Jacques Panthier for improvements to the manuscript.

References

Bell GI, Selby MJ, Rutter WJ (1982) The highly polymorphic region near the human insulin gene is composed of simple tandemly repeating sequences. Nature 295: 31–35

Gill P, Jeffreys AJ, Werrett DJ (1985) Forensic application of DNA 'fingerprints'. Nature 318: 577–579

Jeffreys AJ, Wilson V, Thein SL (1985a) Hypervariable 'minisatellite' regions in human DNA. Nature 314: 67–73

Jeffreys AJ, Wilson V, Thein SL (1985b) Individual-specific 'fingerprints' of human DNA. Nature 316: 76–79

Jeffreys AJ, Wilson V, Thein SL, Weatherall DJ, Ponder AJ (1986) DNA "fingerprints" and segregation analysis of multiple markers in human pedigrees. Am J Hum Genet 39: 11–24

Jeffreys AJ, Turner M, Debenham P (1991) The efficiency of multilocus DNA fingerprint probes for individualization and establishment of family relationships, determined from extensive casework. Am J Hum Genet 48: 824–840

Mariat D, Vergnaud G (1992a) Detection of polymorphic loci in complex genomes with synthetic tandem repeats. Genomics 12: 454–458

Mariat D, Guerin G, Bertaud M, Vergnaud G (1992b) Modulation of polymorphic detection with synthetic tandem repeat variants. Mammalian Genome 3: 546–549

Nakamura Y, Leppert M, O'Connell P, Wolff R, Holm T, Culver M, Martin C, Fujimoto E, Hoff M, Kumlin E, White R (1987) Variable number of tandem repeat (VNTR) markers for human gene mapping. Science 235: 1616–1622

Stoker NG, Cheah KSE, Griffin JR, Pope FM, Solomon E (1985) A highly polymorphic region 3' to the human Type II collagen gene. Nucleic Acids Res 13: 4613–4622

Vergnaud G (1989) Polymers of random short oligonucleotides detect polymorphic loci in the human genome. Nucleic Acids Res 17: 7623–7630

Vergnaud G, Mariat D, Zoroastro M, Lauthier V (1991a) Detection of single and multiple polymorphic loci by synthetic tandem repeats of short oligonucleotides. Electrophoresis 12: 134–140

Vergnaud G, Mariat D, Apiou F, Aurias A, Lathrop M, Lauthier V (1991b) The use of synthetic tandem repeats to isolate new VNTR loci: cloning of a human hypermutable sequence. Genomics 11: 135–144

DNA Fingerprinting: State of the Science
ed. by S. D. J. Pena, R. Chakraborty, J. T. Epplen & A. J. Jeffreys
© 1993 Birkhäuser Verlag Basel/Switzerland

Characterization of canine microsatellites

N. G. Holmes, S. J. Humphreys, M. M. Binns, R. Curtis,
A. Holliman and A. M. Scott

*Departments of Immunogenetics and Infectious Diseases, Animal Health Trust,
PO Box 5, Newmarket, CB8 7DW, UK*

Summary
Canine DNA was cloned in M13 and screened for the presence of $(dC-dA)_n \cdot (dG-dT)_n$ repeats. Oligonucleotide primers were synthesised to the microsatellite flanking sequences and used in the polymerase chain reaction to amplify those loci from genomic DNA. The polymorphism of each microsatellite was estimated in a set of unrelated dogs.

Introduction

DNA microsatellites are short, tandemly repeated sequences which have been identified in the genomes of a number of species and which can be conveniently amplified from genomic DNA using the polymerase chain reaction (PCR). Dinucleotide repeats, particularly CA/GT repeats, are very abundant (Stallings et al., 1991) and have great potential as genetic markers (Todd et al., 1990; Petersen et al., 1990). Many of the microsatellites that have been reported are very polymorphic; the variations in length of different alleles has been shown to arise from variation in the number of repeat units (Oudet et al., 1991). The length of the alleles can be estimated by gel electrophoresis on standard sequencing gels. Most microsatellites behave as single locus markers (Weber, 1990), the locus specificity being determined by the flanking sequences. We report here the isolation and characterisation of polymorphic microsatellites from the dog.

Materials and methods

Canine DNA, prepared from buffy coats with SDS and proteinase K, was digested with *Hae* III and the fragments ligated into the *Sma* I site of M13mp10. After transfer to Hybond N$^+$ the plaques were screened with a double-stranded polynucleotide $(dC-dA)_n \cdot (dG-dT)_n$ probe (Pharmacia) radiolabelled by nick translation. Membranes were pre-hybridised with 0.5 M sodium phosphate, 7% SDS, 0.1% bovine serum albumin, 1 mM EDTA adjusted to pH 7.2 with glacial acetic acid

(Church and Gilbert, 1984) and then hybridised at 65°C for 18 hours with the labelled probe in the same buffer. The membranes were washed for 1.5 hours in 0.5 × SSC containing 0.1% SDS with three changes of buffer and autoradiographed. Positive clones were re-screened and those confirmed as positive sequenced using a Sequenase kit (USB).

Oligonucleotides to flanking sequences were synthesised on an Applied Biosystems 391 oligonucleotide synthesiser.

PCR was carried out in a total volume of 25 μl of 50 mM KCl, 10 mM TRIS, 0.01% gelatin pH 8.3 with 0.42 mM of each of dATP, dCTP, dGTP and dTTP (Pharmacia). The concentration of $MgCl_2$ and the annealing temperature were optimised for each microsatellite used. The reaction contained 350 ng of each oligonucleotide primer with approximately 10–20 ng of M13 single strand preparation or approximately 100 ng of genomic DNA. Samples were covered with 50 μl mineral oil (Sigma) and denatured at 95°C for 5 mins. 2.5 U AmpliTaq (Perkin Elmer Cetus) was added and PCR performed in a Perkin Elmer Thermal Cycler. 30 temperature cycles were used: each cycle consisting of 1 minute at 94°C, 2 minutes at the annealing temperature and 1.5 minutes at 72°C.

The polymorphism of the microsatellites was assessed with a pool of genomic DNA samples from unrelated dogs from a variety of breeds. To detect the PCR products, an aliquot of oligonucleotide was radiolabelled. The oligonucleotide was 5' end-labelled (Weber and May, 1989) but using [^{35}S] ATP γS (Promega Protocols and Applications Guide, 1989) and the labelled oligonucleotide separated from unreacted [^{35}S] ATPγS using a Chrom Spin + TE-10 column (Clontech). Under these conditions about 80% of the ^{35}S can be incorporated into oligonucleotide. The labelled oligonucleotide was mixed with the unlabelled form in a ratio of 14:1 and used as a primer in PCR. At the end of the PCR reaction, 20 μl of sample was mixed with 16 μl formamide-dye solution, heated to 80°C and 18 μl was loaded onto a 5% acrylamide-urea sequencing gel.

Results and discussion

A total of 7 CA/GT repeats have now been identified and characterised from the canine genome (see Tab. 1). The microsatellites isolated varied in length from 13 to 23 repeat units. In man, longer repeats have been shown to be more polymorphic than short repeats (Weber, 1990).

Figure 1 shows the alleles of 101 present in a number of unrelated dogs. On electrophoresis, each allele is seen as a set of bands of varying intensity, as has also been reported for microsatellites from other species (Litt and Luty, 1989; Weber and May, 1989). An intense band can be seen, with other less intense bands above and below it. A product one

Table 1. Canine microsatellites

No.	Primers	Clone	Het.	PIC	Alleles No.	Alleles Size
101	5'CCTTCCATCCCGTTGTGTGT3' 5'GATTTTCTCTCGTCCACTT3'	$(GT)_{23}$	46%	0.72	7	$n = 17$ to 27
106	5'ATGCTTGATGTCTGCGTGCG3' 5'GCCGCCTCGTTTAATGGGGT3'	$(AC)_{14}$	5%	0.07	3	$n = 14$ to 16
107	5'TCCCCGGCCCCTGCCCGGAG3' 5'TCTGTGCCCACCTGTGGAGC3'	$(AC)_{17}$	53%	0.43	3	$n = 17$ to 21
109	5'ACTTTCATATTACTCTACTG3' 5'AACACGTCACTTGCTGTCCA3'	$(CA)_{16}$	41%	0.55	8	$n = 13$ to 22
110	5'CCTGGCTGCTGGGACACACC3' 5'TCTCCCTGTGCCCTTTTATTA3'	$(GT)_{17}$	28%	0.31	4	$n = 15$ to 19
111	5'CCATACCAGGATAGTTGAT3' 5'CCATCCTGAGGCTAGCTGTG3'	$(AC)_{17}AT(AC)_2$	27%	0.60	5	$n = 15$ to 21
115	5'AGAATGAAGTTTCTTTCCAA3' 5'TTCTATATTCATTGCAGAGA3'	$(TG)_{18}TA(TG)_3$	30%	0.42	3	$n = 18$ to 21

Het.: Observed heterozygosity.
PIC: Polymorphism Information Content.
n: Number of repeat units.

At least 19 unrelated dogs were used to assess heterozygosity and PIC for each microsatellite.

The optimal conditions of Mg^{++} concentration and annealing temperature for amplifying each microsatellite were:-

101: 1 mM Mg^{++}	55°C	106: 1.5 mM Mg^{++}	60°C
107: 1.5 mM Mg^{++}	63°C	109: 3 mM Mg^{++}	50°C
110: 2 mM Mg^{++}	55°C	111: 2 mM Mg^{++}	55°C
115: 2 mM Mg^{++}	50°C		

Length of product amplified from M13 clone:- 101: 132 bp; 106: 84 bp; 107: 76 bp; 109: 105 bp; 110: 115 bp; 111: 86 bp; 115: 178 bp.

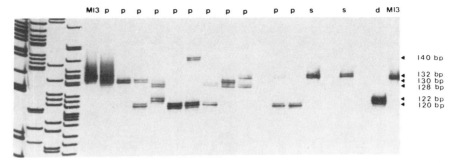

Figure 1. *Alleles of microsatellite 101.* ^{35}S-labelled PCR products from canine genomic DNA samples were separated on a 5% sequencing gel and autoradiographed. Product sizes were calibrated with M13 sequenced using the Sequenase kit (USB). PCR product from a single-strand preparation of the M13 clone containing 101 was also run as a reference. The individual dogs typed were (from left to right) 11 miniature poodles, 2 Irish setters and 1 miniature long-haired dachshund.

nucleotide larger than the main band is consistently present as previously reported (see Litt, 1991). It has been ascribed to the insertion by *Taq* polymerase of an additional nucleotide at the 3′ end of a product (Clark, 1989). Additional bands can be seen below the strong band; these probably arise as a result of a strand slippage mechanism (Tautz, 1989; Luty et al., 1990). We have noted variation from one microsatellite to another in the pattern of extra bands present, as noted for equine microsatellites (Ellegren et al., 1992), but each microsatellite gives a consistent appearance under the same conditions of amplification. The alleles can still be scored, despite the presence of these extra bands. Six different alleles of 101 can clearly be seen in Fig. 1. In all, we have identified seven alleles at this locus (Tab. 1).

The Polymorphism Information Content (PIC) (Botstein et al., 1980), has been calculated for each microsatellite (Tab. 1). By the criteria of Botstein et al., 101 and 109 should be highly informative (PIC > 0.5) and 107, 110 and 115 reasonably informative ($0.5 > $ PIC > 0.25). Table 1 also gives the observed heterozygosity in the individuals typed. The individual dogs which were used to assess the polymorphism were from several breeds, mainly miniature poodles, Irish setters, Chesapeake Bay retrievers and Labrador retrievers. As yet, we have little information on differences in microsatellite allele frequency between breeds. However, pedigree dog populations can be highly in-bred, suggesting that different breeds may vary in the allele frequency at these loci.

To be useful as genetic markers, alleles must be stable and inherited in a Mendelian fashion. In other species, microsatellites that have been characterised have fulfilled these criteria. The segregation of 101, 106 and 107 has been tested in family pedigrees and shown to be Mendelian. Figure 2 shows the segregation of 106 in a family of Irish setters. The

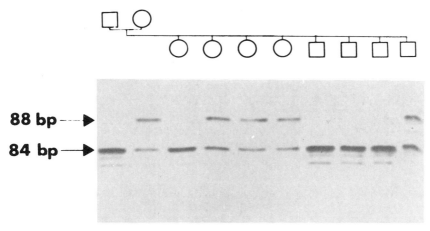

Figure 2. *Segregation of microsatellite 106.* Details as Fig. 1. Samples were from a family of Irish setters, as indicated. Alleles are 84 bp and 88 bp corresponding to $(AC)_{14}$ and $(AC)_{16}$.

sire is a homozygote with an allele giving a product size of 84 bp, and the dam a heterozygote with alleles giving product sizes of 84 bp and 88 bp. The alleles were transmitted faithfully to the offspring.

Acknowledgements
This project is supported by the Guide Dogs for the Blind Association. We gratefully acknowledge the technical assistance of Miss P. J. Rothoff in the collection of the blood samples, and of Miss H. F. Spriggs and Miss N. J. Strange. We are also indebted to Dr J. Sampson for helpful discussions.

References

Botstein D, White RL, Skolnick M, Davis RW (1980) Construction of a genetic linkage map in man using restriction fragment length polymorphisms. Am J Hum Genet 32: 314–331

Church GM, Gilbert W (1984) Genomic sequencing. Proc Natl Acad Sci USA 81: 1991–1995

Clark JM (1988) Novel non-templated nucleotide addition reactions catalyzed by procaryotic and eucaryotic DNA polymerases. Nucleic Acids Res 16: 9677–9686

Ellegren H, Johansson M, Sandberg K, Andersson L (1992) Cloning of highly polymorphic microsatellites in the horse. Animal Genetics 23: 133–142

Litt M (1991) PCR of TG microsatellites. *In*: M. J. McPherson, P. Quirke and G. R. Taylor (eds), PCR A Practical Approach. IRL Press, Oxford UK, 1991: 85–99

Litt M, Luty JA (1989) A hypervariable microsatellite revealed by in vitro amplification of a dinucleotide repeat within the cardiac muscle actin gene. Am J Hum Genet 44: 397–401

Luty JA, Guo HF, Willard HF, Ledbetter DH, Ledbetter S, Litt M (1990) Five polymorphic microsatellite VNTRs on the human X chromosome. Am J Hum Genet 46: 776–783

Oudet C, Heilig R, Hanauer A, Mandel J-L (1991) Nonradioactive assay for new microsatellite polymorphisms at the 5′ end of the dystrophin gene, and estimation of intragenic recombination. Am J Hum Genet 49: 311–319

Petersen MB, Economou EP, Slaugenhaupt SA, Chakravarti A, Antonarakis SE (1990) Linkage analysis of the human HMG 14 gene on chromosome 21 using a GT dinucleotide repeat as polymorphic marker. Genomics 7: 136–138

Promega Protocols and Applications Guide: Promega Corporation, Madison WI, 1989, 53

Stallings RL, Ford AF, Nelson D, Torney DC, Hildebrand CE, Moyzis RK (1991) Evolution and distribution of (GT)$_n$ repetitive sequences in mammalian genomes. Genomics 10: 807–815

Tautz D (1989) Hypervariability of simple sequences as a general source for polymorphic DNA markers. Nucleic Acids Res 17: 6463–6471

Todd JA, Aitman TJ, Cornall RJ, Ghosh S, Hall JRS, Hearne CM, Knight AM, Lovem JM, McAleer MA, Prins J-B, Rodrigues N, Lathrop M, Pressey A, DeLarato NH, Peterson LB, Wicker LS (1991) Genetic analysis of autoimmune type 1 diabetes mellitus in mice. Nature 351: 542–547

Weber JL (1990) Informativeness of human (dC-dA)$_n$ · (dG-dT)$_n$ polymorphisms. Genomics 7: 524–530

Weber JL, May PE (1989) Abundant class of human DNA polymorphisms which can be typed using the polymerase chain reaction. Am J Hum Genet 44: 388–396

DNA Fingerprinting: State of the Science
ed. by S. D. J. Pena, R. Chakraborty, J. T. Epplen & A. J. Jeffreys
© 1993 Birkhäuser Verlag Basel/Switzerland

Application of human minisatellite probes to the development of informative DNA fingerprints and the isolation of locus-specific markers in animals

E. N. Signer and A. J. Jeffreys

*Department of Genetics, University of Leicester, University Road, Leicester,
LE1 7RH, England*

Summary
In this study, the α-globin 3′ HVR (Jarman et al., 1986), the RNA transcripts of 33.15 and 33.6 (Carter et al., 1989), and the human locus-specific minisatellites MS1, MS8, MS31, MS32 (Wong et al., 1987), MS51, MS228A (Armour et al., 1989) and g3 (Wong et al., 1986) were applied to domestic pigs, common marmoset monkeys (*Callithrix jacchus jacchus*) and Waldrapp ibises (*Geronticus eremita*) and evaluated for their suitability firstly for isolating polymorphic VNTR markers from genomic libraries (pigs), and secondly for producing informative DNA fingerprints (pigs, marmosets and Waldrapp ibises).

Introduction

To date the probes most widely used for producing informative DNA banding patterns in many species have been minisatellites 33.15 and 33.6 (Jeffreys et al., 1985). However, there are cases where these marker systems reveal only a few polymorphic loci for instance in cattle, goats, sheep and pigs (J. Hillel et al., unpubl. data) or in populations where inbreeding or an intrinsic low genetic variability is suspected such as in zoo and laboratory animals and in the common marmoset (Dixson et al., 1992). Possible ways to overcome this obstacle include using the more sensitive RNA transcripts of 33.15 and 33.6 (Signer and Jeffreys, 1992), choosing other minisatellite-like probes e.g. the α-globin 3′ HVR and M13 (Vassart et al., 1987) and applying synthetic tandem repeat probes (Ali et al., 1986; Vergnaud, pers. comm.).

The purpose of the present study was to investigate whether it is possible to isolate new marker systems in pigs by using the classical multi-locus probes, and to obtain hypervariable DNA profiles in such distinct taxa as domestic pigs and common marmosets, and in Waldrapp ibises, which had not been DNA typed before, by hybridization to a range of human minisatellite probes not normally used for DNA fingerprinting.

Materials and methods

Blood, semen and/or tissue samples were provided by the AFCR/ IAPGR, Edinburgh and the Pig Improvement Company, Abingdon (pigs), the Institute of Anthropology, Zurich (marmosets) and the Zurich Zoo (Waldrapp ibises). Extraction of DNA, digestion by *AluI*, *HaeIII* or *MboI*, and Southern blotting were performed essentially as described by Maniatis et al. (1989). Construction and screening of a porcine library was done as published by Armour et al. (1989) for human DNA. Sequential Southern blot hybridization to random-primed oligo-labelled (Feinberg and Vogelstein, 1983) MS1, MS8, MS31, MS32, MS51, MS228A, g3 and MLP12 was in 0.5 M Na phosphate (pH 7.2), 7% SDS, 1 mM EDTA at 65°C without competitor DNA (including high molecular weight *E. coli* DNA at 5 μg/ml used as carrier to recover probes after labelling). Post-hybridization washes were for 3 × 15 min in 2 × SSC, 0.1% SDS at 65°C ("low stringency") or 2 × 10 min in 0.1 × SSC, 0.01% SDS at 65°C ("high stringency").

Results and discussion

Pigs

Isolation of single-locus markers. Figure 1 shows three examples of porcine locus-specific minisatellites isolated from a Charomid library of large *MboI* DNA fragments by hybridization screening with α-globin 3′ HVR (in a), 33.15 (in b) and porcine MLP12 (in c) which itself had been detected by 33.6 and then used to rescreen the library ("probe walking"). Interestingly, subsequent experiments showed that this multi-locus probe was extremely useful for DNA fingerprinting not only in pigs (Fig. 1e) but also in common marmosets (Fig. 2a) and in Waldrapp ibises (Fig. 3a).
DNA fingerprinting with human locus-specific probes. All human mini-satellite probes tested cross-hybridized at low stringency to pig DNA. Depending on the probe and the restriction enzyme used, oligo-locus (less than four loci) or multi-locus (more than four loci) banding patterns were obtained. Based on comparisons between profiles with respect to band mobility and segregation pattern produced from the

---

Figure 1. Polymorphic locus-specific DNA markers (in *a*, *b*, *c*) and DNA fingerprints (in *d* to *g*) in domestic pigs. Some alleles of marker SLP12/14 have internal *MboI* sites and show more than one band per allele. Dots in *g* mark four paternal bands which exclude boar 1 from paternity. A mutant band (M, lane 3) was detected by MS51. F0, grandparents, F1, parents, F2, offspring, mo, mother, fa, father. x, bands co-detected by MLP12 and MS1. □, bands co-detected by MS51 and g3 (not shown). *, Band co-detected by MLP12, MS1 and MS51.

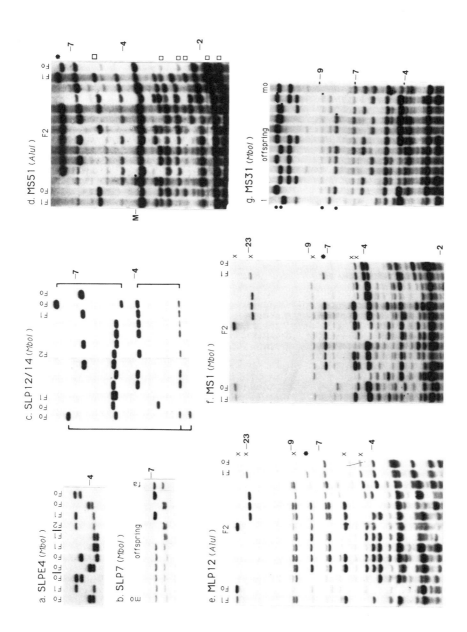

same Southern blot of a pig pedigree, all probes detected several loci independently with only minor overlap between loci above the 4 kbp size range. Exceptions were between MLP 12 and MS1, and between g3 (not shown) and MS51 which co-detected some bands (indicated in Fig. 1e, f and d). The informativeness of the DNA fingerprints varied between probes. For example, MLP12 and MS51 both detected nearly the same number of bands in the lower molecular weight range. However, the pattern of MS51 was better resolved and thus more bands could be scored. As with human DNA fingerprints, occasional mutant bands were detected in pig offspring; for instance, the mutant band detected by MS51 in one out of 30 offspring (Fig. 1d). The power of these probes to reveal new polymorphism not only makes them useful for pedigree testing but also for library screening to isolate further VNTR markers for linkage analysis and genome mapping.

Common marmosets

As in pigs, all human probes tested revealed extensive and mainly independent DNA polymorphisms. Surprisingly, the porcine MLP12 was more informative than 33.15; for example, MLP12 detected two paternal bands which differed between two twin brothers compared with only one with 33.15 and thus giving stronger evidence for assigning the true father (Fig. 2a). Equally powerful in this paternity case were MS31, MS51 (Fig. 2e and d), g3 and MS228A (data not shown). Marmosets normally give birth to dizygotic twins which are haemopoietic chimaeras due to obligatory placental blood vessel anastomoses (Benirschke et al., 1962). As expected, all twins and a rare case of triplets showed identical blood DNA profiles with all probes (e.g. in Fig. 2b, c and f) and could be individually distinguished by DNA analysis of various tissues (except of spleen due to its high content of chimeric lymphocytes; Fig. 2a, d and e, twin partners 1/2 and 3/4), suggesting that chimerism might be limited to bone marrow cells only

---

Figure 2. DNA fingerprinting in common marmosets using DNA from blood (Bl) and different tissues (Br, brain, K, kidney, L, liver, O, ovary, P, placenta, S, spleen, T, testis). Blots in b, c and f show blood DNA patterns from the same family to identify co-born siblings which are connected by brackets. Paternal and maternal bands are marked by dots. In f two human siblings (E, K) are included for comparison. By comparing different tissues in a, d and e the dizygotic twin brothers 1 and 2 could be distinguished and diagnostic bands detected (marked by dots) to determine male 2 as the true father of offspring 3 and 4. Note the leukocyte DNA chimerism between spleen tissue of individual 1 and 2 in d and e. Blots d and e also show a second family with female 6 as the mother and her offspring 1, 2, 8 and 9 and male 7 as the stated father. This male however was excluded from paternity for offspring 1, 2 and 9 based on the absence of the paternal bands marked by x, mo, mother, fa, father, f, female, m, male, M, mutant band.

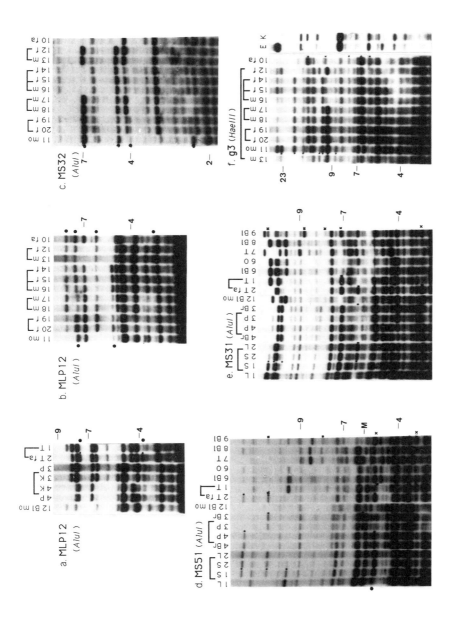

(Signer et al., in preparation). So far, only one single mutant has been detected by MS51 in 17 offspring (Fig. 2d, individual 3, offspring of 12 and 2). Application of such improved DNA typing systems enables us to find more accurate answers to questions on social and sexual behaviour in these primates (Anzenberger et al., in preparation).

Waldrapp ibises

Hypervariable DNA banding patterns could be produced by all the human probes and again by the porcine clone MLP12. In contrast to pigs and marmosets, all probes cross-hybridized extensively to the loci revealed by 33.15 and detected only a few novel loci on their own. However, they were preferred to 33.15 as their banding patterns were less complex and thus easier to score. When compared among themselves, these probes mainly hybridized to different subsets of the DNA fragments detected by 33.15 and could be used either alone or sequentially to maximise the extent of variability. Figure 3 shows the probes that were successfully applied to define the pedigree structure of the entire population (39 birds) which was founded by four males and two females at the Zürich Zoo. Five cases of incorrectly stated paternity (based on behavioural studies) were discovered and the true fathers determined (Signer et al., in preparation). MS31 and g3 also cross-hybridized to a 23 kbp band (marked in Fig. 3c and d) found in all 16 females but in none of the 23 males, suggesting linkage to the W chromosome; this female-specific marker provides a powerful alternative to sexing by laparoscopy. MS228A and g3 co-revealed three band mutations identified as bands absent from the founders but present in some descendents; two of these bands occurred in female 21 (M1 and M2 in Fig. 3d and f) and were transmitted independently to some of her offspring (M1 to offspring 3 and 9, M2 to offspring 6 and 9). A third mutant band (M3) was found in individual 3. Finally, a highly polymorphic single-locus pattern could be revealed using MS51 under high stringency conditions (Fig. 3e), although it is highly unlikely that this single locus in ibises is homologous with the human MS51 locus. This ibis locus seems to be more variable than the one detected in humans (six different alleles in the six *related* founder animals and 81% heterozygosity compared with nine different alleles among 40 *un*related human individuals and 77% heterozygosity) and represents an ideal tool to directly compare genetic variation between different populations and

Figure 3. DNA fingerprints in a Waldrapp ibis colony. The colony consisted of the founder females A and B and males C, D, E and F with their descendants 1 to 22. M1 to 3 denote mutant bands. In male C probe g3 detected a complex minisatellite that was transmitted as a single haplotype of the 8 bands indicated to offspring 4 and 10. For further details see text.

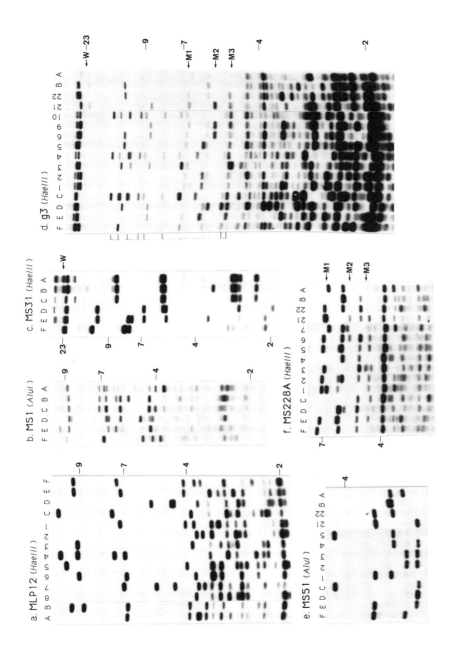

to contribute important genetic information to the conservation programme of this highly endangered species.

Conclusion

In all three species, all probes tested revealed highly informative single-, or multi-locus hybridization patterns to provide a rich source of new markers both for DNA fingerprinting and for the development of new single-locus minisatellite probes in pigs, marmosets and Waldrapp ibises. It is likely that this approach will work well also in other species.

Acknowledgements
The authors are very grateful to Drs A. Archibald, G. Plastow, K. Siggens, A. Mileham, G. Anzenberger, A. Ruebel and Ch. Schmidt for their invaluable help in providing mammalian and bird samples. This work was partially funded by the Swiss National Science Foundation and the Royal Society. The human minisatellite probes are the subject of patent applications. Commercial enquiries should be addressed to ICI Cellmark Diagnostics, 8 Blacklands Way, Abingdon, Oxon OX14, Great Britain.

References

Ali S, Mueller CR, Epplen JT (1986) DNA fingerprinting by oligonucleotides specific for simple repeats. Hum Genet 74: 239–243

Armour JAL, Wong Z, Wilson V, Royle NJ, Jeffreys AJ (1989) Sequences flanking the repeat arrays of human minisatellites: association with dispersed repeat elements. Nucleic Acids Res 13: 4925–4935

Armour JAL, Povey S, Jeremiah S, Jeffreys AJ (1990) Systematic cloning of human minisatellites from ordered-array charomid libraries. Genomics 8: 501–512

Benirschke K, Anderson JM, Brownhill LE (1962) Marrow chimerism in marmosets. Science 138: 513–515

Carter RE, Wetton JH, Parkin DT (1989) Improved genetic fingerprinting using RNA probes. Nucleic Acids Res 17: 5867

Dixson AF, Anzenberger G, Monteiro Da Cruz MAO, Patel I, Jeffreys AJ (1992) DNA fingerprinting of free-ranging groups of common marmosets (*Callithrix jacchus jacchus*) in NE Brazil. *In*: Paternity in primates: Genetic tests and theories. Martin, R. D., Dixson, A.F., Wickings, E.J. (eds) Basel, Karger, 192–202

Feinberg AP, Vogelstein B (1983) A technique for radiolabelling restriction endonuclease fragments to high specific activity. Anal Biochem 137: 266–267

Jarman AP, Nicholls RD, Weatherall DJ, Clegg JB, Higgs DR (1986) Molecular characterization of a hypervariable region downstream of the human α-globin cluster. EMBO J 5: 1857–1863

Jeffreys AJ, Wilson V, Thein SL (1985) Hypervariable minisatellite regions in human DNA. Nature (London) 314: 67–73

Maniatis T, Fritsch EF, Sambrook J (1989) Molecular Cloning: A Laboratory Manual. Volume 1. Cold Spring Harbor Laboratory, N.Y.

Signer EN, Jeffreys AJ (1992) Both "hot" and "cold" transcripts of minisatellites 33.15 and 33.6 produce informative DNA fingerprints in pigs. Fingerprint News 2: 3–7

Vassart G, Georges M, Monsieur R, Brocas H, Lequarre AS, Christophe D (1987) A sequence in M13 phage detects hypervariable minisatellites in human and animal DNA. Science 235: 683–684

Wong Z, Wilson V, Jeffreys AJ, Thein SL (1986) Cloning a selected fragment from a human DNA 'fingerprint': isolation of an extremely polymorphic minisatellite. Nucleic Acids Res 14: 4605–4616

Wong Z, Wilson V, Patel I, Povey S, Jeffreys AJ (1987) Characterization of a panel of highly variable minisatellites cloned from human DNA. Ann Hum Genet 51: 269–288

DNA Fingerprinting: State of the Science
ed. by S. D. J. Pena, R. Chakraborty, J. T. Epplen & A. J. Jeffreys
© 1993 Birkhäuser Verlag Basel/Switzerland

The 'individualization' of large North American mammals

J. L. Ruth and S. R. Fain

US Fish & Wildlife Forensic Lab, 1490 East Main St, Ashland, OR 97520, USA

Summary
The enforcement of wildlife laws and the captive breeding of threatened/endangered species requires the ability to identify individual animals. DNA profiles of a variety of large North American mammals, birds, and fish were generated using ten different oligonucleotide probes. The probes tested were four multilocus probes [33.6, 33.15, JE46, and $(TGTC)_5$] and six 'human unilocus' probes [MS1 (D1S7), CMM101 (D14S13), YNH24 (D2S44), EFD52 (D17S26), TBQ7 (D10S28), and MS43 (D12S11). Each of the probes was chemically synthesized, and labeled by the attachment of alkaline phosphatase; after hybridization, the probes were detected by chemiluminescence catalyzed by the enzyme. Initial screenings against zoo blots including samples of bear, wolf, large cat, wild sheep, deer, birds, marine mammals, and fish indicated that three multilocus probes [33.15, 33.6, $(TGTC)_5$] gave informative patterns containing 15–40 bands for most or all of the animals tested, as did two of the 'human unilocus' probes (MS1 and CMM101). The other five probes appeared informative only in some species (for example, YNH24 against canids). Subsequent screenings of populations within species were used to determine genetic diversity by analysis of observed bandsharing (S). Large heterologous populations, such as white-tailed deer, exhibited highly diverse band patterns $(S \leq 0.2)$. Geographically isolated and/or genetically constricted animals, such as endangered Mexican wolves, Tule elk, and Columbian white-tailed deer, exhibited much higher frequencies of bandsharing $(0.6 \leq S \leq 0.95)$. Comparison of apparent bandsharing on the same individuals between different probes suggested that the loci detected by 33.15, 33.6, MS1, and CMM101 in animals do not overlap significantly $(0.06 \leq S \leq 0.18)$. Databases collected in this manner are being used in national and international forensic casework.

Introduction

Accurate estimates of the magnitude of wildlife crime are difficult. Observations of animal species in the world pet trade include at least 140 mammal species, 85 bird species, and 57 reptile and amphibian species. The global market for illegal wildlife products has escalated into an estimated $1–$2 billion a year business (World Wildlife Fund). Fish & Wildlife Service estimates are $200 million per year in the U.S. alone, a 100% increase in the last ten years. In the US, it is estimated that two animals are poached for every animal taken legally.

The enforcement of laws concerning these crimes is not a simple task. The importation of nearly all wildlife and their parts or products is variously regulated in the US by the Endangered Species Act, Marine Mammal Protection Act, Migratory Bird Treaty Act, Tariff Classification Act, Lacey Act, and the Convention on International Trade of

Endangered Species (CITES). In addition, many species are potential targets of organized poaching interests: black bear (pharmaceuticals), elk (trophy hunting & captive breeding stock), wolf (trophy hunting & predator control) and walrus (ivory). We were interested in determining the extent DNA fingerprint variation could be used to individualize evidence samples from these species.

Individual-specific DNA profiles generated by multilocus (Jeffreys et al., 1985) or unilocus (Nakamura et al., 1987) VNTR probes have been extensively studied in humans. DNA profiles of wildlife have largely been generated with multilocus probes, which crosshybridize (somewhat unpredictably) with many animals (Jeffreys and Morton, 1987; Longmire et al., 1988; Gilbert et al., 1990; Wolfes et al., 1991). In a wildlife forensic setting, techniques to accurately measure genetic diversity are necessary for enforcement of wildlife laws. The ability to identify the smallest units of genetic 'diversity' (i.e., individual animals) also provides basic information for management of endangered or threatened species in captive breeding programs. We were interested in determining the informative value, if any, of both multi- and uni-locus probes in wildlife studies. The work reported here summarizes the preliminary results obtained by screening ten oligonucleotide probes against a number of large mammals (canids, bear, deer, cat, otter, walrus), birds, and fish found in North America. Studies of selected populations were used to establish the level of genetic diversity identified by each probe for a given species.

Forensic casework requires additional considerations, such as assay speed and sensitivity. To address these issues, the work described here was limited to oligonucleotide probes labeled with alkaline phosphatase (Jablonski et al., 1986; Edman et al., 1988; Ruth, 1991), and detected by chemiluminescence (Tizard et al., 1990; Ruth, 1991). Known sensitivities for internally-labeled oligonucleotides are $\approx 2 \times 10^5$ molecules of target sequence (3×10^{-19} mole), or about 50–100 pg of total human DNA for probe 33.6; probes labeled with enzyme on the 5′-end may be less sensitive (Ruth, unpublished results). The application and sensitivities in non-humans were largely unknown.

Materials and methods

DNA was prepared from muscle tissue obtained from hunter-killed animals, or from white blood cells (Jeffreys and Morton, 1987) fractionated from whole blood taken by wildlife biologists from immobilized animals. DNA (5 µg) was digested with 50 units of restriction enzyme (*Pst* I, *Alu* I, *Hae* III, or *Hinf* I) in 20 µl volumes. DNA restriction fragments were electrophoresed through 200 ml 15 × 25 cm long 1.0% agarose gels at 45 volts for 24 hours with Tris-Borate-EDTA buffer.

DNA fragments were transferred to nylon filter membranes (Magnagraph, MSI) by vacuum transfer (LKB VacuGene, Pharmacia) followed by crosslinking with 120 mjoules UV for 30 sec (Stratalinker, Stratagene). Membranes were prehybridized/blocked for 30 minutes at 50°C in hybridization buffer (5 × SSC, pH 7.0, 1% SDS, 0.5% BSA, 0.2% Hammarsten-grade casein, μfiltered). Hybridization was with 2–3 nM alkaline phosphatase-labeled oligonucleotide probe (Edman, 1988; Ruth, 1991; see Tab. 1 for sequences) for 30 minutes at 50°C. Membranes were then washed three times 8–10 min in 1 × SSC, 1% SDS at 50°C, and twice for 5–7 min in 1 × SSC at ambient temperature. Membranes were washed twice in DEA substrate buffer (100 mM diethanolamine, 1 mM $MgCl_2$, pH 10) for 5 minutes at room temperature and then incubated in DEA substrate buffer with 400 μM AMPPD (1,2-dioxetane, Tropix) for 10 minutes. The membranes were exposed to Kodak XAR-5 film for 30 minutes to 3 hours after 1–15 hours incubation in the dark at ambient temperature. For reprobing, the membrane was stripped by washing twice in 0.1 × SSC, 0.5% SDS at 95°C for five minutes and once in 1 × SSC, 1% SDS at room temperature for five minutes.

A semi-automated video imaging system (JAVA, Jandel Scientific) was used to characterize and digitally record each DNA fingerprint profile. All uniquely sized restriction fragments between 2.0–24 kb were scored as to their presence or absence in the individuals being compared. Restriction fragment bands of the same migration (± 0.1 mm) and intensity were scored as identical. Band size was determined by comparison to molecular markers (*Hind* III-restricted lambda DNA and 'Genetic Analysis' ladder, Promega). Genetic variation was assessed in each species by making repetitive pairwise comparisons between the DNA fingerprints of individual samples. This was accomplished with "COM*BAND" a Lotus 123™ macro program (Bruce Taylor, US-FWS Forensic Lab) which calculated the probability of bandsharing or similarity (S) between two individuals as the number of fragments of equivalent length identified in both DNA fingerprints divided by the total number of fragments compared (Lynch, 1988).

Results and discussion

Oligonucleotide fingerprinting with chemiluminescent detection was used to characterize genetic variability in wildlife species. This approach allows blotting, hybridization, and detection in as little as 8 hours, in contrast to the 4–7 days required to record an isotopic result. This greatly reduces turn-around time in forensic casework.

The ten oligonucleotide probes listed in Tab. 1 were screened against 'zoo' blots of isolated DNAs from representative species of wildlife.

Table 1. The oligonucleotide probes below are labelled with alkaline phosphatase on a thymidine base analog (T) (Jablonski et al., 1986) and used as multilocus DNA typing probes. The probes were synthesized on a custom basis by Syngene, Inc (San Diego, CA)

Common name	Human locus	Length	Sequence
33.15	—	32	5'-AGA GGT GGG CAG GTG GAG AGG TGG GCA GGT GG
33.6	—	22	5'-TGG AGG AGG GCT GGA GGA GGG C
MS1	D1S7	26	5'-AGG GTG GA(CT) AGG GTG GA(CT) AGG GTG GA
CMM101	D14S13	30	5'-TCC ACC TCA GCC CCC TCC ACC TCA GCC CCC
(TGTC)₅	—	19	5'-TGT CTG TCT GTC TGT CTG T
YNH24	D2S44	31	5'-AAC AAC CCC ACT GTA CTT CCC ACT GCT CCT G
EFD52	D17S26	27	5'-TAC TAG CAC (AT)(CG)(CT) CCT GG(CT) TAC TAG CAC
TBQ7	D10S28	31	5'-TGC CTG AGC CTT CTC ACA GTC TCA CCT GAT C
MS43	D12S11	25	5'-CCT TCC CGG GGC CCT CCC TAT ACC C
JE46	—	17	5'-CCC CCC GTG TCG CTG TT

Many of the human-derived probes (EFD52, YNH24, TBQ7, MS43, and JE46) hybridized weakly, if at all, with most of the species tested; some reacted with only a few species (example: YNH24 in wolves and birds) under the conditions used. As expected, the multilocus probes 33.6, 33.15, and (TGTC)$_5$ hybridized significantly to most or all species (for example, see Fig. 1). Two human-derived unilocus probes, MS1 and CMM101, also hybridized strongly to all animals tested, resulting in multilocus profiles (for example, see Fig. 2).

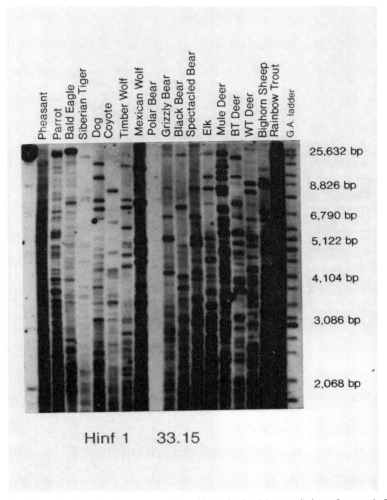

Figure 1. Example of a chemiluminescent 'zoo blot' obtained by restriction of genomic DNA with *Hinf*I and hybridization with an alkaline phosphatase-conjugated oligonucleotide corresponding to the core sequence of the human mini-satellite 33.15. See text for details.

434

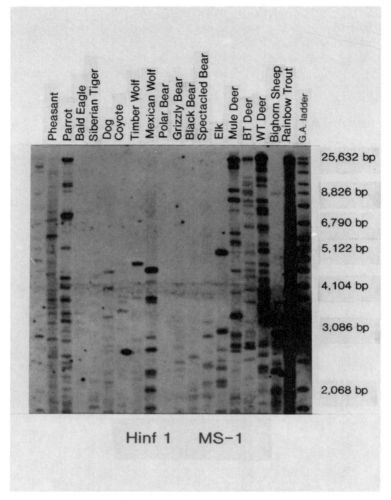

Figure 2. Example of a chemiluminescent 'zoo blot' obtained by restriction of genomic DNA with *Hinf*I and hybridization with an alkaline phosphatase-conjugated oligonucleotide corresponding to the core sequence of the human VNTR MS1. See text for details.

After initial screenings, numerous animals from populations of each species were analyzed, and their DNA profiles compared to establish average similarities (S). The derived similarities for probes 33.15, 33.6, MS1 and CMM101 ranged from $S = 0.2$ to as high as $S = 0.9$, depending on the species tested (see Tab. 2). Correspondingly, the conservative probability ($S^{x/2}$, where x = average number of bands in a profile) that two unrelated animals would have identical profiles using a *single* probe ranged from 5.5×10^{-8} (1 in ≈ 18 million) for mule deer using 33.6, to only 0.62 (1 in ≈ 2) for elk using MS1.

Table 2. Initial results. Large North American and Marine Mammals

Species	Probe used		
	Ave. Fraction of Bands Shared (Ave. band number per individual)		
	33.15	33.6	MS-1
Black Bear (n = 54)	0.55 ± 0.08 (11)	—	0.79 ± 0.07 (13)
Mexican Wolf (n = 4)	0.79 ± 0.06 (21)	0.79 ± 0.06 (21)	0.70 ± 0.07 (12)
Elk (n = 53)	0.61 ± 0.08 (20)	0.52 ± 0.08 (15)	0.91 ± 0.12 (9)
Mule Deer (n = 36)	—	0.29 ± 0.01 (27)	—
WT Deer (n = 72)	—	0.20 ± 0.01 (15)	—
Col WT Deer (n = 18)	0.54 ± 0.01 (16)	0.61 ± 0.01 (24)	0.62 ± 0.02 (27)
Walrus (n = 58)	0.43 ± 0.08 (19)	0.40 ± 0.08 (22)	—
Sea Otter (n = 18)	0.60 ± 0.08 (14)	—	—

Black Bear –	*Ursus americanus* (CITES Appendix II)
Mexican Wolf –	*Canis lupus baileyi* (CITES Appendix II)
North American Elk –	*Cervus elaphus*
Mule Deer –	*Odocoileus hemionus hemionus*
White-tailed (WT) Deer –	*Odocoileus virginianus*
Columbian WT Deer –	*Odocileus virginianus leucurus* (endangered)
Pacific Walrus –	*Odobenus rosmarus divergens* (Marine Mammal Protection Act)
Sea Otter –	*Enhydra lutris* (Marine Mammal Protection Act)

These exclusion powers can be increased in a multiplicative manner by the use of probe combinations, but only if apparent bands ('loci') between probes are not shared. As a measure of overlap, apparent "bandsharing" *between* different probes on the same individuals was determined. In the endangered Columbian white-tailed deer ($S \approx 0.6$), the results *between* all possible probe combinations of 33.15, 33.6, MS1 and CMM101 ranged from $S = 0.06$ to $S = 0.18$; this indicates that any apparently common bands which may exist are indistinguishable from background band sharing. As a result, even species with little genetic variation can be identified with exclusion probabilities of 1 in more than 10^6 individuals, representing adequate discrimination for wildlife forensics.

We have used such techniques and analyses in more than 150 forensic cases in North America. The analyses have involved such species as elk, deer, wolf, parrots, bighorn sheep, eagle, and bear. Such cases generally involve identification of individuals, matching field evidence (blood, tissue, gut pile, etc.) to evidence (such as meat or trophies) in possession of the suspect. Occasionally, parentage determinations are required, as well. It is our hope that the wildlife DNA fingerprinting techniques and results described in this paper will simplify the enforcement of wildlife laws and aid in the conservation of wildlife for the future.

Acknowledgements
We wish to gratefully acknowledge all of the wildlife people, too numerous to name, who contributed tissue or blood for this study. In addition, we wish to thank Dr. Bruce Taylor of our Laboratory for quantitating the similarity comparisons, a tedious and time-consuming job at best.

References

Edman JC, Evans-Holm ME, Marich JE, Ruth JL (1988) Rapid DNA fingerprinting using alkaline phosphatase-conjugated oligonucleotides. Nucleic Acids Res 16: 6235

Gilbert DA, Lehman N, O'Brien SJ, Wayne RK (1990) Genetic fingerprinting reflects population in the California Channel Island fox. Nature 344: 764–767

Jablonski E, Moomaw E, Tullis R, Ruth JL (1986) Preparation of oligodeoxynucleotide-alkaline phosphatase conjugates and their use as hybridization probes. Nucleic Acids Res 14: 6115–6128

Jeffreys AJ, Wilson V, Thein SL (1985a) Hypervariable 'minisatellite' regions in human DNA. Nature 314: 67–73; Jeffreys AJ, Wilson V, Thein SL (1985b) Individual-specific 'fingerprints' of human DNA. Nature 316: 76–79

Jeffreys AJ, Morton DB (1987) DNA fingerprints of dogs and cats. Animal Genetics 18: 1–15

Longmire JL, Lewis AK, Brown NC, Buckingham JM, Clark LM, Jones MD, Meincke LJ, Meyne J, Ratliff RL, Ray FA, Wagner RP, Moyzis RK (1988) Isolation and molecular characterization of a highly polymorphic centromeric tandem repeat in the family *Falconidae*. Genomics 2: 14–24

Lynch M (1988) Estimation of relatedness by DNA fingerprinting. Mol Biol Evol 5: 584–599

Nakamura Y, Leppert M, O'Connell P, Wolff R, Holm T, Culver M, Martin C, Fujimoto E, Hoff M, Kumlin E, White R (1987) Variable number of tandem repeat (VNTR) markers for human gene mapping. Science 235: 1616–1622

Ruth JL (1991) Oligodeoxynucleotides with reporter groups attached to the base. *In*: Eckstein F (ed.), Oligonucleotides and analogues: A practical approach, Oxford University Press, pp 255–282

Tizard R, Cate RL, Ramachandran KL, Wysk M, Voyta JC, Murphy OJ, Bronstein I (1990) Imaging of DNA sequences with chemiluminescence. Proc Natl Acad Sci USA 87: 4514–4518

Wolfes R, Mathe J, Seitz A (1991) Forensics of birds of prey by DNA fingerprinting with ^{32}P-labeled oligonucleotide probes. Electrophoresis 12: 175–180

DNA Fingerprinting: State of the Science
ed. by S. D. J. Pena, R. Chakraborty, J. T. Epplen & A. J. Jeffreys
© 1993 Birkhäuser Verlag Basel/Switzerland

Bovine microsatellites: Racial differences and association with SINE-elements

S.-L. Varvio[a] and J. Kaukinen

[a]*Department of Genetics, PO Box 17, Arkadiankatu 7, University of Helsinki; and Institute of Biotechnology, University of Helsinki, SF-00014 Helsinki*

Summary
Patterns of polymorphism at eight microsatellite loci in three cattle races are described: two large commercial breeds and one endangered landrace. Significant interracial allele frequency differences were found at six loci. The mean heterozygosity was slightly higher in the landrace ($H = 0.75$) than in the others ($H = 0.69$). The difference is smaller than that found by DNA-fingerprinting. Intrapopulation distributions of microsatellite allele size (dinucleotide repeat number) were generally bimodal, with certain intermediate repeat types lacking. Sequencing of individual alleles revealed some hidden heterogeneity: an allele defined by PCR-product size actually corresponded to different sequence motifs in different races. Two of the microsatellites occurred as tails of SINE-elements. In contrast to some earlier reports, the position of one of the amplification primers within a high-copy-number SINE-element did not disturb microsatellite amplification; even multiplex PCR was possible.

Introduction

Highly variable microsatellites currently provide the most informative class of markers for human genome mapping (Weber, 1990). These mono-, di- or trinucleotide repeat polymorphisms are also known from agriculturally important animals (Fries et al., 1990). Animal gene maps are essential tools for identification and manipulation of economically important genes in breeding programs (Fries et al., 1989), but also of interest for studies on the evolution of mammalian chromosome organization (Womack and Moll, 1986). If intrapopulation microsatellite polymorphism proves to be as ubiquitous and polyallelic in animals as in humans, it should largely remove the need for choosing reference populations for linkage studies (genome mapping) on the basis of maximum inter-breed divergence. Rather, the choice could be on the basis of information on the traits of economic interest (Beckmann and Soller, 1990). In any case, a crucial question is, how much genetic variation is related to their inbreeding histories and records of artificial selection.

In this paper, we describe patterns of microsatellite polymorphism and differentiation in three cattle races. Elsewhere (Varvio and Kaukinen, submitted), we have reported on a considerably lower level of

VNTR-polymorphism in commercial breeds than in landraces, although the landraces are currently in low numbers and highly endangered.

Material and methods

Genomic DNA was isolated from a total of 117 individuals of Finnish Ayrshire and Friesian cattle breeds and a landrace (Finncattle, eastern and northern type). The Friesian sample comprised 32 unrelated individuals. The Ayrshire material (41 individuals) comprised 10 calves, their parents (19 ind.), and some maternal grandparents (12 ind.). For allele frequency estimates 22 unrelated individuals were used. The Finncattle material (44 individuals) comprised 27 calves (including 13 sibs or half-sibs) and their parents (17 individuals). The calf sample was used for allele frequency estimates.

PCR conditions and primers for seven microsatellites were as described (Kaukinen and Varvio, in press). In addition, the microsatellite in the sixth intron of the steroid 21-hydroxylase gene (accession number M11267/M13545) was studied (primers in Fries et al., 1990). One to three microsatellites were amplified in a single reaction: HEL1, HEL5 and HEL13 were amplified in one reaction, HEL9 and HEL10 in another one, steroid 21-hydroxylase and HEL12 in another, and HEL11 alone in another. PCR-products were resolved on polyacrylamide sequencing gels (6%, 7 M urea). Some of the PCR-products were sequenced, following Casanova et al. (1990), after purifying the fragments with Magic PCR Preps™ (Promega).

Relative sizes of different alleles (PCR-products) were determined by running sequencing ladders and MspI digested pBR322 in the same gels, and by including the amplification product of the individual, from which the microsatellites had originally been identified by sequencing.

Results

A two-base spacing of fragment sizes was found at all microsatellites, supporting the assumption that the variable repeat unit is a dinucleotide. This was verified by sequencing some PCR-products of homozygous individuals from HEL1 and HEL5.

Four HEL11 alleles were sequenced, in addition to the reference from the original plasmid library clone. The reference sequence (from an Ayrshire individual) was $(GA)_5(TA)_7(CA)_5(TA)_3(TG)_{19}(T)_5CC(T)_9$ and product size 191 bp. Two of the newly sequenced PCR-products were also 191 bp; however, they differed in sequence. One, from Finncattle, had only 14 TG-repeats but instead 5 (TA)s; the other, from Friesian, had 19 (TG)s as in the cloned fragment, but 8 (CA)s. The two other alleles sequenced, 185 bp and 187 bp both had 19 TG-repeats, but we could not read most other parts of the sequence.

Allele frequencies (Fig. 1) were significantly different among the races at six of the eight loci. Chi square test statistics (with d.f. in parentheses) for the individual loci were: HEL1, 11.2 (4) $P < 0.05$; HEL5 70.0 (6) $P < 0.001$; HEL9 15.1 (6) $P < 0.05$; HEL12 9.9 (4) $P < 0.05$; HEL13 13.5 (4) $P < 0.01$; steroid 21-hydroxylase 67.0 (8) $P < 0.001$.

The landrace was, on the average, slightly more heterozygous ($H = 0.75$) than the commercial breeds ($H = 0.69$ in both Ayrshire and

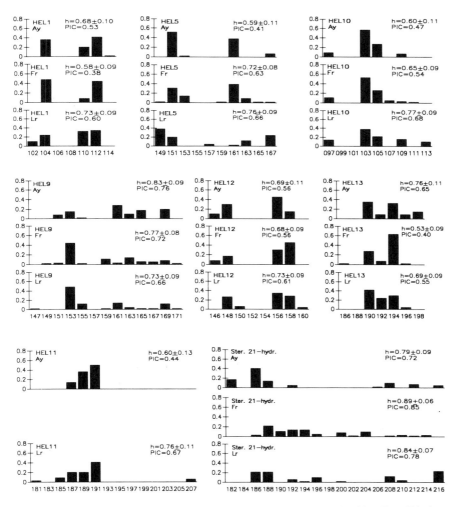

Figure 1. Microsatellite allele frequencies in three cattle races: Ay = Ayrshire, Fr = Friesian, Lr = Landrace. Alleles are designated in base pairs of the corresponding PCR-products. h is the expected (Hardy-Weinberg) proportion of heterozygotes.

Friesian, from the seven loci studied in all races). PIC values at individual loci ranged from 0.55 to 0.78 (mean 0.65) in the landrace, from 0.41 to 0.76 (mean 0.57) in Ayrshire and from 0.38 to 0.85 (mean 0.58) in Friesian.

At most loci, the allele size distributions were bimodal, exhibiting a lack of certain repeat types of intermediate length. This was true for all races, although the races often differed with respect to their prevalent allele(s).

Discussion

The microsatellite motifs of HEL1 and steroid 21-hydroxylase occur as tails of an artiodactyl SINE element (Kaukinen and Varvio, 1992). This SINE element, or retroposon, consists of a tRNA-derived 85 bp sequence (the artiodactyl C-element of Rogers, 1985) followed by a 117 bp A-element of unknown origin (Watanabe et al., 1982; Rogers, 1985). HEL1 is located at the 3′ end of the A-element; one of the primers used for its amplification is situated within the element. In HEL5 the amplified fragment includes a truncated (22 bp) C-element. The steroid 21-hydroxylase microsatellite is also a 3′ tail of the A element, and one of the primers is within the element. Despite the high numbers of the SINE-elements in the genome, PCR of the SINE-associated microsatellites amplifies unique loci without background (Fig. 2). In future it might be possible to select bovine SINE elements in hybrid cell lines as a potential means of identifying highly informative polymorphisms within a restricted portion of the bovine genome. The study of microsatellites associated with SINE elements present in thousands of copies throughout the genome has earlier faced technical difficulties. The placement of one of the PCR primers within a human *Alu* sequence resulted in weak amplification and/or high background (Economou et al., 1990; Beckmann and Weber, 1992). However, we did not encounter any problems with the SINE-associated bovine microsatellites.

We find that cattle races differ considerably with respect to their microsatellite allele frequencies; the prevalent alleles are often different in the races. Moreover, there was an indication of hidden heterogeneity within microsatellite alleles as defined by PCR-product size: such an 'allele' was found to be a composite of different alleles at the actual sequence level. However, only one individual PCR-product per one allele has been sequenced, so far.

In terms of the level of intrapopulation heterogeneity, the differences between races are not great, although an indication of slightly higher heterozygosity in the landrace may be seen. The result is interesting in the context of the widely differing demographic histories of the populations. The actual sizes of commercial breeds are very large, but they

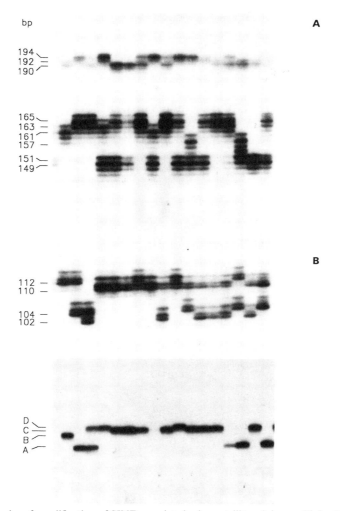

Figure 2. Examples of amplification of SINE-associated microsatellites. A is a multiplex PCR, in which the lowest microsatellite (HEL1), is a tail of a SINE-element (the A-element). The uppermost one is HEL13, and the middle one is HEL5. In B, the microsatellite (HEL8) is a tail of the tRNA-derived SINE-element.

have undergone intensive artificial selection programs, with associated reduction in effective population size and in levels of genetic variation. On the other hand, the total size of the landrace (eastern and northern Finncattle) is currently less than 100 individuals, and the race is highly endangered.

The results showing similar levels of polymorphism in different races, suggest that the choice of an experimental population may have little

442

effect on the efficiency of the basic task of constructing a linkage map. Furthermore, a microsatellite detected in one cattle race is very likely to be informative in others too.

However, it should be noted that greater differences in DNA polymorphism of cattle races have been detected with other techniques. In a study of DNA-fingerprinting by the M13mp9 as a probe (Varvio and Kaukinen, submitted), the average percent difference in band profiles (a measure of intrabreed heterogeneity) within the landrace was 43.9, while the corresponding estimates for the two commercial races were 23.4 and 33.8. It seems that the genetic erosion associated with population reduction in the landraces has so far been relatively minor, and they may be expected to contain important genetic resource even at the intra-breed level.

At most microsatellite loci the allele size distributions are bimodal; certain repeat types are conspicuously lacking in all races. Bi- or multimodality is also a general phenomenon in human microsatellite and VNTR allele distributions (Boerwinkle et al., 1989; Ludwig et al., 1989; Weber and May, 1989; Edwards et al., 1992; Fornage et al., 1992). The mechanistic or population genetic background of such distributions might be partly elucidated by comparative studies of the same microsatellite loci in (closely) related species.

Acknowledgements
The study has been supported by the Academy of Finland and NKJ. We thank Dr. Lars Paulin for oligonucleotide synthesis, Prof. emer. Kalle Maijala for Finncattle blood samples, and Risto Väinölä for critical comments on the manuscript.

References

Beckmann JS, Soller M (1990) Toward a unified approach to genetic mapping of Eucaryotes based on sequence tagged microsatellite sites. Biotechnology 8: 930–932

Beckmann JS, Weber JL (1992) Survey of human and rat microsatellites. Genomics 12: 627–631

Boerwinkle E, Xiong W, Fowest E, Chan L (1989) Rapid typing of tandemly repeated hypervariable loci by polymerase chain reaction: Application to the apolipoprotein B 3' hypervariable region. Proc Natl Acad Sci USA 86: 212–216

Casanova JL, Pannetier C, Jaulin C, Kaourilsky P (1990) Optimal conditions for directly sequencing double-stranded PCR products with Sequenase. Nucleic Acids Res 18: 4028

Economou EP, Bergen AW, Warren AC, Antonarakis SE (1990) The polydeoxyadenylate tract of Alu repetitive element is polymorphic in the human genome. Proc Natl Acad Sci USA 87: 2951–2954

Edwards A, Hammond HA, Jin L, Caskey CT, Chakraborty R (1992) Genetic variation at five trimeric and tetrameric tandem repeat loci in four human population groups. Genomics 12: 241–253

Fornage M, Chan L, Siest G, Boerwinkle E (1992) Allele frequency distribution of the $(TG)_n(AG)_m$ microsatellite in the apolipoprotein C-II gene. Genomics 12: 63–68

Fries R, Beckman JS, Georges M, Soller M, Womac J (1989) The bovine gene map. Animal Genetics 20: 3–29

Fries R, Eggen A, Stranzinger G (1990) The bovine genome contains polymorphic microsatellites. Genomics 8: 403–406

Kaukinen J, Varvio S-L (1992) Artiodactyl SINE-elements: association with microsatellites and use in SINEmorph detection by PCR. Nucleic Acids Res 20: 2955–2958

Kaukinen J, Varvio S-L. Eight polymorphic bovine microsatellites. Animal Genetics, in press

Ludwig EH, Friedl W, McCarthy BJ (1989) High resolution analysis of a hypervariable region in the human apolipoprotein B gene. Am J Hum Genet 45: 458–464

Rogers JH (1985) The origin and evolution of retroposons. Intern Rev Cytol 93: 187–279

Watanabe Y, Tsukada T, Notake M, Nakanishi S, Numa S (1982) Structural analysis of repetitive DNA sequences in the bovine corticotropin-b-lipotropin precursor gene region. Nucleic Acids Res 10: 1459–1469

Weber JL (1990) Informativeness of human $(dC-dA)_n \cdot (dG-dT)_n$ polymorphisms. Genomics 7: 524–530

Weber JL, May PE (1989) Abundant class of human DNA polymorphisms which can be typed using the polymerase chain reaction. Am J Hum Genet 44: 388–396

Womack JE, Moll YD (1986) Gene map of the cow: conservation of linkage with mouse and man. J Heredity 77: 2–7

DNA Fingerprinting: State of the Science
ed. by S. D. J. Pena, R. Chakraborty, J. T. Epplen & A. J. Jeffreys
© 1993 Birkhäuser Verlag Basel/Switzerland

Oligonucleotide fingerprinting of free-ranging and captive rhesus macaques from Cayo Santiago: Paternity assignment and comparison of heterozygosity

P. Nürnberg[a], J. D. Berard[b], F. Bercovitch[b], J. T. Epplen[c], J. Schmidtke[d] and M. Krawczak[d]

[a]*Institut für Medizinische Genetik, Medizinische Fakultät (Charité) der Humboldt-Universität zu Berlin, 10117 Berlin, Germany;* [b]*Caribbean Primate Research Center, University of Puerto Rico School of Medicine, Sabana Seca;* [c]*Abteilung für Molekulare Humangenetik, Ruhr-Universität, 44780 Bochum, Germany; and Institut für Humangenetik, Medizinische Hochschule, 30623 Hannover, Germany*

Summary
Multilocus DNA fingerprinting with oligonucleotide probes $(GTG)_5$, $(GATA)_4$, and $(CA)_8$ was applied in order to determine paternity in one birth cohort (15 infants) of a social group (S) from the free-ranging colony of rhesus macaques (*Macaca mulatta*) on Cayo Santiago. While sires could be identified in 11 cases, all males tested ($N = 19$) could be excluded from paternity for the remaining four infants. Data revealed marked discrepancies between actual paternity and paternity as inferred from the observation of copulation behavior. Thus, a dominant social rank does not appear to be strongly associated with reproductive success. Furthermore, alternative reproductive strategies were found to yield comparable net benefits in reproduction. A second group of animals (M) was translocated from Cayo Santiago to the Sabana Seca Field Station in 1984. They have continuously resided together in a large outdoor enclosure since then. Here paternity assessment was seriously impeded by a reduced number of discriminating bands, i.e. offspring bands which were unequivocally derived from the sires. This was initially held to be indicative of a smaller degree of heterozygosity in Group M, and was attributed to inbreeding due to a lack of male immigration or extra-group fertilizations. However, a comparison of the DNA fingerprint patterns obtained in Group S and Group M lends only partial support to this idea.

Introduction

In recent years DNA fingerprinting analyses have been performed for several non-human primate species (Weiss et al., 1988; Dixson et al., 1988; Arnemann et al., 1989; Ely and Ferrell, 1990; Ely et al., 1991; Martin et al., 1992). However in terms of population genetics and paternity assessments the outcome of this endeavor has not fulfilled the high expectations of primatologists hitherto. With the help of the more advantageous methodology of multilocus DNA fingerprinting using synthetic oligonucleotide probes specific for simple repeat motifs, this situation is likely to change. At least for the island colony of rhesus monkeys (*Macaca mulatta*) on Cayo Santiago genetic relationships could be elucidated. These free-ranged monkeys have been studied intensively by ethologists for many years. However, only matrilines are known, and the interest in getting reliable data on sireship for this colony is obvious. On the basis of a new model for the statistical analysis of multilocus DNA profiles it should be possible to reconstruct the patrilineal pedigree of the Cayo Santiago Macaques (Krawczak and Bockel, 1992; Bockel et al., 1992). The results of such an analysis would allow, for example, to pursue the segregation of several genetic defects that these animals are suffering from.

Material and methods

Cayo Santiago (15 ha island, 1 km off the southeast coast of Puerto Rico) has been populated with rhesus macaques since 1938. Colony size has fluctuated from about 200 to 1200 animals (Rawlins and Kessler, 1986; Kessler and Berard, 1989). In 1989, a total of 1093 animals were organized into seven naturally-formed social groups – including Group S. This group consisted of 54 monkeys at that time comprising 11 adult males and 18 adult females. Behavioral data on these animals were collected as described elsewhere (Berard et al., 1993). Group M, three times larger than Group S, was translocated from Cayo Santiago to the Sabana Seca Field Station on Puerto Rico in 1984. These monkeys have continuously resided together in a large outdoor enclosure since then.

  Blood from the free-ranging animals could only be taken during the annual trapping season. DNA preparation was performed according to standard procedures (Blin and Stafford, 1976; Kunkel et al., 1977). The methodology of multilocus DNA fingerprinting using oligonucleotide probes specific for simple repeat motifs has been described in detail by Epplen (1992). In this study we used the oligonucleotide probes $(GTG)_5$, $(GATA)_4$, $(GACA)_4$, $(CT)_8$ as well as $(CA)_8$. Paternity was assigned on the basis of published likelihood formulae for multilocus profiles (Krawczak and Bockel, 1992).

Results and discussion

Paternity assignment in Group S

Paternity in Group S was studied for the 1989 birth cohort. Blood samples were collected from 15 mother-infant pairs and, with one exception (F24), from all males that were observed copulating during the preceding breeding season ($N = 19$). Of these nine resided in other social groups.

Initially, HinfI-digested DNA was successively hybridized to all probes. The five different DNA fingerprints obtained for each infant were then compared to those of its mother. All bands of necessarily paternal origin were marked and used for a preliminary identification of presumed sires. In additional runs, DNAs of the possible sires were compared directly to the corresponding mother/child dyad in adjacent lanes (Fig. 1).

In 11 cases, paternity was successfully assigned on the basis of the likelihoods of the multilocus profiles. Using the information obtained for three probes, $(GTG)_5$, $(GATA)_4$, and $(CA)_8$, the combined likelihood ratios in favour of paternity exceeded 10^{10}. In the four unresolved cases all investigated males were excluded as sires on the basis of at least three necessarily paternal offspring bands not present in their own profiles. This procedure was performed without using any information

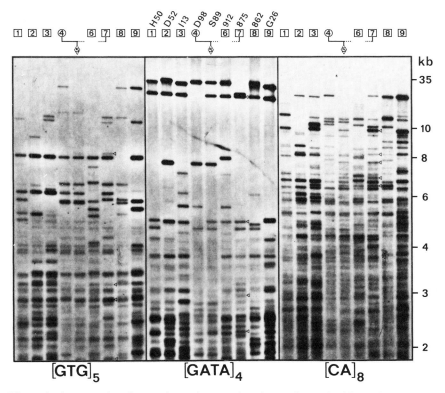

Figure 1. An example of paternity assignment based on oligonucleotide probes $(GTG)_5$, $(GATA)_4$ and $(CA)_8$. The mother is D98 while her infant is S89. Numbers H50, D52, I13, 912, 862 and G26 denote the potential sires. Arrows indicate bands not present in the mother but shared by the infant and the actual sire. The only male to exhibit these bands is 875 which is thus likely to be the sire of S89. In fact, the combined likelihood ratio in favor of paternity was calculated to be 10^{17}.

on dominance relations, social history, mating partners or mating patterns.

This is the first study to successfully determine paternity in a free-ranging group. Other studies faced problems with poor-quality DNA fingerprints on one hand and lack of appropriate statistical management of the multilocus profiles on the other (see Martin et al., 1992 for review).

Behavior and paternity in Group S

In Tab. 1 the reproductive success (RS) of the males observed mating is reported together with some behavioral data. Obviously, a high percentage of extra-group fertilization must have occurred, since four of the 11 infants of known paternity were sired by males residing in other social groups. This portion would even increase if the four infants with unsolved paternity were not sired by F24, the only S-group male that could not be tested hitherto.

Table 1. Reproductive success versus mating behavior

Male	Social group	Rank	Offspring sired	
			Expected[a]	Actual
722	S	1	5	2
761	S	2	1	2
856	S	3	0	0
D52	S (N)	4	0	0
912	S	5	1	0
G21	S (N)	6	0	1
G20	S (N)	7	0	0
B76	S	8	1	1
875	S	9	2	1
F24	S	10	1	?
H50	S (N)	11	0	0
728	T	H	0	0
A84	T	H	0	0
C78	T	H	0	0
G06	T	H	1	0
E92	T	L	0	0
F46	T	L	1	2
G26	T	L	0	1
G41	T	L	0	0
862	Q	L	0	1

[a]"Most-likely sires" were determined on the basis of the ejaculation frequencies during the female's conception cycle. (N) = Natal to Group S.

Rank: The 11 males of Group S are ranked in a linear hierarchy. Males residing in other groups are ranked from within their social group and their ranks are classified as either high (H) or low (L).

? = This male escaped trapping and was therefore not analyzed.

It was of considerable interest to determine whether dominance rank and RS were correlated for the free-ranging male rhesus macaques. The answer is obviously no. Although the alpha (722) and beta (761) males were able to sire two offspring, one low-ranking male (LRM) residing in another social group also sired two infants, and in total only 4/11 infants (most probably even only 4/15) were sired by high-ranking males (HRMs). Furthermore, only 2/9 HRMs had offspring while 6/11 low-ranking males reproduced. Calculation of the Spearman rank correlation coefficient for social rank and reproduction confirmed non-significance. Similar findings have been reported for another vertebrate class, the poeciliid fish species (Schartl et al., 1993).

Observed relationships between breeding males and females have been assumed to predict RS (Cowlishaw and Dunbar, 1991), although paternity data confirming this supposition have been lacking. In this study, a significant relationship between mating success (MS) and realized RS was not observed. The most-likely sires, determined by ejaculation frequency during the female's conception cycle, turned out to be the actual sires in only four cases. When all sires and non-sires were compared for several parameters describing MS, we found that sires (a) did not ejaculate more, (b) fail to have more consorts, (c) overall did not spend more time in consort, (d) have no greater average consort length and (e) do not mate with more females than non-sires during females' conception cycles (data not shown). Thus mating parameters can not reliably predict RS.

Comparison of heterozygosity in Groups S and M

Starting paternity testing in Group M, we had to face the problem of a reduced number of non-maternal offspring bands (Tab. 2a), i.e. bands that are required in order to discriminate between different putative fathers. Therefore the DNA fingerprint data were analyzed for clues as to a loss of heterozygosity in Group M compared to Group S. Following the analysis outlined by Krawczak and Bockel (1992), this was feasible on the basis of the band-sharing frequency (bs) either between unrelated animals or between parent and offspring. This parameter is calculated as twice the number of shared bands divided by the total number of bands exhibited by any two individuals.

Reevaluation of the multilocus profiles revealed a general reduction of the average number of bands per individual in Group M as compared to Group S (Tab. 2a). To our surprise, however, bs between mother and offspring was not found to differ significantly between the two groups but was instead significantly higher than expected under the assumption of complete heterozygosity in both groups (Tab. 2b). Following this rationale, Group S would have to be considered as inbred, too.

Table 2a. Average number of maternal bands (N_m) and of non-maternal offspring bands (N_o)

Parameter	Group	N	Probe		
			$(GTG)_5$	$(GATA)_4$	$(CA)_8$
N_m	M	23	16.3	11.3	26.3
	S	15	23.7	14.9	40.4
N_o	M	23	3.9	2.5	4.5
	S	15	5.1	2.7	8.3

Table 2b. Band-sharing frequency (bs) between mother and offspring

Group	N	Probe		
		$(GTG)_5$	$(GATA)_4$	$(CA)_8$
M	23	0.73 (0.60)	0.77 (0.61)	0.82 (0.59)
S	15	0.75 (0.63)	0.77 (0.61)	0.78 (0.62)
Chisquare		1.097	0.005	2.617
P		0.2948	0.9404	0.1057

Chisquare and P-values result from comparing the M and S groups by a Wilcoxon test. Band-sharing frequencies in brackets are as expected assuming complete heterozygosity.

In a first attempt to clarify the unexpectedly high bs in Group S some unrelated animals from other social groups on Cayo Santiago as well as from other breeding stations were analyzed. The bs values between unrelated individuals within this heterogeneous group did not differ significantly from Group S (not shown). Therefore a higher "species-specific" bs than observed for humans (Reeve et al., 1990; Krawczak et al., 1993) can not be excluded until a genuine outbred population is available for comparison.

It should be noted that deduction of homozygosity from increased levels of bs between parents and their offspring is only valid if each fingerprint band corresponds to a single locus. Thus our apparently contradictory findings (reduced number of bands but equal bs for Group M in comparison with Group S) could also be explained (i) by more than one locus being involved in a substantial proportion of fingerprint bands, thereby increasing the average bs in both groups, (ii) by an increase of homozygosity in Group S at loci not actually visualized under the employed experimental conditions, or (iii) simply by the fact that, at an already high level of homozygosity, a further increase will cause a less than proportional increase of bs between mother and infant.

Acknowledgement
This work was supported by the VW-Stiftung.

References

Arnemann J, Schmidtke J, Epplen JT, Kuhn H-J, Kaumanns W (1989) DNA fingerprinting for paternity and maternity in Group O Cayo Santiago-derived rhesus monkeys at the German Primate Center: Results of a pilot study. PR Health Sci J 8: 181–184

Berard JD, Nürnberg P, Epplen JT, Schmidtke J. Alternate reproductive tactics and reproductive success in free-ranging rhesus macaques (*Macaca mulatta*). Behavior (in press)

Blin N, Stafford DW (1976) A general method for isolation of high molecular weight DNA from eukaryotes. Nucl Acids Res 3: 2303–2308

Bockel B, Nürnberg P, Krawczak M (1992) Likelihoods of multilocus DNA fingerprints in extended families. Am J Hum Genet 51: 554–561

Cowlishaw G, Dumbar RIM (1991) Dominance rank and mating success in male primates. Anim Behav 41: 1045–1056

Dixson AF, Hastie N, Patel I, Jeffreys AJ (1988) DNA "fingerprinting" of captive family groups of common marmosets (*Callithrix jacchus*). Folia Primatol 51: 52–55

Ely J, Ferrell RE (1990) DNA "fingerprints" and paternity ascertainment in chimpanzees (*Pan troglodytes*). Zoo Biology 9: 91–98

Ely J, Alford P, Ferrell RE (1991) DNA "fingerprinting" and the genetic management of a captive chimpanzee population (*Pan troglodytes*). Am J Primat 24: 39–54

Epplen JT (1992) The methodology of multilocus DNA fingerprinting using radioactive or non-radioactive oligonucleotide probes specific for simple repeat motifs. *In*: Chrambach A, Dunn MJ, Radola BJ (eds) Advances in Electrophoresis, VCH, Weinheim, pp 59–114

Kessler MJ, Berard JD (1989) A brief description of the Cayo Santiago rhesus monkey colony. PR Health Sci J 8: 55–59

Krawczak M, Bockel B (1992) A genetic factor model for the statistical analysis of multilocus DNA fingerprints. Electrophoresis 13: 10–17

Krawczak M, Böhm I, Nürnberg P, Hampe J, Hundrieser J, Pöche H, Peters C, Slomski R, Nagy M, Pöpperl A, Epplen JT, Schmidtke J. Paternity testing with oligonucleotide probe $(CAC)_5/(GTG)_5$: A multi-center study. Forensic Science International (in press)

Kunkel LM, Smith KD, Boyer SH, Borgaonkar D, Wachtel SS, Miller OJ, Breg WR, Jones Jr HW, Rary M (1977) Analysis of human Y-chromosome-specific reiterated DNA in chromosome variants. Proc Natl Acad Sci USA 74: 1245–1249

Martin RD, Dixson AF, Wickings EJ (eds) (1992) Paternity in primates: Genetic tests and theories – Implications of human DNA fingerprinting. Karger AG, Basel

Rawlins RG, Kessler MJ (eds) (1986) The Cayo Santiago Macaques: History, behavior and biology. State University of New York Press, Albany

Reeve HK, Westneat DF, Noon WA, Sherman PW, Aquadro CF (1990) DNA "fingerprinting" reveals high levels of inbreeding in colonies of the eusocial naked mole-rat. Proc Natl Acad Sci USA 87: 2496–2500

Schartl M, Erbelding-Dink C, Hölter S, Nanda I, Schmid M, Schröder JH, Epplen JT. Reproductive failure of dominant males in the poeciliid fish *Limia perugiae* determined by DNA-fingerprinting. Proc Natl Acad Sci USA (in press)

Weiss ML, Wilson V, Chan C, Turner T, Jeffreys AJ (1988) Application of DNA fingerprinting probes to old world monkeys. Amer J Primat 16: 73–79

DNA Fingerprinting: State of the Science
ed. by S. D. J. Pena, R. Chakraborty, J. T. Epplen & A. J. Jeffreys

Use of highly repeated DNA polymorphisms for genome diagnosis and evolutionary studies in the genus *Beta*

T. Schmidt, K. Boblenz[a] and K. Weising[b]

Karyobiology Group, Department of Cell Biology, John Innes Centre, Colney, Norwich NR4 7UJ, UK; [a]Institute for Veterinary Medicine, Federal Health Office, Naumburger Str. 96a, 07743 Jena, Germany; and [b]Plant Molecular Biology Group, Johann-Wolfgang-Goethe-University, Siesmayerstr. 70, 60054 Frankfurt, Germany

Summary

A considerable fraction of the genomes of cultivated beet, *Beta vulgaris*, and its wild relatives consists of highly repetitive DNA organized as tandemly arranged sequence elements. These satellite DNAs belong to various classes in respect to their distribution, evolution and molecular structure. Eight non-homologous satellite repeats from different *Beta* species were analyzed. Several of these satellite sequences were used as genome-specific probes for phylogenetic studies and for the detection of alien wild beet chromosomes in hybrid plants. DNA fingerprinting was performed to investigate the distribution and abundance of simple repetitive sequences complementary to the synthetic oligonucleotides $(GACA)_4$, $(GATA)_4$, $(GTG)_5$, $(CA)_8$, $(GGAT)_4$ and $(CCTA)_4$ in the genomes of several *Beta vulgaris* cultivars. All motifs were present, though at different abundance and with a different degree of polymorphism depending on the oligonucleotide probe. The most informative fingerprints were obtained with $(GATA)_4$ hybridized to HinfI-, HaeIII- or RsaI-digested DNA, respectively. This probe allowed clear differentiation of double-haploid breeding lines.

Introduction

The plant nuclear genome contains large fractions of highly reiterated DNA sequences, of which tandemly arranged elements are described as satellite DNA (Singer, 1982). In plants preferred repeat sizes of 150–180 bp and 300–360 bp are observed corresponding to the size of one or two nucleosomes. Considerably shorter are simple repetitive sequences of 2–10 bp (Tautz and Rentz, 1984). Simple sequence arrays are often characterized by a high polymorphism caused by variable copy number and conservation of flanking restriction sites. Using synthetic oligonucleotides complementary to simple sequence arrays these polymorphisms can be detected as DNA fingerprints (Ali et al., 1986; Weising et al., 1991a). Molecular analyses of satellite and simple sequence repeats can provide insight into the evolution of genomes and species, support taxonomic and phylogenetic studies and can be used as specific DNA probes in plant breeding programs. In this study, we summarize and present molecular data concerning the distribution and evolution of several satellite and simple sequence repeats of the genus *Beta*. Within the genus, the section *Beta* contains important crop plants (sugar beet, fodder beet, Swiss Chard, mangelwurzel, beetroot) and wild species. The sections *Procumbentes*, *Corollinae* and *Nanae* consist of wild beets only, which are attractive to plant breeders, because they include several genes for the resistance to beet viruses and animal pests.

Material and methods

Plant material was obtained from the Botanical Gardens of the Universities of Halle/Saale and Frankfurt/Main (FRG). Several wild beets were kindly provided by L. Frese, formerly CGN Wageningen. Hybrid plants and double-haploid lines (DH-lines) were obtained from the Institute for *Beta* Research, Klein Wanzleben (FRG). Standard molecular methods were used (Sambrook et al., 1989). Isolation of genomic DNA, cloning of satellite repeats and oligonucleotide fingerprinting were performed as described by Schmidt et al. (1991, 1993).

Results and discussion

Molecular structure, distribution and evolution of Beta satellite DNA families

From the results of our satellite analyses we can assume that a considerable proportion of repetitive DNA (63% in beet; Flavell et al., 1974) is organized in tandem arrays (Schmidt et al., 1991). Five different satellite repeats were isolated from two *Beta* species. Their size, origin, AT-content and estimated copy number are listed in Tab. 1. The repeats were

Table 1. Molecular characterization and origin of *Beta* satellite repeats

Satellite	Origin	Size (bp)	AT-content (%)	*Procumbentes*	*Nanae*	*Corollinae*	*Beta*
BamHI	*B. vulgaris*	327–328	69	—	—	—	+ + +
EcoRI	*B. vulgaris*	156–159	59	+ +	—	+	+ + +
Sau3A I	*B. procumbens*	158	70	+ + +	+	—	—
Sau3A II	*B. procumbens*	395	65	+ + +	+	+	+
Sau3A III	*B. procumbens*	114	45	+ +	+	—	—
HaeIII	*B. corolliflora*	149	43	+	+ +	+ + +	+ +
HaeIII 1	*B. trigyna*	149	67	—	+ +	+ + +	+
HaeIII 2	*B. trigyna*	162	41	—	+	+ + +	+

Abundance: high: + + +   middle: + +   low: +   not detected: —

designated according to the restriction enzyme site which is conserved in the repeats of the satellite DNA family. Southern analyses including representative species of all four *Beta* sections revealed considerable polymorphisms: (i) The BamHI satellite was present in the section *Beta* only. (ii) The EcoRI and two out of three Sau3A satellites were present in more than one section but variably organized and amplified to different degrees. (iii) One *B. procumbens* satellite existed in all analyzed *Beta* species in different genomic organization and copy numbers. The characterization of three additional wild beet satellites is in progress.

These investigations together with sequence analysis allowed some conclusions on the evolution of satellite DNA sequences in the genus *Beta* (Schmidt and Metzlaff, 1991; Schmidt et al., 1991). In general, the amplification of satellite elements probably occurred through different periods in the phylogeny of the various *Beta* species. The existence of several satellite DNA sequences in more than one section suggests that these repeats might be relatively old (Fig. 1A). In contrast, the BamHI sequence family exists only in the section *Beta*. Since this satellite does not exist in the section *Corollinae*, which is relatively closely related to the section *Beta* as suggested by analysis of chloroplast DNA (Fritzsche et al., 1987), we assume that the BamHI satellite DNA is recent and the amplification of the repeating unit occurred after the separation of both sections (Fig. 1B).

Molecular markers for genome diagnosis in the genus Beta

The application of molecular markers for genome diagnosis in plant breeding research permits faster and more accurate screening of large numbers of individual plants than classical methods. DNA probes with high genome specificity or specific hybridization patterns are suitable for the analysis of hybrid plants. We used one *B. procumbens*-specific satellite for the detection of alien wild beet chromosomes in hybrid lines ($2n = 18 + 1$) (Schmidt et al., 1990). These monosomic addition lines were generated from crosses of *B. vulgaris* × *B. procumbens* aiming to transfer the resistance to beet cyst nematode *Heterodera schachtii* into cultivated beet. After dot blot hybridization of 24 putative addition lines using the wild beet satellite as a probe (Fig. 2A) strong signals were observed for only the lines, which were later proven to contain an alien *B. procumbens*-chromosome by cytology. For fast screening of large numbers of individual plants, we adapted the squash dot hybridization where fresh leaf samples are squashed onto nylon membranes which bind the DNA (Fig. 2B). Detection of alien lines was extremely efficient (Schmidt et al., 1990).

456

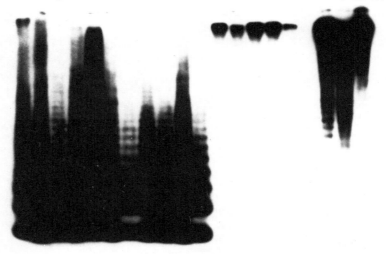

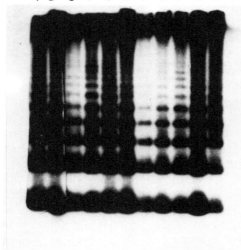

Figure 1. Distribution of the EcoRI satellite and BamHI satellite in the genus *Beta*. Genomic DNA of species of the sections *Beta* (1–11), *Corollinae* (12–16), *Nanae* (17), *Procumbentes* (18–20) and of the related species *Spinacia oleracea* (21) and *Chenopodium bonus-henricus* (22) were digested with EcoRI (A) and BamHI (B), respectively. After electrophoresis and Southern transfer filters were hybridized with the EcoRI repeat (A) and BamHI repeat (B).

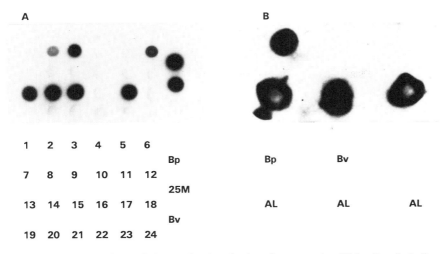

Figure 2. Dot blot and squash dot test for the selection of monosomic addition lines including alien *B. procumbens* chromosomes. Panel A shows the dot blot hybridization of a *B. procumbens* satellite with DNA from 24 individual plants (1–24) of a backcross of a monosomic addition line (25 M) to *B. vulgaris* (Bv). *B. procumbens* (Bp) served as a control. Panel B shows the hybridization of the same probe with squashed leaf material of *B. procumbens* (Bp), *B. vulgaris* (Bv) and three monosomic addition lines (AL).

Identification of double-haploid lines by oligonucleotide fingerprinting

As a first step for the introduction of DNA fingerprinting to analyzing the beet genome we investigated the distribution and polymorphism of simple repetitive sequence motifs in several cultivars of *B. vulgaris* and the subspecies *B. vulgaris* ssp. *maritima* (Schmidt et al., 1993). Our analysis showed that all investigated motifs, i.e. $(GACA)_4$, $(GATA)_4$, $(CA)_8$, $(GTG)_5$ (Fig. 3A), $(GGAT)_4$ and $(CCAT)_4$ (not shown) are present in the *B. vulgaris* genome, though at different abundances. According to the number and intensity of hybridization signals, the most abundant motifs were $(GTG)_5$, $(CA)_8$ and $(GATA)_4$. Except for $(CCAT)_4$, which produced either zero, one or two weak bands depending on the cultivar, all tested motifs gave rise to easily screenable multilocus fingerprint patterns with varying degrees of intra- and inter-specific polymorphism. $(GATA)_4$ proved to be the most informative probe in being able to detect variation within varieties (Fig. 3A). Considerable variation in copy number and polymorphism of simple repetitive motifs has also been observed in other plant species (Weising et al., 1991a, b, 1992). Depending on the probe and species under investigation, oligonucleotide fingerprinting can thus yield information at different taxonomic levels.

Since cultivated beet is outbreeding, rather high levels of hetero-zygosity are usually encountered within cultivars. In order to obtain

458

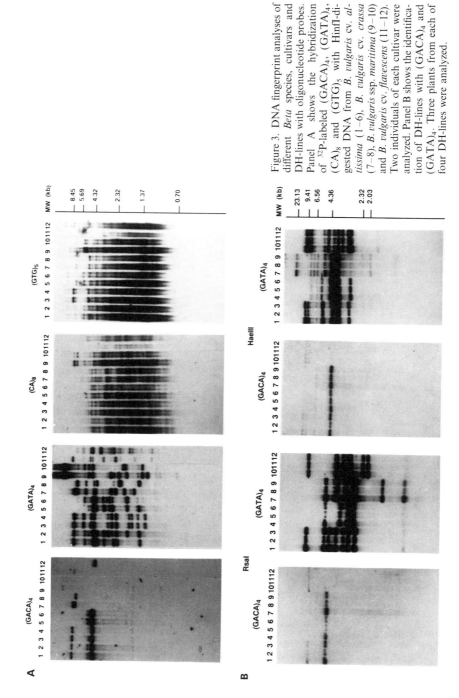

Figure 3. DNA fingerprint analyses of different *Beta* species, cultivars and DH-lines with oligonucleotide probes. Panel A shows the hybridization of ^{32}P-labeled (GACA)₄, (GATA)₄, (CA)₈ and (GTG)₅ with HinfI-digested DNA from *B. vulgaris* cv. *altissima* (1–6), *B. vulgaris* cv. *crassa* (7–8), *B. vulgaris* ssp. *maritima* (9–10) and *B. vulgaris* cv. *flavescens* (11–12). Two individuals of each cultivar were analyzed. Panel B shows the identification of DH-lines with (GACA)₄ and (GATA)₄. Three plants from each of four DH-lines were analyzed.

homozygosity, double-haploid breeding lines have been established. We used the $(GACA)_4$ and $(GATA)_4$ probe, respectively, to characterize different double-haploid breeding lines of *B. vulgaris* (Fig. 3B). While yielding identical fingerprints within each line, $(GATA)_4$ could clearly distinguish between the lines. We therefore suggest that oligonucleotide fingerprinting may become an important tool for estimating the degree of homozygosity and purity in breeding lines of *B. vulgaris* (and probably other crop species), for line identification and protection of breeder's rights.

Acknowledgements
T. Schmidt acknowledges grant no. 40081/15.249.2 of the Stifterverband für die Deutsche Wissenschaft to attend the 2nd International Conference on DNA Fingerprinting. K. Weising is supported by a FAZIT fellowship (Frankfurt/Main). We thank Drs T. Schwarzacher and J. S. Heslop-Harrison for critical reading of the manuscript. The simple repetitive oligonucleotides are subject to patent applications. Commercial inquiries should be directed to Fresenius AG, Oberursel, Germany.

References

Ali S, Müller CR, Epplen JT (1986) DNA fingerprinting by oligonucleotide probes specific for simple repeats. Hum Genet 74: 239–243

Flavell RB, Bennett MD, Smith JB (1974) Genome size and the proportion of repeated nucleotide sequence DNA in plants. Biochem Genet 12: 257–269

Fritzsche K, Metzlaff M, Melzer R, Hagemann R (1987) Comparative restriction endonuclease analysis and molecular cloning of plastid DNAs from wild species and cultivated varieties of the genus *Beta* (L). Theor Appl Genet 74: 589–594

Sambrook J, Fritsch EF, Maniatis T (1989) Molecular cloning: a laboratory manual. 2nd edn. Cold Spring Harbor Laboratory Press, Cold Spring Harbor, New York

Schmidt T, Junghans H, Metzlaff M (1990) Construction of *Beta procumbens*-specific DNA probes and their application for the screening of *B. vulgaris* × *B. procumbens* (2n = 19) addition lines. Theor Appl Genet 79: 177–181

Schmidt T, Metzlaff M (1991) Cloning and characterization of a *Beta vulgaris* satellite DNA family. Gene 101: 247–250

Schmidt T, Jung C, Metzlaff M (1991) Distribution and evolution of two satellite DNA families in the genus *Beta*. Theor Appl Genet 82: 793–799

Schmidt T, Boblenz K, Metzlaff M, Kaemmer D, Weising K, Kahl G (1993) DNA fingerprinting in sugar beet (*Beta vulgaris*) – Identification of double-haploid breeding lines. Theor Appl Genet 85: 653–657

Singer MF (1982) Highly repeated sequences in mammalian genomes. Int Rev Cytol 76: 67–112

Tautz D, Renz M (1984) Simple sequences are ubiquitous repetitive components of eukaryotic genomes. Nucleic Acids Res 12: 4127–4138

Weising K, Beyermann B, Ramser J, Kahl G (1991a) Plant DNA fingerprinting with radioactive and digoxygenated oligonucleotide probes complementary to simple repetitive DNA sequences. Electrophoresis 12: 159–169

Weising K, Ramser J, Kaemmer D, Kahl G, Epplen JT (1991b) Oligonucleotide fingerprinting in plants and fungi. *In*: Burke T, Dolf G, Jeffreys AJ, Wolff R (eds) DNA Fingerprinting: Approaches and Applications. Birkhäuser, Basel, pp 312–329

Weising K, Kaemmer D, Weigand F, Epplen JT, Kahl G (1992) Oligonucleotide fingerprinting reveals various probe-dependent levels of informativeness in chickpea (*Cicer arietinum* L.). Genome 35: 436–442

Subject Index

(The page numbers refer to the initial page of the article in which the keyword occur)

462

466

BIRKHÄUSER
LIFE SCIENCES

Experientia Supplementum

DNA Methylation: Molecular Biology and Biological Significance

Edited by

J.-P. Jost, *Friedrich-Miescher Inst., Basel, Switzerland*
H.-P. Saluz, *IRBM, Rome, Italy*

1993. 572 pages. Hardcover. ISBN 3-7643-2778-2 (EXS 64)

"... This publication is timely and up-to-date and provides a comprehensive background not available in other single sources. ... After reading it, I appreciate what a bargain that was. ... It is so recommended." **John C. Rogers,** Washington Univ., St. Louis, MO, USA
"Cell", May 7, 1993

The goal of this book is to provide a comprehensive collection of reports on the state of the art in DNA methylation. DNA methylation is found in many different genes in bacteria, viruses, fungi, vertebrates and plants. It is involved in the protection of DNA against restriction enzymes, X-chromosome inactivation, imprinting, changes in DNA and chromatin structure, changes in the interaction of proteins with DNA, silencing viruses, and in embryogenesis and cancer.

This book gives students and newcomers to the field a unique introduction to the topic and is also designed to help the experienced scientist to broaden and update his knowledge in this highly topical field. The numerous references cited in the 24 chapters and the many explanatory figures and tables which complement the text will guide and stimulate the investigator to further studies.

Please order through your bookseller or directly from:
Birkhäuser Verlag AG, P.O. Box 133,
CH-4010 Basel / Switzerland (Fax ++41 / 61 / 721 7950)
Orders from the USA or Canada should be sent to:
Birkhäuser Boston
44 Hartz Way, Secaucus, NJ 07096-2491 / USA
Call Toll-Free 1-800-777-4643

Birkhäuser

Birkhäuser Verlag AG
Basel · Boston · Berlin

BIRKHÄUSER
LIFE SCIENCES

Advances in Life Sciences

Transgenic Organisms -
Risk Assessment of
Deliberate Release

Edited by

K. Wöhrmann / J. Tomiuk, *University of Tübingen, Germany*

1993. 280 pages. Hardcover. ISBN 3-7643-2834-7 (ALS)

The genetic structure of organisms is being altered to an ever-increasing degree by molecular genetic techniques. Thus far, more than 500 transgenic organisms have been tested or utilized in the field. The strides forward, however, have been encumbered by persistent and intense controversy. What is happening now on the forefront of genetic engineering? What are its aims, and inherent risks? What is its justification?

The purpose of this book is to offer the reader a firm grounding in the subject by systematically reviewing several basic issues: the interaction between host DNA/RNA and the introduced DNA/RNA; the extent and effect of horizontal gene transfer; the fate in populations of genes inadvertently released into nature; the feasibility and effectiveness of risk assessment; and the manner in which this modern technique can best be harnessed to improve human health. More generally, but perhaps most significantly, the book calls for a critical appraisal of the desirability of the aims advanced by molecular geneticists today.

Please order through your bookseller or directly from:
Birkhäuser Verlag AG, P.O. Box 133,
CH-4010 Basel / Switzerland (Fax ++41 / 61 / 721 7950)
Orders from the USA or Canada should be sent to:
Birkhäuser Boston
44 Hartz Way, Secaucus, NJ 07096-2491 / USA
Call Toll-Free 1-800-777-4643

Birkhäuser

Birkhäuser Verlag AG
Basel · Boston · Berlin